FAITH OF OUR FAMILIES
EVERTON FC: AN ORAL HISTORY
1878-2018

FAITH OF OUR FAMILIES

EVERTON FC: AN ORAL HISTORY
1878-2018

EDITOR
James Corbett

ASSISTANT EDITOR
Jack Gordon Brown

CONTRIBUTING EDITOR
Philip Ross

First published as a hardback by deCoubertin Books Ltd in 2017.

Published as a softback in 2018.

First Softback Edition

deCoubertin Books, 46B Jamaica Street, Baltic Quarter Liverpool, L1 OAF
www.decoubertin.co.uk

ISBN: 978-1-909245-74-7

A CIP catalogue record for this book is available from the British Library.

Cover design and typeset by Leslie Priestley.

Printed and bound by Olusur.

For Joshua, Eleanor and Henry.

And the Reverend Harry Ross,
on the occasion of
40 years as Goodison chaplain.

Praise for
Faith of our Families

Longlisted for the Coutts Football Book of the Year in the 2018 Sports Book Awards

---

'Magnificent... the history of Everton told through hundreds of stories.'
– **Philippe Auclair,** *France Football*

'It's the history of Everton Football Club, told by the people who made it. It's outstanding, it's entertaining – and it's also historically important. Faith Of Our Families is an Oral History of Everton Football Club and it's told by the individuals who actually made that history. Just about every significant living figure in Everton's history has been interviewed - players, managers, chairmen, journalists, fans... Those who are no longer with us have had their words transcribed - making up an utterly enthralling first-hand account of the history of Everton Football Club. If you think you know your history, think again. A criticism? I only wish it was longer.' – **David Prentice,** *Liverpool Echo sports editor*

'Faith of our Families is by far and away the best book that's come out this year... James Corbett has produced some fantastic Everton books over the years but he has surpassed himself with this oral history. It is truly wonderful, full of bits of information that you didn't know and stories you haven't heard. Frankly, if it's not in your Christmas stocking then no one loves you.' – *When Skies are Grey*

'An awesome tome, an incredible production... I'm sure it is going to be recognised for the landmark work that it is.' – **Mike Collett,** *former Reuters world soccer editor, and chairman of the Football Writers Association Books Committee*

'A cracker.' – **Tony Evans,** *London Evening Standard*

'It's heavy, it's weighty, it's absolutely terrific. Loads of Evertonians will want this. If you're a blue you've got to get hold of this.' – **Ray Stubbs,** *TalkSPORT*

'A monster of a book.' – *NSNO.co.uk*

'A superb book… Fascinating inside stories from players, managers, directors.'
– **Charles Lambert,** *former BBC Radio Merseyside sports editor*

'A fantastic piece of work.' – **Matt Jones,** *The Blue Room*

'A history with a difference. 'Faith of Our Families' is an in-depth history of one of our oldest and greatest football clubs – Everton. What makes this tome different from its many competitors – there are at least half a dozen books claiming to be the official history of Everton – is that a story of almost 140 years football toil is told in a series of interviews with the people who were there, saw the events unfold or contributed to them. It features more than 200 original interviews with managers, players and supporters who provide unique insights into the changing fortunes of one of England's oldest League clubs. From the fledgling days as a church team of the 1880s to the modern-day search for a new home Everton's rich history unfolds in the words of many of those closely involved in it... An essential read.' – **Eric Brown,** *Sports Journalists Association website*

'A masterpiece... If you're an Evertonian then you must have your own copy of this magnificent book by James Corbett it really is a must have!' – **John Blain,** *chairman Everton Shareholders Association*

Contents

Introduction

'Once Everton touches you, nothing is ever the same again.'

Alan Ball's famous aphorism is one of the truest things anyone has ever said about a football club. Everton is a club that grips and obsesses, cradles and slaps you around, causes agony and joy. And that's just as a supporter. As a writer who has seen in print countless words about his beloved club new stories and new ideas constantly ferment. It's a subject I can't help but going back to.

Five years have passed since publication of my *Everton Encyclopedia* and nearly fifteen since *Everton: The School of Science* was written. Since the last book to carry my name on the cover I have collaborated with some of the most distinguished figures in the club's history on their memoirs – Neville Southall, Howard Kendall, Dave Hickson and Bob Latchford. But after that work the time seems right to add another, more wide-ranging contribution to the club's chronicles.

Everton appear at a crossroads in their history. After struggling to make an impression in the Premier League era, a new majority shareholder and considerable investment has given a fresh impetus to the club. Its manager Ronald Koeman has spent a lot of money on a lot of new players. The prodigal son, Wayne Rooney, has returned. There are changes in the way the football club is run. And in three or four years time it seems likely that Goodison – the Grand Old Lady, the first purpose built football stadium in the world and home to so many memories – will be left for a new abode on the banks of the royal blue Mersey.

It's a fascinating and fast moving period in the club's history and the changes heighten the imperative to capture something more of Everton's past before it transforms forever. But what else can be added?

Quite a lot as it happens.

In the early-1990s, Radio City put together a 32 part series chronicling the history of Merseyside's three professional football clubs, Everton, Liverpool and Tranmere Rovers. The voices in that series were later put into print in the wonderful oral history of football on Merseyside, *Three Sides of the Mersey*. It tells the story of the game through the voices of the people who made it the great spectacle that it is: players, managers, directors and fans. It wassuch a simple and beautifully executed idea and a work I referred to many times.

The concept was one that stuck with me while I trained as an historian and embarked on a career in the media. What would such a book be like if it focused on the fortunes of just one club? In American sportswriting there is a fine tradition of oral history, but it's one less often used in Britain – this despite Thomas Hauser winning the country's top sportswriting award, the William Hill Prize, for his oral history of Muhammad Ali's Life and Times.

In that work Hauser spoke to no fewer than 176 people who knew, saw and were moved by Ali. His book is an astonishing achievement. My ambitions when starting this project were initially less ambitious. With my colleagues, Philip Ross and Jack Gordon Brown, we initially aimed for 100 interviews – around the same tally as had been achieved in *Three Sides of the Mersey* – but the project soon took on a life of its own. The more people we spoke to, the more layers and stories we built, and the more possibilities opened. It was a little like building a football team and then having that magic realisation that you have something very special on your hands. Our belief that Everton was 'more than just a club' was reaffirmed many times, and we show a complex institution that touches people's lives in many different ways.

In the end we interviewed just about every significant living figure in Everton's history: more than 200 people – players, managers, directors, chairman, officials, supporters – generating hundreds of hours of recordings and two million words of transcripts. Never before has a study of any sporting institution benefited from so many original interviews. Allied to this is significant new research on Everton's early years, utilising lost and long forgotten documentary sources.

I also wanted to show the wider sweep of history and demonstrate the ways in which Everton was 'more than a club'. How has football changed over the lifetimes of the interviewees? To what extent does the game reflect wider changes in society? What of the role of women or those from ethnic or sexual minorities? What of Everton Ladies? It is the conceit of every football fan that their club is somehow special, but I wanted to show how Everton touched people's lives, whether through how they played on the pitch, or via their ambitious and brilliant community scheme.

The resultant book, *Faith of our Families*, is what I believe, an unprecedented study of a football club, charting the inner workings and highs and lows of Everton Football Club, from its inception as a church team in 1878 to its position today as an aristocrat of the English game and one of the wealthiest clubs in the world.

I hope that Evertonians and all fans enjoy this work as much as we all enjoyed working on it. And I hope in years to come it is referred to as an essential part of every Evertonians library.

James Corbett
Liverpool and Ireland
September 2017.

Part 1

The Making
of a Football Giant
1878-1946

Everton became one of the richest clubs in the country, through its measured step towards high-grade football, and building up the stands and under arches for the benefit of their public, together with the signing of good-class players who would play the game for their credit's sake. We had our standards of play and our standards of players.

Will Cuff

The birth of Everton and the road to the Football League

Thomas Keates: When Stanley Park, Liverpool, was opened in 1870, football and golf were referred to in general conversation as games played in Scotland, enthusiastically, scientifically, or by a code of rules. What is now known as the Association game in football was not played in England. The young Scotsmen who crossed the border in search of employment, and found it, had much to do with the spread and development of the sport in England; they were conspicuous players, and tutors in the new clubs. The early local clubs were associated with churches and chapels and were named after them: cricket clubs in the summer, they played football in the winter. One of these can claim the distinction of having been the originator of the Everton Football Club.

Will Cuff: The club grew out of the St Domingo Church followers, and its first playing area was on Stanley Park, where the foundation of Everton's greatness was laid.

Thomas Keates: Soon after Stanley Park opened the youths connected with the Methodist Chapel at the top of St Domingo Vale formed a cricket club and played in the park. In 1878 they added a 'St Domingo Football Club' to the summer organisation. In 1879, as the Club's players were mostly outsiders, it was decided to alter the name to that of the district – Everton.

Victor Hall: Each season in those days was a risk. One bad season might see the best of clubs break up for want of public support. One bad season could be the ill fortune of any club that failed to produce a good playing and winning combination. The secretaries of those days were the mainsprings of every team. There were then no subdivision of duties and responsibilities as there are today. There were, for instance, no 'team managers' to undertake personal control, at all times, of the players. There were few 'ground' committees, looking after turf conditions, turnstile and stand repairs. There were no 'club stewards' to help at big matches, and there were no 'supporters' clubs to run club concerts, and help financially in the many useful ways of those modern concerns. And usually there was no treasurer or finance committee to shoulder the anxieties of the club moneybags.

W.J. Byton: Those were the days when the Everton club was kept alive by the annual subscription of the members. Gates were on the microscopic side, and playing members of the club found their own boots, pants, and jerseys, and paid their 'whack' each week for the rent of the dressing rooms!

Victor Hall: Those were the days when the directors or committeemen of Everton were football enthusiasts in the winter months, and cricketers – playing cricketers – not spectators – in the summer months. They were all Stanley cricketers and Everton footballers.

Thomas Keates: The first playing ground was situated at the south-east corner of the park, nearly opposite 'Stanley House', the residence of John Houlding, one of the first influential non-players and patrons of the club.

Victor Hall: There are still many men living who will cherish, while memory endures, the name of John Houlding, one-time Lord Mayor of Liverpool, and the creator of the Liverpool Football Club. Indeed, with all its proud record, owes more than allegiance to the grand old man who so truly reflected the aims and aspirations of Everton people. It is a long cry back now to the days when the Everton club, playing in Priory Road, invoked the powerful aid of John Houlding, the shrewd, far-seeing business man, who living himself in Anfield Road, had watched the progress the new game of 'football' was making among the young men of his own neighbourhood.

Thomas Keates: Its players were all amateurs. There was neither dressing room nor shelter for the players or spectators, and no 'gate'. The expenses were defrayed by the members. From the Park Lodge in Mill Lane they carried the goal posts, fixed them in sockets, and whitened the lines. The names of these enthusiastic pioneers deserve to be inscribed in the club's roll of honour.

Victor Hall: Mr Houlding had one remarkable gift that is denied to many public men, but which he held in generous measure, and that was the grit of attracting to himself the personal affection of his younger followers. It may have been a form of personal magnetism, or a psychological grit that some men hold by unknown charm, but the remarkable fact is that it did exist, and that in a very remarkable manner in the genial personally of old 'King John'. Those were great days in the growing enthusiasm of the new game, local residents were drawn into the enthusiasm of the players, every Sunday school had its own football club, and every district rivalled each other with a fine spirit of emulation. Everton fought Bootle with all the keenness of an international battle, and rivalries sprang up, as one club tried to coax away the better players from their neighbours.

Thomas Keates: Unfortunately, the venture to Priory Road [after leaving Stanley Park in 1883], for the season 1883/84 did not blossom into anything like a rose. The proceeds of the first gate must have been depressing for the adventurers, and especially to the treasurer. They did not require much counting: the grand total was 14/-.

Victor Hall: [John Houlding] felt that there was a future for the game, and offered the use of the land he had already purchased in Anfield Road at a very modest, indeed nominal rental. That is the ground on which today the Liverpool Football Club play. And so is history made.

Jack Wildman: I well remember the first match at Anfield Road. Charley Twemlow, the treasurer, stood at the gates with a handbag for the coppers. Frank Brettle was secretary. Both Charley and Frank were schoolteachers. Charley I think went to Australia, Frank later, became team manager for Bolton Wanderers for a short time, but what I want you to know is that Everton did not bring Alec Dick to Liverpool. There was a club called Stanley that played on a pitch where Goodison Park stands now, or very close to it, which was composed of nearly all Scotch players. There were no pros then, Archie Goodall, brother of John Goodall, played for them [afterwards going to Preston N.E.] also the brothers Wilson; but they did not get a lot of support. I think the first import was George Dobson from Bolton, then George Farmer from Oswestry, and I think if there is to be a monument on tablet fixed on Everton's ground, George Farmer's name should be in the centre. Farmer was the man that made the people come and take notice. We never looked back after he came. We got two good Welsh boys Jobe Wilding, Abel Heys, then George Fleming. I don't think Alec Dick came till after Stanley broke up. The first team at Anfield Road when we started was C. Lindsay [goal]; Morris, Marriott, Preston, Parry [Capt], Pickering, Richards, Whittle, Jack McGill, Gibson, Higgins. The opening match was against Earlestown, whom we had beaten in the final for the Liverpool and District Cup, the previous season. Our full team did not play for, at the time, rounders held a big away and some of our members were in the Crescent Rounders Club. So that Charley Joiffe was in goal, Jack McGill and Pickering played back.

As for funds we started in a small way, but were not long in laying a firm foundation, which others found easy to build on, and claim all the credit.

Everton enter the Football League in 1888 as founder members

Thomas Keates: In 1888 the most important event in the history of Association Football transpired. The Football League was established. The contrast in the attendances at cup ties and ordinary matches, the trifling interest taken in the latter by the public and the insignificance of the takings had long vexed the souls of club managers. How can we vitalise the torpid? That was the question.

Will Cuff: The Football League's birth is one of the romances of the game. It was born in Birmingham where a Pickwickian character named William McGregor conceived the notion that friendly football matches were all quite well in their own stolid way but a gathering of all the football clans could formulate a scheme whereby each of them would tackle each rival, home and away, and then – here came his biggest golden thought for the day – a league could be created. Played, won, lost, drawn, goals for, goals against, points – just as simple as that. And from that day to the present every form of sport [except cricket, which could not enter the framework owing to abandoned, incompleted and drawn matches] had founded its meetings upon that excellent plan, and league for every manner of sport have been unable to add or take away from the McGregor plan which was the Football League plan.

Everton win their first league title in 1891

Thomas Keates: Everton, in its third season in the League, 1890/91, reached the zenith of football distinction — achieved the ambition of the management and drove its supporters wild with delight, by heading the League table, with Preston North End two points below as runners-up.

Victor Hall: The first eleven of that day read like this: - J.J. Angus, A. Hannah, D. Doyle; D. Kirkwood, J. Holt, W. Campbell; A. Latta, A. Brady, E. Chadwick, A.Milward, F. Geary. Trainer: D. Waugh. Umpire: R. L. Stockton. Secretary: R. Molyneux. There's a team to ponder over! Regard again, whoever, remembers that team in action, just how they played, and the dove-tailing of the combination, by which in attack they were all attackers, and under hostile pressure, every man of them a defender.

Dan Kirkwood: When one of us was cornered another seemed to divine his intention, and it was this sympathetic intuition which enabled us to overcome difficulties, and create anxiety amongst the opposing defenders.

Victor Hall: The personalities of the group of Everton players of the nineties will, to my mind at least, be the combination that brought highest honour to Everton and left a tradition of skill and daring energy that has formed an ideal for every team since that has played in the name of Everton. Let it in not be thought, however that they were 'kid gloves' merchants those Everton players, and Dan Doyle's methods at back hard knocks. Dan Kirkwood, still active with us today, could tell rare tales of their battles by flood and field. Young Fred Geary of those days, the demon goal-getter, was no Sunday school player, and Dan Doyle's methods at the back were scarcely those of a dancing master. But the team as a whole fought clean. It fought to win, and it generally got the verdict, and stayed the distance.

Thomas Keates: In the cherished opinion of many veteran enthusiasts this was one of the best teams that ever played for the Club. Every member of it has some rhapsodic eulogists; Geary for his electric runs, tricking out opponents; Chadwick and Milward [left wing] and Latta and Brady [right], as superb exponents; Hannah and Doyle as giant barriers, tacklers and sensational kickers; and the half-backs as reliable resisters and feeders.

The Split

Thomas Keates: In 1891 a crisis in the Club's affairs loomed up – a smouldering fire burst into flames. When the migration to Anfield Road took place, Mr John Houlding, the President, arranged that he should be the club's representative tenant. As soon as prosperity in the new location seemed assured, the executive found their representative tenant had made himself their landlord, ended their normal tenancy and substituted a rental, with an intimation that, as the Club's income increased so would the rent. It did thus [from £100 in 1885/85 to £250 in 1889/90]. Mr Houlding also insisted upon having a nominee on the committee. A feeling that the club was in for very commercial treatment was engendered.

Victor Hall: When Everton hazarded their future and made the famous trek from Anfield to Goodison Park, there was one among the leaders who was destined to leave a revered name in local football history. Mr George Mahon had been a leading protagonist in the cause of those who advocated a change from the old ground, and when it came to a cold discussion of ways and means, and cool heads were wanted, he came into prominence and eventually was of powerful influence in the fortunes of the old club.

Thomas Keates: Discontent with the affairs of the club had for a long time been simmering among members; they complained, but were afraid to strike. It soon became apparent that the two new members of the committee [Dr Clement Baxter and W. R. Clayton] who headed the poll were unafraid. George Mahon's cooperation was a great asset. His experience as an accountant, and as a member of the Walton Local Board was invaluable in the great venture which he and his associates were advocating.

Victor Hall: Rival forces contending for mastery came prepared to those May meetings to put their forces in array. Presiding, there would be that slender well-known figure, slightly tilted head, the blue eye and boyish bearded face, with that well remembered bating yet incisive speech in which later resolution gleamed below the tentative, halting phrase. How many of these meetings that were going to be so noisy ended mildly with the music as of cooing doves, and the protagonists of an hour ago going home arm in arm? Such was the personality of George Mahon, and that expressed one side of his remarkable personality, there were other equally alluring. His speeches were crisp, witty, full of a wishful humour, and yet brimming over with a blending of sound sense and real hospitality. Most valued of all, too, they were brief and to the point. There was nothing wordy or circuitous about either the man of methods. Straight 'as a die' himself he expected the same measures of simple honesty from those with whom he came into contact.

Thomas Keates: The 'split' involved a considerable sacrifice of time by the revolutionists, mental anxiety, diversion from their urgent business responsibilities, monetary risks, partisan denunciation and misrepresentation. The constructive responsibility entailed was intimidating; the finding of a new ground, the drudgery and expense of levelling, draining and sodding; the formidable items of stands, offices, dressing rooms etc., and of incalculable [in advance] tons of bricks, woodwork, roofing etc., were enough to scare average men from the undertaking.

Victor Hall: It must be clearly understood that each of the other directors of Everton was equally – many more so – pledged financially and in prestige to the support of the club, otherwise the huge undertaking at Goodison Park could never have been carried to its happy issue. Those were the days when to be a football director meant something more responsible than travelling with the team, or attending a board meeting once a week. If often meant going to a bank manager and pledging one's own personal property in security for such advances as the club might have occasion for, and when one realises the claims of family and business finance, it can better be appreciated how those pioneer directors backed their faith and stood by the principles.

Thomas Keates: At the General Meeting necessary to secure the majority of members of the Club, Mr Mahon's judicial and dignified reasoning was enthusiastically applauded, and when he referred to a new ground a raucous voice exclaimed, 'Yer can't find one!' There were roars of laughter as Mr Mahon retorted 'I've got one in my pocket.' Metaphorically speaking he had, for he held an option on the Goodison Road ground.

W. R. Clayton: The result of the efforts of [the directors and committeemen] was the building of the club which stood pre-eminent amongst the clubs of the football world. It was the envy of most clubs, it was looked upon as a club run upon sporting lines, and was respected the world over. The success of the club and its wonderful position caused a number of small-minded but envious men to desire to obtain control of this great organisation, by means of purchasing shares and placing them with carefully selected friends and by all kinds of unfair methods and tactics they endeavoured to undermine the confidence of the shareholders in the directorate. Was there ever a more unsportsmanlike action? [They] had borne the met and burden of the day and by whose thought and energy the club had been built up to a gigantic success, to be dismissed by a few ambitious nonentities. They were successful in their aim.

Thomas Keates: The members and players turned themselves into a gang of labourers, with spades and barrows, boards and hammers and nails. A hoarding of boards was fixed on the walls and rails around the playing pitch. Spectators stood on the intervening sods, a very humble stand crouching on the east side for officials, members, pressmen and affluents.

Victor Hall: When Everton migrated to Goodison Park they had behind them a strong leaven of the old club members who wanted to be up and doing in the new enthusiasm for the club on the new ground. They had started there at Goodison with a solid backing of the old club 'members' many of whom were qualified by years of spade work to numbered in the classic term 'supporters.' They could not all be directors, though from their ranks came later many who did ably fill that responsible position. Still there were plenty anxious to be of service in any capacity; so the idea occurred of nominating a selected number to act as honorary stewards. Their duties were not exacting. They acted in all big matches as assistants in the stand arrangements, they supervised the placing of the turnstile men, and on occasions they received distinguished visitors, and generally acted as orderlies to the directors in their responsive duties. Of the three hundred members of the old club, who became shareholders in the new venture, thirty or forty of the most active were enrolled in the new honorary service.

Thomas Keates: Although they affected to have no misgivings, the undaunted wondered how, in the close season of 1892, before a penny of gate money could be handled, they were going to raise the large amount of money that was absolutely requisite to defray the cost of the inevitable outlay involved. Mr Mahon felt the worry of the financial bogey keenly. Suddenly the cloud he so much dreaded vanished and he was basking in sunshine. One of his colleagues offered to advance all the money that might be required [£1000] and asked for no security and stipulated that the amount must be offered free of interest. The name of this friend in need and friend indeed is Dr James Clement Baxter.

Victor Hall: When Everton immigrated to Goodison Park from Anfield, the club 'gates' almost at once assumed handsome proportions. The lavish enterprise of the energetic directorate of those days in providing handsome and adequate stand accommodation brought an immediate reward in an established patronage of people who came to see football under comfortable conditions, of shelter and seating room, and who liked the game, and kept on coming. As the weekly gates grew, so did the club's resources. Players of ability were secured in rapid sequences, the best was then only good enough for Everton, and the enterprise of the directorates, and the quality of the football fare provided met its just reward, and the finances of the club became so well established as to leave Everton easily the most influential, and certainly the richest club in the League.

Will Cuff: When Everton removed its home from Anfield to Goodison Park it needed men of vision to fashion the Everton future. First of all Liverpool FC attempted to take on the name of Everton FC. That was a case of 'He who steals my good name...' and the Football Association at once gave Everton their nameplate, and Anfield became the home of the new Liverpool FC – a happy way out of the impasse.

The Goodison Park Riot of 1895

Thomas Keates: December 1895 was a harassing month for the directors as they had a riot to contend with when Small Heath were the visitors, Heavy rain had fallen for three days, the ground was a swamp and to play on it seemed an absurdity. The referee, however, ordered the game to be played. After half an hour's play the referee mercifully stopped the game. Quite a crowd remained [after the game's abandonment], and, recruited by an army of street loafers who had entered, a howling mob fronted the office demanding their money back. The Secretary tried to appease the brawling crowd but in vain and retreated when a stone was hurled at him. George Mahon did manage to get a hearing, and, pointing out that it was impossible to tell who had paid and who had not, a free ticket was offered to all the demonstrators for the replayed match.

Victor Hall: There was but one occasion in Mr Mahon's career with Everton when the magic of his speech fell on deaf ears. It was the occasion of what has sometimes been described as 'the riot at Goodison Park.' An unruly number of people had taken from entry of the ground, when the gates where thrown open on the abandonment of a certain match – they had clustered round the official demanding their money back. Most of them had paid nothing, but got in when the gates were thrown open. Mr Mahon addressed them from the balcony of the club pavilion, offering them free tickets for the replayed match, if they would wait their distribution. His voice did not carry very far over their angry cries and it was only when they commenced to pull down the palisades and shatter the windows that the police held in reserve were let loose to deal with the disturbance, which they did accordingly with promptitude and dispatch. That is the only time George Mahon ever spoke ineffectually at an Everton meeting.

Thomas Keates: The howling intensified, with the clamour for money. Stones were thrown at Mr Mahon, one of them smashing the thick glass of the clock over his head. As the situation worsened the policemen on duty called for assistance. While they waited for reinforcements to arrive, 'Showers of stones flew about, every pane of glass in the office windows was broken, and the woodwork was smashed and used as weapons. A crowd made for the grandstand, and a cry of 'Fire the stands' was heard . . . Pandemonium reigned and dreadful damage was imminent. [When police arrived they] drew their batons and at once attacked the mob. A momentary show of resistance was made, but batoned heads and bodies soon affected a panic-stricken rush to the gates, with a clearance from the ground and its vicinity.

Will Cuff: Today [in 1949] the Everton ground is unequalled for covered accommodation, for its government in its gate control, and its 'homeliness.' It has so many features I cannot do more than skirt the main ones, such as the notification of 'Spectators take their own risk of weather.' This became necessary through the abandonment of a meeting of Everton and Small Heath when spectators demanded their money back. Since then every ground has borne this forewarning notification.

Everton's nineteenth century heroes

Victor Hall: The agents whom Everton employed in Scotland to report on promising debutants who were willing to migrate south, were constantly urged to leave no stone unturned to secure the signature for an English League form of those younger men, whose fame had already been recognised by international and other honours in their active Scotland. The agents were paid a fixed fee of £10 for each player of note whom they were instrumental in signing for the wealthier English clubs.

Dan Kirkwood: I had been recommended to the Everton club by old comrade [Dan] Doyle, who had also come to terms with them, and one of the directors – Mr Brooks – came stealthily by night to the village, under his guidance. Doyle pointed out the house where I lived, and taking advantage of the darkness Mr Brooks gained admission unobserved. That night I had gone to a country fair, known as Falkirk 'Tryst,' and my old mother – a typical Scotch dame – was alone in the kitchen. 'Is Dan at home?' said Mr Brooks. 'Nae, he's gan awae to see't 'Tryst.' 'To see Christ!' Gasped Mr Brooks in amazement, whose acquaintance with the Scotch accent was very limited. It required some little effort to make matters plain, but eventually this was accomplished.

Victor Hall: An example of type that was akin to genius – outstanding genius as that, let me recall 'Johnny' Holt, the Everton centre half-back. If you ask in which of these degrees Johnny Holt excelled, I answer at once – 'in all' – and in twice as many!' To give a faint picture of his style. Remember he was not tall. 'Little' Johnny Holt was his pet name – he was four or five inches below the average height, and he often played against exceptionally tall centre-forwards. He enjoyed that. Almost invariably when the opposite side got a goal kick – Johnny got the ball. He generally stood a few yards from the centre-forward, who, conscious of his own height – waited for the goal kick to 'come' to him. Holt made no movement until the ball was in the air – and dropping; then like a flash his body shot up into the air. Most often his hands rested on the startled centres' shoulders for an instant of time – getting an 'impetus' of a 'poise' whichever he needed. And his head headed the ball; often two feet higher in the air than the six-foot 'centres' below him. Holt's 'heading' was miraculously exact – he seldom headed a pinpoint out of direction, but he headed to his own forwards, and straight away his side were attacking again! He worthily served his club and his country, and was never out of form.

Johnny Holt: It cost Everton nothing to secure my services. I played for them for nine years, and then when I wished to make a change they asked for £300 for my transfer. They practically barred me from playing in the north, for naturally a man could not be worth that to any club after having played for so long. I may state that New Brighton offered Everton £135 for my transfer and Burnley were prepared to pay £200. Consequently I had to come south out of reach of the transfer fees. Directly I had signed for Reading I received a telegram from Everton to come and meet the secretary of Clyde Football Club. The two clubs had agreed about my transfer. It had been arranged without my consent, and then it was too late.

Sam Crosbie: At one game we noticed a player circling around as if very dizzy. Jack Bell ran to him, took hold of his head, put his shoulders between his knees, pulled his head with all his might, and in a few minutes the player joined the game. It turned out he had dislocated his neck and would have been a dead man in a few minutes had not Jack Bell adjusted the dislocation.

Victor Hall: The club-fellows of the Dumbarton club stood out, figuratively, head and shoulders above every other contemporary player in Scotland about that time. One was Dicky Boyle a right half back, the other his club mate John Bell, a centre-forward. Boyle was slim in build, but sturdy, and of admirably proportioned physique. Fair to a fault in his play, he never gave the appearance of great speed, and yet he was speedy, and could turn quickly, and get off the mark with the fleetest winger he had to tackle. He was extremely good to judging pace in both ball and man and wise to a degree in weighting up the style of play of his opponents and quickly adapting himself to watch and eventually combat that style. Bell was a forceful and robust physique, of dauntless courage, fleet of foot, a deadly shot and, above all, a skilled tactician and a glutton for work. Added in these natural gifts, he was of regular health and active temperament and devoted to his trade – engineering. Can you imagine the bow every 'agent' in Scotland held an open league form and practically a blank cheque in his pocket-book for the lucky day when he should attach the signature of 'Bell of Dumbarton'? John Bell was at that time easily the most successful and most respected forward playing football in Scotland.

Thomas Keates: Jack Southworth was transferred from Blackburn Rovers to Everton [in 1893]. He has been described by competent judges as the best of all centre-forwards but his outstanding achievement was performed after he had joined Everton, when, within ten days, he was responsible for 15 of 22 goals scored in four matches, including six in succession against west Bromwich Albion. He was transferred to Everton for what was described as 'the handsome sum of £400.' With Geary and Southworth as centre-forwards the position of Everton was enviable.

Victor Hall: 'From the succeeding centre Geary scored, giving the goalkeeper no chance to save.' These lines might almost have been kept in type by the newspapers that reported football matches in the days when Freddie Geary was the idol of every follower of League football in England. Fred Geary was the smallest of them all. Splay-footed, broad-shouldered, this son of Nottingham came, saw, conquered, and to this day has the eye of a hawk when handling his beloved bowls on the green. As to the individual style of Geary's play he generally lay well forward in the centre of the field – never 'offside' – but ready for the first swinging centre that came in either half-back or forwards. As it came towards him he seemed without a glance to know instinctively just where his own forwards where and how the opposing defence were placed, and before the ball touched the ground it was lifted in the required direction for either a colleague to take or for a dash forward 'on his own.' Therein lay another of his gifts. He could get up speed instantly. To say that he was off 'like a shot' may be a figure of speech, but certainly if Fred wanted to take his own forward pass he was through the backs' almost as quick as the ball he had passed; and he was instantly careering towards goal with the defence failed out behind, and his own wing men narrowing in for the rebound or the goalkeeper's 'kick out' if the first time shot should miss.

Sam Crosbie: Fred Geary came with a great reputation for speed and dribbling – a popular idol at once; his runs placing the ball in the net created a sensation.

Victor Hall: There was a personality about the famous 'left wing' of the Everton team of the '90's that led people – especially their own followers – to speak and think of them always as a 'pair.' Just as one would speak of something that together forms a 'pair' and apart, would be just 'odd' ones. So people always spoke of Chadwick and Milward as the 'left wing!' If through injury or illness, or other cause, one or other of the two stood down, then the 'left wing' for that day at least, was not playing, and the surveyor had another partner for that match, but the Everton left wing was 'away' for the day. Yet, individually, each of the pair were brilliant in their respective positions, but when playing together, one could say today, with little fear of exaggeration, their combination and perfect understanding has never since been equally.

Dan Kirkwood: Never have I seen finer forward work than that which was shown by the Everton front rank of those days. Latta, Brady, Geary, Chadwick and Milward were a wonderful combination and I think the best display they ever gave was at Pike's Lane, when we defeated Bolton Wanderers by five goals to none. The Wanderers were a convincing force then, and included such players as Davenport, Brogan, and Bob Roberts, but they were helpless against us. Another famous victory was that at Blackburn, where I played centre-forward in the first half, and Parry took the same place after the change of ends.

Victor Hall: Nothing was more entertaining to the club's spectators than to see Milward at full gallop down the touch line – his arms whirling in a mad ecstasy of sheer delight, outpacing every yard the panting defence with the faithful Edgar loping along fifteen or twenty yards in the rear and slanting in towards goal for the pass he knew would come with mathematical accuracy once Milward had reached the required spot on the goalline. In Milward, Edgar Chadwick found that ideal partner with the necessary speed and dash that gave his own play its exact complement. Without Milward's strategy and impelling forcefulness, most of Chadwick's midfield work would have been wasted, but equally with any partner but Chadwick-Milward might conceivably never have reached first rank, and most certainly would not have retained a premier position for so long. To see Edgar Chadwick in play was to realise for the first time what the art of 'dribbling' really meant.

Will Cuff: Friends have asked me for my stepping stones toward the high station of football life. They began when I was elected a member of the Everton Club in 1890 before the club was formed into a limited liability company. Everton broke away in 1892, and when a move was made to Goodison Park, I applied for and got shares [3]. At the annual general meeting there was a distinct rumpus – there were many collisions of interests from that day to the present – and I was elected to the Everton board in 1895. In 1901, I was elected secretary of the club owing to the resignation of the late Richard Molyneux and continued in that office until 1918, war-time spell, when I resigned through my legal profession growing to a point which made it difficult to carry on with the football club position. The late William

Sawyer succeeded me as honorary secretary, and I returned to the board in 1921, became chairman in 1922, and continued in that position until 1938. In 1948 I resigned from the Everton board. These, then, are the milestones in a football life of intense interest, instruction and enjoyment.

Victor Hall: Bob Kelso had none of the individualisms of some of the more famous of his contemporaries but he had an all-round adaptability that made him a safe player in whatever position he played, and to a selection committee that is the type who is a most valued asset. To be able at short notice to have a player who can 'fit' into whatever position of responsibility comes vacant is an advantage that can be easily realised and Kelso, in most of his playing career at Everton, had that exceptional gift.

10 April 1897
FA Cup final
The Crystal Palace
Everton 2, Aston Villa 3

Victor Hall: Perhaps the greatest game of John Bell's English career was the final English Cup tie against Aston Villa at the Crystal Palace in April, 1897, when Villa won by 3 goals to 2 in the match that has since been often described as the best played final for the last thirty years. For the interest of students we may repeat the Everton team; Menham; Meehan, and Storrier; Boyle, Holt and Stewart; Taylor, Bell, Hartley, Chadwick, and Milward. In the second minute of the game Holt received an accidental kick in the chest from Charlie Athersmith and for the remainder of the game played in great agony. When the fortunes of the play turned against Everton, John Bell played the game of his career, and Peter Meehan, coming up among the forwards, fed and passed, and struggled with Bell and the other Everton forwards to pierce the sturdy Villa defence. But Whitehouse in goal and Howard Spencer and Evans were impassable.

Thomas Keates: The club had got together an array of talented players for every position, except in goal and the weak link in the chain cost the side dearly. The Club met Aston Villa in the famous 1897 English Cup Final, the best played final up to that year. Everton lost 3-2 and, as was generally admitted, through feeble goalkeeping.

Will Cuff: There was nearly a riot in the dressing room through a football smash-and-grab incident. Everton were on the losing end that day and the whole Aston Villa team went into the Everton dressing room after the game demanding the ball be handed back to them. They had seen an Everton player gather the ball and rush off to the Crystal Palace dressing rooms. Everton players declared they did not know where the ball was. Villa players searched boots, the skip, every nook and cranny, knowing the ball must be somewhere around there. Their search was useless, for an Everton player, realising the difficulty of hiding his treasure, had taken out his penknife the moment he got back to the dressing room and slit the ball, and was proudly going around the Villa players taunting them to 'Well, find the ball and you can have it.' Actually he was wearing it under his football jersey – as a chest protector! Years after he mellowed and handed his 'trophy' to Fred Geary the famous little centre-forward of Everton who proceeded to hand it over to the Aston Villa management when they came our way to play a league game. The strange sight of the ball was worthy of your attention – it was a seamless ball, and the like of that ball has never been used since, although many a man of genius has tried to invent a ball without seams. So ended the chest protector in its many miles of travel – in the boardroom at Aston.

Everton ensure Liverpool's relegation in 1904

Alex Raisbeck: The match which sealed our fate was one in which we were not engaged. Stoke, who were running us neck-and-neck, as it were, for relegation had to play Everton at Goodison Park. It ought to have been a pinch for Everton as they were well up in the League and were very hard nuts to crack on their own ground. To the surprise of everybody, however, Stoke won the match and our fate was sealed. The result did not please everyone, as you will imagine, and I heard at the time that a great number of Everton's ticket-holders tore their tickets up after the game and swore they would never go to Goodison again.

Everton challenge for a league and FA Cup double in 1905 – and end up with nothing

Thomas Keates: Shakespeare wrote of 'The uncertain glory of April.' This April is remembered as a shocker.

Jack Sharp: I think the best team Everton had during my eleven seasons as a player at Goodison Park was in 1905, the season in which Aston Villa beat us in the Cup semi-final at Nottingham after a draw at Stoke. We were all over Villa on that occasion. In the same season Newcastle United beat us by one point for the League Championship. Everton were so unfortunate to be so beaten, as the Championship would have been theirs but for the abandonment through fog of a match at Woolwich in which they were leading 3-1 when the game was stopped seven minutes from time. Woolwich [Arsenal] won 1-0 in the replay.

21 April 1906
The Crystal Palace
FA Cup Final
Everton 1, Newcastle United 0

Alex Raisbeck: My best season with the Reds was undoubtedly 1905/06. We won the Liverpool Cup, League Championship and London Charity Shield, while we were only beaten by our near and dear neighbours, Everton, in the semi-final of the English Cup. The Cup tie took place on the Aston Lower Grounds, now the Villa Park. It was a very unfortunate day for Liverpool.

Arthur Goddard: Alex Raisbeck was the most outstanding player in the semi-final at Villa Park. He was magnificent, and so was Sam Hardy, the greatest goalkeeper I ever saw.

Sam Hardy: That was the greatest cup tie in which I have ever played... memories of every kick in the game will remain with me. It was at the same time, the greatest and the most disappointing. Yet, what a game! Think of it; Liverpool versus Everton, neighbouring clubs, and both eager to annex the trophy. Small wonder that 15,000 people travelled from Liverpool to Villa Park, Birmingham, to witness the fight, but, quite apart from local interest the ordinary football loving public were alive to the fact that the game would be worth seeing, and, altogether, there were 37,000 on the ground.

Joe Hewitt: I think I played the game of my life, Harry Makepeace could do nothing with me. I sent across a stream of centres which should have given us a three-goal lead, but in the end we were beaten 2-0 by Everton.

Sam Hardy: The battled ruled fast and furious for sixty-five minutes before a goal was scored. Then, Abbott, the Everton half, had a shot, which West, one of our backs, seeing that it was going behind, allowed to go. Dunlop, our other back, however, as if fascinated by the ball, had a kick, in the excitement of the moment, diverted it into the net before I had a chance to get anywhere near.

Joe Hewitt: I can well remember Everton's first goal. It was a long lob by Abbott, which Dunlop tried to high kick and sliced the ball beyond Hardy, who was left helpless.

Sam Hardy: But for this the ball would have gone behind, and we were all left so astonished that before we quite realised it Everton swept down and scored again.

Joe Hewitt: The winner, I will never forget. Sharp had centred right across the goal face, and Hardman came dashing in to ram the ball home at great speed, and actually followed the ball into the net. It's a wonder the Everton amateur did not break his neck.

Thomas Keates: Newcastle on previous form were fancied to win [the subsequent final]. They were giants compared to the Everton players, who were nearly all on the small side, but sturdy and nippy.

Will Cuff: Newcastle in those days were not bothered with transfer calls; every man was a friend of the other player, and the methodical style adopted by Newcastle made the eleven the most difficult side in the land to beat.

George Bailey: It was a tremendous event for a lad of eleven. It was my first time in London and my eyeballs were popping out when I got my first sight of all the glass. The other memory I have is of the hansom cabs and their drivers opening the roof and shouting down 'Where are you going, sir?'

Thomas Keates: Up to twenty minutes from the finish there was no score. Suddenly sensation intervened. Taylor passed the ball to Settle, the inside left, who sent on to Sharp, the outside-right. In a twinkling it was tipped to Sandy who banged it into the net.

George Bailey: I was too young to have a recollection of the match itself, but all that mattered was that Everton beat Newcastle 1-0. I was left breathless by all the excitement and didn't remember a thing about the train journey home. I was fast asleep but very happy.

Thomas Keates: Arriving at Central Station, a thunderstorm of cheering greeted Jack Taylor, Cup in hand, and his victorious comrades as they stepped from a saloon carriage. After a preliminary reception, on the platform, by the Lord Mayor, surrounded by football directors of Liverpool as well as Everton, a host of officials of other clubs and local notables, the Lord Mayor ascended a gorgeously-carpeted truck, and delivered a neat congratulatory oration that would have swelled the heads of ordinary mortals. But Jack and his comrades were not ordinaries. Conscious, however, that they were having the time of their lives, they were compelled to keep smiling, couldn't help it, if they could. From the station on a four-in-hand [the players outside], Jack Taylor, on the driver's seat, proudly waved the Cup to the cheering thousands that lined the route to Goodison Part, via Church Street, Whitechapel, Byrom Street and Scotland Road. The enclosure was crammed with enthusiasts. The team [escorted by mounted police] had a great reception. More ceremony, more speeches. Refreshments, a lull; fatigue, dispersal; followed by a welcome rest after a prolonged hour of glorious life.

Alex Raisbeck: Everton beat Newcastle so the League Championship and the Cup both came to Liverpool the same season. Our winning the Championship was greatly minimised by Everton's carrying off the Cup. As you know, a greater interest is taken in the Cup in England than in League doings. In fact, one would scarcely have known in Liverpool that we had won the League. Merseyside people went absolutely mad over the Cup coming to Liverpool for the first time.

Will Cuff: The boys of today cannot conceive the return of Everton FC, conquerors of the Cup in 1906. Liverpool went mad. The city had been buoyed up twice, before by 'Finalitis,' once at Manchester in a debating class with Wolves [in 1893] – and once more when Aston Villa won 3-2 at Crystal Palace [in 1897].

Stars of the early-twentieth century

Victor Hall: Few who ever saw Jimmy Settle play will forget the characteristic style of his footwork. There was always a grim whimsicality about his play, a tenacity of purpose, and, withal a suggestion that he saw fun and humour in getting of goals that escaped many of his fellow players. From the commencement to the finish of every game he was an electric needle of energy. The recollection will come back to thousands of memories of those sinuous twists and feints of his, those side taps and sudden turnings by which he missed the opposing players and worked himself into position. What a really enjoyable player, too, to watch in action.

Will Cuff: Sandy Young was a most remarkable young man – he had a Napoleonic strip of hair stretched across his forehead; light, lithesome, sombre, he was, at his prime, the best centre in the world. But he had his moody moments, and although he could recite every line of the Bible, he had other pleasures and sometimes these crossed his athletic path, so much so that at one period, he arrived back from Scotland and his summer holidays in a state that caused us to send him away for a month [suspension] to make himself fit.

Victor Hall: The brothers Bert and Jack Sharp are another instance of individual brilliancy budding and blossoming together in maturity, and associating together with the same club. The two brothers came to Everton together about the end of 1899/1900 season, and were early drafted into prominent playing positions in the league team. Jack, the younger as a forward, and Bert, the elder, in the rear division. The speed of Jack, speedily marked him for a distinguished career as a forward and, as all football historians are aware, that career took him eventually to the star position as a forward in the Everton club, and in 1903 brought his international cap against Ireland, and in 1905 crowned his football career with the international cap against Scotland. Bert Sharp played a long, sturdy and honourable career in the Everton ranks, not always in the League team, but dependable whenever he played, and while he did not attain the international distinction of his younger brother, he certainly left his career as a football player an honoured and distinctive one.

Will Cuff: It is my view that [Tommy] McDermott was the greatest of all inside forwards. His ability to wind himself round on a three penny piece and never lose control of the ball was a football feast served up to Everton followers as a meal-ticket which never failed to satisfy. There is a great joy in the smallish man holding the ball and twirling himself round to the consternation of the half-back. McDermott could also beat his rival without touching the ball, which is Stanley Matthews' greatest feature of forward play.

Victor Hall: It is curious to reflect how all the really great teams have found their soul in the middle line. Cast your memory back as you will to any of the brilliant teams that have shone for a season, or a number of seasons, and inevitably it will be realised that the half-backs line has been a line of intellect and untiring energy. Nothing also can make a team so surely, nothing can break a team so completely, as genius well directed, or mediocrity in the backbone division. In the combination of Tom Booth and Walter Abbott with Jack Taylor, there was the perfect assembly of rugged dour downright grit, with sure defensive instinct. That was Abbott. There was the shrewd incisive cool deliberation wedded to bold, fearless audacity. That was Booth. In Taylor was the gaunt determination to overcome every obstacle to the immediate end in the view, whether attack or defence.

Ernest 'Bee' Edwards: Players such as Settle, Sandy Young, McDermott, and co., were beginning to come to the end of their tether, I had an idea that Bert Freeman would be capable of picking up a lot of good football points from such as Settle and McDermott and that Everton by signing him would do a sensible stroke of business. He would learn more football trickery in five games with Settle and Young or Settle and Tommy McDermott than he would gain in five years with Woolwich Arsenal. Freeman was essentially a goal-getter. I never claimed for him that he was otherwise – then Everton wanted a goal-getter, and I so rammed home in my 'Notebook' the need for Everton to get Freeman's signature till the matter became as obnoxious to me as it did to my readers.

Will Cuff: Freeman was with Woolwich Arsenal, and was the subject of days of special pleading by 'Bee' that he should be signed – he was just what the Everton doctor wanted to replace Sandy Young. Freeman was watched by Director Bainbridge, who felt he was not the Everton style. It leaked out that he 'had scored Arsenal's four goals – but he did nothing else,' which makes rather laughable reading in the days when spectators, starved of goals, are not very concerned how they are made so long as they are made.

Ernest 'Bee' Edwards: Generally speaking the folk didn't fancy him – they laughed at his darts forward and his funny little steps. The critics in certain quarters 'went' for me in a mild way and showed plainly enough that they would not have signed him if the matter had rested with them.

Will Cuff: Even the official programme of the date when Freeman played his second game said, 'We cannot see how Freeman can possibly fit into the Everton attack. Combination cannot be a feature with such a leader.' This was rather harsh foreboding. Freeman went on to break the existing goal record of Liverpool's Raybould – 38 goals in one season. He was duly barracked by the crowd when playing outside-left on an icy turf [after months off with a broken shoulder blade] and he was turned from Everton by spectators and became Burnley's leader, to score the final-tie goal against Liverpool on their only appearance [to date] in the final tie.

Ernest 'Bee' Edwards: Great was the scene when Freeman broke Sam Raybould's record and I shall not forget it in a hurry. But a crowd which had been well fed in the goal line cried for plenty of goals the next season. They did not realise that by making a record Freeman was making a rod for his own back.

His fame fed to his being marked in more than one sense of the term. I stood up for him hard and fast now, for he was asked to do too much and his reasonably good goal crop was not bad enough to be sacrificed. The matter cut another way if Freeman was being watched by more than one man whenever he put down his feet. Where were his co-forwards, and how was it they were not succeeding in splashing? It was not granted that Coleman and some others were showing still further signs of age. No, Freeman was the marked man. By the next season the crowd began to bark at him.

Jack Sharp: Bert Freeman required less help from anybody else than any centre I have seen and used to 'place' his scoring shots instead of shooting hard. He was a wonderful match winner.

Ernest 'Bee' Edwards: Former Everton 'guardians' have told him that they could not keep Freeman at Everton because the crowd had got at him. He had been tried at outside-left and shaped fairly well - he nearly always turned to the extreme left if his solo runs were likely to be baulked. However the plan of playing him in away matches was not tried and therefore the crowd's bark was as hard as its bite, the effect being that Everton decided to transfer Freeman. While Everton were getting knocked out at Glossop in the first round of the Cup Freeman was helping his club to start their famous walk to the 'Sportsman's Final' in 1914. Burnley won the Cup, Freeman scoring the only goal of the game against Liverpool.

20 April 1907
The Crystal Palace
FA Cup final
Everton 1, Sheffield Wednesday 2

William McGregor: I doubt if we have ever had a final in which there has been more loose play . . . [It was] one of the poorest finals.

Jack Sharp: We lost in the final with Sheffield Wednesday through an error of tactics in team selection. Wilson was left out of the side because he would not re-sign for the following season, and the players were very sore about it. He had played in all the other cup ties as partner to Hardman, while Jimmy Settle had been my partner on the other wing.

Will Cuff: I have often been asked to explain the bombshell which arose in one of our three cup final ties. Hence there follows the story of the George Wilson case. Geordie was a funny bundle of physical strength – short, tubby, yet speedy over ten yards, having a cracker shot, having a grand manner. He was one of the greatest inside forwards the game has known. He and his brother David were signed by Everton, and Geordie from Hearts soon fascinated the crowd. We had won the final tie against Newcastle United a year before and arrived at Crystal Palace for the second final issue – two appearances in successive years was something wonderful even in those days. We were keyed-up for this second appearance on the Crystal set. In the inner chambers, however, a little bird whispered that all was not well. Geordie would not sign. We talked with him, reasoned with him begged him to take his chance of a medal – no; he would not sign. Now, the club had ruled that no player could take the place in the final tie who had not signed for the following season. Geordie Wilson struck it to the bitter end, and on the morning of the match we had to bring in Hughie Bolton to fill the gap in the attack.

Jack Sharp: It was an awful blunder to leave Wilson out, as it not only weakened the team but affected morale. I feel sure we would have beaten the Wednesday if we had our best team out.

Will Cuff: We had no option. We had to be fair to all the Final tie side. This caused shareholders to introduce their now infamous phrase of 'Sack the lot.' It has been used at varying intervals ever since. 'Sack the directors!' Players were alleged to have said; 'We were not beaten by Sheffield Wednesday. The big D beat us' – meaning directors. The players said they were so upset at their favourites not being allowed to play they could not do themselves justice. Their hearts were broken. Certainly the Wilson versus directors case became a feud, and by the time the annual general meeting arrived, 90 per cent of the shareholders had their daggers drawn.

Thomas Keates: The Everton players at once evoked applause by their pretty passing, and fine combined movements that were delightfully deliberate and charming to watch; but in Cup finals these are frequently negative by a team which plays the rush game as opposed to dainty and scientific. The Sheffield contenders elected to play in the former style and were successful by two goals to one.

Will Cuff: Teams go out of the cup through the faintest of incident happenings – a throw-in at Crystal Palace cost us a cup tie versus Sheffield Wednesday. I can see burly Walter Abbott to this moment – away on the far side of the field. Not speedy in 1907, Walter refused to kick the ball into play for safety's sake. Walter hung on to the ball to try to skim it along the touchline – to keep play flowing. Walter was a dainty player, but he became leaden-footed, and the ball was snapped up, and straight-way the amateur Simpson of Sheffield, scored the winning goal.

Football business in the early years

Will Cuff: Quite the jauntiest and simplest transfer deal I can remember concerned two great Irish friends. We wanted a broth of a boy named William Lacey. Now we had on our books Val Harris. I went to Dublin, arriving at 7.30am and said to Val Harris; 'Is Lacey here?' 'Yes, sorr,' said Val, 'Bring him in,' The pair appeared in the hotel. 'Would you like to play for Everton?' I asked Lacey, 'I would that, sorr,' said the big boy, 'Sign here then,' said I, and within sixty seconds the deal was done, no argument, no questioning of promises – and that was the quickest transfer I can remember.

Thomas Keates: Transfer fees in the pre-war period were trifling compared with the large sums demanded and paid now [in 1928]. For instance, at the close of the last century, two first class players, one an expert, were transferred to Everton by one of the leading League clubs for £400. Now £3000 for one player is frequently paid. In some cases a much larger amount – even £10,000 has been given currency, paid or not.

Will Cuff: In those days team changes were uncommon, except in the case of injury – a team of 1 September was the team for the season, and local people will recall how the names of Makepeace, Taylor, Abbott, would roll off the tongue; just as the forward formation of Sharp, Bolton, Young, Settle, H.P. Hardman, became famous by their constant appearance in the team-sheet. In those days teams picked themselves, to a great degree, and today it would puzzle any fervid partisan of a club, other than those at the top posts of the league, to rattle off the names of the team that 'plays for Stoke'.

Jack Sharp: Everton have always maintained a good standard of football. You may be curious to know how that has come about. Well, my explanation of it is that they look at a man's character before they take him on. Everton play good, clean football, and the club's traditions in that respect are like those of Aston Villa and Newcastle – as being amongst the most scientific and cleanest sides in the game.

Will Cuff: Everton became one of the richest clubs in the country, through its measured step towards high-grade football, and building up the stands and under arches for the benefit of their public, together with the signing of good-class players who would play the game for their credit's sake. We had our standards of play and our standards of players, and when it was my duty to try to sign a player I generally took along with me one of our players, so that the 'wanted man,' could see our type and our standard.

Outbreak of World War I and Everton's second league title win

Thomas Keates: The situation was bristling with perplexities for everybody. The directors decided to be guided by public opinion, in conjunction with the League and Football Association. To the impulsive, panic-stricken section of the community, the idea of any entertainments, or sporting games being tolerated, was unthinkable. The experienced governing bodies of the country were soon convinced that the wise and sound policy was to carry on, as far as it was possible, as usual. Every suspension would create additional unemployment, undermine the courage of the population, and be commercially and economically disastrous. Diversion and cheering entertainment was found to be the most essential tonic and sustainer for the men at the front as well as for those by the home fires.

Despite winning just eight home games all season, Everton crept to the League Championship in April 1915 by a single point, after their main title rivals, Oldham Athletic, capitulated at the last. Bobby Parker scored an astonishing 35 league goals in his 35 appearances for Everton. By then, however, the Great War was in its ninth month and the death toll was rapidly mounting. The Football League had initially bought into the 'over by Christmas' mentality and did not suspend its programme. But as fighting continued and the country was overcome by jingoism, this became a cause for antagonism and football was dubbed 'unpatriotic' for carrying on when lives were being lost. It is perhaps for this reason that no interview or other documentary first hand account of Everton's second league title can be traced; indeed an entire book has been written on the subject and the author drew a similar blank in finding contemporaneous voices. It is as if Everton's 1914/15 title win was considered a 'dirty secret', never to be spoken of.

William Ralph 'Dixie' Dean

League football resumed for the 1919/20 season, but over subsequent seasons Everton failed to mount sustained challenges at the top of the First Division and at one stage even flirted with relegation. Their fortunes changed in March 1925 with a £3000 signing from Tranmere Rovers.

William Ralph 'Dixie' Dean: I went to a matinee at the pictures and when I got home my mother told me that [the secretary] Tom McIntosh of Everton wanted me to go down to the Woodside Hotel to have a word with him and off I went. I didn't look for a tram… I got shifting, running. It must have been the quickest two miles ever! When I arrived there was Mr McIntosh, the Everton secretary, waiting. We shook hands and he said to me, 'I'd like you to come to Everton.' I hardly believed it. It was the greatest delight of my life. I agreed straight away.

Will Cuff: He had a body balance not given to many forwards. Sturdy of frame, he was brought up on football at his school, and would play three games a day if need be. When at Tranmere he was surveyed by 'Bee' in prophetic words that rang true 15 years after they were written. In my view, Dean was the complete centre-forward, and in heading the ball he had the facility that has come to no one since the days of Sandy Turnbull [an inside forward who played at the start of the century with Manchester City and United].

Thomas Keates: Everton are to be congratulated on their acumen in securing him from Tranmere Rovers in the face of competition from 20 clubs. His remarkable record in league and representative football is well known. He is by no means a selfish player but the question is frequently asked [in 1928]: 'What would Everton be without Dean?'

Will Cuff: I recall that his first game was at Arsenal's ground, and he was described in a Liverpool paper as 'a passenger' – which was not exactly kind or constructive criticism of a boy of 18 who had never seen a First Division match and had never seen London – couldn't sleep a wink at nights through nervous strain. I mention these facts because I feel spectators and press critics should take every consideration with players, and especially with new players, lest they spoil a career. It is sufficient to remind ourselves that Dean and his helpers [the whole of the side] helped to make Everton's fame and fortune.

Dick White: He came in that first season and scored goals straight away. I think he scored 33 goals in that first full season, but then he had a terrible motorcycle accident and we all wondered if he would ever play again. There was a near panic amongst the Everton fraternity. My father and uncle would meet up every Sunday night at our house and talk football and racing. The mood was very gloomy. My father was in the police force and through his contacts knew that this accident was a very serious one. I think at that time everyone was very shocked. Of course he did, but the story going around was that he'd had a metal plate inserted into his head, which added to his heading prowess. I don't think the heading power was down to any plate; he just had a natural genius.

Cliff Britton: Dean was the finest header of the ball I have ever seen. The beauty of his play in the air was his delicacy of touch. He could come to the near post and, with superb judgment of the finest of angles, flick the ball into the net by the far post.

Will Cuff: In heading ability I doubt if anyone could be anywhere near him, because he had the lost art of adding pace to the ball when heading it, and his capacity for turning the ball from his curly locks was monumental. Goalkeepers have told me they would have bet pounds he could not head the ball beyond them 'at that angle' but instead they found he placed the ball better with his head than many modern [players] place the ball with their boots.

William Ralph 'Dixie' Dean: The secret of heading is to catch it on your forehead. If you get it on top of your head it will knock you dead in no time. I was not as tall as many of the centre-halves I have played against, but I never had any difficulty beating them in the air. It wasn't a matter of leaping higher than they could. It was just a matter of going up at the right time.

Dick White: Not only did he score with his head, he used it to bring other players into the game. The ball could be kicked out of defence and with unerring accuracy he could head towards either corner flag to bring into play the wingers. That was part of his game: when he got the ball he didn't just head straight to goal, he brought everyone else in. And of course he was very powerful, he could shield and hold the ball up.

Charles Mills senior: All the teams played with four forwards at that time, at least until Alex James's Arsenal came along, which may have added to his prowess. He had a winger, Alec Troup, who had this ability to hang the ball up in the air, which would give Dean a moment to decide where the ball was going to go. Dixie also had this ability to hang in the air, almost like he was standing still.

Dick White: On the other wing was Ted Critchley, who didn't have the ability to hang the ball in the air, but could cross accurately and with pace. It only needed the slightest flick of the head off a fast-moving ball and it would be a goal.

Will Cuff: Dean's heading prowess was the envy of his comrades. It was not so much that he headed the ball, but that he added pace to the ball, and could flight it, angled toward goal with a surety that led him to be the most dangerous leader goalkeepers faced. He did not make spectacular nods – it was more of an edging that brought him his goals – he looked that way, and said, 'I'll put it there,' and the ball went to the appointed spot – and goalkeepers know there is nothing more awkward for a goalkeeper to save than a header going away from him.

Dick White: We knew that we had a legend. Everybody was talking about him, his name was on every man's lips, even Liverpudlians. I can remember, I used to go and watch a local team in Clubmoor and they had a centre-forward who had shaped himself on the great man, even to the point of his hairstyle — I don't know how he did it — but they used to call him 'Dixie'. He dominated the scene on Merseyside.

Barbara Garner: My father was born in 1904 and was the youngest of eight children living in Everton, so of course they were absolutely passionate about Everton Football Club. He played himself with one of his brothers, near St Domingo's, somewhere up that way. But he didn't actually go to the matches because he couldn't afford to, they didn't have the money. They used to hang around outside. And I think he actually saw Dixie Dean with the team coming back from something where they'd been successful, and he ran alongside with his brother. All the kids were running around shouting to Dixie. He was so impassioned about Dixie Dean. Eventually when I had a son, when I was going off to have this child, I said, 'I'm going to call him after you dad,' and he said, 'No, call him William Ralph Dean.' But I didn't! He was a young lad who just grew up in that atmosphere in that part of the city.

Will Cuff: He scored momentous goals – at Hampden Park, at Wembley, in internationals, at home, and in his record bag of 60, but to my mind the best he scored was that at Aston Villa's ground when he back-headed a ball to beat the Villa's goalkeeper, who had advanced at least 12 yards out of his goal. Dean with his back to the goal, threw back his head and scored what the locals believed was a sheer fluke but to those who knew the man and his accuracy there was never a doubt that this was an intentional headed goal, made by the genius who could do everything with a ball, especially when it was placed towards his head.

William Ralph 'Dixie' Dean: There was nothing like quietening the Kop. When you stuck a goal in there it all went quiet, apart from a bit of choice language aimed in your direction! Scoring there was a delight to me. I just used to turn round to the crowd and bow three times . . . Everton have always been noted for going on the pitch to play football. We got called the 'School of Science' quite rightly. The other lot, the Reds . . . well, they were a gang of butchers! . . . They should have been working in the abattoir. McNab, McKinlay, the Wadsworths. God bless my soul. They'd kick an old woman! I had some great fun, though, with the lot of them.

Thomas Keates: When Everton played their last match at Goodison Park [in the 1927/28 season] their position as champions was secured. It eased the strain that risk of displacement would have entailed; but another motive inspired the team to play for all they were worth – to gain the record of goals by a single player, for their forward, the marvellous Dean.

William Ralph 'Dixie' Dean: There was a bit of fun attached to it. I needed ten goals from the last four games! I thought to myself, 'I'll have to get a move on here' but I just seemed to take it in my stride… I scored one in our win over Newcastle and then I bagged another couple when we beat Aston Villa 3-2. I still needed seven from the last two matches and it was off to Burnley for the next one… I got four before half time.

Thomas Keates: Dean had already astonished football by scoring 57 goals in league matches. Who could wish for more? Where did the incitement come in? It came in here. There was a fly in the ointment. Camsell, a Middlesbrough second division centre-forward had scored 59 goals the previous season.

Dick White: I kept saying to my father, in the week leading up to that game, 'Hey, Dad, we're going to have to be up there early.' My father was never a man to hurry, though. Although he was no longer a policeman he had that majestic, slow policeman's gait — he walked that pace everywhere. And he always insisted that I went up to the ground with him. We lived ten, fifteen minutes' walk away from Goodison, but you wouldn't believe, on this particular day, he still left at the same time and insisted I was with him in case I got lost! We walked up to the ground, along Walton Lane, up Bullens Road and into Gwladys Street. The old boys' pen was on the Bullens Road, just around the corner of Gwladys Street, and my father always paid his bob [1s., or 5p in today's money] and stood under the clock [on the corner of Gwladys Street and Goodison Road]. We got to the corner, he put his hand in his pocket and produced fourpence, which was what it cost to get in the boys' pen, and said: 'Now, at the end of the game, meet me on the corner, by that lamp-post.' I said, 'Yes, all right, Dad, I'll be there.' And off he went and I got in the queue.

William Ralph 'Dixie' Dean: I got off the tram and walked along Goodison Road and into the ground. I got there nice and handy as a matter of fact. As Huddersfield had lost during the week we were champions whatever happened. In fact, the trophy was sitting there at the front of the directors' box ready to be presented to our captain, Warney Cresswell, after the match.

Dick White: When I was within five boys of the front of the queue, disaster struck. The gates shut. I was distraught. I'd been looking forward to this for weeks, months. It was history in the making. I was weeping and all sorts of things were going through my mind. Shall I go home? Or shall I wait until three-quarter time [when they opened the turnstiles]? If Dad comes out and I'm not here, he'll be worried, so I'll have to wait . . . Tears streamed down my face. Then this gentleman was walking along, and stopped, and looked at me. 'What's the matter with you?' he asked. So I unburdened my sorry tale on him. 'How much money have you got?' he asked. 'Fourpence,' I said. 'Well, you need a shilling to get in,' he told me. 'Yes,' I said. 'I know.' And he gave me eight pence! I don't think I even thanked him! I legged it to the nearest turnstile, paid my shilling and fought my way through this mass of people behind the Gwladys Street goal, around to the far side, as near as I could get to the players subway, and fought my way down, almost to the well.

Will Cuff: Dean got one goal from a penalty – how he rushed up to take that spot-kick awarded by the referee from Worcester, as if anyone else had dared to think of taking the penalty kick! Two goals to Dean and still the task appears abundantly impossible. Arsenal would not give him a goal, they didn't want it to be said, 'Dean scored three against Arsenal and thus broke the world record.' Time passed on. One felt like asking the referee to order extra time if need be!

William Ralph 'Dixie' Dean: I needed three goals against Arsenal, who were the greatest club in the land. But that didn't worry me whatsoever. I always used to think, 'I'm better than you.' [After the penalty] I could hear a voice inside me saying, 'Well, that's two you've got.'

Will Cuff: Finally the chance came, and Dean having worked more solo than in any other match in his life, had hardly the strength left in his worn-out body and limbs to take the chance. GOAL!

William Ralph 'Dixie' Dean: Alec Troup took the corner from the left and it came absolutely perfect for me. I ran in from outside the area to head it and the ball flew into the net. That was it. The record.

Thomas Keates: You talk about explosions and loud applause. We have heard many explosions and much applause in our loud pilgrimage, but, believe us, we have never heard before such a prolonged roar of thundering congratulatory applause as that which ascended to heaven when Dixie broke his record.

Will Cuff: Dean's sixtieth goal was one of the outstanding joys of any Evertonian's life. The conclusion of the game was quite the most pantomimical of my memory. Picture the situation, Arsenal, then famous and in the Chapman grip. The last game of the season. A sunny day, ball lively, ground dry and dustyish. Charles Buchan – quite the outstanding personality of play at that date – is playing his last game before entering into journalism and broadcasting. Nearly 70,000 people have gone there to a see a personal triumph. But three goals when needed and when wanted are surely too much to expect. Players don't deliver goals to order, and although every player on the Everton side was prepared to hand the ball to Dean on a golden plate, the match did not travel quite like that.

William Ralph 'Dixie' Dean: Somebody ran on the pitch and stuck his whiskers in my face and tried to kiss me. Well! I'd never seen a supporter run on to the pitch until that day.

Will Cuff: Players leapt to the air. Dean's mother, seated in the press box upstairs, had prayed at the 70th minute that her only son should be granted 'just one more chance.' Many must have felt demented at the joy of their hero making a goal-drop that may stand for all football's history. There were some minutes left to complete this league game. No one cared a brass farthing. The ball? Anyone could have it. Play had stopped to all intents and purposes, and Arsenal players were so bewildered by the brake on the game that they did not take advantage of the chance of winning – they joined in the processes of wasting the moments.

Charles Buchan: There are many who believe that Arsenal sat back and allowed Dean to get the three goals that broke the record. I can assure them that nothing is further from the truth. For myself I wanted to go out on a winning note [it was Buchan's last game before retiring] just as I'd come in back in 1910. The Arsenal players wanted to help me in this by beating the new champions. It was a memorable day, one I shall remember as long as I live. Dean was then at the height of his powers. When he got the third, the Goodison Park crowd rose to him. It was a scene beyond description.

Will Cuff: It was the signal for the pantomime dames and gentry to take up their stance. The crowd raced on to the field, the game appeared as if it would never be restarted. Players leapt into the air, nobody cared a brass farthing for the remaining minutes of the match.

Thomas Keates: Dean's achievement was the dominant theme. The modest way in which he minimised his own success and insisted on his comrades being entitled to a big share of the praise was one of the charms of the fraternisation.

Dick White: I met my Dad after the match at the lamppost. 'Wonderful to see the great man get his record,' he said. 'Yes, Dad,' I replied. 'But I very nearly missed it.' So I told him the story and he stopped, and looked at me. 'He gave you eight pence?' he said. 'Yes.' 'EIGHT PENCE! You know what that would buy? [It would probably have paid for about four pints.] 'Who was he?' 'I don't know, Dad. He just came and saw me.' 'Did you thank him, then?' 'I don't remember.' For weeks after, he'd show me to people and tell the story, and he'd always end it with: 'And this unknown man gave him eight pence!'

1929/30: Everton are relegated

Just two years after Everton's Dean-inspired League Championship win, the unthinkable happened – Everton were relegated to the Second Division.

William Ralph 'Dixie' Dean: The season we went down we didn't play too well. Not by any means. There's no getting away from the fact. As far as I was concerned I still managed to score a few even though I was in and out of hospital and nursing home with injuries. I spent a lot of time in those places. To me, from fairly on in that season it seemed we were destined to go down. We couldn't save ourselves. All our injuries started to take their toll.

Dick White: It was poverty that saw them go down. Poverty of ideas. Everything that could go wrong did go wrong.

Ted Sagar: On the fateful afternoon when Everton went down into the Second Division for the first time in their history, Mr Cuff, the chairman of the club said: 'We will be back next year in the First Division.' It was a well-founded confidence rather than wistful thinking. Mr Cuff never lost confidence in the team. There was no panic at Goodison Park. The spirit of the officials was, 'bad luck, boys. It is just one of those things. You were good enough, but things didn't go right.' There were no recriminations, no scapegoats, and it was the boardroom spirit as much as the play on the field that enabled the Blues to get out of the Second Division after only one season. Football form and fortune are peculiar. Here was practically the same team taking all before them in the Second Division when twelve months previously they could hardly put a foot right.

Dick White: In the final games of the season they reaped an enormous number of points [nine from the last ten available], which, if it had come a few games earlier, would have seen them alright.

In the 1930/31 season Everton lifted the Second Division title with five games to spare, scoring 121 goals along the way and reaching the FA Cup semi-final, which they narrowly lost to West Bromwich Albion.

Warney Cresswell: Second Division football is very hard. There is a lot of rushing football played. A greater amount of that, that is, than in the First Division. The reason for this is that there are more players in Second Division teams who lack experience, and who try to make up by sheer hard work what they lack in football skill. But the side which decides to carry on playing good football is the most likely to get back. The decision to play in the same way when we went down to the Second Division was made by the officials and the players of Everton. To a large extent even the same players were kept in the side. And the policy paid. We got back with something to spare.

Ted Sagar: There was the usual celebration dinner at which Mr Cuff rightly remarked that equally as important as the winning of the championship was the reputation for sportsmanship which the Blues had left on every ground they had visited in the Second Division. Footballers are not known as after-dinner speakers, but several of the boys revealed hidden talents in that direction on this festive occasion.

Upstaging the Great Dixie

Tom [Tiny] Bradshaw: It is usually difficult to remember individual matches, but one can't forget a Liverpool v Everton cup-tie [in 1932]. Everton were then doing very well and scoring a bundle of goals every week in the First Division. We expected to be flattened out and Everton started well when Dixie Dean, whom I had the responsibility of watching, put them in the lead.

Jimmy McDougall: At that time Everton were going great guns, scoring seven and eight goals a match, and our policy was to stop their gallop, but lo and behold Dixie Dean had the ball in our net in a matter of seconds. It certainly looked as though our policy was going to be torn to rags and tatters.

Tom [Tiny] Bradshaw: We eventually settled down and our outside-left, Gunson, made it 1-1 at the interval. There was naturally a very tense atmosphere as we struggled for the lead and there was tremendous enthusiasm among the Liverpool supporters when Gordon Hodgson headed the winner home from a cross from the left.

Jimmy McDougall: It was a hard game, not a great game, just a typical cup-tie – backwards and forwards. Dean was right at the peak of his form, but we managed to hold the scoring machine to that goal. In fact, Everton had a great side out so it was very pleasant to put a stop to their triumphal march.

Tom [Tiny] Bradshaw: There was talk at the time of Elisha Scott going to Everton but he was 100 per cent Liverpool. He was the most excited man in the dressing room at the end, and one of my memories is of Elisha throwing his boots up to the ceiling in sheer joy.

Everton win the 1932 League Championship

Ted Sagar: Late on in the season we beat Leicester 1-0 at Filbert Street and some of the newspapers said I won the match but it was a team victory. No team of individuals can get far. We have had witness of that in many international games, when eleven players, ostensibly the best in the country in their respective positions just fail to weld into a team. Everton's championship belonged to no one player or group of players, but the whole of the playing staff, officials and board.

Dick White: What Everton did do the year they went down was invest in new players towards the end of that season that formed the basis for their future success: Tommy Johnson, Jock Thomson, Jimmy Dunn, Cliff Britton, Tommy White. They had spent money on some very good players. These were the men that would bring them success in consecutive years in the Second Division, the First Division and – who could forget! – the FA Cup.

1933 FA Cup Success

Ted Sagar: After we had beaten Newcastle in the Champions v Cup holders annual match [the Charity Shield] the chairman of the Newcastle team expressed the hope that Everton would follow the United's example and win the cup the following season. His words were to come true. Our league position throughout 1932/33 was comfortable without being as inspiring as the previous season, but somehow we felt that this was to be our Cup year. It is remarkable how a team's hunches do materialize. When we were coming off the field [in the fourth round match v Bury] I picked up a brooch bearing a miniature replica of the FA Cup, I regarded it as an omen and treasured it right up to Wembley. Prior to one cup tie, I had left home when I remembered I had left my charm behind. I dashed back for it even though I was in danger of missing the team.

William Ralph 'Dixie' Dean: Two seasons earlier we'd got to the semi-final of the Cup but lost 1-0 to West Brom at Old Trafford. They beat us with one of the lousiest goals you've ever seen. It cost us the chance of doing the double of Second Division Championship and FA Cup. In 1933 we reached the semi again, this time against West Ham at Molineux. The club knew we had a really good chance of doing something that year so the directors gave the go-ahead for us to go off on special training in Buxton.

Ted Sagar: When we played West Ham on 18 March 1933, they had several personalities including Vic Watson and Jim 'Man Mountain' Barrett, the centre half. We took the lead in the first half through Dunn, but before the interval Vic Watson equalised with a picture goal that almost sent the 'Hammers' supporters delirious. Morton put in a low centre from the wing, and although it appeared to me as though none of the United forwards could possibly reach it. Vic Watson the centre-forward, flung himself headlong and, with his body parallel with the ground, headed the ball into the net. In the second half Ted Critchley put in a centre which beat the goalkeeper, and although Barrett tried to breast the ball away he only succeeded in turning it into the net. It was ironical that Critchley, who scored the goal that put us into the final, should have been dropped for the Wembley game for which Geldard was fit, but Ted was twelfth man and received a medal.

Charles Mills senior: My father had a friend called Vin Nolan, who lived in Crosby. My father had got a ticket for himself – he'd sent one of his workers to go and queue for him; the fella had waited for about five hours – but Vin was without one. He went up to Goodison about three days before the final, and my Dad warned him he would never get one. 'There's thousands of people who haven't got hold of one, you'll stand no chance.' Anyway, Vin went up to the ground and came back quite bumptious. 'I got my ticket,' he said. 'How did you manage that?' asked my father. 'I saw Theo Kelly [then on the club's administrative staff].' 'How on earth did you do that?' 'Well I told the flunky that there was someone quite important to see him, and they led me in. Kelly didn't know who I was, so I said, 'It's me, Nolan, from Virginia Waters [an exclusive golf and country club, renowned for its connections to the nobility], you remember.' 'Ah, it's coming back,' said Kelly, who'd evidently never set foot in the place in his life but didn't want to lose face. Nolan then span him a whole list of imagined escapades – 'You were quite a hit with the ladies!' 'Remember the midnight bathing?'– the upshot of which was he got his ticket; he didn't even have to ask for it. 'You will of course be going to the final?' Kelly ventured. 'I would, but someone has let me down.' 'Oh you must have a ticket!' said Kelly, who proceeded to give him a complimentary one!

Will Cuff: The players in 1933 went into private quarters down south – in charge of them was placed out director, former captain and player for Everton, the late Mr Jack Sharp, who had uninterrupted control until the teams went on the field of play. Mr Sharp was one of them; he had played the game, he knew what it was like to attempt to gain sleep the night before a final tie. Teams should not be harassed by interlopers of any kind, and I can think of nothing worse than officialdom entering into the team's affairs for days before the final tie.

Ted Sagar: About an hour before the game still in mufti, we inspected the Wembley pitch which is perfection in football pitches. We received a greet cheer from the Everton fans who recognised us. Even among those roaring thousands I was able to pick out my wife in the stands and acknowledge her wave. Wembley is an occasion that one will never forget – tier after tier of good-humoured spectators stretching it seems right up to the sky; the colourful uniforms of the massed bands and the flashing glint of their polished instruments and most inspiring of all 92,950 voices raised in that soul-stirring hymn, 'Abide With Me'.

Will Cuff: Cresswell icy cool in a thousand games in his lifetime, found the inside rooms of Wembley a trouble to his stomach muscles. He asked a policeman if here was a private room near by the dressing room where he could have a smoke – 'to settle my nerves, d'ye know man?'. The constable obliged, and Cresswell, breaking all known rules about smoking before a match, let alone a cup final, took out his pipe of intensely-strong tobacco, lit up, and after a smoke went off to rejoin, the Wembley heroes – and played like the rest of the side, just ideally.

Ted Sagar: Smoking in the dressing room is barred before a match and more particularly before a Cup final, but even that strict disciplinarian, Warney Cresswell felt it necessary to have a quiet pipe in the corner of the dressing-room and nobody said him 'nay' [as a matter of fact I had a cigarette with him]. The coolest of us all was Billy Dean, who never throughout my acquaintanceship with him betrayed the least sign of nerves.

William Ralph 'Dixie' Dean: When I went out and got alongside Sam Cowan the City skipper he was holding the ball and you could see how nervous he was. 'The ball's shaking in your hand,' I said. 'Put your other hand on top of it to stop it shaking.' You should have seen his face!

Matt Busby: To play against Dixie Dean was at once a delight and a nightmare. He was a perfect specimen of an athlete, beautifully proportioned, with immense strength, adept on the ground but with extraordinary skill in the air.

Ted Sagar: Manchester City started as though they were going to swamp us, and I think that during that critical period we had to thank more than anybody Willie Cook, who had to face the City 'flyer' and match-winner, Eric Brook. Willie well and truly subdued him.

William Ralph 'Dixie' Dean: Our lads played well and one of the sharpest in our forward line was Jimmy Stein, the outside-left. There was no getting away from it, he was a good player that lad. He was there to put the ball away when the City keeper Langford dropped a cross from Cliff Britton late in the first half.

Dick White: It was one of the first games to be broadcast live on the radio. Before the match they printed diagrams of the pitch segmented into areas so that the commentator could refer you to where on the pitch the ball was – 'It's in square B1, over to A2' . The players were numbered for the first time too – from one through to 22. When they scored the first goal not everybody in our street had a radio, and you would see people running out of the houses to tell a less fortunate neighbour that they'd scored.

William Ralph 'Dixie' Dean: It wasn't long into the second half when Cliff Britton sent another one over. It was a beautiful thing! From about eight yards out I met it and headed it into the back of the net with the goalkeeper Langford lying on top of it. He'd made a last effort to try and grab it but it was right at the back of the net. Our third goal came from a corner by Albert Geldard. He sent a great ball over, little Jimmy ran in and headed it into the net. It was something similar to the one I'd got myself.

Will Cuff: Years gone by the scenes after the final whistle were a disgrace. A player thought if he could gather the ball the moment the signal stopped the game it was his property. This was quite erroneous but it became a habit, and the made scrimmaging that went on to collar the ball become a scandal. In one cup final of our remembrance, Everton v. Manchester City. Geldard was near enough to dash in and collar the ball. He was leaving the cup final scene with this memento only to find an official challenge him for possession. Such a finale to a final was quite undignified and the authorities thereafter stopped the nonsense, by instituting a rule stating that the ball must be handed to the referee at the conclusion of the game, and it was later handed to the captain of the winning club.

William Ralph 'Dixie' Dean: I'll never forget going up to the royal box at Wembley to collect the FA Cup. I received it off the Duchess of York [the late Queen Mother]. She congratulated me and said it was a very good game. She really smiled and said she had enjoyed it. That made me feel so proud. I was walking ten feet tall because it meant I had won every honour in the game. That Cup medal completed my collection.

Ted Sagar: There was a victory dinner that night at the Victoria Hotel, and on Monday the team were taken to a news theatre to see the film record of the final. Naturally there was a lot of ragging about taking up the screen as a career.

Charles Mills senior: My father went and was back in the house at 9.30pm – they laid on 40 charter trains from Wembley to Liverpool. In the interim mother got in touch with the neighbours — they were all women, because all of the fellas had gone down there. They dressed themselves in white shirts and black knickers [like the team] and were waiting for them when they got back — you should have seen my father's face when he saw that lot!

Ted Sagar: On our homecoming on the Tuesday night we were given a tremendous reception by huge crowds who lined the route from Lime Street Station to the Town Hall where we were received by the Lord Mayor and Lady Mayoress. We travelled in triumphal procession in the original four-in-hand which carried the victorious 1906 team and was driven by the same driver Mr Jack Pagenham. Thousands were waiting outside the Town Hall and covering my embarrassment I handed over to a policeman a six-year-old lad who had been passed up to me at the station. He was dressed in a miniature football kit, but with a red jersey! Some Liverpool supporter nearly had the last laugh. We had to appear on the town hall balcony with the Cup and more than one, including Billy Dean himself were in tears at the warmth of the reception. Thousands more lined the route to the ground and it was estimated that 60,000 more were waiting inside the ground for us. Certainly nothing like it – not even the two Armistice nights – has been seen in the city before or since.

Will Cuff: It was a miracle no one was seriously hurt en route from the town hall to Goodison Park because the crushing and swaying made it well nigh impossible to get to the grandstand. One chara in which my old friend, Mr Herbert Barker, was seated, suffered a terrible time, with the doors smashed, the windows smashed and the threat of the burning chara wheels setting the 100 people who clung on to the rafters in grave fear of being burned to death. There is something providential about the way football crowds escape death blows on such occasions.

William Ralph 'Dixie' Dean: I remember coming up Scotland Road and we had to ease up or speed on account of the crowds. This kiddie was screaming and crying and as I bent down to shake hands with the mother she said to the youngster, 'If you don't stop this noise I won't bring you next year!' At any rate, the kid stopped crying.

Players of the 1930s

Will Cuff: When we went to Switzerland there was a snag in the tour arrangements – the local people had come to see Dean, the famous Dean, and he had left us to play in an international match elsewhere on the continent. It nearly ruined our programme. His fame is worldwide and we had no opinion in playing a reserve centre-forward, but they never forgave us for the omission

Ted Sagar: Torry Gillick is the best positional player I have ever seen in my 20 years of football, and one whose uncanny anticipation turned 100 to one chance into magnificent goals. He was always popping up at unexpected moments and I remember that for days Torry was walking around with the loveliest pair of black eyes one could imagine as the reward for one piece of enterprise when he headed a half-chance into the net while the surprised Villa goalkeeper, Rutherford, accidentally landed a punch between Torry's eyes that would not have disgraced Joe Louis. For days after Torry could only glare balefully as the Everton players in passing, whistled innocently: 'Two Lovely Black Eyes.'

William Ralph 'Dixie' Dean: Ted Critchley was a fine player and a great signing for us. He knew how to centre a ball and we harmonised well. Little Alec [Troup] on the other side was an amazing fella and a great ball player… He stood only 5ft 5 inches but was full of bravery and skill. Because of a weak collar bone which kept slipping out of joint he had to play with a strapping on his shoulder every game… I think we had a perfect understanding and I think I have to thank him more than anyone else for the part he played in scoring the goals I did. I'd rate him one of the best wingers there's been.

Ted Sagar: My automatic choice for right-back would be old Warney Cresswell, a great player, a fine gentleman, and an ideal clubmate. Cresswell was a two-footed player with an uncanny sense of anticipation, and an ice-cold brain that carried both himself and his team-mates through the stormiest phases.

William Ralph 'Dixie' Dean: As a captain he had our respect and he was such a great reader of the game that he was rarely under pressure. He saw things before they happened and should have won far more than nine England caps he did get. Off the field he was very careful, too! I think the only time he took his hands out of his pocket was to hold his pipe or his pint. In the pub he'd always be last to buy a round! Sometimes he'd say: 'The beer's no good here… let's go somewhere else.' He'd hope we'd forget it was his round! We never did.

Ted Sagar: Warney was the most stylish back I ever played behind. He was a brilliant reader of the game and always put himself in a position to make things look easy.

Raich Carter: The most devastating centre must always be the one that slashes into the middle before the defence have had time to set their stall out. The player who often finds himself best placed to catch a defence in such a position of vulnerability is the wing-half. Few have demonstrated the force of this argument in such an emphatic manner as Cliff Britton. I have come across wingers who are less effective with their centres than this cultured wing-half-back.

Joe Mercer: Cliff was the exact opposite to me. While I roved and ran and relied on my undaunting energy, Cliff was cool and poised. He had the most educated right foot that I ever saw. We used to work for hours together hitting a ball to and fro. We must have gone through the coaching manual and back again – just two youngsters trying to improve themselves.

Father John Ashton: Ted Sagar was a very good goalkeeper; very vocal on the pitch. How does he rank among Everton goalkeepers over the years? Not as good as Neville but better than Gordon West. That's pretty good.

Eric Moonman: If T.G. Jones was God, then Ted was his caretaker. When he was there we were stood behind the goal and even when things went wrong you didn't blame him. Nobody blamed him. He was marvellous. He had a long long run and without much real challenge. I think his general distribution of the ball was good. He was formidable, strong. I think he ticked all the boxes.

Dick White: There was a right full-back called Ben Williams, a Welshmen, brilliant player, and

I remember going up to get autographs in the summer holidays. The players were there training. When this fella Ben Williams came out you'd have thought he was one of the directors. He had a smart suit on and a gold-topped cane!

Cliff Britton: Jock Thomson was possibly the most underrated player in the team at that time. He possibly got less publicity than anyone else but he was one of the most important cogs in the team.

Tommy Lawton: Geldard was the fastest thing on two legs over ten yards. We had other wingers like Torry Gillick, Wally Boyes and Jimmy Caskie, but Albert had played for England only the season before [he was sold, in 1938] when he'd kept Stan Matthews out of the team.

Charles Mills senior: Geldard was very fast, but, as my father used to say, 'Half the time he doesn't take the ball with him!'

T.G. Jones: The best wing-halves I played in between were Joe Mercer and Jock Thomson. For power, strength and ability I don't think there could be any better than those two. Mind you, Cliff Britton was a fine player, a brilliant player on the ball, but you had to get it for him. Mercer and Thomson could get it for themselves and do plenty with it.

Joe Mercer: After my first game for Everton [a 1-0 win against Leeds in April 1933] I thought, 'Well, I've played. No matter what happens now, no one can take that away from me.' I was brought up to believe Everton were the best team in the world and nobody was going to beat us. The players knew what they were supposed to do and got on with it. We always had fun. I probably learned more about the game at Arsenal, but I learned how to laugh at Everton.

Charles Mills senior: Gordon Watson is someone that is often overlooked. He was never going to be a star, a good passer of the ball, but what a capable player, who could fit in anywhere.

Goodison's Greatest Game

FA Cup Fourth Round replay,
30 January 1935
Everton 6, Sunderland 4

Dick White: In those days the only way you could find out about what was going on in the first team game when they were away was by attending the reserve game [which would be played simultaneously at Goodison]. Where there is now the Gwladys St double decker there was a sort of shed with a lean-to roof. Perched on top of this was a box with all the letters of the alphabet and if you had a penny programme it would have the fixtures with letters relating to this board. In the centre of the box was a cut out where at intervals a chap emerged to update the scores. On his particular day with Everton playing Sunderland at Roker Park – I don't know how he got out of the box, because he was a corpulent man – nobody was really watching the match, they were watching this box for the scores. Anyway, this man came out after about 20 minutes, and puts up that it's 1-0 to Sunderland. There were about 25,000 people in Goodison just watching this little box for an update. But the minutes were passing until right near the end he re-emerges to update the scores. It was 1-1. This little fat fella stood on the roof of this lean-to and like Oliver Hardy does a little dance for the crowd, who are all cheering. That was the precursor to the great 6-4 game.

Ted Sagar: I have been asked frequently what was my most memorable game. The answer to that is easy. Without hesitation I say the 1935 Cup replay against Sunderland at Goodison Park, a view to which the 59,215 spectators who saw it will probably subscribe. Think of all the superlative adjectives that can be applied to a football game, and you will do it only adequate justice. Former international stars who were present at the game and who have spent a life-time in football said they had never seen anything to approach that historic struggle. Thrill following thrill and goals came upon goals.

Will Cuff: This 6-4 replay at Everton came upon a dirty day. Sunderland sent their mascots and their men and women. In the stands they had draped their colours over the grandstand seats. It was a day when anything could happen, when no goal might be scored, when someone might be sent off – no, not that, because every player knew as he stepped on to the field that [referee Ernie] Pinkston would tolerate no nonsense, no word, no arguments. The setting of the game, is well known, but it must be recalled that Everton leading 3-2 saw, to their horror, Bob Gurney, the Sunderland centre-forward, kick the ball over his head into the goal for an equaliser – 3-3! The last kick of the 90th minute. Gurney did not see the ball enter the net, and mention was made in the papers that he was the only one who didn't see it, only to find complaint that the statement was not quite right – there were five blind spectators at the ground. They too, had not seen the goal scored!

Ted Sagar: We thus changed over for the last fifteen minutes still level, somewhat foot sore, and more than a little fatigued. At the 21st minute of extra time Geldard put in a tentative centre which swerved over Thorpe's out stretched hands into the net. We were elated, but what had gone before had prepared us for anything. We began to think that it was in the natural order of things that Sunderland would get an equalising goal, but they had shot their bolt. A minute before the end Geldard clinched the issue with another goal and we won 6-4 amid some of the wildest scenes of excitement that I have ever seen.

Will Cuff: It was at the 90th minute that the drama found its laughing parade. The players awaited their trainers for the sponge, the lemons, the drinks. Pinkston turned them straight round, but before he could restart the game he found a diminutive man on the field of play, which is all against the rules. Pinkston eyed this man [half his massive height] and demanded to know 'What do you mean by coming on to this field of play?' The little man [Jimmy Cochrane] replied, 'I'm the manager.' Pinkston flew flurried words at him; 'I don't care if you're the manager of the best team in the world.' He had not time to finish his 'sentence' when the little man replied, 'But I am, I am, I am!' That manager went home with a 6 to 4 verdict against his side in one of the greatest and most exciting games of my lifetime. The goal thrill was as nothing to the thrill of the completely upturning state of the game, the continual cut and thrust, the certainty followed by the uncertainty that came into everyone's mind. A roaring cup tie with a homely win and homely touch of laughter from the little man from Sunderland.

Ted Sagar: At the end, hundreds of spectators in their excitement surged on to the pitch and mobbed both teams as we struggled to the dressing rooms and the police had to come to our aid to enable us to make our way, one by one, down the subway. I think the players were as excited as the spectators and it was a game that will be talked about for years to come by football fans, who will be proud to say, 'I was there' and who, in turn will hand the story down to succeeding generations.

Alec Stevenson: Being in the side that took the 1939 title was the highlight of my career. But it was a Cup match that brought me the outstanding memory of one single game. That was the famous tie with Sunderland that finished 6-4. People still talk to me about that game to this day.

Interwar years management

William Ralph 'Dixie' Dean: Tom McIntosh was a great man and when he passed away [in 1935] I was very upset. He was someone you looked up to and respected ... When I was made captain we used to have many a chat about this and that and you never had any trouble talking to Tom. He'd always listen and he'd try to do what was best for all concerned.

Thomas Keates: McInosh is the consultant and Father Confessor of the players, a redressor [if it is possible] of their grievances, consulting engineer of the captain and trainer, and prudent adviser and information bureau of the directors.

Alec Stevenson: When I signed Everton had a secretary-manager [McIntosh] who was really involved in the administration side. The players all got together and the more senior ones pointed things out and played the game the way we saw it.

Tommy Lawton: We were paid £8 a week but nobody moaned, we didn't know any better. When they put a contract in front of us, we just signed it. Never read it, we were just happy to be playing.

T.G. Jones: Dixie Dean was Everton. Make no mistake about that. I was an innocent lad, you see, and he was the man who almost picked the team on his own. The story was that he used to go up to the office and say, 'This is the team we're playing [fielding] on Saturday.' I don't know whether it's true or not but that was the story.

Tommy Lawton: All they ever said was 'Make sure you pass it to a man in the same shirt.' That was as close as we ever got to talking tactics. We just listened to what Dixie had to say and went and did it.

Joe Mercer: Dixie never had a negative thought in his head. Tactics? He never worried about tactics. He used to say, 'Get it up the middle to me and I'll knock them in.'

Charles Mills senior: Theo Kelly [who succeeded McIntosh as secretary in 1936 and became secretary-manager in 1939] virtually ran the club. They had a chairman – Cuff – but he was a hands-off chairman, he left it all to Kelly, he was the man who directed operations.

Dixie Dean: This chap Kelly had no time for the older lads. I just couldn't get on with him. He was secretary but I didn't care what he was. I knew what was happening. He wanted to get rid of me and also one or two other people who looked like being in with a chance of becoming manager one day. I didn't want to leave Everton. But Kelly was the reason I did leave. It wasn't on account of Tommy Lawton arriving — it was nothing to do with that. That fella Kelly just didn't want me there long.

T.G. Jones: He wasn't a manager, he was a secretary. He couldn't tell Dixie what to do on the field.

Tommy 'T.G.' Jones

T.G. Jones: I was full of ambition, and I wanted to see things, and I looked forward to it tremendously. Mixing with all the players, great names... it was marvellous actually. I used to look with great respect to these players who were at Everton. I used to think, 'My God, what an honour.' I would go back and tell my parents and my friends. They would look at me and want to hear all about it because going to a football match from Connah's Quay was an event.

Will Cuff: It has never been my pleasure to see the avowed 'stopper' centre half-back whom I rate as a mere chopping block – he need not be a good footballer, he has only to have the merit of heading ability immense leg power and a keen eye to follow the ball, and he will fit most football sides this generation. I have no love for mere stopping tactics that have become the foundation of must modern football sides. Rather would I have on my side the Tom Jones type. Now here is a player who has rarely gone from his pivotal lair, although he has been tried as centre-forward and inside forward. His natural ability would make him prevail if you played him in any position, but he is the natural centre half back by birth and upbringing. He has the height, the flair for sizing up the next move of a forward, eyes glued to the ball, and heading ability.

William Ralph 'Dixie' Dean: [The best player I ever saw?] He would have to be an Evertonian: T.G. Jones, the Welsh international centre-half. The best all-round player I've ever seen. He had everything – no coach could ever teach him anything. He was neater than John Charles. John looked awkward whereas Tommy would get out of a ruck by just opening his legs, letting the ball run wide and all this sort of thing – just letting it run through.

Len Norman: He was first rate, a class act. Of all the centre-halves I've seen play for Everton he was the best. It was a joy to see him play.

Father John Ashton: There was nobody to touch T.G. Jones. He was a wonderful player. He had such fantastic ball control. He was playing centre half – at a time when centre-halves just belted it up in the air – and no matter where the ball came to him he had the most fantastic control of it. He was a revolutionary, because he never just kicked the ball in the air, he always saw that the ball was following a trajectory he had chosen. He was a beautiful player.

T.G. Jones: To say I was overawed is an understatement but I learned a lot from them. If I made a mistake they came down on me like a ton of bricks. And if I made two I was in big trouble.

Tom Gardner: We called him 'Big Tommy'. I think the reason was that there was also 'Young Tom' in T.E. Jones. As a player, T.G. was one of the most perfect centre-halves that I have played with or ever seen. He always seemed to be in the right place at the right time – a very hard man to beat on the field – even in training. He appeared to be slow and I would think, 'He's never going to get there.' But his positional play was unbelievable and he was always there – a hard man to get past. His all-round performance was absolutely superb.

Eric Moonman: T.G. was majestic in his manner and his control. Perhaps if one was being cynical about T. G. Jones they might say that he probably never broke sweat because firstly he could move around and provide a ball. Joe Mercer was the same and it's very difficult for a player in the modern world to actually adopt that pose. I think John Stones was trying to do that but you know the game has speeded up and supporters are impatient and they don't always see what's in the players' minds. But I think T.G. Jones did have the support of the crowd and he also had the skill. I don't ever remember him being in trouble and that builds up a confidence with the crowd.

T.G. Jones: I developed this ability to be able to kill the ball, then bring it under control and beat people by dribbling. Many times I'd bring the ball down dead in the penalty box and then, with a shrug of the shoulders, I'd have two or three people going the other way. Don't ask me how or why – it was sheer instinct. The brain couldn't work quick enough to think about it – you did it instinctively. Today they'd call it talent, I suppose.

Dick White: We were behind the goal, right behind the net, and Everton were under pressure. The ball kept coming over and getting cleared and Sagar was hopping around like a cat on hot bricks. Then this fella came tearing in and was blocked by T.G., who then took the ball. All the while, Sagar's yelling, 'Clear it! Clear it!' Then Jones makes this immaculate pass and the pressure's off. Later when things had died down, somebody shouted, 'Ain't he bloody marvellous, Ted?' Sagar turned, and yelled back, 'He might be bloody marvellous to you, but he's driving me bloody mad!'

Ted Sagar: Tommy Jones, the football artist in anybody's language and one who does – and gets away with – things nobody else would think of attempting.

Dolly Sagar: I think of all the players he played with, T.G. was Ted's favourite. They had an understanding between each other and they worked really well together. The pair of them used to talk for hours before the match about players who they thought could give them problems – and they continued their natter on the park.

Charles Mills senior: What a player. Never made a foul. A strong tackler, but not one to hoof the ball — the way you see now, with endless kicks up the field.

Tommy Lawton: He had the great capacity to stroke the ball around. He also had the best right foot in the business and so complete was his positioning and balance that he always seemed to receive the ball on his right foot.

Exit the Master, Enter the Apprentice:
Tommy Lawton signs and Dean leaves Everton

Tommy Lawton: I signed on New Years Eve in 1936. The fee was £6,500 – a bloody fortune! But I didn't see any of it – it was a record for a teenager at the time and I'd only been a professional since my seventeenth birthday. Anyway, the next day, New Year's Day, I had to report to Everton. Well, it wasn't a bank holiday like these days, it was a normal working day and people were all over the place on their way to work. I caught the train, eight minutes past nine from Burnley to Liverpool Exchange. I was really nervous because I'd never been that far on my own before. There was nobody to meet me at the station either so I asked the porter, 'How do you get to Goodison Park?' He told me to catch a number four tram from down on Dale Street and the conductor just nodded like when I asked him if he went to Goodison. Then when I was waiting to hop off, he was looking at me and I looked away but he said, 'Hey, you're that young Lawton aren't you? And I said, 'Yes.' He just stared at me for a bit and he said, 'You'll never be as good as our Dixie!' So I just said, 'Oh! Thank you very much.' And I got off feeling very small.

Will Cuff: It was touch and go whether we got him to come, and there were in some parts of our boardroom, doubts as to whether we were doing the right thing in risking £6,000 for a boy of his tender years. Would he succeed? Would he fit the Everton front line? The doubting Thomases were answered in the course of time, but the war and his desire to be away from Everton cut his innings at Goodison Park – more's the pity.

Tommy Lawton: At the ground I knocked on the dressing room door and waited and then the door burst open and there was Joe Mercer with that big grin of his and he says, 'It's young Lawton isn't it? My you're a big lad!' And before I knew it I'd said, 'Yes and I can play a bit too!' He just laughed and introduced me to all the first team players, all getting ready to play Preston. There was Jackie Coulter and Ted Sagar, Charlie Gee and Billy Cook – all good players but there was only one that I really wanted to meet and I said to Joe, 'Where's Dixie then?' And at that moment the door flew wide open almost knocking me over and in he came. 'I'm here,' he said and grabbed my hand. He looked a sight as if he'd only just tumbled out of bed. His hair needed a comb through it and he hadn't shaved; he'd a little stubbly beard and he had a pair of old slippers on his feet. He put his arm around my shoulders and took me to one side. 'I know you've come here to take my place. Anything I can do to help you I will. I promise, anything at all.'

William Ralph 'Dixie' Dean: He impressed me right away. He was quiet and listened.

Charles Mills senior: It was sort of acknowledged in the city that Lawton had come to replace Dean. Lawton played as his inside right for a period. Dean, in fairness, took him under his wing and taught him what he knew.

Tommy Lawton: A sort of depression set in [the day Lawton was first picked ahead of Dean in September 1937]. I didn't know what to think. I was at centre-forward in place of the great Dixie. I was delighted, surprised, but sad too.

Alec Stevenson: After Dixie we thought, 'That was it, there can never be another like him.' Well I'm not saying there ever has been but Tommy Lawton went as close as is possible. They are the two greatest centre-forwards ever as far as I'm concerned.

T.G. Jones: Tommy was the complete centre-forward – two very good feet, strong in the air and quick with a great understanding of the game.

Dick White: It was often argued, 'Who was the better of the two.' I think of them Lawton would have better fitted the modern game. He was certainly better looking! I think that statue of Dixie at the stadium flatters him!

Ted Sagar: Invidious though comparisons are, it is impossible to mention the name of Tommy Lawton without someone asking, 'Who was the better – Dean or Lawton?' Billy Dean has always been my football idol, but if I were asked to give my candid opinion, forgetting personal feelings and having played in scores of matches with both, I would have to give the vote to Dean by a narrow points margin. Like the boxing referees I would reserve the right to refuse to disclose my score card. Tommy probably had the edge in his superb footwork and with the possible exception of Tommy Jones was the hardest hitter of a ball since the days of Wilf Chadwick, but Dean's headwork was unique. I don't think anybody before or since could turn a ball on a curl-like William Ralph Dean.

William Ralph 'Dixie' Dean: I'll never forget the Everton fans for the way they treated me, not only when I was playing but long after I left the club,' he said. 'I felt that these fans belonged to me and I belonged to them. I was born and bred an Evertonian and I knew I would never change'

Tommy Lawton: He helped me a lot when I first joined the club. He had his faults, he was a boisterous character, but everyone liked him. He was often black and blue from the harsh treatments handed out by unscrupulous defenders, but he used to take it and never complained.

Will Cuff: William Dean should, in my estimation have concluded his career at Everton, instead of which he went off to Notts County and later to Ireland. He it was he who forced our hands, although he knew quite well my idea of his life at Everton was that it should end at the club which made him famous and which he made famous. Naturally there are divergent opinions about transfer of star players.

Everton's 1938/39 League Championship winning team

T.G. Jones: The year before we won the league, Everton were in a mess and had a job to escape relegation. They brought a lot of young players into the team for the following season: me, Norman Greenhalgh from New Brighton; George Jackson was right-back; Torry Gillick, Joe Mercer, Tommy Lawton and Stan Bentham. Alex Stevenson was inside-left. We were a good side with a lot of young players.

Tommy Lawton: We began to know each other as people, not just players. People with different personalities, faults, varying moods, likes and dislikes . . . a wonderful blend developed between the players, which resulted in a far closer team spirit.

T.G. Jones: We went to Glasgow for a couple of weeks... and all the top Scottish teams were there and one or two English teams. And we got to the final... Glasgow Celtic beat us. It did something for us, that competition, because the next year we walked away with the First Division.

Tommy Lawton: That is where we got our act together – because of five-a-sides, comradeship and friendship.

Ted Sagar: We started off like champions that year, winning the first six games, three of them away, but Middlesbrough put a stop to our run by beating us 3-0 at Ayresome Park. The following match we beat Liverpool 2-1 at Anfield. The other highlights, however, was a double over Arsenal's might. Anybody who could do that in 1938 deserved the championship. We continued consistently to pile up the points without any of those spectators flourishes that marked our 1932 championship season and had the title in our keeping three matches from the end even though we lost at Charlton.

T.G. Jones: That was a truly great side. We never seemed to have to run about. We pushed the ball to each other and everything went like clockwork. It is a great pity that the war broke out because I am sure we would have gone on to great things.

Dick White: Over more than 80 years of watching Everton, that was the team that gave me the most pleasure. Even now the team rolls off the tongue – Sagar, Cook, Greenhalgh, Mercer, Jones, Thomson, Gillick, Bentham, Lawton, Stevenson, Boyes. They would have swept the board for years to come. Whenever I think of Everton, I think of that team.

Tommy Lawton: They were a bloody good side. And the next year we should have won the League again, the FA Cup and the bloody Boat Race if they'd put us in it.

T.G. Jones: Do you know what Everton gave us as a present? A half-day trip to Morecambe! You could take your wife or girlfriend if you so wished. I didn't go anyway; I didn't think it was worth travelling from Connah's Quay to Liverpool to travel to Morecambe for half a day.

Norman Greenhalgh: What happened? Bloody Adolf Hitler, didn't he?

World War Two, wartime football and its aftermath

Tommy Lawton: I don't think anybody expected that the war would come so soon. We just wanted to play. We were the champions. I think that we thought that nobody, not even Hitler, could touch us.

Dick White: They played football on a regional basis because travel was impossible, and they relied upon people who were in the forces but were based in the area. I went to go and see some of it, but it was a travesty compared to what we'd seen in 1938/39. There was no enjoyment from it.

Tommy Lawton: All my prospects of fame and fortune were shattered at one fell swoop. I'd signed advertising contracts for shaving soap and porridge oats, they were cancelled. But there were thousands worse off than me, so I just decided to get on with it.

Eric Moonman: My life changed. My family were in the milk business and not only our business but a good part of the inner city was destroyed on 20 December 1940. You never forget those dates because your life takes a change. I had a big family and fortunately no one was seriously injured but there was no question of staying in the house or indeed the area. We were offered by the council to go to Huyton but we had a sister who lived in Southport and she was able to find us room, but initially there were seven of us in a room. There was then a delay in travel to the games because I was still a youngster and it was different going from Liverpool than going from Southport. Then of course were the wartime games, which of course carried on. Whereas you may see Tommy Lawton once a month you were now seeing him once a week because he got leave. They had disbanded the league, which we thought was pretty tough going and it was regional – north and south. I think that in a way the tribal aspect of the teams we supported was put on ice, that was the feeling I had, because you couldn't very well have attitudes to a player that fails in your team because you knew that he was in the Army and he had just come in at short notice.

Will Cuff: There was no special football training in the years 1939 to 1946 with the result that the new generation of players did not rise, and the older players had an innings showing the younger folk how much they had to learn before they became proficient.

Tommy Lawton: I was one of the fortunates who, by reason of my retention in this country on Army service, was able to get in my weekly game throughout the period of hostilities. And incidentally there was periodical hostility from people who thought it wrong that fit, able-bodied young fellows like myself should be playing football in England while their husbands, sons and sweethearts were fighting in the sun-baked deserts of Libya and the Middle East, were flying out over Europe or were dying in the dangerous seas. I am not going to defend myself, I have done nothing to defend myself against. The war moguls ordered that I stayed in England to do my war job. Football was incidental, but in its way it too played a part. I appeared in hundreds of charity matches for England, the Army, combined services and unit sides. Let me make it clear. I didn't ask to stay in England.

Ted Sagar: Although judged by army football standards, I was still playing well enough to hold my place, I felt I had gone back a mile after my long lay-off and that my First Division career was finished. My reflexes were dulled and I really believed that the last chapter had been written to the story of 'Ted Sagar – Footballer.' There were times when I lay on my army bunk and thought, 'What now?' I was at the crossroads. It was more in fear than in hope that in 1946 in an unmistakable 'demob' suit I presented myself at Goodison Park and asked whether I could be of any further use. Many will have seen that magnificent film, 'The Best Years of Our Lives,' which tells the story of the hopes and fears of four American ex-Servicemen as they seek to rehabilitate themselves in 'Civvy Street.' I think I could have stepped into that film without a rehearsal. Theirs was play-acting; mine was the real thing – no more I suppose, than that of thousands more like me who were returning and wondering what the future held for them. But here and now let me express my thanks to Mr Theo Kelly, whose cordial greeting made me feel immediately at home and more important made me feel that I was 'wanted.' It was something I will never forget. [George] Burnett was playing well and I was not optimistic about getting my place back in the first team however hard I tried to recover my pre-war form. I felt that a run in the reserves might help me to get the 'feel' of the ball, and I felt there was a chance that some of it might come back to me.

Postscript: Ted Sagar was one of the lucky ones in not attracting the opprobrium of the idiosyncratic secretary-manager Theo Kelly. When league football returned in September 1946 Kelly would regularly drop T.G. Jones and had already fallen out spectacularly with Joe Mercer after accusing him of feigning an injury and refusing to have it treated.

Mercer would recall: 'It was a terrible blow for me to go, because I was so crazy about Everton. Mind you I wasn't easy to handle. I was captain of England at the time and had been a Sergeant Major, running my own show. Theo Kelly and I had one or two ups and downs. The funny thing was, he wanted me to play centre-half – Me, a wing-half who used to go diving into the action, when the club had T. G. Jones, the best centre-half of all in my opinion! Things became so bad between Theo and me that one day I went to see the directors at the Exchange Hotel, where they held Board Meetings, and said 'Transfer me, or I turn it in'. The directors said they wanted to me to stay but I was determined and Arsenal paid £9,000 for me.'

Lawton too had by then departed for London, seeking a transfer to Chelsea on account of the capital's 'more clement weather' as his wife Rosaleen was unwell. At least that was the story the newspapers ran; the reality was that he was trapped in an unhappy marriage with a local girl and needed to escape Liverpool. 'On reflection,' he later admitted, 'I should have stayed and transferred the wife.'

Jones remained until 1950 but would never have a harmonious relationship with Kelly and flitted in and out of the side. On four occasions during 1947 alone he asked to leave, and each time met the same negative response. The spat with the management then broke out into a public argument between Jones and the club. 'Could it be,' asked Jones, in the local press, 'that having lost Tommy and Joe, when both might have been kept if different methods had been adopted, they are frightened of public opinion if they let me go?' In 1948 a transfer to Roma fell through at the eleventh hour and Jones remained trapped at Everton. 'From being captain of Everton and Wales I went to nothing. They wouldn't even play me in the reserves.'

To soldiers, airmen and naval officers returning home after years of war and national service they expected their teams to be unchanging, but the reality was that in seven years everything changes in a football team. In Everton's ranks the adjustment was more pronounced than elsewhere, even if expectations remained high.

'It was what you looked forward to all week,' recalled Charles Mills senior, who returned from national service in Palestine in 1946, having previously served as a navigator in RAF bomber crews. 'People were glad of the entertainment.' Upon his return as a belated 21st birthday present he was given his first season ticket by his father in the Upper Bullens stand, thus becoming the third generation of his family to hold such a ticket. The fare on offer in the late-1940s was unbefitting of what he had witnessed in his own adolescence and to the memories of his forefathers.

'From being at the heights,' he remembered, 'We plunged to the depths.'

Everton on the Brink
1946-1961

'Life after the war was difficult. People had lost family members, there was austerity, rationing. But it wasn't obvious; people were awfully good at hiding their thoughts. A lot of them had lost their family, their brothers and their sisters, but somehow there was a religious aspect to football, which meant you lost somebody but you hadn't really lost them. Which was marvellous, really.'

Father John Ashton

Football after the War

For the second time in Everton's history, war changed everything. The players that had lifted the League Championship in 1939 returned from the conflict older, often lesser athletes than those that had enjoyed such success in the late-1930s. In the league Everton would struggle. From challenging for and winning league titles, the rest of the 1940s were filled with worries about relegation.

Father John Ashton: Life after the war was difficult. People had lost family members, there was austerity, rationing. But it wasn't obvious; people were awfully good at hiding their thoughts. A lot of them had lost their family, their brothers and their sisters, but somehow there was a religious aspect to football, which meant you lost somebody but you hadn't really lost them. Which was marvellous, really.

Eric Moonman: People were searching for ways – they were desperate – to have normality. People had lost their loved ones; whether they went through The Blitz or whether it was on the battlefield. People were searching and they weren't sure that it was ever going to be [the same] because it was the first war where it wasn't just happening out there on the battlefield or on the different continents but in fact so many of the casualties were in the streets where they lived and that was quite dramatic. I think it produced [the mindset] 'Let's have a good time, let's forget about it.' Football, more than most things, played a role in normalising things.

Len Norman: The crowds were enormous then, always 40, 50,000, sometimes more. Stupidly – because I only did it once – you could lift your legs up and just go with the crowd and they would carry you because the pressure was so great. You'd just have to hope you didn't fall because you'd get trampled on. I don't know what the safety factors were like then.

David Hart: Two of the early games I went to, with a friend of mine Eddie Martin, we couldn't get in – 78,000, 75,000 – and you were perfectly safe in crowds that size. People behaved, the language was controlled. If there were women there, there was a code. So the behaviour was terrific. We actually sat in Stanley Park, I sat on his shoulders. You could see one goal through the stands, and it was the Arsenal game, they'd just been promoted, and we could just see one goal. We had no idea what the score was.

Dick White: We used to dream of the war ending because we were still living in the shadow of the 38/39 side and it never crossed my mind that six years had passed between the sides playing again – and in 1945/46 it was only played on a regional basis; it was 46/47 by the time the Football League started again. They were decimated by then.

Theo Kelly

Dave Hickson: Theo Kelly was the Everton manager during those years. He had risen through the club administration and, having originally been secretary-manager, was given charge of team affairs ahead of the ill-fated 1939/40 season. He had a reputation as a meddler and for falling out with the club's top players. Dixie Dean, Joe Mercer, Tommy Lawton and later T.G. Jones – some of the greatest players in Everton history – all left after falling foul of Theo. Perhaps because I was only a kid I never saw that side to him. He was always fine with me, although at that stage we really had little interaction with the people running the club. In fact Kelly probably helped me and some of the others in turning professional. Under his management Everton were more concerned with bringing in the best local players and giving them a chance than buying in stars from elsewhere.

Alec Farrall: I used to train with Liverpool when I was a kid, with Joe Mercer. Joe was captain of Arsenal [but still lived on Merseyside and commuted to London for games]. I started playing for the English schoolboys, so I used to train with him. And he used to go to Anfield to train – he didn't go to Everton. I don't think they'd let him in.

Tom Gardner: The manager when I was here was Theo Kelly, and to be perfectly honest he was getting a bit past it. He spent most of his time in the office, you never saw very much of him on the field. Like the managers these days, take the likes of David Moyes; he's out on the field with the boys, he's completely embroiled with them if you like, like all the managers now these days. Theo Kelly was in his office, and you never saw him come out onto the field. I don't think he knew what football was about to be honest, he was just a football manager.

Eric Moonman: We only thought about him in the sense that he was powerful and when things went wrong, as they do in any organisation, it would be relating to him. I don't think he was a kindly man. I think he was out of touch with reality and certainly he might've succeeded today at certain clubs but he wouldn't have lasted terribly long. From where he came and from what he was experiencing he probably thought that this was the right behaviour. But on the other hand he was probably close to the board, he had a good run for what he wanted to achieve. He didn't come with any football background.

John McNally: The worst person – and I think that he ruined this club – was Theo Kelly. He was a terrible one, and the players he bought! They were the worst players. Oscar Hold was one and I can see it now at the Park End, the ball hits the bar, comes down and he made a swipe and missed, and he missed it again, and again. Three times! Peter Farrell was the captain and he was running down the pitch saying 'Come on get up' and that. He couldn't stop laughing and the crowd couldn't stop laughing at him. That's the players we had; that's what that Theo Kelly did.

Dick White: His management was incomprehensible. He would play Jack Humphreys – an honest trier – ahead of the great T.G. Jones, who he even played at centre-forward. It defied all our belief that this clodhopper would play ahead of the great man. Theo Kelly was the ruination of the club.

Cliff Britton

After finishing the first two post-war seasons tenth and fourteenth, Everton started the 1948/49 season in shambolic fashion, propping up the First Division in the early part of the season. The Everton board finally took action and replaced Theo Kelly with the Burnley manager, Cliff Britton, who had been one of Everton's pre-war stars.

Dave Hickson: Cliff had been a pre-war half back at Everton, winning the Second Division title in 1931 and the 1933 FA Cup as well as nine England caps. I remembered him when I first came into the club during the war. He was a fine player, a great reader of the game and for England had formed a famous defensive line with my fellow Portites, Joe Mercer and Stan Cullis, in wartime internationals. I can't ever remember Cliff getting stripped off into his kit and joining us on the pitch at Bellefield, though. He was a collar-and-tie man, watching us from the edge of the pitch in his coat and suit. Cliff would usually get Gordon Watson to do the training with us. He had been a utility man in the late 1930s, winning a League Championship medal in 1939, and would fill all sorts of roles at Goodison over the years. Charlie Leyfield, who had been a winger during the 1930s, also used to help with the training. Harry Cooke was the main one who used to look after us in those days. He was the top man at the time: kit man, physio and trainer rolled into one. He was very strict with the players, very meticulous and very fussy, sorting all the boots out and making sure everything would be ready. He had been a player with Everton 50 years earlier and had seen everything and knew everyone. Sometimes he used to tell us stories about the old days; names like Dixie, Chedgzoy, Sharp and Troup. His grandson, also Harry, joined later on as chief scout, although he was very different and would deal more with the board.

Tom Gardner: Jock Thomson came in for a short while after Theo Kelly finished. Jock was a coach and he took over as manager for a short while. Now he was a different man, a Scots lad, been a good footballer, got on well with the boys, one of those that explained things what he wanted and all the rest of it, whereas Cliff was 'You will do what I tell you', 'Do this, do that', and if you didn't do it you were in trouble. He wasn't there all that long anyway, Cliff Britton, and a left a short while after he came anyway.

Tony McNamara: Cliff Britton, I thought, was a good manager. He used to say 'Get your boots on Tony for a rollicking!' I used to like him, a good manager, better than the ones they got after that.

Tom Gardner: He'd been a good footballer, Cliff, a wonderful footballer, and he knew his football. I felt he was a bit hard. Now whether we weren't used to that kind of thing, I don't know, but he was an 'I'm the boss and you'll do as I tell you' type and very strong. A bit like Shankly really, although Shankly did have a nice way with him as well. Cliff Britton was a bit off-handed, not exactly abusive, but he was the boss.

Mick Meagan: In those days, the manager was kind of a Sergeant Major type of person. I think they were all ex-army men anyway. And you never saw Cliff in a tracksuit, always in the trilby and beautifully dressed, even up in the training ground. They were like, I always thought, a racehorse trainer overlooking their horses. That type of person. They'd call you over after training and have a word with you; what they expected of you and things like that.

Arthur Parker: I met him once and I was in awe of him. He was very much a gentleman and he was well dressed; you only had to look at him and you'd give him respect, just looking at him. And he liked kids. I came back once on the coach and I was really made up with that you know. Getting off the coach, they used to stop the coach outside the ground and they always had kids and that waiting, and I got off the coach and they'd say 'Who's that one there, that young one there?!' They thought I was one of the players and I wasn't going to tell them I wasn't!

Derek Mayers: Personally I thought he was a good manager, a great manager. Everywhere he went he had success. At Preston [where Mayers followed Britton in 1956] we finished runners up in 1957/58 in the First Division, if you can call that success. We never got nothing for it, not even a medal.

Relegation and the rise of Dave Hickson

Although Britton led Everton to safety in 1948, league performances did not improve. Everton finished the 1949/50 season eighteenth, although they made the FA Cup semi-final, which they lost to Liverpool. The next season was an unmitigated disaster. They conceded more and scored less, bar one club, than anyone else in the division. Needing a point against already-relegated Sheffield Wednesday on the final day of the season in order to secure safety, they lost 6-0. Everton finished bottom of the First Division and were relegated.

Tom Gardner: I don't know what went wrong. They had all the same players, and they'd made one or two signings. But football is football, you know you can have a good game one week and then for some reason or another you can fall down the next week. I think it was a bit that way really. There was no actual feeling of everybody not doing their job, not working hard, not doing their best. I think its football, it's just one of those things like life, isn't it? Life has ups and downs, football has its ups and downs.

Dick White: Some of the players that were brought in were useless. There was this player they signed from Portsmouth as a record signing, Albert Juliussen was his name. There was great excitement for his debut [in 1948]; in those decades the *Echo* would have placards with the headline and all the way to the stadium we could see these signs with the headline 'Record Signing Plays Today'. There was great excitement. Until I saw him – because I realised then that I'd played against him in the army with our little battalion team. And he was no good then, either! I thought he was a great big bloody oaf.

Charles Mills senior: They played the last game of the 1950/51 season against Sheffield Wednesday, who had already been relegated, needing a draw to stay up. I listened to it on the radio. They lost 6-0.

Leon Bernicoff: It was upsetting. They weren't run properly, that was the thing that annoyed me about Everton.

Eric Moonman: I think the shock wasn't as big as – to give you a comparison – the worry and the fear years later when we went to that famous game with Wimbledon [in 1994].

John McNally: It was a sinking feeling but it never altered the crowd. When they went into the Second Division the crowds never diminished, as a matter of fact they always had to play a hard game, Everton and Liverpool, because the crowds were that big that the away teams loved coming there.

Dave Hickson: Relegation hurt Everton very badly. It was a terrible thing for the club and luckily one that they've not had to encounter since. Even as a youngster you could sense the hurt from the first-team players. I hadn't played any part in the disastrous run-in, although I had been selected as twelfth man for a visit to Charlton Athletic in March 1951. Back in those days, twelfth man really was twelfth man; we used to push the skips in and help the trainer. There was no substitutes and no chance of getting on the field, unless someone was unexpectedly injured or taken ill in the build-up to the game. Despite their problems I was still in awe of Everton. I wanted to play and I was determined I was going to make it.

Father John Ashton: Hickson was this fellow with tousled hair and a square body. He was strong. Always going for things, never stopped. He wouldn't stop to see if it was political or not; he was going for the ball and he went for the ball. He would fight people out of the way. He was disruptive; he would punch people. But as fans we didn't think about disruption; we thought about Hickson showing the spirit of Everton.

Dave Hickson: Everything that was going wrong for the first team was going right for the reserves. I was selected to play centre-forward against Sheffield Wednesday reserves in a Central League match. It was great playing for the reserves and we always had good gates, because we played at Goodison. We won 7–1 in that game, and I scored five times. The following Saturday I was picked for my first-team debut, away at Leeds United, in place of Harry Catterick. Poor Harry never played for Everton again.

Derek Temple: Dave was an old fashioned centre-forward. You could tackle from anywhere in those days, not like now where you can't tackle from behind. Then, as a forward, you expected to be kicked up in the air as the ball was coming to you and your back was to goal; the defender was going to get you and unless you were quick he was going to kick you. But Dave didn't take to that very well; he used to get a bit upset and he used to lose his rag quite a lot.

John Sutherland: He was Everton through and through and he was always a bit rough. We were playing in the reserves at Manchester City and Dave was having a go at everybody. We were 3-0 down and the referee was starting the game again and Dave says to him, 'Hey Ref why don't we all go in and have a shower and you play with Manchester City?' The Referee said, 'Any more cheek and I will send you off.' 'Yes,' Dave said 'And you can go and run the bath for me!' He was a real character, Dave, but he was a good lad.

Tony McNamara: I remember one incident at Bellefield with Harry Leyland, the goalkeeper at the time. It was just two sided, eleven-a-side and someone had a shot at goal or a pass-back or something like that. Dave went after the ball and Harry came out to pick it up. It was Harry's ball because it was near enough to him, but Dave came sliding in! Even in a practice match he was full of it, you know. Of course Harry got up, and reacted! Cliff Britton said 'If you do that again you're out of this club.'

Eric Moonman: Dave and John Willie Parker were a terrible handful. Everybody was frightened of Hickson anyway and the great thing is if you've got someone alongside you that is equally capable of scoring and has got courage it's always going to win through. The lone guy who's going it alone up front, who's doing his best, is not nearly as good so I think.

George Orr: Everyone's watching the films: Davey Crockett, the Alamo, all these Hollywood stars. And we've got a fella in an V neck blue shirt, splattered in blood, blond hair; we had Hollywood and he was called Davey Hickson.

Bill Kenwright: Dave Hickson I worshipped, just worshipped. It was the time of Roy of the Rovers, the Tiger; and he was Roy of the Rovers. I wasn't alone. You talk worship, it doesn't get better than Dave, I don't think, with Evertonians of my era and a little later. It was that willingness, that apparent willingness, to die for your club. I just thought he would do anything for Everton. As I've said often, if I'm remembered for anything it'll be that I was quite brave and took chances; well, I think that's where I learnt it.

Dave Hickson: I was fearless. Nothing scared or overawed me. I played against some of the greatest defenders there were, like Billy Wright, and also some of the hardest, like Malcolm Barrass. I feared neither type of player. The fearlessness I had in my game was something that was always in me. Off the pitch people tell me I'm quite mild, but on it I just had an absolutely unbelievable desire to win, to score goals. I just wanted to finish; to finish a move with the ball in the back of the net. It was determination, it was never anything personal. When it's all over you shake hands and that's it. Nobody likes getting kicked or punched, but it's what happened in football in the 1950s. As long as we never broke someone's legs, you were okay – and we never did that at Everton. You would go for the ball and the man. It was a hard game, but a good and exciting game. I think it's gone a little too far the other way now. I think the players are too quick to go over and the referees too quick to penalise.

Derek Mayers: Dave was definitely as committed in training as he was in games. There used to be a little pitch at the back of Gwladys Street, where we used to play head tennis; and they used to get matches there, play for a few bob, you know, 30 bob or £1, which was quite a lot in those days. And oh, dear me; the air went blue when he was playing head tennis and he lost. He would knock around opposing defenders when he was in training as he would on the pitch. He played it hard; in five-a-side there was no punching code!

Tony McNamara: If Dave was angry on the pitch then he was angry. In one game the opposition had scored and it'd come back to the centre for kick-off and of course he was the centre-forward at the kick-off. But he stood there and the referee blew his whistle at him and he just stood there. He said 'Are you happy now? You've give it to them have you?' People would say 'Eh Dave shut up.' The referee would say 'I'll have to send you off Hickson, you'd better calm down a bit.' He was that sort of fellow.

Dave Hickson: Why was I the way I was? Firstly, because I wanted to win. But also because I loved the game. I think, looking back, I loved it too much – if it's possible to love anything too much. I just wanted to be out there on the pitch, playing, succeeding, winning. I lived football and I loved Everton. I became really obsessed by them, as I am today. I might be 83 now [at the time of the interview in 2013], but I still play every week with the lads. I'm up there in the stands, playing every single ball. I might do the PR now, but as far as I'm concerned I'm still playing – if only in my own head. There's nobody more gutted than me if we lose.

Mick Meagan: The great thing about Dave, as you know, was that he had a big mop of blonde hair, and he invariably came off the pitch with blood streaming down his face with the heading; getting up and clashing heads. I think that sort of added to the folk stories about him: 'His heads fallen off, the blood's streaming down, and he's carrying on!'

George Orr: There was a determination. They went out there and they ran their legs off. They played for Everton Football Club and they were loved. Dave Hickson's famous saying was 'I'd break every bone in my body for any club I played for, but I'd die for Everton.' That is something that hits the heart strings of every Evertonian.

Life in the Second Division

Dave Hickson: I knew they didn't belong in the Second Division and I wanted to help them. We were under no illusions that the task facing us was going to be hard. Just two teams went up in those days and there were no play-offs. Financially football was run on a much more equal basis, so that big clubs – and we were one of the biggest, despite relegation – found it harder to acquire players from elsewhere. Certainly this was a problem Cliff Britton came up against.

Tom Gardner: When we played it was direct; maybe I'm giving it the wrong way but I felt it was direct football. You had two full-backs, three half-backs, five forwards; that was attacking, and all teams played the same thing, there was no difference. It was only later that the 4-3-3, 4-2-4 came in. Those days you were told point blank to get the ball forward, get it forward all the time. The wingers, for instance, where I was playing, weren't full-backs, we were at the half-way line and forward, and didn't go back; the two full-backs looked after their forwards, the three half-backs looked after their inside-forwards. But the wingers were wingers and you stayed on that wing… Our game was direct; down the wing, slash it across, full whack to the centre-forward; that's why Hickson did so well.

Dave Hickson: I don't know why we found it hard as a team in the Second Division. I think struggle is the wrong word, but we never looked like we were going down again. It always seemed like we were getting it together, but it obviously took time. There were a few young players like me, and I suppose you're learning all the time. Sometimes you need to have that bit of experience to push you over the line. There were times when we'd play exceptionally well and just not get the result we needed. I remember one game in the season that we finished sixteenth in the Second Division and chance after chance after chance came our way. It was unbelievable. And somehow we ended up losing 1-0. We were the best team, but that's what can happen. Nobody ever pointed fingers, or accused teammates of not being good enough or pulling their weight. It wasn't the Everton way. Everyone gave 100 per-cent on the pitch and to each other.

Derek Temple: I was on the ground staff when you had the likes of Jimmy O'Neill, Jack Lindsay, Tommy Clinton, Cyril Lello, Tommy Jones, TE Jones, Jimmy Tansey, Kenny Rea; an awful lot of the stalwarts going back to the early 1950s. Football was evolving quite quickly in the 50s. They were good players in their own right and they did well for Everton, and a lot of them were internationals, especially the Irish. Peter Farrell, Tommy Eglington, very, very good players and they did well for Everton.

David Hart: Ted Buckle used to play on the wing, he always looked a little weedy, gaunt. Not a smile on his face at all.

Barbara Garner: He was on the outside-right and he took a corner, and it was brilliant. Everyone's waiting and it comes over, and talk about a curve ball, right in the net with nobody touching it. We all went berserk. I was near the corner flag that day, I was the other side, just couldn't believe it, we were speechless. Never seen a goal from a corner like that.

John McNally: I think Ted Sagar was a great goalkeeper in his day but I think he was past it after the war. He wasn't a bad goalkeeper but I would say that age must've crept up on him. He was bad tempered as well; he was always bad tempered to the full-backs; effing and blinding. He'd shout at anyone.

Eric Moonman: They were a great combination at different times. Eglington had moments when people loved him but he also had his critics, whereas Farrell pretty well consistently kept on improving. I think it established something that was already there: Everton's link with Ireland, which exists to this day.

Barbara Garner: Peter Farrell was a fatherly sort of figure and shape, and he had a serene, solid sort of nature. And the rest of them, they just seemed to gel together. You felt that they were just one team.

Dick White: Individually some of the players were okay, but nothing more than that. It had been the same since the war. There was Harry Potts, an industrious inside forward they'd signed for a record fee of £20,000 but he was nothing outstanding. Before they went down there was Harry Catterick who was a very ordinary player, but he had a very good inside forward in Wally Fielding. Eddie Wainwright was very quick. Wainwright and Fielding were the only good players until Dave Hickson came along. He was a far better footballer than a lot of people gave him credit for.

Barbara Garner: Wally Fielding always played with his shirt sleeves down, he held the shirt sleeves. Everybody else had short sleeves, rolled up sleeves. He was like a little back entry diddler. He had his hair in his eyes, but he was a terrific inside forward.

Dave Hickson: Cliff Britton probably bore the brunt of supporter frustrations. It's a shame because he had been a good player for Everton and was a nice man. But it was hard getting out of the Second Division. It was hard to play in. I never felt like it was any easier scoring in the second tier than when I played in the top flight. There were only two promotion slots and none of this play-off business you have nowadays. Now, if you're in the top ten or twelve by Easter, you're still in with a chance of going up, but there was none of that then.

Barbara Garner: The games weren't as tense. You were supportive and you wanted your team to win, but there was a lovely feel and atmosphere.

Tom Gardner: It was an exciting time to watch football. I mean to see Bill Liddell go down that left-wing, it was absolutely magic. It really was magic. And we had them. Tommy Eglington, left-winger; he would be down that wing like a shot. Peter Farrell was his mate at left-half, and Peter and Tommy were good. Tommy seemed to know what Pete was going to do with that ball, knew exactly where it was going to go. It was good, it was fast, it was good football. Not the speed that we've got today but more direct. There was very little of the back passing. Harry Cooke used to say 'Don't pass the ball back unless you've got to!' And you wouldn't. The full-back would get in trouble if he was back-passing because the wingers were so quick. I was quick as well. And if the ball was passed back you would be in like a shot.

Mick Meagan: Dave was a very good header of a ball and he had Tommy Eglington on the left wing then, and of course Tommy was very good at crossing balls. John Willie Parker was a lovely touch player. They had a great blend. I was surprised, before I went over from Ireland we used to have English teams coming over here during the summer to play in benefit matches and that, and they all seemed to be big, powerful lads. When I arrived at Everton, I thought that was going to happen to me: after a year at Everton you turn into a big monster of a man. But when I went over and who was there? Nobby Fielding, Eddie Wainwright, Cyril Lello – all small, little fellas. I thought 'Holy God, they're not the fellas that I was idolising.' But great players and lovely, lovely people.

Dave Hickson: In the dressing room we all stuck together. There was never any finger pointing, or feeling that someone wasn't pulling his weight or wasn't good enough. Nobody ever said to Cliff, 'We should be signing this fella.' It's not like it is today with all the transfer talk and speculation. We had no subs or anything, just the eleven players that were changed by Cliff very infrequently. It helped build up a great team spirit.

John Sutherland: I was a great friend of Tommy Eglington. He looked after me when I got there; he took me playing golf – introduced me to golf – and many times he'd meet me where he lived in Dublin. Happy days they were. Peter Farrell was a great player and good quick player a wing-half. He was captain and took it very seriously; he was a good man off the field. Tommy was like a bullet on the left wing. He could run, Tommy Eglington.

Mick Meagan: I think there was about seven of us lads from Ireland: Jimmy O'Neill, Don Donovan, Peter Farrell, Tommy Eglington, Tommy Clinton, John Sutherland and Georgey Cummins. They were all very good to me, as all the players were. You didn't have to be Irish, they just made you welcome, the whole lot and they were a great lot of lads, and I enjoyed every minute of their company.

Barbara Garner: My favourite team, the team that I was really passionate about, was about 1950, 51. Peter Farrell was captain, and I lived in the Old Roan, and he lived in the Old Roan, and being an Irish Catholic he went to the same church. Tommy Eglington was his friend, and he lived there too. I saw them around all the time. They were just friendly, they'd just chat to you. My father played quite a role in the church, so he obviously made very close friends with them. He was also very close friends with Jimmy O'Neill.

Arthur Parker: My brother's [John Willie Parker] biggest mates were the Irish lads, Peter Farrell, Tommy Eglington, George Cummins, Jimmy O'Neill; they didn't half get on well. We only had a two-bedroomed house in Birkenhead and they all used to come to our house for the dinner, and me Mam used to give them egg and chips! Outside there was a big school playground and they'd go on at half four, put the gear on and play the school kids, and were diving all over the place! Leyland's diving all over the goal! They were crackers, it was brilliant, absolutely brilliant!

Gerry Moore: I remember one day I got off the bus at Spellow Lane and I went to buy some sweets in a shop on the corner of one of the streets that lead down to County Road. As I got in there the Everton captain at the time, Peter Farrell, was in there buying some cigarettes. I was surprised to see him but I got chatting to him and he actually waited for me to buy my sweets and then chatted to me as I we walked to the ground and then he went into the players entrance. You would never get that happening now!

Bishop Tom Williams: Most of the priests in the city were Everton supporters because they were all Irish and Everton had a lot of Irish players. It was a bit like when Arsenal had Liam Brady and all of the local Irish people supported them. Most people thought to support Everton you had to be Catholic or the other way around but that wasn't true. A lot of the priests were season ticket holders and mad Evertonians because they knew people from Ireland who played for them. There's a strong link with Everton with North Wales and the North Wales element is anything but Catholic it was very Methodist. Everton was essentially a Methodist Church foundation – St. Domingo's.

David Hart: We had a great following from Ireland, they used to come over in boats. Everton were the first team I think – then United and probably Liverpool – that had a big Irish supporters' club. They'd walk up the river, come on the boat, and walk up to the match. A lot of them, of course, were Catholics, so a lot of clergy went to Everton, had season tickets or whatever, so there was a nice atmosphere.

Jimmy Harris: There were more priests in the stands on a Saturday afternoon than spectators. I think there was a row of about 20-30 priests, because Eglington, Donovan, Tansey, Meagan, Jimmy O'Neill, George Cummins, they were all from Dublin. I think it was only Brian Harris and myself who were Protestants. We used to eat in town in the Exchange Station and then we'd make our own way up to the ground in the car, and one of the Catholics would stop up at that church halfway up Scotland Road. He would go in and get the holy water, and he'd put it all over him to stop him breaking anything.

Dave Hickson: The supporters were always brilliant; they always stuck by us. They could see that we were trying our best for Everton and respected that. If it was quiet you tended not to take any notice, but if they got behind you it really used to encourage you. They were great, even when we were in the middle of the Second Division. They were patient and never heckled. They could see that we were trying to play good, exciting football. Sometimes when we went away you'd get booed or heckled by the home fans before kick off. But that was only because they knew we were going to have a go.

1953 FA Cup run

The 1952/53 season would be the worst league campaign in the club's history, with Everton finishing sixteenth in the Second Division. But in the FA Cup a series of heroic performances saw this team of under-performers enter club lore.

Dave Hickson: We didn't start the 1952/53 season well, losing our first three games and scoring just once. We went to the bottom of the Second Division; the lowest point in Everton history. The mood was not very good at all. I never liked losing. Like me, my teammates wanted to get out there and win. But it was no good feeling sorry for ourselves. We just had to pick ourselves up, that was all. As well as getting out of the Second Division, our other priority was doing as well as we could in the FA Cup. In the days before European football and the League Cup, and with international football still undeveloped, it was a huge thing in those days. In terms of prestige it was, in many people's minds, the equal of winning the League Championship. We hadn't done so well in my first experience of the FA Cup, losing a third round replay at home to Leyton Orient. Second time around, in 1952/53, we did much better. Indeed, the run has gone down in Everton history and my part in it is something I became famous for.

After winning home ties against Ipswich Town and Nottingham Forest, Everton were drawn in the fifth round against First Division Champions, Manchester United.

Dave Hickson: The game did not start as planned. United took a 27th-minute lead when Johnny Berry's shot was palmed by our goalie Jimmy O'Neill into the path of Jack Rowley, and he scored from six yards. I suppose then it looked like the game was going according to form. United's advantage was, however, short-lived. Seven minutes later I played in Tommy Eglington, who took it around Johnny Aston and let fly with a right-footed shot which flew into the back of the United net. Five minutes from the interval came the moment everyone remembers. Jack Lindsay crossed and I dived in, trying to connect with his cross. In doing so I caught an opponent's boot and was left with blood streaming from a wound above my right eye. Harry Cooke led me from the field with a ball of cotton wool affixed to my head. I missed the last few minutes of the first half as, in the dressing room, old Harry did his best to stop the bleeding before the doctor stitched the wound up and put a bandage on it during half-time. But I had to come back on. There was really no choice in the matter. I came onto the field after the break, a few seconds after my teammates. I'm sure there were some people there who didn't think I'd make it back out, but that was never an option.

Leon Bernicoff: I remember the blood pouring from the wound there on his head and he carried on. Everton won 2-1. He was the hero, scoring the winner.

Rev. Harry Ross: I think it was the dedication that made him an idol. I think nowadays if they are injured they just go off the pitch or if they foul they can be sent off but in those days they just continued. It was just dedication: got to get the ball, got to get the ball in the net, doesn't matter if I've got blood pouring out of my head, I'm just carrying on. The dedication and the commitment appealed to me as well as the artistry. I do admire what they do today but there just seemed to be something extra in those days.

Dave Hickson: The win over United saw us drawn at Aston Villa in the quarter-finals a fortnight later. It was a tough draw – Villa were in the First Division – and another big crowd, with more than 60,000 filling Villa Park, including many Evertonians. It was a tight game and Villa had their chances. One thing about being a centre-forward in those days was that you were only expected to attack. Now you see everyone coming back to defend set-pieces, but there was none of that really. So when, fifteen minutes from the end, Everton launched a break, following a scrum in their own area, I was on hand to assist. The ball was hacked clear as far as me, just inside our own half. I switched play to Ted Buckle – who was in the outside-left position – and sprinted forward to take the return pass. Then, holding off the challenge of a Villa defender, I fired the ball home.

Victory brought Everton a semi-final appearance against Nat Lofthouse's Bolton Wanderers at Manchester's Maine Road.

Dave Hickson: I don't know what went wrong in the first half of the semi. It wasn't that we were terrible, more that they just played exceptionally well and Lofthouse – who was a great, great player – was at the centre of everything. Before we knew it they were 4–0 up.

Arthur Parker: Hickson was told by Britton to stay away from Malcolm Barrass, who was a big fat centre-half for Bolton who kicked everything that moved. Hickson was told to stay away from him. And in the first ten minutes, Hickson goes for Barrass and the next thing he's on the floor and he's suffering from concussion. There were no subs or nothing then. It wouldn't have been allowed now, but they let him play on, and he didn't know where he was.

John McNally: You know how a centre-forward used to go into the net sometimes. Hickson was coming back and he was running out and 'boomph!' Malcolm Barrass smacked him. He got away with it as well.

David Hart: Hickson and Barrass, the Bolton centre-half, had a running feud the whole game. Hickson got battered and possibly carried off. And next time Bolton came to Goodison, Barrass ended up in hospital. There was a real feud between them. Our parents used to talk about it, they hated Barrass.

It was Jimmy O'Neill let them down that day. Although he was my favourite, he made a couple of bad errors, possibly under pressure from Lofthouse.

Dave Hickson: Half the time I didn't know what was going on. I'd gone up for a ball that was heading for me and Malcolm Barrass, the Bolton centre half, flattened me. I don't know what had happened, whether it was on purpose or not. The ball was heading to me and next thing I was on the floor, gasping for air. I was really out of it and had to leave the field for 15 minutes. In fact I was only really half-fit for the rest of the game. Shortly before half-time we had a glimmer of hope when a penalty was awarded in our favour.

Arthur Parker: Tommy Clinton missed a penalty about two minutes before half-time but it didn't seem to matter. They came back; my brother scored two excellent headers. I cry when I think about it now – they came back and it got to 4-3 with a quarter of an hour to go, and they pummelled them and they just couldn't get it. And that was the Matthews final and everything, the glory he would have had they been there, but it wouldn't have affected him. It would have done me but not my brother.

Dave Hickson: There was a feeling of devastation in the dressing room afterwards. I never usually looked back. I never reflected on what might have been. I always looked forward to the next game if we got beaten, but this was different. There were lads there that knew they'd never come so close to winning a trophy. I was one of them, it turned out. I never got so close in the FA Cup again after that. My immediate disappointment was dampened by my injuries. I was out of it. I went to stay with relatives in Manchester that night and they didn't recognise me. It was unbelievable. I'd been bashed around so badly in my face. My eyes were filled with blood for weeks and my mum wasn't happy about it at all. I remember watching on Pathé News a few days later being played through. I couldn't believe I missed it. I'm sure if it wasn't for the concussion I'd have scored and brought us back into the game.

John McNally: They did put a good show yeah but you always knew that Everton were going to lose. You could see the players and their heads drop and there was no one in real command. That was the situation until Catterick came as manager, and he was the one that got Everton on the right track.

Dave Hickson: Bolton later played Blackpool in what became known as the Matthews Final, losing 4–3, the same scoreline by which they'd beaten us. I think we'd have won that game. We were good enough. I'll always regret never having the chance to have played at Wembley while I was a professional. It would have seen us make an indelible impression in Everton football history.

1953/54 Promotion

After the disappointments of the 1952/53 campaign, a core of Everton players rallied together and put together a sustained promotion drive. Led by the forward partnership of Dave Hickson and John Willie Parker, who combined to score 55 league goals, Everton spent the majority of the season in the promotion places.

Arthur Parker: When John Willie Parker got into the first-team he couldn't go wrong in the Second Division. He was leading goalscorer in the three seasons they had there. He never got excited, he was the coolest man in the world and he didn't have to act it, that's the way he was. Never did anybody a bad turn in his life.

Dave Hickson: My partnership with John Willie Parker really took off. He was an excellent inside forward. We had a good working relationship and with that you always know what the other fellow is doing. Between us we scored 60-odd goals in the 1953/54 season. People always say that's great, but I always say, 'Well, Dixie scored sixty on his own!' Wally Fielding was a great player, don't get me wrong, but sometimes you didn't know what he was going to do. You'd expect it and he'd turn his back on you, when he should have played the first ball. John Willie was really my partner in crime. We each knew what we were going to do; if I was going for a ball he'd be there waiting for it and I could find him. He was from Birkenhead and played for several years for Everton as an amateur before turning professional later on. We made our debuts around the same time, but he was more than four years older than me so was in his mid-twenties before he made his league bow. Some people said he didn't move around enough, but for me he was always in and out of everywhere. He didn't really have pace, John. He had a long stride on him and he used to deceive people a lot. I used to love setting up chances for John Willie, but it takes two to make a partnership. It gave me great joy to set up chances for teammates; people often overlook that this is, after all, a team game. I could probably have scored more goals if I'd wanted to, if I'd been a bit more selfish, but I didn't. Helping others was always my priority. He gave me opportunities as well. He'd give me one goal and I'd give him one back. He was quite a guy was John Willie; a good worker and a real nice fella.

Eric Linford: The greatest Dave Hickson performance was when we played Plymouth Argyle [on 27 February 1954]. They wore a green shirt and they had a bloke with a beard and Davey Hickson would pull on his beard. It was probably the game I've been to with the most goals: Everton 8 Plymouth 4.

Charles Mills senior: Everton's hour came at Oldham; the last day of the 1953/54 season. We had to win for a return to the First Division. If we won by six we'd be Champions. In a hired charabank with all my mates we arrived at the ground. The gates were shut and thousands outside. The stewards were shouting, 'Sorry lads. The ground is overcrowded already.'

Dave Hickson: Everton were in third place behind Leicester City on 56 points and Blackburn Rovers on 55. With both of those sides having completed their programme of fixtures, it meant that we needed a win against Oldham at Boundary Park to pull level with Leicester and pip Blackburn to promotion. If we scored six, we would be crowned Second Division Champions. They say there were 20,000 Scousers there that night, but I thought it was nearly 40,000. You'd never normally get that at Oldham, would you? They said that they tarmacked over everywhere – literally poured hot sticky tar over the walls – to stop people getting in, but it didn't work. The fans climbed over everything to get in. The place was packed, heaving. It was a fantastic night.

Father John Ashton: They had tried tarmacking the walls earlier to stop people getting in. I climbed a wooden post to get over the wall and there were several priests alongside me, all in collars, because we didn't get rid of the collar in those days; we wore it to go to the match. We were all giving each other a leg up outside of Oldham's ground.

John McNally: They put tar all over the walls on the outside to try and stop us. I never tried anything like that, but they put papers they'd brought and stuck them on the wall and went over the wall.

Charles Mills senior: For the first and only time we joined the mob. The gates crumbled and we all entered in one mad rush. Just in time to see our first goal. Another three came before half time.

Mission accomplished.

Father John Ashton: Oldham were a good side then; they weren't just a rubbish collection. And we had Davey Hickson play that day as centre-forward and he would go through defence lines as if they were not there.

Dave Hickson: We were 4–0 up at half-time. Tommy Jones and I each scored one – Tommy getting his with a shot from our half – and John Willie a brace, but we still needed two more to win the Second Division Championship. Tommy Eglington hit the post and our old teammate George Burnett, who was in goal for Oldham, kept a few out. We had a great chance to go clear of Leicester, but it wasn't to be. The score remained stuck at 4–0. We hadn't won the Championship, but we'd been promoted. At the final whistle, not for the first time in my career, hundreds of Everton supporters invaded the pitch and carried us off the field. We had a celebration in the dressing room and photos taken, before getting the bus home and going our separate ways. Everton were back in the First Division and – although there were a few scares against Wimbledon and Coventry in the 1990s – they've stayed there ever since.

Charles Mills senior: The next plan after the game was to find a pub. Late April, it was still light, but with about 55,000 Scousers well and hell bent with the same objective it seemed hopeless. Outside one pub, with about 100 trying for admission, the manager came out. 'No more in, lads, but I can fix you up in the back garden. Any trouble now and you're out.' We tipped our coach driver who, after our 'natural agreement' led us to the garden and kept his promise of drinking lemonade. That was until about 3am when he managed to get us out with the help of the proprietor. It then dawned on me that 3am was the time that I started work – in Liverpool. Nemesis threatened. I was put down in Queen Square, where I worked at he wholesale market, to be met by my Dad – then my boss. His first words were 'You're late' and 'You've been drinking again.' One of his fellow directors came to my aid: 'Come on Charlie – it's only a one off.' 'It had better be – otherwise he's out,' came the reply.

Leon Bernicoff: It was wild in the city after we got promoted. We've always had better support than Liverpool.

Barbara Garner: My father drove us down to Goodison and we stood in the dark with other supporters waiting for a good hour in the night time, cold with our scarves, waiting for the bus to arrive. And the joy when the bus arrived and all the players got off. Everybody was shaking hands, and they stood in a line for the *Echo* photographers, and we were on it. We were on the photo.

Eric Moonman: It wasn't a coronation at all. If anything it was almost matter of fact. I mean it was different, say, from winning the cup or a great achievement like Dixie Dean scoring his goals. I think the fact that we went down was a shock but coming up really didn't transfer into massive enthusiasm. It was 'We are here now, let's get on with it.'

Barbara Garner: We were so excited that they were coming up – we felt that the door was open then, we had this wonderful team. The team was loved as one man.

Dave Hickson: In some ways we found the First Division easier than the second tier. Early in the 1954/55 season we went top, and although form dipped, it rose again too. After a slow start personally, goals continued to come the way of John Willie and me. Our partnership made such a promising start in the top flight that with ten games left that season, Everton moved up to fourth, four points behind league leaders Chelsea, and with three games in hand. I think we were probably undone by our lack of experience in the end. We lost seven, drew two and won just one of our remaining fixtures, finishing the season eleventh – the lowest position we'd held all year.

Life as a 1950s footballer

Tom Gardner: In those days I got paid £7 a week to start, £8 a week when I made the first-team but that was a little more than the average wage then which I think was about £5 for a worker in an ordinary job. It was nothing like it is now but it was reasonable money.

Arthur Parker: My brother loved Everton but the thing that people don't realise is he made no money out of it. It used to be five years and they'd get a testimonial and it was £750; you used to pay £248 tax out of that and that's for five years service! Everybody talks about the maximum wage but not everyone got the maximum wage. When he played it was £14. Until he got in the first-team, he wasn't on £14, he was on £10, and that'd drop again in the summer.

Dave Hickson: The most I earned from playing was £20 per week at a time when my Dad was on £16. I also got £2 for a win and £1 for a draw. There was always talk of under the table payments at some clubs, but we never got any of that at Everton. The management at Goodison always played everything straight down the line. At the same time you were only ever on a one-year contract. There was no real security. If you got seriously injured you were at the mercy of the club. At the end of the season they would publish their 'retain list' and if you weren't on it, you were finished. You had to play well to get on that list. There was no contract. There was also no freedom of movement, so it wasn't like you could just go and join another club.

Arthur Parker: I remember a joke about Tommy Docherty, when he was at Preston and he was discussing terms and £14 was the maximum wage. Jimmy Milne was manager at Preston and he said 'We've got to talk wages Tommy, what do you think?' And he said 'Well it's £14 maximum wage isn't it?' So he said, 'Yeah but there's only one player on £14 a week at this club and that's Tom Finney.' So Tommy Docherty said, 'Why can't I have it?' He said, 'Because you're not as good a player as Tom Finney.' So they went on and they used to get summer and winter wages. He said 'So what's the summer wages?' 'Well Tom Finney's on £12.' 'Well can I have £12?' 'We've told you you're not as good a player as Tom Finney.' And he said 'I am in the summer!' Because they didn't play football in the summer! They used to have summer and winter wages, you'd get so much when you were playing in the winter but your money dropped when you weren't playing.

Millie Donovan: I knew Jimmy O'Neill, and Jimmy invited my friend Pat and I to a party. So we went to the party and when we come out after the party Pat said to me, 'Did you fancy any of them' and I said 'Well I fancied that one, Don.' She said, 'Well I fancy John.' None of us fancied Jimmy and he'd taken us to the party. That was when we started dating them and she married John Sutherland and I married Don Donovan. I hadn't a clue he was a footballer. My mother said to me one day when it was raining, 'Well, they won't be playing today in the rain, they don't play in the rain' and I said, 'Oh they do 'cos they have plastic macs on.' She said 'Oh, I was going to say they'd have to wear something.' We were all girls, so we never ever went to a match. We didn't know a thing about football. I didn't even know it was a job.

John Sutherland: I lived about a mile or something like that at the most from Goodison and then they gave me a club house, which is now where the Dixie Dean statue is [on Walton Lane, facing Stanley Park]. There was a row of houses and that's where I lived when I got married. Cyril Lello was there and Jackie Grant; a lot of chaps living there.

Millie Donovan: We rented the house off Everton, we didn't buy it. Mabel Farrell [Peter's wife] rented hers and we rented ours next door. We didn't buy it because they gave you a house and I think Don just paid the rent to the club.

Dave Hickson: I was difficult to avoid because everyone knew my quiff! I quite enjoyed the attention, it was good. We had to be at Bellefield at 9.30am to start training at 10am, and my journey would be [from Ellesmere Port] by bus to the ferry terminal, then we'd cross the Mersey by boat and get a tram to the training ground. People were great with me; you'd go to offer your sixpence fare and the ticket inspector would say, 'Put that away, Dave.' Usually I'd meet John Willie Parker on the way. We worked as a pair and we travelled as a pair. He didn't have to pay his fare either!

Derek Temple: In those days there was a bus that used to come to Goodison Park and take the players to Bellefield and then after training shift them back to Goodison, to use all of the facilities, the bathing facilities. There was a little room upstairs, up a spiral staircase. It was like a little canteen where you could go and have a bite to eat, because you'd often be training in the afternoon as well.

Tony McNamara: We used to get invited to different clubs, like church clubs and things like that, and of course there were a lot of people there that were Everton. So you used to see each other every now and again, and that was the only time we saw each other together in midweek. But I think it was very good. They don't do that now so much. Players now, everybody's got a beautiful big car, whereas only a couple of us had a car in those days.

Father John Ashton: Peter Farrell and Tommy Eglington were very good Catholics, and they were very pally with us priests. Farrell was very nice and he of course was captain of Everton. As priests we had a team and for a while I was captain of the team. Farrell and Eglington used to play with us! We used to play Liverpool Police, and this factory – I can't remember the name of it – but Bootle Police was the big game and I remember playing and beating them. After the game they took us for a cup of tea down to the police station and out of the police van – they sent a van, a Black Maria – stepped all these priests, and they made their way into the police station as though they were being copped. It was great! We had a good team. The reason we had a good team was we were non-smokers. We weren't allowed to have much in the way of a cigarette – once or twice a week, you know. And we used to play with them. They came along to our games.

Dave Hickson: Off the pitch I didn't really socialise with any of the players. I didn't smoke or drink at the time. I was married to my first wife very young, and I used to make my way home after the game. Peter Farrell and Tommy Eglington would be the main ones who would organise the socialising among the players. I believe John Willie Parker would go out and have the odd drink now and again midweek. After Wednesdays we were told, 'Don't go drinking, that's it.' One or two used to do different things together, go to the pub or some clubs or something like that, but not me. I went home.

Arthur Parker: John Willie got well known obviously in the press and all that, but he was just one of the lads. He still went in the same boozer; he didn't drink a lot, always drunk bottles of Guinness. Cliff Britton always let him have two bottles of Guinness on a Friday night before a game when he went away. He always said 'Go and get your two bottles of Guinness' to our kid and he'd go and get them. He wasn't like that with everyone! Just special people! He never let anyone do anything Britton, he was pretty strict actually.

Derek Temple: I went on the ground staff, and I can say I served my time on the yard brush. I didn't do it for too long because I went out helping their own tradesman. They had their own men on the staff. They had an old master painter named Bob. I say master painter because then you had to mix your own paint, and he was very good. I used to go out with him, and do the players' houses. I did work on Cliff Britton's house years ago, because he was manager when I first signed. After a while of being on the yard brush, I advanced to the paint brush, and I quite enjoyed it. It was a little bit of a grounding in painting and decorating.

Dave Hickson: We used to play in old hobnail boots. You used to have to hammer them to soften them up. We'd get supplied with one pair to last us the whole season, and if they got broken you had to repair them. When you see what they play in now, it's really unbelievable. All the gear they've got is wonderful: light boots, breathable materials, a much lighter ball. I'd have loved to have played with some of that gear. Some players in the 1950s experimented with new gear. Stanley Matthews, after seeing foreign players at the 1950 World Cup, commissioned his own lightweight boots. But there was none of that for most of us. Very few players were involved in advertising or endorsements back then. If I was a player today I couldn't see myself in pink or orange boots, although there's probably money to be made from it. It's probably accepted now, but I just don't fancy the idea of wearing yellow boots or something like that! We'd get two strips for the season. I believe the players get ten these days, but we just had to make do with the two shirts. One would get washed one week, the other the next. We had an away strip as well, but no third or fourth-choice kits as they seem to do today.

Tony McNamara: When we went away to London everybody had a nice leather bag with all their things in. John Lindsay, the full-back, he came, but he had a brown paper bag instead. We said, 'Eh Lindsay, do you realise who you're playing for? Everton Football Club.' And the lads picked his stuff up, opened the window and threw it out!

Dave Hickson: For away games we would travel by coach or train. There was no flying then! I mean, they fly down from Liverpool to Southampton now, but there was none of that, and remember these were the days before motorways too. There wouldn't normally be overnight stays either. None of us really minded. I suppose we didn't know any better. Typically we would stop off around 11.30am on the away-day journey, stretch our legs and have a light lunch – a bit of fish or something like that. On the return journey it would be straight back.

Millie Donovan: We went to the theatre and we were sat in the row and watching the show and two or three people came along the row to ask Don for autographs. I thought, 'Why are they asking him now for autographs?' and that was when it dawned on me that he must've played and they knew him. He was well known in Liverpool in Spellow Lane. There was a cake shop on the corner and when he went in they all knew him and they also knew him in Ryders. They were mad Evertonians and they all went to the match. After the match we all went into their shop and all the fans came in asking for autographs and that was when I realised that football was a thing that people liked. We weren't a footballing family, we hadn't a clue and none of the family: my father and my brothers didn't; they never went to a match.

Derek Temple: I wasn't the only one of course, but an awful lot of footballers did national service. But I can't remember another full-time professional being in Kenya. I was kidded a little bit. You had your choice of what regiment you joined, and I was asked by one of the recruiting officers at the medical. This chap said to me 'You play football, Temple?' and I said 'Yes.' He said 'If you join our regiment you will be able to play every week, it won't interfere with your career because you're based at Formby, Harrington Barracks.' It was the Kings Liverpool Regiment. It was a very well-known regiment with a good name, an infantry regiment which was probably not the best regiment to join because you're always going to be on the front line. I said 'That's great, if I can carry on my career.' So I joined the Kings regiment and ten months later I was in Kenya!

Dave Hickson: I was posted to the Cheshire Army Cadets in Chester, so I was far from neither home nor Merseyside. Not only that, when I was with the regiment's football team, I had a very special coach: Dixie Dean. We had some good times together while I was on national service. Dixie took us over to Ireland to play some matches – we played Cliftonville, who were a top side over there. The story is that it was Dixie who recommended me to Everton, but that's not true. I'd already been there for nearly four years off and on by the time our paths crossed. I was later transferred over to the North Staffordshire Infantry Regiment and posted to Egypt. Theo Kelly was not in the least bit happy about this and tried everything he could to get me out of it and wrote many letters to all sorts of people trying to get me posted in England. Although I'd travelled around a bit playing football and visiting family in Salford, I'd never been anywhere and certainly not overseas (apart from Dixie's trips to Ireland). It was my duty to go, but at the same time I only wanted to play football. I wouldn't ever say national service was my wake-up to the world because it was just not my scene. I wanted to get back to football. Had Everton got me off the boat I believe I would have started earlier in the first team.

Graham Williams: I played for the British Army ten times. You wouldn't believe the quality. They'd get orders printed from the War Office in London, saying, 'Sapper Williams must be allowed all efficiencies and help to enable him to fulfil his commitment to the British Army Football Team.' Well my Commanding Officer was mad for football and obviously he was overjoyed to help me. I played against the French army, which was advertised as an international between France and Britain. The two star men were Graham Williams 'the definitive outside-left' – I kept the write-ups – and Cliff Jones on the right wing. And Bobby Charlton was my inside left. They had a Scottish International goalkeeper from West Ham. We drew one each, and there were 25,000 spectators.

Jimmy Harris: We just had to go. Everton didn't see me for eighteen months. I'd changed, I got bigger and stronger from being in Germany and then I played in a practice match at Bellefield, and I did quite well. The manager Cliff Britton said 'When are you coming full time?' So I said 'I'm going back to Germany tomorrow for four months, and then I've got twelve months serving my time to finish.' So I was 21 when I came back.

Derek Temple: It was hard work coming back from national service. I always say that the army or national service cost me three years of my career, because I was established as a first team player when I went into the army only nineteen at the time. Who knows what would have happened if I hadn't gone in? I played for England youth team, Under-20s I think it was. I was a goalscorer. I had two years in Kenya where I played, but it was a different standard of football of course. Where I was based in Kenya it was 8,000 metres above sea level so the altitude slows everything down. When I came out it took me a year to get back into the swing of things. I was still retained at Everton, but I was in the reserves. It wasn't bad in one respect, because the reserve team then, there was a lot of established players.

Alec Farrall: I was in the army and I got called down to the office of the colonel in charge of the camp, and he said to me, 'I've had a letter from the War Office.' I'd never even heard of the War Office. And he said, 'They're going to demob six weeks early because you're going to America with Everton on tour, and you're going to make dollars for the country.' Because they were skint I suppose, the government. So that's what happened – I went to America with Everton. One week I'm in the army, next week I'm on the Queen Elizabeth going to America. It didn't seem real.

Jimmy Harris: I was a good player for Everton, I was fairly consistent. My mum and dad used to go: if you've got your mum and dad in the stand you couldn't be having stinkers. He came home one Monday from work as an engineer, and he said 'All the lads were saying how bad you were on Saturday.' I said, 'Yeah I wasn't very good Dad.' He said 'You won't be going out much for a few weeks will you?' I said 'No, dad'!

Changes at Goodison

After winning promotion in April 1954, Everton did well back in the First Division and for a period in Spring 1955 were in sight of an unlikely title challenge. Late season form dropped off and the Blues finished eleventh, four places higher than the subsequent season. However, all was not well off the pitch. Cliff Britton's popularity continued to diminish after he sanctioned the sale of Dave Hickson to Huddersfield and in February 1956 he was ousted as manager after a boardroom spat. The Everton directors initially took charge of first team affairs, before appointing Ian Buchan, a former amateur footballer and PT lecturer at Loughborough University, as manager.

Alec Farrall: Everton always played good football – well they tried to anyway. There was no kicking up and run after it sort of thing; they tried to play decent football, I always thought so anyway. It was drummed into you when you were a kid, when you were 16, 17, to play the way the first team played. Because if you got in the first team then you had to play like they did.

Dave Hickson: I never swore when I was on the pitch. I might have said 'bloody' every now and then, but nothing bad. The Everton management were all right then, but I felt that under Britton maybe that counted against me. When he left me out I was done with him. It set me back a lot. He'd told me I'd play for England. It was a big let down being left out and I didn't want to be unwanted, so when a couple of clubs came in for me I told Everton I wanted to leave.

Mick Meagan: Evertonians were really shocked, they didn't expect him to go. It wasn't a thing that was done very much in those days. Once you signed for a club you were more or less with them; that was your club and that was it. But Dave, whatever happened, it was a big shock, and in those days when there was talk about a player being transferred you sort of wouldn't believe it. But when he came back to collect his boots that would be the sign that you were on your way.

Bill Kenwright: The only close thing to it is when my first girlfriend parted with me at the Pier Head when I was 17 or 18. Your first broken heart is the worst. It was in-des-scribe-able. This is quite well known, quite famous, that I wrote to all of the directors and I said – and this is in a child's handwriting – 'You know nothing, but nothing, but nothing about football. How can you do this?' I wrote to Dave, and when they did my This Is Your Life, he came on, and he had the letter, and he took it out of his pocket and read the letter that I'd sent to him saying, 'I'm praying that one day you'll come back; and until you do, whoever you join, I will support you.'

June Bernicoff: We went to see Huddersfield versus Stoke, to see Dave Hickson play. That is where I made the biggest faux pas I could. Leon [her husband to be] said, 'He's blond, you can't mistake him.' He was all full of enthusiasm waiting for him to come out, and I said, 'Is that him?' He replied: 'Oh for God's sake, that's Denis Law.' I lived to regret that one.

Jimmy Harris: I'd just been playing for England U23's at Sheffield. We were at Buxton doing special training for the sixth round cup tie on the Saturday. England called me up on the Monday, and I went to Sheffield on the bus, played for England against Scotland, scored, came back and they all had newspapers. There's a photograph there. I said, 'What you all reading the same fucking paper for? What's up with you?' They said, 'Oh, Cliff's just had the sack.' I said, 'What?!' Because he ran the place, you know. He ran the directors and told them what to do and everything. He was a pretty stern character, Cliff, so they ganged up on him and got rid of him.

Derek Temple: Cliff Britton left Everton when I was on the groundstaff. They had an interim chap named Harold Pickering who was like an admin officer, but he wasn't the manager, because he didn't know anything. He might have known a bit about football, but he wasn't an ex-footballer. He was an administration officer.

Mick Meagan: Ian Buchan came in. Ian, I think, was more of a trainer rather than a football man. Ian changed it completely. That was when the likes of Peter Farrell and Tommy Eglington, Jack Lindsay moved on. They brought in all the young lads. Cliff Britton seemed to say 'That's my team,' and he used to go for the old, experienced type of player. But when Ian Buchan came he changed it completely, and went in for all the younger lads. Eddie Thomas, Jimmy Harris, Brian Harris… this is how we got into the team then.

Graham Williams: I thought Ian was a wonderful coach. You know the story of how he came to Everton? Everton approached Loughborough College, where he was head of department, looking for a trainer; and he saw the salary that Everton were offering and took it himself!

Derek Mayers: He was an ex-fitness training instructor at Loughborough College. But he didn't know an awful lot about football. I can remember one time, we played I think with Chelsea at Goodison and we got beaten 3-0. He said, 'I'm not going to talk to you now lads; I'll see you at Bellefield on Monday, we'll sort it all out then.' Well, I'm not kidding, nothing went right. Pre-plan free-kicks went wrong, throw-ins went wrong; nothing went right at all, so we thought we're going to get a right bollocking at Bellefield. So we get down to Bellefield and we all gather in the practice room, and Ian comes in and he says, 'Well lads – I've thought a lot about that game on Saturday, and for the life of me I can't think where we went wrong!' We all fell about laughing. Everything went wrong and he couldn't even see it.

John Sutherland: He was a fanatic with new ideas. When you were playing away you'd get off the coach early. Say if you were going to Sheffield you'd probably get off at Chesterfield and walk the rest of the way.

Charles Mills senior: Ian Buchan was a dead loss, but then Cliff Britton – as a good a player as he had been – was too!

Tony McNamara: We had a spell where we had the directors in charge of the club. You used to get things passed down from the captain of the club, Peter Farrell, and a couple of the other fellows used to be asked into the directors' box when they were having discussions in the evening in midweek. They were picking the team and that sort of thing. They used to tell us the stories, it used to come back through the players. There was one fellow there whose advice was always 'Give him a kick!' That was his idea of the game, 'Give him a kick!'

Derek Temple: He was a nice man, Ian. He came from Loughborough College; he was a physical education lecturer. He'd played, but for Queens Park in Scotland, an amateur team who played at Hampden. He gave me my debut. He didn't last long, but he had us tremendously fit. He built a gym on the Gwladys Street End, in the corner of the stand underneath and he had us really, really fit. When things started to go wrong – I think he had us top of the league just after Christmas – we got a few injuries and a loss of form, and he didn't know how to handle it then. Maybe we didn't have a strong enough pool, that's possible. He got the push and he later worked for John Moores, at Littlewoods. He was killed a few years later at Scotch Corner in a car crash, which was tragic. I liked Ian a lot, he was a good man.

Although Ian Buchan's time in charge of Everton was widely derided, the return of Dave Hickson from Huddersfield Town in August 1957 came under his charge.

Bill Kenwright: The great joy about breaking up is when you're making up, as Neil Sedaka said. And the day I heard he was coming back – oh my God – the world changed. You must know that he played in the practice game, which we started the season off every year, and over 30,000 came to see his return. I can think of no-one in my lifetime, and this is memory talking, that's had as big an impact.

Dave Hickson: No one wanted to be at Everton more than me. When the transfer went through [in September 1957] it was a great homecoming at Everton. I really enjoyed it, but then how could you not? They were my club. It was the happiest day of my life when I returned to Goodison.

Jimmy Harris: I think we settled down when Dave returned. We had a good relationship playing on the pitch. But Dave was a head case. He was popular with the crowd because he was that type. At Goodison he would kick anybody, but they were all waiting for him when we went away. Once he got on the pitch he just went into this red mist. I remember him trampling on Billy Wright at Goodison one day, and he said 'Get up, there's nothing the matter with you, you're hopeless! Like the Beverly Sisters!' Billy was married to one of them!

Mick Meagan: The great thing about was that the chap you knew when he went away, when he came back he was still the same Dave. No change, no nothing. When he came back he was still the same character – great, great character. That was the wonderful thing about it.

Derek Temple: When Dave Hickson came back to the club, he went centre-forward, I went inside forward to Dave, and I was still getting goals, because he was the big strong guy, I was the smaller fella, he was knocking balls down and I was knocking them in, so it worked out. Unfortunately, national service came calling.

Dave Hickson: Results didn't go Ian Buchan's way, but I liked him and thought that he was a good manager. A lot has been made of his background as a sports lecturer, but I don't remember anything different on the training ground. It was mostly the same as it always had been; lots of lapping, head tennis, five-a-sides. At Everton we were brought up to play good football. I liked to get stuck in, but playing attractive football was very important too. There was only so much anybody could ever teach us. Although I was number nine, there was competition for my place. Ian Buchan brought in new signings in an attempt to redress Everton's decline. Jimmy Harris, who usually played as inside forward, was sometimes tried in my place and Alec Ashworth and Peter Harburn were brought in, tried and discarded. I didn't like not playing.

Everton lost seven of the opening eight games of the 1958/59 season and Ian Buchan was sacked. While the club awaited his successor, Johnny Carey, to see out his notice period at Blackburn Rovers the club signed the Celtic inside forward Bobby Collins, won three out of four of their games, including a famous 3-2 win over Matt Busby's Manchester United. That, however, came just a week after the club's record defeat, 10-4 at Tottenham Hotspur.

Dave Hickson: While the board deliberated on Ian Buchan's replacement a three man sub-committee picked the team. It didn't really get much better without him – although I did score my best ever goal during this period! We were playing West Bromwich Albion at the Hawthorns and my second of the afternoon was the winner in a 3-2 win. I ran from the halfway line with their centre half, Ray Barlow, chasing me. There were three or four players bearing down on me and I passed them all and scored. I was absolutely shattered at the end of it. I should have kept on running because the other players all piled on top of me and almost crushed me to death in a mad celebration. People always remember my goals in the 1953 FA Cup run, but that was the best.

Jimmy Harris: The directors took over and started running it, which was an absolute shambles. Then we had the PTI, Ian Buchan; and an Army Sergeant Major from Aldershot who hadn't got a clue, Harry Wright. They muddled through and we managed to stay up a few times. During that period between Cliff Britton and Harry Catterick they didn't have a clue, they didn't know what they were doing. The directors ran it and bloody hell, some of the teams – how we stayed up I don't know. Some of the teams – I've looked in the programmes I've got – how did that bloody team win? How did we stay up? But we managed.

Dave Hickson: On 11 October 1958 we went to White Hart Lane, which was always one of my favourite stadiums. We came in on the back of three straight wins. What unfolded was one of the most extraordinary afternoons in English football history as fourteen goals were shared between us. Unfortunately 10 of those went Tottenham's way.

Jimmy Harris: We got beat at Tottenham 10-4. I scored a hat-trick. The following week we played the Manchester United team – Charlton and all them – and we thought 'How many is it going to be today?' after the 10-4, and we beat them 3-2. We run them daft a bit that day, and it was said 'from chumps to champs.'

Dave Hickson: Against Spurs we should have had ten ourselves. Jimmy Harris scored a hat-trick but I should have had five. John Hollowbread, the Tottenham keeper, was in unbelievable form, and so was Bobby Smith, the Spurs forward. It should have been 15–10 to Spurs because Bobby was unbelievable that day. It was a frustrating game because with our new signing Bobby Collins in the side we were developing into the sort of team that could score lots of goals. We just couldn't keep them out.

Johnny Carey

In October 1958, the Blackburn Rovers manager, Johnny Carey, was appointed Ian Buchan's successor. As a player he had enjoyed an illustrious career as Manchester United and Ireland captain and was highly regarded throughout the game.

Dave Hickson: Johnny Carey came in as manager from Blackburn Rovers. I had come up against him when he was a player with Manchester United. He was a nice fella, probably too nice to be a manager in some ways.

Dick White: Johnny had been a very very fine footballer. He had John Moores' money and he spent it, in my opinion, very wisely. He bought well, but he did not have the dynamism or forcefulness with the players, the sort of attributes he would have expected in his own Littlewoods organisation. He expected it at Everton too. But the football they played in that Everton team was absolutely superb.

Mick Meagan: Johnny came, and Johnny was more a real football person. I suppose the older players won't have been too disappointed to see Buchan leave, but the younger lads who he gave the chance to play in the first team, we were all disappointed to see him go. Johnny had a wonderful name as being a great technician and a wonderful footballing person. He was unlucky, Johnny; I think he was just a year too late. Johnny's team, that was probably the team that won the league in 62/63 and Johnny was just gone a year before he could get us organised.

Eric Linford: When Ian Buchan was manager Everton were just staying in the division, bottom third, and he was no great shakes. But in those days the managers didn't have the same profile as they had later. When Johnny Carey came there was John Moores and there was money, which, as I got a little bit older, I began to appreciate more. As we got into the 1960s the corner had been turned and Everton were becoming a force again.

Jimmy Harris: I didn't like him, and he didn't like me, or Derek Temple. I suppose he was doing the switch of the local lads we had in the team to bringing his team together. I was in Everton's team, and Frank Wignall had just come in the team, so I played my last few games as outside-left. We were third from top of the league when I left [in December 1960]. I could have gone to West Brom on the Thursday, but I wanted £1,000, they wouldn't give it me so I said, 'I'm not bothered, I'm still in Everton's first team.' On the Saturday we beat Sheffield Wednesday to go third, I scored and got brought down for a penalty. We beat them 4-2. The reason I fell out with Carey was when he was at Blackburn he signed Matt Woods and he wanted me. I met him and said, 'I wouldn't go to Blackburn, I only play for big city clubs.' I can't imagine myself saying that, but I must have said it. And he was manager of Everton a month later. That day we beat Wednesday he walks past me and he stops. We're all getting changed. 'Jimmy,' he said, 'You know that big city club you want to play for? Meet them in the Adelphi at 8pm.' I met Birmingham and got a few bob off them, and had four good years there.

Derek Temple: I thought he was a very sarcastic man, and that's not just my opinion, a few other players thought the same. In football though you could get somebody with a halo around their head and one of the players wouldn't like him. That's part of it.

Ken Rea: He was a terrible manager. People might say he was okay but he wasn't; he was a funny man. He'd come up to you at half-time and say 'I want you all to listen to this' – but he never told us anything! I think at Arsenal, we were losing about 2-0 or something, and he said, 'I want you to go out there and meet the ball and play football.' But I thought that was part of the game!

Dave Hickson: The key man, for me, was Bobby Collins. We had signed him from Celtic in the period between Buchan's dismissal and Carey's appointment. He was an inside forward and probably the best player I ever played alongside. We had a year or so together before I joined Liverpool and he was great. Bobby would play the early ball: he would get it and know exactly what you were doing, and play it where you wanted it. He was so clever. You couldn't ask for anything else from an inside forward. It was nice when you could get an understanding going with the rest of your forward line. Bobby was also a winner. All of our players, in their way, were winners, but Bobby was the real deal. He was like me. He'd dive through crowds of players to get where he wanted and was ridiculously brave. He was hard. Although, like me, he was gone by the time Everton started lifting trophies under Harry Catterick, he helped bring a winning ethos back to Everton and also brought it to Leeds United, where he encountered lots of success.

Derek Temple: Bobby was very, very influential. He was the best player I played with, Bobby Collins, a tremendous player. A little bit ruthless on the field, he could look after himself, let's put it that way. But he was a great player, and unfortunately I think he fell out with John Moores and moved on to Leeds. Of course Leeds then became the team known as the cloggers, I don't know whether Bobby had an influence, I think he might have done. But he was an excellent player and I had a lot of time for him as a footballer.

George Orr: Bobby Collins was 5ft 3inches tall. He was tiny. He'd get all his clothes from Mothercare. But if you want to talk about a player who is as tough as nails and full of determination then that was him.

Mick Meagan: Bobby Collins to me was one of the best players you could play with. A terrible player to play against. But to play with, he was a mad football person. He would go out and he'd run, and he'd kick. Bobby was a nasty little player. Now this was against the opposition. But [as a teammate] he was a brilliant player and he had a lot to do with bringing the likes of myself, Eddie Thomas, the Harris's, Derek Temple through. He was a great player and hard as nails.

Dave Hickson: I'll always remember playing against Brian Labone for the first time. It was a few weeks after my return to Goodison, in the Blues v. Whites match, which they used to have those at the beginning of the season. Brian was seventeen and only a month out of school. Now they go all over the world for their pre-season matches, but this was a big thing at the time and you used to get a lot of people going along. And Brian Labone was a young lad in the second team at the time and he played centre half against me. You could see straight away that he was going to make it, he was so steady and cool. He reminded me of John Charles, who was a fantastic centre half as well as a great centre-forward; he was probably one of the best I ever played against really. Brian's positional play was good, like Charles's; he was very very hard to break down. He had me baffled, to be honest. There were some defenders that had a certain thing about them; they just knew the game and you had to pit your wits against them. Brian and John Charles were those sort of players. Then there were those who'd go head to head with you. They'd do you. Hurt you. I didn't mind who I was playing against – I just wanted to play.

Graham Williams: Brian was just out and out gentleman. Quiet, unassuming giant of a man. And a giant of a player. Superb in the air; powerful ground player; great tackler.

Mick Meagan: Brian was great. Another very nice chap, a lovely person. He was always a big, strong lad; always in control of himself; never seemed to be doing anything, but was always there. He was good on the ball, a good passer of the ball. It was great playing with him. A fella would smack the ball over your head and there'd be a chase on, and who'd be stepping out to cover you? Only Brian. You were never left on your own, and vice versa, if you were supposed to be in covering him.

Dave Hickson: One of the developments in football at this time was floodlights. Night games were the most dramatic. Everton introduced floodlights in 1957, four tall lights on stanchions in each corner of the ground. I played in the first floodlit games at Goodison and Anfield in 1957 in rare Mersey derby encounters in this period. After they built them and we'd play at night something would happen to the crowd. They were electrified. It was magical. I looked forward to them greatly, I'd be lying awake the night before looking forward to it. I couldn't wait for it to start. Once you were on the pitch you were all right. It was that build-up. The crowd were fantastic.

Jimmy Harris: I think we played Red Star Belgrade in the first game under our lights to open them. We had some great nights at Goodison under the lights, cup replays, very good. It was a great atmosphere, compared to what it is now. There's no thrills now in football, though I still go to it. In our day there was no cameras, the games just flowed.

Dave Hickson: You go to Goodison now for a night game when it's full and there'll be 38 or 39,000 there. Imagine doubling that? It was unbelievable. I'll always remember playing Charlton Athletic in the fourth round of the FA Cup in 1959. We drew 2–2 at their place and brought them back to Goodison the following Wednesday; 74,782 filled Goodison that night and the lights were on, not that all those people could have seen much. Thick, dense fog filled the pitch. We won 4–1 after extra time, having drawn 1–1 at 90 minutes; I scored a couple but there was just confusion. People were shouting out, 'Davey, who scored that one?' Even I wasn't sure!

Charles Mills senior: By the end of the 1950s they had a good team again, they were good to watch and played good football. But they were never going to win anything.

John Moores

The Littlewoods Pools magnate, John Moores, had first bought into Everton during the Second World War. Only in the late-1950s, however, did he start to make his huge wealth count at Goodison, firstly lending money for floodlights in 1957, then underwriting several big money transfers, including that of Bobby Collins in Autumn 1958. In the summer of 1960, Moores' role at the club was formalised when he became chairman.

Lord Grantchester: He was a great sports fan anyway. He was very keen on all sorts of sports, especially boxing and cricket. I can remember that he always wanted to know what the test match score was, even when being played overseas in winter. He was very interested in investing in a football club, and Everton was his strong favourite that he wanted to get involved with, but he was approached by others. I do know that Blackburn Rovers was one that approached him at one stage, but he said 'No, I'm going to put my money into Everton.'

Dave Hickson: Football by the late 1950s was starting to change. You could sense it. There was a bit of money coming into the game, and things were being run a bit more professionally. John Moores, the Littlewoods tycoon, had started to put a bit of money into Everton. Goodison was a fine old ground, but it started to get better, with floodlights and so on. His investment had an impact on the pitch as well, with new signings. There was a sense of change, but you could never have envisaged it would be the way it is now. There was a board, a manager and they were in complete control of the club, the team, and your destiny; it was strict and you had to abide by it.

Jimmy Harris: He sent one of his leading men from Littlewoods to do the survey for him. John then came in, sat us all down and told us that he was the chairman and that there would be changes, and a lot of people would be going.

Dick White: As supporters I don't think we were as aware of the inner workings of the club as in the modern game. I can't say I even knew about John Moores's involvement until it was announced that he'd bought the club.

Eric Moonman: I think that the difficulty with John Moores running was his general attitude to business, which was never discussed really. He might've been suitable now in certain clubs but he was a businessman. I think that was the worrying thing. We know that his Merseyside roots were deep and all his business dealings, [the question was] 'What would be the next thing that he would do?'

Keith Tamlin: He was a successful businessman. He could be very supportive, very kind... but he was a businessman and he expected the same standards from other people round him. I was a great fan of his but he was a complete contrast to his brother Cecil. Cecil Moores had a great sense of humour, worked hard, played hard and he was quite a joy to be with. I knew him very, very well and of course he played football as did John Moores in one of the old Zingari leagues.

George Telfer: My Mum and Dad worked for Littlewoods Pools. I was born in Radcliffe street in Everton and my Father came down from Scotland just after the Second World War and became a policeman, but the money wasn't great in those days so he joined Littlewoods on security. My Dad got a job as gamekeeper for John Moores on his estate in Troon in Scotland and my Mum ran a convalescent home for the Littlewoods Pools girls. We were there five years and I used to play with all the Moores children, so we got to know John and [his brother] Cecil Moores very well and Mum used to look after them. John was always very nice; he always looked after my mum and dad. Cecil Moores was always a very nice man and all the Moores family. They used to come out in big parties and go hunting and fishing and my dad always used to prepare the fishing gear and the guns.

Graham Williams: When I signed, John Moores took me into Liverpool, he bought me a watch. I haven't got it now, but he just took me into the jewellers and he said, 'Pick a watch'. He didn't say, 'What price?' or anything; and I was so naïve then I wouldn't pick one with a high price; you know, £50 I'd have gone to. But he didn't stipulate which one to buy. You didn't really mix with the directors in those days.

Derek Temple: Footballers are a bit phlegmatic about things, but we thought it was good. In the end, for most footballers it's about how much money you can make while you're playing. It gave us a chance. He did put money into Liverpool as well, so he was fair in that respect, but it was unknown at the time. We were known as the 'Mersey Millionaires', because it kept seeming to be Everton players who were publicised. Later, Harry Catterick used to disappear for a day or two, and he'd be in Scotland. He would come back with a player, and they would be good players too, very good players, players who could go straight into the First Division side and play. I don't think you can do that so much now.

Eric Moonman: He was never Everton's Abramovich. I don't think he tried for that either. He was a businessman. He was also working for two teams on Merseyside.

Mick Meagan: They were never involved in the football as much, they might come in and have a little chat and things like that every now and then. But one story: We had just arrived in America, New York. We had no dollars or anything, so John Moores handed over a few dollars, and Billy Bingham sort of took charge; 'I'll look after the dollars, you'll each get five dollars', until the spending money was sorted out. Some time that evening Mr Moores, came over to Bingham and said, 'Billy, have you any change for me?' and he wasn't very pleased. He was expecting some change out of it! That was the type of man he was.

Sale of Dave Hickson

As Johnny Carey sought a winning formula at Goodison, players came and went, most controversially Dave Hickson, who was sold early in the 1959/60 season to Liverpool. The transfer met outrage and remains one of the most controversial incidents in the club's history. Many Evertonians even went to Anfield to see Hickson play. As the Moores money began to take an effect on the fortunes of the club more exciting new signings joined the Everton squad, including Blackburn's Roy Vernon and Hearts' Alex Young.

Dave Hickson: Football does take unexpected twists. Johnny had dropped me early in the 1959/60 season and shortly after, Phil Taylor, the Liverpool manager, called me up and said, 'We'd like to sign you.' It was like the time I joined Villa. I was out of the side and just wanted to play. 'We'll play you every week,' he promised, and he did. That's how the move to Liverpool materialised. As far as I was concerned it was quite straightforward. Because I was a professional I accepted it to a certain extent, but of course I was bitterly disappointed by this because I knew I'd have to move on again. I didn't want to leave. I came back to Goodison because I wanted to finish my career there. I think what did for me again was my disciplinary record. Everton didn't like players who were booked or sent off. That wasn't the image the directors wanted to present. My record, in fairness, wasn't that bad, given that football was a very physical game at the time and I was a physical player.

Eric Moonman: It was a shock, yes. Everything about Hickson was. He was part of the crowd. Of course, what happens is it's such a shock that people say, 'That's it for me I'm off now.' I think you lose supporters when a great player goes. It happened with Tommy Lawton. You might say, 'What sort of loyalty is that?' Well, I think it's not temporary loyalty but I think people need time to settle in their minds why he has gone and they often come back. The affection for him, his goal scoring ability, his determination; everything about him was picked up.

John McNally: I don't think it bothered me personally. The thing was, he was getting past it.

Dave Hickson: Despite the controversy there were huge queues waiting to get into Anfield for my debut against Aston Villa. With an attendance of nearly 50,000 Liverpool had 11,000 more fans than at any other league match so far that season. I scored two goals and I think that helped win a lot of Liverpool supporters over. I remember one fan running onto the pitch and saying, 'You're one of ours now.'

New signings

Derek Temple: The thing about the Scots – and I got on well with all the Scots – they had this wonderful attitude, this never-say-die attitude. There were no lost causes. Another lad who came to Everton and wasn't recognised at first as the player he was because he took over from Bobby Collins, was Dennis Stevens. He was English but he had the Scottish mentality: no lost cause, he would chase anything down and tackle anybody. He wasn't recognised by the spectators but he was recognised by the players. He was a first class player.

Mick Meagan: Bobby Collins was a great leader, Bobby wouldn't stand for any of this nonsense. Bobby was a footballer, you were a footballer, and Bobby would always be there to help you, to talk to you and have a great bit of fun with you. That was the great thing about it, there was never any, 'Oh you're only a reserve player,' there was none of that at all. There was great encouragement from all the lads.

Graham Williams: The day he signed, I met him in the first team dressing room and said, 'Hello Bobby, welcome to Everton; I'm so pleased you've come. I'm not the smallest player in the team now.' Well, he whacked me in the chest really hard! He said, 'You are now!' I'm not kidding, I went two yards backwards. But he was a hell of player. He'd kick his grandmother; but what a player.

Derek Temple: I think Alex Parker was in the same situation as me, in the forces. So they couldn't stamp their authority on games because they weren't there, and when they did come in it took them time to settle and build up to the pace of the game, because it was a lot quicker in England than it was in Scotland, and I would say that's probably true now. It's closed up a bit, but it is a higher standard.

Mick Meagan: The minute Alex Young walked into the club, you would just look at him and say 'This is a great player.' He was just that type of lad, the curly blonde hair, and he was ever so gentle.

Later, I don't think that Catterick was ever a true lover of his, whereas Carey would have idolised Alex, because that's the way Alex played. A lovely, lovely touch player; it didn't matter where you sent the ball to, he never seemed to have any problem taking it down and playing. He was just a wonderful player, you'd play a ball, whether it was head high, chest high or down the ground, he'd always manage to control it and have the ball, and set something up.

Mick Meagan: Roy Vernon for a fella that was a great player; he smoked, liked his drink. He overstepped the line at times. With Alex Young it was the chalk and cheese kind of thing. Roy must have loved football to do what he did do, but I would say that he didn't bother too much about it, whereas Alex Young would want to be a real star. They were a great partnership because they were so different.

By Christmas 1960 Everton were being spoken of as title challengers and reached as high as second place in the league. However, Carey's team were more entertainers than winners, capable of beating the Champions Burnley one day, only to lose against the same side the very next. A seven-match losing streak in winter 1961 convinced Moores that Everton would not challenge under Carey and he moved to replace him with the club's former centre-forward Harry Catterick, who was at the time Sheffield Wednesday manager, infamously sacking Carey in the back of a taxi.

Mick Meagan: I suppose John Moores was a little bit of a hard man. To make money as he made it he must have been. I think this is probably why Johnny Carey was sacked. He felt that Johnny a laid back man, as he played his football. There never seemed to be any hurry, any problem, and I think Moores wanted a little bit of noise. Carey was so calm in his play, and of course Catterick was a great name at Sheffield Wednesday for his toughness and his ability.

Lord Grantchester: I wouldn't have said it was typical of him as a businessman. He didn't have meetings in taxis. It's become, over the years, quite an event, hasn't it? It happened down in London when they were trying to organise a get together round an FA meeting. He was trying to meet up with Johnny Carey and obviously not being able to fit it in. The situation was developing and changing, and so it turned out that he only had this opportunity. I'm sure it wouldn't have been something he'd planned at all. That's just seemed to be the way it came to pass.

Derek Temple: He was a successful business man, very successful. I think successful people in business have to be ruthless. Again, you don't have to be the one firing the bullets, but you certainly make them and hand the gun to someone else to do it – delegation that's called, isn't it? I was still in the army when Carey got the sack, he was supposed to be fired in the taxi, I don't know if that was true. Then he brought in somebody who he thought was more of a disciplinarian.

Mick Meagan: Johnny Carey was very, very much a footballing person: You don't just kick it, you pass it. Everything was you pass it. What you do is you enjoy doing it. That's the way Carey played. At Manchester United he was a man that wanted to play football and do things; a credit to the game. Not just the big rush down the middle. But he was very good. He didn't say an awful lot, but he'd have a little whisper in your ear, 'Now you didn't do that well,' or 'Why don't you do more of the other thing?' He'd have a nice little chat with you. He had his team but he was just a year too late. He went, and then the next year the team won the league.

Everton's Golden Era
1961-1970

'It'll forever stick with me, Bally passing me on the pitch. 'What's it like to win it? What's it like to be the best?' 'It's brilliant, isn't it?' I laughed. 'It's absolutely brilliant.'

Howard Kendall

Harry Catterick arrives as manager

After being put on notice by John Moores, Johnny Carey was allowed to see out one final match as Everton manager, at home to Cardiff City on 15 April 1961. Moores' appearance in the directors' box shortly before kick-off was greeted with boos, slow hand clapping and chants of 'We want Carey.' Just before the team left the dressing room to come on to the pitch, the captain Bobby Collins made a speech thanking Carey on behalf of the players and expressing their regret at his departure. Everton won 5-1 and the following Monday the Sheffield Wednesday manager, Harry Catterick – who had played for Everton as a centre-forward after the war – was appointed Carey's replacement.

Charles Mills: At the Cardiff City game I was in the Bullens Road stand with my dad and granddad and John Moores was being berated by the crowd for sacking Carey. Carey was a very popular manager, and Catterick was seen as being rather dour. He hadn't been much of a player whereas Carey was a majestic player. Then Catterick came. His secret was his secrecy I suppose, in the transfer market. He was very astute in transfer market.

Tony Kay: We had a lot of success at Sheffield [where Kay was Catterick's captain at the time of his departure]. We were unlucky when Spurs won the double in 1961. We were the only side to beat them, 1-0 or 2-0 at Sheffield, and that year they won the league with a record number of points. Under normal circumstances we would have won it.

Derek Temple: Harry Catterick came in, and he gave everybody a chance, had a look at everybody and then started strengthening in his mind. He had a knack of getting a player, maybe a local lad, and converting them. Tommy Wright was a forward when he first came to Everton, Joe Royle was a centre half. The careers they had, and that was Harry, he converted them and saw things in them.

Roy Parnell: We didn't really know him coming from Sheffield Wednesday. He was the manager and things were going to change. We didn't know things would change as much as they did. We had some terrible rows with him.

Tony Kay: Harry was always his own man, he had his own way of going about things. If you were doing right by him he would leave you alone, but if you weren't he would get in your ear a bit. I was lucky at Sheffield Wednesday; I must have been doing what he wanted me to do because he never bothered me at all.

Derek Temple: He was a disciplinarian; he delegated everything. He was strict, but I think he was fair: if you did your job he was okay with you. A very, very deep man, he didn't want to make friends with anybody. He hated journalists. Hated referees. He was alright Harry. If you did your job he was okay with you.

Dick White: He wasn't the sort of person to excite adulation. But he bought exciting footballers. He bought winning footballers.

1961/62: Everton evolve under Catterick

Catterick quietly asserted his influence at Goodison during his first year in the job. His first signing wasn't until February 1962, when he signed the Blackpool goalkeeper, Gordon West for £27,500 – a record fee for a goalkeeper. West replaced Albert Dunlop, a mercurial figure who was disliked by his own teammates. Next in was Bolton Wanderers' Dennis Stevens, whose arrival heralded the end of the highly influential Bobby Collins, who was sold to Don Revie's Leeds. Everton would finish the 1961/62 season fourth, five points behind Champions Ipswich. At the start of the following season Catterick made just one more signing, Liverpool's left-winger, Johnny Morrissey.

George Sharples: I first came across Gordon West when Everton Youth were playing Blackpool and I think we beat them. When he come for the ball bloody big Gordon, Christ he knocked everyone out the bloody road. That's what I don't understand with goalkeepers, they're not like big Gordon now. He used to come out knees first and boom, you just got out of the bloody road when he were coming. He were a good keeper Gordon West.

Tommy Wright: Gordon was a laugh. He was very agile around the box and coming out for corners. He commanded the box. He was an outstanding 'keeper, Gordon.

Roy Parnell: The goalkeepers have all got screws loose, haven't they? He was a good lad Westy; we had some laughs with him. But he was a good goalkeeper and he was only young as well. He'd shout at you and tell you what to do, not like little Albert. Albert would throw the ball to you backwards when you weren't expecting it. He did that to me once. He'd come out with the ball and he was running up as I was running up and he'd throw the ball from behind his back and I went 'Oh bloody hell Albert!' Albert's having a little laugh you know.

Keith Tamlin: Dunlop was a character as a player. When he was on his form I thought he was brilliant. He did speak his mind because at times and he would exchange views with supporters.

Colin Green: Albert Dunlop did a nasty trick on me. I was called into Harry Catterick's office and Harry asked 'What's this in the paper?' There was a story about me wanting to leave, but I knew nothing about it. I knew very well who it was. Albert used to get a tenner off the papers for giving them a tip, but this one wasn't true. Harry said, 'Well if you don't tell me I'm putting you on the transfer list' thinking he was calling my bluff. I didn't want to say anything. I didn't want to drop Albert in the cart. I went up to Aberdeen to play for the Welsh U23s and on the way back I read in the paper that Birmingham were after me. You see Harry didn't mess about, he just said, 'Okay fine, if you don't want to tell me off you pop.' And off I went.

Roy Parnell: Bandit was what we used to call Albert Dunlop when he was in the team.

Joe Royle: Westy was the union man, he used to have all the kids singing to him and about him. He was like most goalkeepers, insane when it suited him, but nicely insane. He was always up to some practical joke. Him and Labby were a duo and very funny; the life and soul of the dressing room.

Howard Kendall: As a goalkeeper Gordon was undoubtedly one of the best in the game; as a character he was one of the biggest too. He was a truly great goalkeeper; when you talk about Neville Southall, very rarely can you think about a goal that was conceded and he was responsible for it. The same was as true for Gordon. He was absolutely brilliant in the dressing room too, which shouldn't be overlooked. He could lift us up with a laugh and a joke. We used to get the call to go out of the dressing room for training and he would be stood next to the door and he used to stand at it and say, 'Nobody goes out until Westy goes out.'

George Sharples: Bobby Collins he conducted the orchestra. I was a half back and when I won it I gave it to our best player, so I gave it to Bobby Collins.

Charles Mills: In hindsight it probably wasn't a mistake of Catterick's to sell Collins [to Leeds United in March 1962] because he replaced him with Dennis Stevens from Bolton Wanderers. Collins went on to revitalise Leeds; Leeds were getting that very good side, but Stevens was actually one of those players that we've had throughout our history who were rather undersold and underrated; if you think of the likes of the Joe Parkinsons of the world, he was that sort of player.

Roy Parnell: Dennis Stevens was a good player. He done all the running for Vernon. Catterick knew one thing about Vernon and Young they wouldn't do much running but Dennis would run his balls off all match and get no credit for it. He would also never get a bollocking off Catterick because Catterick knew what he was doing.

Mick Meagan: Dennis Stevens more or less came and took Bobby Collins' place. I think Dennis was a wonderful player to play with. You were never, never on your own; if you were in trouble you'd look up and Dennis would be there around you.

Mick Gannon: He had a reputation as a tough guy, but he wasn't really; he should've been a Parson or a Priest! He used to say thank you and I never heard him swear. He was a sound player, a good workman; up and down, up and down. I think he took over from Bobby Collins but he was nothing like Collins. I preferred Bobby: he was everywhere; he was like a little termite; a great player.

Mick Meagan: It's a pity that Bobby went, I was disappointed. I thought Bobby would have been a wonderful person to bring on the young lads. I thought he was a wonderful player, I admired him tremendously. He wouldn't mollycoddle you, he'd tell you 'You want to start fucking doing something.' He'd say to me, when I'd be out of the first team, 'Why don't you go and have a talk with the manager?' You'd say you couldn't be bothered and he'd respond, 'You bloody Irish, you've had it so good over there in Ireland. If you had been born in England or Scotland in the war you'd have to fight for your crust of bread, you've had it too easy over there.' He was very clear about that. 'They would have made men out of you, you're too bloody soft.' I thought he would have been great to look after the likes of Joe Royle and Colin Harvey, all these lads that came through. He would have been a great model to have amongst those lads.

Roy Parnell: He had more ball players Carey, better ball players than Catterick. Catterick had a few hard men, which wasn't wrong – that's the way he wanted to play it – but Carey always wanted you to play football all the time. He always wanted to do that but Catterick didn't he just wanted the result.

Colin Green: In our day it was left to the players to sort things out on the pitch not the people on the touchline. That changed but Everton seemed to do that even after I'd gone. They were still doing it, still sorting out on the right side for themselves.

Derek Temple: We had players who could play football without being coached. Now I think that if you were a First Division player, and you need coaching, you shouldn't be playing in the First Division, you should be able to play without somebody telling you how to play. Systems you play as a team, but not as individuals. All those players could play – you knew where to move on the field, you've got to think all the time. You can't just stand still and then suddenly say, 'I better go there.' You've got to be thinking ahead of the game. All these players could do that. When you see a team playing well, what people don't notice is how hard they're working. That's what it comes down to. We had players who just moved into position, could get the ball.

Mick Meagan: Before the match you'd be looking at each other and you'd be talking. 'Now Mick,' this would be Labone, 'You better cover for me.' I'd say: 'If your man goes up the wing and gets by me you better be out here.' Derek would say: 'I want the ball played early.' It was your own little team talk. Just to build up confidence, or to make you feel better. 'Of course we can do it,' we'd say, 'If we stick to our little game plan, of course we can do it.'

George Sharples: I think we'd have still won the title with Johnny Carey. They make too much of managers to be honest with you: it's just blokes on the pitch that play football. The manager just shouts his head off on the bloody bench and picks the team.

Johnny Morrissey: I was shocked when Everton signed me. At the time Everton were a bigger name [than Liverpool, from where Morrissey was signed], especially with the John Moores thing. I was euphoric, it was unbelievable. And to go to the first team straightaway. As it happened it was just a dream come true.

Mick Meagan: Johnny was a tubby little fella, but oh Jesus he was hard; bloody hell he was as hard as nails, but great to play with. He would stroll on the ball and go by defenders and defenders tackle Johnny, and you'd hear defenders roar. No bothering Johnny. Johnny was born in Liverpool during those years where you had to fight for your crust of bread. He was a nice person, very dry, but by God you wouldn't want to cross Johnny.

Johnny Morrissey: Shanks wore his heart on his sleeve, he really did. I mean his man management was brilliant. Even though I wasn't in the side I loved him, that's very rare for a player to say that about a manager. But Harry Catterick didn't communicate a lot, didn't say a lot. Didn't even speak to the press. I mean to be honest, about Catterick, he's as successful as most managers. He's won the cup, two league championships, but he's never talked about in them tones, of being a great manager, because he wouldn't speak to the press. He used to lock the press out of the ground, be awkward, make them wait for him and then he'd sneak out the back. Catterick was a disciplinarian, which I'm a believer in to be honest. I can't say I liked him the same as I liked Shanks, but he got results, and he got me at Everton so I can't complain.

Alex Young and Roy Vernon

After showing signs of promise under Johnny Carey, the forward partnership of Alex Young and Roy Vernon began to prosper under Catterick. The pair would score 40 league goals between them in the 1961/62 season and Young, in particular, assumed legendary status among Evertonians.

George Sharples: One of my favourite forward lines was Billy Bingham, Bobby Collins, Alex Young, Roy Vernon and Tommy Ring. It was one of the smallest football forward lines, but honestly it was superb; it was like poetry in motion. Alex Young and Roy Vernon were like Mutt and Jeff [A famous American comic book duo].

Bishop Tom Williams: I was always with my dad because he said the boys' pen was a bit too dangerous. We were playing Man United and he said, 'Just watch their number ten he's the best player I've ever seen.' It was Denis Law, so I spent the whole match just watching Denis – where he ran, the position he was playing. But Alex Young was the same. He ghosted in.

Colin Green: Alex absolutely glided. He was ever such a slightly built lad but God he just floated over the ground. I remember a match at Goodison when it had been pouring with rain and it was so muddy. Alex scored two goals and when he came off his shorts were as clean as when he went on. He looked immaculate. Nobody could get near him. He didn't seem to touch the mud, he seemed to float over it. He was absolutely wonderful.

David France: Alex Young was a love affair that continued forever; it continues until this day. Alex Young just had skill, he did things on a pitch that people wouldn't even try in training in front of teammates. He had that incredible natural skill; it's a God given thing. There were two Goodison Gods: there was Dixie Dean, and he is measured by the number of times that he put the ball in the net, and there is Alex Young, and he is measured by the number of times he took our breath away. He would do things which made you forget about the game, about who scored, but you remembered when Alex Young did that – just a piece of skill that sent somebody tumbling in the wrong direction, and you'd go 'Wow.' You'd talk about that in the days before you had television and repeats. The great crime is the fact that there is a very little footage of him.

John Corbett: I didn't see Alex Young until near the end of his career; in fact I probably saw his last goals in an Everton shirt in 1968, but he was a hero to me. It was about the time that the Golden Vision film had been produced by Ken Loach; I remember seeing that on television at the time and you begin to associate with the fact that, 'Oh, I've been there.' Although it was a black and white film – everything was in black and white at that time – you tended to feel that this was part of a team that you watched, and all the characters in the Golden Vision started to become, if you like, larger than life. Particularly interviews in that film with people like Gordon West, Alan Ball and so on; they resonated with the sort of person that you remember seeing playing on the pitch.

Jimmy Husband: I remember one of the first times I saw him play, it was a Tuesday or Wednesday evening kick-off, Everton v Arsenal, and the Arsenal centre-half at the time was the Scotland centre-half, Ian Muir; a tall gangly centre-half. Alex Young ran rings around him, a scintillating performance. I hadn't seen Alex Young play many games because obviously when he was playing normally I was playing somewhere. On that evening I realised what a genius he was. He just ghosted past players, and had that unique skill of holding the ball up. He could dribble. He could head a ball by hanging in the air – I'd never seen that before, because Alex was only 5ft 9inches, or something like that. But when he went to head a ball he was as good as being 6ft.

John Hurst: He had that wonderful technique. He wasn't tall but he could hang in the air. It sounds stupid but he would jump early and he used to hang in the air where everybody else would be jumping and struggling.

Mick Gannon: He was brilliant. If he went up for the ball it was like he was waiting for the photographer: 'Hello I'm up there now.'

Len Norman: They called him the 'Golden Vision'. He oozed confidence. He would get the ball and you'd know something would develop from it.

John Hurst: His movement was unbelievable. Later everybody talked about George Best, who had a bit of aggression with his skill. Youngy never appeared to give out that energy. We used to class him like a Rolls Royce that just purred along. That was Alex.

Johnny Morrissey: Certain players feed each other and blend. You never know when you're going to buy a player to play alongside someone, but them two had it, whatever it was. And of course tremendous ability, especially Alex Young, he was fantastic. His control, his balance.

Roy Parnell: I liked the way they used to help you and move. You didn't have to look for them they'd look for you. You'd give them the ball and they'd do what they do. They were excellent at that, really good.

Howard Kendall: Alex was the Goodison idol, and it was easy to see why. I didn't play with him for very long, but his technical ability was absolutely fantastic. He was so silky; his movement brilliant. You could understand why he was called the 'Golden Vision'. He combined the skill with magnificent aerial ability; he had great spring for his size. It was an unusual combination, this grace and power, but the fans loved him for it. When you talk about Everton you talk about skill and you talk about quality; Alex certainly had those in abundance.

Colin Harvey: If you were thinking of a modern day player to compare him with, it would probably be Dennis Bergkamp; he was that type of footballer. He was great in the air for his size. Really outstanding footballer, very clever, dropped off and kept the ball, and could score goals.

Tony Kay: Those two were excellent, they played so well together. With the skill of Alex Young, the finesse, and Roy was a superb finisher. One of the best finishers I've ever seen. He was comparable to Greavsie and Denis Law, people like that. He was a good player and a good finisher.

Peter Mills: I think Vernon was fantastic. I never heard him criticised; he was always very a popular player. Alex Young has gone into mythology; one of my memories of Alex Young was that he got all this stick off the crowd. I think all that's forgotten about; he was a Fancy Dan player really. Hugely popular to a lot of people; I just remember him getting a lot of stick from the crowds when I was a kid. I remember Colin Harvey getting a lot of stick from the crowd. But Vernon was something else.

He was like lightning, and a really good finisher.

Colin Green: Roy Vernon was the quickest bloke over ten yards I've ever seen in my life. In the box he was like greased lightening but if you asked him to do 100 yards you'd need a calendar not a stopwatch. But from A to B six, seven yards, Jesus he was quick. He also smoked about forty fags a day but Roy was a good player.

Derek Temple: When you look at Taffy he didn't look like an athlete did he? But he was a good 'un, cool under pressure, great penalty taker. No nerves really, it didn't bother him. Bang.

Johnny Morrissey: My main memory of Roy was when he took penalties. You know you see them now and they're side-footing them and all that. Roy, he used to crash these penalties, and he was a great finisher. There's something innate in strikers, and that was Roy Vernon. Didn't do a lot, stayed up the field most of the time. We got the ball to him, but it worked.

Tony Kay: Roy was a very patriotic, very heavy smoking Welshman. He did what he had to do and he did it well, with great aplomb. Youngy reckons he's never ever seen him miss a penalty, and he used to torture Gordon West in the practice game. Westy could never stop a penalty off Roy Vernon.

Gerry Glover: Roy was a bit of a lad. As apprentices we were in the dressing room gathering the kit up and doing various jobs and he was a heavy smoker and after training or after matches he would go into the bathroom get in the bath or the shower with a cigarette and he would come out and the cigarette wouldn't be wet. The cigarette would stay dry. I don't know anyone who could do that; who could get showered or washed and the cigarette was still dry.

Mick Meagan: Roy had this thing about tracking back. Roy would let you know, 'It's your job to get the ball and give it to me, or give it to the front lads. It's not our job to run back there like headless chickens. It's your job.' Johnny Morrissey was the same. If you ran by Johnny with the ball, Johnny would sort of look at you, 'What the fuck are you doing up here? Your job is back there, serving me the ball.' That was the great thing, they were all specialists in their own little areas.

Derek Temple: They could both play. They hit it off very well. Their control was great, they used one another. They wouldn't necessarily always get the ball to each other, they'd go to give and then drag round or something to make an opening or have a shot. They both did this, they used one another. When they did link up they were unstoppable.

Roy Parnell: Roy Vernon was the boss. Roy Vernon always bought your tickets off you. You always got a Wembley football ticket, every player, and Roy would be outside the room buying them all off you. £3 tickets they were. He'd give you a fiver, especially the groundstaff lads because we got one as well. As soon as we got them Roy would know and he'd have them off you. He used to take me to the Races; him and Alex Young, Haydock and Manchester. Me and Mick Gannon went with them and we were made up going with these two superstars.

John Hurst: Alex had the worst feet you've ever seen. He used to suffer terribly from blisters. You would see him after a game and the physio Norman Borrowdale would be having to bathe his feet and be having to put pads on his feet. He'd come out with the hugest blisters you've ever seen in your life.

Roy Parnell: Alex got terrible blisters. They couldn't get rid of them. In the middle of the season he got them with the hard training and all that running. People were sending him doctors prescriptions and all that. He got loads of them, boxes full of cures for these blisters.

Catterick's Iron Rule

From the moment he took over as manager Catterick imposed strict discipline throughout the club. Starting on Everton's end of season tour in 1961 when he sent home his captain Roy Vernon for a discipline breach he always kept a tight rein upon the squad.

Derek Temple: When he sent Roy Vernon home from the tour of the US he was stamping his authority on the team. Roy was a great player, but he was out of order. He knew what the rules were and he broke them, and Catterick made an example of him. He was stamping his authority as a new manager: you didn't step over the line, otherwise you were in trouble. He got shipped out and then everyone else toed the line.

George Sharples: I remember Roy Vernon put a list up in the first team dressing room of Harry Catterick's 'Rules'. Taffy used to come in every Friday and he used to cross them off – 'Done that one, there's another one.' That was his rebellion. After that he got rid of the players that disagreed with him. If you weren't on his side you were gone.

Gerry Humphreys: He was an imposing man and not somebody you could get close to. I think a lot of the young pros and apprentices were a bit frightened of him. He was such a strict disciplinarian type manager. In a lot of cases you were mainly under the coaches there: Gordon Watson, Les Shannon, Ron Llewellyn and Tommy Casey.

Roy Parnell: What's your first bollocking like? I got many. It was on a Monday morning and it all depended on how the first team got on. If you were in the reserves and not in the first team he wasn't usually interested, but we'd have to pay the penalty if they lost: Ten laps round Goodison. He'd take it out on us or anybody else in the A team. The first team would be on their day off! On this day something had really upset him and after we've done ten laps he'd sent Tom Egglestone for us. 'The following people up to see the boss.' And you think, 'Oh Christ I hope it's not me.' 'Roy Parnell, Mick Gannon so and so and so and so.' You'd get up there and you had to queue outside his door. He'd get you in and he'd sit right opposite you. 'I got told you're the most promising player here,' and I put my head down. 'But we've got nothing but complaints everywhere you go, especially over the water [on The Wirral] and don't think I don't know what you get up to over there as well.' I was frightened to death. 'Get out and pull yourself together.' The following week he pulled me in. 'Do you know the trouble with you Parnell? The 3 Bs.' 'What's the 3 Bs boss?' 'Birds, Booze and Betting, you don't give a shit about football.' I said, 'You've missed 1 B out.' 'What's that?' 'Bollocks!' I said and got out walked out and the lads are saying, 'Oh go back, go back!' I said 'I'm going I've had enough.' He never sent for me after that. Well he couldn't do anything because I wasn't frightened of him anymore.

Mick Gannon: There weren't that many nightclubs but we used to go to a little nightclub by the tunnel called The Royal Tiger. Harry Catterick put a stop to it in the end. He used to hide outside and see who was coming out. He caught me one night. I only lived up the road in Scottie Road. 'Where are you going?' he asked. 'Well I'm just going for some fish and chips for me dad,' I fibbed. 'There's no chip shop open after nine o'clock' 'I told me dad…' I said, and went home.

George Sharples: Everton and Liverpool got paid on Thursday and all went to The Tiger Club. Harry Catterick was clamping down and when you came in on a Friday you signed in the book and you went to your dressing room. This particular day Gordon Watson said to me, 'Upstairs the boss wants you.' I thought, 'Fucking hell what does he want now?' I went upstairs and Catterick said, 'It's come to my notice that you've been seen with this blonde girl in here and there,' and he named all the places I'd been in with her. At the end he says, 'What have you got to say about that?' I said, 'Well you've got most of it right boss but she didn't have blonde hair she had black hair!' That went down like a lead balloon.

Roy Parnell: If you come in late you got fined. I was getting a bus a train and a bus to get to Goodison. That's what I had to do, unless you had a car and nobody had a car in them days. If the bus was late you were late, or the train was late you were late. You got to the ground and they'd have a book and you'd sign it. Tommy Egglestone was his right hand man and he had a red line. If you'd put your name under there you were late and you got fined. I was late one day – less than five minutes late – and I walked in and the red line was here. I said, 'Sorry I'm late Tom but the bus was delayed.' 'Oh the boss wants to see you.' The boss says 'You've been late again haven't you.' I said: 'It wasn't my fault, it was the bus. I get the bus, train then bus and if they are late I can't help it. You see, you some lads are late behind me.' He said, 'No it's not good enough. Tell me what time did you leave the ground yesterday?' I said, 'The usual time, 12 O'clock.' 'So you've had from 12 O'clock yesterday to get here for 10 o'clock today and you still can't get here.' I paid the fine.

Mick Gannon: In the end I asked for a move. I didn't have to move. We had a big squad then there must've been about 70 with the first team, reserve team and whatever. Half an hour later Catterick said 'Jump in the car' and took me to Stockport. When we got there he jumps out goes in this terraced house. He was in there about 20 minutes, comes out. He still hadn't said a word about what he's doing so I thought I'd call his bluff. He said, 'We are going to Scunthorpe.' I said 'If you don't mind but where's that?' They were second division then. We met their manager Dick Duckworth. After I'd signed he gave Catterick £50 in cash. He give me £20 and said, 'Here get yourself a meal.' He kept the other thirty for himself!

Colin Green: There was a good cop, bad cop dynamic with his assistant Tommy Egglestone. Tommy was more the 'arm around the shoulder' one.

Gerry Humphreys: Catterick wasn't that type of manager to put his arm around you. I think because you were playing for Everton it was expected that you were to perform. You were very lucky if you got a well done or a pat on the back from him. He'd come down on you like a ton of bricks if you didn't do well, but you never got praised when you did well.

Joe Royle: He wasn't a coach, he was an old fashioned manager. He seldom put a tracksuit on, he was mostly in his office. But he watched everything and he never missed a trick. He was very astute tactically, and a great judge of a player. You look at who he brought into the club – Kendall, Ball and Harvey together for a start. His purchases of players were hugely astute.

John Hurst: He's not a manager that you could imagine managing now. I suppose you could say that about every manager in the league in them days; very rarely you saw him on the training ground.

The only time you saw him with a tracksuit top on you'd know that the TV or somebody was coming up to interview him because he'd have his tracksuit top on with his collar and tie underneath and he'd come out. You've got to give him his due, he did wonders for Everton FC. He knew how to build a team. He dismantled the team that won the championship in 1963; three years later he's got a completely different team that won the FA Cup; and then two years later another completely different team that went on to win the league in 1969/70.

Roy Parnell: I was very sorry to leave Everton but I was glad to get away from Catterick. Everton are great, Catterick was dreadful, especially when you're young and frightened.

The Great Freeze

Everton started the 1962/63 season with a 3-1 win over reigning champions Burnley at Turf Moor. There followed two victories in a week over the Manchester United of Law, Best and Charlton as well as a 4-2 trouncing of Catterick's former club, Sheffield Wednesday. There seemed to be a new resolve about this Everton team, but the season was rudely interrupted by the harshest winter of the century. Between 22 December and 12 February Everton went without playing a league game. It delayed the debuts of two new signings: the wing-half Tony Kay, Catterick's former captain at Sheffield Wednesday; and Rangers' winger, Alex Scott.

Johnny Morrissey: Brian Labone was a tower. Jimmy Gabriel was good, I think Alec Parker was good for a while. It was a good all-round team, Young and Vernon, what a combination. They were tremendous. Dennis Stevens, good player, Brian Harris, who lost his place to Tony Kay, was too. It was just strength all round, I think to win the league you need that. You don't have to have tremendous stars, but we had two or three that were outstanding players. But the whole team was competent.

Mick Meagan: Burnley were a wonderful side then, Tottenham were a wonderful side, Wolves were a wonderful side. They were all great sides.

Johnny Morrissey: I think we were quite a few points ahead before the big freeze. We'd go training on the beach, because the tide would come in and keep it defrosted.

George Sharples: When we were training we had to go to Formby Beach because everywhere else was frozen.

Roy Parnell: We used to run in the stands because we couldn't run anywhere else because of the ice. You'd get more injuries than anything.

Mick Meagan: We were still training, and I remember little things that stand out. You used to get pellets to put in the ground to soften the frost. This is for training. But one or two of the lads were allergic to these bloody pellets, and they used to come out in lumps. They'd all come out in these blotchy red marks.

Johnny Morrissey: Footballers wanted to play. And in them days I don't know if there was any underground heating – I don't know if Everton had it and it didn't work. But everybody was just laid off, it is just frustrating.

Tony Kay: Harry was a realist. He knew what he wanted: he wanted skill and he also wanted bite. Therefore, he bought Alex Scott, who was a very quick and fast winger. He bought Dennis Stevens who could bite, and me who could bite as well. He was quite astute in that respect.

Mick Meagan: Alex Scott was lovely, very quiet. Alec would play and say nothing, but by God he could run. Give Alec the ball or play it over the top and he was after it. Not a word out of him.

George Sharples: He was a hard knock, Tony Kay. He was like a tiger. He was a hell of a good player.

Tony Kay: I was on £20, maybe £30 at Sheffield Wednesday. Harry came in for me two or three times, and I said 'I don't want to go, I'm a Sheffield lad and I've just moved house.' But he kept on coming back. The last time he convinced me, how do you think he did that? He offered me twice as much money, which was £60 a week, two grand in cash. So I said 'I'm yours.'

Mick Meagan: Tony was a different type of player. Tony was a real flamboyant type and would smoke his big cigars. He was another great player. Once again, you could say it about them all. Tony would come up to you and say 'don't worry, don't worry, I'll be here to cover you. Don't worry at all, just give me the ball.' There was so much confidence given to you. You felt as if you were the star and they weren't, they just had this lovely gift of making you feel so important. Playing football, Tony would say to me 'For fuck's sake Mick,' as I was very slow. We were playing Spurs and he said, 'Don't worry Mick, we'll kick him, he won't be able to run.' And of course someone smart like Labone would say, 'It's no use kicking him on one leg, you want to kick him on the two legs, because he will still outrun him.'

Tony Kay: I'm quite a strange person, I like to do something well and if I don't do it well I won't do anything untoward like go for a drink or anything. When I first came in it was the great freeze, and I was here six weeks before we played. All the boys would go and have a drink; I used to go out with them but I wouldn't have a drink, I used to drink orange juice. They would say 'come on,' but I would say 'I'm not having a drink until I've played my first game, and proved that everything is alright.'

Mick Meagan: There was always great humour. We still were training, and the great thing about it was we had great fun training in the snow. I tell the lads here now, we weren't allowed tracksuit bottoms – 'Get out there and run around, get warm yourself.' But it was a great era, and luckily enough the snow all cleared up and we were able to carry on.

Tony Kay: My role in the side was to gee people up and to make sure that if the ball was there I would get it. That was my job. I remember one day, I was playing alright, it was Arsenal or somewhere like that. I got the ball and I was really enjoying myself, I was knocking little balls here and little balls there. I got in at half time and Harry said, 'What do you think you're playing at'? I went, 'What do you mean?' He said, 'You're not here to knock the ball about, you're here to get it and deliver it. Do that.' I said 'OK'.

Johnny Morrissey: I think some teams had had games, catching up with us, because they played games when we couldn't play. And I think we went to Leicester for our first game and they beat us 3-1. The gap narrowed, but then we came again after we found our feet, and then we took off again.

Closing in on a sixth League Championship

Everton 1, Tottenham 0
20 April 1963

Tony Kay: Tottenham were always a good side, they always had good players: Johnny White, Jimmy Greaves, big centre half, big centre-forward, Maurice Norman, they had a very good side. But with the additions that Harry made Everton were a bit invincible, it was hard to beat Everton, especially at home.

David France: Everyone talks about the goal he scored at Tottenham, that decided the title in 1963. He was only about 5'8, and he rose above the Tottenham defence to score the winning goal. Tottenham were second. It wasn't the final game of the season, but it was the decider and Everton won 1-0. We battered them but couldn't score. I remember the goal, but I remember the reaction of the crowd and the reaction was this great belief that we're now going to win this – we can beat the best team in the land. I just remember the noise. They say that the noise was so loud that it knocked people off their bicycles in Bootle, that type of thing. I'd never heard Goodison react like that before.

George Orr: Young jumped up and the header was just fantastic. My brother was a Kopite but he said that from miles away he could hear the roar so he knew. It was just a feeling that we had won when we scored that goal. It was something I've never seen.

Eric Linford: My one abiding memory of the Golden Vision was from that game. I got to the ground very early for the game against Tottenham and all I can remember is Everton getting a corner in the fourteenth minute and somebody taking the corner straight onto the Golden Vision's head. Back of the net. 1-0. Championship done.

George Orr: I've still got the match report to this day. The reporter said: 'I've never seen a smaller man jump higher' and it was like he was hovering in the air. He had the ability to judge a ball coming over.

David France: I've actually seen the goal on tape and it's nothing like as good as I thought it was, and that's maybe the sentimentality of it.

Leon Bernicoff: My wife June was in the maternity hospital having our first daughter and she was the only one there without a visitor. I was at Goodison watching Everton and Alex Young got the winning goal; now there's a player. I brought her flowers in that night and was so excited, coming in with an Everton programme and shouting 'Alex Young.' I wanted to know what our daughter was going to be called. We named her Helen Kay – after Tony Kay.

Mick Meagan: I remember the game we played against Tottenham at home [on 20 April]. We beat them 1-0, and then [a few matches later] we played West Brom away, I think we won 4-0, and they were the two matches where it was a case of, 'It's now or bust; if you don't win now it's gone.' The last match against Fulham, we were odds on to win. I think we won it with matches in hand in the end.

Roy Parnell: Gordon West was injured and Albert Dunlop returned for the last four games of the season. It was the end of his career. Albert was too old to alter but Catterick was really worried about him with them last few games. He'd go over to Albert and say, 'Well done Albert.' We'd think 'What's going on here like?' He praised him because he was frightened of Albert more or less losing the match really or doing something not quite right. He was worried about Albert and Albert couldn't give a shite.

Colin Harvey: On the day we played Fulham [on the last day of the season when Everton lifted the First Division trophy] I was playing in an A team game at Bellefield, kick off 2 o'clock. I played, we won the game, my dad was at the game and we just drove straight down to Goodison. I got in through the late entry turnstile watching them go round with the championship trophy and everything. You just think 'What an occasion this is.'

Roy Parnell: I'm in the photograph. You'll see two people with suits: one's Westy – because Westy was injured – and I was twelfth man on the other end drinking champagne. I remember Labby coming up to me and saying people keep asking who that guy is on the end cos nobody knows you. I was only eighteen. Labby told people, 'It's Roy Parnell, it's a lad coming up.'

David France: Alex didn't take the mickey out of people, he didn't embarrass people, they embarrassed themselves. But he didn't intentionally embarrass people. He scored about 24 goals in the championship season with Vernon, and Vernon was a great asset to him, because he had that incredible pace over a short distance. He was very small, very thin, like a whippet type of a runner. But he had that incredible acceleration over 10 yards. With somebody like Young who could control it however it came to him, he could just play it off to him. It was the days before assists, but I imagine Roy's goals were all assisted by Young. They were an incredible twosome.

Mick Meagan: It was a great time to be in Liverpool. Everton won the league, Liverpool got promoted and The Beatles were on their way up then, so Liverpool was really buzzing. It was a great, great place to be. I loved every minute, and the great thing about Liverpool and Dublin, the people are identical, they're great characters, and most of them are a little bit mad. But there was always fun; always fun.

Everton in the European Cup

League Championship won, Catterick gave his men the double goal of retaining it the following season and winning the European Cup. Everton had had a brief adventure in Europe during the title winning season, but suffered the ignominy of being knocked out in the first stage of the Inter City Fairs Cup by Dunfermline. Their opponents in the European Cup in the 1963/64 season were, however, a different proposition: Helenio Herrera's Inter Milan.

Derek Temple: We played them at Goodison. Roy Vernon scored what I thought was a decent goal, I couldn't see much wrong with it, but it was disallowed, we drew 0-0 and went to Milan and played them in the San Siro.

Mick Meagan: They were a good side. Discipline was their biggest thing: discipline, discipline, discipline. You will do it, you will do it for your teammate, you will do it for him.

Tony Kay: I think in those days the difference between English teams and European teams was that defensively they were superb. They were always great at defending. They must have started the game off by saying if we defend, nobody will score, and they were absolutely superb. On top of that, when we played against Italian sides, even if it was the under 21s or under 23s, we were always told by the manager, 'If you go down don't pick them up, because they will poke you in the eye.'

Derek Temple: They do things that you don't get in English football, you don't realise, the fans don't know. For instance they had this thing, you would push the ball past them and they'd body-check you, very frustrating; they'd just walk in front of you. Very often the referee wouldn't even give a foul, and they'd get away with it. Then they would knock you down, tackle you, you'd go to get up and it looks as though they are patting you on the head, but they're not, they're pulling your hair. You get up and you're angry and the crowd start to go, 'Look at that' – that's their crowd of course. They were very cynical in their attitude to the game. They did win an awful lot: whether you could say that is the way to win, I don't know. It's not my way of winning.

Roy Parnell: I played the match before against Ipswich away and who got star rating in the paper? There was only one paper that gave a star rating in them days it was *The People* – Roy Parnell 8/10. I had a good game there and I thought 'Bloody hell I must be playing next week against Inter Milan, gotta be playing but I don't trust him that Catterick you know.' When we went to Italy, it was the same team that played – me in the eleven – plus a lad called Barry Rees and Colin Harvey, who'd never been with the first team before ever. We got round this table in Milan in this big castle we were staying in. All the reporters travelled with us then they were all in the bar all the time. We got round the table and then, 'The team for tomorrow is: So and so in goal, Brian Harris move to left-back from left half' – and I thought 'that's my position' – and then 'So and so right-back and Colin you're coming in wing-half' and he went white. I went red with embarrassment and then Catterick said, 'Roy you're twelfth man.' I said, 'Oh fucking hell I can't believe this' and walked out. I kicked these bloody doors on the way out – you should have seen these doors in the castle nearly twenty foot high I nearly broke my foot on them – and pushed the doors open and of course all the fellas at the bar were all the reporters. 'Eh Pancho what's wrong?' I said 'I'm not playing. I'm twelfth man.' They said 'God we were at Ipswich, saw you played well. Who's playing?' 'Colin Harvey.' 'Colin who?'

Colin Harvey: We had a team meeting after lunch. Jimmy Gabriel was injured, so Catterick said 'Dennis Stevens, you move back to four [Gabriel's number], Colin you come in at number 8.' It was quite clever of him actually, because I had no time to think about it, we were playing that night. I went out quite relaxed, which is quite unusual for me, because if I was relaxed I wasn't happy, because you needed to be wound up a little bit.

Derek Temple: Colin Harvey made his debut and played tremendously well. Didn't phase him at all, it looked like he'd been playing there a long time.

Colin Harvey: I didn't notice the crowd. There was 80,000 of them, and it was a cauldron of noise, but all I did was get on with my job, and play football. I really enjoyed it. I did alright.

Derek Temple: We ran them very close again, we lost 1-0 and that was us out. They went on to win it. We couldn't have been a bad side when we ran them so close. With that little bit more belief we might have done it.

Colin Harvey: Inter ended winning the European Cup that year and they won it the year after; they were a really great side at the time. So I did alright. On the Thursday we travelled back, went in Friday morning, and I was back in the reserves! The reserves were playing Liverpool reserves at Goodison, and the first team were over at Anfield. So I was back in the reserves at Goodison, played in front of about 15 – 20,000, actually, because people who couldn't get into Anfield came over to Goodison to watch the game. It was a reality check!

Harry Catterick's quiet war with Alex Young

Although they remained in touch with the top of the table, Everton largely struggled for form in the first half of the 1963/64 season. In March Catterick shocked English football by smashing the British domestic transfer record when he bought Blackburn Rovers centre-forward Fred Pickering for £85,000. Pickering, a converted left-back who had led the Blackburn attack, had a dangerously hard right-foot shot, which had earned him the nickname 'Boomer'. To many observers it marked the end for Goodison's idol, Alex Young.

Derek Temple: Harry, if he won something, would break the team up. I thought he had the idea that people would become complacent if they had won something. I don't know if that's the case or not. Very often it would give you the reason to go for more – you've enjoyed the success winning – and a lot of players would want to more. But Harry had the idea that it would make you complacent, and nearly every team that has won something, he would break it up if you look back in history to when he was there.

John Hurst: Youngy was unbelievably talented; everybody knows that. He had a nickname though – 'homer' – a lot of people reckoned he only played at home but away from home sometimes they would think he is a bit limited. He wasn't a great worker. He didn't put defenders under pressure, but he was an absolutely wonderfully talented player and a dream to play with when he was on top form.

Howard Kendall: I think that there was a physical side he didn't want to get involved with too much. Away from home he could go missing and Harry was never one to shirk in criticising a player. Harry Catterick used to have team meetings every Monday lunchtime after a game. Alex, however, had trouble with his hearing and if he had played at home, scored a couple the hearing aid would be in. 'Alec, you were superb, well done; great goals,' Catterick would say. But play away from home, knee deep in mud, Alec would be the first one he'd point the finger at. 'You didn't try a leg, you didn't run up and down, you weren't interested.' Alec would have the hearing aid out; and Catterick would finish his speech and whoever was sat next to him would nudge him. 'He's talking about you, you know.' 'Oh was he?!' he'd say obliviously.

Fred Pickering: I'm not sure Harry always got on with Youngy, he wasn't his type of centre-forward. Harry was one of the old do or die types, stick your head in where it hurts. Youngy was a bit more finesse and skill.

Johnny Morrissey: I think Alex was on his way out then. Catterick was never really fond of Alex, he was unfair to Alex. Catterick liked muck and bullets in a way, besides ability. He just felt, in my mind, that Alex was too peripheral. But he wasn't, he was far from it as a player. You learn more about the game when you're finished as well, watching, and Youngy was a great link man. Vernon enjoyed a lot of pleasure from playing with Young, creating goals for him and all that. But Youngy and Catterick never got on.

Charles Mills: I thought Alex Young literally walked on water. I thought he was man of the match every single game that I watched. So no, I didn't understand why Catterick didn't like Alex. I didn't fully get the antagonism towards Young.

Fred Pickering: I was better on the left side than on the right side because I was brought up as a full-back: I was a left-back and for some reason I went up as a centre-forward. When I went to Everton I had to start to learn how they were playing and to change my positioning places with Derek Temple. He was an out and out flying winger so you had to leave that space for him. He created a lot of crosses and I scored a lot of goals through that. I had to change a little bit to keep him in his position because when I first went to Everton I think he was top goal scorer at that time. The day I signed for Everton they had played the week before at Spurs and beat Spurs 4-1 and Derek Temple had scored two and Alex Young had scored two and I thought, 'Well what's the point in signing me?' I was in the England squad in Sheffield for training before the Scotland-England game and Jimmy Greaves was saying ;'You're going to going to Goodison? They've just battered us. You'll never get in the team.'

Colin Harvey: He inherited Alex. He wouldn't have signed him himself, because he was a centre-forward himself; robust, have a go, whereas Youngy was more touch and technique.

Fred Pickering: When I played for Rovers down at Goodison Park we beat Everton 4-2 and I scored three goals. That was October time of that season. Then I came in March and I scored a hat-trick on my debut at Goodison. I'm the only one that's ever got back to back hat-tricks at Goodison Park.

Derek Temple: Fred came in as a converted full-back – converted not by Harry but by Blackburn – and his nickname was 'Boomer' because when he hit the ball it would go 'boom'; he could strike a ball. He belted them. He did well. His first game he scored three. A fella comes from Blackburn like that, bang, three goals, and you think here is something special.

Fred Pickering: I wasn't replacing anybody; I was there to buck them up. I was replacing Alex Young and Alex Young was going to replace Dennis Stevens and they didn't like it. He was a grafter and you needed that type of player for that team with Vernon and Young at the side of him. Gabriel used to be the midfielder but they wanted Youngy in as a player and playmaker. I was there because I was a goal scorer; Alex Young wasn't. I played about 110 games for the first team and scored 70 odd goals. Alex Young he was a goal scorer up in Scotland, it was a lot harder down here than what it was up there. He wasn't a big scorer but he was a class player, unbelievable player. I was more of a Hickson type of a centre-forward; knock 'em about a bit.

Challenging for the 1963/64 title

Pickering's debut hat-trick against Nottingham Forest in a 6-1 drubbing put Everton second. A week later they went top after Derek Temple's late winner against Pickering's former club, Blackburn. Indeed, with five games remaining Everton remained top. Although they subsequently faltered, what remaining title hopes they had were dealt a further blow on Sunday 12 April 1964 when the Sunday People printed allegations that a number of players had received bribes to 'throw' games. To the astonishment of everyone involved with Everton, Tony Kay was named as one of them.

Fred Pickering: It was just coming out in the *News of the World* that I'd asked for a transfer at Blackburn and this *Daily Mirror* sports correspondent from Liverpool rang me up and said, 'You don't want to be going to Everton because they could be banned from playing football because of what's gone on with this.' I asked: 'Why what's happened?' and he said, 'Oh you'll read it in the paper...'

Derek Temple: If you're gambling or throwing games, or trying to influence the results of games that you're taking part in then it's completely wrong. We've always believed that when there is a match on in England it is straight, and I think it generally has been and it still is. I can't think of any games that are suspicious. I haven't seen any.

Tony Kay: I was in the Royal Tiger on Manchester Street. A friend of mine said 'You're in trouble. Your name is right across the front of *The People*.' I said 'What about?' He said 'This match fixing thing.' The next day I was in the office with Harry and he said to me 'What's happening?' I told him all about it and left it at that. The day after that the FA said we're stopping you playing.

James Mossop: Tony Kay was in the Royal Tiger club and gestured as if to say 'Don't talk to me.' Not in a nasty way, but he knew he was in trouble. Bronco Layne and Peter Swan were the others involved in the scandal that blew up. It was mainly dealt with by the news pages and they got a lot of stick from the crowd. We all felt sorry for Tony Kay. That was him finished.

Johnny Morrissey: The Sunday papers came, and that was the first I knew of it. And Tony Kay wasn't mentioned then, I don't think, it seemed to be second, third division players at the time. And it broke that it was David Layne, Peter Swan and Tony Kay – they were the big names of whatever happened. Then it was an ongoing thing, nobody knew if they were banned. But it wasn't spoken about because you can't speak about it. I think that's how you had to go about it, isn't it? What can you say? I don't really know the ins and outs, but the players never discussed it. Never discussed it.

Fred Pickering: It was nowt to do with Everton but these people were thinking Everton were involved with it. The way these journalists were talking it looked like they were going to be in a lot of trouble but then Tony just got suspended. If it had been today it wouldn't have happened. None of the lads said, 'Well you're an idiot for doing this, that or the other.'

Kay was accused by Jimmy Gauld – an inside forward who had played 26 times for Everton in the 1956/57 season – along with two other Wednesday players, Peter Swan and David Layne, of accepting a bribe to throw Wednesday's match with Ipswich Town in December 1962. Ipswich had indeed won 2-0, but Kay had won the man-of-the-match award and even they acknowledged that he had 'put up a fine performance.'

Tony Kay: We'd never won down there for two or three years, and somebody came up to me and said 'How do you fancy it?' I said, 'No chance of winning whatsoever, no way.' He said, 'I tell you what if you give me £50 I'll get you 2/1.' That was it. For that I got four months in prison, banned for life, and fined £150. So would you not feel hard done by if that happened to you?

Mick Meagan: Tony was going to be an England player for a long time, and I felt very sorry for him.

Tony would be the likes of a fella that if you offered something he'd say 'Yeah, I'll take it,' but no way would he sell a match. He might sort of take the money and say 'Well fuck you that's alright, but I'm not going to sell any match.' He was a lovable rogue. He loved a big cigar and a Crombie.

Gerry Glover: I've always thought that Tony Kay would've played for England in the 1966 World Cup winning team instead of Nobby Stiles. He was a better player than Stiles, he was as hard as Stiles if not harder. Stiles was reputed to be hard but Tony Kay had skill as well. He was a magnificent player.

Derek Temple: It was quite a shock. My memory of that is in 1964 we went to Australia, and I can remember us all meeting at Goodison to get a coach to the airport and Tony was there, but he couldn't come with us and that was sad. He should have been coming to Australia with us but he was banned.

Tony Kay: They were just going to Australia. I was at St Georges playing fields in Huyton, playing football and all these players were walking across. I said to one of them 'I could have been on that, they're going to Australia and I'm stuck here playing in Huyton with you.'

James Mossop: There was talk in one of the papers – I think *The People* and it was a bloody scandalous thing – that the Everton players were on 'purple hearts' [amphetamines]. When Everton turned up to play at Anfield a lot of the Kop had these big purple heart things on and so when that came out the London office were sending news reporters – 'We need to get to the bottom of this.' So, as a follow up we went to see Roy Vernon at the Royal Tiger where they all used to go in Liverpool. I went down there and they didn't tell us very much at all. They reckon it was all rubbish. Well they would say it was all rubbish, wouldn't they? Nobody ever got to the bottom of it and it was actually a story that had been in another paper, so we didn't get very far. But they were embroiled in that for quite a while.

1964/65: Catterick reshapes Everton

Everton finished the 1963/64 season third and would end the following season fourth. After Kay's demise Brian Labone succeeded him as captain, while the England left-back Ray Wilson – a signing from Huddersfield – replaced Mick Meagan. Catterick's testy relationship with Alex Young persisted, while Pickering replaced Roy Vernon as the team's main source of goals, scoring 27 league goals in 64/65. Young players also started to emerge and stake their place in the Everton first team, notably Colin Harvey and Tommy Wright, but also John Hurst, Jimmy Husband, Andy Rankin, as well as a plethora of other talented young players who would lift the 1965 FA Youth Cup. The First Division was, nevertheless, changing, with newly promoted Liverpool and Leeds – under the management of Bill Shankly and Don Revie – immediately emerging as forces. When Everton faced Leeds United at home on 7 November 1964 the game became notorious as 'the Battle of Goodison' with Sandy Brown sent off and Derek Temple injured by an horrendous chest high tackle by Leeds' Willie Bell. As furious spectators showered the pitch with bottles the referee withdrew both teams for a 'cooling off period.'

Roy Parnell: Jimmy Hill [the PFA chairman] came out with this law that removed the maximum wage [in 1961]. I think it was £30 a week the first team players got from the £20 [maximum] which was like a 50 per-cent rise. Alex and Roy had argued for it but Labby never argued about anything, he just signed. 'It's Everton' he said and just signed. He told me he didn't even look and just signed for what they offered - £28 or something like that. After Roy and Alex got better terms, Catterick sent for Labone again and said 'I've decided you need more than them other boys. I've given you £30. I thought I'd give you a bit less than Young so I'm putting you on the same wage.' So he got £30 with the rest of them.

Tony Kay: Brian was a good player, but a gentleman of course. Harry came up to me one day and asked 'What do you think of Brian?' I told him I thought he was a good player, but he needed a bit more devilment in him; that he could do with putting it about a bit. So Catterick said, 'You tell him.' So I told him. I said, 'Do you fancy getting stuck in a bit, Brian?' So he tried it. We came in at half time and I looked at Harry and Harry looked at me and he said, 'Brian, forget it about it... just carry on as normal.'

Johnny Morrissey: I call him a 'Battle of Britain pilot.' You'd hang your hat on him. We used to play against Burnley and they had a player called Andy Lockhead, a big brute of a lad. And Labby would have belts on his eyes, but he'd still be up heading the ball. But he never spoke. He was a funny lad, you'd have a laugh with him in the dressing room, but on the field he wouldn't say to anyone 'Do this, do that.'

Jimmy Husband: Brian was a superb captain, a father figure to the youngsters. He didn't go round ranting and raving, anything like that. He led by example – great centre-half. Again he had come through the youth system, albeit a few years before the likes of Joe Royle, John Hurst, myself and Colin Harvey. He was great in the dressing room and an excellent player. Technically he was a better centre-half than Jack Charlton, but in Alf Ramsey's mind Jack Charlton was probably a better pivot next to Bobby Moore as opposed to Brian Labone. Maybe Brian Labone, who tried to play football from the back, and Bobby Moore might have been too similar.

Howard Kendall: Sandy Brown was the butt of a lot of Labone and Westy's fun. It was a shame that everyone remembers him now for his derby day own goal, because he was a very good player. He was as fit and hard as any player I ever knew. His stomach was like a washboard; it was all muscle. He used to say in his thick Scottish accent 'Punch for punch', challenging you to hit him so he could wallop you back. 'You can have a free one, if yer like' he'd add; meaning he didn't do it back to you first time around. Not many people took him up on it.

Colin Harvey: Ray Wilson was probably one of the most vocal in our group in terms of people talking behind you and telling you what to do. He had a good football brain, and it helps if someone behind you gives you a little shout about something you can't see yourself, and you just need a little reminder.

Len Norman: They only got Wilson fairly late in his career, but he was an absolutely amazing player; he was almost a full-back-cum-winger at times. What I liked about him was that if he made a mistake – which didn't happen very often – he would put his hands up and acknowledge his error to the crowd. He was a spotless player. He was the sort of player who would go off with his trousers still clean.

Peter Mills: I just loved Ray Wilson because he was class; everything he did was class. When the full-back had passed the ball back to the goalie he would always chip it back to Gordon West so Gordon wouldn't have to bend down. Just things like that always showed a touch of class.

Derek Temple: We saw the young players training, we knew they were going to be established players pretty quickly. You're seeing them every day in practice, you know their strengths, and generally you would only see strengths not weaknesses, they were good, and you knew they were going to be top notch. The other thing is that it is like a jigsaw. You can bring top class players in, they might not necessarily gel, they might not fit in. But if you get the right one and they get in that jigsaw, then there's another piece. If you get the lot together, you're going to win things.

Colin Harvey: John Hurst was probably very unlucky to be playing around the time of Bobby Moore, because he had been a striker, and then he had been a midfield player, and then he had been a back four player. He was very accomplished on the ball, so it was very easy. He would come out with it and you would just position yourself and he would give it to you.

Derek Temple: When Leeds came to Goodison it was always going to be a battle. The thing about it was they could play good football, they had good players. But Bobby Collins got them so competitive, and they were cheats really in a way because they would foul people and then go down in agony as though you had kicked them. The referee would be thinking 'What has happened?' But there was nothing wrong with them. They'd really kicked you or whoever you were playing.

Tony Kay: Sandy Brown was a hatchet man. We used to say to him 'kill', and Sandy used to kill. I wasn't like that. I used to get involved, but nearly every time I played against opposition, other than Denis Law, anyone who was a bit lively, I used to say, 'What we playing at today?' And they would say, 'What do you mean?' And I said, 'Are we kicking one another or are we going to play football?'

Derek Temple: That game we played them that day, I remember Brian Labone hitting a ball out to me, I was out on the far touchline by the Paddock. I had to turn and go back because he hit it behind me. The next thing I remember I had just been hit in the back, he threw himself apparently, feet first. He hit me in the kidneys at the back, and I went down.

David Hart: I was in the Paddock when Willie Bell hit Derek Temple with both feet about hip high right in front of us. It looked as though he had broken his back. The crowd was already livid because the referee had just sent off Sandy Brown for an incident that was caused by Johnny Giles; they reckon that Johnny Giles grabbed Brown on the floor in a position and Brown reacted and the referee from the half way line sent Brown off which made the crowd angry. Then this tackle went in so the referee took both teams off because he said he couldn't control the game but he was frightened of the crowd. I hated Leeds after that, they were filthy.

James Mossop: As they were treating Temple, Willie Bell went down as well. The Leeds trainer was saying 'Stay down, stay down.' There was nothing wrong with him, but he shouted to the stretcher people 'Stretcher, stretcher over here.' One of them that was supposed to go on said, 'Get your own effing stretcher' because they knew it was all acting.

Johnny Morrissey: I played against a lad called Paul Reaney, a full-back. There was a throw in down the line, I went to head the ball, and I got clouted in the head. I then got another belt off this lad. That's the way they were. Jack Charlton and Norman Hunter, they all kicked. Billy Bremner wasn't vicious, but he'd be at you and pulling you and all that. Johnny Giles. They'd brought 'professionalism' into football, because they'd be speaking to the referee and all that. We never spoke to the referees.

Derek Temple: I remember that Ken Stokes wasn't a good referee, he was weak. He'd already sent Sandy Brown off for chinning Giles, who had upset Sandy by kicking him in the goolies. It's a nasty thing to do. I remember being in the dressing room, and I heard the voices of the two managers and the referee. Revie and Catterick were saying 'What have you done?' He said 'I've called the game off, there's going to be a riot.' They said to him 'There'll be a riot if you call the game off. You've got to get out there.' Anyway the game finished, we lost 1-0, and big Jack Charlton, he always scored against us, like a giraffe at the near post. It was good play by them, they fired the ball in and they couldn't get near him to defend it. He just touched it in.

David Hart: I'll never forget the battles between Johnny Morrissey and the Leeds players in the years after that. I used to watch a lot off the ball. My brother used to say 'Will you watch the game' and I'd say, 'I'm watching off the ball.' I could always see if the other team got a corner Alan Ball would always grab one of their big players off the ball. On this day Everton had a corner from the right and Leeds had been hitting Alan Whittle in the ribs with stiff fingers; Norman Hunter, Willie Bell and Billy Bremner hitting him in the ribs with their fingers and Whittle was really getting a rough time. The ball came over and Morrissey ran in from the left before the kick and the next thing big Jack was on the floor flat out and on his way into Walton Hospital's Brain Unit. Morrissey had just run in and butted him but nobody saw it. It was brilliant but we shouldn't say that! I think Jack had done something to one of the Everton players in a previous game, so Morrissey thought 'Oh, we'll sort this one out.'

Joe Royle's notorious entrance

Everton started the 1965/66 season sluggishly. They were knocked out of the Inter Cities Fairs Cup in the second round and lingered in mid table. Meanwhile the Goodison idol, Alex Young, was in and out of the first team. Supporter unrest with Catterick climaxed after an away defeat to Blackpool in January 1966 when the manager was allegedly 'attacked' by Evertonians for picking a 16-year-old named Joe Royle ahead of Young.

Gerry Humphreys: Alex was idolised by Evertonians. In my eyes he was one of the best players and that's what stood out for me as a youngster watching him. I used to watch him in training and we used to play a match sometimes on a Tuesday, first team versus reserves. To watch him up close on the pitch and to watch how he used to glide past people and you knew he was a top top player.

Joe Royle: My selection was a surprise. I got two buses to the game with all the fans and they didn't know who I was. By the time I arrived I got all the autographs on the coach from the players. I played, and I was an old fashioned inside right in those days. Instead of being the link from defence to midfield, which I had been as a schoolboy, I spent most of my schoolboy days as a centre half.

George Orr: In those days Everton reserves would be playing at Goodison while there was an away match, so you never got to see the reserves. You didn't know who they were because they played on the same day. We were thinking 'Who's this Joe Royle?' Alex Young was considered to be a God. He was a God!

Johnny Morrissey: Joe was never sixteen! Joe was born at 20, it was one of them things. Joe was Joe and he still is the same, conducts himself well. At sixteen he was very mature. I think that's why Catterick felt he could put him in at that age. He wasn't fazed and he proved Catterick right, because he turned out to be a great player, didn't he?

Gerry Humphreys: I suppose it was a shock that he was dropped. Maybe it had something to do with the fact that him and Catterick didn't see eye to eye. I'm sure Joe would've had a bit of a surprise to find at sixteen he was in the team. It does happen on occasions but not that often at that age.

Joe Royle: Against Blackpool we were dominated. It was a skating rink, a frozen pitch, and there was this little ginger haired chap floating around it called Alan Ball, and I'm pretty sure Catterick made up his mind that day that he was going to sign him.

After a 2-0 defeat a small crowd of Evertonians waited outside Bloomfield Road to berate the team. As Harry Catterick made his way onto the coach he was jostled, fell and – according to the following day's newspapers – attacked.

John Hurst: His foot slipped on the foot rest as he was climbing up and he stumbled. But it got all changed into, 'Catterick attacked by supporters.' It was actually that he just missed his footing.

Gerry Humphreys: I was in the squad that day up at Blackpool when that happened. I didn't play in the game - I was twelfth man or something like that - travelling with the squad and then we were just sat on the coach waiting for Catterick to come from the boardroom. As he came out a crowd of people crowded round him and the next thing apparently he was on the floor. I couldn't actually say if anybody gave him a kicking.

Johnny Morrissey: Alec Young was an idol and when idols are dethroned, people don't like it. Young Joe came in, and as we were going to the coach after the game they were all waiting for Catterick and harassing him. I think he got shoved or pushed or something, and maybe played it up a little, I don't know, and it made news.

Joe Royle: I was on the coach; nobody was aware of any kerfuffle afterwards, it was a shock to everybody when we read in the papers the next day that Harry had been accosted, and he was a clever old fox – I'm sure he wanted everyone to read that instead of Everton losing 2-0 at Blackpool.

Jimmy Husband: I'd been playing in the reserves some place, but obviously I heard about it, and it was discussed in the dressing rooms. It appears that it was perhaps blown up a little bit, I don't think there was any big scuffle or anything like that. It was a generation away from hooliganism and all that. I think a few supporters verbally had a go at Catterick. I think that's about as far as it went, really. I don't think there was any pushing or shoving, or anything like that.

Joe Royle: The next week Alex Young was back in the team. There was a few left out that game, but as the press do they never let the truth interfere with a good story.

1966 FA Cup run

Derek Temple: We had a couple of good results. I think we had Coventry at home, we had Sunderland at home, in between we were away at non-League Bedford Town. Harry built them up to be a top class side. They tried to kick us. We were strong enough to see them off. I got a couple that day at Bedford. Then of course you're into the quarter-finals, only a couple of games off the final.

Charles Mills: The thing I remember is listening to the cup draw at lunchtime on a Monday. Someone at St Mary's College [in Crosby] would have a little transistor and we'd be listening. And then the nervousness as to whether we got a ticket because there were so few tickets given out to supporters. My Dad was the ticket man; he managed to get tickets for virtually everybody. The same people you went to school with were the same people you went to church with and the same people you went to the match with. The Whites, the Flemings, the Normans, the Mills's. It was very much part of our faith really as much as anything. That's the best way of describing it; it really is an actual faith. You didn't have a choice and you wouldn't chose anything else; nor would I want to. Nor do my children, nor do my grandchildren.

Derek Temple: The quarter-final game against City was hard. They were a pretty useful side. We got a draw at Maine Road, and then there was another draw at Goodison, so we ended up going to Wolves. I think it should have been at Blackburn but I think there was something on. When they started off, the first 25 minutes, half an hour, it looked like they were on drugs or something, they were running, they were tackling, they were going like the clappers. We hadn't got a kick, honestly. But then we started to play the way we can and it just turned. We got a free-kick on the right, Scotty swung it in. I was at the far post and I was running in, I was going to head it and I slipped. It was coming across me and I just swung my left foot and I slipped. I volleyed it and it flew in. It gave us great impetus and next thing Fred banged one in. We came out of that winners, and that was probably our hardest game in the lot.

Fred Pickering: I had this knee problem. I missed the quarter-final against Man City, which they drew 0-0. I was fit the week after in the replay and we drew 0-0 again at Goodison. City had a fair side in those days; the centre half for City was a lad called George Heslop and he was a big strong cumbersome type of centre half, but he was hard. I was a bit match fit for the second replay down at Molineux and we beat them 2-0; Derek Temple and I both scored. Then we went Sheffield United in the league and my leg went again, it meant I couldn't play in the semi-final and Mike Trebilcock played in my place.

Mike Trebilcock: We're having lunch and Harry Catterick gets a little board out and he goes 'Ray Wlison, Brian Labone, Brian Harris, Tommy Wright, blah blah, blah – and Mike you'll play instead of Fred' and I'm going 'He just didn't say that, did he?' because I was just sitting there listening to what was going on. I was playing in the semi-final against Manchester United the great Man United a team I'd only read about and I was going to play against the great Denis Law and Bobby Charlton and all those guys! I'm going 'I can't believe this.'

John Hurst: My biggest memory is of the semi-final at Bolton when Colin scored. I was thirteenth man and I was on the bench. I was there with Tommy Egglestone and the physio; there was only room for about four of you in those little dug outs. When we scored Catterick came steaming down from somewhere but couldn't get in so he threw me out and I had to go and stand somewhere else while he sat down. Not many goals stick in my mind but Colin's bobbler is my abiding memory.

Tommy Wright: There was a lot of people who didn't think we'd beat United and the goal was a big boost. I didn't play in the semi as I'd done my back in in training; Sandy Brown played instead.

Derek Temple: We hadn't conceded a goal, and then of course we got Manchester United, beat them. That was the only game I didn't score in actually. There's luck involved in winning the cup, they're one off games. If you've got a strong defence, a team with a strong defence has a good chance of winning.

They're one off games and if you keep a clean sheet you're in with a shout aren't you? The game at Burnden Park against United, I think they just come back from a loss in Europe. So we got them at the right time. That's the luck of the draw. We beat them 1-0, Colin knocked one in, bobbled one in. But it counted, it doesn't matter.

Mike Trebilcock: There were 55,000 people there and they were hanging off the floodlights. You couldn't believe the scenes.

Charles Mills: Afterwards in the crowd outside there was a bottleneck in the road, a huge crush, and a car stupidly trying to inch its way back. My trouser pocket got caught in the handle of this car and I had my trousers ripped off; so I was standing there with no pants. I had to wear my dad's mac for the rest of the journey! We stopped at some pub, in Blackrod, or somewhere like that, and all the coaches were tooting as we were waving our flags and scarves outside this pub.

Colin Harvey: I was an Evertonian as a kid, I used to watch the games from the old boys' pen which is up in the corner of the Gwladys Street. For a little time we lived in Leta Street, which is the one behind Gwladys Street. It's being rebuilt now, but it's still called Leta Street. It was the old two up two down, toilet in the back, it belonged to my auntie and uncle and their two sons, and it was just after the war, so everybody used to take everybody in then, so we lived there for two years. It was great for my dad, because he just walked around the corner and he was on Gwladys Street. So to go from that to actually playing and playing in a cup final, it was unbelievable.

Derek Temple: Fred Pickering got injured in the cup run we had when we got to the final. He wasn't fit, we all knew that. You've got this history of the turf at Wembley finding people out, it's energy sapping, and if Fred would have played he wouldn't have finished the game. Catterick had a choice to make and he put the little fella in, Trebilcock, for the semi-final and he played very well, he didn't let us down and of course he did very well in the final.

Fred Pickering: I wasn't fit. Between the quarter-final replay and the semi-final it looked like it was as bad as I thought it were, but then leading up to the final a couple of weeks before it went again in training. Catterick decided then I wasn't playing.

Eric Linford: I remember queuing for my cup final ticket. It was based on programme vouchers, which you cut out from the programme. You can write a one in many different ways and the way it had been written there was no end of forgeries on voucher number one. I was a student at university and on the day they were selling the cup final tickets I had two sets of vouchers. It was one set of twelve for one ticket and you had to have two people if you wanted two tickets. I remember going to the ground on my way for lectures about 9:30 am and the queue was lengthy. So I went to the university, parked my moped and went straight back to the ground. My brother came up after school and he found me in the queue. I'd spent from about 10 o'clock in the morning till seven or eight o'clock at night queuing for a ticket. I think the ticket was 7s 6d or ten shillings.

Mike Trebilcock: On Friday lunchtime [before the match] the trainer went over to Sandy Brown and then he came to Tommy Wright and he says 'Tommy the boss wants to see you in his room after lunch.' Then he turns to me and says, 'And Mike he wants to see you as well.' John Hurst said 'You must be playing Trebs.' When I got in the room Fred Pickering was there and I just couldn't work out what

Fred Pickering was doing there, and the boss says, 'Look at a time like this decisions have to be made and I'm the one that's got to make them. Sandy I'm leaving you out and putting Tommy back in – which we all knew anyway – and then he said, 'Fred I'm leaving you out and putting Mike in.' If the saying is you could fall off the back of your chair that's what I felt like because I thought I was only going down there to help put the gear out. The boss said 'You two can leave because these two guys might want to say something to me afterwards.' So Tommy and I went outside and we threw our arms round each other and hugged each other.

Tommy Wright: I was made up, but I felt a bit sorry for Sandy. He was alright about it though; he took these things in his stride.

Johnny Morrissey: I played one of the games against City and I missed out on the final. Whatever people say, it's about yourself, and I was sick. I told him I wouldn't kick another ball for him. I said 'I'm finished.' And that changed my whole attitude. Whether the message got home, because from 66 onwards after they won the cup I was regular until I finished. It was frustrating at the time, everybody wants to play in the first team.

Gerry Humphreys: I went down for the FA Cup final. I wasn't in the squad but we all went down as a club and stayed in a hotel in London and we had a really good weekend. If I remember we were on one of the sides on a bench and were all given tickets.

Johnny Morrissey: I went down to Wembley at the last minute, but I must say it was a great day, because I'm emotional – I'm a winner. I'm a winner and I want to win. When I wasn't playing I was disappointed. We went to see Dr Zhivago at the pictures the night before!

1966 FA Cup final
Everton v Sheffield Wednesday
14 May, 1966

In the final, Everton were facing Catterick's former club, Sheffield Wednesday. Everton went 1-0 down to Jim McCalliog's early goal and although Alex Young found the net it was disallowed after a contentious offside decision. Then, on 59 minutes, disaster struck. David Ford scored Sheffield Wednesday's second: 0-2. With only half an hour left, Everton's task seemed hopeless.

Fred Pickering: Like anything else if I'd have been fit and everything I might've scored three or four. I was lot better player than Trebilcock and he hadn't had a kick before he scored the goals. It was like he was lost and the trainers, Tommy Egglestone and Ron Llewellyn, were saying 'We should've played Fred.' If I'd have been fit there wouldn't have been a problem.

Mike Trebilcock: The story really is that once Sheffield Wednesday scored then the rest of the day the Everton spectators were going 'Harry's got it wrong, shouldn't have played Mike, should've played Fred' and I'm sure that was going through all spectators' minds until it got to 2-2 then that all changed.

Derek Temple: We were firm favourites, because we'd already beaten Sheffield in the league [5-1 at

Goodison in August]. But they did well, they came out the blocks, like City earlier. They got the goal, that was the first thing we conceded in the competition which was a bit upsetting. But you just carry on playing, you've got confidence in your own ability and your teammates. Harry said to us at half time 'Just keep playing to your system. You're doing alright.' Then they got another one and I was thinking 'This isn't in the script.' We're going to have to come back next season to do it for the fans, because the fans were great.

Two minutes after Wednesday's second goal, Mike Trebilcock entered Wembley lore.

Mike Trebilcock: The first goal was straight from the training ground. I mean we did it every week. When you work with two strikers you always work on the theory that one comes short and one goes long; that's the theory you always work on and whichever side the ball is on that player comes short, the other player goes long; that's the basics. So Brian Harris got the ball on the right and I was the nearest striker to him, so I came short as quick as I could and I went, 'Yes' . When I came the Sheffield Wednesday defender started to come with me and when Brian knocked it to Derek Temple the defender turned to his right to see where it was going and I turned to his left and when Derek knocked it down it just bounced once and I went 'I'm going to do a Jimmy Greaves here and I'm just going to put it in the near post.' I knew Ron Springett was a top class goalkeeper and the theory is when it comes in from one way you knock it back across the other: that's always the theory with strikers. But I'd watched Jimmy Greaves and I loved Jimmy Greaves – the best goalscorer ever – and I said 'Now near post.' But it just bounced up and I volleyed it straight into the near post and he was dead.

Derek Temple: That's 2-1. If you get a team that's winning 2-0, everything is hunky dory. If you get one back and it goes to 2-1, they suddenly start panicking thinking they're under pressure, and they shouldn't really, it's still like winning 1-0. But anyway it did unsettle them, and next thing we have a free kick and Labby nodded it back and again he is there, bang, 2-2.

Mike Trebilcock: The second one [three minutes later] was a classic. When Malcolm Allison first came to Plymouth he told me as a striker when you're in the box you've got more time than you think. We got a free kick on the right hand side and Labby went to the far post and we knew that Alex was going to knock it to the far post. So I thought, 'When that ball goes to the far post I'm going to head for the penalty spot.' Alex took it, back it came, I headed to the penalty spot and it landed right in my stride and Malcolm Allison's words came back to me – 'You've got more time than what you think.' I've hit the sweetest half volley you've ever seen and I said to myself, 'Don't worry about scoring hit the target keep your head down put as much leather on leather as you can and just hit the target.' When I looked up Ron Springett was lying on the ground with his face down and the ball was just rolling out the back of the net like I never saw it go in. I've never seen it go in until this day. Nobody can show the replay it went so fast.

Everton were suddenly level with Wednesday. But the best was still to come in the eightieth minute.

Derek Temple: Colin hit a ball out of defence. I was a left-winger but I'd ended up in the inside right position, because I wasn't governed. I wasn't told to stay on the wing, I moved round. This is about thinking about the game, you get into positions where you think you can be dangerous or have an impact.

Gerry Humphreys: I can remember Gerry Young miscontrolled the ball and it went under his foot and

Derek ran on to it and took it through. It was him against the keeper and he could've done a number of things really because the keeper advanced a bit.

Tommy Wright: Derek was quick and he was a good finisher. We were watching him and thinking, 'He's going to win this for us here.'

Derek Temple: I ran towards Gerry Young, who was the sweeper and the last man. It was only just inside their half but I thought, 'Oh well, if it bobbles off him I'll have a chance to get it.' He went to trap it and it went under his foot. He was the last man so I had a clear run then. He couldn't turn quick enough, I was away. It was from the right wing so I had to go infield, take it in. I had a chance to look up and I was thinking 'He hasn't come off his line so I can't chip him,' so I just kept going. His angles were alright, and that's what it is all about in a one-on-one like that. The goalkeeper tries to get his angles right. Just on the edge of the box when I was running the ball came up right, about a foot off the ground for me to strike it. I just aimed for the far corner which is always the way.

Gerry Humphreys: He could've tried to take it round him but there were no defenders around. He was clean through one against one but he got to the edge of the box and decided to hit it and it flew into the corner. It was a tremendous shot and a tremendous goal.

Mike Trebilcock: When Derek Temple took off I was going after him and I'm saying, 'You shoot, let the keeper save it and I'm going to be there for the rebound.' But he just put it straight in the corner.

Derek Temple: I think he got his fingertips to it but it didn't change the direction. It went in, sort of hit the side netting, I think. People say, 'What did you feel like?' I just say, 'Relieved.'

Mike Trebilcock: The Wednesday players were shattered, they were drained. I mean when it was 2-0 they would've been going to take the cup home to Sheffield, they were going to shake Princess Margaret's hand and get the winners medal and all that and then Bang, Bang, Bang and all those dreams were gone.

Charles Mills: We had had the famous incident when Eddie Kavanagh ran across the pitch celebrating Trebilcock's second. It was one of the funniest things I've ever seen in my life. Four police officers grabbing his coat and he's squeezing out of it.

David Hart: I always think that Brian Harris won that game for Everton. I remember him picking up that policeman's helmet and starting larking about [after Eddie Kavanagh had been apprehended]. When you're losing at Wembley and you've got the mind to do that kind of thing the others must think we thought we were winning. I think that turned the game.

Mike Trebilcock: After the game Fred just walked off the bench, put a fag in his mouth, put his arms round me and said, 'Well done Trebs.'

Johnny Morrissey: There was a reception at the Grosvenor Hotel. Anyway, I wasn't going. We were in the hotel room, knock at the door, it was Ray Wilson and Alec Young. 'Look you're part of our team, come on, come.' I said, 'No, I'm not going.' And they talked me into it. I went and had a good night.

Charles Mills: We had this epic coach journey home, which became famous locally for one of the fellas on it – Jack Fleming – 'Walking' all the way back from Wembley, because he wouldn't sit down. Up and down the aisle he'd go with this cake his wife had baked.

Len Norman: Our bus driver arranged to stop at a pub near Harrow. The landlord had set aside a room for the children and bottles of lemonade, and we went into the bar. The pints flowed. We were probably there until around 11pm and set off again back to Liverpool. The landlord gave us a crate of ale to see us on our way, which was very good of him. But we hadn't gone very far when we had to make a toilet stop, so we pulled up on the side of the motorway and there was this scattering of men running off into the bushes! We set off again, but we'd only been going another 45 minutes when the tyre burst.

Charles Mills: We didn't have a proper jack, so Jack Fleming set off down the hard shoulder to call for help. However he'd had a few pints and lost his footing and disappeared down an embankment. We lost him for two or three minutes before he made his way back up. Eventually we got back on the road and I think we got back about half five the next morning. We had a few hours sleep and got up to watch the victory parade on Queens Drive. A memorable, memorable day that was. One of the great days. One of the great cup finals.

Dick White: For so long Catterick came across as cool and unemotional, but when the team came back to Liverpool to parade the FA Cup we saw a different side to him. There were thousands and thousands of people on the streets to greet the team, and when the trophy was handed to Catterick he held onto it – no one could get it off him.

1966 World Cup

1966 was also the year that England hosted – and won – the World Cup. Ray Wilson was part of the winning team, but Goodison also played a big part in the tournament, hosting games until the semi-final stage. Bellefield played host to the Brazil team of Pele, Garrincha and Tostao and received a much needed upgrade for the occasion.

Colin Harvey: Bellefield when I first went there, it had been the Co-op's old sports ground, and it was like a pavilion. It was quite dilapidated. We never used to report there, we used to report to Goodison, and then we'd bus it to Bellefield and bus back afterwards for your bath and what have you. But it was 1966 when they did completely revamp it, and at the time it was state of the art. We used to report straight there every day then, you would only report to Goodison on match days.

Lord Grantchester: Getting that all organised, all of that investment was crucial. So that the youngsters had an affinity to the Club. Young players came through the ranks to support the team.

Jimmy Husband: Bellefield changed into a self-contained training facility. Players didn't go to Goodison in the morning and get changed into their football kit and then get on a bus. We started going to the training centre at Bellefield where you had your physiotherapy. Every Friday, I still remember his name, Dr. Irvine, would come in on Friday to check in on anybody who'd got any sort of ailments or injuries. [The physio] Norman Borrowdale was on hand to deal with any problems. This was all self-contained at Bellefield. It was great. We had all the best quality baths and showers, all the facilities you could wish for. And of course we had one of the first indoor playing areas, roof and walls around it, where if it was atrocious weather we could train.

John Hurst: I went to quite a few of the games. It was good and exciting. It was a wonderful occasion to watch some of the games. Pele got kicked out of the game against Portugal. It was absolutely horrendous some of the tackling. It wasn't tackling it was just kicking people. It was assault; he got kicked everywhere.

David Hart: We had Brazil, Bulgaria and Hungary in Liverpool. Brazil were knocked out. That was a cracking game, Hungary v Brazil. And then Portugal played North Korea in the quarter-final so we had that one. We had some great games. Portugal had Eusebio at the time; they had half the Benfica team: they had Coluna, Jose Augusto, the big fella Torres. They had some great players did Portugal, they should've won it, although I have to say England played some very good football in that World Cup. Ramsey was a good manager.

Peter Mills: Those games were all televised, so to see Eusébio, Pelé, Beckenbauer, and the Hungary team – who were unknown and they had fellows like Flórián Albert and Ferenc Bene – just fellows who were producing football that was like something you'd never seen before; it was wondrous to watch that at Goodison.

Leon Bernicoff: I went to those games; I went to West Germany v USSR and of course we all supported Russia. 'Bury him Jimmy, he bombed our house' – that was the classic. Nobody supported Germany, we all supported Russia. It was good to accept though that Germany really won the final; that was no goal from Geoff Hurst.

The Holy Trinity

Again, Catterick had not made a significant pre-season signing in 1966, but two days after watching his Everton team outclassed by Liverpool in the Charity Shield he entered the transfer market again. The man he brought to Goodison was Blackpool's 21-year-old World Cup winning midfielder, Alan Ball. Once more Everton broke the British transfer record, shelling out £112,000 for the midfielder.

James Mossop: Bally said that there was talk of Leeds being interested. He lived in the Manchester area at that time and one day there was a knock on the door and Lesley, his wife, answered and this fella gave her an envelope. He said, 'This is for Alan Ball.' So she took it in and they counted out £100 in notes 'What's this all about then?' and it happened every week. Bally said he didn't know whether to take them to his Dad [Alan Ball senior, a coach and manager] or whomever and then one day he got a phone call telling him that it was an 'investment'. It was from Leeds United. So, of course, he did tell his Dad. Then the Everton interest came in and he said 'Everton or Leeds?' Knowing what they knew about Leeds and they used to go and watch Everton midweek when Blackpool weren't playing they decided they were going to Everton.

Jimmy Husband: We'd joke about Harry Cooke, the chief scout, being asked about his best signing. 'It was Alan Ball,' he'd say. 'Where did you first spot him?' 'Oh I first spotted Alan Ball when he was in the World Cup final.' 'Oh yeah, good spot.'

Colin Harvey: The minute he walked in the place you knew you were in the presence of a great player. And he just pushed everyone, he raised the bar. You're never going to be as good as him, but to be nearly as good as him you worked that much harder again. He's the best. Obviously Dixie Dean's record is unbelievable, but of all the Everton players I watched and played with, he was by far the best.

Johnny Morrissey: He was an atom bomb. Great in the dressing room, great on the field. Best player I've ever played with. Bally was brilliant. He was a 5ft 6inch giant. You can't eulogise him enough.

David France: The Holy Trinity were better than the Leeds team at the time: Bremner, Giles and the like. Alan had agreed to go to Leeds – he had taken a backhander to go to Leeds – and he decided not to. So I'd hate to think how good Leeds would have been had he gone there. But he was a great acquisition – when you get the star of the World Cup final joining you, you believe great things will happen.

Howard Kendall: Bally was a once in a lifetime player, someone who was incomparable. The 20 goals a season we would get from him were the difference between us being a very good side that were in the mix and an outstanding one.

Joe Royle: Alan was great, lively, noisy; most of the time a bundle of fun, a great guy. A terrible loser, as poor a loser as you will ever see, sometimes on the odd occasion when we lost he would be crying, throwing his boots around the dressing room, an awful loser. It's just as well we didn't lose so often. You would always make sure you weren't the first in the showers if Bally was ranting and raving. What he was and still is, is the best player I ever played with, and a great guy and friend.

Peter Mills: I went to the Charity Shield when we played Liverpool after they'd won the League and we'd won the FA Cup; and they battered us 1-0 at Goodison; absolutely battered us. And then a couple of days later we signed Ball, and about two weeks later they played again at Goodison when he made his debut. I didn't go but my dad came back and said, 'Oh, they've got some player there.' Whenever you saw him he just stood out. He was a little fellow as you know, with red hair, and fiery, and ran about all over the place but very, very skilful. But he'd sit on the ball, or tap the ball with his arse, or do something to make him stand out. He was our George Best; he was our hero.

Howard Kendall: Alan was definitely the best player I ever played with. He was so consistent. The disappointments he had earlier in his career [Ball was rejected as a schoolboy by his hometown club, Bolton] had a profound effect upon him and he never wanted to fail again. Even when he was a World Cup winner, he kept pushing himself and pushing himself, believing that he would make it. There were times in a game when we'd be losing and he'd run 10 or 15 yards to kick somebody. Everybody in the ground knew what he'd done, and he'd get a caution. And Alan would just turn round to the rest of us and say, 'You don't care as much as me'. We did; we just weren't as silly as he was.

Jimmy Husband: Alan was quite vociferous and opinionated, which was great, because we already knew he was a great international footballer. He was a great addition to the Everton squad; a tremendous addition.

David France: Bally, as we all know during his early days was outstanding, because he'd contribute 20 odd goals a season from midfield. He had unbelievable stamina with that fantastic touch. When it comes to talking about teammates, Alan had a positive and not so positive impact: you either liked him or you didn't. He was so demanding and so critical, that he sort of alienated people in the dressing room. He told me this and I knew him well. He wasn't the sort to let you into his life, but once he trusted you he was a very good guy.

John Hurst: He was a great lad Bally, bubbly, effervescent; he was just a great lad to have. On the pitch he was enthusiastic, off the pitch he was enthusiastic. Even in training he was the same. In five asides he was competitive. He never wanted to lose anything. It just fed off onto other players when you were out on the pitch. Sometimes he used to snarl at players unduly because someone made a mistake. They didn't make a mistake on purpose and he'd be on their backs and then two minutes later it'd be forgotten with. He was a hell of an asset.

Johnny Morrissey: Sometimes you go out and you've lived the right life, but you've got like lead boots on. You feel heavy-legged. Sometimes you'd go out like that and Bally would say, 'Come on John, what's happening?' I'd say 'Bally, I'm knackered.' He'd say 'come on. I'll stay over here for five minutes, do a couple of one-twos.' And that's Bally all over the field. Just besides his own game he was helping everybody else.

James Mossop: There was an FA Cup fifth round tie against Liverpool [in March 1967, played at Goodison but also screened live at Anfield]. The ground was full and Anfield was full because they had a big screen and Everton won [Alan Ball scoring the winner]. People leaving Anfield were quite emotional and one of them was Jimmy Tarbuck and someone shouted, 'It's alright Jimmy it's only a film.'

Derek Temple: I can criticise Harry Catterick for changing a team, but he invariably changed the team for the better. It worked for him, he was given money to go and break British transfer records, and he was buying top class. Bally was man of the match in the World Cup final, and we've got him coming in. Then we got Howard.

Howard Kendall: By 1967 I had been in the Preston first team for three years. At that stage I just wanted to play at the top level. I was very honoured to be linked with Liverpool and there seemed some inevitability about the transfer. I'd even been over to stay with Peter Thompson at his digs for a weekend. It was a matter of if I was moving I was going there. By March the transfer deadline was approaching and the transfer talk hadn't quietened, despite Liverpool signing a similar kind of player to me in Emlyn Hughes a month earlier. The Preston chairman had been upset by some off-the-record comments I'd made about my failure to secure a transfer that had been made public in a national newspaper. I hadn't fallen out with the club, but the situation wasn't great. One evening there was a knock on the door. It was the manager Jimmy Milne. It was my Dad he did all the talking to. 'I've got a club for your lad; we're going to let him go,' he said 'Is it Liverpool?' my Dad asked. 'No; across the road.' There had been no hint whatsoever that Everton were interested in buying me. Not a whisper.

Derek Temple: I was in training and Harry Catterick sent for me, and he said, 'I've got Jimmy Milne from Preston coming over, he wants to have a word with you.' I said 'He wants to have a word with me? I don't want to go anywhere.' I knew what he was on about. I said 'I don't want to leave Everton.' And he said, 'No, and we don't want to lose you. But you might as well have a word with him, he's on his way over.' Did he think I was thick or something, stupid? We don't want to lose you? Rubbish. What happened, I was part of the make-weight for the Howard Kendall deal, but he wouldn't let me go at that time. But obviously he said, 'Let's see how it goes, and when we're ready you've got first option sort of thing.'

Howard Kendall: I'd come in to replace Jimmy Gabriel who was popular among the players and supporters and had been crucial to the league and FA Cup successes. I'd seen him play and he was an absolutely tremendous wing-half. He could tackle, get forward; he was the perfect wing-half, a superb player. It can be difficult, sometimes, coming to take over from someone who has such a bond in the dressing room and on the terraces, but he was fantastic with me. On the day of my debut there was a telegram waiting for me; it was from Jimmy wishing me luck. I think that was the measure of the man.

David France: Howard was a tackler; he had a wonderful skill where he could go in, tackle and win the ball. He was another player who was a sensation and played in the cup final as a baby, I think he had nappies on in the cup final against Preston [he was aged 17 – the youngest player in an FA Cup Final until Paul Allen – when Preston lost the 1964 final to West Ham]. Everyone knew about HK, and he came to Goodison instead of Liverpool, he was going to sign for Shankly. He was an exceptional talent. He had a great long game, whereas somebody like Harvey would play a short passing game. Howard's strength was that he could tackle well and release long balls. He didn't have pace, Howard, but he had a great mind.

Jimmy Husband: After England won the World Cup playing 4-3-3, Catterick decided that was what he wanted to do. I was put out on to the right-wing with a free role – go where you want. Johnny Morrissey was kept on the left as a more traditional left-winger, so he kept the balance on the left hand side of the pitch and on the right I used to wander round anywhere I wanted to go. I think that was quite effective, because the full-backs that were marking me, they never knew where to go. If I made a run to the inside of the pitch, right across, the full-backs never knew whether to go with me or try to pass me on to another defender. Quite often that caused confusion for the opposition. Of course I had a lot of pace; quite often they didn't have time to make decisions of who was picking me up.

Joe Royle: We had a young, virile, hard-working but talented side who could all handle the ball. We had lots of pace in the side, good size with Brian Labone, John Hurst and myself, and an international goalkeeper. Catterick knew the formula and he knew what he wanted, but first and foremost he had the players and found a system that suited him.

John Hurst: People don't realise that when you go through the team Tommy Wright, myself, Colin Harvey, Joe Royle, Roger Kenyon, Labby came through the ranks. Johnny Morrissey cost ten grand or something. We had the name Merseyside Millionaires but half of them had come from school and through the A team.

Gerry Humphreys: I would have thought in the 1960s Johnny Morrissey was probably one of the most underrated wingers. He never received a cap of any kind but he was a top notch player and as hard as nails. For somebody to be a winger and to be as tough as John is not heard of very often because it's usually the full-backs that leave the wingers writhing on the ground.

Johnny Morrissey: Catterick was losing me. [After missing out on the 1966 FA Cup Final] I had no intention to play for him anymore. In fact, I trained on my own in the 1966/67 close season with

Stuart Shaw. I stood up for myself and Catterick brought me back into the fold. I think history shows it was the right decision.

Joe Royle: Johnny Morrissey was a workaholic, he was underrated anyway, as well as being as tough a winger as you will ever see. Nobody messed with Johnny, that was for sure. But he would work back and help the full-back.

Colin Harvey: Whoever played on the right, whether it be Husband or Alan Whittle later on, they acted as an auxiliary striker, whereas Johnny was an out and out winger. My first job according to him was to give him the ball. So as soon as I got the ball, if he was available, I had to give it to him.

Johnny Morrissey: I was the 'get out' man in our team. If it was tight, I used to be deep and they could get the ball to me, and I could hold it up. I had the strength to hold it up so we could reorganise. The system was like that; I was always known as the get out man for the ball. A lot of the time, if we were under the cosh we went four across the middle.

Colin Harvey: Howard and I were not holding midfielders, but we were sort of the base, and Bally played off whoever the striker was, mostly Joe. And his goalscoring record is something like 80 goals in 240 games, which is one in three. For a midfield player it's absolutely amazing.

David France: Harvey was outstanding. In my time at Everton when it comes to skilful footballers, and this includes Wayne Rooney, he would come only after Alex Young. Colin had bite, he could tackle, and he was just dominant. He suffered from injuries after he reached his peak but Colin was outstanding, I'd seen him in the reserves, he'd played against Inter Milan when he was 17 or something like that. He was like Peter Reid with pace. The old midfielders who tackled, won the ball and released the ball. He could do everything but shoot, though strangely he scored two of the most famous goals in the club's history. One was the winner against United at Burnden Park when we went to Wembley in '66. It was a bit of a bobble on it but he scored then.

Howard Kendall: One time at Bellefield the coach Wilf Dixon decided to get himself involved in our play. 'You give the ball to Colin; Colin give it to Johnny; Jimmy, you start off your run, put it back to Colin; Howard I want you to go round there. Colin, try and pick Howard out in that space over there because the fullback's gone with it.' We just laughed: 'Wilf, we do that.' That's not meant disrespectfully, but it was something you didn't need to coach. We all knew what we were doing and it was a good balance. I think that's the thing, the balance of it; and by making the signings and promotions from the youth team that he did, that was Harry Catterick's great gift to Everton.

Johnny Morrissey: I think players changed the system. He had Bally, who was a crackerjack. Bally could afford to be in midfield and go deep, because he had that much energy, he could get up there and support the forwards. I mean he scored goals. He wasn't a great tackler, but he'd be at you and nibbling like a little dog at your feet and all that. So player's changed the system. You had Kendall, Ball and Harvey, and I was there as well. I used to drop deep. I could play defensively as well, so a lot of times Catterick would come to me and say, 'We're playing away from home, I don't want you to go over the halfway line this game. Stay deep, keep things...' But then if you got on top and you were winning 2-0, your possession dictates that you push forwards then. But sometimes he'd say to me, 'I don't want you to go over the halfway line this game.'

Joe Royle: I had a great affinity with Bally, particularly from free kicks. We worked between the two of us. There was no coaching in those days – we weren't coached, we were trained, and by God were we trained. With all the modern science that goes on now about under training as well as over training, we just ran until someone was sick and then that was it. Bally and I used to do a couple of free kicks, mostly of his inception. He was always a thinker about the game. Colin Harvey was a great thinker about the game. Howard, not so much at the time, but became a great thinker about the game. But they were all great lads together, and they were all top players.

Howard Kendall: Harry Catterick had a very ruthless way of discarding players. When someone had performed well for him but he felt there was need for a change, very rarely did a player move locally. The risk that Harry saw was that a player would maybe do well for a club in the same area so Evertonians would be reminded of it every other day. He sent Alex Young to Ireland; Jimmy Gabriel, Southampton; Mike Trebilcock to Plymouth. They were going all over the place, as long as they weren't in the area. You tend to accept the hand that is dealt to you in football, but it showed quite unequivocally where the power rested within a club in those days: the manager.

Colin Harvey: There were other good players in their own right – like Gerry Glover and Frank D'Arcy – who rarely made the first team. To be honest with you, if I had been them I would have moved, because at the end of the day if you're a footballer you want to play first team football don't you? You don't want to be a standby. I thought they were good enough to go to decent clubs in their own right.

Frank D'Arcy: I used to go up and see Catterick about once a month and ask could I move because I had no chance of getting in the first team at full-back. You know you're talking about Tommy Wright and before him Alex Parker; and there was Ray Wilson and Mick Meagan before him. I used to say to Catterick, 'Boss is there any chance of me moving somewhere?' He'd be looking out of his window and I'd be sitting behind him and he'd turn round and he'd go, 'Hmmm. Harry come in please!' And Harry Cooke would come in and he'd ask, 'How much is Frank on?' Harry would get my contract out say 'He's on around about £30 plus two thirds of the first team bonuses.' Harry would say: 'Put another £10 on his basic money.' And he'd just look at me and go, 'Is that okay?' 'Alright Boss, yeah,' and I'd walk out. That must've happened about five times. His idea was that if you're going to win leagues and cups. We'd want about sixteen or seventeen in the squad. He'd say 'You're one of the squad players' I said, 'Yeah I know that but I'm only getting two or three games a season.' He'd reply: 'You're happy here aren't you? You've got a nice car outside which Everton paid for, you're on good money driving round in a white sports car. What do you want to go for?'

Howard Kendall: Slowly we built momentum as the footballing relationship between myself, Bally and Colin began to flourish. Our brand of football was about retaining possession, passing quickly and incisively and moving into space. It was largely intuitive, perfected over endless games of five-aside in the Bellefield gym. It came easily to us, naturally. There were no get togethers where we thrashed out what we were going to do on a Saturday. We knew instinctively what we'd be doing. It just happened.

1968 FA Cup run

Howard Kendall: When the 1967/68 season kicked off I was still just 21, Colin, Bally and Tommy Wright were 22; even Westy was still just 24. Joe was 18, Jimmy was 19. The average age was just 22. We were exciting and effervescent, if not lacking experience. As spring came we hit a rich vein of form. We won 12 of 13 games, including nine on the spin. The run carried us through to the semi-finals of the FA Cup after we dispatched Southport, Carlisle United, Tranmere Rovers and Leicester City. It set up a semi-final at Old Trafford with Leeds United, a side Catterick's Everton teams had struggled against since their promotion in 1964. They were hard, ruthless and dirty.

Johnny Morrissey: We feared Leeds. To be honest, when we drew them in the semi-final of the cup we were sick, because we didn't have a great record against them. Bally was suspended, John Hurst got jaundice. I think Tommy Jackson got in and Roger Kenyon.

Jimmy Husband: I had a big hand in the goal. It was something actually that me and Joe Royle had worked out in training. We'd noticed by watching films of Leeds games – this was back in the days when goalkeepers had to bounce the ball and they could only go three or four yards, or whatever it was, before they actually had to release the ball – that every time Gary Sprake had the ball in his hands and he was about to kick it that quite often if any player had [stood in front of him] he was quite often kicking the ball a good 20, 30 yards short of the halfway line, from his hands actually not very far, as opposed to a normal goal kick. And sure enough it paid off; Joe forced Sprake into a blunder and I could see the ball was dropping way short of their midfield players so I nipped in, got it under control fairly quickly and then I could see Sprake was way off his goal line, so I chipped it, and it was going right in, expect Jack Charlton was back peddling, and he handled the ball over the bar, which gained us the penalty.

Joe Royle: I was penalty taker up until then. I wasn't in particularly good form going into it, and I remember saying to the coach on the day before that I would be happier if someone else took it, should we get one. Johnny Morrissey took it and scored.

Johnny Morrissey: As we were deflated getting Leeds, with West Brom we were elated. Nobody performed on the day, nobody performed. We missed a bagful of chances, don't get me wrong, we still were creating quite a bit, but we were under-par on the day.

Joe Royle: The game is a bit of a blur to me. I was eighteen, on my way to Wembley in my first full season in the team, I was leading goalscorer and I was very nervous as we all were. We froze on the day. I didn't have a particularly good game, but none of us reached our best form that day.

John Hurst: We were huge favourites but you just have games sometimes – and that was one of those games – where I think they could've taken the keeper off and we would never have scored. It was one of the few occasions you can honestly say that we never played to our potential. I can't put my finger on it but we could've played them the following week, beaten them by three or four goals, but this was just that one game on that one day that we missed fire altogether.

Joe Royle: We'd beaten West Brom twice in the league that year, 6-2 at the Hawthorns and 2-1 at home. We were odds on to win it. You might say that as a young side we froze on the day, which is quite possible, but they were very physical and shall we say got about us, and even then we still had the chances to win, had we taken them.

Colin Harvey: The ball wouldn't go in the net. Jimmy Husband must have had about three or four gilt-edged chances, and he just had one of those days. He wasn't a clinical finisher, Jimmy, he got a lot of chances because he was really quick, but he wasn't a clinical finisher. He'd need four or five chances to get a goal, but generally speaking he was quick enough to get there. He just had one of those days when he couldn't put the ball in the net.

Johnny Morrissey: Maybe you can say we were naïve, I think maybe a bit overawed as well. Bally wasn't because he'd played for England, but most lads would be naïve.

Howard Kendall: Four minutes from the end I burst forward and sent a diagonal ball across the Albion penalty area. There was no one to meet it, but Johnny Morrissey retrieved it on the left and sent another cross into the six yard area where Bally and Jimmy Husband were both unmarked.

Jimmy Husband: I was never famous for my headers. It wasn't my best attribute. Johnny Morrissey made a lovely cross; I could see myself getting on the end of it, but I knew Alan Ball was coming in the side, and I think I sort of hesitated just enough for me to get under the ball and not over it. I missed an excellent chance.

Howard Kendall: Jimmy, with time and space, got to it, but he was underneath the ball when he headed it, and while he should have buried it in the back of the net, it floated harmlessly over. He said later that he could have 'swallowed it' and that Bally put him off by yelling for it – both of which were probably true. If only he had left it, though, you would have put your house on Bally finishing it.

Colin Harvey: It then went to extra-time and I remember the ball hitting me and bouncing back to Jeff Astle on his left foot. I remember thinking, 'Hit it with your left and it will go in the stands', and he hit it with his left and it went right into the top corner. That was it.

Jimmy Husband: It's probably my saddest day at Everton, really. Most of the other players had already won a cup medal in 66, so it maybe wasn't quite disappointing for them but for those of us who hadn't played in the 66 final, it was really sad.

Howard Kendall: We were devastated. We hadn't covered ourselves in glory, but we had been the better team. Sometimes you don't mind losing if you've played badly, but defeat is always harder to take when you know you've edged a match. We repaired to the Grosvenor Hotel and drowned our sorrows, taking comfort in the assumption that as young players our chance would come again. I think we would all have been shocked had we known then that of the eleven of us, only Bally would get another stab at Wembley glory while still a player.

John Hurst: You've lost so you're despondent. It doesn't matter who's there, nobody's going to cheer you up. Everybody reacts differently to defeat; some people sit there head down and not everybody reacts the same. Mostly it's just a glum dressing room. I think the thing that was the worst wasn't losing; we were more disappointed because we hadn't performed on the day and that was our big disappointment.

Howard Kendall: The following Tuesday we returned to Goodison to conclude our league campaign. We put in the sort of performance we should have done at Wembley and trounced Fulham 5-1. It ensured we finished fifth, just six points off champions, Manchester City. We'd won nothing, but the crowd sang and chanted our names as if we were the champions long after we'd left the pitch. After the end of the match, Catterick ordered us to leave the dressing room and return to the pitch. There, in a rare display of showmanship, he addressed the crowd himself, promising that the brand of football they had witnessed that night 'would be the pattern of things to come.'

1969/70 League Championship win

Joe Royle: By the time 1969/70 season arrived we had become a winning machine, I think we only lost four games that season. For many a season that was the record points scored in winning the league. Even now if you rearrange it with the extra/less games it's still a very, very high total points total that we had. I think it was just a natural development.

Charles Mills: The 1969/70 team was absolutely majestic, although curiously enough a lot, me included, have actually thought we played better football in 1968/69, where we came third but the football was just unbelievable. One particular game against Sheffield Wednesday, when they won 3-0 [in September 1968] we were unplayable that day. A young left-winger called Gerry Humphreys scored; there was an iconic picture of a former England goalkeeper, Ron Springett, standing still as the ball hit the top corner of the net in the Gwladys Street end. He didn't even have time to move. 1968, 69, 70 that was a great side.

Mike Hughes: I used to go with my friends around 1968 and the following season I started going a lot, more or less every home game. Even Joe Royle will back me up on this, during the 1968/69 season Everton probably played better football in 1968/69 than they did in 1969/70, which is deemed to be one of the finest Everton teams ever, but only because there was something tangible at the end of it.

David France: Their dominance came in the year before they won the title. They were absolutely incredible, particularly at Goodison – I don't think they lost that season. They just tore teams apart continuously. Teams couldn't get out of their own half because they mopped up. They also played this great short passing game on difficult pitches, not like the ones now. They played in mud, quagmires.

Terry Darracott: If you look at a lot of teams now in the Premier League, and around Europe, they play 4-3-3; and when I got in the team at Everton they were playing 4-3-3 in 1968. They had two wingers, Jimmy Husband and Johnny Morrissey; they had Joe Royle as a centre-forward, Bally in behind Joe Royle, and two older midfield players – Harvey and Kendall. So you could say they were ahead of their time really; that's down to the manager – he sets the tactics. He sets how you're going to play and he got the right players to do it as well.

Colin Harvey: Leeds were probably just about at their peak around that time as well, and they were a good side. And Liverpool generally around that time were a good side. But we played a quicker game than anyone at that time. Quicker into passes and quicker movement.

John Hurst: Our first two games that season was Arsenal away and then Manchester United away. They were two of the hardest games you've got to start with, both away from home we went and won them both. When you've won them two something is telling us we were going to do well this year.

Colin Harvey: We knew we were a good side. You know that yourself without being told it. But we'd beaten those teams, and we went to Arsenal and it was a really tight game and John Hurst scored the winner. On the Tuesday we went to Manchester United and won 2-1. You started to think, 'We're beating the good sides, in not brilliant games, but we were out-battling them as well, it maybe this is our year.'

Joe Royle: I scored two against Leeds [in Everton's seventh game of the season, all of which took place over just three weeks at the start of the season], which was hard. They were on a long, long unbeaten run at the time when we beat them. And we'd gone 3-0 up and they pulled two goals back. I never quite saw it that way, I scored a header at the near post I think, and I scored one from the edge of the box. You just went on, you played – if you were in the side that was great, if you weren't in the side you worked hard to get back in.

Howard Kendall: Bally kept getting sent off and served a five week ban. When he returned, Catterick claimed to have pulled off one of his tricks. Brian Labone had been struggling with injury and so, in his place, he appointed Ball captain. What Catterick was saying to the press was that it was a move to positively channel Bally's aggression, but you'd never do that with Alan. He didn't need to be captain. It wouldn't raise his game, because it didn't need to be raised. It didn't change him because he was unchangeable and uncompromising. He carried on the same as he always had done: relentless, demanding, hotheaded, sometimes irresponsible. As a captain he was not a good example to follow, but his infectiousness rubbed off on us all the same. Claiming that making Alan captain was some sort of masterstroke was typical of Harry – taking credit for something that hadn't really changed anything.

Colin Harvey: That season, 69/70 season, I had an inflammation on my optic nerve and I didn't train for about five or six weeks because I was on steroid injections to reduce the inflammation. Luckily during that period there was quite a few games postponed because of the weather, so I didn't miss too many games. And then obviously I didn't train at all, I had to go in every day and have a steroid injection, and just walk around the outside of the training area. It took me another month to get fit again because I hadn't trained for five or six weeks.

Joe Royle: We'd had a quiet spell around Christmas, we only lost four games all season so it couldn't have been a disastrous spell, but one of the games we had lost was against Liverpool at home. We went to Anfield and won, when we all knew that we had to win. Even if we won the league, we would have lost to Liverpool twice, it would have been somewhat tainted. So we were right up for it for the Liverpool game at Anfield, and we won 2-0.

Frank D'Arcy: He signed the England left-back Keith Newton from Blackburn. I think they paid something like £40,000 for him. When I went in the next day I didn't even bother getting changed into my training kit. I went to see Catterick. I said, 'Boss look this is starting to get ridiculous with me. I've got Tommy Wright in front of me, Sandy Brown, Ray Wilson – who was just at the end of his career – and now Keith Newton. I've got no chance.' He did the same as he always did. 'Harry! How much is Frank on?' Go on go out and train.' I didn't bother going in to get changed into my gear I just got in me car and went home, but he never fined me. I knew the potential that I had, but it didn't work out.

Colin Harvey: There was a little spell where we weren't playing particularly well. We were getting the odd draw and the odd win, but we weren't playing particularly well. He had a meeting Catterick, and he said, 'I want to make changes over the season.' He actually dropped Jimmy Husband and brought Alan Whittle in. Alan just added a little bit of something all of a sudden.

Johnny Morrissey: We weren't as fluid as we had been, Jim Husband got injured, Whitt came in, and he won it for us. That year I'd say he got us over the line. He got important goals when we were struggling, and once you get a goal, it may not sound much but it lifts the whole team, a bit of euphoria comes in and you go again. Whitt was great, he came in and did a great job.

Colin Harvey: I think he scored eleven goals between then and the end of the season. We then took off, and you just thought it was impossible to get beat at the time.

Jimmy Husband: It was extremely disappointing for me. I only suffered a niggling injury, which meant I missed two or three games. Alan came in and in those two or three games he scored two or three goals, so when I was fit again, Catterick decided that he didn't want to change a winning team. I thought well, 'I'll probably be in in another couple of weeks.'

John Hurst: Alan came in and took over from Jimmy Husband. He played in that wide right position. He came in and he was a revelation. He played exactly the same as Jimmy had done playing wide on the right and coming in and linking up alongside Joe. He loved running at people with the ball. He was such a live wire. He was absolutely electrifying.

Johnny Morrissey: Nothing against Jimmy: we'd gone stale, we were tired, because we were a running team, and running teams use a lot of energy. Towards the end of the season you get tired, it catches up with you. But that's no reflection on Jimmy, it was the whole team. And when he got injured Whitt came in, and luckily enough it's what we needed, it energised everything.

Jimmy Husband: Catterick kept the same winning team. It was very disappointing for me to miss this part, but on the other hand I can understand the manager's decision. In fact he actually brought me in for the last game of the season against Sunderland away, which was a nice touch by him, because I'm in the north east where I come from. Alan wasn't injured or anything. We still had something to settle because if we'd have beaten Sunderland we would have broken the record number of points to win a title. As it happens we drew, so we equalled the previous record.

Colin Harvey: We played Stoke on the Monday, and that was a tough game, we won 1-0. We got on the bus, and Harry Catterick said, 'We're going straight to a hotel.' This wasn't preordained or anything, he just said, 'We're going to a hotel.' We stayed out by Chester, and we had to go into Chester and buy new shirts and underwear, things like that. We had to phone home and say, 'I'm not coming home.' Then we went straight to the game against West Brom on the Wednesday, and they came out all guns firing. They weren't going to lie down. I remember getting about five or six stud marks down the back of my leg early on in the game. They did really put a game on. It wasn't like, 'These are champions, we're just going to lie down and die.'

John Hurst: The West Brom game was just a wonderful occasion. It was a night game and you remember it well. It was just a great feeling because it's nine months work. We knew we'd sew it up that night.

Colin Harvey: Whittle scored and then with 25 minutes to go I remember picking the ball up and just going on the run. Next thing I was just going past two or three people and I thought, 'I might as well have a shot at the end of this.' I just hit it and it flew in the top corner. It wasn't something I was normally associated with, but I see it every now and again on YouTube or something like that, and it was a spectacular goal, even if I do say so myself.

Howard Kendall: From then on, we knew the title was ours. The remaining 25 minutes were played out to non stop chants, of 'Ever-ton,' 'We are the champions,' 'We're on our way to Europe,' 'Send our team to Mexico' and even a couple of choruses of, 'When you're smiling.' The sound of the final whistle was the prompt for thousands of supporters to run onto the pitch, chanting, 'We shall not be moved.' We returned to receive the Championship trophy.

George Orr: Everyone's on the pitch and it was the last game of the season so everyone's taking up a piece of the pitch. I had a little piece of Goodison turf and I took it home. My Dad wasn't a football fan and I said, 'Eh-ah, look at that Dad. What do you think of that?' He just replied: 'It looks like one soft sod holding another soft sod!'

Howard Kendall: We played against Sheffield Wednesday on the Saturday, three days later. Some of the lads had been drinking solidly since the West Brom game. It was by far the worst preparation for a game I'd had in my life and I'm sure I wasn't alone in that. We shouldn't have done it then either. But we were flying and we knew we'd won the League. I pulled a hamstring after about 20 minutes; while half-a-dozen players were running off beer. They hit the bar. They hammered us. But we still won and we condemned Wednesday to relegation. It'll forever stick with me Bally passing me on the pitch that day. 'What's it like to win it? What's it like to be the best?' 'It's brilliant, isn't it?' I laughed. 'It's absolutely brilliant.'

George Orr: Harry Catterick never got the praise that he should've got. He took over Everton and, yes, we were the millionaire's club, we were the Chelsea or the Manchester City of the day and we bought the great players and he formed a great team and we stormed the league and won the cup. But then in 1967 the money didn't quite dry up; John Moores gave the support but didn't give the money that he used to give. Harry just looked and the likes of Jimmy Husband, John Hurst and Joe Royle – all those players coming through – and thought 'This is a great team'. Within two years they won the league and apart from Sandy Brown it was a totally English team. That was what we used to sing in 1969/70, 'send our team to Mexico', because of the World Cup. I thought that 1962/63 was the best team and still think it was the best team I've seen, and 1969/70 was also a fantastic team.

Joe Royle: The team I played in, the 67-70 side, was exceptional. There are still people that argue we have never had a side anywhere near as good since. That includes Howard's 85 side. That's for other people to comment on, but it was an exceptional side, and great memories, lovely smiles.

Everton Overshadowed
1970-1981

'The 1971 FA Cup semi-final defeat was a catastrophic day for Everton Football Club. That was the day that we handed the baton of Merseyside football supremacy to Liverpool. We've dented that here and there since then, but we've never challenged their supremacy for a sustained period of time despite our best attempts.'

Howard Kendall

Everton defend their League Championship

After winning the 1969/70 League Championship with a record number of points, an England team featuring four Everton players – Brian Labone, Alan Ball, Tommy Wright and Keith Newton – had reached the World Cup quarter-finals in Mexico. Reunited with their teammates in England, the Everton team were expected to dominate English football for the next few years and there were high hopes for the European Cup challenge. After winning the Charity Shield with a 2-1 win over Chelsea, Everton embarked on a slow start to the season.

Howard Kendall: The great mystery was not how we won the Championship in 1970. It was how we didn't win more in the years that followed. Bally had said after we'd won it: 'I can see five great seasons ahead. This team is certain to go better. We have lots of skill and every player works hard for each other. With that behind us, how can we fail?' He was right though. Really, we should have had a dynasty, in the way that Liverpool under Bob Paisley later did. Instead we won nothing.

Charles Mills: That 1970 team, it's a mystery why that didn't happen. I remember the first game of the following season and we played Arsenal, we drew 2-2. I was immensely disappointed, I just thought we had everything going for us. There had been the World Cup of course; we were represented by four players at the World Cup – Bally, Labone, Tommy Wright and Keith Newton. And that may have had something to do with it. But it was a mystery why it didn't happen for us or we didn't kick on.

Charles Lambert: What was a bit baffling was how quickly that happened, from being league champions and supplying a third of England's World Cup team in 1970 and all of a sudden, they were back among the also rans. One theory I've heard, that may have had something to do with it, was because Everton had so many players involved in the World Cup squad and that really incapacitated them for the defence of that league title the following season. That was the World Cup in Mexico and this was an era before sports medicine was anywhere near like it is now and playing and training at such altitude as Mexico was very, very demanding, especially after a long season here.

Joe Royle: We were slow out of the blocks the 1970/71 season. I honestly couldn't tell you why, I don't know. The team didn't fall apart in one season but all of a sudden everything that had been free-flowing and easy the previous season wasn't.

John Hurst: I think it was a hangover from the World Cup. We had Bally there, Labby had gone, Keith Newton had gone, so did Tommy Wright. Whereas nowadays they come back and they have a long rest, they came straight back to pre-season training with us. They never said, 'Have a couple weeks off longer.' There was a hangover from the fatigue of those players without a doubt, but you can't say that was the one reason.

Howard Kendall: I don't know whether it was fatigue or complacency or the injury crisis that would soon engulf us, but we started the 1970/71 season as if we were preparing for a relegation battle rather

'The club grew out of the St Domingo Church followers, and its first playing area was on Stanley Park, where the foundation of Everton's greatness was laid.' The oldest known photo of Everton, from their Stanley Park years. [*David France*]

'In 1888 the most important event in the history of Association Football transpired. The Football League was established.' Everton's team from c. 1889. [*Getty*]

'The Club met Aston Villa in the famous 1897 English Cup Final, the best played final up to that year. Everton lost 3-2 and, as was generally admitted, through feeble goalkeeping.' [*Getty*]

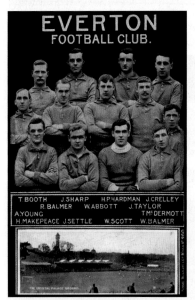

'I was too young to have a recollection of the match itself, but all that mattered was that Everton beat Newcastle 1-0. I was left breathless by all the excitement.' Everton win the FA Cup for the first time in 1906. [Getty]

'We lost in the 1907 final with Sheffield Wednesday through an error of tactics in team selection.' George Wilson's omission, due to a contract dispute, was blamed for Everton's defeat. [*Getty*]

Everton play Tottenham Hotspur at Spurs' White Hart Lane ground, London, 2 September 1912. [*Getty*]

Everton's 1915 champions. No first hand account of Everton's second league title can be traced. It is as if Everton's 1914/15 title win was considered a 'dirty secret', never to be spoken of. [*Getty*]

'We knew that we had a legend. Everybody was talking about Dixie, his name was on every man's lips, even Liverpudlians.' [*George Chilvers*]

'I'll never forget going up to the royal box at Wembley to collect the FA Cup. I received it off the Duchess of York. She congratulated me and said it was a very good game. She really smiled and said she had enjoyed it. That made me feel so proud.' [*George Chilvers*]

'Tommy was the complete centre-forward – two very good feet, strong in the air and quick with a great understanding of the game.' [*Getty*]

Heroes and villains: Everton's legendary chairman and committeeman, Will Cuff; and Theo Kelly, the notorious secretary and manager, whose influence would prompt the exits of Joe Mercer and Tommy Lawton. [*Colorsport*]

The original number 1 and number 9. William Ralph 'Dixie' Dean watches as Ted Sagar claims a ball in the 1933 FA Cup final – the first time players wore numbers in an official match. [*Getty*]

'It was upsetting. They weren't run properly, that was the thing that annoyed me about Everton.' Everton players in training ahead of a promotion push, having suffered the indignity of relegation in 1951. [*Author's collection*]

This and next page: 'Life after the war was difficult. People had lost family members, there was austerity, rationing. But it wasn't obvious; people were awfully good at hiding their thoughts. A lot of them had lost their family, their brothers and their sisters, but somehow there was a religious aspect to football, which meant you lost somebody but you hadn't really lost them. Which was marvellous, really.' Behind the scenes with Everton in 1946. These pictures formed the basis of a Picture Post photo essay, published in the year after the war. They offer a revealing insight into life at a football club. [*Getty*]

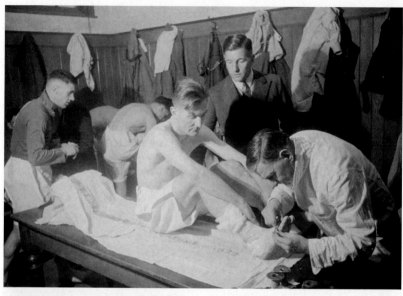

'My father drove us down to Goodison and we stood in the dark with other supporters waiting for a good hour in the night time, cold with our scarves, waiting for the bus to arrive. And the joy when the bus arrived and all the players got off. Everybody was shaking hands, and they stood in a line for the Echo photographers, and we were on it.' Barbara Garner [second from the right] joins Dave Hickson, Eddie Wainwright and Peter Farrell after Everton win promotion in 1954. [*Author's collection*]

Left: T.E. Jones – Everton's captain in the late-1950s. [*George Chilvers*] *Right:* 'There were more priests in the stands on a Saturday afternoon than spectators. I think there was a row of about 20-30 priests, because Eglington, Donovan, Tansey, Meagan, Jimmy O'Neill, George Cummins, they were all from Dublin.' Everton's popular Irish internationals, Peter Farrell and Tommy Eglington. [*Colorsport*]

'You talk worship, it doesn't get better than Dave, I don't think, with Evertonians of my era and a little later. It was that willingness, that apparent willingness, to die for your club. I just thought he would do anything for Everton.' [*Author's collection*]

'Ian Buchan [right, pictured with Harold Pickering] was a fanatic with new ideas. When you were playing away you'd get off the coach early. Say if you were going to Sheffield you'd probably get off at Chesterfield and walk the rest of the way.' [*Colorsport*]

Clockwise from the top: Derek Temple, who would find immortality in the 1966 FA Cup Final. [*Getty*]. Johnny Carey, who brought a pure attacking creed to Goodison but not success. [*Getty*]. Sir John Moores, the paternalistic pools millionaire, who was the defining influence in the club's running for 30 years. [*Getty*]. Harry Catterick, the ruthless and highly successful manager who defined Everton's golden era. [*Author's collection*]

'Young jumped up and the header was just fantastic. My brother was a Kopite but he said that from miles away he could hear the roar so he knew. It was just a feeling that we had won when we scored that goal. It was something I've never seen.' Alex Young heads Everton to a sixth league title against Tottenham in 1963. [*Colorsport*]

'Brian was a superb captain, a father figure to the youngsters. He didn't go round ranting and raving, anything like that. He led by example.' [*Getty*]

'I used to say, 'What we playing at today?' And they would say, 'What do you mean?' And I said, 'Are we kicking one another or are we going to play football?'' An angry fan remonstrates with Billy Bremner during the so-called 'Battle of Goodison' in 1964. [*Mirrorpix*]

Top left: Ray Wilson congratulates Mike Trebilcock after his heroic display in the 1966 FA Cup final. [*Offside*] *Top right:* Harry Catterick holds aloft the FA Cup with Fred Pickering on the steps of St George's Hall. Catterick had omitted Pickering from the 1966 final. [*Press Association*]

'It was an exceptional side, and great memories, lovely smiles.' Jimmy Husband and Joe Royle celebrate a goal against Crystal Palace in front of a half-built Main Stand on their way to the 1969/70 title. [*Offside*]

'The Holy Trinity were better than the Leeds team at the time: Bremner, Giles and the like. Alan had agreed to go to Leeds – he had taken a backhander to go to Leeds – and he decided not to. So I'd hate to think how good Leeds would have been had he gone there.' [*Colorsport*]

'We went one goal up, Alan Ball scored a goal, and for an hour we outplayed them. And then Brian Labone did a hamstring injury, and Sandy Brown had to go to centre-half. That was the difference then.' Sandy Brown and Alan Ball look on as Liverpool go on the attack in the 1971 FA Cup semi-final. [*Getty*]

'Letting our best player, our talisman go at that stage was on reflection a big mistake.' Alan Ball and Arsenal manager Bertie Mee after the midfielder's shock move to Highbury in 1971. [*Getty*]

'The local journalists used to ask me, 'What have you done to Bingham?' He was, I was told, always complaining about me, telling them that he didn't rate me.' Captain Howard Kendall with Billy Bingham after the latter's appointment as manager in 1973. Eight months later Bingham would sell Kendall to Birmingham as part of the British record transfer to bring Bob Latchford to Goodison. [*Offside*]

Stars of the 1970s. Clockwise from top left: Martin Dobson. [*Getty*]. Dave Thomas – in his rubber soled boots and with his socks around his ankles. [*Getty*]. Bob Latchford celebrating his famous 30th league goal of the 1977/78 season [*Everton FC*] and Latchford with captain Mick Lyons. [*Mirrorpix*]

than the defence of our league championship. Of the first league six games we drew three and lost three, and although form picked up a little, we hardly ever in the top ten, never mind challenging for honours. For a period, it seemed as if Harry Catterick was questioning my value to the team too. In October, he signed Henry Newton from Nottingham Forest for a club record £150,000.

Henry Newton: Catterick wanted me in midfield and he was going to move Kendall. He saw Kendall more as a back four player and that's the way it was going to go. Howard was going to play in the back four but of course the club was decimated by injuries almost straight away. In fact, before I got there, injuries were mounting up to key players so it never really happened.

Howard Kendall: Henry was a right-sided midfielder and it was clear to a number of observers that he was there to replace me. When he made his debut against Arsenal at Highbury, it was John Hurst that dropped out and I moved to centre-back – a position I'd never played in my life. Arsenal had John Radford and Ray Kennedy up front and slaughtered us. We got absolutely stuffed, 4-0, and I never played in central defence again, thankfully.

Henry Newton: I thought we were a better side than Arsenal. Even with it being an awful game and an awful debut I still felt that we were a better side and we would finish above them. We never felt inferior to them at all but clearly the side was showing signs of fatigue. I just thought that once everyone had got to know each other better or got things established again that we would finish above Arsenal. In fact, I still thought that there was a great chance that we would win the league, but we just couldn't get on a run. Every time something good happened something bad would happen. It was one step forward and two steps back.

Everton in the European Cup

John Hurst: The thing is you never used to see these European teams. There was no European football on television or anything. You'd send someone over to watch them and you might see the odd international and think, 'Oh he's played for them.' It was just a question of people going over and watching them and saying, 'This is the formation they play and try and combat it.'

Gary Jones: I should have made my debut in a European game against Keflavík in Iceland. I don't know whether it was a change of climate, but the night before I was sweating up all night in bed. I missed that game. That was a big disappointment, because I think they won the first leg 8-0 [it was 6-2], so it was probably a good game to introduce a youngster, knowing full well they weren't going to take a lot of chances.

Frank D'Arcy: We were playing in Iceland in the European Cup and we're getting the flight home straight after the match. The next thing the coach driver pulls in to get more diesel or whatever and the *Liverpool Echo* correspondent, Mike Charters, who was reporting on the game got off to make a phone call to the say that Everton had won and file his report. Catterick is sitting there with John Moores and he says to the driver, 'Go!' The driver tells him, 'You have a reporter there making a call.' Catterick replied, 'I've got a million pounds worth of players here! Now, go!' And he left him there. That's how strict he was. He said, 'I'm not waiting for him' and in the end he had to get another flight home.

After beating Keflavik 9-2 on aggregate, Everton were drawn next against the West German champions, Borussia Monchengladbach.

Johnny Morrissey: The best player I've ever played against was the German international Berti Vogts. The first leg was away from home. We got to Monchengladbach and he was the marker for them. I thought he was going to be on Bally – he was on me. The only kick I got was on the legs. He was too good for me. I was at my peak, but he was brilliant. I never got a kick. We drew 1-1, Howard scored a great goal at the end, a spectacular goal. We drew 1-1. We go to the second leg, and I wasn't looking forward to it to be honest, at Goodison. Alan Whittle had played over there and he'd had a blinder. So, when we come out for the second leg and Vogts was playing against Whittle, he left me alone! I had a blinder, Whitt never got a kick! We drew 1-1 but won on penalties. However, I remembered Berti Vogts. I had nightmares about him.

Joe Royle: We felt like we'd beaten the best side apart from ourselves in there, and we probably had. Borussia were a top side. Playing on the Borussia pitch when we did was awesome, because the pitches were heavy in England – they certainly weren't what they are now. We all thoroughly enjoyed that. Of course, we brought them back to Goodison and it went to penalties. I became the first player ever to miss a penalty in a European shoot-out but we won out in the end.

Peter Mills: Goodison was bouncing. We were in the Gwladys Street stand for some reason, which is behind where the penalties were, and that was manic. They were a good team. I only remember Bertie Vogts and Gunter Netzer. It was the first ever penalty shoot-out. You didn't know what to expect. It was very exciting. Andy Rankin making that last penalty save. I've got memories of a guy in the front row, Gwladys Street stand, just leaping up and down like a lunatic trying to put off whoever it was who took the kick.

Having beaten the tournament favourites, Everton progressed into a quarter-final the following March against Greek champions Panathinaikos.

Joe Royle: I wouldn't say we were over-confident, but we felt that there was no one left with our quality in it. We played Panathinaikos in a game where we absolutely outplayed them without being convincing. They had one attack and scored, and then David Johnson came on as sub and got the equaliser in overtime, if not the last minute.

Jimmy Husband: It was like one of those games where you're just playing against a 10-man defence. They did an assassination job on me, their captain took me out Dave Mackay-style, and we ended up drawing 1-1. When we went to Greece, Harry Catterick actually took me with the squad even though I had no chance of playing, I'd done my knee ligaments or my ankle ligaments from this foul, but he wanted them to think that I was going to play.

Joe Royle: The away leg was just a nightmare.

Howard Kendall: We went into the second leg in Athens with an away goal against us. We faced the worst sort of intimidation on that trip. The plane was not able to land until the early hours of the morning.

The hotel was circled by cars beeping their horns well into the following night. The club secretary, Bill Dickinson, received a death threat before the game. Things didn't get much better once the game got under way.

Henry Newton: I remember that when we went to train the night before the game their supporters were trying to turn the coach over when we got to the ground. They were rocking the coach and trying to turn it over. It was quite intimidating and sleeping was almost impossible because they were riding round on motorbikes, their horns blasting and everything. Obviously, they knew where we were staying.

John Hurst: The style of European teams varied greatly. We played some of the inferior ones. The Icelandic team, they were just like playing a third division team... and then the top teams, like the top Italian teams, were just a bit better than ours at the time. They were more organised and the Italian teams were the most defensive minded. But it was the tactics they did on the pitch; the poking, the treading on you, the nasty side that you could do in them days. You just watch a game from the 1960s or 1970s, of the tackling and things like that. You got away with murder in them days and they were past masters of it. Disrupting play; they had that off to a fine art. You'd never really get booked or sent off in them days. It was just a completely different game.

Joe Royle: They had the reputation at the time, they were long unbeaten at home, they were managed by Ferenc Puskas. When we got on the pitch it was strange – every tackle we made was a foul, they were pulling hair, poking eyes, it was the school for dirty tricks. The Greek players were running round and saying things like, 'You Will Die'. The 0-0 draw that we got there, put it this way, if that had been the first leg I'm sure we would have beaten them in the second leg.

Howard Kendall: We were spat at and all manner of abuse and missiles rained down from the pitch upon us. John Hurst had his eyes gouged by an opponent. It was incredible, really. We were absolutely robbed by the referee with a dodgy decision; without a shadow of a doubt. The whole thing stank. Having seen Greek football as a manager and the corruption and fixing that goes on there, I think it's quite likely that someone manipulated the outcome of that match. We drew 0-0 and were out on away goals. Ajax beat them 2-0 in the final, although I'm quite sure we would have posed a more significant challenge if given the chance.

Joe Royle: It was just a horrible experience. The whole stadium was caged at that stage because of crowd problems. There'd long been talk of corruption in Greek football, it just wasn't a nice experience. There was spitting, prodding, pulling hair, there was all kinds of stuff going on off the ball. It was hard to get any rhythm to our game. I will say it again: the 0-0 that we got there was as good as it got at that time, it was a battling performance. While we could battle when we had to, we were at our best when we were a free-flowing side and there was never any rhythm in that game.

Howard Kendall: Harry Catterick didn't exactly cover himself in glory afterwards. You'd expect him to come in and say, 'Bad luck lads, it didn't go our way, the referee made some bad decisions.' Instead he came into the dressing room and announced, 'You bastards have cost me five grand tonight.' That was his bonus. It was also the extent of his post-match team talk.

Everton v Liverpool
27 March 1971
FA Cup semi-final

Everton had no time to contemplate their exit from Europe. After returning from Greece in the early hours of Thursday morning they had had barely 48 hours to prepare for an FA Cup semi-final against Liverpool at Old Trafford. Ill health would keep Harry Catterick away from the match and the Everton trainer, Wilf Dixon, took his place.

Joe Royle: Harry Catterick took ill on the plane home, and when we went into the game against Liverpool at Old Trafford on Saturday in the cup – on 24 March – it was the day my first son was born. I came back and we went to the hotel in Lymm, and we had a good talk about it amongst ourselves, the senior boys. We all got in one room and had a couple of beers, nothing silly, and a few home truths came out. We played on the Saturday and until Brian Labone got injured, it was probably the best we played all season.

Colin Harvey: There was a bit of a bug going around the club, we all had it, and we got back from Greece and Harry wasn't well. Myself and four or five others were suffering a little bit, and we went to Old Trafford and he didn't come.

Howard Kendall: We knew this was our final, final chance to redeem something from the season. It was a frenetic start, but Bally put us in front on ten minutes. The turning point came when Brian Labone went off injured with a thigh strain in the fiftieth minute.

Colin Harvey: We went one goal up, Alan Ball scored a goal, and for an hour we outplayed them. And then Brian Labone did a hamstring injury, and Sandy Brown had to go to centre half. That was the difference then.

Joe Royle: I'm sure if Harry Catterick had he been there it would have been different. He had much more tactical nous than Wilf Dixon, who was a trainer, not a coach, and he sent Sandy Brown on. Sandy wasn't big enough to deal with John Toshack. I hope and I think that Catterick might have said to me, 'go and play centre half, we're 1-0 up.' I'd have certainly competed with Toshack a lot easier than Sandy found it. Toshack won two big headers, put Alun Evans in and we lost the game. The whole season and probably the team had fallen apart in four days.

Charles Mills: It wasn't a good day that at all, to be beaten by Liverpool like that in the semi-final. I think there was probably some dodgy stuff about the Panathinaikos game as well. But that was a week that changed everything.

Howard Kendall: The defeat destroyed us. We only won one more of our remaining eight league games, finishing the 1970/71 campaign fourteenth. For Everton that was a disaster. I think the fact that it was Liverpool was psychologically very damaging. It didn't take long for an outsider to realise what it means to a local lad on Merseyside. We had the likes of Tommy Wright, Colin, Joe, Andy Rankin who would take derby defeats far, far harder. But even for the rest of us it wasn't nice, because you become one of them; a Scouser and an Evertonian.

Henry Newton: They were the two defining points there: the loss to Panathinaikos and then the loss to Liverpool, especially after dominating the game against Liverpool. I was injured and couldn't play in that but that was one of the worst experiences I've had in seeing the lads play so well [and lose]. I'm not saying we were confident of winning but it looked like there was only one team going to win it. I can't remember the goals but we dominated the game and were the better side. I remember Bally was everywhere. Joe Royle he was really cut up about that after that game, he was going mad about Larry Lloyd about the confrontation they'd had. It decimated the season absolutely, finished it. That really was a low point. That was terrible.

Howard Kendall: It was a catastrophic day for Everton Football Club. That was the day that we handed the baton of Merseyside football supremacy to Liverpool. We've dented that here and there since then, but we've never challenged their supremacy for a sustained period of time, despite our best attempts.

The sale of Alan Ball

Everton finished the 1970/71 season in fourteenth place. Harry Catterick, who was beset with health problems, tried to change things around by entering the transfer market and promoting young players, like David Johnson and Mick Lyons. None, however, could halt the decline. After a poor start to the 1971/72 season, Catterick stunned English football by selling his talisman Alan Ball to Arsenal.

Gary Jones: Bally will always be to me and my friends, Terry Darracott, Mick Lyons, Steve Seargeant, an absolutely unbelievable human being. Not only a fantastic footballer – the best I've ever played with certainly at Everton Football Club – but he always looked after us all. He would ask us if we wanted to come back in the afternoon to do an extra bit of training with him, which was fantastic and I couldn't wait to get back on the bus home to tell all my mates down the road that Bally had just been coaching us. I couldn't say enough about Alan Ball as a human being and as a footballer.

Frank D'Arcy: He was a character. He lived up by Billinge, he had a house there; I think it was an Everton house. Our son-in-law's Dad used to have a pub up in Billinge, the Stork Hotel. So, one or two nights, especially on a Monday or a Tuesday, me, Bally, Roger Kenyon, Colin Harvey we used to meet in the pub up there, have a few drinks and go home. One evening we went there and the next thing he started crying. We're standing there looking at him going, 'Alan! What the hell's wrong with you? What are you crying for?' He said, 'They've told me that I'm going to Arsenal' I said, 'You're joking.' He said, 'No. I don't want to go, Catterick's said I'm going.' Even though he didn't want to go yet he went. Whether it was the money I don't know, but he didn't want to go. I just remember him crying, saying, 'I didn't want to go.'

Howard Kendall: I found out about Alan's sale in the most unexpected manner. Very late at night I received a call from a supporter and good friend of mine called Joe Murray. Him and his mates had got word of the deal and were devastated by the news. 'My boys' can't sleep Howard,' he said. 'Bally's gone. They can't sleep.'

Joe Royle: Alan Ball came out of Catterick's office, and we always thought he was his blue-eyed boy, he had taken the captaincy off Brian Labone to give it to him, and then he came out with tears in his eyes. Bally was an emotional person. We said, 'What's up?' and he said, 'I'm off.' We said, 'Where you going, we're training this afternoon', and he said, 'No, I'm off to Arsenal.' That was it.

George Orr: The biggest mistake was making him captain. There was a romance about Alan Ball and he was a great player, but I saw Sandy Brown have a go at him, Tommy Jackson smack him, other players threaten him, grab him around the throat. I've even seen Kendall go for him. Ball's last game was against Derby County away and we got beat 2-0 and we weren't playing well. But Kendall was having a blinder, which he always did, and I think he did one bad pass and Bally went waving his thumb and for the first time ever I saw Howard lose his rag and go up to him. You could see him saying, 'I'll knock you out.'

Howard Kendall: In a lot of ways it didn't surprise me. Not long before, we were having a practice match that Wilf Dixon was in charge of. I'll always remember Wilf stopping the play and saying, 'Alan, what's wrong with you?' You could see Bally wasn't going at it. He was sulking, or having a strop. He put his hands out, and said, 'How can I play with this lot?' Most of the players he'd not long ago won the league title with were standing there, looking on. Harry Catterick was standing behind the goal and I thought, 'What's he doing out here?' He'd come out to see Bally. He went straight back in his office and I'm sure the deal was done to sell him to Arsenal that day.

Colin Harvey: Looking back now it probably wasn't the wrong decision. At the time, I thought it was the wrong decision, but when I look back at everything that was going on at the time, and Alan's game wasn't the same, and his goal ratio went right down, Catterick I [later] thought made the right decision. Not at the time I didn't.

Joe Royle: We were all astounded that he had given him up. There were all kinds of rumours about Bally owing money, and about trying to work his ticket to Manchester City, and Bally always dramatically denied that, he said it was nothing to do with that. But letting our best player, our talisman go at that stage was, on reflection, a big mistake.

The last days of Harry Catterick

Howard Kendall: Harry – or those around him – made a series of bad signings. Probably the most notorious of these was Bernie Wright. We played Walsall in the FA Cup in February 1972, and I think the scouting report had gone in and said, 'Big strong lad, the centre-forward, have to be aware of him on the day.' Somewhere, somehow down the line this was translated as 'We must buy him.' Catterick was having one of his spells of ill health and the decision was taken by the board in his absence. It wasn't Harry's signing, but it was an indication of how the side was becoming disastrous.

Charles Lambert: I remember Bernie 'The Bolt', Rod Belfitt and the other players that came in. They just weren't of the same standard of the Joe Royle's and people like that, they were supposed to be replacing or competing with.

Howard Kendall: Bernie wasn't, frankly, the brightest of players, not helped by this thick Brummie accent. 'What are you going to do when you finish playing, you?' we'd say to him. 'I'm going to be a dropout!' he answered, deadly serious. The end for Bernie wasn't long in coming. Every year all the players got Christmas hampers from Littlewoods. There was an A and a B hamper, and the first team squad got the A hampers and it was bottles of port, and a bottle of sherry, and biscuits and sweets. The next day Bernie came in with his bottle of port into the dressing room. He'd clearly been working his way through the hamper since the end of training the previous day. 'When Bernie drinks, everybody drinks,' he announced in his thick Brummie brogue. This was before training! So, we told him to piss off and went outside to warm up. Bernie joined us with his bottle of port and began trotting around with it, taking swills. Before Harry Catterick caught wind of it, Westy went after him and tackled him to the ground. He was then seen on the back of a lorry going into Liverpool with his kit on, still swigging from his bottle. That's the last any of us ever we saw of him.

Joe Royle: We had great faith in Gordon West. We had a superb number two in Andy Rankin as well, who saved the penalties in the Monchengladbach game. But Westy was humorous, was strong, was dangerous. Sometimes we'd look at Westy and you would see a dark side in him. You didn't mess with Westy, there was no messing round, but he was strong and we had great faith in him. He was a fantastic reflex keeper and a very funny man, we laughed our way to the Championship in 69/70, with him and Labone, they were like a comedy TV duo.

George Telfer: Westy was one of the biggest characters we used to have. Before training he'd come down to the apprentice room and get hold of one of the lads and say, 'What's Telfer been up to? He's got new undies there. New undies? Flowery ones? That's definitely a criminal offence.' So we'd have a trial and he'd put a towel over his head as the judge and then he'd pass sentence. Sometimes the sentence was that you got thrown in the cold bath with your kit on just before you went out for training so you'd be scrambling round looking for a new kit to go out in. Another thing was the initiation on the first day, which totally terrified me, was to go in front of the first team players and sing a song. I remember doing 'Ob-La-Di Ob-La-Da' as Westy was jiving. Later, I remember playing with Westy in the reserve games and he had a thigh injury, so he didn't kick the ball out he threw it. The person he threw the ball to every time was me and I'd be wandering round the pitch and he'd just throw it to me. The opposition would be getting wise to it and he would still throw it to me and he'd be laughing. I'd say, 'Westy don't effing throw it to me' and he'd just laugh.

Howard Kendall: Westy was in and out of favour, but Everton – not just Harry – struggled to replace him. In fact, no one really did until I became manager and signed Neville Southall. I do think Everton suffered because they lacked a great goalkeeper between Gordon and Neville. It's the number one position. I think it was very difficult for anyone to come in and match the qualities of those two; very difficult indeed. It's not easy for the manager to go out and find them either. Harry brought in David Lawson for a lot of money from Huddersfield. He was no Gordon West. He had no shoulders. The comment from the dressing room was that they'd have to nail his braces on to keep them on. He was an alright keeper but it's who you're following that you're judged by; if you're following somebody exceptional it's very difficult for the players to come in from lower leagues and immediately be a success.

David Lawson: The big thing about my move was the shock it was me. I dropped the wife off at work in Huddersfield. It was after the season had finished and I usually picked the paper up and just dropped it on the seat next to me. In the headlines on the back page was 'Everton Want Lawson.' And, of course, there was a Jimmy Lawson who played for Huddersfield as well, the forward; and I thought, 'Oh, that's a good move for Jimmy.' And it wasn't till I stopped at the traffic lights that I realised, 'Oh my God, it's me!'

Howard Kendall: Then there was Dai Davies. The fans dubbed him 'Dai The Drop'. I think by the players Dai would be remembered as not being consistent; liable to make a mistake every now and again. Because of this the players in front of him lacked confidence with him. I remember the ball going into the penalty area; it's the keeper's ball, but he's left it and the defender's left it and then the goal is scored against him. Apparently, that was the defender's fault, but it happened so often. Dai certainly had some good attributes; he was a big lad and could be commanding. He was just prone to some terrible errors.

Joe Royle: I had great respect for Brian Labone. He was a very intelligent man and I loved him to bits. I idolised him. He was a grammar boy himself, and they used to make great fun out of us two being the grammar school boys in the team. But we weren't the only ones, Colin Harvey was as well and there might have been others. Labby was a leader in the dressing room as well as on the pitch, but he wasn't a talking leader on the pitch, he led by example, whereas Bally was talking to everyone on the pitch, but he did that anyway, whether he was captain or not. I would never have realised it at the time, but looking back I think that tactically making Alan Ball captain as opposed to Labby might have been a slight mistake. It didn't change Bally's attitude on the pitch anyway, but I'm not sure it went down overly well with Brian and one or two members of the team.

Howard Kendall: We also had some good young players come through, but perhaps because they didn't have the stability a previous generation had enjoyed and they didn't make the same impression. Like a lot of the young players at the time, they all had something to offer or they wouldn't have been at Everton Football Club. But like the situation with the goalkeepers, it was just a case of them being compared with what had passed before. It was unfair on them. Some of the players couldn't live up to what was expected. The crowd could be very demanding as indeed they still are. On the other hand I think they do give the local lads a chance; they don't really set about criticizing if you've come through the ranks. But if you've been bought for a certain amount of money and you're disappointing, they're more likely to get on your back.

Henry Newton: Mick Lyons was a monster. He was one of the fittest lads I'd seen and he was one of the best trainers I've seen and so, so dedicated. He sort of made the most of what he'd got. It was lovely to see a young lad come through and he probably hadn't got the skills of John Hurst and Roger Kenyon, but sheer enthusiasm drove him through and he became a very important and valuable player.

Jim Pearson: I called him Mr Everton. He used to head the roof and punch the walls and everything. The man's not right in the head but he was Mr Everton. I'm an Evertonian now from outside but I've become an Evertonian. He was brought up an Evertonian. To be brought up and to play for them must be fantastic.

David France: Howard's greatest contribution – besides being a manager – was after the Holy Trinity was broken up, and we were going downhill and he kept us going for a long time, and he took on the role as the best player of the club.

Howard Kendall: As Everton's fortunes nosedived, so mine rose. I was club captain and playing well, even amidst the decline of a once great side. Some said that I was responsible for keeping Everton in the First Division during this time. I wouldn't go that far, but I was named Merseyside Sports Personality of the Year the year Liverpool won the title and UEFA Cup. I took that as an enormous personal compliment, even though I would have swapped it for Everton to be doing better.

John Hurst: We were obviously aware that Harry wasn't well, but I don't think it affected us when we went out to play. You've got your own personal pride and that makes you want to do well. Sometimes adversity makes you come out better. It was just a difficult spell that we went through. But I think the changeover was very quick from being such a successful team to struggling and then Kendall, Harvey, Ball splitting up.

Howard Kendall: One of the things about Harry that worked against him after the League Championship success was his cool relationship with the media. When he was successful he didn't think he needed the press. He was naturally aloof, and wasn't forthcoming with information about the team or players, or anything like that; he just kept everything to himself. He was that way. Whereas Shankly was a dream for the journalists. But when things started to go badly the pressure built up on the back pages. Harry didn't really have an outlet or a friendly face he could turn to. You could see the pressure starting to build up on him.

Colin Harvey: You're a bit rudderless, aren't you, if the manager isn't there. He had an air about him, when he walked in the place, that you did sit up straight. He was a bit like a headmaster in that sense. He wasn't a great communicator, but you knew if you worked flat out he'd be more than pleased with you. If he helped you off with your shirt at the end of the game, you'd think to yourself, 'I know I've had a good game!' Because he just didn't mix, if that's the right word, or he didn't communicate to say you'd had a good game.

Howard Kendall: His illnesses were well known about and it was really just a matter of time. The 1972/73 season was a transitional year – we finished seventeenth in the league – and we were really just waiting for him to go. I remember him cornering me once, and telling me, 'They're waiting for me to die.' The end for Catterick was inevitable.

Joe Royle: People like Colin, myself, Howard Kendall, John Hurst, Jimmy Husband all respected him and thought the world of him, even though he was a disciplinarian. We all knew that if you didn't buck the trend or buck the system he would be there for you, and all of a sudden, we'd lost our manager that way. We were still a comparatively young team, so he was going to be missed. When a new manager comes in he has to prove himself.

Billy Bingham

On 11 April 1973 it was announced that Harry Catterick would move to an unspecified executive role at the club and that the search for a new Everton manager was under way. Bobby Robson, Bill McGarry, Brian Clough and Don Revie were the names in the running to replace Harry. Billy Bingham, the club's winger in the 1962/63 League Championship team, was the surprising choice as successor. His appointment came on 26 May 1973.

Keith Tamlin: The Chairman George Watts telephoned me and asked me to accompany him to Manchester Airport to pick up Billy Bingham. The airport in those days was large in size but not like it is today, and it was possible to drop persons or stay for a short period. George went into the International Terminal where he remained and left me to drive his car, a Rolls Royce around the airport perimeter several times. Quite an experience as I had never driven one before! Billy arrived and we then all went to George's home in The Wirral, where we discussed terms. Billy proved to be a good negotiator. Terms were eventually agreed. George rang Mr – as he then was – John Moores and he invited us to his home in Formby for a meal: sausages and mash, which turned out to be Mr John's favourite dish and it was very tasty. Everyone shook hands and we took Billy back to Manchester.

Charles Mills: I wasn't disappointed, I thought he was a good appointment. I'd liked him as a player. I'd met him and he'd been very nice. He was an interesting man. People didn't really question his lack of experience, it wasn't like today. He was a prodigal son coming home, so we were going to be all right. He'd been in a championship side, but I was quite happy with Bingham. I thought he was a good appointment. I certainly didn't want Revie. Clough would have been interesting, I have to admit that; but not Revie. Revie was detested at Everton. And Leeds were as well.

Howard Kendall: I was captain at the time and drove down to Bellefield to wish him all the best. I knocked on his office door and was beckoned in. 'Congratulations Billy,' I said. 'I hope things go well.' He cut me short and hissed, 'It's boss, not Billy.' There was nobody else in the bloody building! I backtracked, and said: 'When the lads are here I'll call you Boss; but we've met before and I called you Billy then...' 'It's boss now,' he said, 'Okay?' I knew at that moment that my time at Everton was drawing to a close: Bingham was going to sell me.

Colin Harvey: I knew more or less right away that he wanted me out, or he wanted me replaced. It was just a matter of time. New manager, new broom, what are you going to do? You're going to get rid of Harvey, Kendall, they'd been here a long time, they're not my players, I want my own players in. It's quite understandable.

John Hurst: He just wanted to change everything. The attitude was that he didn't want anything to do with the Catterick era, even though he played under Harry when he was a player. When I first went to Everton, Billy was still there, but all I remember was that he never trained, he was always injured and he would play on a Saturday. As a manager, the first thing he started was a fitness regime, 'Oh you're not fit, you need to do more running! Down to Ainsdale sand dunes!' I remember thinking: 'Hang on you never did a tap yourself!' But he just wanted to change things and have everything from the Catterick era out of the way and build his own dynasty.

Cliff Marshall: Bingham was always out on the training pitch. He was more hands on, he'd have his trackie on, he'd be watching and he'd be getting involved himself. He was still kicking the ball, running around and having a go playing in the five asides and all that. Catterick never did any of that. There was no messing with him. Pre-season we used to go to Southport for a week. Bingham's hill we called it. You've never seen so much vomit in all your life. He punished us for a week and for that week we played on the sand so when you got on a proper ground we were fit.

Duncan McKenzie: Bingy asked me when I came in [in December 1976]: 'Don't you want to do any gym work?' I said 'What do I want to do any weights for?' So he said to me, 'Well, you're not very strong are you?' I said: 'I'm supposed to be playing them at football, not fighting them'

Jim Pearson: There was a fair bit of running. He brought in a lad called Steve Burtenshaw who was more of a coaching type. If you remember them days, if you look at the bench you had the manager, the physio and the trainer. Now there is about 84 people on everybody's bench today, it's unbelievable the way things have changed. It was kept to a minimum. But after his training methods we were a fit team. We used to train on the beach at Ainsdale, the idea being that if you run on sand it would be much easier to run on grass. Good in theory but not so sure it worked in practice. There could've been a bit more skill work, but it wasn't too bad.

Terry Darracott: I can remember a lot of running – a *lot* of running. With Catterick our first week in pre-season was spent at Ainsdale Beach, running up and down sand dunes; and even from a young age I thought, 'If I ever stay in football I'll never do that to footballers. I'll never do it, because we play on grass; we should train on grass.' You have to go in the gym and do different things in the gym, I understood that, but as a really fit lad you quite enjoyed running, it wasn't a problem to me. I didn't like training in soft sand; I just thought it was crazy. And then Bingy came in and he did the same; I thought, 'Oh not again.'

David Lawson: We used to go to Pontin's at Ainsdale, when I just lived up the road. And I used to go home at lunchtime and I used to be on my bloody knees. You used to train all the way down the beach there, and you got so far and there was this bloody hill, this sand dune, and up and down that sand dune. And you'd go from the sand dune into the wooded area and do laps round there, all against the clock; and then you had so much time to get back to Pontin's after you'd finished. And me and Westy, they used to send search parties out for us! And, of course, the last day – all week you were allowed to run on the flat sand, where cars had been and everything, it was just like running on the road – but the last day you had to come over the dunes all the way back to Pontin's. By God, it used to kill me.

George Telfer: We played in a pre-season tournament in Holland. Apart from the training, which was ridiculous, we got the wooden spoon and there was a celebration afterwards. Billy was going to it, but we couldn't go because that was the punishment because we got beat. Eventually he says 'You can have two beers each and then go to bed' Dai Davies put his hand up and asked, 'Can I have a cup of tea?' Bingham shouted: 'Are you taking the piss out of me?'

The signing of Bob Latchford

On Valentine's Day 1974 Bingham concluded a shock British record transfer to bring Birmingham City's centre-forward, Bob Latchford to Goodison. As part of the £300,000 transfer his captain, Howard Kendall, along with the full-back Archie Styles went to St Andrews. While the arrival of Latchford was welcomed, the sale of Kendall prompted outrage.

Howard Kendall: The local journalists used to ask me, 'What have you done to Bingham?' He was, I was told, always complaining about me, telling them that he didn't rate me. I was the club captain and had just won the Merseyside Sport's Personality of the Year so I can't have been that bad. Newspaper speculation started to appear linking me to a move back to the north east. Bingham, the stories said, wanted to part exchange me for Sunderland's Dennis Tueart. Everton were a team in transition and the 1973/74 season was a personally frustrating campaign for me. I picked up a nasty knee injury just five games in and spent nearly five months on the sidelines. I was just coming back to fitness and had returned to the team in February 1974, when I was summonsed to Bellefield on my day off. I knew, straight away, that something was up. 'A club has come in for you,' announced Billy. The papers had been full of stories about Tueart coming to Everton and there had been contact with Bob Stokoe the Sunderland boss. I was certain I would be moving to the north east. I was wrong. 'It's Birmingham City.'

Bob Latchford: I was called early one morning by my manager at Birmingham, Freddie Goodwin. 'Everton are interested in talking with you,' he announced, 'I'm coming to pick you up.' Within a few hours he had collected me and we travelled up the M6, where we met the delegation from Everton at a hotel midway between Liverpool and Birmingham.

Howard Kendall: To say I was surprised was an understatement. The reality was that I was a chip in a complicated deal, which involved Bob and Archie Styles. With £80,000 on offer as well, the deal was worth £300,000 - a British record fee. Everything hinged on my decision.

Bob Latchford: I'm as surprised now as I was then that Birmingham got Howard. Archie was Archie; he was another body, another player, but Howard was a big capture. He was the Everton captain, part of the acclaimed 'Holy Trinity' midfield that had brought Everton the 1970 League Championship, and many considered him the finest English player never to have been capped by his country. Birmingham's problems were defensive and they were always leaking goals. While Howard may not have offered ready answers to those issues he had leadership and experience and was a terrific player. I'm sure Freddie saw him as someone to knit a side around.

Howard Kendall: Because of the passion that football generates, there tends to be a lot of sentiment attached to relationships with the clubs. I had become an Evertonian and had grown to love the club, but actually, as a player, there's little room for sentiment. It's your job, and the same factors apply to your work as a footballer as they do in most other workplaces. If you're unwanted by the boss, there's no place for you there. So while it was a sad to have to leave a club I had served for seven years and a wrench to uproot my young family, the decision was actually an easy one. I wasn't wanted at one club, but another team sought me. I would become a Birmingham City player.

Peter Mills: I loved Kendall as a player, we won the league and then in the early '70s Kendall kept us in the First Division on his own one season. He was just immaculate in everything he did, and hard-working, good shot. And he was one of those players that other teams, supporters, always acknowledged. Kendall would be one of my all-time playing heroes. I was heartbroken when Kendall went in part exchange for Latchford, but to come into my affections was a sign of how good I thought Latchford was. He would score big goals, relatively big goals – League Cup final and Cup semi-finals and things like that.

Bob Latchford: The main thing I remember was that it was the first time I ever met Howard off the pitch. I recall passing him as I went into one room and he went into another room; we nodded at each other and smiled. When I came out, Howard was on his way back from his talks with Freddie. 'Everything okay?' I asked. 'Yeah, and you?' 'Yeah, thanks.' And that was it. A brief, inconsequential, perfunctory chat marked the end of my association with my boyhood club and Howard his with an institution with which he was synonymous. We never got the chance to play together, or I under him when he turned to management, but our paths would cross many times in the years afterwards.

Howard Kendall: One of the first dates in Birmingham's upcoming relegation battle was at Goodison Park. Naturally it was going to be an emotional day for me when I returned to the stadium in which I'd enjoyed so many memories. But I also had a job to do and that was to save Birmingham. I had my role as a player, but as a senior member of the team too it was to instruct my teammates and make sure they did the right thing. I knew plenty about my old teammates, but I also knew that Everton's danger-man was their old colleague, Latchford. Bob was a terrific player, but there were times when he played within himself. Because he is by nature placid and laid back, sometimes his personality would be reflected in his play. As an opponent you wanted him to be calm, because you knew you stood a chance with him. If he was wound up he was a different man. He was like the Incredible Hulk. On a nice day he'd be a real gentleman and he wouldn't even think about it; great player. But if you wound him up or upset him, he was a Hulk. He even kicked his brother, Dave, who was our goalkeeper at Birmingham. That day at Goodison we had Joe Gallagher, who was a Liverpool born centre-back, marking Bob 'Joe, when you go out there with Latchford; just ask him how he's settled in; where is he living and how's the family,' I said. 'Be nice to him. Don't for Christ's sake kick him.' 'Okay,' replied Joe. In the first minute, Joe whacked him from the back.

Bob Latchford: There was no sentiment shown whatsoever. I got a kick early on and I and my new teammates went to war.

Howard Kendall: Latchford was like an animal after being wound up. He ran us ragged that afternoon and scored twice as my old team won 4-1; their biggest win of the season.

Bingham shapes his Everton team

Through the rest of 1974 Billy Bingham continued to make his own imprint on the team. A British record cash fee of £300,000 was paid for Burnley's elegant midfielder, Martin Dobson, and £100,000 was paid for St Johnstone's Jim Pearson. Meanwhile, stalwarts of the Catterick era retired or were moved on.

Bob Latchford: Martin Dobson was a terrific boy, a very good player, highly talented. He could do so many things. If you needed somebody to calm the situation down Dobbo was the man; he'd just keep the ball and play to his rhythm. He was the one cog in the team that could dictate the tempo of how we all played, was Martin. If he wanted to slow it down he'd slow it down and if he wanted to quicken it up he could do that too. He was a big lad; as big as me, if not bigger and he could get forward and score goals too.

Martin Dobson: As soon as I came to Everton it was like, 'Wow.' It's a different complexion. I felt at that time that everything would be better at Everton: bigger crowd, bigger stadium, players better and all this. And I left a very, very good side at Burnley, good young players with some senior players, but the way we played the game was terrific. I must admit when I came to Everton there were very good players, but I felt we were playing a different way, it took me a bit of time. I hoped that at the time I could just settle in and play my natural game with the players around me, but it didn't quite work out that way.

Bob Latchford: The one other player Everton should have broken the bank for was Peter Shilton. Between the end of Gordon West's career and the ascent of Neville Southall in the early-1980s, this was always the club's problem position. Shilts was attainable: if you look at his career path – Leicester, Stoke, Forest, Southampton, Derby – it's not as if he ever played for a truly big club. At the time there were few bigger than Everton and he would have jumped at the opportunity. Funnily enough Billy had told me after signing me, 'I'm going to be signing Peter Shilton; I'm going after Shilton and will be signing Peter Shilton.' Whether he was just telling me a story I don't know, even to this day, but for whatever reason neither Billy nor Gordon Lee ever went for him, or at least signed him. Instead, in November 1974, he joined Stoke from Leicester. Had it been Goodison rather than the Victoria Ground what happened later on that season may have been very different.

Martin Dobson: What was so interesting for me – because they had Bob Latchford and Joe Royle – was what a threat we've got up the top here now. If I'm going to be creative, we can get people in wide areas, and balls in the box and these two will get shedloads of goals, that's my thinking. But as soon as I walked into the dressing room Joe said, 'No Dobbo I'm going to be away.' Straight away I'm thinking what's that about.

Joe Royle: Billy sold me in the end, and I couldn't blame him for selling me, I was playing quite poorly at the time. He briefly entertained the partnership I had with Bob Latchford, and I thought we were doing well enough together – I think I got three goals and Bob got five in the first seven games. He said at Coventry, 'I'm going to give Jim Pearson a go today.' It was after we'd played a League Cup replay against Aston Villa, and I think we'd lost the game, and I'm pretty sure it was Jimmy Hill on television who said he couldn't see Royle and Latchford as a partnership because they're both similar old-fashioned big centre-forwards. It might have been coincidence, or maybe he was just thinking the same thing. I played one game more that season, and Billy persistently told me that Birmingham City wanted to sign me; where he'd sold Howard Kendall and Archie Styles to take Bob Latchford; where he was to sell John Connolly and Gary Jones later on. I would have been the fifth player sold there. I didn't want to go there. I knew that Manchester United and Manchester City were both interested, so it was a waiting game really. I went down to Birmingham to bring the thing out into the open, because he'd never really readily admitted it to me that they wanted me, but I knew it through contacts. In the end he relented, on Christmas Eve 1974 I signed for Manchester City. I was devastated.

David Lawson: He got rid of players that I would never have got rid of. He signed Bob Latchford, and I don't know how many games him and Royle played together but they were fantastic together. When he sold Joe Royle I just couldn't believe it, because Bob Latchford was not a target man; he played off a target man, and, of course, once Joe Royle went he was the one who went upfront. I was really disappointed when Joe Royle left because he was a great player; he was a great lad, he was a great club lad. I couldn't believe it to be honest, but Billy Bingham wanted his own team and he bought in a lot of players.

Bob Latchford: I think there was maybe an element of getting rid of these players a little too soon. Joe, for example, earned an England recall at Maine Road. But I think at that stage Billy wanted to clear the decks of players who were associated with the championship winning side; he wanted his own players in there, which is understandable. A lot of managers are like that. In my view it would have been better from a playing point to have them around for a year or two more. Although he is only twenty months older than me, Joe had an awful lot of playing experience that could have been very useful. He knew what it was to win things – and lose them too. In a title race you can't put a price on that and, John Hurst aside, we had nobody with comparable experiences. I understand the reason why Billy got rid of them, but I think it would have been better for the squad and the team to have that experience around for longer. I think it was short-sighted: short-sighted to sell him, but also not to replace him properly at the time.

Gary Jones: Billy set up his teams very, very defensively, and players like myself who liked to express themselves did more defending than going forward. It wasn't a big thing to me because I could do that sort of stuff anyway, but when we nearly won the league [in 1974/75], we should have won it. We were very methodical and there wasn't a lot of flair going on. We just dug in deep. I didn't enjoy it, I must admit, because I wasn't really that type of player who liked to constantly do that. I was more of a flair player. Some players, good defenders, enjoy that sort of stuff, but at the end of the day it's all about getting results.

Bob Latchford: Quite a lot was made at the time about Billy Bingham's 'scientific training techniques', but I think that was really just a lot of spin. Billy was essentially an old school manager, albeit that he could talk a good game. My old Birmingham manager, Freddie Goodwin, was far more innovative and tried to introduce ideas from other disciplines – such as yoga and dance – into our routines, which were practically unheard of ideas in the early-1970s.

Jim Pearson: It was rigid at the back to a degree and it was 'Do this, do that' and then once you got forward he allowed you to do bits and pieces. It was a bit more negative than I was used to I was used to playing 4-2-4 up in Scotland. That was always trying to win games whereas this to a degree was making sure you didn't get beaten. We were winning games but I'm not sure how great we were to watch up against somebody who was flying forward and attacking.

Bob Latchford: Why did we draw so many games? Was it because we weren't quite the finished article, or was it due to the competitive nature of the First Division? In my view it was definitely a bit of both. We certainly weren't the finished article. We definitely were lacking one or two players in certain areas. It was also a very competitive league. There were probably seven or eight teams capable of challenging for the league title. We're not talking what we'd consider by today's standards big clubs either. Manchester United were in the second division, Chelsea would end up relegated and Spurs nearly went down. Instead, the top of the table was dominated by the likes of Derby, Ipswich, Stoke, Sheffield United and Middlesbrough. How many provincial clubs could you imagine challenging for the title today? It's inconceivable now.

John Corbett: My memory of that particular season is going to games and being rather horrified that the silky School of Science, which I'd been used to, was now slowly disintegrating and the sort of players that Everton were employing were more workmanlike; they were more utilitarian rather than the artists that had been paraded round in 1970. So, losing to teams like Carlisle, who more or less got in your face and, if you like, pushed aside the playmakers, that was something that we were starting to get used to.

Bob Latchford: A few days before Christmas, Carlisle United came to Goodison. They were rock bottom of the First Division and remained there nearly all season long. They were a team that you would expect to beat, both at home and away. With just over half the game gone, everything was going according to plan. I'd scored twice and we were cruising, cementing our place at the top of the league. Yet what happened in the 14 minutes after my second goal, on 51 minutes, still gives me nightmares more than 40 years later. We imploded. Joe Laidlaw scored twice in five minutes to bring the game level.

Then Les O'Neill, who'd worked his way up from non-league Blyth Spartans to the top flight in a long career, scored an improbable winner. What on earth happened? Was it inexperience? Complacency? Very possibly both. Because of what happened at the season's conclusion, it's still a bugbear now, something that I still ponder. What was the reason? Why? I keep asking myself, rolling over memories of that night in my mind, and I still can't come up with any answers.

Gary Jones: I thought personally in them games, thinking back, that there was certainly some players in the team that could have done a bit more. If you want to use the term 'take your foot off the gas', I think that's what happened in them games, and I think perhaps if certain players would have given a bit more then we would have done a little bit more that season. That's what let us down really, them couple of games. Because I mean we went to Leeds and drew with Leeds, the great Leeds team, and I remember talking to Billy Bremner after the game, and he said, 'It's yours to lose now.' And we did!

Martin Dobson: I always feel you finish where you deserve to finish in the league. It's a long season. We did lose at Carlisle, 3-0, [in the away fixture on Easter Saturday] it was a poor performance up there. Around about Easter time – we came back on the Easter Monday – and we played Coventry City. Billy had put the names up on the board and you see you're playing. I scored a 20-yarder against Coventry, Neil Ramsbottom was the goalkeeper. Pick that out, 1-0! That took us back top of the league. So again, you talk about Carlisle being the main games that season, they beat us twice so probably right, when you reflect on it but in the next game we did get back on track and we were top of the league.

Bob Latchford: The following Friday evening, we faced Burnley at Goodison; the match moved to accommodate the Grand National the following day. It was another scrappy game, but just before the hour mark I calmed some nerves by sending a looping header into the back of the net. We seemed to relax and for the first time in weeks started to play as we could do. We could – and should – have had two or three more goals, and maybe things would have turned out very differently if we'd have found the back of the net again. But with eleven minutes to go Peter Noble, on a rare foray up field, headed an equaliser. We were still top, but it was another point dropped.

Everton travelled to Luton Town on 9 April in second place and needing a win to put them back in the mix. Bob Latchford put them 1-0 up on 20 minutes, but Everton then conceded two goals shortly before half time and were unable to avoid defeat.

Bob Latchford: From being top we had now dropped down to fourth with three games remaining. We ground out a win at Newcastle to keep the pressure on Derby, who were now top. We faced Sheffield United at Goodison and probably played some of our best football of the season. We were 2-0 up at half time, but then – just as we had on several occasions that season – we surrendered. By 73 minutes United were level. At this point the crowd really turned against us. It was nothing more than frustration, but it did have an impact. I think you try very hard for it not to, but I think subconsciously it eats away at you. I think it can have an effect on your performance. Sometimes you are totally oblivious to it but under certain circumstances you become aware that the crowd's a bit edgy. They do have an impact and they did that afternoon. The winner – which probably, at that stage, seemed inevitable to the home crowd – came with five minutes to go from Tony Currie.

Martin Dobson: Why couldn't Bingham the manager replicate the title success of Bingham the player? Well you would have to ask Billy that. He's the man isn't he? Whether he could look back on selections or formations, or was it just the fact that players went off the boil, the injury situation, only Billy knows himself. Would he have done anything different on the training pitch? I'm not so sure.

John Hurst: I don't think it was the manager. I think a lot of times it's the players. The players we had in the 69/70 team could handle that pressure. They were all competent, they could assess things on the pitch, sort things out. Maybe in 1975 it was just the lack of confidence in the players, getting up there and they started panicking. We were always thinking 'Oh if we lose this' whereas we never thought about losing games before. All we wanted to do was go out and win the game. With Billy you started with a point and went out and made sure you didn't lose that one point. Whereas in 69/70 we looked at it as if we had one but you'd want two. If you get negative it's harder to play.

Charles Lambert: It's hard to explain why Everton faded because when you think back to the fixtures they were losing to teams they should've trounced – Carlisle, Sheffield United. Really Everton should've won the league that season, no question about that, and how they threw it away I do not know. I can only think that it was something in the mentality: they were just not resilient enough. They saw the top of Mount Everest and they ran out of oxygen.

Mick Lyons: At times we flattered to deceive. I remember what really let us down was getting beaten beat by Carlisle twice. If we had won those two games then I think we would've won the league. It was really disappointing to get beat by Carlisle twice

Bob Latchford: I still look back upon that season with such great regret. We weren't the finished article, but rarely will you get so many chances of winning a league title. People always fix on the two games against a doomed Carlisle team – two matches that had we won would have seen us lift the title – but there were other missed chances too. Even had we beaten Sheffield United and won our final game against relegated Chelsea [Everton drew 1-1] even after all those wasted opportunities we would have edged the title on goal difference. Failing to win a trophy at Everton is the biggest regret of my career. There would be other opportunities in later years, but the 1974/75 League Championship was the one we should have won. Had we done so it would have set the tone for the rest of the decade. I'm sure we would have won more, possibly much more. Instead, it set the tone of a 'nearly' team: we nearly won the FA Cup, we nearly won the League Cup. It set the tone for the rest of the 1970s where we came close but not close enough.

Everton in the UEFA Cup

Everton finished the 1974/75 season fourth which, with the exception of a seven-hour period in April, was the lowest league position they'd held since Christmas. Derby County were champions, just three points ahead of Everton. Nevertheless, Everton returned to Europe for the first time in five years. The UEFA Cup draw, however, wasn't kind and they were drawn against AC Milan in the first round.

Gary Jones: You talk about the pressing game now, they were doing that then. They were very tight all the time, so you had to try and create a little bit of space for yourself to turn and take people on. They didn't give you space, as long as we'd known the Italians played like that, very defensively. Don't get me wrong, Italian teams can attack as well, but they've always been very well known for being very, very good defensively. So it was always hard to play against them sort of teams, and the

Germans as well are similar, very dogged in the way they set themselves up.

Bob Latchford: It was a terrific atmosphere that night at the San Siro, not just because of the size of the crowd – at 66,000 it was the largest I'd played in front of at that time – but because a significant contingent of Evertonians made the journey. It was a time when travel was less convenient and far more expensive than today and they were magnificent. Unfortunately, we were also facing a twelfth man in the East German referee, Rudi Glockner. Decisions went against us all night. We played really well against a team of genuine quality. We had two clear penalty efforts turned down, firstly, when Gary Jones was fouled only for a free kick to be awarded outside the area; later, when Jim Pearson was knocked over. It was ridiculous. Then he awarded a penalty against us on 67 minutes for handball, which Milan converted! Late on Dobbo nearly scored with a header, which would have seen us through on away goals. It wasn't to be.

Jim Pearson: The Italian teams could defend properly but used to kick lumps off of you too. I remember going to Milan and walking on the pitch there was netting on the side and they used to spit at you, it was just horrible. I played directly against a lad called Romeo Bonetti who was as hard as nails, I had a fight with him. Anyway, we did alright and he was a strong dirty lad tough in that game. I can't remember but I got brought down in the box. Gary Jones is adamant it was the most blatant penalty he'd ever seen, but you didn't get them in those days if you were away in Italy.

Gary Jones: That was a great experience, the noise when we come out the tunnel and flares going off. You had to really compose yourself and say, 'right we've got a game on here.' But I think we did fairly well in that game, I was quite happy with the way I played. I think we should have got a penalty, my shirt was dragged off my back in the penalty box and we didn't get one. So that was disappointing, but a fantastic experience. They were up to all dirty tricks the Italians; spitting in your face when the referee couldn't see, and all sorts of stuff that you had to deal with. But great memories.

Billy Bingham's team in decline

Although Everton were unlucky to lose over two legs to Milan, the match resembled a turning point of sorts and the team's form fell away. Everton remained in mid-table for the remainder of the 1974/75 season, finishing eleventh, and were knocked out in the FA Cup third round. Discontent at the manager began to grow and sometimes bubbled over on the pitch. In an away defeat at Leeds in November Gary Jones became embroiled in a touchline spat with Bingham.

Gary Jones: I was pissed off, and I shouldn't have took that into the game, bearing in mind you're playing against a great Leeds team. I didn't show enough commitment during that game, the manager did the right thing in taking me off, he shouldn't have played me in the first place because I was already having a dispute with him. I threw my shirt at the bench when I came off, and he suspended me for two weeks and fined me two weeks' wages. I regret that as I got older, but it should never have come to that. He should have just given me what I wanted. It certainly wouldn't have broken the bank.

Bob Latchford: Billy usually seemed averse to the pressure. He was as cool as you like. He was never a shouter and if he took it out on players I don't recall him doing it in public. Outwardly he seemed like he could handle pressure. I think it manifested itself in what we did during the week that became more and more negative and physical. In other words, he ran us. The worse we were doing, the more we ran. The more we ran, the greater our resentment.

Charles Lambert: In those days, it was the custom for whoever covered the match for the Liverpool *Daily Post* and *Echo* to travel with the team to away games, but Billy banned me from travelling on the bus because he didn't approve of the way I was writing up my Everton match reports. He thought I was too critical. Funnily enough somebody else who thought the same thing was none other than Bob Paisley, which is amazing when you think about it. I used to have a lot of trouble with Bob and I didn't really understand why he didn't want to talk to me, but a few years later when we started getting on better he explained that he thought my write ups on Everton were too critical and that it was the job of the local reporter to be supportive of the team.

Charles Mills: That was the year the cushion throwing started. That went on into the mid-80s really. There was certainly frustration in the terraces. A lot of that had to do with Liverpool winning everything. It was sickening to be in the city when that lot were winning everything and we weren't.

Despite a disappointing previous campaign, Everton started the 1976/77 season brightly, briefly topping the table. By late autumn, however, confidence had started to ebb and attendances were at their lowest levels in half a century. The signings of Duncan McKenzie and Bruce Rioch failed to arrest the decline.

Martin Dobson: We weren't winning enough games, we weren't playing well. It is one of those situations where there is demand on the chairman, and the directors. There was a similar scenario with Howard a few years later, of course. Sir Phillip backed Howard and what a great decision that was. Because again, those guys are under pressure and he has backed him 100%, and he was under tremendous pressure, both Howard and Sir Phillip. But the directors at this stage thought it was right to make a move and a change. So that's how it developed.

Bob Latchford: Shortly after Christmas 1976 I was called in to meet the chairman, Alan Waterworth. As players, we had little to do with the club's executive management, so it was an unexpected summons. I didn't know what he wanted, but he came straight to the point. 'Bob, now please be honest with me: what is your opinion of the manager?' As a person who sometimes struggles to contain his emotions, it wasn't something I was going to be able to lie about, even if I'd wanted to. 'Billy's got go,' I said simply. 'He's lost the dressing room, lost the players.' That was pretty much the extent of the conversation. I wasn't the only player called in. A few days later, on 10 January 1977, Billy was sacked as manager of Everton FC.

Duncan McKenzie: We beat Stoke in the third round of the FA Cup and they sacked him straight after, which was quite bizarre. Colin Harvey turned round and said sometime afterwards 'I knew they were sacking him. If it had gone on any longer they wouldn't have been able to they can't get rid of him if the results were improving.'

Charles Lambert: I was still travelling with the team and we were on our way back from Ipswich and stopped at a pub to go and get some chips or something like that. Steve Burtenshaw was the acting manager before Gordon Lee was appointed and Steve went in at the head of the group and all the players trooped in after him and the guy at the bar could see them coming off the bus and said, 'Sorry sir we don't serve coaches.' Andy King was standing alongside him said, 'No, he's not the coach anymore, he's the acting manager!'

Gordon Lee

Billy Bingham's successor was the Newcastle United manager, Gordon Lee. His first tasks on taking over at Goodison in late January 1977 were to get Everton through an FA Cup fourth round replay against Swindon and, more pressingly, a League Cup semi-final second leg against Bolton Wanderers.

Bob Latchford: Who would I have liked to see succeed Billy? I think Brian Clough would have brought a certain edge to the club. He would have energised the players and brought the sort of commitment and innovation on the pitch that would have made us contenders. His record, even at that stage, was phenomenal. But I don't think the Everton directors would ever have stood for a Brian Clough. Cloughy was the type of manager who would want total control and no interference, and the directors of Everton would not have been open to that. I feel maybe they were a bit like the FA – who overlooked Clough for the England job – in a lot of respects: conservative, a little controlling. They wanted a certain type of manager that would toe the line to an extent, and I'm not sure Cloughy would have fitted their mould. Billy's eventual successor was more their type: decent, hardworking, uncontroversial.

Duncan McKenzie: They were talking of having Brian Clough as the new manager, they were talking of Bobby Robson; Don Revie – who was never going to be in the frame but he was also mentioned. We're talking huge names and they all turned Everton down. I spoke to Brian Clough sometime afterwards and he said 'I couldn't work for Sir John Moores. Nothing wrong with the guy but I want to run the club that I'm at' and he wouldn't let him do that. The sad or bad news for me was they signed Gordon Lee.

Keith Tamlin: Enquiries were made by Bill Scott, the Chairman, and George Watts and others. Gordon was presented in a most favourable way to us. Personally I knew very little about him at the time but was impressed by the reports we had received. He turned out to be a delightful person with a great family and it was a pleasure to work with such a splendid character who always had the Club's best interests before him in the performance of his job.

Gordon Lee: I think when you're a manager and you go into any club, the important things are first of all you have to be honest, and secondly you have to be open. Players, generally speaking, react to how you treat them, and I was just a safe old bloke who treated them as mature, good, players, professional players, and I expected the same to come back from the players. I was always honest and open with what I did, there was no underlying stuff with me, I was open and honest, and I always worked that way. The trademark was that it created a good dressing room, it created a good spirit among the players, and hopefully that goes on to be successful on the field.

Martin Dobson: He made it very simple, did Gordon, he even got back to passing the ball accurately. You're thinking 'Wow, you do that with eight and nine year olds; control the ball, pass, control the ball pass.' But I'm thinking straight away because of where I've come from [Burnley] 'Yeah, that's what we need. Pass it to a blue shirt. Get the ball down and pass it to a blue shirt.' So it's two touch football: control the ball and pass and move. Control the ball, pass and move. Don't complicate it, because all of a sudden you get the confidence in the team, and I thought that was terrific. Very simple, but that's your starting point isn't it? Then you go to the back four and what they need to do, keeping clean sheets and how you're going to create chances, but I thought that was terrific. From there we started building results. You wouldn't say Gordon was the greatest coach in the world, but he had his qualities, and that is what he was looking for in his team: togetherness, keep together boys, get on the front foot, get wide, get crosses in, and be creative. If you make a mistake, don't worry about it. You've got to entertain as well, but you entertain by keeping possession of the ball and creating chances. So that was terrific for me, I really enjoyed it.

Bob Latchford: Gordon's biggest problem was that he wasn't media friendly. He always had a problem relating to the media and the press, and they gave him an image of being very dour and very sour mannered. Physically he was very gaunt, looking a little like Uncle Fester from The Addams Family or the 1990s sitcom character, Victor Meldrew, which I think added to this perception as an austere disciplinarian, but he really wasn't like at all. he was probably the total opposite of how he came across in the media. He was somebody completely in love with football, a passionate man and obsessed with the game. He thought about football 24 hours a day. Sometimes he was a little bit too intense, too focussed on the game rather than the real world. But he was honest and down to earth; a man that you thought you could get behind and believe in what he was saying. That's an important thing as a player, that you can believe and trust in what a manager is saying to you, that you have a sense of doing the right things and going in the right direction. It was just unfortunate for him that his image was such that people got the wrong impression of him.

Duncan McKenzie: I scored the winning goal at Cardiff in the FA Cup. Granted, it was a little bizarre but I was a little bizarre I suppose. I've nicked the ball from the centre half, a guy called Albert Larmour, and I'd gone loping through this ploughed field that was Ninian Park. They had a little goalkeeper called Healy who'd previously been at Manchester City and had a low centre of gravity and I've tried to dribble him and he stayed on his feet and I thought, 'Cor, he's a better defender than most of their defenders.' Ultimately he went down but nobody's come to take the ball off me, they've all run to the goal line which has three or four defenders on it and it was like watching a table football match. I've shaped to shoot and they all danced across the line and then danced back again and I started laughing. As I've swung my boot the ball rolled over a divot and I miskicked it and it went in through somebody's legs but nevertheless it went in and it was a winner. Afterwards I came in and Gordon said, 'What on earth do you think you're doing? What were you doing then?' I just replied, 'I know you would rather have seen me run through hit if first time and it'd gone over the bar.' He said, 'I would.' In the corridor afterwards this guy from the *News of the World* has said to Gordon, 'Well Gordon what do you say now? You're always having a go at Duncan but he's got thirteen goals for you' He's said, 'Twelve.' The journalist says 'No, thirteen' He's said 'Twelve' He said: 'You're not counting that one he got today are you?' Gordon replies: 'I'll be ringing up the FA. I want it taking off him!'

Charles Lambert: The vast majority of players liked Gordon Lee and that included Duncan McKenzie, who is portrayed in the media as being at daggers drawn with Gordon and their footballing philosophies were miles apart. But as men they got on well, they would nearly always sit together on the bus going to away games and they were playing cards nonstop and Gordon would quite often defer to Duncan in Duncan's wider knowledge of matters to do with the world at large. When it came to football of course the boot was on the other foot and Gordon would not be backward in coming forward and telling Duncan that he shouldn't be messing around and trying to dribble past players in his own penalty area and things like that.

John Bailey: I knew Gordon when I was a young apprentice at Blackburn and he was manager. Gordon was great; all he knew was football. You mention anything that was going on in the world and Gordon wouldn't know anything about it. There was a trip away to Israel and we had a day trip to Bethlehem and he didn't really know where it was, 'What are you going there for and what are you buying?' I think I bought a carved statue of the Last Supper for my mother – I'm from a Catholic family – but other than football Gordon was a bit three-sheets-to-the-wind. But he was a great fella and I owe a lot to him because he signed me as an apprentice.

Mike Pejic: I remember Gordon pulling all the lads together and he was sifting through the squad and sifting the team out and everything. He said to everybody 'What have you actually won?' He was quite blunt about it. We all looked at each other and thought, 'Right, this is where it starts!' There was a scramble for places and a scramble for positions, and a fight for every ounce of that pitch you could when you played. That was start really of getting a great team spirit together.

1977 League Cup run

Martin Dobson: We went to Manchester United for the quarter-final. I scored the first goal, a 20-yarder outside the box - dipped my shoulder and put it right into the bottom corner. I always used to score against Manchester United, I enjoyed playing against them. I think Kingy scored a couple of goals too. If you look at the video clip I'm shaking my backside in celebration. Someone showed it me the other day and said, 'Dobbo what's all this about?' I don't think anybody copied it for a goal celebration.

Bob Latchford: We played Bolton Wanderers in a two-legged semi-final. The first match, under Steve Burtenshaw's caretakership, typified the malaise we were in. On an edgy night at a packed Goodison we were leading 1-0 through a Duncan McKenzie goal, but had seemingly done enough to hold onto the win. Then, two minutes from the end David Lawson took more than the six steps goalkeepers where in those days allowed to take with the ball; an indirect free-kick was awarded inside the area, from which Bolton equalised and all our hearts sank.

Martin Dobson: Bolton were the team that released me as a 19-year-old. I was going back there as an international, a £300,000 player, playing in a semi-final. For me it was really important we got through. I played the first game at Goodison, and it was only a draw, one apiece, a bad pitch. Then we played the second leg over there, under a bit of pressure. I remember a throw-in down the left hand side, it was crossed in and Latchy gets on the end of it, we were in 1-0.

Gordon Lee: Bob Latchford was one of those lads, if he was at it, when he was in the routine of scoring goals, he had everything. He could run, he was strong, he could head the ball, he could play with players; he had all the things going for him. When he was in that frame of mind I thought well he'll score again next week and the week after, and he did. He had the little spells of scoring when everything went right for him. At times, when things didn't go so well, he was a little bit the opposite, he'd lose a bit of whatever he had. If things weren't going well, or he wasn't playing well he'd be down on confidence. But when he was on form there would be nobody better in the country than him as a centre-forward.

Martin Dobson: It was a comfortable 1-0, if you can say that. We got into the final and it was great in the bath afterwards, because that's the bath I used to be in all those years ago when my career was going nowhere, and the manager doesn't tell me he's letting me go to my face, he sends me a recorded delivery letter from Bolton saying thanks very much, goodbye. All of a sudden it comes back doesn't it? You knock them out and you're going to Wembley.

Bob Latchford: The final was three weeks later against Aston Villa. They weren't a bad outfit and had Andy Gray – who would end the season double PFA Player and Young Player of the Year – leading their line, but they held few concerns for us. We felt that we were a stronger unit, despite the struggles we had encountered under Billy. Being a Birmingham boy there was added impetus for me to get one over them. For Gordon too, I'm sure there was a great incentive to win. Having served Villa for such longevity as a player, six weeks into his managership of Everton he was leading out his new club against them at Wembley.

Gordon Lee: The preparation wouldn't be anything different, I don't think. The only thing I would have made sure of is when we were going out to play the game, my theory was get your mind-set right, I know your families are here and it's a lovely day, but get your minds on the job. This is a game of football and we want to win. A lot of people are out there, it's Wembley, they look up at the stadium and they get carried away a bit, I think you've got to be focused completely on the match itself. It's difficult because there's a lot of people watching the match. It's not easy for them, but it's a big day and that's what you've got to do. I always used to have this thing in me: when you play a game of football at whatever level, I used to say to the lads, 'Don't forget lads, we kick-off at three o'clock, not quarter past three.' In other words, don't start slowly. On the ball straight away, don't let them get a foothold in the game. Be the first to get your foothold on the game. Don't play soft, easy football because all of a sudden they will score and you're chasing the game. I always liked them to start well.

Martin Dobson: The first game I really enjoyed it, even though it was 0-0. Then I got a bang, a hip injury, somebody whacked me in the second half. We should have won the game in the first one. I thought, we were the better side.

Bob Latchford: Four days later we met again at Hillsborough for the replay. Dobbo was missing with a hip injury and we perhaps lacked some of the composure he brought our team. The game looked as though it would be heading for another stalemate when, ten minutes from the end, Roger Kenyon, who was playing his first match since Christmas, ran the ball into our net. It was inexplicable, as a lot of incidents were at key moments for Everton over those years. How on earth do you explain that? Roger was one of our most experienced and dependable players and yet he made such a big and basic mistake at such a huge moment. The pitch, it must be said, was horrible – a complete quagmire and mud from it covered my shirt and hid my number nine – and I think the ball just got stuck under his studs. Big Roger's error focussed some minds and galvanised our attack. We sent waves of attackers forward as we tried desperately to gain an equaliser. These efforts were rewarded in the dying seconds.

Jim Pearson: I think I came on as sub in the second game and I flicked on a corner and guess who scored? Latchford!

Bob Latchford: It was a bit of a tap in, if I'm honest, but the range of emotions you feel at such a moment almost defy explanation. Relief, ecstasy, elation; you feel all of these things, but putting words onto paper to describe what you went through in front of 55,000 screaming people, under floodlights, will never do full justice to the moment.

Gordon Lee: We were good enough to win it I think, but maybe we just didn't do it on the day in the third game. We were 1-0 ahead when the Villa centre half Chris Nichol, I don't think he'd ever scored a goal in his life, equalised. He was on the halfway line I think and he didn't know what to do with the ball. He took pot luck with his left foot, and how it got in I don't know. You could say it was a goalkeepers' mistake, but it went in, and that's the sort of thing that happens in cup football. It was their time to win and it happened. That's how I look at it. I since played in golf competitions with Chris Nichol, and I usually take the mickey out of him – the only goal you've ever scored. The picture I have of it, it was right by the halfway line where I was sat, and I'm pretty convinced that he didn't know what to do with the ball – he was a centre half – and he just kicked it and that was it. That's the way it goes I suppose.

Bob Latchford: We were briefly in disarray. Within a minute Brian Little was played in; nobody tackled him and although David Lawson came out he seemed to shoot through his body to put them in front. It was unbelievable really.

Mick Lyons: The ball hit the crossbar and it came back to me and I was there and just headed it in. Matches like that they're just over too quickly; it's like when you play the derby it's over too quick.

Bob Latchford: It went to extra time. And then, 90 seconds from a penalty shoot out, another of those freak moments. A sweeping crossfield ball was played to Gary Smith on Villa's right wing. His cross deflected off Ronnie Goodlass, wrongfooting Terry Darracott who should still have cleared it. Lawson scampered after the loose ball, but wasn't quick enough and Brian Little tapped home the winner at the far post. We were destroyed. It was a conspiracy of errors.

David Lawson: There was obviously a misunderstanding. There was a cross came in and I shouted to Terry Darracott, 'Away – clear it away.' And he for some reason he always said that Brian Little, who was behind him and scored, said, 'Leave it.' And he did. Then Little just slotted into the corner. But to this day he always said somebody shouted, 'leave it.'

Martin Dobson: I don't want to criticise people but it was two soft goals. I remember Chris Nichol, he hit it from 40 yards, one of them, and you're thinking, 'Wow, he's never scored in his life.' He just whacked it and you're thinking let him shoot from there, it's gone in the bottom corner. And then there was the winner, and it's so sad because I always feel you need to get that first trophy under your belt to go on, and that was the nearest point apart from the Liverpool semi-final.

John Corbett: It broke everyone's heart the game at Old Trafford against Aston Villa. I think both sides were rather weary, but there was a feeling of inevitability that it would be a mistake by one side or the other that would settle it. It was a bitter disappointment because it seemed to cap off a decade of bitter disappointments.

Gordon Lee: I was disappointed for the players and the fans of course because we got so close, and we'd got things going. It's an even bigger disappointment when you think you're going to get there and you're going to do it. People say it's easier to lose the semi-final, but I think when you get to Wembley and you don't win, it's still a big disappointment. As you say Everton hadn't won anything for a bit, so it would have been nice.

Bob Latchford: We were completely forlorn, but I don't remember any finger pointing. Nobody blamed Terry or David. If you listen to stories of the great Everton teams of the 1980s, or Liverpool too, the players would completely slaughter each other even when things were going well. Some of those players say it was a symbol of how comfortable they all were in each others company. Maybe that was the case. We didn't have that. Maybe we were poorer for it. Perhaps if there had been that openness it would have lifted all of our standards.

1977 FA Cup semi-final

In the midst of the 33 day long League Cup Final saga, Everton had progressed to the FA Cup semi-final. Awaiting them, as in their previous semi-final appearance six years earlier, were Liverpool.

Gordon Lee: I was optimistic by this time. I think we were a good side. I think we could handle the big occasions, whereas perhaps when I first went there I wasn't so sure about that, because I hadn't been in it before. But having had a taste through the League Cup, I think when you get there with Liverpool, we were ready yes.

Mike Pejic: We were competing in the league, doing really well in cup matches, and then the FA Cup came along, and we were ready for it. We were ready now to compete against the great Liverpool side of that time. We were up there with them, so there was no inferiority complex about us at all. We were well and truly up there with the best, and going in there to that FA Cup semi-final, we felt really confident of winning it and getting into the Wembley final.

Martin Dobson: I had a groin strain, and I had a cortisone injection in my groin before the game, unbelievable. I didn't train all week, but the manager wanted me to play, of course. I had this injection in the doctors' room at Maine Road before the kick off, and it absolutely lashed it down. I got through the first 60 minutes and I had to come off.

Bob Latchford: That afternoon there was a definite sense that they were for the taking. Whether it was complacency or merely an off day, they could not find their rhythm. Even when they went in front, which they did twice, first through Terry McDermott, then Jimmy Case, we sensed that we could get back, which we did from Duncan and then Bruce Rioch.

In the closing stages of the game, and with the scores balanced at 2-2, Everton's substitute Bryan Hamilton became embroiled in one of the most notorious incidents in Merseyside derby history when what seemed like a legitimate goal – and winner – was inexplicably disallowed by the referee, Clive Thomas.

Bryan Hamilton: I'm not bitter in any way, shape or form, but it wasn't the right decision. I've tried to understand why he didn't give it. He said an infringement, but I don't think he really knew. I looked over at the linesman, I looked over at the faces of the Liverpool players, they knew it was a goal and for some reason or other the referee came from a distance and gave an infringement.

Gordon Lee: I think that is the most cruel, and worst, moment of my football life. Without doubt. I can see it now, I'll take it to my grave, and I can tell you everything about it. We were two each, and all through the game something told me it was our day to beat Liverpool. I had that feeling watching the game that it was going to be our day. And then the ball went into the net, Ronnie Goodlass crossed it, and Bryan Hamilton knocks into the net. I'm now at Wembley aren't I? We've won the match. I looked down the bench, to see Bob Paisley and his group of staff on the bench, and their heads went down. Their players' heads were down as well because they thought it was a goal. That was abnormal in those days, because if you've just lost a goal you might want to brain somebody, or think it's not a goal, or it's offside or whatever. But I looked at Bob Paisley's face and if he was alive today I'm sure he would say 'That was a goal and you won the match.'

Mike Pejic: I was the closest to Clive Thomas, I was the closest player to him. When we cut the ball back Bryan knocked it in with his hip past Clemence. Nobody on their side said anything about it. It was a goal, and he gave offside. That was the initial decision, because he pointed and he said 'offside', and then he turned, looked at the linesman, the linesman was on the way back to the halfway line. It was a goal, and he changed his mind on the spot and gave handball. I actually ran after him.

Gordon Lee: The thing was the linesman took his position for the goal, the Liverpool players I'm sure had accepted it, and we thought – well I'm at Wembley aren't I? But, little Clive Thomas, yes it was the advent of television, and here was the guy that I am convinced to this day – and I will take it to my grave – he thought that the game was about the spectators coming to watch him referee, instead of the players playing. And nobody will ever, ever change my mind about that.

Bryan Hamilton: To this day I've never had a satisfactory answer for why he didn't give it.

Mike Pejic: I don't care what anybody says, it was cheating. I'll stand up in court and say that. It was cheating, and he cheated us out of it. To this day it hurts, even more. Decisions like that change people's lives.

Bob Latchford: Clive was an international referee, an uncompromising Welshman who thought more of himself than any other referee I ever encountered. Clive was Clive. You took him as he was, but I've never known a referee who liked the focus on him like he did. He's done things in football that defy comprehension. This is somebody who, a year later, in the last minute of a World Cup game between Brazil and Sweden, awarded a corner and in the time between the ball being crossed to the head of Zico and crossing the goalline – the flicker of an eyelid – blew for full time. Clive did that sort of thing because Clive could. He was the referee and his authority was absolute.

Bryan Hamilton: It's a hard job refereeing. You have to be absolutely sure when you give a decision. I always say referees get 99% of decisions right, but it's the big decisions you have to get right. I think that was a huge decision and he didn't get that right.

Martin Dobson: He didn't really know what he was talking about, because he was hoping that it was either offside or handball, but it wasn't. He flicked it in with his hip, did Brian, and that was it. You know Liverpool, if there was an infringement they would all be up, so it wasn't offside genuinely, it wasn't handball, it was a legitimate goal, last minute and he didn't give it.

Mike Pejic: He had the audacity to come into our dressing room and start talking, and I give him a right roasting. And then the match after, the replay, in the first half I went up for a ball in the penalty area with David Johnson, and Dave used to go up early and hang, and I went up straight and we made contact but it wasn't a foul or anything, you're challenging for a ball for goodness sake, in the air. I went up fair and square and he gave a penalty against me. I still believe to this day it's because of the two incidents I had with him.

Bob Latchford: Bryan's disallowed goal is a massive incident in Everton's history of that era. It robbed us of an opportunity to have played in an FA Cup Final against a team – Manchester United – that we were more than capable of beating. Liverpool had gotten out of jail for free and knew it. They hadn't played well and there was no way that Bob Paisley was going to let them play like that again in the replay. When we met again at Maine Road four days later there was really only one team in it. Paisley's Liverpool didn't pass up second chances and won 3-0.

Mick Lyons: Clive Thomas was a showman referee. I remember after that game the first time we had him after the semi final – I think we played Villa at home – and he give us everything. But it was all too late then.

Gordon Lee's new team

Martin Dobson: Andy King was a character. He came into the club and he was fantastic, so full of confidence. The interesting thing with all the guys was that they love Everton football club. Andy has been to a few clubs, and he came from Luton. All of a sudden he came straight into the first team as a 19-year-old, and he took it by storm. He was scoring goals and he was great in the dressing room, a bit like Duncan McKenzie. Maybe if you lose a game on a Saturday you don't want everybody to be too serious on a Monday morning, you need people to lift the dressing room with the attitude, 'Right let's get back on track, get into training next week and look forwards to the next game.' Andy was one of those, super guy, he just loved life as well.

Mike Pejic: Andy King was jovial all the time. He was a great guy. He was probably a coaches' nightmare, because he was so crazy. He was like a loose cannon, you could say. But what a player, so spirited and effective.

Bryan Hamilton: I remember this cheeky young player coming in, very confident, quite arrogant; but I thought 'What a special talent.' When Andy came to the club he was really my competition for a place and I just saw someone who was very special, very gifted player. I just saw the potential that Andy had and what he was going to give to Everton for years to come and I just saw it being difficult for me to be better than him: he was much younger, he was the future.

Bob Latchford: Andy King was always mouthing off and bantering away. He always had a word for everybody and his larger than life personality made our dressing room hum. We were coming back from an away win against QPR and he was going on and on, messing around, trying to bait me 'You weren't half the forward you are today until you started playing with me!' 'The fans all love you, but you're nowhere near as good as me!' 'There's no better finisher at Everton Football club than me, sorry Latch!' On and on he went for the whole length of the journey. I wasn't rising to it though. I just ignored him, but Andy wouldn't shut up. In the end I had enough of him and walked down the carriage, picked him up and hung him from a coat hook. His feet weren't touching the floor! The lads fell about laughing as Andy dangled there and the train made its way back north.

Martin Dobson: Dave Thomas was a brilliant player. He was exceptional as a 16, 17-year old at Burnley, because he could have gone anywhere. He could have gone to Manchester United, to Leeds United. He was already at Burnley as an apprentice when I arrived, so he is two or three younger than me. Talent wise he was brilliant: goes both ways, balance, ability, whips them in, he can stand them up to the far post, he was just a natural footballer. So when he came to Everton I thought that's fantastic. I was playing left side of midfield at that time and Dave was on the left flank as well. I'm thinking I'll be able to find him, we've got a good relationship, I'll dip my shoulder and come inside and then knock it into him. He was just a terrific footballer, and his attitude as well, he wanted to play the right way.

Bob Latchford: I first saw Dave at a schoolboy international at Wembley when I was fifteen. For some reason, I just noticed him on the pitch when they came out and picked out his name from the team sheet. He had a style and a verve that attracted me to him as a player. He could do things on the pitch with the ball, like juggling the ball with both feet, that few other players at that level could manage. I remember thinking at the time, 'He's got some ability, this lad. He's going to be a player.' Sometimes you can recognise players who are going to make it to the very top and so it was with Dave. From that day on I followed his career, from Burnley to Loftus Road and a short spell in the England team; and here we were some ten or eleven years later playing together at Everton.

David Lawson: It didn't matter how wet the pitch was, how muddy the pitch was, how hard the pitch was, Dave wore rubber soled boots. He never wore studs. Now how can you keep your balance? How he raced down the wing and bloody hit crosses in the way he did, I will never ever know. He was just a fantastic crosser of the ball; absolutely brilliant.

Martin Dobson: It's funny because one of the clubs he went to before, he played with his socks rolled down. He played in rubber moulded boots and no shin pads, but that was the only time he could do it. Apparently at Wolves he played in studs and he wasn't happy, he had to have his socks rolled up and shin pads, and he didn't feel good. Of course, Gordon Lee was like. 'Play in whatever you want, play in your underpants if you want, no problem at all.'

Dave Thomas: I always used to wear rubber studs and no shinpads, and they [Wolves] tried to get me to wear boots and to pull my socks up. I played for Alf Ramsey and Don Revie and they never told me. I was quite stubborn looking back, but I wasn't going to alter for them.

Mark Higgins: I couldn't believe how he used to stand up, because Dave never used to wear any studs, he used to wear the rubber moulded boots whether it was muddy or whatever. But he managed to stay on his feet.

Bob Latchford: We called him Tizer, after the soft drink, because he was so bubbly. He had two magical feet. I've always said about Tizer, that while Glenn Hoddle also had two terrific feet, Tizer had the same qualities and could do anything with the ball, but also do things at speed, which Glenn couldn't. Glenn was a little bit of a stroller, directing things in midfield, pinging balls around. Tizer had the same sort of technical ability but could do it at speed with both feet.

Mike Pejic: He used to take players on all the time. He'd get whacked up in the air and he'd go back for more. He'd go past them the next time, and he'd cause no end of problems. He was a brave lad and what a crosser of the ball he was. The brains there was Martin Dobson, he kept everything ticking over, he read the game so well on both parts, both attacking and defending. The three of us had a great understanding. We played almost every match I think for a long period, and we had a really good understanding together. We functioned really well on the left-hand side. It was a pleasure to play. We were just so fluent, and that understanding was there every match. It was second nature; we just did everything automatically. The rhythm was there, the understanding.

Bob Latchford: Mike Pejic was a hard as nails left-back who had all the attributes that you would want from a great defender: tough, hardworking, very aggressive, but also technically very good. We used to call him Farmer Pej as he lived on an isolated farm in North Wales, where Kevin Keegan had once lived, and would turn up to training in a mud-splattered jeep and wellington boots. He's exactly a year older than me, but even in his mid-60s you can still see that supreme fitness and toughness. He hasn't changed at all. He has taken up Taekwondo and competes at international level, in 2014 coming third in the World Championships in Mexico. Can you imagine? Back then you had to work hard to get past Pejy, and he had a very good understanding with Tizer down the left.

Jim Pearson: Pejy was smashing, a good lad. He was a bit of a farmer and he came in on his first day in his Land Rover. Gordon West, who's a funny man, said 'Excuse me why are you here?' Pej replies 'I've just signed for Everton' West says, 'You may well have, but I don't know you. You move that car from here now, it smells. Would you get out now.' So Peji just took his car and parked it on the road and Westy just shook his head. Westy used to slaughter people.

Mike Pejic: When Gordon bought George Wood we used to say we've bought a blind Scottish goalkeeper. But what a character he was, he was a ginormous character and so funny and great to play with. He was nuts, absolutely nuts. I used to call him a Cadbury's Fruit and nutcase, he was nuts. Typical goalkeeper.

John Bailey: Georgey was a character. He was blind as a bat and wore contact lenses. Anything inside the 18 yard box he could see but if you hit one from outside the box you know he'd get dazzled by the lights and that. He was in the 'F Troop' and when I signed for Everton Gordon said to me 'We've got a group called F Troop – like that series on the telly with all the lunatics on a bender: stay away from them.' It was Kingy, Georgey and a few more like Trevor Ross. Of course, I joined up with them, but that's when players could have a good time, not like these millionaires there are now. Woody was a tremendous fella, he was Andy's minder and if anything went wrong you would hear 'Woody, Woody come and help me.' He had a good career; he was different class, a character. They were all characters.

Geoff Nulty: George's problem was that he couldn't see. I played at Goodison in the 4-4 match in 1977 for Newcastle and I remember Tommy Craig hit one from 35 yards it went over George's head into the net. Big George went round the back thinking that the ball had gone over, he couldn't see it. Mickey Burns had played with him at Blackpool and he said, 'Shoot from 25 yards, shoot from anywhere and he won't see it coming!'

Bob Latchford: I think Gordon wanted a certain type of player and personality at the club. He liked the game played in the right way. Some players he just didn't take kindly too. Bruce Rioch was one of them. Off the pitch he was a lively, engaging and likeable member of the dressing room. On it he was something else. He was one of the most frightening players I've ever seen on a football pitch. He would go into tackles at 100 miles an hour from a standing start. He was at times frightening to look at. But the thing is with Bruce, he would kick you in training as well. You were happy if you were on Bruce's side in five-a-side, because he wouldn't back out of any tackle, even in training. Bruce was just one of those where tackling was just part of his makeup, but he could be frightening at times. I've seen him go in thigh high, knee high, into tackles. We played Middlesbrough in a League Cup tie in October 1977, when he took their left-back, Ian Bailey, out. It was horrendous; it was one of those where you turned your eyes, even as a teammate and thought 'Bruce; that's awful.' He was about five yards away, and went flying in and took the lad out. Ian was taken off on a stretcher. Bruce wasn't even booked. Nor was he challenged in the dressing room, not even by Gordon. Gordon dealt with it in his own way. He played Bruce just one more time and then sold him back to Derby County a few weeks later.

Paul Lodge: His Dad was in the army and you could tell really. Bruce was leaving to go to Derby and he was never very nice to me. I had a cupboard where all my boots that I cleaned went. Bruce was number twenty and he was the same size as me so he had about three pairs of the same boots. I never had any intention of stealing them, it's just in those days pros didn't know whether they had one pair or two pairs as long as I cleaned them. I knew Bruce was leaving that day so I took a pair of his boots out of his number twenty slot and put them right in the top thinking I'd 'misplaced' them. He went up to see the manager and came down; got me by the throat and pinned me up against the wall, and said 'If those boots aren't in my hand in a couple of minutes I'm going to get you sacked you little...' Oh he was terrible! Whereas Terry Darracott, Steve Sergeant were hard lads but they loved you, Bruce was someone I was genuinely scared of.

Mike Pejic: We had a solid back four. Roger Kenyon was a joy to play with. He read the game so well, and I would say an underrated player of his day, he was solid. He used to push me forward all the time, because he was so confident of dealing with things at the back. Lyonsy was mad, and then Terry Darracott was even madder, so we had a daft back five you could say, and not a lot got past. That was a solid base, truly.

Mark Higgins: Mick Lyons was Everton through and through. He was captain as well. He loved the club. He loved to play football, he loved Everton, and he wore the shirt with such pride, which rubbed off on me as well. I was lucky to come through as a kid and that is something that you learn, and that's something the kids now don't understand, if you take the derby game. I played in the B team, the A team, the reserves, all the way up to the first team, and you realise what it's about. You're walking through the streets as a young lad and families are split, they don't speak all week. You just realise how much it matters, but when you come through the club you realise it more.

Gordon Lee: At Everton there was a core: Roger Kenyon, Mick Lyons, Terry Darracott, Ronnie Goodlass. Two young lads as well, Steve McMahon and Paul Lodge. There was a core of what I call the steel of the club and the steel of the dressing room. If things go wrong in the dressing room, and they often do at every football club, the people you look to rely on are the local lads. I found that very, very good, because you always have sticky times. So the likes of Mick Lyons and that type of player at the club, they are invaluable. I think it is missing now, one of the things that I don't like about the game now. I think the supporters of Everton and any other football club, they like to relate to the players on the field. That's how I feel anyway.

Martin Dobson: Mick used to head butt the ceiling to get himself psyched up. I remember one game, the bell had gone and we needed to go out, and Lyonsy couldn't reach it. We were like 'What are you doing here?' He was doing it for ages and the bell rang again. So me and Latch picked him up and that was it, he could head it then. He was a great lad, and he had the superstitions. I think most players do. Lyonsy had sweatbands, because in August and September it was boiling hot, and he had that short-sleeved shirt. So he played well during that time, and in winter and pre-season it would be the same – sweatbands and short-sleeved shirts. He was a real Evertonian of course, came through the ranks, had seen the team on the terraces. To be captain, fantastic. He gave it 100% commitment, and he epitomised to all of us in the dressing room what it means to play for Everton. Lyonsy was ideal for the captaincy, it was a shrewd move by Gordon or Billy.

Mike Pejic: Gordon was a very down to earth guy, and all he wanted was hard work and honesty. That's all he asked, no less and that's all he wanted then and that was fair. With Steve Burtenshaw around him and Jim McGregor wise-cracking all the time, they kept that great feeling around us. It was superb. Again when Bruce Rioch came into the side as well, he was a silent assassin, and he we had Trevor Ross on the right hand side as well, he was another assassin. So we were a really tough, hard side to compete against. But we also had that skill and brains behind us, and we weren't far off.

Geoff Nulty: Gordon was very good at looking at an opposition seeing what made them tick, seeing how we could maybe change things a little bit. But he never changed everything, he changed a little bit just to take account of what their strength was and then hopefully you'll play your own way and still be successful.

Martin Dobson: In that time we did have a very good side, and we worked hard and won games. However Duncan McKenzie frustrated Gordon, and sometimes the players. Duncan was pissing about and nutmegging people, and flicking it over their shoulders and all this type of stuff. So the crowd loved it, but if he gave the ball away we were like 'Duncy, Duncy, what you doing?' With Andy King and Duncy you come in and enjoy life. Duncy had a smile on his face and had a good laugh, and the fans loved him. 'We all agree, Duncan McKenzie is magic', that was the song. And in the big games he stepped up, the semi-final against Liverpool, he scored a goal at Old Trafford when it was lousy weather conditions. He was super confident with his little strut. We were all different and he was great for the dressing room.

Mike Pejic: I think again nowadays Duncan would be a genius match in, match out, because there's no tackling. He would be allowed to do the things he'd love to do. He would be a crowd pleaser every match. Things would nowadays come off for him, because of this no tackling affair now. Nowadays players are so over-hyped because of what they are allowed to do. They wouldn't be allowed to do it then; it would have certainly tested their character.

Trevor Ross: You could never tell with Duncan. You couldn't see Duncan for 70 minutes and then all of a sudden boom, boom, boom, boom, boom: where did he come from? You'd be shouting, 'Come on you lazy bastard get something done' and Duncan would just turn it on, but that was Duncan. That's how Duncan played. He was the same in training.

Gordon Lee: Duncan had ability to do things but I think if we'd had been a good side, a good team, then I think you could get the best out of him. If you're a good team and you're in the penalty area and you're a good team pressing the opposition, his unexpected things that he did would have maybe got you some goals. I don't think he was an easy player to play with, and I don't think he was an easy player to play against. But if you've got a good side I think he would be successful. But if you are an ordinary side and have to have half your game defending or a poor side, then I think you're not going to get the best out of him. Unfortunately, the way I looked at it, that we weren't good enough to have him to get the best out of him, because we were a struggling outfit, when I first came in particular. If you were top of the league, then I think there would place for him. He would have shown his best ... rather than in a middle of the table team. That was my opinion, but he was a good lad, intelligent, no troubles at all, but to get the best out of him, I don't think I ever had a team good enough to show.

Martin Dobson: I just think at that time that Gordon maybe could have handled it better. I know it's difficult as a manager, but I just felt that because Duncan was such a favourite on the terraces, and he was likeable in the dressing room and we had a very good side, I think that extra bit of quality in around the box might have got an extra one or two goals. Because Gordon made it clear that maybe he wasn't working hard enough, there was a bit of criticism there, and that maybe reflected on the terraces. For a club to be successful, everybody needs to be together. I thought Gordon could have realised, we've got a good side here, we could include Duncy in there to do the other little bits and the special moments that maybe just get us over the edge as well. But it was a fraught relationship between them, and maybe we didn't need that if we were going to go for success in the league.

Charles Lambert: One day I was sitting on the team bus getting ready to go on the long journey to Ipswich or Norwich or something like that. The bus was parked outside Bellefield and the players were getting on board and Gordon got on board and he saw me sitting there and he came up and he had a copy of the *Football Echo* from last Saturday in his hands and he slapped it down in front of me and he jabbed at it looking really angry and he said, 'I want an explanation for that' and I'm thinking 'My God what have I done now?' and I looked at the piece and it was a completely innocent feature about Duncan McKenzie's wife, Dot, who had opened a florist's business. For the local paper it was a nice little story 'footballer's wife opens a business' and to make it more interesting she'd opened it right opposite the Kop at Anfield. I said, 'What's wrong with it?' He said, 'Why have you written a piece about Duncan McKenzie's wife. Why haven't you written a piece about Jimmy Pearson's wife? Why don't you write a piece about Mick Buckley's wife?' and I said, 'Well, Gordon, they haven't opened a business let alone a florist shop outside the home of your closest rivals.' He couldn't understand that. For Gordon it was the Duncan McKenzie red rag thing again. It was Duncan grabbing headlines and Gordon wanted the headlines to be grabbed by the people who he thought made a better contribution to the team, like Mickey Buckley and Jimmy Pearson, who worked like the Devil all day long but didn't get many headlines. That was typical of Gordon and it showed how he would champion the players who would run through the brick wall for him. He would absolutely back them to the hilt and that was one of his great qualities. But as a journalist it could be quite frustrating because you knew if you wrote anything about Duncan McKenzie you were going to get it in the neck the following week.

Gordon Lee: As a manager on a Friday night when I go to bed and I pick the team, if I've got a team and I know exactly how they will all play, then I fancy my chances. If I've got one or two players where I'm not quite sure how they will perform, I'm not too happy. He was unpredictable, he had his good points, but I didn't think we could get a team good enough. It's a bit like Rodney Marsh going to Man City in the olden days. He went to Manchester City and they were a good side, top of the league, but it didn't work out. They're not easy players to play with, and the unexpected things they do sometimes look very good. I can understand the public watching the match thinking 'That is very good.' That pleases them, doesn't it?

Bob Latchford's *annus mirabilis*: 1977/78

Ahead of the 1977/78 season, Britain's bestselling newspaper, the Daily Express, offered the prize of £10,000 to any footballer who could score 30 top flight goals – no player had managed to do so since 1971, when Francis Lee's tally was inflated by the number of penalties he took. What started as a tabloid marketing ruse captured the public's imagination in a way that seems almost inconceivable four decades later.

Mike Pejic: We always used to have a go at Bob in training. We used to say, 'you lazy so and so', but you could always find him because he'd be in the right place at the right time, and that's what he used to do. He wouldn't exert his energy in going out in wide positions or running back, he'd stay up there and cause problems to centre-backs. We could always find him and he would be the centre point of our forward play.

Martin Dobson: Latchy was just a great goalscorer, he could score all types of goals, it was just natural for him. The relationship he had with Dave Thomas, whether it was whipped into the near post, he could cushion volley at the near post, if it was stood up at the far stick Latchy was on the end of it with a header.

Gordon Lee: The team set up and the team pattern I wanted to play with was width. David Thomas was possibly the best one in that particular situation, whereby you could get the ball out to him, he'd get down the wing and cross you a good ball. Going back to when I was a young man and things were happening, that was the thing that spectators in those days liked. They liked the winger near the touchline, running down there, beating the full-back and crossing it on goal, they loved that. David Thomas gave them that. That particular season I had Mick Pejic behind him and Martin Dobson and we had a triangle. And even though people watched us play and knew what we were going to do, they couldn't stop us, because that particular triangle in that team was very good.

Mike Pejic: The three of us had a great understanding. We played almost every match for a long period, and we had a really good understanding together. We functioned really well on the left hand side. It was a pleasure to play. We were just so fluent, and that understanding was there every match. It was second nature; we just did everything automatically. The rhythm was there, the understanding.

Bob Latchford: I scored a hat-trick early in the season at QPR and in what seems a rather antiquated gesture, my reward was a case of Scotch whisky. Can you imagine giving a top-flight footballer a crate of spirits as a reward for sporting prowess today? I think it probably says a lot about football back then, when alcohol consumption was a big part of the dressing room team building. I've never been a whisky drinker, so it was shared out amongst my teammates, but I had to pose for the obligatory photo.

Mike Pejic: Bob wouldn't waste his energy, he would save it for the things you wanted him to do, and that was score goals. He used to work those yards around the centre-backs and he used them to good effect, especially around that six to twelve-yard spot where you needed to be brave and Dave used to find him quite a lot and we used to thread balls through to him quite a lot.

Martin Dobson: He was a terrific goalscorer. We used to say to Latchy, keep in the box, we didn't want him outside the box too often, we'd make the chances and he gets on the end of them. If you look at him now, and he looks better physically than when he was playing. He had a big bushy beard, but he was great as well in the dressing room – a quiet guy, a family man. Again, a really good pro, he wanted to do well for Everton. He scored shed loads of goals for Birmingham before he came up, and then he came to us and was consistently good. It was a joy to play with him, and he's a top pro and top person.

Bob Latchford: I scored another hat-trick at home to Coventry in November. The grand finale came two minutes from the end. Martin Dobson hit a perfectly weighted ball for Tizer to run-on to. He was still deep in our own half, but in acres of space. He just ran and ran and ran; the full length of the pitch. As he approached the byline, he looked up and floated in a beautiful cross. I was unmarked at the back post and finished with a left-foot volley to complete my hat-trick. I didn't score many volleys during my career, but this is one I will always savour. The headlines were all about me, but the plaudits really belonged to Dave. I'd scored three times but he contributed four assists. Goodison was rocking and the fans sang: 'We're going to win the league.' On ITV's Big Match, Brian Moore proclaimed, 'That's the goal of a Championship side.' And we players believed them.

Gordon Lee: We were quite experienced, I don't think I had many young lads in to be honest. All those lads you mentioned there, Martin Dobson, Mick Pejic, David Thomas and Bob Latchford for that matter, they were all over 25 and mature, and knew what the game was all about and knew the First Division quite well. I think that was the key to it. Very mature, experienced players.

Bob Latchford: At Christmas 1977 we were second and unbeaten since August. Confidence swelled in our ranks. And yet we knew how hard it would be to be crowned champions. At the top of the table were Brian Clough's Nottingham Forest, who had stunned us on the opening day of the season. They looked well organised, had very solid and good technical players; they played good football and were scoring goals. Above all they were tight and didn't give much away. That as much as anything through the 1970s was the key to success; certainly it was Liverpool's. They didn't ever look like they were going to crack. There wasn't much in it at that stage, but it meant that there was little margin for error. There could be no slip ups. On Boxing Day, Manchester United came to Goodison. They were 12 places and 12 points below us. A week earlier they had been turned over 4-0 by Forest at Old Trafford. This wasn't a vintage United side. In goal they had the novice, Paddy Roche, deputising for Alex Stepney, and the teenage forward, Andy Ritchie. We were never complacent, but we felt we had little to fear.

Duncan McKenzie: Do you know what? We were the better team I'm watching this game and they had six shots and they flew in [Everton lost 6-2]. Some were unbelievable. Gordon Hill scored from the left wing and it was a volley. Lou Macari got a hat-trick. He scored from outside the box. The ball dropped out the air and he's gone whoomp! All I could think was, 'Why us? Why pick on us?'

Gordon Lee: It's funny because Everton usually did well at Man United. I honestly can't remember that day. But I think it takes some getting over losing 6-2, when you've had such a good run. We may have been a little bit short of strength in depth. We had a squad of 15, 16 players, then a gap to the young lads. Whether our squad was big enough to take care of the injuries or suspensions or whatever I'm not quite sure, possibly not.

Bob Latchford: The following day we went to Leeds – where we never got anything – and lost 3-1. From being two points behind Forest, within barely 24 hours we suddenly found ourselves five in arrears. It was a gap that we never looked like making up. There was a time in March where we were a point behind Forest, but they had four games in hand. All season they lost just three league games and were undefeated at home. We waited for a slump, but it never came. They finished nine points ahead of us and seven ahead of Liverpool, who were runners up.

Dave Thomas: It was quite special really. The fans were all aware of it, and they all got behind him, and the players as well. It's not only Bob, it's the whole shebang. They put that reward out at the start, and it was good publicity for them. All of it just gelled together really.

Mike Pejic: To get 30 league goals, blimey! Even nowadays to get 30 league goals… The other thing is we used to play every game then, not like nowadays where there's this rotation lark. The pitches were heavier obviously, and everything else. Tackling from behind and tackling from neck high was evident. You had to put up with that! That's not only from defenders to attackers, I'm talking about attackers to defenders! All in the wash.

Gordon Lee: I think again it's the sort of thing the spectators like. They like the way you score the goals, they like the player to pass the ball out to the wing, the winger goes down and crosses it and people like Bob Latchford get on the end of it, they love that, you know? It doesn't matter how good the opposition is, we can still do it, because Bob Latchford on his day – in terms of the box when the crosses came in – he was as good as anybody. It's one of those things, rapport I think with the spectators. I think they sensed that when David Thomas was on the ball and he went down the wing, that we would get a goal. And they like to see that type of goal, don't they? Well in those days they did anyway.

Bob Latchford: When I woke on the morning of the day of destiny, 29 April 1978, I always knew I was going to score the two goals I needed. I don't think I can think of another situation during my career where I knew for certain something good was going to happen. But I certainly woke up that morning not feeling nervous for the first time ever over a football match. There's always some nerves or butterflies bouncing around, but I woke up that morning feeling mentally calm. I knew with utmost certainty that I was going to score the two goals, no matter what went on in the game.

Gordon Lee: When he was on his game he had practically everything. He was strong, he had good feet, and he was good in the air. When he was on his game he had a good touch, he could power past people because he was strong, and he believed at that time that he was going to score goals.

Martin Dobson: We were all desperate for him in that last match of the season against Chelsea to get those two goals which he needed. Of course, the first goal came across, I headed it, underside of the bar and that's 1-0. Then Neil Robinson scored, and then Billy Wright scored, so we're 3-0 up and Latchy's not scored! Come on, Latchy.

Bob Latchford: Teammates were setting up chances, almost tripping over themselves to hand me opportunities to reach the target, but nothing was forthcoming. On 72 minutes, Mick Buckley crossed the ball into the box, Lyonsy flicked it on and I rose above Steve Wicks to head the ball into the Gwladys Street net. Goodison exploded.

Martin Dobson: It gets to 4-0 and he just needs the one, and it's funny because Lyonsy scored the fifth goal. Lyonsy jumps up and he says to the referee 'Hey I was fouled there ref! It should have been a penalty.' He said, 'You've scored!', but Lyonsy was still adamant he wanted a penalty.

Bob Latchford: I'd never heard a reaction like it. You could almost hear a groan echo around Goodison

Park. Mick, who is perhaps the biggest Evertonian to pull on that royal blue shirt, was bereft. Never in my life had I heard a player celebrate a goal with the word 'sorry' before.

Mick Lyons: You don't really think about things like looking for a penalty; you just play the game naturally and sometimes the referee gives something and sometimes the referee doesn't give it. It's against you also sometimes too; you'll get decisions going for you and sometimes it goes against, but I'm just happy we got that decision that day. Mickey Droy, who was a big lad, shoved me and we got a pen.

Bob Latchford: Dobbo took me aside as the Chelsea players continued to protest. 'Just keep your head down and blast it,' he whispered. I knew exactly where I wanted to put the ball – to Bonetti's right side. There were no nerves. When the referee's whistle shrilled I blasted the ball with my right foot. The roar of the Gwladys Street signalled that I'd fulfilled my task. I ran to the fans and sank to my knees. Fans and players raced towards me. I'd done it.

Jim Pearson: It was the worst penalty kick I've ever seen! He's just slapped it, miskicked it and it went in! But in those days to score 30 goals was great.

Bob Latchford: It was the 50th anniversary of Dixie Dean's 60 goals that week and the great man had come to see the game. As I was leaving Goodison, a lift door opened onto an atrium and there – with his family – was the great man himself. Dixie. 'Well done lad, I'm very pleased for you, very happy.' I was gone at that stage, I'd had too much to drink. Dixie wasn't going to get any sense out of me. So, I thanked him and shook his hand, anxious – perhaps too anxious – to make my leave. He turned to leave to go back to his family and get in the lift. I was about to go down the stairs. He half turned back to me and the 60 goal hero still had this smile on his face. 'Just remember one thing though lad,' he said. 'What's that Bill?' 'You're only half as good as I was.'

Kings Drive

Not only were Everton without a trophy since 1970, but they had been eclipsed locally, nationally and internationally by Bob Paisley's Liverpool during the 1970s. Liverpool, in October 1978, were back to back European Champions, while Everton hadn't even registered a goal against them in two years and a win against them in seven.

Peter Mills: Once Liverpool started to win things they were relentless. The thing about them was that you could never see why they were relentless because television was just coming on then really. You'd see their European matches and they had a lot of average players over the years: Ian Callaghan, Phil Neal, Chris Lawler, Sammy Lee – so many of them who were average players – who probably played about six hundred games each and won loads of cups and loads of trophies; and you thought, 'How could they do that?' But they had a methodical style of play and they were just relentless. They were a machine. Even when they were playing poorly they'd pick up the League Cup, or pick up the Inter-City Fairs Cup or UEFA Cup. I've never hated Liverpool; I've certainly disliked them, but I think they've always earned anything they've got. I don't think they've been lucky, I think they've been great; and they've had shrewd fellows there behind the scenes – Paisley and Fagan; they know football. And they were magnificent there; they played a very simple system, but they could see players. Those average players that I've been talking about, they could see that they were good solid players who could perform week in, week out, get seven out of ten every week, eight out of ten. And they would have top class players, the likes of Souness and Dalglish – they got rid of Keegan and then signed Dalglish to replace him. Dalglish was probably the best footballer I've seen – a magnificent player; just heartbreakingly so.

Jim Pearson: We had so many 0-0 draws against Liverpool because of the fear of losing, especially in those days with so many Scousers playing. We've got Mick Lyons at the back and they've got a Phil Thompson at their end and I'm in the middle watching this ball going backwards and forwards. It wasn't so great that they were going so well at the time either.

Duncan McKenzie: Did I enjoy derby games? You're joking aren't you? I mean in those days you had six or seven Scousers in each team; you had Mick Lyons heading the toilet door on the way out. I'm amazed they bothered kicking off for the first twenty minutes to be honest with you. The first twenty minutes everything got kicked except the ball.

Dave Thomas: At Anfield you were lucky if you got out your own half, they had this way of pegging you back – they steamrolled you. Great side. People use that word great, they were a world class side.

Charles Mills: I hated them. There were some nasty players there. Tommy Smith was a nasty player. Jimmy Case was not fit to be on a football pitch. There were some fine players too – later Hansen and Lawrenson were very, very good players – but I detested the Liverpool team. I still do. Some people mix things and say, 'I don't mind Liverpool, I want Liverpool to do well.' I don't. I never want them to win.

Gordon Lee: Two weeks before you play them, there's a thing when you say, 'Hey we're going to beat you.' If you go into the shop and buy a paper it's 'Hey we'll do you Saturday.' It builds up for two weeks. So therefore when the game is in progress, it's 100 miles per hour which is what it's all about anyway. It's pushing, shoving, running, fighting, scrapping, whatever. It's amazing insofar as it's difficult to play slow football. It's got to be quick action, all action, forward balls, no back passes, no side passes.

Martin Dobson: I was captain on that day, because Micky Lyons was the captain – he was either suspended or injured on that day – and I was vice-captain. Kenny Dalglish was captain of Liverpool of that day because I think it was Thommo who was captain, similar kind of situation. We came out together and the roar, the noise level is unbelievable when you play in those games. Straight away you know there's no hiding place. To win the game you've got to be on top form, and we were both in the top three at that time, and I think by doing that we got to top position, and it's so important that you get off to a good start, and I had even more responsibility as captain as well.

Bob Latchford: Surprisingly for a derby it was a really good game. We had lots of chances and played well throughout. On a different afternoon we could have had three or four goals. I think I probably had my best chance of scoring against them while in the blue of Everton. Played in one on one with an onrushing Ray Clemence I tried to loop a header in from the edge of the penalty area when I should have tried to blast it. But maybe it wasn't meant to be.

Martin Dobson: We got this free kick, Pejic put it in, I knocked it down and of course Andy comes in and volleys it in the top corner. I always had a laugh with Kingy after that and said, 'You shinned it didn't you?' He said, 'Sweet as a nut Dobbo.'

Gordon Lee: When I first went there Everton hadn't beaten Liverpool in God knows how long. But we beat them 1-0, and Andy King scored the goal. It was not so much for me, it was for the fans I felt – the fans would love to beat Liverpool, and that was always in my mind when we beat them, it was such a big thing. We hadn't beaten them in such a long time, and it was a tremendous strike. Because of that Andy King was a hero, wasn't he? And he remained a hero. He had the ability to do that. He had a beautiful right foot, beautiful control and a quick eye. A very sharp lad.

Bob Latchford: It was like a hoodoo had been broken. It was a great afternoon and it became a great evening. We celebrated in the way that we knew best: lots of alcohol and lots of talk of doing it all over again. We drank because that's what players did then, but we drank to switch off and forget. If you're in a stadium with 50,000 people baying for you to win and you actually go and do that, the adrenalin rush, the energy that that gives you is phenomenal. We didn't need reasons to drink on a day like that, but if you're looking for an excuse, one of them would be to switch off.

A failed title challenge: 1978/79

Everton were top of the table as late as February 1979, but their late season form faltered and they finished fourth, seventeen points behind champions Liverpool.

Mark Higgins: Nowadays you get three points for a win and one for a draw, back then it was two and one. We had too many draws in the end. I think with the team we had we really had the chance to go the full way, but it just wasn't to be.

Trevor Ross: I can't recall anybody thinking that we were going to win the league. We would think that we were in with a good chance but you would never think it. In those days everything was a little bit tighter; there wasn't eight, thirteen, fifteen points difference then. It wasn't as distant as what it is now. I suppose in a different way you would always hope that you could win the league. We used to say, 'If we keep going as we're going we're in with a chance.' I think that was the way we would've put it about: that we were in with a chance.

Geoff Nulty: I hate to bring him into the conversation but Bob Paisley said, 'All you think about is the next match and not get carried away.' I didn't get carried away. We might be winning this or we might be winning that, but just look at what's in front of you because you know while you're looking at that there might be something down here and you trip over it. All you do is concentrate on the next match and hope you're going to be in it.

Charles Mills: The difference between Everton and Liverpool in this era was the goalkeeper. Clemence and Lawson. If we'd have had Clemence we'd have won. But in the 60s Liverpool had very ordinary players as well. Shankly won the championship '64 and I think they only used just thirteen players. Shankly made them believe in themselves. They were very ordinary players. Even the likes of Roger Hunt was a workmanlike player; effective. They always seemed to have the rub of the green at the right time too. It wasn't easy being brought up, going to school with that lot in those days, having it pushed down your throat all the time. There was always the feeling the press had a Liverpool bias for some reason. There's still that feeling now I think, isn't there?

Dave Thomas: I think where Everton went wrong is that they should have bought Trevor Francis [Francis joined Nottingham Forest in February 1979 and would score the winner in that season's European Cup Final]. Latch obviously played with him at Birmingham. It's not only about Bob though, and you want at least fifteen to twenty goals from the other striker, and that never happened. Trevor Francis was a good player; I played with him at youth level. But sadly – and no disrespect – they bought Micky Walsh from Blackpool. They paid a club record fee of £325,000. Poor old Walshy, it didn't work out for the lad. He was under a lot of pressure. I don't think that goal helped him – when he won goal of the season on Match of the Day against Sunderland – and it seemed as if the price went up after that. Gordon Lee bought him, and he just didn't have that knack. Even today players get transferred for a lot of money, and sometimes it doesn't work out for them for all sort of reasons.

Gordon Lee: We briefly topped the table in February 1979. I do think we were in the title race. I can't remember the match, something went wrong and we lost it. I do think I was very disappointed that year, I thought that was probably the best chance we would have, and it turned out to be right. We finished fourth. I think that was the stage where we could do something.

Decline or Progress? Investment in youth 1979-81

Having topped the table as late as February 1979, Everton finished the 1978/79 season fourth, 17 points behind champions Liverpool. Barely 23,000 fans turned out to see Everton's final Saturday home game, against Birmingham City. Off the pitch there was discord, with senior players in dispute over contracts – Britain was beset with high inflation at the time – and unhappiness over the coaching regime. By early in the 1979/80 season senior players like Mike Pejic, Colin Todd, Martin Dobson and Dave Thomas had moved on. Liverpool, meanwhile, continued to cast their shadow.

Martin Dobson: He always got a bit of criticism, Gordon, but the players, I've got to say, loved playing for him, because it was on the front foot, with Dave Thomas one side, Gary Jones maybe on the other; Andy King and Trevor Ross in midfield, with Bob Latchford and maybe Duncan McKenzie up the top, or Jim Pearson. Mike Pejic at the back. All of a sudden, we had an excellent side, and we were playing the right way, on the front foot trying to score goals and I got a lot of enjoyment, because we were an excellent side. We finished third then fourth in the league, but we were always under pressure, because of what was happening across the road. They were not only the best team in the country but the best team in Europe.

Duncan McKenzie: Liverpool were a great team. Let's be honest, whatever your allegiance is you have to accept it was a phenomenal team. I made my debut for Leeds in the Charity Shield game when Kevin Keegan and Billy Bremner got sent off and to see those teams lining up you think 'How can anybody beat any of these?' If you looked at those two teams they were pretty much unbeatable in Europe never mind in Britain.

Bob Latchford: The turning point, I think, in Gordon's managerial reign was the loss of Steve

Burtenshaw, who became Queens Park Rangers manager at the start of the 1978/79 season. It took some months for this to manifest itself, but a key part of the balance at Goodison had been lost. Steve and Gordon complimented each other very well. Gordon was so intense, so wrapped up in things, whereas Steve was an easy going Cockney and we responded well to him.

Mike Pejic: The big thing for me was letting Steve Burtenshaw go. It broke up that relationship, that partnership. I felt quite strongly about it because he was the main one for me in that relationship. I thought that's when it started to break up, because I thought although his replacement Eric Harrison was good with youth players, he didn't quite know how to handle senior pros, certainly international pros. I thought that was a big let-down, it didn't work out with a few of us with him. You have to look at his character. I think he felt more at home with youth players, where he maybe could be a bit more vocal with them and it didn't suit quite a few of us the way he handled us seasoned pros. I thought he had an agenda in getting his youth players through to the first team and I thought he lacked a little bit of respect for us who had gained so much for Everton at that time in rebuilding the club. I thought he was disrespectful and I voiced my opinion on that, on a number of occasions!

Geoff Nulty: Eric only played for Barrow and Halifax and there was this thing then the players used to say, 'What's he saying? He's never played for anybody; what does he know about this?' It's an excuse but players are like that at times if you rub them the wrong way.

Charles Lambert: Gordon and Steve worked together superbly because they were so different. Gordon was passionate down to earth a man of football and nothing else. Steve was much more urbane who had a wider experience of life was much more phlegmatic and laid back and the two of them I thought were really, really effective. When Steve left Eric Harrison was promoted and Eric is a brilliant coach and a top man – he proved what a good coach he is when he went to Man United with the kids there [Harrison is credited with bringing through the so-called Class of 92, including the Neville brothers, David Beckham and Paul Scholes] – but I didn't think as a partnership that he was as effective with Gordon as Steve. Gordon and Eric are peas from the same pod, they were just too similar. You didn't get the same imagination for want of a better word. The football they were playing and the way things were being done was too blinkered, whereas Steve, with his experience at Arsenal and with just a totally different attitude, would bring in things that Gordon would never think of. But once he'd gone that didn't happen any more.

Geoff Nulty: When he was at United them young lads, the sixteen-year-olds or eighteen-year-olds, they said, 'There's your man who's going to get you where you want to be.' The same Eric Harrison who didn't make a difference there might have made a difference then because they're so keen and they couldn't go to the manager and say, 'Excuse me a second, I don't like this bloke, he shouts at me.' Maybe that was why Eric was successful there because he taught them, 'Do this, do that, do the other' and they'd all say, 'Yes sir, three bags full.' Of course, the manager picked them because Eric would be very much like Alex Ferguson. Ferguson was a tough guy, he didn't back off anybody; Eric would be the same.

Bob Latchford: I remember one morning at Bellefield, after training, when one of the young apprentices came into the dressing room and told me Gordon wanted to speak. I went into the manager's room and Gordon was in the shower, stark bollock naked. I leant against the door. 'Latch, what's wrong? Tell me what's wrong,' he said. 'Gordon, you know what's wrong, don't you?' He made a sort of groaning noise. 'Yeah, I do,' he answered. But that was it. He knew and I knew, everybody knew what was wrong, but he didn't do anything about it. Whether he could or he couldn't change his coaching staff I don't know because I never pressed him on it; but he knew what the problem was.

Kevin Ratcliffe: I wasn't even eighteen and I always remember getting a little bit of a kick in the teeth when they got a drubbing. Colin Harvey [then youth team coach] was a hard taskmaster and the reserves were training on the next pitch. Colin turned around to us and said 'See that lot over there? That lot there can't get in the first team, they're not good enough.' The first team had just lost heavily. And we looked at Colin and he said, 'You're here with me. So where does that leave you?' He was more or less saying 'Up your game.' Then I realised if that group doesn't move on we don't move into that group. Colin really kept us on our toes day in day out.

Martin Dobson: Micky Lyons used to come in sometimes, and he said, 'Dobbo we'll have to go out on a Tuesday night and have a few bevvies.' I'm talking about the squad here and Lyons is captain. And I said, 'Why's that Lyonsy?' And he said, 'Well Liverpool do it, they go out on a Tuesday night when they've got no game and they don't get rat arsed, but they have a few bevvies and get together, and it's good for morale, togetherness with the team.' I said 'Lyonsy, they're winning things, if we're finishing third and fourth in the league and we're seen out in Liverpool, maybe the Evertonians will think that's the reason why we're not number one.' I was thinking about it from a different perspective back then. When you start reflecting on it now, you think maybe that was just one thing that might have given us an extra five per cent, you're always looking for that to get better. Let's face it, a dressing room it is like a work place, but it could be that when you socialise, you get to know them a bit better, and then all of a sudden, things start happening.

Bob Latchford: In one pre-season game at Hertha Berlin all the anger and frustration boiled over. Colin Todd was being played out of position, again at right-back. We knew he wasn't happy about this, and we were aware of the madness of the situation. He'd played all his life as a centre-half, and was a terrific central defender. In that position, he was one of the most difficult players I ever played against. That afternoon something snapped. The game was going on and all of a sudden Toddy was just walking across the field. He got to the touchline, took his shin pads off, threw them down, took his shirt off and proclaimed, 'I'm not playing there. That's it. I'm not a full-back and I'm not playing there any more.' It was chaos in the dressing room at half time. People were shouting and arguing and suddenly Eric started on Dave Thomas. Tizer was one of the most unassuming and placid members of the Everton squad. I don't know why Eric chose to have a go at him, but he started ranting about his rubber soled boots: 'You should be wearing fucking studs; get your stockings up, get your shin pads on.' Tizer for the first and only time I'd ever known, blew it. He swore – Tizer never swore – he was swearing, and his boots came off, his shirt came off. 'Fuck this and fuck you; I'm not playing.'

Paul Lodge: It was genuinely about money. The lads felt as though they got really close that year, quite rightly, and they asked for pay rises. I think a lot of them were out of contract at the same time which, again, the club were at fault. It left the club in a vulnerable situation and I think the club and Sir John Moores called their bluff. He wouldn't pay them want they wanted but didn't think they would leave and they did. We lost a great team overnight

Dave Thomas: I loved my time at Everton. We had a good side, I liked the manager. The only reason I left Everton was because I was in a contract dispute. That's all. In those days, there were no agents. My contract was coming up for renewal, and Bill Shankly used to come into Bellefield every morning.

I'm quite a private person really, and I thought I might ask for a bit of advice from Shankly. I've never been a guy who had an agent. I always did [contract negotiations] myself or my wife did it; even in my day I was very wary of people in football. These agents – there's good and bad everywhere – but they are just parasites, the lot of them. Why would I want them to negotiate on my behalf when I can do it myself and get some support with the PFA and pay them 20% or whatever. Shankly said no problem as he used to live round the corner from the training ground. So he said 'Yeah come round', and I wish I didn't tell the football club. He gave me some advice, because he was familiar with Liverpool and the players of my era. I'd had two great seasons at Everton, but there was no ill-feeling with the football club whatsoever, Gordon Lee, and obviously he gave me a guideline of what to ask for you see. So I went to Gordon Lee and he said would you like to meet the chairman, it was a guy called Philip Carter, a lovely man. So he had a meeting at his Littlewoods Office, and nothing came out of it, so in a funny sort of way I thought 'I will put in a transfer request.' And Everton allowed me to go.

Despite struggling in the league – Everton would finish the season nineteenth - they reached the semi-finals of the 1980 FA Cup against Second Division West Ham.

Bob Latchford: We were drawn in a semi-final at Villa Park with West Ham. Our opponents were then in the Second Division and we really fancied our chances. It said a lot about the season I was having that I only started from the bench, but from the dugout I could see that we had the measure of our opponents. We took the lead two minutes before half time through a Brian Kidd penalty and had West Ham cold. I couldn't see a way back into it for them. The game turned in the 63rd minute. For reasons only he can explain Brian got involved in an off the ball tangle with Ray Stewart that developed into a fight. It was inexplicable and inexcusable and cost us dearly. He was sent off. Seven minutes later Trevor Brooking broke down the left and cut in from the byline to set up Stuart Pearson for an easy goal. Gordon to his credit still went for the win, bringing me on in place of Gary Megson, but from a winning position we were now left with a replay at Elland Road the following Wednesday.

Kevin Ratcliffe: Obviously we'd lost a striker and the day of the replay I'm coming out the lift in the team hotel with Joe McBride. Me and Joe have been talking; Joe's going to be playing, I'm not even thinking I'm going to be on the bench. So we go to go down for pre-match lunch, and as we get into the lift Gordon Lee is walking out. As he walks out, we get in the lift, and just as the double doors are shutting Gordon turns back and say to me 'You're playing' and to Joe, 'You're not.' And before Joe can actually have a go at him for not playing, the doors are shut! Joe was devastated. But that's just how Gordon was!

Bob Latchford: Elland Road, where the replay was staged, was never one of the happier grounds I visited. The replay was a tight and testy game that finished goalless after 90 minutes, but we should have had it won by then. In extra time, Alan Devonshire put West Ham ahead with a superb solo goal. We had to pull on all reserves to try and retrieve something and we did just that. Billy Wright broke down the right flank and sent in a low hard cross; I dived at the near post, made a connection and the ball flew past Phil Parkes into the back of the net, right in front of the Evertonians. It was a brilliant moment. I climbed onto the security fences, my hands aloft, as supporters charged forward trying to touch me.

Kevin Ratcliffe: What Gordon decided to do once again was move Billy to right-back. People say 'What did he do with John Gidman?' And I say 'John Gidman was supposed to do a man to man job on the lad Alan Devonshire, which he did.' But Devonshire scored, so he mustn't have done it that good!

Bob Latchford: We were heading for a second replay, but then one of those freak moments that typified this era for Everton struck. Ninety seconds from the end, a long cross from Ray Stewart was headed back across our penalty area, and who should be there, but the right-back Frank Lampard, who headed home the winner. He hadn't scored in a year and I don't think he'd scored with a header in his entire life. It was unbelievable. I sometimes think about like Mario Balotelli and his famous t-shirt emblazoned, 'Why Always Me?' That's how I felt back then. But it kept happening to us over a period of time. Carlisle, Clive Thomas, Chris Nicholl and now this. It wasn't just one thing, it was a catalogue of misfortune.

In the summer of 1980 Andy King and George Wood joined the list of Goodison departees. Lee, who had given debuts to young players such as Kevin Ratcliffe, Graeme Sharp, Martin Hodge and Gary Megson the previous season pledged to invest his faith in youth. On the opening day of the 1980/81 season his team included Ratcliffe, Megson, Sharp, as well as the winger Joe McBride and Steve McMahon. In total there were six home-grown players in the starting XI. Everton lost that day at Sunderland, but by October were as high as third before their form started to slip away. They would end the season fifteenth.

Gordon Lee: I said to the chairman 'I'm not going to go and try and sign any more players, particularly in that age group, the mature age group. I'm going to put the young lads in the side. I had Graeme Sharp then, Kevin Ratcliffe, Stevie McMahon. I put the young lads in the side. I thought to myself, the best chance we've got is maybe in the cup, because in the cup you only had to play well every three or four weeks. I was a bit worried if you've got young lads, what they're not going to do is play 40 matches on the trot all up to scratch. We started off the season very, very well, and I think Stevie McMahon might have got an U21 cap or something like that. We then went into the cup matches. On the whole we had tough cup matches but did well.

Paul Lodge: I just couldn't believe it. I was only a young lad and I felt, 'Where are all the players going now?' Initially I thought it was going to help me but I know for a fact when I broke into the first team [in the second half of the 1980/81 season] if I would have been surrounded by more experienced players I think it would've helped me 90%. I came into a team – and I'm not making excuses up because I still have nightmares about it – that was in free fall. 15,000 people at Goodison booing. You could hear everything. You'd rather be playing in front of 40,000 instead of 15,000 and that affected me badly.

John Bailey: I can remember when we were having a bad time and Gordon was under pressure. We got a lot of seat cushions thrown from the stands at our heads. Me and Bob Latchford had to run for cover. Can you imagine a cushion coming from the top balcony at Goodison? So they weren't happy days, no.

Gordon Lee: I think it was a tall ask and a tall order, but to be quite honest when I did that I was fed up of the difficulties of dealing with 28 to 30-year-old players. I said 'This is where it goes now, I've been successful for a period of time at Everton with a mature side, and now I'm going to go the other way and put young players in.' I said to the chairman, 'It might not be the best thing for Gordon Lee, but I think it will be the best thing for Everton Football Club,' and the lads I think they went on to do well. Unfortunately, time is against you sometimes in football, you haven't got time for the young lads to get there, you've got to be successful all the time.

Paul Lodge: You go back to the Alan Hansen quotation, 'You can't win anything with kids.' He got caught out with that, but in our case he was right. We were all good players but we could have done with that extra year and certainly with experience around us.

Gordon Lee: Graeme Sharp probably was the best signing I made. I think I paid about £80,000 for him from Dumbarton. When I think about it, he played 11 or 12 years for Everton, he was very successful when he played, and they sold him for £500,000 to Oldham Athletic. That's got to be the best signing that certainly I ever made. You get 11 or 12 years' service and you make all that profit on him. It wouldn't happen now. He was good and he did very, very well. When I first took him I met his parents and his parents were lovely people. The only worry I had was whether he would get used to the rough and tumble of being alone in Liverpool. But in fairness to the lad he did very well, worked very hard and became a very good centre-forward.

Graeme Sharp: Gordon Lee was a lovely guy. I remember speaking to him at Dumbarton, he phoned me after a game and told me he had been at that game. The scout Harry Cooke was a regular visitor to watch me play for Dumbarton and then Gordon got the chance to come up and see me one night. We played Arbroath at home. I think we got beaten. I managed to score but Gordon had left by the time I'd scored. I got the call the next morning and I spoke to Gordon and he invited me down. I had no idea; I was naïve because I had been down to Aston Villa before with Dean Saunders. I trained with them. But Gordon invited me down, but it wasn't to train or anything else. I thought I was just going to see the place and look around, having no idea that I would be driving back up to Glasgow that night as an Everton player. But I came down and signed.

Gordon Lee: Graeme had this mixture of neatness, tidiness, but he could also mix it. He was a good football player when I first saw him. When he first came to England in the First Division, I thought if he learns how to mix it, take care of himself physically, then he would be a very good player. When it happened I went up with Harry Cooke to see the team play and I only saw him for 10 minutes and I said to Harry we'll try and sign him. He looked like what I was looking for, and at the same time I was looking at Ian Rush. I had a vision of Graeme Sharp playing with Ian Rush, but in fairness we couldn't afford both, and in fact we went for the cheaper one. Liverpool were always that bit better in terms of finding a bit more money, you know? They paid about £300,000 for Rushy from Chester, but at the time I thought I'd love to have those two together. It was just a vision I had about Graeme and Rushy, because I thought Rushy was a very good player. He was a very good forward as well, different type of player.

Bob Latchford: Kevin Ratcliffe was the other youngster that stood out a mile. He had presence as a defender, but also as a man. Even as a teenager you could tell that once he established himself he would be a leader. The success that followed for him never surprised me at all. Steve McMahon too was a good little player, a hard worker, who achieved great things, but in a Liverpool shirt.

Gordon Lee: Kevin Ratcliffe had two outstanding assets, one was that he was left-footed, which is a bit of a balance on the football field, but he also had tremendous pace, particularly the early pace; even though he wasn't tall for a centre-back, his pace would get him out. When you are an opposing forward you know you aren't going to beat him for pace. If you're playing against a slow player as a centre half and you're a forward, you think I'll beat him, but Kevin Ratcliffe...

Despite facing strong opposition – Arsenal, Liverpool – who were memorably beaten by an Imre Varadi winner – and Southampton, Everton reached the quarter-finals of the 1981 FA Cup and were handed a home draw against Manchester City in the quarter-finals.

Gordon Lee: We were winning 2-1, and I remember ten minutes from time and the left-back gave Imre

Varadi a daft back pass, trying to get it to Joe Corrigan. It went straight to Imre, and he could have put it in with his back side, and he missed it. The thing is, Imre Varadi was one of those lads if he had a lot of time, he'd make a mess of it, if he hadn't much time he'd score. He had so much time that he could have gone off and come back on and scored it. Anyway he missed that, five minutes from time, I thought they had packed up. At that stage we weren't playing well, we were winning 2-1 and I thought we're through anyway. They kicked a long ball down the middle, it went over Mick Lyons, he let it go, and Paul Power chasing a lost cause poked it in the net. 2-2, and we lost the replay. That was the beginning the end of me.

Mark Higgins: I think you do see it coming when you don't get the results and you're not getting the things what the club want. It's a tough job.

Howard Kendall: In reality I knew I was coming home months before the end of the 1980/81 season. I'll always recall one Sunday morning when a gentleman turned up on my doorstep claiming to be representing an unnamed First Division club. I invited him in and we had a short chat, but I think the purpose of the visit was to check on me; see what sort of person I was; make sure I had a stable, family background – which, of course, I did.

Gordon Lee: I knew that when we got beat in the cup, I knew then, I thought then that was my only hope. If we had beaten Man City and got to the semi-final and got to the cup final that might have been me okay. But once we got beat in that game with Man City and put that with the inconsistent performances of a young team which was down the league, then that was the time where I thought, 'Well that's it.' It didn't surprise me, let's put it that way.

John Corbett: It seemed to be an almost robotic series of results season after season, whereas Everton tended to be doing what Everton do best – they raise your expectations only to dash them down again within a few months. Liverpool seemed to just steamroller on. And you had other teams of course who would now begin breaking Liverpool's sequence – teams like Nottingham Forest, Aston Villa [who won the title in 1981 and the European Cup a year later], and you began to think, well why can't we do that? The period from 1970 to 1984 was an incredibly frustrating period; it seemed to go on forever. And the fact that you had managers, such as Billy Bingham, who talked a good game but couldn't deliver on the pitch made matters even worse.

Peter Mills: The 1970s were pretty drab really, although there was some fun. I went to quite a lot of away matches in the seventies and I enjoyed them, because they still had some entertainment, particularly in the late 70s, with McKenzie and Latchford, Thomas, and even fellows like Jim Pearson, quite skilful players. They looked like they were almost there. There were a lot of near-misses in the space of 14 years, from 1970 to 1984. We're looking now [in 2017] 22 years since we won something. And that was only 14 years and there was a lot of near-misses condensed into that time. How bad did it get? It didn't get as bad as it has done since, because you were always just within touching distance.

Gordon Lee: It's a good club, you're proud to be the manager, the people are good people, the supporters are good as well, but I just wish – and it will be me dying wish probably – that we would have won the match against Liverpool and won the cup. That's probably my only downside, I would have loved to have won the FA Cup for them, but if your name's on it your name's on it, and I don't think it was unfortunately.

The Edge of Heaven
1981-1990

'The football, if you could afford to go, took you into a world where there was hope. It was Everton Football Club, they were still playing, there was still hope. No matter what Maggie Thatcher did – she may have closed the factories and the mines and the steel works – she didn't close Goodison Park.'

George Orr

Howard Kendall appointed manager

Within days of the 1980/81 season drawing to its disappointing conclusion, Gordon Lee's departure as Everton manager was confirmed. In his place Howard Kendall was appointed player-manager.

Howard Kendall: I knew I was coming home months before the end of the 1980/81 season. It was a done deal irrespective of whether Blackburn were promoted or not. Gordon Lee's contract was coming to an end and the Everton board were not going to renew it. I knew that the opportunity of managing a club like Everton wasn't one that arose every day. Indeed the chance of managing your club was one that came to few players, and only then once in a lifetime. Everton, I should be clear, were my club at that stage. Once you're bitten by the Everton bug, nothing is ever the same again.

Keith Tamlin: Howard's reputation as a player was second to none as was his reputation as a progressive up and coming manager. There was unanimity in approaching him to become manager. Philip Carter, one of our greatest Chairmen, conducted the negotiations and we were fortunate to obtain the services of one of our most successful managers.

Howard Kendall: The trophyless years had gnawed away at every fan, but been worsened immeasurably by the fact that Liverpool had comprehensively overtaken their great rivals. Since 1970 Liverpool had won the League Championship five times and an FA Cup, but had also started to dominate in Europe, winning the European Cup and UEFA Cup twice apiece. They also had a third European Cup Final against Real Madrid in Paris looming. My intention, I told the press, was to match Liverpool. I knew if we were to achieve this we'd be one of the best teams in the world.

Kevin Ratcliffe: Howard was like a breath of fresh air, although I didn't dislike it under Gordon. Like at the start of pre-season, you got five and a half weeks to get fit, not five days, but it was still competitive. It was little things that he was instilling, team games in training. Although I never figured early on, I could see what he was trying to do and I was thinking, 'Hold on a minute, this suits me, I like this.' Although I maybe had my differences with him for leaving me out and not putting me in, there must have been something there that he liked about me.

Peter Eastoe: We used to have a lot of ball work which was completely different and five aside games, which were like FA Cup ties. They were absolutely superb and suited me. I loved playing the five-a-sides; they were top class and you've got Colin Harvey and the gaffer playing too. You had one on either side; what a great game you used to have. I tell you what, they were better than on a Saturday if you'd have seen those games! It was wonderful.

Alan Ainscow: The work was done in the week, the fitness side, and by the time you got to Thursday, Friday you become a bit more technical, i.e. you'd play forwards v defence or you'd play a bit of shadow to get yourself into a pattern. He liked to play a lot of eleven v elevens because that's what happened on a Saturday and it makes sense.

Howard Kendall: I brought Mick Heaton in from Blackburn as my assistant manager. I'd developed a very close relationship with Mick at Ewood Park, promoting him from reserve team coach to first team coach. He knew the way my mind worked and brought tremendous enthusiasm to the training pitch and dressing room. One member of Gordon's backroom team that was going nowhere was Colin Harvey, who was initially in charge of the reserve team. Together we would reprise our old partnership with enormous success.

Neville Southall: Colin, for me, epitomised what a Scouser is and personified that wide array of heavy expectation. Footballers have to be aggressive in the right way and Colin was just that: he was aggressive in his training, he was aggressive in his play, he was aggressive in chasing what he wanted. Off the pitch he was mild mannered and charming, but on it he was different. He had been a great player but was forced to retire through injury five years earlier. You could still see that style about him on the training pitch, that he had a good football brain in his head, that he could use both feet; that he was the sort of stylish player that the club had once been synonymous with. He led by example. He trained and trained and trained. Players looked at him and were inspired by what he did. Even years later, when he was in his fifties and was having to get plastic hips put in, he'd get bollockings off the surgeon for training when he should have been resting.

Howard Kendall: Colin was such an intense presence. If you ask many of those players who wrote their name into Goodison lore just a few years later, they will point to Colin's coaching as being integral to their success. When he came into the coaching room to talk to you on a Monday, you knew he'd been deliberating and thinking about things all weekend. We didn't have modern technology in those days and he would play the game again and again on a VHS player. He'd stop the tape, write the counter number down, make a note and start again. I had words with the players after the game but he used to get them in individually on a Monday morning and go through it again. 'What were you told after the game?' he'd ask. 'Have a look.' He would stop the tape at that particular point, and show them where they'd gone wrong, or how they could improve. He'd watched the game all weekend long; he knew it inside out, and the players too. He was a great worker; an absolutely fabulous worker and would be crucial to me and Everton Football Club.

John Bailey: I remember getting a man of the match award. I carried two or three bottles of champagne home on a Saturday night after a game at Goodison and I thought I was the bees knees. I went into Bellefield on the Monday morning and the finger came from the coach's room, 'Come here Bailsy.' He sat me down and showed me a video of the match. [To him] I had a nightmare. That was Colin: he picked and picked.

Derek Mountfield: Colin had everything. He was a fantastic footballer, he still had the best touch in the game. His first touch was fantastic. But he had the patience, and what he did do a lot, which a lot of youngsters appreciated – people like Gary Stevens and Kevin Richardson and other players who were trying to come through at the time – when we had a training session on a Tuesday he'd say 'Right then you're back later, you're back, you're back' and we're going, 'Oh no.' Then he would go to the senior players and go 'And you, and you, and you are as well.' So people who weren't involved in the first team, like Mick Ferguson, Alan Biley, Alan Ainscow, Alan Irvine, Jim Arnold – came and trained with the young lads in the afternoon. Straight away I'm working with experienced first teamers.

Neville Southall: Howard was a football manager in the true sense of the word. He wanted everything done with the ball. On a typical day we'd arrive at Bellefield between 9am and half-past. We'd play some head tennis and go out. We did a warm up, a little circle, a game of some sort; probably a bit of shooting, maybe a few little sprints, and that would be it. We'd be finished by quarter-past or half-past twelve, maximum. Sometimes we did some running, but not very much. Howard believed that if you were successful you didn't need to run on the training ground. Playing 70 games a season was enough and you just needed to do enough to tick over.

Howard the player

Kendall also returned for first team duties, playing six times in the 1981/82 season and regularly turning out for the reserves.

Kevin Ratcliffe: He actually got persuaded by Mick Heaton to play. I don't think he wanted to, but I think we were such a young squad and I don't think he fancied the older pros; didn't trust them. Howard had a standard. I think the older guard were getting pushed out a little bit because the manager viewed this is as game for a lot of the younger people. And I think that is what was happening, slowly but surely. But for him to pick himself, an old guy, I think that was more as an education to the players. I remember playing against Coventry with him. It was great when you had the ball, but when you didn't have the ball Howard was an absolute nightmare. Training sessions were the same. He was at an age where he never gave the ball away.

Alan Irvine: Howard was great for the young players. I came in, I didn't expect to play for Everton that season [1981/82], because of the jump [from Scottish football where Irvine played in the lower leagues with Queens Park]. But as it happens, Howard played in a lot of the reserve games, and there were a number of us in that reserve team at that time – Graeme Sharp, Gary Stevens, Kevin Richardson, Alan Harper, Kevin Ratcliffe. A whole load of lads who became first team players and very, very important players for Everton. And what we had was Howard Kendall, who was kind of playing in there with us and coaching us as we were going along.

Colin Harvey: He had a style of playing at Blackburn, and he brought the idea with him. He was having problems adapting it, or the Everton players were having problems adapting to it. He said, 'Do you think I should play to do it?' And I thought 'No'. Because I'd watched him in training, and although he still had his touch, he didn't have the fitness and mobility he'd had, and to go back into what was the old First Division then, I didn't think he was up to it and I told him. He played a couple of games and said I was right!

The signing of Neville Southall

Kendall made seven signings in summer 1981. Most of the so-called 'Magnificent Seven' were destined for Goodison failure, with one significant exception.

Neville Southall: In July 1981 Liverpool was ravaged by some of the worst inner city rioting seen in the twentieth century, arising from long-standing tensions between the city's police and the local black community. In nine days of riots centred on Toxteth, hundreds were injured, more than 500 people were arrested and scores of buildings were razed to the ground. It was quite a change from sleepy Llandudno or Bury. When [the Bury manager] Jim [Iley] drove me in to sign the city was literally on fire.

Howard Kendall: I got some stick about my signings, dubbed the 'Magnificent Seven' [Alan Biley, Mick Ferguson, Jim Arnold, Alan Ainscow, Neville Southall, Mick Walsh and Mickey Thomas]. Perhaps some of it was fair; but Neville Southall was my number one buy, so how can you criticise me on the other six?

Neville Southall: There was no great ceremony or anything like that. I was just a lower league signing, one of seven players Howard would buy that summer. There was hardly even anyone at Goodison, just Howard, Jim Greenwood the club secretary, and Jim MacGregor, the doctor. I don't think anyone else knew who I was. There's a famous story about Tommy Lawton, the great 1930s centre-forward signing for Everton and getting the tram to Goodison. He was spotted by a conductor who came up to him and asked if he was Lawton, the new signing. 'I am,' said the young striker. 'You'll never be as good as Dixie,' came the blunt assessment. But afterwards when I got on the bus and went back home to Bury nobody even recognised me.

Mark Higgins: He came into the club and we didn't bat an eyelid, he's so laidback now. As a player, I can see it now, the amount of times the ball went over my head, and one thing about Nev was that he would come through and clatter me and hit everything, but he would punch or go and catch the ball, that was the good thing about him. He was so hard to beat in training as well. No one would dare to take the mickey because he would chase them round the pitch.

Howard Kendall: I first got a whisper about Neville a year earlier from a very good friend of mine called Norman Jones, who had a public house in Llandudno. Neville was playing for Winsford United in the Cheshire League at the time and Norman told me that he was a local phenomenon and that his father drank in his pub. I asked him what the pub was called, and he said it was The Neville. I knew then that we were fated.

Kevin Ratcliffe: Jim Arnold was fantastic for Everton. He was the one that maybe gave Nev that breathing space to be the keeper that he was. Jim was a great shot stopper.

Howard Kendall: I knew Neville wasn't quite ready for the first team, but that it was only a matter of time. So I signed Jim Arnold from Blackburn as well, who I knew I could depend upon. I knew it would be a bit much to jump from non-league to the First Division in barely a year and I saw Jim as a short-term answer to my problems. But I never doubted Neville.

Alan Ainscow: He was always out twenty minutes before and he used to get told off at times because you know you're not properly warmed up. There was always a goal at the back of the gym and you'd start firing them in and Neville would be there and he would go for everything. It was like he'd just make sure that nothing was going past him no matter what. That was his attitude.

Peter Eastoe: In five-a-side games in training, Neville used to be in goal at one end. My word, you used to hit some balls, which used to go flying in the top corner and you'd think, 'That's a goal.' I'll tell you what he used to pick it out out the top corner. He was an absolutely superb goalkeeper, Neville.

Howard Kendall: We played [for the reserves] at a near-empty Goodison, which was always a privilege, but there was none of the pressure accompanying me. I was there to help the young players in our ranks, and what a bunch we had. The most naturally gifted among them was Neville. I could tell he was going to be phenomenal. Some of the saves he made were superlative. Contrary to what he and other people think I don't think he's ever been shy. He used to ask me for a lift back from training because he couldn't drive at the time and I lived near his home in Ramsbottom. You wouldn't have asked Harry Catterick for a ride, but you could ask me; I was more of a player's manager than a manager upstairs in an office. You'd congratulate Neville after a reserve team game where he's had probably one save to make and he'd reply, 'Bored. I'm bored,' and slouch off back to the dressing room. Some keepers do work harder in training than they do on match days, but it's the decision making on match day which is most important. Neville at that stage perhaps didn't have that; he lacked experience. But it was only really ever a matter of time.

Stuart Rimmer: Neville helped me because I was training against him every day. He used to hate me scoring against him or anybody scoring against him in training. He was unbelievable. You could tell straight away as soon as they signed him; it's surprising nobody else did to be honest. He was in the Central League team for about a year with us but you could tell he was going to be a good goalie because he had everything. He was a modest guy. First into training and he stayed later because he'd ask some of the young lads to do shooting practice with him every day. If you could get past Neville you could get past anybody.

Neville Southall: By the start of 1982 I was the only one of Howard's 'Magnificent Seven' regularly getting a place in the starting line up. Alan Biley was loaned out to Stoke and then sold at the end of the campaign to Portsmouth, where the goals flowed again. Mickey Thomas was kicked out and sold to Brighton after he was supposed to have refused to play for the reserves. I couldn't really see that to be honest; Mickey's not one to have bust ups. Like me he just wants to play football and if he's not he's a nuisance. I think Howard was just looking for someone different. Neither Jim Arnold, Alan Ainscow, Mick Ferguson or Mike Walsh could get a game, and all except Jim would be gone within a year or so. I was finding my feet, but to be fair so was Howard. He used 27 players that season; a huge number at a time when there was only one substitute allowed.

Howard Kendall: That first season at Everton was one of quiet evolution. I learned a lot about the players that I inherited and the ones that I bought. None of the 'Magnificent Seven' barring Neville lasted more than a couple of years at Everton. I was always quick to move players on if I could see that that they didn't have a role to play. I was never one for having players toiling endlessly in the reserves; it did neither them, their market value, nor the squad any good at all. Far better to move them and bring someone else it.

Everton in the early-1980s

Howard Kendall: The manner in which Everton was run was very different to Blackburn. It was professional. The board were mostly comprised of the directors of the Littlewoods corporation. They were top business people, running the football club as a business. That came from the very top: the old man, Sir John Moores, wouldn't have it any other way. The Financial Management Committee of the board would set targets and my budget would be set accordingly. For example, there'd be a target of an average gate of maybe 18,000; and I'd be told that. And then they would decree that that covered all the expenses and wages and everything else. Anything over that would be given to the manager to spend on the players, anything beyond the third round of the FA Cup was given it to the manager. As long as the fundamentals of the club were run on an even keel, it was given to the manager. It was so much simpler then than it is today. In fact it was a lovely way of running it.

Lord Grantchester: Sir John kind of backed away from being too active in the Club, is probably the way to put it, in that he stepped down from being chairman. With all the fuss with Maxwell and the ownership of Pools as well as a football club he stepped out from being involved in the day-to-day management of the Club. He always put the chief executive of Littlewoods onto the Board and others he had confidence in. He populated the Board and he had faith in them to run the Club. Sir Philip Carter was obviously one which we all know and was there a long time and who was successful in not only bringing Littlewoods on and helping develop Littlewoods, the stores but also Everton and involvement in the Football League. Sir John was very happy to talk to the various people whom he respected who then got on and did it for him. I don't know Abramovich but I'm sure he would be similar at Chelsea. He wasn't then on the Board but was there in the background, providing stability and making sure things were running well.

Kevin Ratcliffe: He was trying everything Howard, when you look back. He was always the first into the football club. You'd go in and every light would be on – 'Why are the lights on today? It's a sunny day.' He wanted to make it as bright as possible, not gloomy. Training never changed; it never changed. He believed in what we were doing was the right thing. For me it was all about getting the right sort of formula on the pitch – everything off the pitch was spot on. But I just think he couldn't get that; that right midfield selection. He tinkered about with that so much, playing himself. And then all of a sudden it clicks, doesn't it?

Howard Kendall: If I wanted to buy a player I'd contact the secretary, Jim Greenwood. The two of us virtually ran the club together and we'd be talking constantly. Jim would then notify the chairman and the chairman would go around the directors, and they'd sanction it. Philip Carter was managing director of Littlewoods at the time; a huge job in its own right, but if I ever wanted to speak to him I'd simply have to pick up the telephone. He was always there when I needed him. But, as I say, I would know the financial position and wouldn't ask if I didn't think there was a realistic chance of getting.

Neville Southall: If you look at the team it was good. It just wasn't gelling in the way that Howard wanted it to gel. We ended the 1981/82 season with a flourish, winning five of the last six games and drawing the other and finished eighth, which, for a team in transition, was okay. But Liverpool were miles ahead of us, winning the title and finishing 23 points in front. So the pressure was really on.

Howard Kendall: What did I learn from those first days in the Goodison hotseat? That pressure and expectation were high. That many of the players I'd bought and inherited were not talented enough to take the club to where I wanted it to be. But also that we had some good young players, who were going to mature into top class professionals. Neville, who played in just over half our league games, was the prime example, but there were others too.

Neville Southall: People look at this as a difficult period in the club's history and maybe it was. Home crowds were often below 20,000, while Liverpool were riding high, winning League Championships and European Cups. But we had a good young team too, one that was learning quickly and gaining experience that would stand us well a few years down the line. By the end of the season several players, who many would consider among the greatest in the club's history had broken through.

Howard Kendall: I first saw Kevin Ratcliffe when he was playing in the Everton reserve team at Blackburn. I tried to sign him in an exchange deal with a centre-forward I had called Kevin Stonehouse that Harry Cooke was ringing me about fairly often. Everton came back and said no, but my loss as Blackburn manager was to be my own long term gain. Kevin was a fabulous captain and centre-back. He was initially playing left-back but wasn't making an impression as he was more technically suited to the centre, where had more space and options. He had tremendous pace; I was trying to build from the back with the change of pace in Gary Stevens and Ratcliffe and I thought it really was vital in the way I wanted to play it.

Neville Southall: He brought back an old favourite, Andy King. Andy was a much, much better player than anybody gave him credit for. He was one of the best finishers I've ever come across. He was just magnificent in training; he could bend it, smash it, he had real quality. Lots of people think he's a bit of an idiot because he used to mess about, but when he put his mind to it he was brilliant. But second time around I think it was wrong time, wrong place. I think Howard wanted someone who would take on more defensive responsibilities. He worked hard enough but to me he was another free spirit, he lacked the sense of responsibility Howard sought.

Howard Kendall: Adrian Heath was someone I had signed after I'd missed out on Bryan Robson. I'd played with Adrian at Stoke and he was a record signing for Everton. I looked, constantly, for what the paying public would consider an 'Everton type of player'. By that I meant men who liked to go forward, have a crack at goal and entertain the fans. Adrian was one of those players, but perhaps mindful of his price tag not every supporter took to him straight away. He had a bit of a slow start and took time to develop, but he was still only 21 and although he wasn't scoring bagfuls of goals he was getting into some tremendous positions. It was all about learning; progress; atuning to the pressures of the First Division.

Neville Southall: He was another one of those players – we had a few of them at the time – that was full of energy. He was a terrific little player, super-confident and brave little bugger too. He didn't mind getting hurt and with his pace it meant we could put pressure on defenders at the other end.

Howard Kendall: Liverpool's reserve midfielder Kevin Sheedy was a player that Colin Harvey had spotted. I went to Preston to see him play for Liverpool Reserves with Colin and you could see his potential. His left foot that was like a wand; his technique glorious. But I didn't think he had what it took. 'Superb effort but I think he's lazy, Col,' I said. 'Take him,' he said. Colin was only ever forthright about the very best players. It was an important part of our partnership; appreciating his opinions and knowing when he was right, even if doubts crossed your mind. 'Alright,' I said. 'We'll take him.'

Everton 0, Liverpool 5
6 November 1982

Howard Kendall: In the week before the derby we were unsettled by an injury to Mark Higgins. In his place I brought in Glenn Keeley on loan from Blackburn. He was a good centre-back, who I trusted, and he had some big game experience while playing for Newcastle in the mid-1970s.

John Bailey: I remember Howard pulling me to one side at Bellefield and he said 'I've got Glenn on loan.' I said, 'Glenn who?' He said, 'Glenn Keeley.' So I went, 'You what?' I'd played with Glenn at Blackburn. He'd played for Newcastle and played in the League Cup final for Newcastle so he was an experienced player so I thought he can handle it. But unfortunately he was up against Dalglish. And we know what happened, don't we? He turned him inside out.

Mark Higgins: Howard and I had had a word, and I was dropped for that game. I sat in the stands alongside Kevin Ratcliffe. Glenn Keeley was brought in on loan and played in that game, but that was his one and only game. I saw Howard on Monday at training and he said, 'Don't say a word to me you're playing the next game.'

Howard Kendall: Glenn was sent off after 37 minutes with Everton trailing to an Ian Rush goal. Rushy scored another three times and Mark Lawrenson added a fifth. It was a shocking afternoon. People ask me if the 5-0 defeat to Liverpool was the lowest point in my managerial career, but I can truthfully say that it wasn't.

Neville Southall: How good were Liverpool? I knew how good they were, but in my mind that was them over there. Anfield might as well have been the moon for all I cared. They were nothing to do with me. I only worried about the things that I could actually control and the only thing I could control was me and doing what I had to do to stay in the team and help it do better. If Liverpool won the European Cup it was nothing to do with us. The troublesome neighbours weren't my interest or problem.

Howard Kendall: Of course you want the final whistle to blow about half-an-hour earlier but we were down to ten men, and Liverpool had a fabulous side at the time. As a manager you had enough of a challenge playing against them with eleven men. To be down to ten men so early was a killer, you just want to get home. It was a low point and you could say it was one of my mistakes in management, bringing in Glenn Keeley from Blackburn and putting him straight into the team like that. But he'd already played for Newcastle in the top flight; and I knew him. I'd managed him and played alongside him. I knew he would give his all. Luck also conspired against us. I believe that was the first game of that first weekend that the ruling whereby someone is sent off automatically for denying a goalscoring opportunity. Just my luck that the first incident would involve Glenn and Ian Rush.

Neville Southall: Even all these years later I've never watched a video of the game, so I can't say if I was to blame or not. I don't think I played that badly; I certainly don't think I was absolutely shocking. It wasn't that I was bitter or because I hated losing (which I do), I just didn't like watching myself on the telly, whether I'd had a good game or a bad one. If I made a mistake I usually knew why I made it.

Roger Bennett: The darkest point was 1982. Kenny Dalglish and Ian Rush knocking them in. The fact that [Rush] was an Everton fan, a boyhood Evertonian is just a dragonglass to the heart. I remember watching that game and I was still young enough to believe in football clichés and that football cliché that it only takes a second to score a goal. Until there were four seconds left in the game, even when there were five seconds left, I still believed Everton would somehow score five and turn that game around. That was probably in my lifetime the most humbling – not just a footballing loss – life lesson. Even talking about it today I can recover the agony, the disbelief and the sense of not just losing a game but feeling personally utterly defeated.

Southall himself was also one of the victims of the post-derby cull and after being dropped in favour of Jim Arnold was sent to Fourth Division Port Vale on loan.

Neville Southall: During those months in the wilderness I didn't accept my fate. I refused to. I did everything I could to get back in that first team. I trained as if my life depended upon it. I told myself I would not be one of those players who thought, 'I think I'll do alright today, I'll just have a jolly little train, fuck about; go home, fuck about, and come in tomorrow and fuck about.' You can't do that with sport. At home I rested and planned how I would be better the next day. I obsessed. I wanted to improve. By improving I knew I could play for Everton again.

Peter Reid

In December 1982 Everton signed Bolton Wanderers midfielder, Peter Reid for just £60,000. Gordon Lee had tried to sign him two years earlier for ten times that amount, but Reid's career since then had been ravaged by injury.

Colin Harvey: If I didn't have a game on a Saturday afternoon I'd go to watch a game to do some scouting, and I went to watch him while he was at Bolton. We got him for £60,000, which was next to nothing. I saw him play about four or five times, and Howard said 'What do you think?' I said, 'Sign him. He'll give us something we haven't got.'

Howard Kendall: I signed Reidy just before Christmas 1982, but it was a struggle. The club's financial predicament was such that we had to change banks to an institution that would extend our overdraft to cover Reidy's acquisition. We weren't talking vast sums either: just £60,000 secured a player who would be vital to the club. It was a fine show of faith, but we weren't initially convinced of the dividends.

Mark Higgins: I remember when Reidy came from Bolton, because my father played for Bolton when they won the cup in 1958 against United. Reidy came from Bolton and I remember one time my father talking to him and he just said 'Get your head down because you've got a good chance here,' and he did.

Neville Southall: Howard had got him on the cheap as everyone thought he was finished, and his doubters might have had a point. He played a handful of games for Everton, got injured and was then out for six months. He played a handful more games early in the 1983/84 season, having missed the start, and was then injured yet again. By the time he came back into the team around November I think I'd only played alongside him four or five times. But as far as I was concerned whatever baggage he had stopped at the door. You can only judge someone when you've seen them.

Howard Kendall: I recall, vividly, sitting in a hotel room in Carlisle with Colin soon after. We'd be to see a game up that direction and were waiting for the team coach to pick us up on the way to a friendly in Scotland. 'Sorry about Reidy,' he said. 'Colin,' I said, 'We all make mistakes.' The two of us were convinced he was finished. Pressure was mounting and it was understandable. We lost another derby, comprehensively at the start of November 1983. It was a year to the day since the 5-0 annihilation. This time it was only 3-0.

Neville Southall: Reidy was a good player; a lively lad as well; another character in a dressing room that was becoming a louder and louder place to be. And a more ruthless place too. The banter and stick that went around was absolutely horrendous at times, particularly from him. He was a good laugh, but there was a side to his comedy that was very dark. But then if you want to survive on the pitch, you have to off it.

Howard Kendall: Peter Reid was also starting to put his injury problems behind him. Reidy was clever; he adapted his game so that he would be less vulnerable to injury. He learnt how to go about playing football without going into crunching tackles. He intercepted balls. He used to close down opponents, and then read where the ball was going. He never went into a block tackle because he knew of his knee. Not sliding tackles; not crunching tackles; he blocked it. In evolving his game he was very, very clever, and Everton would soon reap the full benefit.

Kendall under pressure

Colin Harvey: His initial period wasn't very good, and in fact the crowd had turned against him after a while. There were brochures about getting him out, and I think he'd had things written on the garage. It doesn't matter how good you'd been as a player, if you weren't doing it as a manager, the crowd let you know. It's as simple as that.

Howard Kendall: Things were difficult and supporters were making their unrest known. Before one game photocopied leaflets were distributed bearing the message 'Kendall and Carter Out: Bring Back Attractive Winning Football to Goodison Park.' Gates were really low and some of the media were on my back. I fell out with the now-disgraced broadcaster, Stuart Hall, who wrongly reported that the Wales manager [Mike England] was sat in the director's box ready to step into my job.

Neville Southall: Although training was good, and the atmosphere in the dressing room was good, on the pitch things weren't so great. We were the sort of team that could lose 2-0 at home to Norwich and then go to Old Trafford and win in front of 40,000 people, which was a big crowd at the time. But because we were struggling for goals and struggling at home and because we were in Liverpool's shadow Howard was coming under serious pressure from those fans that were still coming to Goodison. Returning home from training one afternoon he found his garage daubed with the spray-painted words 'Kendall Out' with the same slogan sprayed on a wall further down his road. Leaflets demanding 'Kendall and Carter Out. Bring back attractive winning football to Everton' were also distributed outside the stadium.

Keith Tamlin: Some newspapers from time to time contained reminiscent articles regarding the time when Howard's continuing position was in serious doubt but that his position was saved by the sole support of Philip Carter. The latter was indeed a strong supporter of Howard but he was not the only supporter on the Everton Board. I, for one, was and I cannot recall anyone who wasn't of that view. Certainly, the articles in the newspapers caused some annoyance to some members, including myself, and I recall the late Allan Waterworth, a previous Chairman, remarking 'Can't this continuing comment be corrected?' Philip Carter replied, 'It will simply add further impetus to the continued printing of this comment.' He was, of course, right, but it was and is incorrect.

Colin Harvey: I could tell he was worried. It's like everything else, if you're not doing your job, or people perceive you to not be doing your job, you've got problems. And he had problems.

John Bailey: If you're up and you're winning everything, like we did later on, you couldn't wait to get back to training. But if you're on a low and the crowd's turned against you and things are not going well you're a bit slower getting out of bed of a morning not looking forward to going in. It's a different thing.

Kevin Ratcliffe: It doesn't sit well, does it? I suppose you're too young to realise that. You're more concerned about your own performances than the manager. You're really oblivious as to what the manager is getting – as long as you're not getting it. It's when the criticism starts coming to you, then the chairman decides, 'Well I've got to do something about this.' It hadn't got to that stage where the chairman was getting stick. It was just about to; you could sense the manager's going to be in trouble if the crowd turns on the chairman. But while they're at the manager, then the chairman's getting away with it. So you're happy as a person.

Neville Southall: To be honest I didn't feel under any pressure myself. Looking back it probably wasn't right, but I didn't worry about anyone else other than myself. I was selfish because I thought you needed to be selfish to be successful. Being so preoccupied with what I did was an important part of what made me succeed on the pitch. As a goalkeeper you can't make things happen in front of you; it's just impossible. Once you start trying to do that you're likely to mess up big time – and the one thing you don't want to do in a struggling team is to mess up for them. Let people do their jobs in front of me and then if I have to I'll do my job was my view. I couldn't atone for a lack of goals, or a stray pass in midfield; but I could stop goals from being conceded and bring solidity and confidence to the defence. Those were the things that I worried about. I was oblivious and impervious to the woes of others.

Howard Kendall: You're never going to stop Everton fans supporting their club. They're not supporting the manager, they're supporting the club. The manager appreciates that and I appreciated that on the day. You select a side and you live and die by it. Was it particularly hurtful because of my record as a player? At times yes, even though I was usually unemotional on that side.

Mark Higgins: Sir Philip backed Howard. He was a lovely man. I had great respect for both of them. But he was superb, he was a really good chairman, a quiet man but he said what he wanted done and he did back Howard, and credit it to him because we wouldn't have won everything that we did under Howard.

Kevin Sheedy: I think Howard's relationship with the press helped. He was very good with them, he gave them stories and he would always deal with them correctly. I think that brought him a bit of extra time. They weren't on his case, they weren't like 'Kendall out' or anything. His general man management and of the media was top drawer.

Kevin Ratcliffe: Howard tried everything. We were going down to Goodison to train, to get a feel of Goodison because you're there once every fortnight, or twice a fortnight if you have a midweek game. Were we used to the stadium and were we used to the atmosphere? But the problem with the atmosphere was there were only 18,000 there! 9,000 there for the Coventry game. It's a different type of atmosphere. It's harder to play in front of 18,000 at Goodison than it is 40-50,000.

Peter Mills: What it would have been like today on ToffeeWeb or social media? I don't remember there being any appetite at all for Kendall to be sacked. But after the Coventry game, we used to listen to Sports Report on the radio coming back in the car from the match, Stuart Hall was saying that Mike England had been spotted at Goodison, and we were just gutted. There was no triumphalism over getting a new manager; it was heartache. It was absolutely heartbreaking that Howard might get the sack.

John Bailey: You know you're having a bad time. You look around: Gwladys Street half empty, Paddock, the stands, you know you're doing something wrong. Unfortunately the manager always gets the brunt of it when it's going wrong.

Stuart Rimmer: The atmosphere was awful. I was going to all the games – you had to as a pro go to all the games – and the atmosphere was dreadful. The crowds were well down; it wasn't a good time. I actually thought Howard was going to go at one point but he stuck at it and everything turned out great. Howard never really changed the training we always kept going the same as we always did he obviously had belief that things would change and he was right.

Derek Mountfield: I'd only been in the side sometime in November I think it was, away at West Ham in the Cup. Come Christmas time we were struggling, we'd hardly won a game. We played at home to Coventry on Boxing Day and drew 0-0 in one of the most boring games you will ever see. Straight after that we got on the coach to Wolves, to play on the 27th – the following day – and got beat 3-0. Wayne Clarke, who joined us a few years later, said 'You were the worst team, you were rubbish' and we were. We came at home again, and I think it might have been Sunderland. There was only 12,000 in the ground, and the leaflets were saying 'Kendall must go, sack the board blah blah blah.' It was awful, there was cushions raining down from the seats, boos everywhere, but all credit to Sir Philip Carter, he stuck by Howard. We knew Howard had a long-term plan.

John Corbett: The point of despair was reached probably in December 1983. It was an away game at Wolverhampton Wanderers, which we all went to as a family group. It was a cold day; there was snow on the ground. Wolves I don't think had won a game all season. A friend of mine who was a Wolves supporter, joked, 'What's the difference between a triangle and Wolverhampton Wanderers? A triangle has three points.' Everton played a full strength side with the exception of a young fullback, and were beaten decisively by Wolves on their own ground. At that point we felt it couldn't get any worse. We just had a mediocre start to the season, we're heading in the wrong direction in the First Division, and we were beaten by probably the worst First Division side that I've seen in 40 years. Coming home from that Wolves game you begin to think it's time we got rid of Howard Kendall. Leaflets were being printed, handed out before home games. We still had cushions in the stands which people could hire, and famously they were thrown on the pitch at the end of most home games.

Howard Kendall: I think if I hadn't been connected with the club before my managerial career that I may have been sacked by New Year. I think there was more patience because of my connection with Everton; it was something I was forever grateful for.

Merseyside's economic nadir

The 1980s coincided with severe economic problems on Merseyside: mass unemployment, deindustrialisation and depopulation. After the inner city riots in Toxteth in 1981 the Conservative Chancellor, Geoffrey Howe, even urged the prime minister to abandon the city and put it into 'managed decline.'

Kevin Ratcliffe: What you've got to realise in those days is that the city was very gloomy. There was a deep depression going on. You've got Maggie Thatcher denouncing football as much as she can, and I think Liverpool and Everton gave everybody in the city something to talk about, to be happy about. That's what people forget. The city was on its arse, there were all sorts of things happening.

George Orr: It might sound strange to say it but the eighties under Maggie Thatcher were as bleak as the Second World War and the First World War. There was nothing. I know myself. It's not like now when you're unemployed now and they give you some agency job that's crap but at least there's a chance to get some money. Under Maggie there was nothing. You signed on and that was the minimum you had and you were totally devastated and skint. I remember the only thing you'd buy was eggs, bread and beans, because with an egg you could have an omelette, you could have fried eggs, it was so versatile and a cheap food to have. That's how you got through. The football, if you could afford to go, took you into a world where there was hope. It was Everton Football Club, they were still playing and there was still hope. No matter what Maggie did – she may have closed the factories and the mines and the steel works – she didn't close Goodison Park.

Charles Lambert: You could say that that was the last knockings of the previous order of football and society, where you could get on the Gwladys Street, you could get on the Kop, and it didn't cost you an arm and a leg. You didn't have to book weeks in advance, the ordinary person could still come. The culture of football was still the working man's culture. I remember there was a scene in 'Boys From the Black Stuff' where Alan Bleasdale had scripted this scene where the lads go to a bar and bump into Graeme Souness and Sammy Lee. I cannot imagine that being scripted these days, not working lads off a building site or off the unemployment. Football has gone into a different orbit now.

Andy Gray signed; Colin Harvey promoted

In November 1983, Kendall entered the transfer market again. The signing was another veteran many considered to be past his best: Andy Gray. The same month Colin Harvey replaced Mick Heaton as Everton's assistant manager.

Howard Kendall: We were struggling for a striker and the board had told me to make a shortlist for our next meeting. I wasn't exactly sure how much they'd let me spend. So I made a few enquiries and drew up a shortlist: Ipswich Town's Paul Mariner was available at £600,000; Andy Gray was £300,000 and Bob Latchford was available on a free transfer. I then did a cross-section of the pros and cons of bringing of Bob back from Swansea; signing Andy Gray who had had well documented injury problems but had played in twenty-odd games the previous season, and the one before that as well. Mariner, I knew, was a quality player and a regular part of the England squad. I went into the next board meeting and presented the options to the directors. Bob coming back didn't feel like the right move. We didn't have £600,000 to sign Mariner, so the board suggested I went for Andy. I progressed with the transfer, but when it got to the medical his knees were an issue. We got a specialist in who looked at the number of games he had played over the previous two years and said that if he developed his quad muscles in his legs and kept them strong to stabilise the knee joints then there was no reason he could turn around and fail his medical.

Andy Gray: I'd had a couple of bad years at Wolves – we'd got relegated and then got promoted – and I wasn't sure where I was going from there, I have to say. So when Everton came along it was a wonderful opportunity, because Wolves were in a bad place, they'd gone into liquidation, the club was in turmoil, just ruined. No one knew who the owners were going to be, it was really bad. So to get the chance to move was taken very quickly with me as soon as I met Howard, it wasn't a problem. I knew that's what I wanted to do. I was 28 years of age, coming up 29. You wonder whether you've got it, and I would be lying if I said when I arrived at Everton I wasn't at my most confident, but neither was I a shrinking violet.

Mark Higgins: I played Andy when he was at Villa, and I had some really good tussles with him. I can remember one game at Goodison he actually got a bit of a knock from the full-back at the time and he came back on. Back in those days you could tackle properly and I went through Andy and he was stretchered off, which made my game easy against Villa because I didn't have a centre half to mark. When he signed for us he actually said to me, 'Higgy, you were the one player I vowed to do.' I said, 'Andy, welcome to Everton.'

Kevin Sheedy: Andy was a massive gamble. He had major problems with his knees, but Howard quite rightly took a gamble on him. Reidy was the same, he'd had lots of injuries and at first Reidy couldn't get in the team. It was no coincidence that when he finally broke into the team, we were doing okay but then it just seemed to kick on again.

Howard Kendall: I'll always remember Andy meeting the press for the first time. He was asked why he had come to Everton. 'To win things,' he answered without hesitating. When they told him that they'd heard that sort of things many times before, he told them: 'You've never heard it from me.'

Andy Gray: I was genuine. I got laughed at a little bit, I remember that. I think they were a little bit surprised, the supporters and people I talked to. They were struggling in the bottom half of the table: Everton, what do you mean you've come to win things? I genuinely meant it. I felt that as long as I was there, however long it was, whether it was two, four, six years, I felt that I could win things with Everton.

Howard Kendall: Such self-confidence had a great effect on the dressing room. He was loud, cocky; always spurring his teammates on. On the field he was brilliant, leading by example. He was absurdly brave, putting his head in places where others would have shirked at putting their boots.

Neville Southall: Vocally he made a great deal of difference and his bravery was ridiculous. He wouldn't stand for any shit, which helped make everybody else play well. When you get a good team they demand a certain amount of quality out of the players around them.If you haven't got it they can slaughter you. You have to be quite strong; you have to provide quality to people when you're passing or crossing or shooting or saving; and you have to demand it too. That outlook always brings up the standard of everything else at a football club. I think Andy brought up the standard of play around him, because he wasn't going to settle for anything less. He wanted the ball exactly where he wanted it delivered, and if not he slaughtered you.

Kevin Ratcliffe: We played Coventry in the League Cup [and came from behind to win 2-1 in front of just 9,080 spectators] and the next day Howard promoted Colin Harvey from first team coach to reserve team coach. And then on the Thursday he signed Andy Gray. All of a sudden with Andy coming in, from what we'd done in the week, coming from a goal behind, it's amazing what that can do to you. When Andy came in we could really see the type of character that the manager's brought in. We've got this £1 million player in his time coming in through the doors and being as bold as brass. Couldn't whisper over three fields could he, Andy? He was supposedly, like Reidy, finished. He must have been some player at nineteen or twenty.

Andy Gray: I signed on the Friday, and they played Coventry in the midweek, and I think there was about 9,000 there at Goodison. I mean that was the state of affairs, it was as low as it could get. Everton stumbled past Coventry that night, and then I think they'd got thumped the week before by Liverpool in the derby, 3-0. They were very close those games. Howard was coming under increasing pressure, and then I came along. I wasn't exactly the marquee signing I'm sure that Everton fans were looking forward to greeting. I had a couple of injuries, they were signing me for £150,000. They weren't signing a £10 million player. So they must have thought 'Goodness me, what have we got here?' But I knew what I could offer, I knew what I was good at, and I knew that I could get people going as well as myself, so I was fairly confident that it would work. But I can guess the Everton fans at the time must have thought, 'What the hell is Howard doing?'

Neville Southall: Above all, I think it took a bit of pressure off Sharpy as well. He'd come in as a bit of novice and done really well at first. But carrying that centre-forward burden can be difficult for a young player. He needed someone to feed off every now and then. But when the two played together they could be a pair of battering rams too.

Graeme Sharp: People say when Andy came in I become more aggressive. I think at times early on in my career when I was playing against experienced players, it was a case of getting bullied. My brother [Richard] used to play professionally up in Scotland, he played for Rangers and Kilmarnock, and he was probably a better footballer technically than me, but he was a bit soft. So I always remember my Dad saying, 'Don't be like Richard, you go out there and make sure you look after yourself.' So that was the case, and I was coming up against players like Kenny Burns, who was at Leeds at the time, who was a hard Scotsman. They'd threaten you – 'I'm going to do this to you and I'm going to do that to you.' I then had to say 'Right, okay, I can sink or swim here. I can either shy away or face them up.' And I just faced them up. Then Andy came in, and the two of us were really difficult to play against, and I think we just kicked on from there.

Andy Gray: Certainly I taught Graeme how to jump properly for the football and make life difficult for centre-backs. I think he'll admit that, that I spent a bit of time with him, showing him what I thought was a good flick and how to do that, and he liked it.

John Bailey: Reidy was the biggest winner you could ever meet in football. Andy was the same. Andy Gray brought Sharpy up to what he was, showed him a few tricks, not skill wise but how to look after himself, put himself about. It just all seemed to fall into place.

Derek Mountfield: They were both winners, they wanted to win everything: a game of cards, a game of pool, a head tennis match, they wanted to win. Andy Gray is full of confidence, you see it on the telly, he's a confident lad. I think that helped us, there was a lot of youngsters. I was only 21, Trevor Steven was 20, Gary Stevens and Kevin Richardson were only 21. Neville was probably only about 23. Ratcliffe was 24 and captain. Sharpy was 23, 24 – it was a young side. Gray and Reidy came in around the ages of 28, 29 and they had a bit more experience and a bit more life skills around a football pitch than we had, and we were struggling at the time. It didn't just happen the minute they arrived; they were in the side and we still struggled for a while. But they had something about them that made us realise 'We can do something here.' I think Andy and Reidy saw that as well.

Andy Gray: It was a natural thing, because we were good pals off the pitch. We spent a lot of time together socially. We spent a lot of time going to games sitting and talking about the game. We would talk to players, always on the pitch. If anything needed to be said, or a bollocking needed to be given, then Peter and I would invariably give it. Kevin, as captain, was Kevin. He wasn't a vocal captain, he led by example, he was terrific at what he did, but if somebody needed to be told then I would tell them, and if I didn't then Peter would. And in the right way, only to make the team better and to make them better. So that was done, but we never thought, 'We need to take these guys aside.'

Kevin Ratcliffe: I think then all the lads started to really believe in themselves, and it brought a lot of character out of us that was hidden. Us thinking 'This guy's 28 and he can say this, he can do that, well we've got to be a bit more like that.' I think he helped in that way – helped the dressing room as in camaraderie, and when we were going away, the togetherness of the lads.

John Bailey: Colin was in charge of the reserve team. I think I was part of it then and we went ten out of ten wins, unbeaten, top of the Central League. Mick Heaton was Howard's assistant and knowing Howard was always looking for something to change put Colin in his place and that was it. Colin had so much respect. Things just gelled unbelievably.

Alan Irvine: We had a really promising young [reserve] team [and] Colin Harvey was in charge. Colin was very, very influential for me certainly, and I would think that most of the other lads would say Colin was very influential. And Colin moved to the first team, and it wasn't long after Colin moving into to work for the first team that a lot of our lads moved up with him. I think we were unbeaten in the league at the time. There was an exciting group of young players there. But I couldn't tell you exactly what people behind the scenes were thinking. We all were enjoying our football, and we all seemed to be moving in the right direction.

Colin Harvey: Howard moved me up to first team coach, because the reserves had started the season and we'd won ten games on the trot. I was coaching the reserves a bit different to how he was coaching the first team, which you did then. There wasn't a club policy of playing the same way through and he said, 'What are you doing?' I remember one of the games we were at Wolves, and he came to the game, and what we were doing was pressing high up and leaving the space behind the back four. But we had a couple of quick players; Ian Marshall was one of the centre-backs, who was quick and obviously if the ball was knocked over the top they were quick enough to get back and deal with it. So he said 'Would you try that with the first team?' I said, 'It's up to you, if you want me to come and do it.' So he did, and that was how we started.

Alan Ainscow: You could see the quality in training. Some of the finishes Sharpy used to do you used to think 'Wow.' The games are a continuation of the training in some ways and if you're doing things like that in training fairly constantly it tends to go that you'll do it again on Saturday if you get similar opportunities. Sheeds was very classy on the ball great left foot, pick a pass, not the quickest in the world but he didn't need it because he had good skills to beat players with skill rather than with pace.

Howard Kendall: Throughout all this time I remained confident that we'd turn things around. I had utmost confidence that some of the players I'd brought in – Southall, Steven, Sheedy – were class acts, and that others would come good too. The atmosphere in the dressing room was good as well. And I'd see things on the training ground that weren't being translated on the pitch. I remember one morning at Bellefield, bringing Harry Cooke, the Chief Scout, to the window. I wasn't out on the training ground that day, and I said, 'Harry, have a look at that quality.' We were flying on the training ground but it just wasn't happening on match days. 'Have a look at that quality,' I said. 'We're not far away, are we?' I suppose as much as anything I needed a member of staff to turn around and reaffirm my belief. In front of us were players like Kevin Sheedy, Trevor Steven, Neville Southall; some of the finest players to ever wear an Everton shirt. 'We're not,' agreed Harry. 'We're not at all.'

Kevin Sheedy: It was just putting the performances into games. In training you knew how good the players were, you trained with them every day. We made each other better. Neville, for example, when we were doing finishing, shooting exercises, if you didn't put it right in the top corner he was saving everything, he'd get a little tip on to the bar. So as an individual he helped me improve my finishing. You're playing up against good British defenders – Gary Stevens, Kevin Ratcliffe, [later] Dave Watson. They're testing you every day as well. I think we helped each other to become better players and then the team clicked and we went on a great run.

Turning point

Andy Gray: I think there were three things really important at that time, round about November, December [1983]. That was Colin was promoted to be first team coach; Reidy finally nailed down a place in the team permanently; and Howard signed me. And I think those three decisions, without a doubt, along with Howard's enthusiasm and terrific man management skills, were pivotal in Everton turning that season around and then going on to have the couple of seasons we had after that.

Neville Southall: We played Coventry on the last day of 1983 and drew 0-0. Just 13,659 turned up, but their boos were loud at full-time. But we hadn't lost and Howard wasn't likely to start the new year looking for another job. What's more I'd kept a clean sheet and played pretty well. Because I was a bit insulated from the rest of the team and really just focused on myself and improving I went in at full-time with a big grin on my face. Howard saw this and came up to me. 'What the fuck's wrong with you? Why are you smiling?' I said nothing and just stood there with a grin on my face. I think if it was anyone else he would have gone mad, but he knew when to leave me alone. He knew that I'd done my job well, done everything that was asked of me and enough to keep my place in the team. He knew that's why I was happy, so he left me alone.

Andy Gray: Most Evertonians look at Oxford away and Kevin Brock's back pass that Inchy nipped in on and stuck in. And yeah that was a big game. There was another game before the Stoke game, funnily enough, a league game against Birmingham City at St Andrews [2 January], that was maybe the week before Stoke. I remember Howard sitting us all down and he said, 'Listen, I've been really loyal to you boys, I think you've all got a chance, but if today goes against us, I'm seriously going to have to make big changes in the team.' And we've all kind of sat there and gone 'Okay.' And we went to Birmingham and we won 2-0 . Then we played Stoke [in the FA Cup third round].

Peter Mills: That was a form of madness that day against Stoke. I don't know how many people were there but I've never ever known an atmosphere like it. We said, 'This is all going to go wrong today.' I've never known anything like it – how it came about, why it came about, no idea. No idea where it came from. But something got into everyone that day. Maybe it was because it felt so hopeless after Wolves.

John Corbett: We travelled again as a family group. People were still on holiday so a lot of people who arrived at Stoke City were, shall we say, the worse for wear for drink. We had a seat behind the Everton goal and the place was absolutely buzzing. People were bouncing up and down on their seats; fans were doing hilarious and outrageous things prior to the game.

Mark Higgins: Howard opened the window and went, 'Listen to that...' You could hear the fans. He had a good way of bringing the best out of the players, and I think when you do start to get that winning feeling, it does tend to rub off. I remember watching the lads play when I was injured and they went on to win everything. I've spoken to Rats and Sharpey, and they do say that you get to a stage where you don't think you're going to lose a game.

Howard Kendall: It was like their last stand. The noise was ferocious. In the Victoria Ground dressing room I didn't really have to give a teamtalk. The atmosphere among the players – despite the shaky form – was great. It was increasingly vociferous and full of character. In Reidy, Rats, Andy I had some real leaders. There was the bubbly, wisecracking Bails; the dry wit of Big Nev; and players like Sharpy and Adrian Heath always made their feelings known. On this day I went around the changing room and all you could hear were Evertonians singing and chanting. I opened up the windows and simply said to my players, 'Just listen to that. Are you going to let them down?' They knew what they had to do.

John Bailey: He never gave a team talk; he just opened the window and said 'Listen to them, do I need to say any more' and that was it. Off we went, as simple as that.

Derek Mountfield: There must have been 8,000-10,000 Everton fans in there, and they were just singing and singing and singing. He said, 'Listen to that, go and do that for them.' We won the game 2-0. He just said, 'Go and win it for them' and the crowd was superb.

Neville Southall: In terms of utilizing that as a motivating tool Howard rarely used the fanbase; or rather he picked his moments carefully. This was one of them. It was a brilliant piece of psychology. We just sat there listening to the shouts of 'Everton! Everton! Everton!' We got caught in a swell of positivity and by five to three we couldn't wait to get get on the pitch. To be exposed to all that hope and expectation, there was simply no way we were going to lose. And we didn't. Goals by Andy Gray and Alan Irvine saw us through to the fourth round.

Howard Kendall: Some people say that the Stoke match was the turning point in Everton's history. People talk about turning points and look for them too. To my mind it came a couple of weeks later when we played Oxford United in the quarter-final of the League Cup. I think there would have been a lot of pressure had we not won it. Although they were in the Third Division they were a good side and had beaten Manchester United in the previous round. The Manor Ground was a difficult place to go to; it had a sloping pitch and Oxford were on the rise. Within 18 months they'd be in the First Division.

Kevin Sheedy: Oxford was a real difficult place to go to, the Manor Ground, a sloping pitch, they had real experienced players. Two centre-backs, really strong old fashioned type centre-halves. They were flying, particularly at home, so we could have easily got beat that night and it might have been a different thing, but we got a fortunate break.

John Parrott: I actually remember the fact that we had the worst tickets in the world. They were white, just printed with a Stabilo pen across them and there were about 15,000 Evertonians in the same seat because someone had just bought a Stabilo pen and was selling the same seat. So we were next to the poor fella who thought he was the only one in the ground that had the right one, but they were packed to the rafters.

Howard Kendall: We were missing Andy Gray and fell behind to Bobby McDonald's goal on a cold night. We tried, but we just couldn't seem to break down our opponents. Then, with just nine minutes remaining, a miracle. Kevin Brock passed the ball back to his goalkeeper, Steve Hardwick. He was actually under a llot of pressure from Peter Reid, which tends to be overlooked, but nevertheless Adrian Heath read it superbly, ran onto the loose ball, took it past Hardwick and, from a tight angle, struck the equaliser.

John Parrott: It was a horrible blustery terrible night. The team had been terrible, the crowd had been calling for Howard Kendall's head, the team was struggling. Nothing seemed to be working right. We looked like we were going to go out. All of a sudden Kevin Brock makes the infamous short back pass, Adrian Heath steals in nips round the keeper, 1-1, the roof comes off.

Keith Tamlin: I recall well, as I'm sure many Evertonians do, a match against Oxford United in mid winter. Our team had, prior to the fixture, run into a bad patch and the manager and the team were attracting criticism. The weather during the match was dreadful, driving wind, snow, rain, a difficult pitch—name some hostile element that wasn't present. The Chairman of Oxford was I believe Ghislaine Maxwell, daughter of Robert Maxwell. Despite the elements, the home crowd and the efforts of the home team, our boys showed great spirit, determination and no little skill in overcoming all these factors and we won when 'Inchy' seized a misplaced back pass and scored . The result turned round the club's season and we didn't look back.

Gary Stevens: I think it kicked off at Oxford. I talk about that game; things just went from strength to strength. There were good characters on the pitch and we enjoyed ourselves off the park and it just went from there... In a strange way everything came along very very nicely – a domino effect – but we all worked very very hard on the park and very hard in training and I think it paid dividends. Howard Kendall wanted to copy Liverpool, the way Liverpool played and I think in the end we did it better than Liverpool for a couple of seasons and usurped them.

John Parrott: From that minute it all turned round. We just found a system and how to play and the team all improved. Peter Reid was probably the catalyst.

Derek Mountfield: Something happened, whether it was the Birmingham game, opening the window, drawing at Oxford in the League Cup with Inchy's late goal, something happened in a short space of time and we developed this incredible self-belief in ourselves. When you've got that half the battle is won. You see negativity in clubs now on the pitch; we went from being a team lacking in confidence to one full of confidence in a matter of weeks.

Neville Southall: The turning point couldn't have been that great, because we were taken to an FA Cup fourth round second replay against Third Division Gillingham. They were hard games and close games. Gillingham might have been two divisions below us but they had some really good players, like Steve Bruce and Tony Cascarino. We went more than 200 minutes without scoring (or conceding) a goal against them. The [venue for the] second replay was decided on the toss of a coin and we were sent back down to Kent, where you could say that we were set up to lose. Priestfield was a hard place to go. It was a small stadium and because of its proximity to the coast always windy. That night it was windy, raining and the pitch was heavily sanded. There was a big crowd for a ground like that. It was a Monday, so a bit different to our usual routine. In short it had all the makings of a giantkilling. But for once I enjoyed myself there; a brace by Sheeds and a goal by Adrian Heath eased us into the fifth round.

Howard Kendall: We faced Aston Villa in the League Cup semi-final first leg at Goodison on 15 February. It was seven long years to the day since Everton had last reached Wembley when they beat Bolton Wanderers to reach the final of the same competition. Kevin Sheedy put us in front with a goal on 28 minutes after a mix up in the Villa area, but it was the unsung Kevin Richardson who was the key man that night. Early on he had fallen and hurt his arm quite badly. He was insistent that he wanted to play on, despite being in considerable pain. It said much of the spirit we had engendered by that time that his bravery overcame his common sense; nobody wanted to let anyone else down, or give up their place in the team lest they lose it long term. Eight minutes from the end Kevin struck a fantastic second goal sweetly on the volley. Even then Kevin wasn't done, and he blocked a shot on the goalline with a couple of minutes left. The Villa players said he handballed it, but the referee saw it differently.

Jimmy Martin: As coach driver, if you won the first stop was the off-licence, put a few beers on for all the lads and all that. You couldn't do that nowadays; Everton is so much more monitored, nutritionists and all that. I'm not into all that kind of stuff; I'd rather have the old regime. They all liked a few beers. The good thing about it was they'd be in the next day and they'd train hard and they'd run it off, but there'd be nothing after maybe Wednesday. They'd be ready for the weekend.

Howard Kendall: So much had happened over just a couple of months, but a team that had appeared to the world to be on its knees at Christmas now had its first major final since 1977.

Neville Southall: The [FA Cup Fifth Round] Notts County game is famous for an absurdly brave header by Andy Gray just after half-time. We were drawing 1-1 on a muddy pitch, with the wind and rain lashing around, when we got a free kick. Sheeds lifted it in and the ball evaded the challenge of Sharpy, falling to the back post where Andy slid in, nose almost touching the ground to head home our winner. Andy was always better heading the ball than kicking it, which I think is why he went in head first.

Andy Gray: As it was coming over I kind of misjudged it, because I didn't think it was going to dip as quickly as it did. I'd half-committed myself to the header and suddenly it was kind of dipping in front of me and bouncing. I just thought, 'Get something on it.' I put my head on it and I'm not saying I picked that corner and I steered it in there all on my own, no. I wanted to get it on target and I was fortunate enough that I got a really good contact, and it went across the goalkeeper, who I think was surprised as anything. He was beaten more by surprise than the power of the header. But it found the bottom corner, and again it was a big goal for us, and a really tough cup tie away at Notts County.

Kevin Ratcliffe: If he had a chance of scoring a goal with his head, he'd throw his head in there and his head would get battered – he wouldn't even think about getting hurt. He scored that half-volley header against Notts County, which I've never seen in my life before. He's half-volleyed it with his head into the top corner.

Andy Gray: I often see in the modern game the ball comes across the face of the goal and players stretch at it with their feet. It just goes past them and the chance is missed, about waist height or chest height. And I've always believed that if the ball's in front of you, you have more chance of getting to it if you actually launch yourself forward to head it. I mean it's natural, because you're springing off your feet and you're pushing your body forward, whereas when you're stretching with your leg, you haven't really got any forward momentum. So my theory has always been, if anything comes across the face of the goal and it's in front of me, I'm going to dive and head it.

Everton 0 Liverpool 0
25 March 1984
1984 Milk Cup final

Roger Bennett: Everyone always talks about how one in four Liverpool males invaded London to savour that first ever derby in a final at Wembley. It felt less like a game of football and more like a delirious celebration of the city itself. The cries of 'Merseyside, Merseyside, Merseyside' rang out not just across Wembley but also across London the entire weekend.

John Bailey: I couldn't get enough tickets for friends and family; it was unbelievable. You don't think of it then. It's not till afterwards you go, 'Christ I played in the first all Merseyside cup final.' It was unbelievable: both sides of the City going down there and to walk out in front of them it was like walking out in Liverpool city centre; both sides all friends and mates.

Neville Southall: For me the 1984 Milk Cup Final represented a turning point in Everton history. Because we matched Liverpool every single step of the way, it affirmed my conviction that we were the best team in the league. In fact because Liverpool were the best team in Europe it put us on the same pedestal.

Howard Kendall: When I was first appointed Everton manager I said that my target was to match

Liverpool and over two games and 210 minutes of football I felt that we did just that. In the first game at Wembley, which ended in a 0-0 draw, we had enough chances to have won 3-0.

Gary Stevens: What do I remember of the game? You mean other than Alan Hansen catching the ball and kicking it down the park from standing on the goal line? No that's all I remember about the game! That was an outstanding glaring error by the referee, linesman, whoever you want to blame.

Neville Southall: The first game at Wembley – a 0-0 draw on a muggy afternoon – hinged on a goalline clearance by the hand of Alan Hansen, after Adrian Heath had dispossessed Grobbelaar and hooked a shot in. Had it gone in or we'd have scored a penalty Everton's barren streak would have been at an end.

Colin Harvey: It was a handball, wasn't it? How the referee missed it I don't know. But the fact that we played as well as we did against them, that give us a great deal of belief.

Neville Southall: What did I think of Hansen's handball? I think everything ultimately evens itself out in the end. Those sort of decisions can kill you on the day or save you – as might have happened in the semi-final when Kevin Richardson got away with a similar offence. But the good teams always get more decisions; that's partly why they're good teams.

Howard Kendall: We played the replay at Maine Road just three days later. It took a superbly struck goal by Graeme Souness to beat us, but once more there was not much in it. We were disappointed to lose, but the fact that we'd matched the best team in Europe told us how far we'd come. The belief that we had in ourselves, we felt, was starting to be matched by the fans. They were the important ones, our target. They'd seen enough in those two games to recognise we could compete with the best.

Andy Gray: We went close, it took a replay and a Graeme Souness thunderbolt to beat us in that game. And I think when you look at the quality of the Liverpool side, who were all seasoned, they were all great players, and they were the benchmark for most teams, then absolutely I thought, when I watched those two games, 'We are close.'

Kevin Sheedy: It was a tight game, and the replay was a tight game. The players, when you get to your first final, get confidence from that knowing that you can reach a final. Then obviously getting to the final and winning it, so I think the confidence was there for the start of next season.

Roger Bennett: Even in that final we were shafted and inextricably, Alan Hansen was diving full length to save the ball with his hand [in the first match at Wembley]. I mean everybody could see. I just remember driving home seething in silence. I mean not just losing but being shafted. We didn't lose honourably, we weren't defeated by the better side but just feeling like doom. It's a repeat motif.

Neville Southall: All this was less than 17 months after the 5-0 annihilation and more recently the dark days of Christmas 1983. The transition from no hopers to contenders had been incredibly swift but in other ways it didn't surprise me.

Kevin Ratcliffe: We competed on an even keel with them. I think that game give us that belief, and then to lose narrowly at Maine Road in the replay, I think that just give us the belief that we can compete. Because if you ask anybody at the end of that season: what do you want do next season? What's your ambition? It was to finish above Liverpool. And everybody's saying 'Well what an ambition that is?' And we're saying 'Yeah, well if we finish above Liverpool we'll win the league.' And that proved the case.

Everton 1, Southampton 0
14 April 1984
FA Cup semi-final

Neville Southall: A fortnight later we met Southampton in the FA Cup semi-final at Highbury. It was a good ground to have the game on; everyone packed closely to the pitch. It seemed to me at the time as if there were only Evertonians in the stadium. The ability of Scousers to get anywhere and everywhere in colossal numbers never ceased to amaze me and that day it was as if they had colonized north London. They helped galvanise us on those occasions for it was often like playing at home. The crowd never discernibly impacted my play, but I think we all sensed the expectation. Subliminally they must have made an impression on me.

Howard Kendall: Southampton were a really good team and only narrowly missed out on the league title that year, finishing runners up and just three points behind champions Liverpool. We knew we'd have to be at our best. I dropped Graeme Sharp to the bench and played Terry Curran on the flank. My instructions were to get the crosses into the area as often as possible and see what either Andy Gray could do, or hope that one of Peter Shilton's punched clearances would fall kindly for us. The tactic worked reasonably well, and we enjoyed a lot of domination but Southampton had the best chances. Fortunately Neville, as he was on so many days, was in inspired form. Nothing was going to get past him.

Derek Mountfield: We had to work hard for it. I remember after the game the delirium amongst the fans. I know there was a lot of aggravation, a lot of violence, but we never saw it. We just got the celebrations.

Howard Kendall: The tension was incredible. The crowd at Highbury, like Goodison, was very close to the pitch and there were no security fences at Highbury during that time. Deep into extra time, Peter Reid's free-kick was nodded on by Sharp – only on as a substitute for Trevor Steven – and Adrian Heath headed past Shilton. The crowd roared and streamed onto the pitch, and the last few minutes were played out with hundreds of Evertonians lining the sidelines, watching the club that they and I loved so much confirming their path back to Wembley.

Peter Mills: When it went in that was possibly the biggest goal I've ever seen us score; in terms of disbelief and ecstasy, and thinking my head was going to blow up. That moment was something else. For a single individual goal, I can't really remember one that had such a profound impact. And that was when we started thinking 'Something's happened here.' I think we all knew we were going to win the cup final.

Neville Southall: It was absolute bedlam. Highbury was one of the few grounds at the time that didn't have fences and fans poured onto the pitch. I was elated because I knew that with just three minutes to go we were heading back to Wembley, but at the same time I was trying to keep my concentration because you're often most vulnerable after a goal. I knew that those last three minutes may well feel like an hour and I had to focus on that. But at the same time I was aware of the noise and the supporters and their joy, which I shared, although I tried to keep my emotions in check. The pitch was eventually cleared; the Highbury terraces, rocking and cheering the name of our club, and before we knew it extra time was up and we were Wembley bound once more.

Howard Kendall: On the way back to Merseyside we told the coach driver to take it easy, as we savoured every moment of our victory. We watched car after car of jubilant Evertonians, scarves hanging from the windows head north. The beer flowed, our joy uncontained. It's a big thing being responsible for bringing so much happiness to so many people.

Everton 2, Watford 0
19 May 1984
FA Cup final

Derek Mountfield: It was absolutely unbelievable that we'd got to Wembley again for the FA Cup final. Then you get four weeks between the semi-final and the final, and you just can't wait for the game because there's so much going on between that time. There's meetings, there's media, there's pictures – you get your cup final suit and your song. By the time the game comes you can't wait for it to start. The biggest issue is tickets; people think you can get tickets. [As a club] You only get 20 odd thousand now, but people think [as a player] you can get hundreds. My friends and my family got sorted out, but people didn't get tickets because we didn't have enough. I could have sold Wembley out myself.

Howard Kendall: In the weeks leading up to the final, against Watford, we played some lovely football. We were peaking at just the right time, and the potential that I'd watched during those hard winter months on the training ground was now being replicated on match days. At times our football was exuberant. Players like Trevor Steven, who had had a slow start to his Everton career, were starting to show their ability. Goals, previously a problem, were no longer an issue. Until New Year we had scored just eleven league goals, in the second half of the campaign we managed thirty-three.

Colin Harvey: We'd got such a head of steam that we fully expected to win. I remember the same feeling when I was playing, you got a head of steam and you thought no matter what we do today we're going to win. It was very much the same feeling.

Howard Kendall: Because of what I saw, I was so optimistic about our chances in the final against Watford that I had to contain myself. I didn't want this to seep through to the players and breed complacency.

Andy Gray: We had unbelievable belief, I mean to the extent that if any of the press asked them it didn't matter, the game was won. We were beating Watford. Now I thought that in my head, but because I was more experienced than them, I wasn't prepared to say it. I would say 'Of course we feel confident, but they've got people like Maurice Johnstone, George Reilly, John Barnes in their side. These players can hurt a team.' And I'm turning my ear and listening to the other guys, Inchy going 'We'll beat them easy, they can't cope with us, we're too good. If they get one we'll get two, if they get two we'll get three.' And I'm going 'No boys you don't say that!'

John Bailey: I was rooming with Andy Gray and we used to have a rule that the junior partner always got up in the morning and made the tea before we went down to breakfast or pre match meal. We just heard laughter outside and I went, 'What's going on here?' and we opened the window and there was Freddy Starr. He was kitted out in this old fashioned football kit and all the boys were hanging out their windows just in hysterics for twenty minutes. Until we got away from him on the coach we didn't think we were in a Cup Final.

Kevin Ratcliffe: I always remember him looking up and seeing Andy Gray and saying 'Andy! People say to me that me and you look alike, but I can't see it that way because you're such an ugly looking man.' He was doing all this and funny walks, and it really relaxed us. You see him on TV at 11 o'clock, it was a full day! The FA Cup was just a full day. I remember Michael Barrymore was at the Watford hotel, turns around on live TV and says to Freddie Starr, 'Freddie, how come you've got more supporters there than I've got here?' And he says, 'That's because I'm a bigger star than you.'

John Bailey: When we did get to Wembley there's Freddy again, he came onto the pitch with us and into the dressing room.

Kevin Ratcliffe: He wasn't acting the fool, he was just staring at Neville Southall with his mouth open. Now all he was saying was 'You're unbelievable.' This was early in Nev's career, and all Freddie Starr could say was 'You're fucking brilliant, you are. You are absolutely... do you realise how good you are?' And Nev was getting embarrassed.

John Bailey: We were trying to get changed and Howard had to say to him, 'Eh, Fred we're going out in about twenty minutes.' He took your mind off things; we were just in giggles we didn't realise you're going to a cup final.

Gary Stevens: I don't know whether you get to a cup final and you think, 'Well as long as we just enjoy the day.' I'm sure that Watford had a desire to win. We were there to win and you wouldn't take anything away than the fact the opponents were there just to make up the numbers. They were a good side in their own right.

Kevin Ratcliffe: The big thing for me in the game, there was a big turning point in the first-half where John Barnes gets through, passes the ball or shoots, it goes past Neville and John Bailey gets back, clears it off the line. Slides in and just gets a touch. The referee didn't see the touch, didn't give the corner kick. He gave a goal kick. And I honestly think that's a big, big turning point. Bailsy just touching that ball, it was 0-0 at the time.

Neville Southall: Watford had some early chances, but once Graeme Sharp put us in front on 38 minutes our superiority was never in doubt. I don't remember being called into action much. There were a couple of testing crosses I had to claim but that was it.

Kevin Ratcliffe: A big thing for us, a big advantage was that their left-back Wilf Rostron was suspended or injured. That weakened their side for me, and Trevor Steven had an absolute blinder; he tore the left-back inside out. They actually changed the left-back; Kenny Jackett went there in the second half, and he did the same to Kenny.

Gary Stevens: I'm a full-back and my job that day was to mark John Barnes who was up and coming; younger than me actually. I didn't play against too many players who were younger than me at that time. I think the ball broke out to twenty, maybe twenty five yards out and it was a bit of a foot race between John Barnes and myself and whether it was a tackle, shot, pass doesn't matter. It ended up at Graeme's feet and the rest we always talk about. That was nice, nice to be involved in that final little piece of play; a precision pass shall we say.

Howard Kendall: Sharpy in a single movement stopped the ball, turned, and shot off the inside of the post into the Watford goal.

Graeme Sharp: It just came out to the edge of the box and Gary kind of mishit it. More than anything else it was like a block tackle, and I was watching it. It fell to me and my first touch was good with my left boot, I turned, and then shot inside the post. They were complaining a lot for offside, I think they weren't too happy about it, but at that stage and at that time you don't really think about that. The most important thing is to get your shot on target, and I was fortunate enough to see it go in off the post and past the goalkeeper. It was fantastic for me, fantastic for the players. Watford had their chances, and it was just at the right time to score. I think that settled us down.

Neville Southall: Andy Gray put the game beyond Watford six minutes after the half-time after heading home a Trevor Steven cross. His goal was considered controversial because he clattered the Watford keeper, Steve Sherwood, while rising for the ball, but it was just a collision of the kind you get in every game; there was no foul, and the referee was right to allow it.

Andy Gray: Had it been the winning goal then I'm sure it would have caused even more controversy. I think the fact that it was the second helped. But it was a goal that won it, without a doubt, because at 1-0 you're always a bit edgy. The second goal went in and we knew they couldn't score two against Neville, that was certain. I just remember that Trevor Steven was going down the right wing, I knew he just wanted half a yard and he would sling it in. What I had to choose was whether I was going to go near post or stay back post. Invariably sometimes when you have to dig it out, because he was under pressure, when you dig it out it goes long, so I decided to hang behind, I think it was [Steve] Terry, big centre-back, and Steve Sherwood who was in goal, and as he floated it I had a good run on it. And I can remember going up for it and Sherwood was stretching, really stretching, and he kind of got both hands to it, and my head came through just as he was collecting it, because Terry didn't jump, because he felt his keeper was getting it. So I kind of jumped over him, and as I got to the ball the keeper was just about to close both hands on it, and I just put my head on it, and because we were so close to goal, it didn't need a lot of power, and I just nodded it out his hands and it just dropped over the line. I said it at the time, nine times out of ten that might have been given as a free-kick, because it would have looked bad, but what I never did, if you look at it, is make contact with the goalkeeper bodily, because I jumped past him. I managed to get my head to the ball because he was at full stretch and I knocked it out of his hand. When I saw it rolling over the line I think we all knew – you just had to look at our celebrations then – it was game, set and match.

Kevin Ratcliffe: I've never played in a more boring cup final than the second half. Mo Johnston and the lad Riley, we caught them offside, me and Derek, that many times. I think the worrying part is you're dominating the game so much that they'll get one chance and score. Then that ball that floats over and

Andy heads in. How can somebody can actually say it's a foul I just do not know, because if you look at it time and time again, he doesn't touch the keeper. It's their player that touches the keeper and he gets his head to it, and that was Andy all over.

Derek Mountfield: Next thing I know, the whistle goes, me and Rats have a big huddle and I go, 'Shit, I've won the FA Cup.' I'm looking up at the steps at the old Wembley thinking, 'I'm going up there in a minute, and I'm coming down with a medal.' There's a great picture of Howard looking up at us in his suit, and that was a sign of somebody really enjoying what he has produced.

John Bailey: I just sank to my knees. I looked up to the sky. I can't describe it; I can't believe it, it's something a kid dreams about; what I dreamed about. I turned around and the first one I saw was Big Nev and I just jumped into his arms. I think there were a couple of supporters on the pitch; they grabbed hold of me and you just don't know what you're doing. I went over to Colin, the boss and that's it and then I remember getting a top hat.

Howard Kendall: These were the days before the managers received winners medals and I stood on the Wembley pitch, looking up as my captain Kevin Ratcliffe took the trophy from the Duchess of Kent and raised it aloft. Having been up those famous steps twice before to collect losers medals and experienced that agony, I was so happy my players were going up as winners.

Kevin Ratcliffe: Howard said when they won the league under Harry Catterick, that Harry Catterick wouldn't take his hands off the cup, and he never let the players enjoy it. So Howard stepped back and let the players enjoy it. Which was nice because the players have done it. He's only picked the team hasn't he?

Mark Higgins: Kevin tells me to this day that if he had his time again then he would have taken me up to get the cup, because I was captain as well, but they didn't do it in those days. If you see the photographs, I didn't even go on the pitch for the photographs, I walked back in the dressing room, because I didn't play.

Neville Southall: I didn't mind getting the medal but I didn't want to traipse all the way up to the Royal Box to get it from the Duchess of Kent. I just wanted to get the medal and go. I found it all incredibly embarrassing and always did. I never watched it afterwards on television; it just wasn't me. Even the lap of honour I found very awkward. I was very happy, but for me if you go to work and you do what you're supposed to do, nobody jumps around for you, do they? It might be nice but we'd just done what we were supposed to do, which was win.

John Bailey: The top hat came from a place in Aintree. I got my medal, came down the stairs and a fella just threw it at me. I didn't put it on then. I went down the stairs and I just ran round with it put it on and someone threw a pair of Elton John glasses. I wish I had a £1 for everyone who asked me about it; I'd be a millionaire by now.

Graeme Sharp: You've seen it happen so many times before with other people, having the enjoyment of it, so we were delighted to go up those steps. I always tried to follow Kevin up the steps; we all tried to get second spot. Coming back from the game the champagne's popping in the dressing room, everybody's on a high. And then it's a case of 'Where do we go now?' We had an after-match party arranged in London. The staff had arranged it back at the hotel prior to the final, and it was a case of 'Who's taking the trophy?' Howard wanted to take the trophy to the staff do, the players wanted to take it to the players' do. We eventually won at the end and we got the trophy back. [We went] into London afterwards and then go to the nightclub, Stringfellows was the name, and we were drinking champagne in Stringfellows from the cup. It was something that all winning teams used to do, so we thought 'Why not? We can't break the habit.' We had a great night with our families and friends.

Andy Gray: Everyone says the first's the most difficult, it's not really. The second's the most difficult, because anyone can win a trophy. Middlesbrough won the League Cup a few years ago, but never really went on to win anything. Coventry won the FA Cup, they didn't really move on and win anything. What I've always said is the first one is difficult, but a lot of teams have won the first one. The really good teams go on and win the second one quickly after it, and that was important for us. We had won the FA Cup, it gave us a boost, it gave us great belief in what we were doing, and it sent us into the summer so looking forward to the start of the next season, it was unbelievable.

Neville Southall: All this was down to Howard and the jigsaw he had created. Some players had been tested and hadn't worked out. There were gambles, such as Andy and Reidy, who would pay off in the end. But I think his real quality was the strength he had in his own convictions. He made his decision and stuck with it. He never came out and criticized; always backed his team, which was a major thing in building up loyalty and a sense that his team would do anything for him. He was a proper old school manager, but had some very modern and progressive ideas on the training pitch. I don't know how much of this Philip Carter saw and I think it would have been very easy for him to have sacked Howard when things weren't going right. I don't know the conversations the two of them had, but obviously Howard convinced him enough to say 'carry on.' And thankfully it was the right decision.

Howard Kendall: The first trophy is always the best. It's something no-one can take away from you. You've made an indelible mark in the history of Everton Football Club, that you were the manager when the FA Cup has been lifted. Whatever else happened in my life and career I was the manager when we won something. Joe Royle would feel the same way too. Nothing would ever feel as good as that first trophy, but more were to come.

Derek Mountfield: You come back home on the Sunday, get off the train on an open top bus, and you realise then what it means to the fans. Everton fans have watched Liverpool fans parade trophies around the city for years, and all of a sudden it was us. It was magnificent to do that, one of the highlights of my career.

Neville Southall: The next day we had the victory parade around Liverpool, which, again, I was not really very easy with. I just found the attention embarrassing and always would; it was something I never grew out of. But happily for Evertonians I was to be posed with plenty more awkward moments over the next few years.

The players of mid-eighties

Howard Kendall: One of the players I knew straight away that I would do anything to sign was Trevor Steven. I went to Burnley a number of times to watch and he always shone for me. He looked an

Everton player, and when I say an Everton player I'm talking about an Alex Young-type player – that standard, that level of class. Whatever club he went to fans would love him, but especially Evertonians given the tradition they enjoyed with such players.

Gary Stevens: Technically Trevor Steven was fantastic; very very quick feet; he was pacier than I think people give him credit for. But if you look at it as a kind of partnership down the right he'd always do the opposite to what I would do; so if I was forward he would defend. We were a very difficult team to break down on the right hand side. We shared a room and we knew each other very well on and off the park so it does make for a good partnership when you get on with a player. You know what he's going to do and you've got the confidence to know that if you go past him and you don't get the pass he isn't going to lose it, he's going to keep it. We called him 'Tricky' because he had very very good feet and it was very difficult to get the ball off him.

Howard Kendall: When I promoted Colin to first team duties, one of the additional jobs I gave Mick Heaton was to work with the full-backs. That was Mick's position when he was a player and I knew his experience playing there combined with his excellence as a coach would benefit the players. The one to profit the most from Mick's input was Gary Stevens. He had been a left-winger or left sided midfield player when I went to Everton and I transformed him into a right fullback because of his pace and his athleticism. Mick worked with him after training and gave him special coaching for the fullback position. He'd been in and out of the team during my first two seasons as manager, but now seemed set to make the number two shirt his own.

Kevin Ratcliffe: People don't see what Kevin Sheedy did, but because he'd make sure he was in the right position, then he didn't have to do any work. I always think that Bob Latchford did exactly the same, and that's why they were called lazy and they didn't do anything else but score goals and create goals. But Kevin was by far one of the most talented players I've seen at the club, and I've never seen a left foot like his. I still haven't as of today. Messi, okay, but it's a different type of left foot. He could do anything.

Derek Mountfield: Howard Kendall did things differently to what I'd seen previously with my previous two managers. You run with the ball, you play with the ball, so why would you run miles and miles without the ball? You need your basic aerobic fitness and that was your 20-25-minute run, everything else was done with the ball. That's the thing I noticed, straight away it was ball work. I became a far better player very quickly, because the ball was constantly with me: he liked his head tennis, his 1 v 1's, his 4 v 4's, his 5 v 5's, his big games. Because the ball was with me more I became a better player very quickly, and a lot of that is down to Kendall and Harvey.

Howard Kendall: I think Kevin Ratcliffe's role in that great side is sometimes overlooked a little bit. He wasn't the most technically gifted player, but he had pace, character, aggression; he was left sided, which is always an asset to a manager. As a captain he controlled the dressing room. When someone stepped out of line he made my job a little bit easier by imposing discipline upon them. Reidy, Sharpy and others were big personalities, but Kevin was my main man. I could rely upon him completely.

Andy Gray: We had a lot more of the football that I had been used to at times, a lot more short-sided games and things like head tennis. Very much team bonding, they did a lot of things outside of the game as well. Howard believed in not over-coaching. So he was the motivator, Howard was the man manager, he took part in training and got involved that way, whereas Colin would take you away to the side, maybe after a game, and he'd take you upstairs to his room, and he'd have the TV and the tapes on, and he'd just show you a few things. He'd say 'Listen: this, this, this and this,' and it was the first time anyone had done this to me, taking me aside like that. People had talked to me about the game, but they hadn't shown me on videos what we were doing wrong and what we might change. Between them they had a terrific partnership that gelled beautifully. One was the very outgoing manager and the other was quieter, very thoughtful; both magnificent football men though. They complimented each other really well.

Howard Kendall: When I was at Stoke as a player-coach [in the late 1970s] they didn't have an apprenticeship scheme, didn't have any youngsters coming through at all. Reviving their youth scheme was something that Alan Durban started off. What he did was contact local amateur leagues to ask them about their best young players, and he brought in about twelve players during the summer for us to have a look at. It was essentially to start off an apprenticeship scheme and we agreed that we'd sign six out of the twelve. From the trials we picked out five of the six players and then there was a vote on the last one. The youth team coach and myself voted for one, but Durban disagreed. But because we had two votes, we won and the young kid was given an apprenticeship at the Victoria Ground. That player was Paul Bracewell.

Neville Southall: Paul brought calmness and an ability to tidy things up to the side. He made his living for the first couple of seasons passing back to me and getting a round of applause from the Goodison faithful for it! He was a great foil for Reidy; they went in pairs and they closed down well. Brace had a good brain on him too. I don't think he was particularly the quickest player in the world but he had a touch of class.

Howard Kendall: I signed him from Roker Park for £250,000 and as with Trevor Steven it was a great bargain. All Paul had needed was just that little bit of luck to get him started, but he was a great player for us. For eighteen months or so he was absolutely magnificent with Reidy. They were on the same wavelength. Reidy went in and closed down; Bracewell followed him. Bracewell goes and closes, Reidy was following him. I think it was a superb partnership.

Gary Stevens: As a coach now Kevin Sheedy's always going on about getting in there and tackling, running and I think, 'Where did he get that from?' Sheeds never really had any pace but he had so much time. Left footed players always look the part; they always have a gift. He had a wand of a left foot and all the time he had he was fantastic and he provided a lot of ammunition for the strikers.

Neville Southall: A couple of months into the season Howard made another new signing, bringing the left-back Pat Van Den Hauwe from Birmingham City. Pat came in for John Bailey, who I thought was very unlucky to lose his place. I knew John inside out and he was a much better all round player than most people gave him credit for. He was a fine attacker. He was honest. He could tackle. I wouldn't say he was a cleverer player than Pat but he at least looked like someone who naturally played on the left side and got a good cross in, whereas Pat was more of a pure and simple defender.

John Bailey: It was upsetting at the time. I mean, Christ, you've just won the cup. The Boss believed in playing a right footer at left-back. I don't know if he was a better defender than me but it was hurtful at the time.

Howard Kendall: I loved the bones of Bails; I think he's an absolutely fantastic character. I've employed him, I've sacked him; I think he's absolutely brilliant. He was constantly cracking jokes. We were playing Liverpool and Craig Johnston ran down the left hand side, crossed the ball; Rushy nipped inside Bails, past Neville and scored. Neville in his typically blunt manner yelled, 'Where did Rushy come from?' Bails replied, 'I think it was Chester.' That was the type of character he was. But I felt that he wasn't as good a defender as I wanted. I felt I needed another left-back, and so I sent one of my coaches, Terry Darracott, down to Birmingham to double check on Pat. My reason for sending Terry was that he was a full-back, so knew and understood the position, which I felt was something very important. Terry came back and reported, 'Not too sure about the left foot; but he can defend, there's no problem on that.' That was good enough for me.

Pat Van Den Hauwe: My job was simple. Howard said to me if you could just win the ball, give it to Sheeds, he'll do the rest. I said well that's alright, that'll do me. Sheeds, one of the best left foots, at the time, in the First Division. He could spray it anywhere, 30 yards, 35 yards, he was different class. Scored free kicks for us.

Kevin Sheedy: I think I got more of the ball off Pat because he was a right-footed left-back. Bails had a great left foot and he tried to make the passes that I would have tried to make. So from a selfish point of view Pat gave me a lot more service than Bails, but Bails was a great full-back as well, so I was fortunate to have great players playing behind me. He took a little bit of weight off me defensively, I was able to focus more on my game, which was creating and scoring goals. They were two good players to play in front of.

Neville Southall: Much has been said and written about Pat, who has attracted his own mythology. But for me, the 'Psycho' sobriquet has been overstated. Pat was always a bit of a pussycat as far as I was concerned. There's two Pat's; there's the Pat that trains every day and the Pat that's had a drink. I always found him to be nice as pie; never a threat to anybody. He could be a nuisance sometimes, but I never found him threatening, nor that way inclined. To me Pat's aggression covered a lack of confidence. He wanted to be liked and built up an image that I don't think anywhere near reflects who he is. He's got a reputation of being a hard man but I just didn't see that in him.

Howard Kendall: Pat's nickname was Psycho, but his reputation as a hardman was overstated. There were some tough players at Everton then, but none had a reaction like Pat. It was his reaction that got him the nickname, rather than doing something dirty or crude or something like that; it his look.

Neville Southall: Pat was openly aggressive in his game, I'll give you that, but I never found him to be stupidly aggressive. He'd front people up, but it's easy to front people up on the field because somebody always breaks it up. It's like in school when the teacher's round the corner, where they stand up to each other, start pushing each other, then the teacher comes and they all run off. He didn't like anybody taking liberties, and he would kick people. If someone wanted to fight him he'd stand up for himself. But all of them did. But I don't think he ever sought out trouble, really.

Kevin Ratcliffe: Pat was a good defender. That's what he's been brought in to do; he was quick, he was aggressive, he was 6ft 1inches, good in the air, played right the way along the back four. Limited going forward, but didn't have to because he had Kevin [Sheedy] in front of him, who was exceptional. Howard just needed somebody to back him up really, and I thought he worked a treat.

Neville Southall: The season opened with a return to Wembley for the Charity Shield match against Liverpool, who were League Champions. We placed a lot of importance on it. It was partly a revenge match and partly another chance to use them as a yardstick. We put in a commanding performance that was settled when Sharpy broke into the Liverpool area, took the ball around my opposite number, Bruce Grobbelaar, and when his shot was blocked on the line by Alan Hansen it rebounded back off Bruce and into the net.

Colin Harvey: Going into the 1984/85 season we played Liverpool in the Charity Shield. We beat them, and gave them a real good game. The season started, and we got beat 4-1 at home by Tottenham after dominating the game, then went to West Brom on the Monday and got beat. But you could see, even though we got beat in those two games, we were the better side After the game I just said, 'We've got 40 games to win the league now.' And sure enough we did.

Neville Southall: Two of the most memorable games in the autumn of 1984 were against Liverpool and Manchester United. Liverpool had had a really bad start to the season but even though we – as a team – knew we were as good as them, for the fans there was still a hoodoo. They were our nemesis. But this was to end in spectacular fashion.

Graeme Sharp: Howard had us training the week prior with those Adidas tango balls that Liverpool used. We knew by training with them that they were very light, and if you hit them right they would fly all over the place, and it was difficult for both the goalkeepers. Howard had done his homework, and allowed us to practice with these footballs.

Neville Southall: When Gary Stevens hit a long punt upfield, Sharpy was on the end of it; he flicked the ball past Alan Hansen, then volleyed into the top corner of Grobbelaar's net from 30 yards. It was a fantastic goal, and the win it earned us reinforced how far we'd come.

Graeme Sharp: Gary knocked it long, I managed to get a decent touch on it and take it away from Mark Lawrenson, and if I'm honest I'm thinking, 'I'm not going to win a race with Mark Lawrenson,' because he was a quick defender. As my touch was good, it bounced up for me and having had all the practice the week before in hitting these balls I thought, 'Well why not?'

Derek Mountfield: Once that goal went in and we won the game, everyone sort of went 'Yeah we are as good as them, we can match them', and Liverpool realised as well. I think they realised that there was going to be a nice competitive element on Merseyside for a few years to come. With luck it would have been a lot longer. We never saw the league title coming with five or six games to spare and 90 points, but something happened that game and it gave us a bit more belief.

John Corbett: It was the only time I've seen fans supporting one side fighting amongst each other. It led to an outbreak of fist fighting in the Kop, literally. They could not believe that Everton were winning by such a spectacular goal. And the walk across Stanley Park afterwards was absolutely amazing because people were very excited by it; Liverpool fans were more or less heading off in a kind of funereal haze. But it was an incredible goal. And the expectations that came from that were, 'Well, we can do this twice every season now.'

Neville Southall: For me there was an added edge. Every time we played Liverpool the 5-0 always came back to my mind. That's all I ever thought back to every time I played them: You cost me so many months of my career; you beat us 5-0 and you basically fucked my career up for a bit. I never needed much motivation for any match, but that gave me an extra edge.

Howard Kendall: United were tipped as one of the title favourites and had a team that cost six times what I'd spent on my Everton team. What followed that afternoon wasn't so much a win, but a rout.

Neville Southall: We came off the pitch at Anfield thinking things can't get any better. But when we played United at Goodison a week later they did. United were top of the league and title favourites. We beat them 5-0 with a performance that was flawless. We couldn't play any better and it would have been hard to pick a fault. When you come off the pitch you normally say 'I could have done that, maybe done that.' But that day it was impossible to pick up on anything. There were lots of games like that by the season's end. We scored a variety of goals; different people scoring goals; we defended well, we attacked well; we just had a whole thing going. We put pressure on people and made them make mistakes. We had some open games where we scored fantastic goals; we scored a lot of goals at times.

Kevin Ratcliffe: The big thing was the Man United game, because they'd gone ten games unbeaten at the start of the season and were talking about winning the league. People would sort of say 'It's Man United's...' To which I'd say: 'How many games are left by the way?' You don't win the league within the first ten games of the season. It might dictate the way you're going to be, but then for us to go and win that with the run that they'd been on, and absolutely pummel them. 5-0, but maybe it could have been eight or nine. I had a penalty decision turned down, when I've skinned Gordon McQueen. Sharpy was once again unplayable; Sheeds was throwing his head in where he'd never thrown his head in before. They couldn't live with us.

Kevin Sheedy: That was the turning point, the 5-0 against Man United, because they were a good team. They were going for the league as well. I think probably that was the best performance from a team I've played in, because it was 5-0 going on 8-0. We just absolutely battered them. I remember scoring a header from the edge of the box, which was a rarity for me, but just the quality of football that we played, everybody probably played to their maximum on that day, there was no stopping us. After that game you're looking in the dressing room and you then realise now when you go out and play against teams, if they're not so good you can play at 70, 80% and beat them.

Derek Mountfield: We won two games 5-0 in the space of five weeks, we beat Forest 5-0 as well. But that United game, people say that's the best performance they've ever seen at Goodison Park. We demolished them. It should have been a lot more than five.

John Corbett: At that stage we began to feel rather arrogant; the sort of feeling we had in 1970 was starting to come back again. The confidence that any team coming to Goodison was liable to be dealt a lesson in football.

Colin Harvey: Even better than that, we went there on the following Tuesday and beat them 2-1 in the League Cup. We took a pounding, Bryan Robson was at his most powerful, went through every player like he could do, and we beat them 2-1, and that was more satisfying than the 5-0 one. Bryan Robson was steaming after the 5-0 game, and he came out all guns blazing. It was one of the best performances I'd seen from a player. Physical and football wise.

Andy Gray: Sharpy and Inchy became arguably the best front pair in the country at the time; they were terrific together. Watching them play was a joy. I mean I was frustrated, but it was an absolute joy to watch the two of them. Brilliant combination play, they got on well with each other, they were opposites in the way that Graeme was a target man with great skill and Inchy buzzed around him. And then I came back in the team and for ten games I was on the bench. I think it was November that Inchy got a terrible injury against Sheffield Wednesday at Goodison, did his cruciates. I think that everyone thought, 'Well that's it, that could be the end of our challenge,' because Andy's totally different to Adrian. Graeme and Andy might be too similar. I think Graeme and I knew that there were one or two questions, and we talked about it. We said, 'We need to show that we can do this,' and I always felt that we could. We might have been similar in the way we played the game, but we were intelligent footballers. We weren't tripping over each other to get to the same ball. I was more experienced than Graeme, and I used that experience, and it ended up that it couldn't have worked any better. We went on a great run. As you know the rest is history, it was an unbelievable finish to the season we had. We hardly lost a football match, and it gave me great satisfaction because I was taking over from someone who had lit up the First Division in the opening ten or fifteen games.

Kevin Sheedy: It was a major loss. It was only maybe Andy who could have stepped in that we had at the club. Adrian was on fire; his movement, his understanding of where to be and the runs he made. He was a goal scorer as well. If we hadn't have won it, we could have looked back and said that would have been the difference. Andy came in, and obviously he was chomping at the bit because he couldn't get in the team. It was his opportunity to win a league. Again going back to Howard, that's good man management, forward thinking. He needed an extra striker just in case, took a gamble on Andy and it paid off.

Howard Kendall: By November 1984 we were top of the First Division and besides a brief spell over Christmas we remained there until the end of the season. I had a similar problem as I experienced at Blackburn five years earlier: we just couldn't stop winning. How do you motivate players when they're winning? Send them out there. Don't bore them. How do you stop them from getting complacent? Other players stop them from getting complacent. It wasn't down to me.

Kevin Sheedy: Obviously the better the opposition you have to play better, but certainly at that time we were oozing confidence. You just look at Nev, it would take something special to beat him. The back four was solid, you could play a high line because Rats was the quickest defender in the country at the time. The midfield, you had Reidy and Brace, every time they went in for a challenge I knew they would win the ball 99% of the time, so that allowed me to step forward in front of whoever was marking me and I'd get a pass because I knew they were winning the ball. I had a great understanding with Adrian Heath. I knew when he wanted the ball short or his movement in behind, and as the ball is coming to you, you knew exactly where he wanted it. You've just got that relationship, that understanding, all over the team. Gary Stevens and Trevor Steven, they had a great relationship and understanding of playing down that right side. All over the pitch you had your pairs, and it all linked and gelled into the team.

Neville Southall: It was quite difficult sometimes because you've got to concentrate on what you're doing without getting caught up in it all. It was for the same reason that I didn't watch Match of the

Day because they just go on and on about this, that, you could do this, this could happen. I didn't really want to hear it. All I wanted to know was what was thought on the training ground and in the dressing room. That was enough to focus on. I never thought about the last game, only think about the next one.

Andy Gray: The system didn't change and neither did the players, I think that was the secret. You could pick that back four, obviously John Bailey had moved out and Pat Van Den Hauwe had come in, so you could virtually name that team. Southall in goal, Stevens, Ratcliffe, Mountfield, Van Den Hauwe, Steven, Bracewell, Reid, Sheedy, Sharp, and as it was me taking over Inchy. The team hardly changed. Great players like Kevin Richardson couldn't get a game. They played in the odd game, and Alan Harper contributed hugely, both of them. But when Howard needed a team, he picked that team that I've named. And that was the team that basically saw the season out.

Kevin Sheedy: Game to game the same players played – if you were fit you played, so he obviously eased on the training ground, we did very light training sessions building up to games. You didn't want to be playing because of the atmosphere, particularly at Goodison, the atmosphere was fantastic and you didn't want to be sitting on the bench, you wanted to be out there. It's a short career. I know they have the rotation in place now because they've got much bigger squads, but certainly at that time if you were fit and you were playing well you stayed in the team.

Howard Kendall: To be honest, it was easy to manage in the second half of the 1984/85 season. You knew what you were getting; you knew who was going to be on your team sheet. Every Monday morning, there'd be a 'knock knock' on my door; I'd say, 'Come in Kevin.' Because I knew exactly who it would be. Richardson. 'What have I got to do man?' he'd ask. 'What have I got to do?' He scored two at Southampton and I dropped him; left him out, for Sheedy. Sheedy was safe. The other one was Harper. 'What's happening?' he'd ask. I said, 'I've got to pick my best eleven. You're a very good player and I want you; but I've got to pick my strongest team, I'm sorry.' I think they got the chances though; they played the games because it wasn't a 20-man squad or 22-man squad; it was 14 or 15; and that was enough back then. They knew they were going to get the chances.

Colin Harvey: It was the same feeling I had during the 1969/70 season. We played a game in that season at Coventry and we won 1-0. We played absolutely rubbish, but we won 1-0, and when you come away from a game like that and you know you've been rubbish and won you know it's going your way. It happened in the 85 season – I forget who it was – we played away from home and we won. And Howard said to me afterwards 'Do you remember a game against Coventry?' I said 'I certainly do.' He asked, 'Does that remind you of something today?'

Andy Gray: It was the unity, it was that we liked each other off the pitch as well as on it, there was a drive, there was a determination, there was a desire. They had all that as young boys, and I had it as an old guy because I didn't want it to end, I was enjoying it hugely.

Kevin Sheedy: I think you're in a position you've not been in before as a player. You don't want to not win it once you're in a winning position. I think just think the players that we had, the professionalism that we had, the training, the intensity of the training, the quality of the training was always just going into the games. We didn't have a great deal of injuries or suspensions, so we had the continuity of the same team. Everyone was just playing to their maximum, full of confidence.

Howard Kendall: Winning the League Championship was down to so many factors. People ask me what the key component was in that team, and the answer is simple: goals. Without them you won't win anything. It's fine having a tight defence, but you need to do more than simply shut out your opponents; you need to beat them. Five players – Trevor Steven, Derek Mountfield, Graeme Sharp, Kevin Sheedy and Adrian Heath scored more than ten league goals, a sixth – Andy Gray – scored nine.

Gary Stevens: If you look at a montage of goals from that season – fantastic stuff – and we scored from all over the park which was a nice thing. You get your centre half getting double figures. I was at the dizzying heights of two, three a season at that point as well, so goals came from all over the park! It was very enjoyable. At the end of the day football was my job, it was my day at the office, and if you could go to the office and have a good time – I was living every schoolboys dream.

Derek Mountfield: I was a centre-forward until I was about thirteen, nearly fourteen – I'd been a centre-forward all my life, so I just liked the glory of scoring goals. I moved back and people say to me 'you scored a lot of goals.' I scored 60 odd in my career, and I guarantee most of my goals came from free-kicks and corners. If you get quality delivery into boxes – and I had Trevor Steven and Kevin Sheedy, I went to Aston Villa and had Gordon Cowans – you're going to score goals.

Andy Gray: The way the league was set up, I think Tottenham had ten games to play, six of them home. We had a lot of away. And we went there [on 3 April], and they were classing it as a title decider. And there must have been nearly 50,000 in White Hart Lane that night, it was absolutely packed. Packed. And I think they came to see us get beat, but, like most teams at that time, we were good enough. Again, it was a big night, we played really well. Defended well, made the most of the chances we had, and when Mark Bowen made a mistake and Trevor Steven nicked in, and when he made it 2-0 we thought 'Yeah, this is a big statement.' But then they got one back, Graham Roberts smashed one in, and I don't think anyone who was at Everton then or played in that team will forget the save Neville made from Mark Falco in the last couple of minutes to keep it at 2-1. It was just unbelievable, out of this world.

Neville Southall: The moment that everyone remembers came three minutes from the end. Glenn Hoddle crossed the ball into the area and from point blank range Mark Falco headed towards my top corner. I stretched for it and tipped it over the crossbar. What more can I say? It was straight at me really and I'd saved plenty like that on the training ground. I always knew I was going to get it. For many people that was the moment we won the league title. Maybe they're right because we held on to win 2-1 and Spurs eventually finished the season thirteen points behind us. But at the time you never think of the significance of what you've done, or say to yourself 'That was a great save.' My teammates certainly didn't congratulate me. Ratcliffe yelled at me: 'Why didn't you catch it? Why are you fucking giving a corner away?'

Howard Kendall: Where do you begin with Neville? Neville became the world's best, for me, but it never changed him. He was still grumpy and down to earth. There were none of the things that you associate with a famous footballer and he still cycled to training from his home in West Derby. But his success and recognition were all fully deserved. Although he was shy in many ways, he was also very vociferous on the training ground. He was a great example of a player helping me as a manager. He'd dictate how he wanted the defence organised for set pieces. 'I want someone on the back post, I'll deal with anything that goes anywhere else but I can't do both,' he'd say. 'I can't protect my near posts as well as my back post.' So we got a defender to go back when the ball was about to be taken, to go back on the back post so the goal was protected. And the rest of it was down to Neville. To be honest, that wasn't my idea of coaching; that was the goalkeeper telling me what to do. But if he's telling me what to do and he's comfortable about that, then you do it.

Pat Van Den Hauwe: He was first in, last out. Trained like a dog. He was there three quarters of an hour, an hour before the rest of us, and he was already doing his work, then he'd join in and do bits with us.

Andy Gray: Neville was best in the world at the time. There was no other goalkeeper in the world that I would have rather have had in goal for us than Neville Southall. He was sensational. Sensational. Unbelievable. He worked so hard at his game, and I mean the year before that they'd almost played a game each: Jim Arnold, Neville, Jim Arnold, Neville, Jim Arnold, Neville, Jim Arnold, Neville. Howard couldn't quite make up his mind who was his number one goalkeeper. And then he did, and he made the right decision, without a doubt. He was terrific.

Derek Mountfield: Neville was unique. He struggled early on in his career like a lot of us did, but when he got in the first team and got that run in the side, he made goalkeeping look easy. Some of the things he did in training that people never saw, but he made things look easy. He used to dive in training and head the ball away, or chest it away, he wouldn't even use his hands. But some of the saves he made were phenomenal. I've seen him make mistakes, but some of the saves. People talk of the save at Tottenham from Falco, but he made a save at Sheffield Wednesday from Imre Varadi [on 4 May] which was just out of this world for me, fantastic. It's quite strange to think that we won the league at a canter, and we have Graeme Sharp scoring 25 to 30 goals, Andy Gray, Trevor Steven, yet our goalkeeper gets the FWA Footballer of the Year award. What he had to do, he did absolutely magnificently. But when he was quiet, when he had nothing to do, he still had to be on his toes all the time. Something could come and he would have to be alert to it. But for a goalkeeper to win the FWA award when the team's won the league title, at a distance, showed you how good he was. When he did things he was superb at it. Now he's just big Neville.

Neville Southall: Soon after the Spurs match I was named the Football Writer's Player of the Year. It's the older of the two player of the year awards and in winning it I was the first Everton player, the second Welshman (after Ian Rush) and only the third goalkeeper (after Bert Trautmann and Pat Jennings) to ever do so. No goalkeeper or Welsh player has won it since. It was nice to get the recognition but part of me felt a little uneasy to get all the plaudits when the players in front of me had also done so much. I went down to an awards ceremony at London's Savoy Hotel with Howard Kendall, but I was hardly able to speak having contracted laryngitis after all the shouting I'd been doing on the pitch. These dinners were never my thing anyway so I told Howard to do the speech for me. Unfortunately he fell off his chair and off the stage and ended up splitting his pants. He had to get them sewn up backstage, before saying a few words after I'd collected the award from the former FIFA president, Sir Stanley Rous.

Everton in the European Cup Winners' Cup

Neville Southall: In the European Cup Winners' Cup first round we played University College Dublin – a student team, basically. Everyone expected a walkover, but they held us to a goalless draw in Ireland

and in the last few minutes of the second leg at Goodison had a shot that clipped my bar. We were winning 1-0 at the time, but had it gone in they would have gone through on away goals.

Andy Gray: They nearly beat us, I think they hit the bar in the last minute at Goodison, had that gone in that would have been it.

Neville Southall: We went to Czechoslovakia to face Inter Bratislava. This was of course behind the Iron Curtain and to step into a communist country was to step back 20 years in time. The journeys were always ridiculously long, because there were a lack of direct flights or – if you were on a charter – airports at which you could land. Then there was loads of bureaucracy at the borders, and all you wanted to do was get to your hotel and get some rest and start preparing. As for the opponents it's not like now, where you can turn on the telly and watch a million games on Sky. People had to go and watch them. You had to really do your homework. That said we just played our way; we didn't change for anyone. Inter Bratislava weren't the best of opponents. We went there, got a 1-0 win, and at Goodison two weeks later turned them over 3-0. We always had our away matches first, which was always a big help. After that match there was a five month gap before our next European tie.

Andy Gray: When we played Sittard [in the quarter-finals] we were playing well, of course we were, we were flying. Terry Curran played that night; he played some part that night, I remember it. It was brilliant to get a hat-trick, it really was, particularly at the Gwladys Street. That's something I'll never forget: all very different goals: the first one I scuff in when the goalkeeper dropped Peter Reid's shot, the second a diving header in amongst feet, arms and legs, and the third one I smashed in from about twelve yards.

Colin Harvey: [In the semi-final against Bayern Munich] We played in the Olympic Stadium in Munich, which was their old ground. We had a couple of injuries, and Kevin Richardson played wide right, and Alan Harper played wide left, and the two of them did fantastic jobs, just real hardworking, do as you're told jobs. I remember thinking after we beat them at Goodison that those two probably set that game up for us, because of the discipline and hard work they'd shown in the Olympic Stadium, which meant we drew 0-0.

Neville Southall: They were one of the great club sides in European football; a club that had won the European Cup in three successive years in the mid-1970s. They had famous players like Lothar Matthaus, Dieter Hoeness and Klaus Augenthaler in their line up. By contrast, I think, hardly anybody outside England knew who we were. We didn't let this phase us. We never let anything bother us, ever. We just played our game. Reputations counted for nothing. When we travelled to Bavaria for the first leg Kevin Sheedy and Andy Gray had picked up injuries. We didn't have a large squad, but we had a close one and we trusted the players that we had in reserve implicitly. So when Alan Harper and Kevin Richardson came in for Kevin and Andy we knew they would do a job. And they did just that. We played with maturity and commitment, like winners, although I didn't think I played that well myself. I was beaten on one occasion by Michael Rummenigge, the younger brother of Karl Heinz, but Richardson was there to clear the ball off the line and to safety. We drew 0-0 and we knew we'd get them at Goodison.

Andy Gray: They were the big boys. We were the ones that were going to be the whipping boys. It was the princes and the paupers that were supposed to playing that night. They were the elite of Europe, all the best players, fantastic club, great tradition and history, and we were ragtag and bobtail at that time. Although we played for a great club, no one really in Europe had ever heard of any of us. We'd all heard of them: Michel Pfaff in goal, [Soren] Lerby, [Dieter] Hoeness upfront for them, all sorts of good players playing for them. Ludwig Kogl as well. Great players, great players. I think Lothar Matthaus played in those two games, so this was a brilliant team, and we kicked their butt. We kicked their butt. Our job was to get to the final, because we knew this was the final. We thought we'd beat Rapid Vienna, and we all knew – I think Bayern Munich knew – whoever won the semi-final was going to win the final.

Neville Southall: We knew the immensity of the occasion, that this was our final. If we beat Bayern we would beat anyone. On the day of the match we had a short training session in the morning, something to eat, and then went for a rest in the afternoon. It was a typical match day routine. But when we got to Goodison we knew that this was very different. There were people everywhere, singing and dancing and chanting our names. The team coach took 45 minutes to drive around the ground to the players' entrance. It was unheard of. The place was mental. I always loved playing under the Goodison floodlights, but this was different; this was really, truly something else. The crowd never normally affected me in any way, but on this night – the only time in my life – they worked as twelfth man. We could see how much it meant to everyone there and we wanted to win it for them. But the crowd also intimidated our opponents, jostled and battered them and in the second half almost seemed to suck the ball into the Gwladys Street net. You can beat 11 men, but you'll never beat 50,000 of them. I'd never seen anything like it before and never will again in my lifetime.

Howard Kendall: The danger, however, when playing amidst such enthusiasm and passion is that you lose your heads and make an error. A slack moment in the 38th minute saw Kogl played in behind the Everton defence by Matthaus. One on one with Neville, Southall blocked his shot only for Hoeness to put in the rebound past two defenders on the line. It was unfortunate for we had played much of the better football and held a level of dominance. But such is the danger of European football. One slip and your dreams are over.

Kevin Sheedy: That was just the best atmosphere I've ever played in. I've been fortunate enough to play in FA Cup finals. I played in the World Cup quarter-final in Rome, 80,000 people. But that night, just hitting the top step and coming out, the atmosphere was just electric. The noise levels seem to have lifted, and you could hear when they scored to go 1-0 up, you could just hear a pin drop. It was just deadly silent.

Andy Gray: We were really determined to get there. We didn't want to spoil it, and when we were 1-0 down it was a big fifteen minutes for Howard, and he handled it great. We went back out and we threw everything, and I mean *everything*, at them. We went long at times, we had long throw-ins; our first two goals came from long throw-ins. You know, there's more than one way to skin a cat. Not everybody plays the way Manchester City do, Barcelona. You can win big football matches in various ways.

Howard Kendall: My half-time talks were always brief. Fifteen minutes is a long time to fill, but I never spoke for more than a couple. I told them that the Gwladys Street would help 'suck it in.' That they had to be direct. It was not the most attractive way of doing it – long throws, aggression – but it worked. I didn't tell the players to rough up their opponents, or do anything like that; they knew what they had to do themselves. Fortunately we had players who were capable of understanding what we needed.

Kevin Sheedy: I've always said the turning point for us at half-time – we were kicking towards the

Gwladys Street – and Howard said at half-time 'They'll suck the goals in for you, just get them on the back foot.'

Kevin Ratcliffe: It was starting to get a little bit naughty. And I mean naughty. Even when they were down they were trying all the tricks in the book. Augenthaler was trying to elbow me in the box when he had a free-kick, to try and get a penalty. They were desperate. He was trying to elbow me, he was pushing me, standing on my toes. You've just got ride your luck and get on with it.

Pat Van Den Hauwe: We always believed that if we could get a result away from home and bring them back here, we'd have a very good chance. But as things turned out, they scored first. We all knew deep down that that's okay we could deal with that. And once we levelled the scores the crowd went absolutely fucking nuts. The noise, it's the best I've ever experienced at Goodison Park. It just gave us a major lift, and we all knew.

Howard Kendall: Andy seemed to go to war in that second half. The Germans just couldn't deal with him. At one stage a Bayern defender was off getting treatment for bloodied nose and Udo Lattek leaned out of his dugout and screamed, 'Kendall, this is not football.' The reaction from myself, the coaching staff, the substitutes, the physio – there must have been about 18 people who stood up – was unanimous and instant: 'Fuck off!'

Kevin Sheedy: We started the second half with a real high tempo, got a couple of throw-ins from Gary Stevens, which we hadn't practiced. It was just his adrenalin probably, he launched them in the box and Sharpy got on the end of one, Andy Gray got on the end of another one, and then the game opened up.

Andy Gray: I was going to test them, that is an absolute certainty. I'd made up my mind. I nearly got sent off in the first 20 minutes. Somebody came through the back of me and I turned and had a wild swing at him, and had I caught him I probably would have gone off, and who knows what would have happened. But I missed him and the referee took some sympathy on me. In those days you could be a bit physical and if people didn't fancy it you soon found out. There were a couple of incidents in the game, it's fair to say, and I remember Peter Reid playing with a sock that was just red because he'd been kicked, a big hole in his shin, and he didn't bother going off, he just stuck some cotton wool in it and just carried on. But by the time the game had finished he had one red sock and one white sock!

Kevin Ratcliffe: I think they might have been a little bit surprised about the way that we went about it, as if we were like gladiators going in and thinking that we've got to kill to survive. Because that's what it's like playing at Goodison in those type of atmospheres; you do fear you're not going to get out of there! It's intimidating, and we used that. I don't they'd expect that type of crowd, especially in a country like Britain. You might go to somewhere like Turkey, where it might be hostile, but to go to Britain and you've got that ground shaking…

Charles Lambert: My favourite memory of Goodison Park was the goal I never saw. I was producing for Radio 2, the outside broadcast, and that was the game where the emotions see-sawed. They were winning 2-1 with about ten minutes or so to go and I get the word in my headphones from London saying, 'Charlie you're going to do the post-match interviews get downstairs now so that you're in position for when the players come off the pitch.' So I got up and as I was making my way down the concrete staircase at the back of the stand I heard the most almighty roar and what felt like an earthquake taking place and I thought 'Something's happened' and 'Please God, it's an Everton goal.'

Kevin Sheedy: There was always going to be another goal. I remember getting the ball in the left-back position, I was waiting for Andy Gray to make a run, there was 55,000 Evertonians shouting 'man on.' I put it into Andy, he's fed it on to Trevor Steven, who scored the third goal. There was an eruption of noise, I've never heard anything like it before. That was us through to the final.

Howard Kendall: Andy was at the heart of our third and final goal. Paul Bracewell played a ball to him just inside the Bayern half. Andy played the ball first time, without looking up, into the path of Trevor Steven who raced clear and calmly drew Pfaff out of his goal as he advanced unchallenged, then stroked the ball past the exposed goalkeeper and into the bottom corner of the net.

Kevin Sheedy: There was no love lost in the game. There was tackles going on that were just X-rated. I remember Reidy taking his shinpad off and he had a big hole in his shin where Soren Lerby had gone over the top on him. Reidy just put a sponge on it and got on with it, it was that type of game. If that game had been played now it would probably end up five-a-side. It was just a crazy night. We knew what was at stake. They had some great players in their team so we really had to give it everything and more. Every ball was challenged for, and I don't think they had come into arena with the intensity from both the supporters and the players, that's why they lost their heads a bit I think, going to the bench: 'This is not football.' Well actually this is football.

Andy Gray: I remember getting interviewed by Elton Welsby after the game. I was stood there, and I could see Uli Hoeness, who was their Director of Football or whatever, stood there, and I thought he was going to say, 'Congratulations, good luck in the final!' But when I finished I turned around and he went, 'You, Gray, that is not football, that is not football, you are a disgrace.' I said, 'Piss of Uli, we're in the final! Do one!'

Neville Southall: It was an unbelievable night and something that will probably never happen again. It was a perfect storm; an inherent understanding between the players and the crowd. For me it was better than winning the league, better than winning the cup, better than anything that happened before or since.

Derek Mountfield: I remember going to watch Andy King score his winner against Liverpool and Latchford get his thirtieth. I'd experienced good nights in Goodison as a fan, but on the pitch that was by far the best atmosphere I've ever known in a football stadium. I played not far off 600 games, but for a one off atmosphere that was just incredible. I don't think it was the best of games, but the atmosphere will be the best atmosphere I have ever played. I'm taking all the finals away, that one game – the Bayern Munich game – the atmosphere was absolutely magnificent, it really was. It was amazing to think there was only 51,000, it felt like there was 151,000 in the ground; it was packed, it was busy, it was noisy and in the end we got the right result and it made it even better for us.

Howard Kendall: Afterwards I headed into Chinatown with some of the journalists that had been covering the game and reflected on hugely momentous night in my life and career. I'm not sure if anything has ever lived up to that experience. Back at home when my children came downstairs the following morning they found me and the Daily Mail's Colin Wood replaying a video recording of the game and drinking brandy and coffee. There was no way I could have slept that night, with the adrenalin surging through my veins.

Andy Gray: That will always remain the greatest game that I've ever played in ever. Not just at Everton but ever. I'll never forget that night, and I don't think there's an Evertonian alive who was at that game that would not put that down as his best ever night as an Everton fan.

Neville Southall: After that night what happened was, in a strange way, anti-climatic. We still had ten games to play in all competitions and we carried on doing what we'd been doing all season: winning. Victories over Norwich City, Sheffield Wednesday and Queens Park Rangers brought us the club's eighth League Championship.

Howard Kendall: It's funny looking back because we had still not won anything other than the right to play in the final. Rapid Vienna had won the other semi-final 4-2 on aggregate meaning we would meet in Rotterdam three weeks later. I immediately flew out to Austria to run the rule over them and on my return to Bellefield had to suppress my delight from the players. I was almost certain we would win the final, but I couldn't betray that confidence.

Derek Mountfield: Howard never told us, 'You're the best, you're going to win this', he would always set us up right. He would say these can do this, this and this, but if you do that, that and that you will beat them.

Neville Southall: We travelled to Rotterdam knowing that we wouldn't get anything less than a win. It would have been impossible after Bayern Munich. There was no way Rapid Vienna were going to get anything from the match; no chance whatsoever. The De Kuip Stadium was packed full of Scousers. Their ability to get places in huge numbers, even when the city was on its knees economically and unemployment raged, never ceased to amaze me. I'm sure there were always a few scallywags among them, but there was never any sign of trouble. Evertonians wherever they went were always loud, passionate and good-natured. English fans at the time had a reputation as troublemakers, but Evertonians were just never like that. On the day of the final they were playing games of football in Rotterdam's squares with Rapid fans and the local police.

Rev. Harry Ross: It was my son Philip's eighteenth birthday and I thought I would ask Jim Greenwood if there was any way of getting tickets. He said, 'Well yes and you can come on the plane with the team. So I wasn't going to say 'no.' They flew out from Liverpool airport which, of course, in those days didn't look like it does today. I remember after we checked in we followed the players to a prefab room that was similar to what schools used to use as classrooms. Philip and I hadn't flown before so, to be honest, we were too nervous to mix too much with the players save for the odd hello. Anyway the first sign that my big boss was on our side was when we went to get on the plane and I remember it had the papal crest on it. Apparently Pope John Paul II had used the plane when he toured Holland and Belgium as it was a KLM flight. So that immediately made me think, 'Okay things are going to be fine.' Then John Bailey took over as only John can do. As the stewardesses were doing the safety instructions there was John at the back of them copying everything they were doing; typical John and just what we needed. The flight was awful: up and down, not good for first time flyers; we were glad to get off it. We stayed at the Marriott in Amsterdam but the team stayed somewhere else. I remember in Amsterdam we went sightseeing and I was getting known as 'The Chaplain' then and I had my collar on, but that didn't stop many an Everton fan saying, 'Eh Father do you know where the Red light district is?' Well I genuinely didn't know where it was then so I could innocently say, 'No!'

Peter Mills: It was the first time I'd flown when I went to Rotterdam. I'd been abroad, but things like EasyJet and cheap flights were not around. I had a young family so it cost a lot of money. That season was very expensive, just cup ties and away games, and going to the match. I couldn't afford to travel, or couldn't get a pass really before then. That was a very exciting day; a big day in Rotterdam. That was the heartbreaking thing about it, just for the joyous atmosphere and how well-behaved everybody was, compared to what went on a fortnight later. That's where the bitterness really started and whether the bitterness is ever justified I don't know but I can fully understand it.

Pat Van Den Hauwe: I think in the dressing room in the days going into playing the game, we had self-belief, all the players. The manager didn't have to say nothing. No words. We went out with the mentality that we're going out to win this game. We're in the final and we're going to win it, and we did it for Everton Football Club.

Neville Southall: The thing people ask me about most regarding the final was my goalkeeper shirt. It was red, a colour many Everton fans consider sacrilegious. But there was an odd logic to me wearing it. Because Rapid played in green and white stripes I couldn't wear my usual colour, nor white. Black was out because that's what the referees played in, and so was blue for obvious reasons. Yellow was also out because that was only allowed in international matches. Which didn't really leave an awful lot more choice. Later at Everton I wore orange and pink and I think now you can wear whatever you wanted. But back then it was a bit more straightforward: primary colours, which pretty much left red.

Kevin Ratcliffe: I think the biggest disappointment was we came in at half-time and it was 0-0, and we've had that many chances that you think you've ran out of chances here, you've used them all up. I think Derek missed a couple of headers from set pieces. They broke on us a couple of times in the first half, and nothing worried me. I always knew. If I was a little bit hesitant about somebody because they had a bit more pace or whatever, but I never really felt in any danger of conceding a goal in that game. And we did, and it was late on, but other than that I never really felt that we were going to concede.

Derek Mountfield: We came in at half-time and I'd been flagged offside for a goal. I headed it back and Andy Gray scored, and Howard ripped me: 'You don't be offside.' I said, 'I wasn't offside.' He said, 'You were!' When he saw the replay after he came back and said, 'Sorry son you were right you weren't.' I was about two yards onside when the ball was played, but when I actually headed it I was offside. He said, 'No, take it back mate you were onside.'

Neville Southall: I think the most surprising thing was that it took us so long to get in front. Andy Gray put us ahead on 57 minutes after Sharpy latched onto a bad backpass to set him up. Trevor doubled the lead 15 minutes late after a scramble from a corner. Annoyingly the Austrians pulled one back through Hans Krankl with six minutes to go, but within a minute Sheedy had restored the lead. Don't get me wrong, it was a good night, but after Bayern Munich it was an anti-climax.

Derek Mountfield: I'm one of the eleven players who played a European final for Everton. You can't take that away from me. It's amazing that this little lad who grew up locally and played a lot of sport and then grew up a blue, all of a sudden is playing and winning a European final – I find it hard to believe still to this day. But what memories.

Kevin Sheedy: Myself and Gary Stevens got called in as we walked off the pitch to do a urine sample. As everyone knows you can't do it straight away. I think we were in there for about 45 minutes to an hour before we were able to do it. Got back to the dressing room to join in the celebrations and it was empty, there was no one there, they'd all showered. We'd missed out, so that was a little bit of a disappointment, but I can look back with a smile…

John Bailey: We got on the plane and we had a couple of bottles of champagne and when we got back to Speke we didn't go out. We drove home and we just got asked to report back to Bellefield on Friday ready for the match at Wembley on the Saturday. Man United. Some of the lads might have gone for a drink and celebrating – You've just won the European Cup Winners' Cup! – but we knew we had the final on the Saturday and so we all just took off and that was it. On Friday we got back into training, little run, five-a-side, head tennis, and back on the road to Wembley on the Friday, all back to normal. But it must've been tiring for the lads. I was on the bench then but it must've taken a lot out of them.

Andy Gray: We couldn't rest, that was the unfortunate thing. I don't think there was another team since that has had to do what we had to do. That's play abroad on a Wednesday night, a late kick-off in a European final, arrive back in their country about four in the morning. That's now Thursday. Go to bed for the day basically, rest. Get up Friday, go into training, basically have a jog, a warm down and a massage, get on a coach, drive to London, check in a hotel, get up the next morning and try and win a football match, an FA Cup final. It was too much; it really was a game too far. And it's a pity, because to win the treble would have been what that team deserved, because we were that good.

Everton's 1985 FA Cup run

Howard Kendall: We met Ipswich Town at Goodison and it was in many respects the perfect cup tie. The drama began after just five minutes when Kevin Sheedy scored twice from the same free kick. With the first kick he bent the ball over the wall into the right hand side of the Ipswich keeper, Paul Cooper's, net, but unfortunately the referee hadn't blown for the kick to be taken. Sheedy kept his cool and chipped another shot over the wall to Cooper's left!

Kevin Sheedy: It was a free-kick about 22 yards out, and I always used to try and get on the ball quickly so that if there was an advantage to be gained I could score. I did this time. The wall wasn't properly lined up by Paul Cooper, so I put it in his top right hand corner. The referee disallowed it, so Peter Reid picked the ball up and said, 'What are we going to do now?' I said, 'Get out the way and I'll put it in the other corner.' Paul Cooper had moved a step too far because he knew I could put in his right hand corner, so he left a gap on his bottom left so I was able to lift it over the wall. That's high on my list of favourites.

Derek Mountfield: In the semi-final against Luton we were 1-0 down, we played very poorly. We were getting back into the game and with about ten to go Howard gave me the nod, 'Up you go son.' I went upfront, I won the free-kick. It was only a little touch, but I made it into a big touch, and Sheeds scores from the free-kick and we're back in the game. I was regularly sent up late on in games if we were losing to try and get something for us. But that's the way.

Howard Kendall: Our tiredness showed and it seemed as if [Ricky] Hill's goal was going to be enough to put them in the final. With three minutes remaining we got a free kick after a foul on Derek Mountfield, who we'd pushed up front to give us some presence. Sheedy stepped up, and with his deadly left foot curled a shot wickedly around the Luton wall and it bobbled beyond the grasp of Les Sealey. We were ecstatic on the bench and as I celebrated I said to Colin, 'That'll do. When's the replay?' Colin was perplexed. 'We've got extra time Howard, there's still another 30 minutes to go.' In the excitement and fatigue I'd slipped into a state of confusion and forgotten what we'd been through twelve months earlier at Highbury.

Neville Southall: Derek was a key man on many occasions. In the Luton semi-final we pushed him up and he caused mayhem in and around the opposition box... In extra time we got another free kick: Sheedy crossed, Derek headed home and we were heading back to Wembley.

Derek Mountfield: I had a striker's instinct at times I think, I didn't try and lash the ball into the net, I tried to place it. Some centre-halves get a bit 'ahhh' and throw their feet at it, their feet are all over the place, but I tried to be a bit more controlled and patient, and I got the goals because of it.

Andy Gray: We had beaten Manchester United [who Everton were to face in the final], 5-0 at Goodison, I think we'd knocked them out the League Cup at Old Trafford, we drew 1-1 in the league at Old Trafford – they couldn't beat us, and Big Ron [Atkinson] knew that. But on the day we were tired. And the spark wasn't there. The effort was there, but the sharpness wasn't. The desire was there, but it was dulled, because it was going that extra yard. It was tough, and we found it really hard.

Kevin Sheedy: We had the Indian Sign over United. Obviously they'd had a free week leading up to the final. The Rapid game, you look back, and it does take it out of you physically, probably mentally as well, you don't realise at the time. We got back in the early hours Thursday morning from Rotterdam, went home and then reported Friday morning to travel down to Wembley. So we didn't really do any training because we wanted to save our legs. I remember walking out at Wembley and it was like the hottest day of the year, which didn't help us.

Howard Kendall: The game swung Manchester United's way when Kevin Moran was sent off for a foul on Peter Reid. It was a foul, but lacking malicious intent and because he caught Reidy off balance it looked worse than it was. I don't think it was a sending off and I don't think Kevin deserved to be the first player to be dismissed in an FA Cup Final. His sending off seemed to galvanise his teammates – as so often happens when a side is reduced to ten men – and it became even harder for us.

Kevin Ratcliffe: I think the big moment was when Kevin got sent off, then Frank Stapleton went from striker to centre half and had a great game. Never gave Andy or Sharpy a kick.

Andy Gray: Then it went to extra-time, and even though they only had ten men, we normally would have dominated teams who had a man less than us, and would have kept them penned in, wouldn't have let them out. But we couldn't do that on the day, for whatever reason.

Neville Southall: The final probably came a day too early for us. We had plenty of chances to win the match and hit the woodwork twice. But the energy and verve that had carried us through the previous six months wasn't quite there in the same quantities. United took us to extra time and we seemed to be heading for a replay when Norman Whiteside cut inside Pat Van Den Hauwe and curled a left footed shot past me.

Pat Van Den Hauwe: I said to Whiteside, 'Come on then', take me down the line, because I knew he was going to beat me with pace. That yard, as he's gone that way I went with him, and he clipped it back onto his left and whipped it in. I'm always interested to find out whether he meant to score that goal or was it a cross? Because I blamed myself for that goal, Neville blamed himself after the game for being too far on his near post, and it hit the far post and went in. I hold my hands up to it, Neville held his hand up, and Howard came up to both of us and said, 'It's none of your fault, it's just one of them things.'

Kevin Ratcliffe: For me it was Nev's fault, I've always said it. He was so close to touching the ball, but if you have a look at his positioning, he was actually right on the post. If we have been maybe half a yard, not even half a yard, he would have touched that, because he nearly got a fingertip to it. You'd like to think that it was a fantastic goal by a fantastic player. There were plenty of bodies. We always got told to bring players inside, when they were coming from the wing because when you take them inside there's bodies. In hindsight, maybe somebody like Norman, should take him down the line, because he's not going to do you for pace. I can't even remember if Norman was left footed or right footed; he was so good with either.

Neville Southall: I thought it was my fault, but no one blamed me and I haven't looked at it since. Norman later told me he'd practised that technique again and again. It was enough to win the match for United and it ended the most extraordinary season in Everton's history on a flat note.

Norman Whiteside: When I joined Everton a few years later I got on well with Big Nev. He was a real football man and a great keeper. We re-enacted the '85 goal many times over!

Pat Van Den Hauwe: I personally felt I had let the supporters down, and Neville did as well. Because it was the treble wasn't it? We wanted to win that as well, you know what I mean? But it was a bit hard that, I didn't really sit too well after that game. It was hard for me. Neville was looking at me and I was looking at him. Howard was fine with it, we did the best we could.

John Bailey: That was it, bingo, they couldn't recover; too tired. They were knackered. When I went into the dressing room after the medal presentation; they were just shattered. I was trying to say 'You should be proud of yourselves; you've just won the the league and European double.' They were okay after a few beers.

Derek Mountfield: That was probably one of the lowest points of my career that night. I was devastated we didn't win the treble, it would have been a fantastic achievement. You come back on the Sunday, you're down, I turned my ankle, so I couldn't play, I'm on crutches. You get on the bus at Goodison and you start driving round, and the fans are there in their thousands again. I remember seeing this one sign that said 'Don't worry boys, two out of three isn't bad.' And you think 'Yeah, you've got a point there.' They would have been delighted just to win the one trophy, but to win two, and have a chance of winning a third, it brings it back into perspective.

Andy Gray: We came up a game short, but it was tempered by the fact that we'd won the league and we became the first Everton side to win a European trophy. No one can take that from us. If somebody says to me, 'What would have you rather done? Would you have rather lost and done the double?' And it's a good question, but I would be rather be remembered as a member of a team that won Everton's first European trophy. I know the double would have been exceptional, but I don't know there's something nice about winning in Europe.

Heysel

Howard Kendall: Hooliganism was a problem that beset English football throughout the 1970s and 1980s. Domestically it was a huge blight on the game, contributing to declining attendances and dilapidated stadiums. Internationally it reaped shame on the country. Seldom did an overseas England international pass without major disturbances, which dominated the press not just in this country but far beyond. Everton, like all clubs, had a tiny minority of troublemakers, but wherever we travelled in Europe there were no real concerns about anyone misbehaving or bringing shame upon our great football club. Wherever we went our supporters followed us with passion and good behaviour. The final of the European Cup Winners' Cup in Rotterdam was a case in point.

Neville Southall: The following Wednesday all eyes were on Liverpool again, when they played Juventus in the European Cup Final. It was Liverpool's fifth final, Juventus's first. Liverpool had never lost at that stage of the competition before. They had that sort of winning mentality that we now also believed we had. But what happened that day was one of the most notorious episodes in football history. I watched at home on my television with rising disbelief and anger.

Kevin Ratcliffe: Unfortunately, it was the team across the road that was playing in that game, but when that happened I had a very good friend playing for Liverpool. My first thoughts were about his wife and kids. And that's Ian Rush. So I'm not looking on it as, 'Red shite have caused us the problems.' I'm looking at it from a friends' point of view. You know it's serious, especially when the captains are coming out and asking for calm and everything. But to this day I can't understand why Italy weren't punished as well, or why they haven't had a ban. There were two sets of supporters in that ground, not just one. We became a victim as well, and we weren't even there.

Howard Kendall: The match should never have been played at that venue. It's worth noting that the Liverpool chief executive Peter Robinson raised concerns about the choice of venue and arrangements on the day, but was ignored. That proved very costly. I was watching the match at home, completely incredulous. The loss of human life was just dreadful.

Neville Southall: History has blamed the fans because they're an easy target. I think sometimes it's very easy as an Everton fan to look at Liverpool and blame them for Heysel. I don't blame them for Heysel whatsoever. I blame other people for Heysel. I've seen inside how UEFA sweep stuff under the carpet at first hand. Anybody who caused any grief they'd just get rid them, because that's their way of doing things. And look at what happened after Heysel, a tragedy that started with them? Maybe Liverpool fans bore some of the responsibility, but too little attention has been focused on the true causes and UEFA's responsibility. Why was the game played at the Heysel Stadium, which was completely unfit – it was utterly substandard – for such a match? Why was drinking allowed to take place all through the day leading up to the game? Drinking makes people want to fight at the slightest hint of grief, and unlike the Dutch police – who were great prior to the Everton game a fortnight earlier – the Belgian police have shown themselves to be incapable of defusing tense situations. I think the final, disgraceful decision to play the game after all those people died showed just how incompetent and devoid of reality UEFA were. If they were capable of making such an appalling decision, then you do have to wonder how many bad decisions they might made when planning that match? Obviously people died and the tragedy has always got to be remembered in the context of those lives lost. But from a footballing perspective what followed next was one of the most disgraceful, disgusting episodes in the game's history.

Howard Kendall: When you look back on it, it was an horrific punishment for English football – and only English football, despite other countries having a culture of hooliganism – and terrible for the game that our country had been made an example of. In the five years that the ban stood, Everton missed out on qualification to the European Cup in 1985 and 1987; the European Cup Winners' Cup in 1986; and the UEFA Cup in 1988, and probably 1990, when reduced entry meant that sixth place was no longer high enough for qualification.

Pat Van Den Hauwe: We knew that if we had the opportunity to go into something like that [the European Cup] we'd stand a very good chance of winning it. You'd have to ask the rest of the players, we had the self-belief, we knew we could do it. We was playing that well at that time, it was like this belief, indestructible, it was amazing just to come and play here and when you go training. Everyone was like buzzing all the time.

Neville Southall: The British government was also culpable, putting pressure on the FA and bowing to UEFA's every demand. They wanted to tow the line and didn't want to have the British shown in a bad light. But it didn't make it right. It was a complete disgrace and all sorts of people who had no part in this horrible tragedy were punished. As a player to not have the right to compete with the best clubs in Europe was a devastating, bitter blow. You look back and you see careers destroyed by that European ban. I'm sure it must have been awful for a fan as well. It was also to have appalling consequences for Everton at a time when we were considered the best club side in the world.

Keith Tamlin: The Football Association withdrew English Clubs from participation in the European Champions Cup following the dreadful events at Heysel. This decision prevented our participation and many felt that not being able to influenced our future performance. I'm not critical of the decision in the light of the immediate aftermath but it is so ironical that two weeks before Heysel, we had played In Rotterdam again Rapid Vienna in the European Cup Winners' Cup and won and our supporters were praised by the Dutch authorities for their exemplary behaviour; they even played football against the police in the centre of the city earlier on match day.

Gary Stevens: I think it must've been frustrating for the fans and it is for the players not to have had the opportunity and the chance to find out 'actually' how good we were. Yes we won in Europe and we beat some good sides in the run up to that European win but we still want to play the Champions. You talk about that, but people lost their lives so it doesn't matter about the football. It's just a shame that happened.

Derek Mountfield: We were disappointed, we felt we shouldn't have been banned. I think you look at teams like Luton, who won the League Cup, Coventry won the FA Cup, they never competed in Europe, so it didn't just affect Everton. You feel a little bit like 'It shouldn't be us.' The decision was made, I don't think it was UEFA's, I'm sure the government at the time under Mrs Thatcher had a major say in the decision. But that team in 84/85 could have gone on to even bigger and better things I feel. You could have found Merseyside being the hotbed of European football for x amount of years afterwards. It could have gone to be magnificent, but unfortunately the ban stopped us playing in Europe so in their infinite wisdom, the Football League thought they'd bring in this Screen Sport Super Cup in. It was an absolute joke. Rubbish.

Howard Kendall: It was a horrible feeling knowing we wouldn't get a chance to compete with the best. The fans had enjoyed Europe. The players had enjoyed Europe, and so had I. It was particularly hard to take because Everton were considered not just the best team in England or even Europe, but the whole world. Later that year I would travel to Zurich, where the FIFA president Joao Havelange presented me with the World Team of the Year award. We were on a high but never got a chance to prove that status on the pitch.

Derek Mountfield: Disappointments in my career are very few and far; I've got no regrets. But to never compete in a European Cup, despite winning the league twice, it frustrates me when you see teams aiming to qualify fourth to qualify for the Champions League. You had to qualify as League Champions in the 80s to play in the European Cup, and we did it twice, and I never got the chance to play in the European Cup. It's a massive disappointment in my career. We could do absolutely nothing about it, it was totally out of our hands. As much as we could complain, moan and groan, we had nothing to do with it, the decision was made by the hierarchy of UEFA and our government. The Everton team lost the chance to be regarded as one of the finest teams Europe has seen. I think we could have gone on and done really well in European football for four or five years, it might have kept that team together. Once we lost it, Howard gave it a year, got tempted by European football and Bilbao, Gary and Trevor Steven went to Rangers, Lineker had already gone. If that team had been kept together by playing European football, could we have gone on? I think we could have done, I think we could have made a fist of European football for three or four, five years. Howard would have had more money to bring in other players, so I might have left, you don't know who he would have brought in. I thought that European football ban stopped Everton being or becoming one of the greatest European teams of all time.

Keith Tamlin: We did look at the legal side but I don't think public opinion would've carried us. The board decided that in the end that – balanced overall –taking it to the courts would not be in the interest of the club. I think we would've been criticised anyway and in any case what would be the basis of our case? The fact of the matter is that if the Football Association had not taken the step it did, which under its rules it was entitled to do (although that decision could be challenged by a participating club), the European and international organisations would've banned us anyway, even though we were completely innocent.

George Orr: When that ban came in, we knew we were the best team and we got voted the best team in the world by *World Soccer* magazine. Heysel spoilt all that. But at the same, if you take the bitter and blue out of it, in 1969/70, when we won the league we thought, 'The 70s was going to be ours, this team was unbeatable, this was the team that was going to be the England team and we will walk through everything.' Yet back then, Ball gets sold and within two years we are fighting relegation.

Charles Lambert: We have to put everything in the context that we know people lost their lives and everything else pales into insignificance. But just in the sporting context, Everton had reached a point under Howard where they weren't the finished article. They knew how to win the cup, they knew how to win the league, they won in Europe; they should've been going on to play in the topmost European competition. But because they didn't and because the European ban was not just one season – it lasted several seasons – people couldn't see light at the end of the tunnel. So, if they wanted to progress their careers like Trevor Steven, Gary Stevens and Howard himself they had to move on, and they moved onto teams where they could play in Europe. I think that was absolutely devastating for Everton and I think you could make an argument to say they haven't actually recovered from it.

Howard Kendall: I wasn't at Everton when the ban was lifted, but I felt that the club should have been the first to be invited back, irrespective of where they had finished. I don't think that the club pushed enough for that then.

Kevin Ratcliffe: Only two clubs in Britain suffered from Heysel, and that was Everton and Liverpool. And Liverpool got back in at the first opportunity, we never got invited. Which we should have in my eyes, when I look back. We should have been invited back into the European Cup once that ban was lifted.

Exit Gray, Enter Gary Lineker

Andy Gray: To have such an affinity with the fans, it was just extraordinary. How Evertonians still think so highly of me, I'm honoured that that's a fact. And it's a measure of what we did as a team: not me but what we all did. Everton will never have an eighteen months like that ever, ever again. They just won't. To win the FA Cup, to lose narrowly in the Charity Shield, to win the league, to win the European Cup Winners' Cup, to just fail in retaining and winning the treble and the FA Cup on the last day of the season; that's things that dreams are made of.

Neville Southall: Howard was a great manager and although it was sometimes hard to take when confronted by it, one of the things that made him great was his ruthlessness. He was quick to judge a player and if he didn't fit his plans he was swift to move them on. He kept the squad fresh and us players on our toes. But that didn't mean we had to like or agree with his decisions.

Derek Mountfield: The best managers always try and improve their team every year with one, two or three players. You can't go from season to season with the same squad, complacency will set in. We were all shocked when Andy went, very shocked, because he'd been such an important member of that team for 18 months. He was crucial in what we did. Who'll ever the diving header at Notts County away, when he was like two inches off the floor? He got the hattrick against Fortuna Sittard or the first goal in the final in Rotterdam. He scored some important goals for us, and was a massive, massive part of the team.

Howard Kendall: Andy was very good about it. There was no anger or frustration; if anything there was an appreciation about what I'd done in terms of setting up the deal with Villa. I don't think at first it was a particularly popular deal with Evertonians. They deluged the local press with letters protesting at Andy's sale. But as a manager you are paid to make difficult decisions and this was one of them.

Andy Gray: I was gutted, I didn't want to leave: why would I have left? It's exactly what I said to Howard when he came to my home that summer, and I knew, he doesn't come to your home in the summer to do anything but tell you he's thinking of selling you, so I knew what was coming when his car pulled up.

He said, 'Listen, do you want to stay? Everything Okay?' I said, 'Of course I want to stay, why wouldn't I? We've just won everything; why wouldn't I want to stay?' Then he uhm'd and ah'd a little bit and then he got to it and said, 'Well I've got a chance of signing Gary Lineker so I think I'm going to sign him.' I said, 'Well I can't stay. I've had too good a season, too good a 20 months to go back playing reserve team football. I'll make it easy for you, I'll go.' And I did. I never caused Howard any trouble, why would I? He gave me a wonderful opportunity and I loved him as a man. And he had a football decision to make, and he made it. He made it and he brought Gary in, and I went. And it was with great sadness that I went, great sadness.

Howard Kendall: Gary was unlike anyone I had at Everton at the time. He possessed a blistering turn of pace, which was my main reason for wanting him. Neither Sharpy, Andy Gray nor Adrian Heath were particularly quick, relying instead on their guile and bravery. Gary by contrast was like lightening. I don't think that there were any First Division defenders at the time that could have lived with his pace. In the penalty area he was fantastic. He had that sublime knack of being in the right place at exactly the right time. He had his weaknesses: he couldn't head the ball, he wasn't much use outside the area and was a bad trainer. He used to have a warm bath and do stretching in the bath before he went out to play; but he was as sharp as a razor from the first whistle. I bought him for £800,000 and he did very well.

Neville Southall: There was never any sentiment with Howard. Once you were done you were done and as soon as he thought he could get Gary, Andy was finished. Maybe he thought we'd change the way we played as well. It's hard to know what was in his mind, but I'd have rather kept them both to give us a different combination of pace and aggression. With fresh legs and competition Andy probably would have lasted and done better. But the proof's in the pudding, and Gary scored 40 goals while Andy never reached the same heights he managed at Goodison again.

Howard Kendall: We'd had the best two years we could ever get out of Andy. He'd been absolutely fantastic for us, but he was nearly 30 and I didn't want him to spend the rest of his days with us as a substitute and not play one week and then ten minutes the next. I didn't want him to be a reserve or a fringe player; he deserved better than that.

Andy Gray: Gary was an individual success, but did he contribute enough to the team? I know people who say, 'Well he got 40 goals, wasn't that enough?' Well sometimes it isn't. I wouldn't know how many goals Graeme got that year, but when you look at the front two positions when we won the league the first year: Graeme got 30, I got fifteen, Inchy got fifteen: we had 60 goals between us from two positions. That's a lot of goals. So Gary individually was successful without a doubt.

Neville Southall: Gary gave us a different dimension and we could play more directly with him in the side. He was a bit like Rushy at Liverpool; if we were under pressure you could just boot the ball over the top and he'd get on the end of it and score a goal. He was a great finisher, every bit as good as Rushy. The difference was that Ian was a brilliant defender too – Liverpool and Wales's first line of cover – but Gary never really defended. As goalscorers I thought they were both top class, but Rushy had more to his game overall.

Pat Van Den Hauwe: It give us another option. For a midfield player or a defender like me or Gary Stevens, Derek Mountfield. He'd come to the ball and signal to me, and I knew what he meant, so I'd just go bang over the top. And once he turns there's not a player that would ever catch him in that first division then. Des Walker was pretty quick then but not as quick as Lineker.

Howard Kendall: Gary changed the style of our play. We became more direct. His pace was such a good outlet that sometimes it was just too easy. We would ping a long ball forward knowing that he could outrun just about any defender. I don't think we became one dimensional or even overly reliant on his goals – Sharpy scored 24 in all competitions. But the focus was much more centred on our strikers, whereas the previous season the goals were shared around. Back then Trevor Steven had scored sixteen in all competitions, Derek Mountfield fifteen, Sheeds had got seventeen. This time there wasn't the same spread of goals from those not in forward positions.

Neville Southall: There wasn't much to his game and you could spend months and months trying to analyse what he did. Essentially he just had an almost subliminal knack of being in the right place at the right time; a great understanding and awareness of what was going to happen. He didn't score many from outside the box. But inside the box, he could finish anything. It didn't matter whether it came off his arse, his face or his knee, he'd score a goal. He'd be quite happy doing nothing else, but when you look at his goal-scoring record it's difficult to fault that outlook.

Gary Stevens: If you've got someone that has Gary Lineker's gifts perhaps you're going to go earlier forward because of his pace. I played alongside him for England and he scored very very good goals for both England and for Everton. You're looking for excuses and that's maybe one of them, but for a couple of poor results that season we would've gone on and taken the title.

Colin Harvey: Gary was never fit, Monday to Friday. There was a slipper bath at Bellefield, about the size of that settee, maybe a little bit longer. He used to spend Monday to Friday in hot water, and Howard used to say, 'Go and check if he's got webbed feet, will you?'

Derek Mountfield: We were surprised when he sold Andy and brought in Gary, but our system and style of football changed a little bit because Gary was a goalscorer. He had pace. All credit it to him he scored the goals, but unfortunately we managed to finish runners-up on two occasions, which again was a massive, massive disappointment.

1985/86 season

Neville Southall: That season was one of the most open and competitive campaigns in years. Obviously there was Liverpool and Everton fighting it out at the top, but West Ham had the best season in their history and might have won the title. Manchester United, Sheffield Wednesday, Chelsea and Nottingham Forest were all really good teams; George Graham's Arsenal were also an exciting and talented young side who would go on to do great things a few years later – although we smashed them 6-1 when we met at Goodison in November.

Howard Kendall: When we were beaten by Luton Town on their AstroTurf pitch on 22 March it was the first time we had lost a game in more than three months. I firmly believe that that game cost us the league title. We were leading 1-0 with just eight minutes to go, but Steve Foster and Mike Newell scored late goals. It was just a slip, but a costly one at a time when Liverpool's form was incredible.

Neil Pointon: Most players will say you don't really look over your shoulder, because you want to look at the teams you're playing against in the next game. And obviously if you keep looking behind you, you will eventually make mistakes because you're worried about them.

Howard Kendall: The destiny of the League Championship was still in our hands, but four days later I had more bad news. I received a phone call at home to tell me that Neville Southall had been badly injured playing for Wales against the Republic of Ireland in Dublin.

Neville Southall: Ireland's footballers shared their stadium with the country's rugby players and you can imagine what the pitch was like, coming not long after the Five Nations rugby championships (as it then was) in one of the wettest cities in Europe. It was a mudbath and Mike England criticized it beforehand, calling it 'diabolical.' We were winning 1-0 through a first half Rush goal when, in the 66th minute, I went up for a routine high ball with John Aldridge. As I came down my foot landed in a pothole and I ended up in a heap on the floor. I was unable to get up and the physio and the doctor and all the other players were standing over me thinking I'd broken my leg. There was no break, but I'd dislocated my ankle and torn all the ligaments. It's funny: it was the worst injury of my career and I felt no pain at all.

Howard Kendall: There were fears of a broken leg, but the injury was perhaps even harder to treat: a severe dislocation and ankle ligament damage that was to keep him out of contention for the remainder of the season and for the start of the next campaign too.

Colin Harvey: Bobby Mimms didn't do too badly, but there's a difference between a good keeper and a world class keeper. Neville won games for you, Bobby didn't.

Kevin Ratcliffe: You're taking away your Maradona. The best player I've ever played with. I don't know how many points a year he would have saved us, but if you're looking at three points per game then it's easily fifteen a year.

Kevin Sheedy: Bobby was a good goalkeeper. Neville was the best in the world. So that says it all. Things like that happen in football. Bobby was a good goalkeeper; I wouldn't put him to blame for us not doing the double.

Neville Southall: During what was left of the season Bob only conceded four league goals, plus the three in the FA Cup Final, so I don't really think you can say he was responsible for anything. I look at what he did for the side and thought about what I could have done and I don't think that the outcome of the title race would have been any different. Goalkeeper was definitely not the weak link.

Howard Kendall: Over the previous 27 months our league form had been extraordinary. In our 100 previous matches we had won 64, drawn eighteen and lost eighteen, scoring nearly 200 goals. Gary Lineker had just won the PFA and Football Writer's Player of the Year Awards and had bagged 35 goals in an Everton shirt already. If we won our last four league games we would retain the League Championship. Everything was in our hands. The following Wednesday we travelled to Oxford United, scene of where our renaissance was sparked two years earlier. If we won, and followed it up with victories in our remaining fixtures at home to Southampton and West Ham, we would be champions by at least a point. It was a thoroughly depressing evening. Peter Reid had failed a morning fitness test and

Kevin Richardson took his place. Gary Lineker, who could simply not stop scoring all season except for that night, missed three or four decent chances. We lacked a killer instinct. As we pressed for a win Oxford hit us on the break and struck a late winner. At the same time, Liverpool were playing Leicester at Filbert Street where Ian Rush and Ronnie Whelan goals gave them a 2-0 victory.

Alan Myers: The night of the Oxford game was horrendous, because it was a late winner. I was sitting there listening on the radio, and Liverpool were beating Leicester but needed us to get beat that night. And I'll never forget when the goal went in, the Oxford goal. I had five of my brothers and my dad – they were all Liverpool fans – and they all jumped on top of me. You can imagine how gut wrenching that was getting battered by them.

Kevin Ratcliffe: Gary Lineker missed a hatful of chances in that game [Oxford]. He scored 40 goals that year, and missed a few chances in that game. We were actually two games from winning the double. Oxford, and Liverpool at Wembley. It was frustrating, because we knew that we'd blown it. Because since we beat Liverpool [on 22 February] and I scored Liverpool hadn't lost a game until the end of the season. From that moment.

Howard Kendall: It meant the Championship was now in Liverpool's hands. All they needed was a win at Chelsea the following Saturday, which they duly got. Of the final 36 points available, they won 34. In most ordinary years our tally of 86 points – two short of Liverpool – would have brought us the title.

Kevin Sheedy: They won the league down at Chelsea and we played Southampton at Goodison. There was a big roar. Nothing was happening in the game, it was 4-0, it was over. A big roar went around Goodison, someone had got the wrong information that Chelsea had scored. We were thinking they might have slipped up here, so it was that close. Same with the final, it was a close encounter, it was just their year.

1986 FA Cup Final
10 May 1986
Everton 1, Liverpool 3

Howard Kendall: Our best play came early on and I believe the final result would have been very different had we been awarded a penalty when Steve Nicol wrestled with Graeme Sharp in the Liverpool area on eighteen minutes. The irony that the man who turned down our appeals was Alan Robinson of Hampshire – the same referee who had somehow missed Hansen's handball in the 1984 League Cup Final – was lost on no one. Ten minutes later my disappointment eased when Peter Reid struck a superb through ball that Lineker raced onto. He took the ball around Bruce Grobbelaar and put us in front. Things were so bad for Liverpool that their players were arguing amongst themselves. At the time I could only envisage one winner and that was us.

Kevin Sheedy: We battered them, and goals change games. I can't remember how the scoring went, but certainly we were totally dominant from what I can remember. Needed the second goal, and then they get the equaliser and the game changed on its head.

Howard Kendall: It was against the run of play that Jan Molby – Liverpool's best player – latched onto Gary Stevens' poor crossfield ball shortly before the hour mark. The Dane played in Rush – who else?

– and he sidestepped Mimms and pulled Liverpool level. Liverpool had never lost a game Rush had scored in before, suddenly my optimism looked misplaced.

Gary Stevens: There was a lot happened after the poor pass, and I was sort of nutmegged with a cross a little bit after which was a bit of a disaster. I was substituted a bit after. What can you say? That was a bad day at the office.

Kevin Sheedy: It was just one bad pass, a loose pass from one of our lads and they capitalised and equalised. The game changed on its head.

Gary Stevens: I think you have regrets every time you play badly like the cup final. You regret playing below par. I played in a cup final in Glasgow and one of my backpasses was intercepted and Celtic scored a winner but in that game I was man of the match so sometimes it doesn't tally. But in the Liverpool game it was a bad pass but I also played badly and that was a big regret. I've got regrets about the Hand of God game because I don't think England played well on the day. So you have little regrets about not performing or the team not performing and when it happens in the really important games you haven't got time to put it right and you're on the way home.

Kevin Sheedy: He was a prolific goal scorer, Rushy, and he always had the Indian Sign over us. He always managed to score goals. Rats was a top defender, so it showed what a top player Rushy was. If he got half a chance, then he buries them. Unfortunately, he scored too many against us.

Pat Van Den Hauwe: I played in three finals, lost all three. Horrible that. Not funny. We got put on the same plane as those red gits in 1986. What a nightmare that was. I remember getting on the plane and they were on the back holding this big cup. Someone really messed up there. Oh dear me, that wasn't a particularly good trip home.

Howard Kendall: The worst aspect of our cup final defeat was having to travel home with our conquerors the next morning, and then traverse the city on an open top bus. It was an initiative agreed before the game to show the unity of the city, but not everybody agreed. Much to my annoyance, Peter Reid refused to take part and went absent without leave. Watching at such close proximity our greatest rivals celebrate two trophies we had been so close to winning was devastatingly cruel.

Andy Gray: There was a little bit of – not satisfaction, that would be wrong, because I'd never want Everton not to win, and it wasn't like, 'I told you' – I don't know what it was, it was a funny feeling. And then I knew when Inchy and Graeme started playing next year that they'd win the league again. I just knew it. Again, maybe what Inchy gave the team and what I gave the team; it might be 20 goals less than Gary, but maybe for the greater good of the team it was better and more important. The stats will tell you that because we won everything when I was there and won the league again with Inchy, and in the interim they won nothing with Gary, but they finished second in the league, second in the cup. So they went very close to achieving the double, but they didn't. Whatever happened that season was a strange one for me. It took me a while to get over leaving Everton, because I didn't want to. Simple as that.

Howard Kendall: They won the double, but in the end we had lost it by just two games. Such are the margins between defeat and football immortality.

Sale of Gary Lineker to Barcelona

Gary Lineker ended the 1985/86 season with 40 league and cup goals and after playing a leading role in England's progress to the quarter-finals of that year's World Cup came back with the Golden Boot. By then, however, it seemed clear that for the second successive year Everton would sell one of their man strikers after accepting a £2.8million bid from Barcelona.

Kevin Sheedy: We had to change the system. [Gary Lineker] was lightning, he was rapid, and we played a lot more long balls then. So when I received it I just put the ball over the centre-halves head and he just got onto it. He got 40 goals that season, Sharpy got 26. None of the midfield got many goals because we were too far behind the play, so it was either a ball over to Gary, he either scored or it was a ball over Sharpy and he linked with him and Sharpy scored. We had too much ground to cover to get there. That season we finished runners-up in the league and runners-up in the FA Cup, I think we fell short on goals. To win the league you have to score 85 to 90 goals. We came up short with the goals to win the league, then you obviously get to the cup final, that's a different thing, and get beat in that. So to come out runners up in both and Liverpool to do the double, that was a hard pill to swallow. It was still a good season, but we didn't get the rewards.

Derek Mountfield: I personally had no problems with Gary. I think the fans had more of a problem with Lineker than the players actually did. They thought that when he came we changed our total style of football. We did change our football a little bit, but we still put ourselves in situations to either win or win a couple of trophies, and unfortunately we never did, but people look back and say, 'Oh you won the league before, and the league after him' but Lineker was a goalscorer, and his record proves that. People say he was too greedy, and he looked after himself a bit, but I have no issue with Gary at all. I thought we did change our style a bit, but when you score 40 goals in a season you can't say anything about him, full stop.

Howard Kendall: I often get asked if the sale of Gary to Barcelona was linked to my possible arrival there as manager. I can unequivocally state that that is not the case. The deals and the timeframes involved were completely different. In any case, I would never – under any circumstances – work against the interests of a football club I was managing to further my own as a manager elsewhere. That just wasn't the way I worked.

Champions again: the 1986/87 Season

Howard Kendall: After some of the injury problems we had encountered I felt we needed some experience and versatility. The previous season I'd been to see Manchester City play at Watford. It was a horrible mud bound pitch and not a very good game. But almost gliding around it was the City captain, Paul Power. He was in his early thirties, but he was as fit as anything and was the best player on the field. I called the City manager, after the game and inquired about him. 'He's the one player everybody asks about,' he said, 'I could sell him ten times a season.' Paul was due a testimonial at Maine Road, but I managed to persuade him to come to Everton. I think a few fans my have been a little underwhelmed, but Paul soon showed them wrong.

Paul Power: I'd just signed a one-year contract at Manchester City and the manager had almost encouraged me to speak to Howard. The manager at City at that time was Billy McNeill, and they had Andy Hinchcliffe coming up through the ranks who was much younger than me, and would have been the future for the team. That really encouraged me to go and speak to Howard in the first place. Then my dealings with Howard were excellent, he gave me the impression that he wanted to sign me because he bent over backwards to solve a couple of problems that I had.

Howard Kendall: On the eve of the new season it became clear that the injury problems Derek Mountfield had suffered over the previous year were going to remain a problem and that I couldn't rely on his fitness. The man I wanted was Dave Watson from Norwich. Like Alan Harper and Kevin Sheedy he'd been at Liverpool as a young professional, but hadn't made the breakthrough. He went to Norwich and worked his way up to be captain, and played for England too. The Norwich manager Ken Brown didn't want to sell, saying it was 'like cutting off my right arm.' Money, however, often talks in those situations, and we had a lot of it. It took a club record to sign him - £900,000 – but I think over the next thirteen years Dave repaid every penny of that.

Dave Watson: I came through the system at Liverpool. It wasn't an academy system back then; I got picked up at fourteen or fifteen. I used to go training a couple of nights a week. I was a right-back. I was a little skinny kid. As time went on I got moved into centre-back and that's where I stayed. I had good years there. I progressed from what was the B team to the A team and to the reserves really quickly. I must have played about a dozen reserve games and then Norwich came in and bought me. Bob Paisley called me into his office. I thought: 'Fucking hell I have to go and see Bob Paisley.' I knocked on the door and he said, 'Come in son.' He didn't even know my name. He said, 'There's club interested in buying you,' I said, 'Who is it?' He said, 'Norwich.' I didn't even know where Norwich was. I said, 'Yeah, is there any chance in having a bit of time to think about it?' He went, 'Listen son, it takes you five hours to get there on the train, how long do you want to think about it?" I thought, 'I'm going here!' That was it. I was on my way. I was at Norwich for five years. I had a fantastic time there. Ken Brown was like a father figure to me. I played with Steve Bruce. It was an eventful five years. The first year I was there we got relegated. The second year we got promoted. The third year we got relegated. The fourth year we came up as champions and in the fifth year we won the Milk Cup against Sunderland. I didn't think so at the time but it was a great learning curve. Bobby Robson was manager at Ipswich so he used to see a lot of our games. I got selected for England because of Bobby possibly watching. It really just fell into place.

Derek Mountfield: Howard called me and said we're going to have to sign a defender or two, I'm not sure yet, but we're going to have to sign someone. I didn't know it was going to be Dave Watson – I hoped it would be a right-back or a left-back – but he signed Watson. When you're paying nearly a million pounds for a centre half, compared to £30,000 for this scrawny kid from Liverpool, you know your chances are pretty limited. I tried my best to try and break back into the side.

Neville Southall: This was another sign of the manager's ruthless streak: Derek Mountfield had had his injury problems the previous year, but hadn't done much wrong besides being injured. Dave would go on to be one of Everton's greatest servants and he captained the club for many years. He was an incredibly brave and aggressive player and probably better in the air than Derek. But he didn't score as many goals as his predecessor, nor was he as good in possession. In some ways it was replacing like for like: one fantastic centre half with another. It was a nice dilemma for a manager to have.

Howard Kendall: Only two players – Neville and Brian Labone – have appeared more times in an Everton shirt than Dave. When you sign a player I don't think you look at their leadership qualities; it's not something you see until you're in the dressing room or on the training ground with them. Some players, they give their maximum and they're not able to give any extra. Others seem to have this natural – almost subliminal gift – of guiding other players around them. Dave was one of those players, and not just on the pitch, either; he was an example to everybody at the club in terms of how you go about your training.

Dave Watson: I made my debut against Nottingham Forest and we won 2-0. Kevin Sheedy scored two. On the debut I actually got booed because I took over from Derek Mountfield. 'Number one Neville Southall, number two Gary Stevens, number three Pat Van Den Hauwe, number four Kevin Ratcliffe, number five Dave Watson', Booooo! I was on the pitch. It was a nice welcome! It didn't make me nervous. I go the other way. I see it as a challenge. I'll show you. I'll show you how good I am.

Paul Power: I think probably the Man United game at Goodison [on 21 September] was a tremendous performance. I remember a fantastic goal by Sharpy; a header from the edge of the box. I think after that the confidence built. But the best performance for me of that season was Newcastle away. Trevor Steven was unbelievable that day. I think he scored but he certainly made opportunities, and every time he got the ball he was just a real handful. That was the performance for me that made everybody believe that we were a really good side still.

Derek Mountfield: There was a run of games where we won six, drew two and lost one and then he dropped me. I remember the Norwich game [on 6 December] particularly well. I was told I wasn't playing so I never went the game. The fans were booing Dave every touch, and they won 4-0. But I have nothing against Dave at all. It was a football decision, Howard made a decision.

Dave Watson: It took a good few weeks to get in the style Everton played. They played a high line. They had pace with Gary Stevens, and Kevin and Pat. I wasn't the quickest to be honest. Things turned out great and we went on to win the league. It was the high line that was more of the problem. Me staying on the right and Kevin on the left, that's fine, we could deal with that. Further up the pitch we go, there's space behind me and there could be a problem. I had international players all round me and Neville Southall, who was a fantastic footballer as well as a goalkeeper, he could read situations. We had the best goalkeeper in the world at the time. We held firm for most of the season.

Howard Kendall: I'd spotted Ian Snodin playing against us as sweeper for Doncaster Rovers in the FA Cup a couple of seasons earlier, and his career had progressed following a move to Leeds United. I was impressed by his pace and tenacity and in January I spent £825,000 on him. To the delight of Evertonians he chose Everton over Liverpool. I think Kenny wanted him to play wide right in the midfield, and I wanted him to play in the centre. I think that swayed him because financially he was going to get what he was wanting from both clubs. He was a good athlete, a good reader of the game and two footed. He added some fresh impetuous at an important stage of the season.

Ian Snodin: I knew I was joining a top, top team and the confidence couldn't have been any higher. It were a matter of how many they were going to win by, not if they were going to win at the time when you were going out to player. They were a great bunch of lads, the atmosphere in the dressing room every day, training was fun. It was great to go to work. It's classed as work, but being a footballer is the best thing in the world. But it was a pleasure going in every morning, you had a laugh, you trained hard, and then come Saturday you were going to get the result.

Paul Power: Ian Snodin was tremendous at making forward runs from midfield. Neither Peter Reid or Paul Bracewell were. Snods added a little bit of that, he could break the opposing defences down by making runs beyond them. He wasn't the best finisher when he got there, I've got to say, but he actually then made his England debut I think at right-back, so that showed his versatility as well. I'm sure that was down to a lot of work that Howard and Colin did with him.

Howard Kendall: The other very important signing I made close to the transfer deadline was Wayne Clarke from Birmingham City. He scored some hugely important goals for us, but I felt he never got the recognition that he deserved. I don't think he was ever fully appreciated by the players or fans. He had this lazy look about him; it was as if the fans could look at him and say, 'Well, he loses it and doesn't chase back to win it back again; or there was a lot of jogging in his game rather than a sprint and a rest.' But technically he was absolutely fantastic and did well for us.

Wayne Clarke: I always had faith in my ability, even on the first day of training. I remember Peter Reid coming up to me and saying 'You don't look out of place here mate,' and that was obviously a big boost as well. But, I was banging goals in left, right and centre at Blues, so I was full of confidence anyway, and I just literally carried that on in the remaining games that I obviously played for Everton.

Kevin Sheedy: Personally it was my best season. I always wanted to play in the middle of midfield, I just felt I could be more creative but obviously Reidy and Brace were in there. They were injured so that gave me the opportunity to play in there, mostly I think Alan Harper played in there as well. I got seventeen goals, I got in the PFA Team of the Year. So I really excelled that year.

Howard Kendall: I often think the psychological aspects of management are underplayed. In January 1987 we went to play Queens Park Rangers on their dreaded AstroTurf pitch at Loftus Road. Jim Smith, who was in charge of Rangers at the time, was a master of little ruses. Rangers' pitch was particularly bad; it was basically carpet on top of concrete, an awful surface, which gave the home side a considerable advantage. Just before we were about to go out the QPR trainer came into the dressing room with a big jar of Vaseline and said, 'You better put this on your lads, because if you go down it's going to scrape all your skin off, and it'll burn.' And I thought, 'You clever sod. That's no courtesy; that's to dissuade our lads from tackling.' We won that match 1-0, a rare victory on plastic and it increased the conviction that this might be our year again.

Paul Power: All we concentrated on was doing well in the next game. We lost against Watford at the start of March. Most managers I would have played for, if we'd lost a game that we were expected to win would have said, 'Right, you're in training tomorrow.' Howard on the way home said, 'There'll be no training tomorrow, but everybody meets for a Chinese meal at Mr Lao's in Southport.' That was it. You had to be there, it was a team bonding thing; but not just the players, the team doctor was there, all the coaching staff were there – Lyonsy and Terry Darracott and Colin. It was a team bonding effort if you like. There was lots of alcohol, which was fairly standard then. Whatever team I played for they all knew how to socialise and enjoy themselves. Nobody more than Howard to be fair. It was good camaraderie and good fun, and it just helped players to relax.

Ian Snodin: The game against Arsenal [on 28 March] was a pivotal one, it were a great victory, and we realised we have got a hell of a chance here.

Wayne Clarke: It was a tough game playing away at Highbury, there's never any easy games there. I remember the ball obviously coming to me off John Lukic and I knew in my mind straight away what I was going to do with it, even before I got my first touch, because I knew he was stranded outside of his goal area, and I just needed the right first touch, second touch or whatever it was, and then just put the ball in the direction of the goal, and thankfully it dropped in and that was to set me on my way. But it was a vital win for us of course, because Liverpool lost to Wimbledon the same day, so.

Neville Southall: The key match was at Stamford Bridge against Chelsea [on 4 April] when Alan Harper showed the world what a good player he was by unleashing a 25 yard thunderbolt to win us all three points and send us top.

Kevin Sheedy: Alan Harper was more the sitter, so that allowed me to get forward, score and create goals. It really freed me up and I was able to go into different positions that I hadn't been able to on the left. It was a really challenging and really enjoyable season for me. He was just a real intelligent footballer. He could play left-back, right-back, centre-back, midfield. He was a manager's dream, and he played all that season because there was different injuries. But he mostly played alongside me in the midfield.

Neville Southall: By the time we played Liverpool at the end of April we effectively had the title wrapped up. They beat us 3-1, with Kevin Sheedy famously giving the Kop the V sign as he grabbed our consolation.

Ian Snodin: He scored an unbelievable free-kick, and he says that if they had three or four keepers in that day, they wouldn't have saved it, and they wouldn't. He smashed it with his left foot in the top corner, then he went running to the Kop, give it the old. He got in a bit of trouble. Went down to the FA. Fantastic finish.

Kevin Sheedy: It wasn't a pre-planned action. I hit a free-kick right into the top corner at the Kop end, and in those days it was like half Liverpool half Everton supporters anyway. I've just gone to the Kop and put my two fingers up. That was probably one of the best things I've done, because it still gets talked about now. Even the Liverpudlians don't give me any stick, they even laugh about it. It wasn't meant as anything, it was just one of those things that I've done.

Ian Snodin: We just had the momentum, we really did. We were going out every week thinking, 'Yeah we're going to win this', and if we kept winning we wouldn't be caught, it's as simple as that. I just think the team spirit got us completely through. Howard was fantastic in those crucial couple of months; kept everybody calm, kept everybody on their toes, kept everybody smiling and laughing in the dressing room. I think it's important when you get to that stage of a season, that you've got a manager like that. He's seen it, he's done it before, and I just thought his mannerisms, his demeanour around the training ground and on a match day were fantastic, just to calm you, just to get you through the game. He needed a massive pat on the back. His man management skills were second to none. All through his career his management skills were brilliant, but I can remember in those last couple of months that he just made us so relaxed before we went out there. Fantastic.

Neville Southall: Nine days later [on 4 May] we were champions after a rare Pat Van Den Hauwe goal was enough for us to beat Norwich City and make us untouchable.

Paul Power: It was a close game. I just think we all thought it was going to come. We'd won the league with two games to go: we had two home games to go: One against Tottenham, Luton the other one.

Ian Snodin: We had thousands, thousands of fans that day. We knew the atmosphere, it was dead tense, we knew we could beat them, and to get a goal as early as we did were fantastic. We came under a lot of pressure that day after we scored early doors, it wasn't an easy game. We didn't sit back and think, 'We'll defend that.' We tried to attack and we tried to get a second and third, but Norwich were great on that day. Norwich certainly put a great performance on, but we managed to hold on, we managed to beat them 1-0 and it were fantastic. I remember fans running on and the gaffer grabbing me. I realised, I'd come to win a medal and I'd got one within five months of joining Everton.

Wayne Clarke: It was just unbelievable on the journey back, knowing what we'd done and what we'd achieved. More so for the players who had been there for the season, because of how many points they were behind before I'd got there, and the injuries they'd had as well. It was pretty much a unique way of winning the league, because a lot of people had started to write us off by early March.

Paul Power: The best thing about winning the game at Norwich was the journey back. The journey back was unbelievable. It was about seven hours back from Norwich then, and we stopped off at a pub on the way back, and Terry Darracott was like the compere. He had the mic from the front of the coach and everybody had to do a turn. Pat Van Den Hauwe never ever sang or did anything where he might embarrass himself but Terry said, 'You're doing it,' and he forced him. Whether he did boiled beef and carrots, some cockney song or whatever, he did the little rendition and everybody just had a fantastic time on the way back. It was just brilliant.

Ian Snodin: The bus journey home was absolutely fantastic, Terry Darracott took over. They called it Everton radio, and he was DJ Terry, and he invited all the lads up one by one after every couple of mile on the way home. Champagne was flowing, the drink was flowing, everybody was drunk. We were all having to go up and get on Terry's mic and sing a song for Everton radio. We could have gone on for hours. I remember I was travelling back to Doncaster, and my wife was picking me up at Burtonwood services. I used to get a bit of stick off the lads for my gear, and I still do, my clothing. I remember buying a new suit for the game, and wearing it on the way back. I got absolutely drunk. I like a little sing song myself so I went up three or four times on the mic. Unbeknown to me, I'd fallen asleep on a four table and when I woke up I remember the lads saying, 'Snods we're at Burtonwood, your missus is here to pick you up.' I'd got up and they'd cut all me gear, fucking scissors and everything. I stood up and my clothes just dropped off me. I walked to the front of the bus and Jimmy Martin, the coach driver then, opened the door and my missus was in the car waiting to take me back to Donny. I got back to the top of the stairs and I basically had no clothes on. I just had my boxer shorts on and my shirt cut to hell. She said, 'Get in here', and Howard just said, 'Make sure he gets home safe.' It was a fantastic journey home!

Derek Mountfield: I was one game short of my medal. On the Monday we played Tottenham in the last game of the season, and they were playing Coventry in the cup final on the Saturday. He put me on the bench and I'm thinking, 'Alright.' Then he said 'Go and warm up son', and he said, 'You're going upfront.' As the substitution came on, we're defending the Street end, I ran towards the Park end, and someone shouted, 'Degsy you're going the wrong way' and I managed to score the winning goal on the day. My last ever goal for Everton at home to Tottenham at the Park End. I got my medal. I'm proud to say I've got two league title medals. I played my part in winning those medals.

Neville Southall: In a way winning the league title the second time was more rewarding and satisfying than it had been in 1985. It was so easy first time around; we just won games for fun. 1987 was more of a struggle, or rather a series of battles. Firstly it had been such a battle to overcome the injury and then there was the continued element of uncertainty that it may reoccur too. I was constantly tired but I wanted to play all the games I possibly could because I didn't know when it was going to happen again. There were injuries to a lot of other players too. Gary Stevens, Peter Reid, Pat Van Den Hauwe and Sharpy all missed long stretches of the season. Too little credit is given to the likes of Paul Power and Alan Harper who came in and filled variety of roles really well and also to Howard who unified all these players in a winning formation. It was all incredibly fulfilling. But everything was about to change.

Gary Stevens: It was more eked out that season. We didn't get anywhere near the good football we played a couple of seasons before or even the season before. We got a little bit more back to basics. We were always a side that could either mix it, like the Bayern Munich game where a couple of their players ended up with rather sore noses, or we could play football and we were a side that could do whatever needed to be done on that particular day. We didn't play particularly good football the second time we won the championship but we eked it out, we were difficult to beat.

Derek Mountfield: Howard's shrewdness won us that title. Signing Paul Power, signing Paul Wilkinson the year before, signing Kevin Langley. Who had ever heard of Kevin Langley when he came to Everton? Nobody had, but he played a crucial part in the early part of the season. I played right-back a couple of games that season when Gary Stevens was injured. The pictures when everyone is on the pitch, there's Paul Power on his crutches, there's me, Neil Adams, Neil Pointon – we've all got our kit on but we haven't played.

Kevin Sheedy: There was Neil Adams, Ian Marshall, Kevin Langley, Bobby Mimms. We played as a team. I can't think who got the goals. Totally different. In '85 the team was mostly the same, '87 was one week it would be one team and another week somebody else would be injured. You're looking at what's going on behind the scenes with Howard, his management skills and picking the right team.

Howard Kendall: Winning the league title for a second time as manager was almost completely dissimilar to 1985. I wouldn't say it was more rewarding, because the first time is always the best, but it represented a very different challenge. It wasn't an easy process as had been the case a couple of years previously. There were more challenges and the season was a far greater examination of my abilities as a manager. Winning had been easier before and my teams had largely picked themselves. Injuries to key figures now meant I was forced to adapt. It was much harder and as a manager I was tested more. We used a lot of pieces and components to earn our success. Some of those players weren't necessarily big names and it didn't work out for them long term at Goodison, but they did a good job for a crucial period of time. Full credit to them for rising to the challenge.

Kevin Sheedy: I think it's a different type of satisfaction. The first one was one of Everton's best ever teams, and it showed. And I think '87 showed the flexibility of the individuals and the squad to be able to keep performing with so many different changes at the time. It was equally as good an achievement.

Howard Kendall joins Athletic Bilbao

Howard Kendall: My decision to leave Everton in June 1987 and manage Athletic Bilbao was the culmination of a process that had started – in my mind at least – when I first received an approach from Barcelona a year earlier. Being approached by the Spanish giants whetted my appetite and served as a reminder as to what I was missing out on in European competition.

Colin Harvey: The season before Howard had arranged with Barcelona, and he said, 'Do you want to come?' I said no, because my daughters were only about sixteen and fourteen, and the youngest was about six or seven. I said, 'There's no way I'm going to live away for a year or two years while they're still growing up.' So he more or less said, 'Well I'm going.' Anyway it fell through because Terry Venables stayed an extra year, then when Bilbao came up he said it again, and they were only a year or so older, so I said 'I'm not going.' That was that.

Howard Kendall: Kenny Dalglish, the Liverpool player-manager, had been the top target of the Bilbao board. Yet when [Bilbao general manager] Fernando Ochoa contacted the Liverpool secretary Peter Robinson to approach them over Kenny, he was given short shrift. Kenny would not be leaving Anfield under any circumstances, he was told. He did have, however, someone else that they would recommend. That person was me.

Neil Pointon: I remember we went to New Zealand and Australia on an end of season tour, and there were bits of speculation that he was going, and it didn't come out until we got back. A few of the senior players I think, Kev Ratcliffe and Dave Watson, Sheeds and Sharpy, all had an inkling. It was a blow because Howard had set everything up, but with Colin taking over, everybody thought that it would still keep that momentum, but one or two things didn't materialise.

Wayne Clarke: I'm never shocked at anything in football, even back then. I could understand why he did it. Obviously, if there hadn't been a ban I think we would have had a good tilt at the European Cup. We may have strengthened even more during that season, but I think at the end of that season that possible he'd taken the club as far as he could in terms of honours. He needed a tilt at Europe, and unfortunately for Everton there was the ban at the time. I know he had a good two, two and a half years in Bilbao, I know he enjoyed it there. As I club I think it really suffered with Howard leaving.

Howard Kendall: I was leaving Everton in the strongest position possible and Colin Harvey was unanimously considered the right choice as manager. The assumption was that he would continue the success he had already been such an important part of.

Neville Southall: In Howard's place came Colin Harvey, who appointed Terry Darracott as his assistant. I was delighted that were would be continuity between the two managers, but also because it was a person who inherently understood Everton. Colin was the club on legs. Even during Howard's reign it was Colin who set the tone and knew how everything should be. I didn't want anybody else coming in because I didn't want anyone else to ruin what Howard had built. I also thought at the time that we were only a couple of players from being a really world class team again.

Derek Mountfield: We were all shocked when he went, we had no idea at all. But the best man for the job at the time was Colin Harvey. Howard wanted to try European football, he wanted that. Does he regret going? He probably doesn't, because it was a learning curve for him going into Bilbao.

Pat Van Den Hauwe: Colin was more of a disciplinarian. You couldn't mess around too much with Colin. It was a strange feeling, but the players that were still there went out and did their best for Colin and the football club and that lot out there. I think I let him down a couple of times, didn't I?

Derek Mountfield: For me Colin was the greatest coach I've worked under, he was magnificent. I think Colin found it hard to handle being called boss, but he was the right man for the job at the time. But that European ban certainly was the death knell for that squad of players long-term. If there'd been European football, I think that team would have gone from strength to strength, because Howard would have had the funds to buy other players to develop other players and keep that squad as strong as it was.

Neville Southall: Colin was a different type of person to Howard; probably a little bit more stern. I always found Colin great, a man in tune with the way I saw the game. Howard knew how to handle me, but Colin understood my obsessiveness and relentless desire to be the best. As I've said before, he really embodied Everton's Nil Satis Nisi Optimum motto and so did I. We were like peas in a pod.

Ian Snodin: Every player will tell you that Colin Harvey wasn't a Howard Kendall. I don't think there's another Howard Kendall in the world. He was totally a one off, Howard, the way he treated players, the way he went about his man management, he was fantastic. But Colin Harvey had a different demeanour. He was more stubborn, he was harder, there was no question about that. That's why they got on so well together as a management team. There's no good having two people that act the same way. Good cop bad cop as they say.

Kevin Ratcliffe: Colin was a great coach. He had great enthusiasm, he was a great Evertonian. But I think his man management wasn't the same as Howard's. He's not a very talkative person. If you get him on a one· to one basis he's great. He's talkative. But he's not an easy person to talk to. And as you're a manager you've got to be a little more. I think that's what he found the hardest: his communication with the players wasn't great. You need to speak players when they're dropped, what they need to do to get back in the side. Colin really wasn't one of them.

Neil Pointon: Colin was a great coach, and a great motivator, but he didn't have that management style that Howard had, and maybe that little bit of calmness at certain points. We had quite a few coaches who came on board as well: Mick Lyons came back in, Paul [Power] had gone on to the coaching side, Terry Darracott had come back in. I would say from my point of view there were too many voices, whereas Howard was the main voice when he was there and that was with a little bit of back up from Colin. These two were like your Brian Clough and Peter Taylor if you want. We had a good run, but never really hit those heights that we had as a group really.

Neville Southall: His desire to win and bring the best for Everton also saw frustration mount within him. As that first season progressed I could see it rise as he couldn't quite find the right mix and balance. We knew we had decent players; we just couldn't find a way of winning games. It wasn't for the want of trying because I don't think anybody has worked as hard for Everton as Colin. It was hard to see because I don't think anybody's more pro-Everton than Colin.

Dave Watson: He was such a passionate fella, Colin, defeat really hurt him, more than anyone. He couldn't get over it. If you're a coach and you're like that it's not too bad. You have the manager put your arm around you and say, 'Lets go again.' Colin took the responsibility of being coach and the manager and he tried to do too much. He was well respected throughout the club. He did a good job. We got to Wembley in 1989. He had a good go.

John Ebbrell: Colin's legacy is very much still being felt around Everton today [in 2017], certainly in the way I coach, and I'm proud of that because his standards were unrelenting. How important is that? Lots of his disciplines and standards stayed with me as a player, and I'm passing them on now as a coach. Certainly all his best traits I had, I'm trying to pass on as a coach.

Colin Harvey: The buck stops with the manager, without doubt. You can have all the input you want as coach, but it's the manager that has the final say, and if anything goes wrong, he's the man in charge. It was the same for me.

Kevin Sheedy: It just showed the difference between being a great coach and being a manager, totally different skills required. I witnessed that – I went to Blackburn as a youth coach, and Kenny Dalglish had just won the Premier League with Blackburn. He'd moved upstairs and Ray Harford, he was the first team coach there – he was a great coach – went in as the manager and found it really difficult. It's totally different to being a coach where you're just out with the players. As a manager you've got everything that goes with it: dealing with player's problems, the media and all that. I think Colin was the same, he was a great coach but it just showed the difference needed to be a manager.

Neville Southall: We finished the 1987/88 season fourth and had the best defensive season in the club's history, conceding just 27 league goals in 40 matches. Not that I set any stall by that. If you judge your career by clean sheets you're frankly going to struggle. As a team we played well. We reached the semi-finals of the League Cup, knocking out Liverpool along the way. They knocked us out in the fifth round of the FA Cup and won the league by a mile, but we had some small consolation by preventing them from beating Leeds United's 29 match unbeaten start to the season. Not that it mattered. We wanted trophies, not bragging rights over our neighbours.

Break up of the mid-eighties team

Derek Mountfield: I just wanted to play first team football. I didn't like getting carted round on the first team coach to QPR away on a Tuesday night, to come back at four o'clock on Wednesday morning, to play in the reserves Wednesday night. It was doing my head in, I wanted first team football, not watching the first team from the stands, and then playing reserve team football. It was probably the toughest decision of my career to leave Everton, but I did it purely for footballing reasons. I look back – I left in 1988 – I finished playing eleven, twelve years later. So I had a decent career and I can't complain.

Neville Southall: We'd brought in some decent players in the meantime, but you wouldn't call them world class. Ian Wilson, Colin's first signing, was a good grafter but he didn't catch the eye.

Wayne Clarke did a good job for us and scored some vital goals, but he was never going to get you 30 or 40 goals a season. But then you look at the players Liverpool signed in the same period: John Barnes, Peter Beardsley, John Aldridge. They were improving rapidly while we were, at best, standing still.

Paul Power: I think the club ought to bear as much responsibility for that as the manager, because they allowed that team to break up far, far too quickly. To allow Gary Stevens, Trevor Steven, Peter Reid to leave. They didn't support the manager at all I think. The board might have been thinking of cashing in on players.

Wayne Clarke: Without naming names, I don't think some of the purchases were Everton type players. I very much doubt that Howard would have bought quite a few of them. But you know, one era's gone, Colin was setting up his claim as manager, and he wanted to do things his way. It didn't quite work out for him, but you don't know that at the time, do you? That's the thing. He thought he was doing the right thing.

Gary Stevens: I think that would've been on my mind but I'd been at the club since I'd signed as an apprentice in 1979 so I'd already been at the club two years before that and I felt a bit stale. I'd had a bit of a fall out with Colin too. He was a fantastic coach and out of everybody in football he's got the most respect from me and if it hadn't have been for Colin I would not have got where I got to, but we had a bit of fall out and I felt a bit stale and I felt it was the right thing. It wasn't a massive amount to do with Europe but of course people will look for a reason and they want a reason and that was what they came up with. It wasn't really because of that.

Kevin Ratcliffe: I just got this feeling that it had come to an end too soon. You know if you're losing your manager then you're losing your better players and then you're bringing in what is nowhere near the quality that's going out. You get rid of Peter Reid and bring a player that is younger than him, but Peter Reid goes and plays on for about four years after that, and is quite an influence in them teams that he is playing for. Things were changing and not for the good.

In the summer of 1988 Colin Harvey broke the British transfer record to sign Tony Cottee for £2.2million and spent a further £2 million on Stuart McCall, Neil McDonald and Pat Nevin.

Tony Cottee: I think the pressure was on me right from the moment I signed for Everton [in July 1988], because it was a British record transfer. Gazza had gone for two million, I went for just over two million, and I think there was a huge weight of responsibility on my shoulders really. I felt that.

Kevin Ratcliffe: The quality that was coming in wasn't anywhere near the quality that was going out. You're sort of sensing that this is not the same. There was a big change around. I've heard Colin say that the lads, maybe the elder statesman like myself and Graeme and people, never really made them feel welcome. We made them feel more than welcome, but I think there was a big change in wages happening. Mortgages was a big one. I honestly believe that some of them didn't have enough money, believe it or not, even though they were footballers, to actually go out and relax. People had gone from £50,000 mortgages to £200,000 mortgages in the 1980s. The wages for some of these lads were better, but I just think when you're paying 14% on £200,000... I think it stopped a lot of that sort of team building and getting together; things that maybe Colin was still trying to carry on from Howard, just weren't happening. And I think they were of a different mentality than what we were. They were different.

Wayne Clarke: There was never a divide in the dressing room prior to Howard leaving. The season after and the season after that, there was. Some of the lads used to talk about it. And there were little cliques which you can't have in dressing rooms. Howard would have never have let that fester. He would have got rid of the bad wood and got the players in, but that's how it was unfortunately.

Colin Harvey: They were all good players. But the problem was, and it sort of came all of a sudden, there were two sets of players. There were the ones who had been there that long, and these new ones coming in, who probably weren't accepted, for want of a better phrase. There were three teams, because Paddy [Nevin] was another man apart! Lovely fella and a great professional. He'd finish training, go out and do a bit extra, a bit more. He was like a glorified student, but a lovely lad.

Pat Nevin: I adored Colin from the first time I had seen him. I put a lot of stock by the people I trust, the people that are honest. To walk into someone like that, and to be honest you will meet quite a lot of sleazy people that go into management, and people that aren't trustworthy. Sometimes for good reason, because they have to lie as part of their job, make up things. But I looked at and listened to Colin, and I thought, 'This guy is straight, straight up and down the line. If I'm good enough for his team then he will play me, if I'm not good enough he won't play me and then tell me.' I kind of liked him as a person anyway, he's also quite an interesting person. Yes he was a football man through and through, but if you talked about things like music he was fine, cool.

Kevin Sheedy: I saw a quote off Tony Cottee that we'd won medals and trophies before he came, won nothing when he was here and then won trophies when he left. I'm not pointing the finger at Tony. If you look at the team in 85 the players were 100 per-cent together. The squad here wasn't 100 per-cent together, and you're missing that little spark out on the pitch, in training, in the dressing room.

Neville Southall: We started the 1988/89 season in brilliant fashion. On a sundrenched August afternoon we took Newcastle United apart at Goodison, 4-0, with Cottee grabbing a hat-trick on his debut.

Tony Cottee: Unfortunately, in a way, the best thing I ever did at Everton was the worst thing, scoring after 34 seconds and getting a hat-trick on your debut. I wouldn't swap that for the world, it was one of the best days I've ever had and one of the best feelings I've ever had as a footballer, but unfortunately as a result of that the fans expected more and to be honest I put pressure on myself to do more as well.

Pat Nevin: That was maybe even the best couple of days in my time at Everton, because the new players played: Stuart played, I played, Tony played and Neil McDonald played, and we destroyed Newcastle. The football was brilliant. I got a lot of the ball, created quite a few chances, and really without taking the mick, showed a few skills and thought, 'Right okay this can be good, I can grow into this.' There was the nice feeling about the place, it was a beautiful sunny day, the fans were ballistic, they could feel the buzz as well. I suppose at that time there was no higher moment.

Neville Southall: The following week we beat Coventry to go top, Cottee scoring the only goal, then we drew with Nottingham Forest, who were a good team. And then, inexplicably, we sank from the top of the table without a trace.

Tony Cottee: We didn't have a particularly good season the first year, even though we got to two finals, we didn't really play consistently well, and I struggled with my form. I had a couple of good games and then a couple of bad games. All the time you had that 'Oh, two million pounds,' and everyone singing 'What a waste of money' at you when you had a bad game. Eventually it does wear you down a little bit.

The Hillsborough Disaster

James Mossop: I was in the press box and I could see there was trouble in the crowd. Then somebody said, 'There's two dead.' I said, 'Don't be silly, don't exaggerate.' Then you saw people climbing over and then the vivid memory I have was of a kid on a hoarding on one of the advertising hoardings as a makeshift stretcher, and I went down to the front and I thought, 'He's dead, the kid's dead, he's dead.' A policewoman was giving him the kiss of life, another one was pumping his chest and he suddenly sprang to life and all the crowd on that side cheered then he just ... that was him gone with a slump. Afterwards they were laying out all the bodies in a gym in the far corner of the ground and the relatives were going to identify them. I nipped around there, where I wasn't supposed to be, and seeing all these bodies lying out. It was horrific.

Eric Brown: As as a football journalist you set from home on a lovely, sunny day, thinking 'This day's going to end with me seeing a team at Wembley.' You don't expect to be writing about a tragedy and people dying and people who are dead, people who have lost their lives. That certainly seems surreal. I set off to drive up to Hillsborough for a day and come back, but in fact I was still there four days later because I was covering all the aftermath; the visit of Margaret Thatcher. Charles and Diana turned up, the police press conferences. It was absolutely horrendous. I don't know how these war correspondents see people shot and blown up every day. It wouldn't suit me I'm afraid.

Bishop Tom Williams: It was always a threat. If it hadn't have been Liverpool supporters it would've have been Everton. I remember going to an England game at Wembley in the early 1970s and we went into the old Wembley. We were going through this tunnel and it was no higher than a ceiling and we were about twenty deep. There must've been about five hundred in this tunnel and we nearly suffocated before we got out; that's just going through from the underground into the ground. We were treated like garbage by the police. It was awful. There was an idea that if you were a football supporter, you were therefore a hooligan.

Pat Nevin: It was another beautiful, sunny day, the Everton fans we were loving it because we played well that day, we battered Norwich [in the FA Cup semi-final at Villa Park]; Norwich were a good side but we passed them to death and created chances, and boy we looked fast and sharp, and just brilliant. We played really well that day. And that was part of it as well. I scored a goal as well, that's nice for me, we've got to the cup final that's fantastic as well, this is exactly what I've come here for. Maybe that's another little false dawn.

Neville Southall: It was a good game against Norwich and it said a lot about how our fortunes had changed that they finished well above us in the league that season. I was always confident in semi-finals though, and besides the two-legged League Cup semi against Arsenal the previous year never lost one in my entire career. It was a close match and in the end Pat Nevin's goal was enough for us to win it. We were all delighted, jumping around and quite oblivious to the dramas that had unfolded at the day's other semi-final.

Kevin Sheedy: We'd heard there'd been an incident, but we didn't really get told the full facts. You look at the media and what's available now. It was only on the way back when you realise what's actually happened, and then you see it unfold when you get home on the television. That was a sad day for football.

Tony Cottee: At the end of the game, again I still had no idea. At the end of the game I was celebrating with the Everton fans and I threw my shinpads in the crowd, I was jumping up and down, I was really excited because I had worked for seven years as a footballer and hadn't got anywhere near a cup final and then first season I had got to the Cup final with Everton. So I was celebrating and then when I eventually jogged towards the tunnel, I got to the tunnel entrance and there was like a Chief Inspector with like a flat cap on, a policeman, and he stopped me and his words were, 'You're out of order.' I said to him 'What you on about? I've just got through to the FA Cup final.' He said 'You're out of order, you're a disgrace to football' and all this. And he had a right go at me, and he was manhandling me, and in the end I just pushed him off – get lost sort of thing – I thought 'How dare you spoil my day', because he was spoiling my celebrations. The only reason I can think of, and the obvious reason, is the fact that he knew what was going on at Hillsborough and I didn't. He obviously thought that I was trying to encourage the crowd to get on the pitch or something. I don't know what he thought I was doing.

Colin Harvey: I watched the first half from upstairs and then I came down to watch it from the bench. I didn't hear anything. As soon as I came out the pitch, [journalists] Colin Wood and John Keaton were there, and said, 'Have you heard what's going on at Hillsborough?' I said 'No, what's going on?' They said, 'There's been some crowd trouble.' Now that's all we knew at that time, right after the game. It wasn't until 45 minutes later that we started to hear that there had been fatalities and then on the coach going home the full impact was coming through then.

Ian Snodin: There was nothing coming through, there were no mobile phones then really, so nothing was really getting fed through to us, and it wasn't till we won. And it was unbelievable, fantastic in the dressing room. Everybody was jumping round, and then Colin Harvey went, 'Can we just sit down a minute?' I'd just burst in the dressing room to congratulate the lads. And he just said, 'There's been a major disaster at Hillsborough.' It hit everyone in that dressing room, we just went from euphoria to just numbness. The journey home we were just listening to radio reports. Casualties that were going up and up and up every two miles of the journey. It didn't mean anything that we'd won the semi-final to be quite honest, because you know what a tight knit city this is, Liverpool. Whether it happened to Liverpool fans, Everton fans, collectively they get together. It was a very, very sad day. From being up there getting to a cup final to realising what happened, it was unbelievable.

Wayne Clarke: My first thought was, 'Oh there's been crowd trouble.' Violence and stuff like that. Of course coming back from Birmingham, I only lived junction 11 off the M6 so I got off fairly early, three, four or five junctions up. It wasn't until I got in the house and I put the television on that I could see the tragedy that it obviously was. I just couldn't believe it, it was awful.

Kevin Ratcliffe: Don't know until you get back into the changing room after the game. So you're celebrating that you've won and everything, but there's a little bit in the air that you're not quite sure, that's there's been something that's gone on at Hillsborough. But you're not aware of exactly what's gone on, there's been a delay. There's been a delay, not that it's been postponed. To actually think that there's deaths involved and things like that, we don't really know until we get [on the bus] and then you hear, 'Oh, some people have died.' Died? How can people have died? What's happened? Straight away you're thinking about what happened at Heysel, or there could be a bit of trouble. The last thing you're thinking of is that it's trouble between two sets of supporters and there's been deaths then, but then you realise that the death toll is getting higher and higher. With at least 20, and then that 20 goes to 30, 40, 50. And then it ends up the next day or a couple of days later at 96.

Pat Nevin: It was certainly one of the high points of my career, and they're lost within ten minutes. Walking off that park I was happy as I've ever been walking off a football park in my life, because we were in a cup final. But when that happened, it's a really odd thing to be absolutely honest with you when you come off. People often talk about your brain not being able to compute things, to be fair you ask any Evertonians and Liverpudlians as well, what they felt the moment they heard, everyone will say, 'Horror.' But if you really think about it did you really get how serious it was? Did it really sink in? So you take that and also add in the fact that we were on the biggest high in the world, as we were walking off, it must have taken me about thirty seconds to a minute before it really struck. I was told before the start of the interview on BBC Radio, because I was interviewed after the game and it just fell apart during that interview, because it just sank in. So it was this shunt of emotion, and I don't want to ever hear that interview again, but I know how I ended it. Because we were vaguely talking about scoring a goal, and vaguely talking about the game, and Mike Ingham who was interviewing me; he was looking at me and I was looking at him, thinking, 'What the hell are we talking about this for?' The third question I just said 'Listen I'm really sorry mate, but I really don't want to talk about this anymore.' And I think he said, 'Neither do I' and handed back to the studio as if to say, 'Let's forget about all of this. Let's get back to the real story, let's talk about more important things.'

Ian Snodin: The journey home I recall we were just constantly listening to the radio, and we were just sat there thinking, 'Wow, a football game, people going off to watch a semi-final and not even coming home.' So there were no celebrations whatsoever, because as I say we had a long journey back from Villa Park, which usually takes an hour and a half, and it seemed forever. It was one strange, sad journey home.

Neville Southall: The full enormity of what had happened only struck home when we reached the M62 on the last leg of the journey home and were joined by cars and coachloads of devastated Liverpool supporters. A good day turned into a nightmare.

Pat Nevin: You almost need to be a football fan to understand it, but you kind of need to have been in Liverpool – an Evertonian or a Liverpudlian – to know the feelings. I do remember, because I went straight home to Scotland after the game and later the next night I drove back down. I've never seen a day like it – I drove through Liverpool because I had to get something from Bellefield, and there was people just milling about all over Liverpool, just staring into space, it looked other-wordly. There was so many people that had suffered so badly, and you know you can't explain how bad it was, but I think over the years people have understood it.

Dave Watson: We played Spurs away the following week, before we went we went to Anfield to lay a wreath and it was full of supporters. As we walked out in our tracksuits on, it was rapturous applause. That was really touching. Football goes out the window.

Paul Power: My most emotional moment ever in football or in my life – apart from having my two children and being at their birth – was when we went to Anfield and we formed a circle around the centre circle at Anfield and all the supporters were coming in and paying tribute, laying their tributes at the end of the stadium. Colin Harvey walked into the centre circle and put a floral tribute to all the people that had died, and then everybody round the stadium just started applauding. There had been no sound when we had walked to the centre circle. There was no sound whatsoever. Then Colin just laid this wreath and we all just sort of stood round the centre circle in prayer, and then this spontaneous round of applause came. It was unbelievably emotional. To think that those Liverpool fans appreciated the gesture by the Evertonians. It was really quite emotional. Everybody felt the hurt of that situation.

Kevin Ratcliffe: We'd gone over to Anfield and half the pitch was covered in flowers. That's the first time I've ever been clapped Liverpool supporters. We all went there, were dropped off outside, walked in, lay some flowers and realised 'Wow.' It doesn't bring people back, but you're thinking then, 'This is not going to go away. This is not going to go away, how's this football club going to react to this?'

It took two separate enquiries, two inquests and 28 years before criminal charges were finally brought against police officers who were either negligent that day in Sheffield or involved in the cover up that followed the tragedy.

George Orr: My son and my daughter were at Aston Villa that day. I'd given them the tickets so I didn't go, I wanted them to see a semi-final and Everton get to the final. Hillsborough happened. It could've been them. They came out of that ground at the Villa and they didn't know where they were because they were only fifteen and seventeen and they went up to a policeman and they said, 'Excuse me do you know where all the Everton coaches are?' and he said, 'If you don't know, how should I know?' and walked away from them. When I heard about this later, I thought 'That's the attitude.' That was the attitude when you went to a football match in the 1960s, 1970s, 1980s. There's been times I've been to away matches like Wolves and I was in a suit and tie because I was going straight to a wedding when I got back and I'd be pushed and thrown because I'd just strayed into an aisle that I shouldn't be standing in. It didn't matter if you were a woman, kid or a fully grown lad; to the police you were scum. You could be the local magistrate and you'd be treated as the local criminal.

Emy Onoura: Hillsborough and Heysel were accidents waiting to happen. I remember feeling around every ground was kind of pent up, I had my hands in my pockets, more because you'd be squeezed up tight and you didn't want anyone to rob anything out of your pockets. There was loads of dippers around. But I remember lots of times being squeezed against the wall, squeezed up on the terraces, by police horses sometimes, squeezed up against the wall in tight spots, herded around and all this kind of stuff. In hindsight they were just accidents waiting to happen. If we had drawn Forest perhaps we'd have gone to Hillsborough. We might have been the ones who were herded in.

1989 FA Cup final
20 May 1989
Everton 2, Liverpool 3

Pat Nevin: Initially I didn't think it should go ahead. If you had asked me to make the choice I would have said no. But when the families said they wanted to go ahead then yeah, absolutely it goes ahead, and it goes ahead with us giving everything. So that's not a problem, that was absolutely fine, we got on with that. There was no feeling on the day that we shouldn't be doing this, because we weren't the people to make that choice. The right people made that choice. Or certainly were asked about it, and they decided to go ahead with it.

Kevin Sheedy: I think we were always going to be the underdogs because of everyone's feelings towards Liverpool and Hillsborough. I think at the end of the day it puts things in perspective – football's football, people lost their lives. Obviously you go out there as a professional and try to win the game, but it was for Merseyside that day.

Neville Southall: For Everton it was a really difficult situation to go in to because you want to win the FA Cup, but you're playing against somebody who morally deserved to win it. I think that was the hard bit. Obviously I had won the cup before but we had some lads who had never played so far in the cup. We had to be true to ourselves and our supporters, but also keep in mind that for Liverpool it was more than just a game. Dalglish was obviously a great manager and held everything together. It must have been even more difficult for their lads, given what the club had experienced and that some of them were playing to bring a sense of closure to the dreadful events.

Kevin Ratcliffe: We're on a no win situation, we're going into a game where even the songs felt as if they were all Liverpool songs leading up to the kick off. You've just got that negative thing going through your mind that in the end should you be here? But you've got to realise there's two teams in this final, there's two teams that have earned the right to be in this final. But there's only one team getting the credit. It was very hard to play in, and take; the build-up about it was just weird.

Pat Van Den Hauwe: All I can remember about that one is escorting one of our supporters back into the stand. He's coming on and shouting, 'We can still win it.' I just grabbed him and said 'Get back in there before you get nicked.'

Ian Snodin: It was a great game. And when the game were going off both benches and fans were cheering as though nothing had happened a month before because it was a game. Stuart McCall got two, and I remember being sat on the bench, probably four deep because I wasn't playing, I was in my suit. I remember running onto the pitch when Stuart McCall equalised. It was gut-wrenching, the highs and the lows of the game and Rushy scored a couple of goals. Topsy turvy game, but then after the game and the disappointment of losing, the reality again struck what had happened.

Paul Power: Stuart McCall scored a couple of goals didn't he? And then Ian Rush was the absolute bane. I just can't understand how Kevin Ratcliffe and Ian Rush could be such close friends and play together for Wales, and Ratters being such a good defender, but Rushy always scored against Everton, and that was the case in the final. But I think because of what had happened in the semi-final, the result was maybe secondary, although both teams wanted to win it.

The end of Colin Harvey's managerial reign

Kevin Ratcliffe: Sharpy was up front. Tony Cottee was in the side, Peter Beagrie was there, Stuart McCall, Pat Nevin. The balance just wasn't quite right. I didn't feel the same player myself. I didn't feel as if the manager felt that I was the same player, and in hindsight I think I should have moved on. That's how I look at it, but stubborn as you are you want to do well for Everton, you've always been there. It's in your blood. It was far from my mind in one way, but in reality when you look back and thinking for me to get more out of my career maybe I should have moved on. Because I could see that maybe I was going a bit stale at the club at the time and needed a fresh challenge maybe.

Neville Southall: Some of the players Colin had signed underachieved. For a while Tony Cottee just couldn't get a look in; he'd gone from being the most expensive player in Britain to a Central League striker within a year. Pat Nevin was good but unpredictable; you didn't know what you were going to get from one week to the next with Paddy. Neil McDonald was a player who should have played for England. He was very accomplished, good on the ball, versatile, could pass it over five yards or fifty, but it just didn't seem to work out for him. Maybe it was because he didn't get the breaks, or maybe – a little like Bobby Mimms – he just lacked that bit of desire that would have made him a great player.

Neil Pointon: The 89/90 season was a little bit like we're trying to find something again. There wasn't quite the same buzz amongst the players, and everybody's looking over their shoulder, [wondering] 'Who's going to start?' Everton before you knew who was going to start because that was the best team, and you were waiting in the wings. At that moment it was, 'Well, am I going to play or is he going to play?' There wasn't that continuity about who was playing and who wasn't playing. 'That's the best team, no it's not the best team.' I think Colin had a hard task in saying, 'Where is he going to go?' I don't think he quite knew or the coaches quite knew which was his best system. Disjointed is the word I'd use.

Neville Southall: On the opening day of the 1990/91 season we played newly promoted Leeds United at Goodison. It was shit. We were shit. By half-time we were 2-0 down and conceded a third not long after. At half-time I needed to get out of the dressing room and get my head together, so I left and went and sat down in the goalmouth. People went on about it and said it was a protest, but it wasn't at all. At worst it was badly timed, coming around the same time as my transfer request. I certainly wasn't protesting against Colin, who didn't even know about it until that evening.

Ian Snodin: I was having treatment on my hamstring, I was getting a dressing attended to at half-time by the doctor, and Neville came in. I was getting a dressing done and he just started moaning on how crap we were. Was it 3-0 at half-time? 3-0 and he's saying we're this and we're that and we're that. I said 'Come on big man, if you're down in the dumps, imagine everyone else. We need you more than anybody.' He went 'Ah, I'm going out, I'm going out now.' I said 'Going where?' He said, 'I'm just going on the pitch.' I thought, 'What's he on about?'

Colin Harvey: You know how big the dressing rooms at Goodison are? You go in, you say, 'Get them washed', sit down for a few minutes, then go through what you think should happen in the second half. We're getting beat 3-0, so I've gone through everything that I think might just help in the second half, and I thought no more of it. Go out get a couple of goals back, and nearly get a third.

Ian Snodin: The lads were all in the dressing room getting a rollicking or whatever, next thing I hear a big cheer and I turned round to the doctor and said 'He's gone out.' I didn't realise he'd gone and sat by the post until I went up to the stand and realised he had. He was sat down, cap on, sat by the post. But that was just Nev, you couldn't expect anything else. When he said he was going to do it I don't know why I questioned it. It's him all over.

Neville Southall: I'd actually done the same before at Wimbledon a year earlier and nobody had said a word about it then. It cleared my head and allowed me to focus on the second half. But coming when it did it propelled me to the back pages.

Colin Harvey: Clive Tyldesley said, 'Will you do an interview after the game?' So I go out, the cameras start rolling, and the first thing he said to me was 'What do you think about Neville coming out and sitting on the goal?' I said, 'Woah, hang on a minute, what happened?' He said, 'He came out and sat on the post.' I didn't know; this was the first I'd heard about it. I thought he had gone into one of the other rooms because the dressing rooms are big, and there's little rooms off them.

Paul Power: Colin Harvey came to me at the end of the game saying, 'Did you know that Nev wasn't in the dressing room at half-time?' I said I didn't have a clue. Neither did he, neither did Terry Darracott. If we had have known about it, obviously we would have done something about it.

Neville Southall: Colin phoned me that evening at home. He wasn't a happy man. 'What the fuck are you doing? he asked. I explained my reasons and he seemed to calm down. But the next day he called me back to tell me that he was fining me two weeks wages and suspending me. I could be awkward as well, so I phoned my agent and told him that I was suspended for a fortnight. 'If I'm not allowed to come in, ask him if I can go on holiday,' I instructed him. Me, on holiday! I hated holidays. That's how absurd the situation had become. Colin was soon on the phone again. 'Come in on Monday,' he said. 'We'll talk again.' On Wednesday, when we faced Coventry City at Highfield Road, I was in the starting line up, as ever.

Colin Harvey: I said to him on the Monday, 'What were you thinking?' He said, 'I was just feeling shit.' I thought 'Typical Neville like, probably wasn't thinking.' Just wandered out and sat on the post. Why he wanted to do that? Well that was Neville.

Dave Watson: It was totally disrespectful. I didn't totally agree with that. Keep it in house. Neville is Neville. He had a major influence in the great teams of Everton. He'd be on your case if you weren't doing your job. People were frightened of him. He's a top lad, he really is. He has a great passion for it. Never missed training. First into training playing head tennis at 8 in the morning. His feet with the ball was magnificent.

Paul Power: Nev was just a one off. He was an individual. The goalkeeping position is an individual positon, but he was mentally an individual as well. He would do things that suited himself. He was tremendous, he was the best keeper around at the time, but he was always likely to do something a little bit idiosyncratic,. But maybe that would have summed up the tone of the dressing room at the time. He's gone and done an individual thing like that; the togetherness that had always been there in the past was starting to dissipate anyway.

Pat Nevin: In the second half we had a right go back, and it was a travesty that we never got a draw in that game, because we battered the living day lights out of them in that second half. We absolutely battered them, but that was an odd one, because it then started us off on a difficult run. We played Coventry the next game, and we played really quite well. I scored a goal, again, and we got beat, and I thought, 'We're miles better than them.' Having played two games and played really well, and I'm walking about thinking 'Well I'm on form, I'm scoring, I'm creating.' But in the midst of it none of it matters, because you're too busy worrying about not getting results. And we had a right hard start to that season; nothing really went well for us, that was a horrible start. We weren't getting hammered by anyone, we were quite often the better team.

Norman Whiteside: Alex Ferguson and I had already had a chat about my future and he informed me Everton had been watching my progress after I had a Achilles tendon problem. Then he give Colin Harvey permission to speak to me. Colin telephoned me and I meet him in the car park at the Rocket pub before we went to Goodison to do the deal with Jim Greenwood. The mood in the dressing room was upbeat as Colin was assembling a decent team. I thought we had a great chance of success because we had some very good players.

Kevin Sheedy: Norman had problems, he started playing in the World Cup when he was 17, so wear and tear. When he did sign he did have a knee problem. He had a run of games – I think he scored seven goals in ten games. You could see when he was fit, the goal he scored against us in the cup final, that was what he was capable of doing on a regular basis, but just unfortunately he had to retire. Similar to Andy Gray he was a bit of a gamble because of the quality of player he was, but that one didn't come off.

Neville Southall: From Aston Villa came the centre-back Martin Keown, who was probably the best of all of Colin's signings but a very funny guy. People say that I'm grumpy, but then they don't know Martin, who was born moaning. He was like a little old man. Martin's the only person I've ever deliberately kicked in training because he got on my nerves. I like him, but he's one of them people that can rub you the wrong way for no reason whatsoever.

Kevin Ratcliffe: There were one or two players who were at fault for it, and very hard to get on with. As in their personalities were quite hard to actually live with. Even some of the players that were brought in were seeing it and thinking 'There's a conflict here between two sides.' I won't name names, but because of the lads had come in under Colin they'd stuck together, and obviously the lads that Howard had brought through were together. We were a lot older, but it was very hard. Martin Keown was a big problem.

Neville Southall: I think it was harder for Martin than any of the new players because he had been brought in to replace Rats. I think he felt the pressure more than anybody else. It was a difficult time for him, but being the person he was he constantly sought reassurance. He was strong mentally in some ways, but needy in others. He shouted at his keeper, namely me, which didn't go down well and we had a little bit of a row about it. He could be abrasive. But at the same time he was always looking for encouragement. He'd be passing the ball back and asking 'How do you think I'm doing?' Or at half-time following you into the toilets asking the same question. I think he soon learned that if he asked me he was asking the wrong man. My stock response was: 'Fuck off you idiot!'

Pat Nevin: He bought in Martin Keown, Martin was as good a marker as you will ever see. But there was a bad feeling towards Martin. I thought that was unfair. He's an unusual character, but that's not got anything to do with anything, he can play, he can do a job.

Neville Southall: I didn't really mix with one group of my teammates or another, but I was there the night that Colin took us out for a Chinese meal to help clear the mood. This was one of Howard's famous ploys, and it always seemed to work – we never lost after one of our get togethers. But this time it backfired spectacularly. Kevin Sheedy had a really dry sense of humour and was goading and taking the piss out of Martin Keown. They just rubbed each other up the wrong way, but Martin didn't react at first. Then Sheeds said something about Martin's brother, who was out with us, and it all went off. Punches were thrown and Sheeds ended up with four stitches.

Colin Harvey: Apparently he was having a go at Keown's brother, 'What you doing here? Who said you can come?' and all that. Anyway, Keown just said to him in the end 'Leave it out.' And he wouldn't, so Keown gave him a belt, and you wouldn't want a belt off Keown.

Neville Southall: I used to sit down in the afternoons and try and work out what we were doing wrong. But I just couldn't manage it. We were good players; Colin was there; we had all the right components – and yet it just didn't click. We were doing okay in games; we were a decent team, but just weren't doing what we were supposed to do. I had no idea why. It mystified me and it befuddled Colin. I think he tried everything; tried everything anybody could do to make it change. There wasn't one thing that was abundantly wrong with the set up. It was a number of things that just didn't quite click.

John Ebbrell: It was like almost an impossible job really, looking back. But when you're actually there and involved in it, it doesn't seem impossible. If you look at the cards he was dealt, five or six top players from a very small squad leaving, the expectation of the crowd was we're going win or win the cup; it was very difficult. Being part of that I was trying to be selfish about myself in terms of, 'I need to survive here, no one's going to help me, I've got to fight to become good enough, and better myself each day.' But at the same time we weren't winning often enough. Off memory, we were doing fine at Goodison, we were winning a lot of games at Goodison, but we couldn't win away from home. Ultimately, Colin lost his job because of that.

Neville Southall: We didn't win any of our first six league matches and were bouncing around the wrong end of the table. On 30 October we went to Sheffield United for a League Cup tie. It was an awful game and we lost 2-1. Within 48 hours Colin was sacked as Everton manager.

Altogether Now:
Highs & Lows
in Football's New Age
1990-2002

'Football's ever-evolving. So, I remember walking out, I think it was at Coventry, for my first Sky game – there was dancing girls and there were fireworks – and thinking, 'What the hell's all this about?''

John Ebbrell

Howard Kendall returns as manager

On 31 October 1990, Colin Harvey had been sacked as Everton manager. Six days later Howard Kendall returned to Goodison for a second spell as boss, with Harvey also returning as his assistant.

Paul Power: I remember when we went back to the club [after the Sheffield United League Cup tie on 30 October]. In those days it was the staff that got all the kit off the bus and everything – the players just got in their cars and left. So, there was myself and Colin who took all of the gear off the bus. I still had to drive home then to Knutsford, where I lived. Col said, 'Are you having a drink lad?' I said, 'I'll have one drink Col but I can't have a lot because I've got to drive home now.' I went and had a couple of glasses of wine with him in the dressing room; not even in his office – this was in the dressing room at Bellefield. I knew that he wouldn't go home, because I said to him, 'Look' – there was a bottle of wine between us – 'Don't finish it, get yourself off home.' He said: 'I'll phone the wife, I'm alright. Just leave me, I'm fine.' I knew then that the writing was on the wall.

Neville Southall: I was gutted when Colin Harvey was sacked as manager. I didn't think it was the right thing to do; he should have been given more time. I was devastated for Colin, who lived and breathed the club. There should have been more faith and patience shown in him by the board, as there had been with Howard seven years earlier. Sometimes these situations just need a spark to reignite a winning mentality.

John Ebbrell: I can't remember how I found out about Kendall and Harvey's return, but two things. My first thought was, 'No chance, that's just been kept so quiet, this can't be happening.' But then they were both in front of me within an hour, and I couldn't believe it. My next thought was, 'Great, this will work, it's worked in the past, can't wait.' And I have to say, for the first few months when they came back together it was brilliant, because all the old feelings came back. But it's very difficult to replicate, and the players weren't the same players, and it just didn't quite reach the heights of what we wanted.

Kevin Sheedy: That was the dream team when we were successful, so why not give it a go? Obviously it wasn't as successful, but only Howard could have come back. It was just disappointing that it didn't work out, but at the end of the day he's one of Everton's greatest ever players and greatest ever manager, so he was entitled to have that.

Colin Harvey: I'd actually finished. It'd been about a week, and Bill Kenwright was not long on the board and he rang me up and he said, 'Would you come back in if Howard was manager again?' I said, 'Well it's a hypothetical question, he's not going to come back, is he?' He said, 'There's a possibility.' Anyway Howard rang me up and said, 'Would you do it?' and I said, 'Yeah.' And I shouldn't have done it. I should have just stayed out of it altogether.

Howard Kendall: I had absolutely no doubt about inviting him back as my assistant manager. Although there was no hesitation in his accepting my offer, I'm sure he must have been greeted by a confusion of emotions, having just days earlier been shown the door. Certainly, I thought it was a brave decision to return, but it was a mark of how highly everyone at Everton Football Club thought of him that he was welcomed back unquestioningly.

Tony Cottee: It was all a bit weird really, and I knew – and I think all the younger players did too – that as soon as Howard took over, that he was going to revert back to playing the more experienced players and the ones that he was familiar with. We all knew that was coming and it made it really difficult for the young ones.

Howard Kendall: I arrived back in November 1990 to an unhappy dressing room. It was cliquish, and I just felt there were two different groups going out to play together, going out to train together, but changing in the same dressing room. The split was between the, 'Old guard,' whom I had managed previously, and the newer crop of players Colin had brought in. One or two players straddled the divide, but there was a definite division. It was my job to try and do something about that. You could point the finger at both sides in that situation. There were the ones who had done it, had won trophies and caps and written their names into Goodison lore, and they would turn around and say, 'We've got no chance of doing it again with what we've got at this club now.' Then I would look at the other ones who were saying, 'What chance have we got, because Howard is going to come back and he's going to select the Ratcliffes and the Sheedys and people like that; we've got no chance of getting in. They've done it for him before so he's going to be loyal to them.'

Kevin Ratcliffe: I remember having a little chat with him on the coach and he said, 'We'll get this back.' I just turned to him and said, 'Maybe in two years.' He went, 'Nah, one.' I said, 'It'll take you more than two years to get this back to where it was.' You knew that there was that little divide between two sets of players, and you just knew that there was a lot of things; a lot of shifting people out, a lot of shifting people in. I knew that I wouldn't be there at that time, I knew that my performances weren't the same. I never had the pace that I had, so I knew my time was coming slowly. I thought I could have done a job, but obviously other people think different.

Neville Southall: He hadn't changed at all, but then people don't over a few years, do they? As a person he was probably slightly less tolerant; or expected better. When he didn't get it he was a bit more sarcastic this time than he was the first time round. But otherwise, he was just the same old Howard. For me it was good because it meant that I could keep doing things my way.

Ray Atteveld: I didn't have a good connection with him. I didn't like his way and his attitude towards people and towards players. What was quite quickly noticeable was that he was willing to bring in his people. I call it 'his people' because I noticed he took them from club to club.

Andy Hinchcliffe: I remember people laughing at the time and saying, 'There's the manager that just sold you,' and within a short period of time he's come back to the club where he's been massively successful. Having the relationship we did, it was never going to be easy, and even as I got older and played for England, our relationship never really changed. It was never spoken of really; it was never really discussed. He never came in after he joined and said, 'This is what I needed to do, or this is why I did what I did.' It was never really talked about, we just kind of rubbed along together and got on with it.

Tony Cottee: I knew that was going to make it difficult for me personally with Howard, and I think all the younger players felt the same. As it proved as well, because I think he went with what he knew to start with. I sort of fell out with Howard, he chucked me in the reserves, the famous game where I played against my window cleaner against Morecambe, all of which is rather funny looking back on it now. We had a few chats, me and Howard, he had his own individual style of how he did things. But I'm pleased to say eventually I won him over and he gave me a three-year contract. Then he resigned about three months later! It was just how it was really.

Howard Kendall: The only times we came into conflict were when Tony let out his frustrations to the press. I remember one interview in which he said, 'How am I expected to score goals if players around me are not giving me the opportunities?' I sat reading that in my office and my immediate thought was, 'He's having a go at his fellow players.' So I got them together downstairs and just said to Tony, 'You've got two choices; you apologise to these lads here, or you train with the kids.' 'I didn't mean it,' said Tony. 'I was misquoted.' 'Hey, I'm sorry, lad, you said it.' 'I don't want to train with the kids,' he said. 'You've got to train with the kids, or apologise to your team-mates and take them out for a Chinese.' I sent him off to play with the A team at Morecambe, but he quickly backed down. I think he was shocked after realising one of his opponents was his window cleaner!

Neville Southall: I think he wanted a bit of Andy Gray in every player. It wouldn't matter what happened off the pitch as long as they performed on there. But the likes of Tony Cottee and Pat Nevin were conscientious; good pros, but probably didn't have enough character or charisma for Howard. He'd look at them and think, 'Well, is that it? Is that what you do?' It was unfair in some ways because they were good players, but that was never enough for Howard. Team spirit was always an integral part of the way his teams had operated. He believed that if you stuck together, then your good team spirit and strong characters would see you through. During the glory years we won some games we shouldn't have won on team spirit alone.

Pat Nevin: For the rest of the season it was pretty up and down. I think he brought Robert Warzycha in, and I'd been scoring fairly regularly, I think I was getting up to double figures – and I'm not really a scorer, I'm a creator – and then it became quite clear, 'We don't want you, you'll be second in line.' And I tried to fight it and say, 'Look, I'm going to show you how good I am.' Colin was there and he would say, 'Look, he's a good guy, he's a hard-working guy, his reactions will always be incredibly professional.' And it was a mistake, I maybe shouldn't have done that. In retrospect if I had known, I would have just gone in politely and said, 'Do you think I should leave?' and he would have probably said, 'Yeah,' and everything would have been better, but I decided to fight. I remember I scored a couple of goals in the new season I scored against Chelsea and Spurs, I thought, 'I can still do this, I'm still doing alright,' but I suppose in my heart I knew that he didn't rate us, and that was it. We finished the season much better, we did alright.

Colin Harvey: Neither of us was the same person. He'd been in Bilbao and then at Man City. He'd changed a bit and I'd changed a bit, so neither of us were the same, and it just didn't work anymore.

Dr David Marsh: The good thing about him was we used to meet for board meetings and he was there to answer questions from any director. Therefore, you had a direct relationship and he stayed on and had dinner with us afterwards and that was a good way to talk off the record. We talked about all things football, obviously about Everton and others as well and that was the time that I really got to know him.

Howard Kendall: Off the field so much had changed at Goodison in barely more than three years. The disharmony in the Everton dressing room was matched by discord in the boardroom. Everything had been so much easier in the old days, when it was a simple axis running the club: me,

'For him to pick himself, an old guy, I think that was more as an education to the players.' Howard Kendall returned as player manager in 1981, turning out six times for the first team through the 1981/82 season. [*Mirrorpix*]

Everton's young guns line up in December 1982. From left to right: John Bailey, Kevin Ratcliffe, David Johnson, Gary Stevens, Kevin Richardson, Adrian Heath, Kevin Sheedy and Steve McMahon. They would form the core of Everton's greatest ever team a few years later. [*Getty*]

'Reidy was a good player; a lively lad as well; another character in a dressing room that was becoming a louder and louder place to be.' [*Getty*]

Howard Kendall and his mid-1980s backroom team. From left to right: Terry Darracott, John Clinkard, substitute Alan Harper, Kendall, Mick Heaton and Colin Harvey. [*Getty*]

'When it went in that was possibly the biggest goal I've ever seen us score; in terms of disbelief and ecstasy, and thinking my head was going to blow up. That moment was something else.' John Bailey and Adrian Heath celebrate Heath's 1984 FA Cup semi-final winner against Southampton at Highbury. [*Mark Leech/Offside*]

'Everton fans have watched Liverpool fans parade trophies around the city for years, and all of a sudden it was us. It was magnificent to do that.' Gary Stevens and Derek Mountfield parade the FA Cup in 1984. [*Getty*]

'People talk of the save at Tottenham from Falco, but Neville made a save at Sheffield Wednesday from Imre Varadi which was just out of this world for me, fantastic.' [*Press Association*]

'It was a good night, but after Bayern Munich it was an anti-climax.' Neville Southall and Andy Gray celebrate winning the European Cup Winners' Cup against Rapid Vienna. [*Mark Leech/Offside*]

'We had to change the system. Gary Lineker was lightning, he was rapid, and we played a lot more long balls then.' Gary Lineker scored 40 goals in his single season at Everton, but left without winning a trophy. [*Getty*]

'In a way winning the league title the second time was more rewarding and satisfying than it had been in 1985. It was so easy first time around; we just won games for fun. 1987 was more of a struggle, or rather a series of battles.' [*Getty*]

'It was certainly one of the high points of my career, and they're lost within ten minutes.' Pat Nevin celebrates scoring the winner in the 1989 FA Cup semi-final. That joy soon dissipated on learning of the events at the day's other semi at Hillsborough. [*Getty*]

'At the end of the game, again I still had no idea. I got to the tunnel entrance and there was a policeman, and he stopped me and his words were, 'You're out of order.' I said to him, 'What you on about? I've just got through to the FA Cup final.' He said, 'You're out of order, you're a disgrace to football.' Tony Cottee on the moment he learned about Hillsborough. [*Offside*]

'For 120 minutes the momentum ebbed and flowed between the two teams in a night of high drama.' Everton's 4-4 1991 FA Cup fifth round replay draw with Liverpool draw is considered one of Goodison's most dramatic matches. [*Getty*]

'When you're winning you feel confidence, when you're losing you get yourself in a rut and confidence is low. We just struggled, it's as simple as that.' Everton's early 1990s stagnation was symbolised by a game at Wimbledon, played out in front of just 3039 people; a record low in the Premier League. [*Offside*]

'I looked almost surprised. It was like, 'Did that happen? Oh yeah, alright, I better do something now.' And I went.' Paul Rideout on the moment he scored Everton's 1995 FA Cup final winner. [*Getty*]

'Archie and I were of the same mind that Everton were a traditional club, a football club that you respected from the outside. That for me was a big attraction.' Walter Smith (*second from the right*) with his backroom coaching staff: Dave Watson (*far right*), Archie Knox (*centre*), Chris Woods (*left*); Jimmy Martin is seated behind Woods and Knox. [*Offside*]

'Kevin came and scored goals straight away. He was the nicest man on earth, a really good guy. Successful from day one.' Kevin Campbell celebrates after scoring the winner in the 1999 Anfield derby. [*Getty*]

'Gazza was obviously a big name with probably his better years being behind him. But he was still a character, he was fantastic in the dressing room. He was a brilliant guy.' [*Getty*]

'When I took over I had a feeling that finishing just outside of relegation, avoiding relegation and staying up was going to be acceptable. And I could smell it. I smelt it round the club, and I felt that was one of the reasons why I had to try and make a much big change.' David Moyes on his early days as Everton manager. [*Getty*]

'He was a flippin' Roy of the Rovers at that level. Some of the stuff he could do; he would just get the ball and run right through the other team. From the half way line or something, run straight and score.' A teenage Wayne Rooney at Bellefield. [*Getty*]

'From the minute you kicked off you just knew. From the changing rooms, leading into the game, you just knew, he'd tell you he was up for it, no matter what. And you just knew, 'Wow, we're going to get a game from Fergie here.'' April 2005. Duncan Ferguson heads Everton into the Champions League. [*Getty*]

'As much as the four days that broke Everton in the seventies being pivotal, that decision by supposedly the best referee in the world actually set Everton back who knows how far.' Duncan Ferguson heads home the goal that never was in the 2005 Champions League play off against Villareal. [*Getty*]

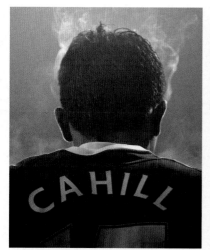

Top left: 'He had the passion and he loved Everton.' Tim Cahill was a pivotal signing for David Moyes. [*Offside*] *Top right:* 'I've always said, from the day I stepped through the doors at Everton in summer 2006 it felt like home.' Tim Howard would play more than 400 times for Everton. [*Offside*]

'There was an incredible understanding between Pienaar and Baines.' [*Getty*]

'It shocked me straight away when I realised I was the fourteenth manager of Everton. Sometimes in the modern game, clubs go through that number of managers in five years.' Roberto Martinez followed manager 13, David Moyes, into the Goodison hotseat in June 2013. [*Offside*]

'Bill was very picky. We've talked to lots of people over the years. He was very picky who came in, and I think he got the right guy in the end.' Jon Woods (*left*) on the new investor Farhad Moshiri (*centre*), with Bill Kenwright (right). [*Getty*]

Everton legend and Everton under-23 manager David Unsworth. After leading the Under-23s to the Premier League 2 title in 2016/17 he served some of the following campaign as caretaker manager of the first team after Ronald Koeman's dismissal. [*Getty*]

Ronald Koeman was appointed Everton manager in June 2016 amidst much fanfare. But despite qualifying for Europe in his only full season as boss, the standard of football was disappointing and the Dutchman failed to connect with the club's fanbase. He was sacked in October 2017 after a poor start to the new season. [*Getty*]

The return of the prodigal son. Wayne Rooney celebrates scoring on his second Everton league debut, v Stoke City in August 2017. [*Getty*]

In May 2018 Denise Barrett-Baxendale was appointed Everton CEO. This was followed several weeks later by the appointment of Marco Silva as manager. The former Sporting Lisbon, Olympiacos, Hull and Watford boss followed the unpopular Sam Allardyce into the Goodison hotseat. [*Getty*]

Jim Greenwood and Philip Carter. In the first board meeting that I attended in my second spell, they were talking about finances, which never came up in the past. Previously the directors always had a separate financial meeting before the official board meeting. But finances were discussed this time and the club's debt was brought up. Philip Carter joked, 'Nothing changes, Howard, does it?' I always remember that statement: 'Nothing changes, does it?' But it had changed.

Dr David Marsh: I was pitched in in a difficult time [as chairman]. I remember attendances falling and trying to get finance when I was chairman. Jim [Greenwood] and I went on various trips to try and arrange finance. You could get the finance, but the people who were prepared to give it would not have been approved by the rest of the board or probably by the FA. You needed millions not, just the odd few hundred thousand, and that wasn't enough. They were very difficult times for finance.

Colin Harvey: Whatever had gone on before, the chemistry we had, it wasn't the same.

20 February 1991
FA Cup fifth round replay
Everton 4, Liverpool 4

Howard Kendall: For 120 minutes the momentum ebbed and flowed between the two teams in a night of high drama.

Ray Atteveld: It was a quite amazing game to be playing in, because I think in all four situations we were one goal down and got back up every time, that was the spirit that was in the team in this game. It's always very strange, very unique to play the same team in the city and the crowds are mixed, not segregated crowds; one colour is there and the other colour is there. You see them sitting next to each other – that for me was a unique experience in these games.

Andy Hinchcliffe: It's one of those things where you have to watch it back to fully appreciate. When you're stuck in the middle of a game like that and you're flying around, and the goals are flying in, and the emotions... That's what I do remember of the game itself, the emotions involved; the noise and the colour. It was just crazy, but then when you watch the game back and realise what you've been able to do. To be behind four times and to keep pulling it back and keep pulling it back, it was an extraordinary game and one you have to re-live and re-watch to understand what had gone on, because it was like a whirlwind. I'd never experienced a game like it.

Howard Kendall: I watched this unfold from the dugout, where alongside me I had my last substitute, Tony Cottee. I'd used Tony infrequently since returning three months previously, but I told him to warm up and with four minutes to go brought him on for Pat Nevin. With just seconds remaining, and just one previous touch to his name, it paid off. Stuart McCall flicked the ball on and Cottee ran in to tuck it past Bruce Grobbelaar. Three-three. Extra time. There were further twists to come. Southall saved brilliantly from Rush and Venison, before John Barnes put Liverpool ahead with a curling 30-yard shot into the top corner. Many sides would have crumbled, but Cottee was in inspired form. Six minutes from time he equalised again to set up another replay a week later, again at Goodison.

Tony Cottee: It was just one of those games where I was in the right place, right time. It's quite funny really because I travel around the world, around Europe and around the country, and a lot of Evertonians say, 'Oh that must have been the best game you ever played in.' I say, 'Well I didn't play in the game,' because I didn't. I didn't come on until 84 minutes on the clock, and then everyone remembers me scoring the two goals, but I didn't start the game. What's even funnier is the Liverpool fans say, 'Oh it's your fault Kenny Dalglish resigned.' I say, 'How'd you work that out?' They say, 'Well you scored two goals, we drew four all and Kenny resigned.' So I get blamed for that by the Liverpool fans.

Andy Hinchcliffe: Even watching it 10 years on you get a sense of what the game was all about. People call it the most extraordinary cup tie ever played, because you just don't see matches like that. To play in it was a bit of a whirlwind.

Neville Southall: It was a game that had everything: goals, saves, tackles, a brilliant crowd; it was a proper old-fashioned game of football, one of the best I've ever played in.

Pat Nevin: You couldn't forget those ties. It's a shame because as a footballer you want to remember the real positives. I would argue that was the worst season, we finished in mid-table, whereas with Colin we were disappointed with sixth, so it seemed a bit odd! It was a pretty mid-table team by that point, you think wait a minute, 'Are we really any better?'

Ray Atteveld: The speed of the game, the pace of the game was enormous. My wife, last week put a video on Facebook and somebody responded with sending her part of this game. She said to me 'Ray, wow this is so quick!' Even in that era it was quick, it was going up and down. That was amazing to play in and be a part of it.

John Ebbrell: They'd scored four great goals, proper goals, they'd footballed us, and we've tackled the ball into the net, they've had mistakes, we've bundled the ball into the net, it's 4-4. I'm an Evertonian, I don't care. It was just amazing, an amazing night.

48 hours after the replay, the Liverpool manager, Kenny Dalglish, shocked football by resigning as Liverpool manager.

John Ebbrell: I can remember being at Bellefield and we were just running round as we did, and a fella just popped his head over the fence and said, 'Have you heard? Kenny Dalglish has resigned!' It's amazing going back thirty years and how it's all changed, you couldn't do that here now like. A fella has just popped his head over, and I didn't know. I'm running around thinking, 'Jesus,' and Graeme Sharp's just said something like, 'Oh yeah the Pope's dead as well you know.' Graeme had a real great sense of humour, it was a cutting remark. He obviously knew but I didn't, but I pretended I did as I ran round. I was gobsmacked. Absolutely gobsmacked.

Kevin Sheedy: I wouldn't say it was the pressure because Kenny's played and managed at the top, it was just a personal decision. It was a strange one, I think it caught everyone by surprise when Kenny announced, but he's a shrewd man so there was reasons for it.

Neville Southall: I think that Merseyside football lost something more intangible the day Kenny left Anfield. Because he was such a great man and such a defining figure, the whole city struggled to come to terms with his departure. He had been a giant through Hillsborough and everyone respected him for that. He brought dignity and class to Merseyside football. As Everton players we measured ourselves against him and what he'd achieved at Anfield. To beat Liverpool with Kenny in charge was a great achievement; he elevated the Merseyside derby to a different plateau and I don't think that the rivalry between the two clubs has been the same since.

Howard Kendall: Although Liverpool have fared better than Everton since then and have continued to win cup competitions, league success has remained elusive for both teams. It was really the end of an era of winning for Liverpool that you could trace back to 20 years earlier and that dramatic FA Cup semi-final defeat of the Everton team I was playing in.

Everton returned to Anfield a week later for a second replay. The game was settled by Dave Watson's early goal.

Dave Watson: It came quite early in the game. It bounced down in the box and I've battered it with my left foot. I thought, 'Oh no, I've woken them up and they'll come at us now!' It was a hell of a strike and it was great to score the winning goal. I was with [the caretaker management team of] Ronnie [Moran] and Roy [Evans] at Liverpool. I knew Kenny as well. When you see the job get to people it shows how much it means. We loved it and I was made up we beat them and I got the winning goal, but when it settles down, and you see people have left their jobs it's a bit touching. The victory for the team is the most important thing. It's nice to get the winner.

Iain Jenkins: Dave Watson was a warrior. If we were training every single day he was on the bike and on the machines forty five minutes before we even trained. He was the fittest, he was a powerhouse, he was a machine. There weren't a lot of home grown players there, but Waggy was a Scouser; he was born and bred in Liverpool and knew about the city where some others didn't. He was excellent.

Peter Beardsley and the players of the early-90s

In summer 1991, after missing out on Derby County's Dean Saunders, Howard Kendall signed Liverpool's Peter Beardsley in a £1million deal.

Howard Kendall: Graeme Souness, who had succeeded Dalglish, said to me, 'He won't sign for Everton; he hasn't got the bottle to move across the park.' But Peter proved him wrong.

Stuart Barlow: I remember the first day he came. I don't know what training session we did but I can take you to the spot where we had the goals and he was just doing things you'd only see on the telly. You thought, 'No he can't be that good.' You're seeing things and the passes he's picking and you think, 'How's he putting a pass through those two players?' And the little jink he had; the little swivel of the hips. He was just doing it day in day out.

Pat Nevin: Peter Beardsley came in, and I played with him at training, and I just thought, 'I'm enjoying playing with you more than any player I have ever played with in my entire career. I have got utter and complete understanding of everything you're doing, and your understanding of what I am doing is amazing.' He would do things in training and I'm thinking, 'I've not had this quality before.' For me I thought he was world class.

Andy Hinchcliffe: To see Peter day in, day out, and the kind of guy that he was as well; you need to see people in training to fully appreciate how consistently good these people are. And with Peter, what I realised is that he was so quick in his head, the ball was gone before it had even arrived at his feet. He didn't have to think about controlling the ball, because he knew he was going to do that and he was thinking about where the ball could be played. So you never got close to him; even in training you realised how good a player he was, because you never got a foot on the ball, because he never allowed you to get close enough to make that happen.

John Ebbrell: When Peter came I remember being in this team thinking, 'Right, I feel like I am one of the key members of this team.' Whereas when I started at Everton I looked around and thought: 'Top player, top player, top player, how am I going to get into this?' It then evolved to looking round and thinking, 'Thank God Peter Beardsley's come in,' because I don't see where else the goals were coming from. I didn't really see where our spark's coming from.

Neville Southall: Peter was a truly great player, probably too brilliant for us at the time and frankly far too advanced for the players that we had. He would play passes that nobody else could see. He loved creating chances for his team-mates, but he often ended up giving the ball away because the others couldn't see what he could see.

Ray Atteveld: He didn't only change the way the team played, he also changed the dynamics in the dressing room with his work rate, with his humour, with his no-nonsense behaviour. Because he was such a big name but he didn't have the behaviour of a star. He was a real genuine guy, and he had no stuck up nose. He was approachable, he was helping you, he was advising you. It was the start of a little bit of a different dynamic in the dressing room as well.

Iain Jenkins: He was the ultimate professional; he would give his time and effort and honestly he was fantastic. I remember when we went across to Ireland on a pre-season tour and we were given a night out by Howard. I'm with the first team squad and sat with Dave Watson of a night time having a few pints of Guinness and Peter just took me under his wing. He said: 'Jenks don't get caught up with this drinking, we are away pre-season and we've got to do it right.' He didn't really have to do that and it wasn't that the other people were dragging me down with them, that was my decision, but to come over and pull me in front of the other senior pros I felt was brilliant. Then he came the next morning to make sure that I'd gone to bed and to get me out of my bed and make sure I was there on time.

Howard Kendall: Billy Kenny broke into the first team in the 1992/93 season and was outstanding. He had great potential and gave a man of the match winning performance in the derby. Unfortunately, it was a difficult time for the club and for Billy. There were excuses coming in, absences, which we checked up on and found out that they hadn't been truths. It emerged later that he was involved in not just serious drinking, but also recreational drug use. We couldn't have that going on at the club, and we came to an agreement on his contract. Joe Royle took a chance on him and took him to Oldham and he was let down as well. It was a terrific blow because the lad certainly had great potential; he was a very good young midfield player and had a great future ahead of him.

Barry Horne: Howard loved him, promoted him, and would have played him whenever he could have really. He had massive potential. He always had time on the ball. That's the key to being a good player, isn't it? That's what all good players have. We will never know. I don't know what to say about Billy but it was a shame for him and Everton.

Howard Kendall: Colin had signed Stuart Barlow from local amateur leagues when he was working as a butcher. He had pace to burn and could have been a local hero. There were so many times he was through on goal because of his speed, and nothing came of it. He got the nickname 'Jigsaw' because he went to pieces in the box. It was a little unfair on him but it's what people were seeing. He was a smashing lad and a dream to work and missing all those chances didn't put him off getting there. He'd keep going, he'd outpace defenders, and he would get one on one with goalkeeper. And miss. I remember a derby game at Anfield and he was put through a couple of times. He could have written his name into the history books, but the chances went. Liverpool had a similar player in Ronnie Rosenthal, but the difference was when he came on you had the old sinking feeling in the dugout; indeed he punished us one particular day.

Adam Farley: Stuart was lightning quick and even later on in his career when he played for Fleetwood I played against him and he was still a great player then; he must've been something like 38. He was a good man to have around, he was a local lad, he came through the ranks. He had everything Stuart; I know he missed chances but you've got to get in that position to miss them.

Iain Jenkins: Neville never shut up. He never stopped and you didn't have to turn round to try and understand your position and where you should be because he had you on a piece of string. He would talk you through the game and you didn't have to turn around. You talk about his training methods; I remember one time there was a sandpit at the back of Bellefield and that's where the goalkeepers used to train with Jim Barron, and Neville pulled us over. He put us in the sand pit and he made us work and for about fifteen, twenty minutes, I came off and I was nearly dying; I couldn't breathe. It was basically his way of having a go at us.

Howard Kendall: There wasn't a great deal of money to spend, so I had to be careful with what I had. In the summer of 1992 I bought Paul Rideout. I'd always remembered Paul playing as a schoolboy international at Wembley in the early-1980s. He was considered the outstanding talent at the time, but his career never really took off the way it should have done. He was a bit slow but technically very adept. He had started to play as centre-half at Rangers, and I thought he had more to offer as an attacking threat. He didn't do too badly for me, but then when you look at what he did afterwards for Everton you realise his importance.

Neville Southall: Barry Horne was the most intense man I've ever met in my life. He was my room-mate and the sort of person who was so clever that he could watch TV, read the paper and listen to the radio at the same time. His mind never stopped. Normally the night before a match we'd have a cup of tea and a sandwich about 9pm and I'd try to go to sleep by 10pm, but Barry would still be up in the small hours of the morning. I, however, always posed him a few problems. Because of my bad back I'd sleep on the floor and block his way to the toilet. Come the morning the teapot would be filled with Barry's piss.

Beginning of the Premier League era

Dr David Marsh: I was there at the beginning of the Premier League. Twenty chairmen and chief executives met and decided how we should run it. I believe it's basically the same sort of set up as it was then, I don't know how many more times money there is. Billions. I don't know if any of us could've foreseen that amount of money.

John Ebbrell: Football's ever-evolving. So I remember walking out, I think it was at Coventry, for my first Sky game – It would have been well into that season, and there was dancing girls, and there were fireworks – and thinking, 'What the hell's all this about?'

Tony Cottee: There were good players leaving and some of the ones replacing them weren't as good. The ones we were linked with – good players – they didn't always come to the football club. It was a frustrating time for everyone.

Graham Stuart: I think it was a difficult time to join the club, and for one reason or another it just wasn't happening for us as well. As soon as you start to lose a few games, it's the same as when you're winning. When you're winning you feel confidence, when you're losing you get yourself in a rut and confidence is low. We just struggled, it's as simple as that.

David Unsworth: I remember some people saying at the time sometimes you have to go down to come back up. Which is an absolute load of rubbish, because we've seen the change of a manager can improve your results overnight. So I never bought into that one little bit, and Everton in the Championship, or Division Two, then it just doesn't work, just doesn't fit.

Tony Cottee: We had players like Stefan Rehn, Ray Atteveld, we were experimenting and dabbling in the foreign market. I think most clubs were; one, two or three players was common really. Now you've got probably 23 foreign players at a club so it's obviously different, the money's completely different as we know. I think it all changed with the advent of the Premier League, but it didn't change quickly enough for me because I didn't get the money that the boys get! There's no doubt it's been good for the game; it's certainly been good for the players.

Neville Southall: Stef was great, a lovely lad who went on to have a top career, playing in World Cups and being made Swedish player of the year. Stef was decent in training. You would look at him training you'd think he'd be far better in the games. But it didn't work out and Colin, despite signing him, just didn't fancy him. He brought him on as a sub in an away game at Millwall and took him off again 15 minutes later and that was the last the Everton supporters ever saw of him. It was a shame.

Ray Atteveld: You saw the role of players coming in, [Dennis] Bergkamp coming in, playing in between the lines at Arsenal and stuff like that. Things were changing. Liverpool under Dalglish were bringing back players that play in a different position and not a fixed 4-4-2 system. So it was already showing a little bit there, and later with the foreign managers, it was more and more happening.

John Ebbrell: I think other clubs were becoming more professional. There was a foreign influx starting. This is Everton, so this is how we do it. At that time, I'm not sure we were embracing the new technology, the new sports science that was just starting. I just think the analogy I would use, we were just caught on the blocks a little bit, other teams would fire out the blocks and we'd been caught sleeping on the line.

Howard Kendall: When you look at foreign players I think you're always better trying to get them on loan and seeing whether they settle in. But sometimes a loan deal can be a little bit false. I experienced that with the Polish international Robert Warzycha, who joined the club in spring 1991. He came over on a loan basis from Gornik Zabrze and what a player he seemed at first. I remember one game at Villa Park when he scored twice and he was just exceptional. Then all of a sudden the problems started – the family had to come over and settle. I think now you would have someone finding them a property and opening bank accounts, and finding schools for the kids, but there was none of that then; it was just Jim Greenwood and I. Hhis performance just dropped. As soon as he signed that contract his performances went down and down; and yet to this day I don't think any manager would have not signed him after seeing what he could do during his loan spell.

John Ebbrell: I remember sitting on the bus with Robert and he'd absolutely set the league on fire for a month. Anyway three months later I'm sitting the bus, we're having a laugh, and I'm saying to him, 'Fucking hell Rob, what's going on lad? One month of goals and setting them up, on fire, what's happening?' So we were talking about this. 'What you doing tonight?' And he says, 'McDonalds.' I said, 'You what?' He said, 'I like McDonalds.' I said, 'Is there any others you go to?' 'KFC. I like KFC.' So anyway this conversation was about Rob finding fast food. He'd put half a stone on, and that was it. It's as much what stopped Rob in my view. He'd come from Poland which I'm sure at that time wasn't the richest place in the world. McDonalds wasn't on every corner and he had all this money and he could eat all he wanted. He was a great player for a short space of time.

Neville Southall: We had a player like Robert Warzycha who was everything that Preki wasn't but couldn't get a game. Howard had signed him not long after he returned and after having a great start he faded from view. He was a Polish international and super-fit; a great player. He couldn't get over English football. In his homeland they trained three times a day in pre-season, whereas we'd go away on tours and half the team would be up drinking most of the night.

Charles Lambert: The goalposts moved and they were moved by a guy called Jack Walker who came into Blackburn Rovers around about that time. Jack put £100 million into Blackburn Rovers and as a result of that Blackburn built a new stadium, they won promotion, they won the league, they could hire Kenny Dalglish, they could buy Alan Shearer and they were doing things that other clubs couldn't dream of. It seems incredible now when you think the bill for that is £100M; that's ridiculous, isn't it? But in those days that was enough money to put Blackburn Rovers head and shoulders above all the rest, including Everton. And Everton were not even the best of the rest. I don't think that Everton responded in finding the investment that they needed to keep pace.

Howard Kendall: I looked again at the transfer market. It was a centre-forward we so desperately needed; someone with a bit of guile, who could make things happen in the box. There wasn't much money, however, and I had to sell before I bought. Crowds were disappointing too, often below the 20,000 mark, and we failed to make inroads in cup competitions, so the likelihood of a windfall was slim. So I had to look at my most saleable assets.

Andy Hinchcliffe: Again, you feel responsible for this, because you're at the club while these things are happening. So, whatever you put it down to, the fans don't want to hear that it's about the dynamic between coaches and players; this is Everton Football Club. You need to sort this out and get this right, and they're absolutely right to think that way, because they deserve the very best. They were voting with their feet, and you can understand completely that what they were seeing, the football they were seeing, was poor. We weren't getting results and we were in big trouble.

Howard Kendall: One of the players I tried to make a move for then was Duncan Ferguson, who was at Dundee United. I called their manager Jim McLean about him. 'He's going to Rangers,' said Jim. 'But he's been down at Leeds United,' I said, knowing that he'd spoken with Howard Wilkinson. 'He went for talks at Leeds.' 'Yes, but he's going to Rangers.' 'Can I talk to him? If Leeds United talked to him can I talk to him?' 'No, he's going to Rangers.' And that was that. Everton was becoming such a hard sell I wasn't even getting in the door with the top players. I looked at Niall Quinn, Mark Hateley, Mark Bright and Brian Deane, but clubs either weren't prepared to sell or asked for silly money.

Phil McNulty: I think there was a lack of leadership and direction from the top: Philip Carter wasn't the chairman anymore; he had a great partnership with Howard. When Everton were very successful, the club was run by three people, which was Howard, Jim Greenwood, and Sir Philip Carter. They made all the major decisions; they were a great team, if you like, and there was just a period of stagnation, when John Moores was very ill, and then, of course, he died [in September 1993]. He was the great driver of the club in the 1960s and the early 70s. There was this vacuum at the top of the club. David Marsh to me was maybe more of a figurehead; he wasn't a fiercely-ambitious, driven chairman to get things done. I think the club did go through that period of stagnation. I just suspect when Howard came back, he was hoping the club would be pretty much the one he left behind, but I think things had changed.

Lord Grantchester: You've got Sir John getting older and older. As you may or may not know, he suffered a break-in at home with him home at the time. It affected him tremendously, when he had done so much to help Merseyside, help people, a successful business, putting his money back into the communities in so many ways. He was very upset to be attacked in that way. That hastened, I think, a lot of deterioration in his health, his relationships, all sorts of ways. He slowly had more and more health problems anyway, getting older.

Dr David Marsh: I think in the days of Sir John the Moores family was highly powerful. He was still influential, but financially, other than his shareholding, he wouldn't come and say, 'Well I'll give you £100,000 to buy X player.' So, from that point of view we knew we had to survive and we had to generate the money without his actually going into his pocket and giving it. That simply didn't happen. He was influential in that he came to the matches until he was too poorly to come and he was quite influential in many ways with [fellow director] Desmond Pitcher who was also at Littlewoods. I used to play cards with the old man, we'd play bridge every Sunday evening, so I knew him quite well, but I never ever asked him for a penny of his money and nor would he have given it to me. It was just an unwritten rule: you don't ask, he's done his time at Everton and we move on until he's too poorly to come.

John Ebbrell: I remember one pre-season we were at an awards sort of dinner, something for the supporters. And Howard, he did brilliantly because we hadn't made a signing, not one signing. And we'd finished mid-table the season before. It was one of these where everyone had to go up on the stage, one at a time, and I think that he sensed within the room, 'What's the fresh hope?' What he did in his own humour was he introduced the 'new signing', the new John Ebbrell. What he talked about was how these players trained, how they would be better and fitter this season. So, he introduced every player as the 'new', and it was quite funny. But it also dampened a few flames that could have been in the room. But that's where we were at – the same team, no fresh signings, no money, so we were drifting really at that point. It wasn't a great time to be playing, around that time.

Barry Horne: He had been a manager for a long time, he was a very experienced manager, so he would never let his guard down, he was never unprofessional. I'm sure he had confidants within the squad that he would talk to about what was going on, the lads who had been with him a little longer, but he would never let slip, or he would never talk to the group about the politics of what was going on. But, of course, players are not stupid, they pick up. Football humour is ruthless, everything is dealt through mickey-taking. You can imagine some of the comments about why we were struggling and how we were struggling, but that never came from Howard.

Howard Kendall: One player I was definitely interested in was Dion Dublin. The centre-forward had been fantastic for John Beck's Cambridge United as they made it to the brink of the Premier League, a notion that seems inconceivable two decades later. I'd tried to buy him a year earlier when their promotion bid failed, but at the last moment – having failed to sign Alan Shearer – Alex Ferguson had bought him for Manchester United.

Neville Southall: Dion was an aggressive centre-forward; a good player, a good character, a good pro who also had that bit of devilment and leadership quality in him. But I think it was getting to the point where the board no longer trusted Howard's judgement. They couldn't see Dion Dublin being worthwhile for us. When they vetoed his signing Howard handed in his resignation an hour after leading us to a 1-0 win over Southampton [on 4 December 1993]. Just 13,667 had come to see it, the lowest league attendance in a decade.

Howard Kendall: I was confident of finally getting my centre-forward. At the end of November we played Manchester United in a midweek League Cup fourth round tie at Goodison. They beat us comfortably 2-0, but afterwards I resurrected the idea of a deal for Dion Dublin with Alex Ferguson. To my delight he was quite receptive and we sat down and agreed a transfer. In the past I'd have simply phoned Philip Carter and Jim Greenwood and the transfer would have been waved through. Now, however, things were different. I called David Marsh the next day, the Thursday, to tell him about the transfer. He neither said yes or no and that was that until the next morning when I received a call at Bellefield. I was preparing for a league match against Southampton. It was Marsh. 'We don't like the deal,' he said. 'The deal's off.' 'I've agreed everything with Alex,' I protested. 'We don't like the deal,' he repeated. 'The deal is off.' 'As far as I'm concerned then I'm no longer the manager of Everton Football Club,' I answered. 'See you.'

Andy Hinchcliffe: It happens, doesn't it? Managers feel 'I need someone, I need X to come and do a job,' and they don't get allowed to buy them. It's maybe different now because the dynamics at clubs have changed. Managers like Howard were the be all and end all; they were the driving force, they really made the decisions and the owners would listen to the manager. Things have changed dramatically now. But Howard maybe thought, 'Wait a minute, I've always worked this way, if I'm not getting the support in terms of who I want to sign then maybe it's time to think about moving on.' So it might of well been a mutual decision between the owners and Howard.

Howard Kendall: I turned up at Goodison the next day for the Southampton match and walked out across the pitch with Marsh. 'I meant what I said yesterday,' I said. 'Yes,' he replied, and then turned to me. 'You will be professional today, won't you, Howard?' I was surprised he would ever doubt my professionalism. 'As always,' I answered. And that was that. After the game, which we won, he asked me: 'Are you serious about this?' 'Yes,' I replied. And then I went to meet the media and announced my resignation as manager of Everton Football Club.

Phil McNulty: Howard was one of life's great optimists as far as Everton is concerned. I think Howard was a realist, but always had at the back of his mind good times were around the corner. But I remember the day he resigned, and I was at the game against Southampton. Everton won 1-0, and he had done his main press conference; he had come up very professionally as he normally would, he had come up to the press room at Goodison, spoken to the media about what was a rather uneventful, rather dull game played in front on a very small crowd, and then he went back downstairs, we never thought any more about it. We were hanging around, just checking what we had for the following Monday. The next thing, Howard returned with David Marsh and we're wondering what's going on, and he announced that he was resigning. We were absolutely gobsmacked. He just said a few brief words and went back out of the door, and that was the end of it. There was certainly no lead-up to it, where we felt he's on the point of walking out.

Neville Southall: Just as I never had any inkling that he was coming back to Everton three years earlier, so I was in the dark about Howard's decision to leave us. After the Southampton game he never told us his intentions and I didn't know he had quit until I read about it on Teletext later that evening. I was aware of his frustration, but it wasn't as palpable as Colin's had been. Howard was a different fish and would never show his feelings. He got a bit tetchy now and again, but not usually with the players.

Phil McNulty: I know he used to get very frustrated and upset by bad home results. He was such a driven manager and a great Evertonian, but there was certainly no lead-up; you didn't think he's going to do this any moment now. I remember ringing one journalist who'd left, on his mobile, saying, 'You'd better come back; Howard Kendall's resigned,' and he just thought I was joking. 'You're having me on.' But I said, 'No, no, it's serious.' Howard's just come back up the stairs with David Marsh and announced he'd resign.

Mike Walker and a journey towards the abyss

A month after Kendall's resignation, in January 1994, Everton appointed the Norwich City manager, Mike Walker, as his replacement. Walker had led Norwich to the brink of the Premier League title a year earlier and subsequently knocked Bayern Munich out of the UEFA Cup.

Neville Southall: When I first heard Mike Walker was going to be Everton manager, I thought it might be okay. He'd nearly won the Premier League with Norwich a year earlier and was a former goalkeeper. He was Welsh as well, from just down the road from me in Colwyn Bay, although he never played for Wales. His son Ian was Tottenham's goalkeeper and a good player. When I first met him he seemed like a nice man. Scarcely could I have imagined that he would oversee one of the most disastrous episodes in Everton's history.

John Ebbrell: When he came in, he was the first non-Everton coach that I'd ever had. So it was a clean slate, open mind. Norwich had come to Goodison [the previous September], with Efan Ekoku… we were 1-0 up, we hit the bar and I'm thinking, 'We're going to batter these here, they're rubbish.' Counter-attacking football, so we had the ball, they pinched it, scored five. It was never a 5-1 game, but their European run and that got him the job at Goodison. Then he tried to instil mainly a counter-attacking style, which hadn't been our way of playing.

Graham Stuart: I don't think it was a surprising appointment. He'd taken a Norwich side and they were doing terrifically well in the Premier League, they'd gone into Europe and done well. Obviously the game that stands out is Bayern Munich when they won in the UEFA Cup. So Mike's stock was as high as anyone else, probably in the Football League at the time. It wasn't an appointment that surprised me.

Neville Southall: Managing Norwich and managing Everton are two entirely different propositions. At Norwich you don't carry the same insatiable burden of expectation and nor do their players. I talked about Howard struggling with the lack of characters at Everton; well, he would have hated a club like Norwich where it was a bunch of 'Yes sir, no sir, right away sir' type players. By contrast the characters that we had at Goodison – even if they weren't enough for Howard – were too much for Mike to handle. I include myself in that equation.

Graham Stuart: I think Mike struggled to get his head around Merseyside, in a similar vein to when I first came up. It does hit you. Because Mike had come up from Norwich, which is a lovely place, full of really, really nice people, and it was a terrific football club. But as soon as you come to Everton you're on a different level, you're on a different plain straightaway. I don't think Mike ever really got his head around it fast enough to save his job.

Tony Cottee: Mike did very well at Norwich, there's no doubt about that. I just thought when he come in at Everton, he wasn't a coach at all. He brought in Dave Williams who put on training sessions that I'd been doing as a 14-year-old, so I didn't enjoy the training. The training wasn't good. Tactically there wasn't a lot really happening in terms of preparation for the games and changing things in the game, and the signings weren't particularly ambitious.

Dave Watson: Mike had done great at Norwich. He came up to Everton and he tried to get them to try and play what you'd call a good type of football, playing out from the back and I don't think we actually had the player at the time to do it. We gave daft goals away. He persevered with it. He did his best but he had a group of characters that were not having him. He wasn't a player's manager. He kept himself to himself. He'd leave you waiting on the bus for a couple of hours after a game in his own time. These things matter to players. They're waiting to get out or get home. if you mess the players about you're knackered. He didn't have the relationship a Joe Royle or a Howard Kendall had. It might have been accidental on his behalf. He had Dave Williams working with him, he was a school teacher and he used to have battles with players. The players were stronger characters than Dave. He was telling them to do things they already knew. Mike managed the youth team and reserves at Norwich and them kids followed him up. You come into a disgruntled dressing room and you need to be able to relate to the players and Mike found it difficult. He could have made an effort. It was like, 'I'm the boss and you do this.' He didn't have one to ones with the players. You couldn't have a laugh or a joke. You have to enjoy going into training.

Neville Southall: When Dave Williams came to Everton as coach, he did everything on the training ground. He was very methodical in what he did, but training was just incredibly boring. Everything was circle work. We might do a few doggies, but that was too easy. There was no reward, no fun; it was monotonous, tedious. Walker was never anywhere to be seen until five minutes before the end of a session when he'd pull up in his Jag, make his face seen and then bugger off again.

Joe Parkinson: You didn't see him often. You saw him more if it was nice and sunny. He'd be out there with his shorts on and he'd be seen sunbathing at the training ground, and these are all things that as a manager you just can't do. I just don't think he knew what the club was all about. It's easy for people to have a go, but it's hard for me to do because he bought me.

Tony Grant: Mike bought good players. One of my favourite players was Vinny Samways, I'm a big fan of Vinny's, I thought he was a great player. Everton never saw the best of Vinny, simple as. But he bought some good players, and he had a great idea of how he wanted to play, it was just that he was probably so laid back and maybe he left too much to his coaching staff.

Phil McNulty: Mike wasn't the complete and utter disaster that people made him out to be, because when he was there, he signed Joe Parkinson, Anders Limpar, and brought Duncan Ferguson to the club – although many thought that Peter Johnson was behind it. I think the problem with Mike Walker was that he was flavour of the month at the time; he'd had some very good results with Norwich; he'd had that famous win away to Bayern Munich in the UEFA Cup, and he had a very good public image when he appeared on TV – the old silver fox – and he spoke well, and his team was doing very well. People look back now and say, 'How on earth could they do something like that?' but I don't remember any groundswell of opinion at the time saying Everton had made a terrible mistake appointing Mike Walker.

Anders Limpar: We had great players, but that system Mike Walker played didn't suit us. He had a system that he didn't have the players for. We were frustrated, and we certainly did our best, but we didn't click those first couple of games.

Neville Southall: He changed the pattern of playing, which didn't do us any favours. We just weren't good enough to play the kind of football he wanted us to play, which was a continental-type game, lots of passing from the back. It wasn't suited to Everton at the time and it wasn't suited to English football. We'd pass the ball 50 times without it leaving our half, give the ball away and our opponents would score.

Anders Limpar: I signed for Everton because of him, because when I sat down and spoke to him his philosophy with football, that was exactly my philosophy: the passing game. Then he actually swapped around and changed around a lot. He didn't play with the same team and the consistency wasn't there. You have to have the consistent players playing every game. When you're struggling as a manager you do crazy things, you do stupid things instead of putting your head down and believing in yourself. But he obviously didn't do that. I can actually think that he felt the pressure more than the players.

Of Everton's last ten games before the final day of the 1993/94 season against Wimbledon, they lost seven, drew twice and won just once. That dismal run included a 5-1 defeat to Sheffield Wednesday, and 3-0 drubbings from Norwich, Leeds and Blackburn.

Dave Watson: Week by week you're slipping down and then it becomes a worry and then you think, 'Have we got enough characters in the dressing room?' It fizzled out to the last game against Wimbledon. Everyone knew. The media was very hyped up. It was a massive thing for Everton. They'd been in the top flight for all their lives. It was a bit of a nervous situation for some players. What it boiled down to: 'Have you got the bollocks? You got us in this situation. Get us out of it.'

Anders Limpar: We all were really shitting ourselves to go down – nobody wants to go down. That made us a little bit stronger – can you believe it – every game. The thing we had at that time was the character in the team, strong mental character, but we didn't have a system that fitted that character. We had some unbelievable players football-wise, but I have to say that the system didn't work for us.

Barry Horne: I can't remember the table off the top of my head, I'm sure most fans can, but there was a feeling that a draw might be enough to keep us up. But I absolutely knew that we had to win. There was never any doubt that we had to win, even if a draw might have been good enough. I never thought that we could take that chance, I thought all the way through leading up to it that that was a game that we had to win.

Dave Prentice: People were ringing the *Echo* sports desk and we'd been acting as counsellors to fans in the buildup to the game. People were ringing up absolutely panic-stricken seeking reassurance, which we couldn't really give them.

Graham Stuart: Walker kept saying, 'I just know we're going to get out if it.' Even to the very last day he still had that sort of arrogance, if you like, to turn round at the end of it, coming as close as we did on the final day of that season, to still have the arrogance to say, 'I just knew we'd get out of it.' It's the boldest quote you've ever heard, 'I knew we were going to get out of it.' From a manager's perspective that's probably not a great way to be going about your business with the players, to keep turning around to everybody saying, 'We'll be alright, I know we'll get out of it,' and stuff like that. There was sort of an air of complacency about it, and if you got it from the manager then it transmits itself to the players and we all know how close it was.

Rev. Harry Ross: I opened St Luke's Church for fans just to go and say a prayer or to sit quietly because I realised that most of them were worried about what was happening to Everton. Everton is such a big part in people's lives and so where there is a worry it's important that the church recognises that and tries to help people in whichever way it could.

Tony Cottee: I think it was a bit scary, because we all knew what a massive club Everton were, we all knew we shouldn't be in that position. I think it was just one of those games where you weren't really looking forward to it, but you knew you had to go through it, and you knew above all else that we had to win the game and hope for the best.

Ian Snodin: Coming into that game we knew we had to do one thing, and that was to win. It was as simple as that. Of all teams you're paired up against, the last team on the earth you wanted to play is

Wimbledon, because they'd have loved it, to send Everton down. A big, big club like Everton and a little club like Wimbledon, they would have loved it with the personnel they had in and around that time.

John Ebbrell: I remember in the lead up to the game thinking, 'We're in big trouble here.' I mean big trouble. Especially playing them, because we're soft. I know Everton, I know Everton teams and thinking: 'We're soft and they're as tough a team as we're going to play. Every set piece is going in our box with quality, with a 6ft 4 inch player coming to head it. They're going to turn us all the time. It's going to be a bobbly pitch. The crowd are going be anxious. They're going play for throw-ins, corners...'

Neville Southall: I never ever thought we were going to lose the Wimbledon match. A game of such importance, I never thought we were going to lose, ever. For me, back then, Everton getting relegated was just completely and utterly inconceivable. Even when things got particularly bad, which they soon did.

Dave Watson: I got a card before the game, I don't know if it was from a Liverpool fan. It said, 'Let's hope you're like the captain off the Titanic!' That made me realise how big it was. Top flight all these years and I'm captain! Taking Everton down! Who was the captain who took Everton down? It wasn't going to happen.

Graham Stuart: There's always been this talk about the game being fixed and all this sort of stuff. Obviously, we know the shenanigans the night before with Wimbledon's team bus and all that sort of stuff. But Evertonians were going to do everything possible to make sure we had some kind of advantage on the day. You'd never have believed after 20 minutes when we were 2-0 down!

Neville Southall: Lots of mud has been thrown around about our win against Wimbledon that day, with some saying it was a fix and a conspiracy. It's certainly true that the Wimbledon bus was burned out the night before by some scallywag Evertonians. But knowing some of the Wimbledon players I'm not sure they'd have been too unsettled by that or the raucous atmosphere at Goodison.

Ian Snodin: Looking back and people were saying it was a fix, you only had to be in the tunnel before that game at ten to three to realise that it wasn't. There were a lot of shouting, ghetto blaster at full blast, they were pumping it to high heaven. If it had been a fix they wouldn't have been carrying on the way they were carrying on before we even got to the pitch. You knew you were in for a game, simple as that.

Neville Southall: I spoke to Hans [Segers] about it a few times and I know what he's like. He's not one of those players that is going to chuck a ball into the net for you. He's just not that sort of person. In any case, it's harder than you'd think just to let goals in.

Barry Horne: It was a clear day, bright blue skies, very still. That was the thing that struck me. In amongst all this turmoil everything just seemed to very calm and very, very, very still. I always used to get there very early because I had a morbid fear of being late for kick-offs. Neville was always first in, then I was pretty much always the next in. And even as I was driving in, there were people hanging around the ground. And, of course, the other odd thing about it was that there was no Park End. It was all boarded up, so we could see trees in Stanley Park. There was people on roofs. My overriding thoughts were we had to win and just how calm and how serene everything appeared to be.

The game hardly got off to the best of starts, with Anders Limpar giving away a penalty in the early stages for handball. Dean Holdsworth converted, and 16 minutes later the visitors were 2-0 up, as Gary Ablett deflected Andy Clarke's mis-hit shot into his own net.

Anders Limpar: It was a stupid thing; I was so pumped up, worked up to win that game, so I was everywhere and nowhere. We were actually running like headless chickens to win the game, and if you do that and you don't think about what you're going to do on the pitch, you run everywhere and your teammates don't know where you're running.

Neville Southall: I've no idea what he was doing there, as he hardly ever came into our half, never mind our box. He wasn't even anywhere near the goal when it happened.

Anders Limpar: Suddenly I was down in the defence and I took it with my hand, and that's the worst start you can actually have. You need to win the game and suddenly they have a penalty and they scored. Gary Ablett, bless him, he scored an own goal, and to be 2-0 down after 20 minutes when you need to win the game, to swap that around shows the character of the team.

Dave Watson: We went a couple of goals down and the writing was on the wall. They hit the post. We thought, 'This is it.' The atmosphere wasn't the best because a stand had been knocked down behind the goal. It was like playing on a cricket pitch.

Neville Southall: It was a catastrophe of errors but even then, when we were 2-0 down, the thought of losing never entered my head. Don't ask me why because I don't know. I never panicked, never worried; I always thought we were going to win; somehow, some way, I always thought we were going to win. I just don't know why; I can't explain it. I've never had that feeling before.

David Unsworth: So before you know it you're 2-0 down; possibly could have gone 3-0 down and then we get a lifeline – Anders win a penalty.

Stuart Barlow: We got lucky, Anders Limpar come out with a great dive won us a penalty. And I take my hat off to Graham Stuart to have the balls to stand up in that situation – you're 2-0 down; I think it was a couple of minutes before half time; and you think, 'We've been battered here' – you can't speak any higher of him for doing that.

Dave Prentice: Neville picked up the ball and started marching down the pitch holding the football. Everyone's thinking, 'What's going on now? Is Neville going to take it?' And Diamond walked towards him, took the ball off him and there was a ripple of applause around the ground.

Neville Southall: [Mark] Wardy wasn't playing and I could see that Tony [Cottee] didn't fancy it, so I took the ball. And why not? I was the most experienced player and after my goal in the Full Members Cup shootout seven years earlier I had a 100 per cent penalty record. I'd said before kick-off that if there was a penalty I'd be taking it, but I don't think anybody took my pledge too seriously until we were faced with that situation. I think seeing me take the ball shamed some of the other players. I'm sure that's what spurred Graham Stuart into action.

Graham Stuart: I do remember Neville walking, and I knew I was taking the penalty, there wasn't even a doubt in my mind. I knew I was taking the penalty. But I just looked at him and thought to myself, 'We all know he's mad, but is he actually mad enough to walk all the way to the end of the pitch?' And he probably would have been, but I said, 'Give us it here Nev, give us the ball,' and he threw the ball to me and that was it. I remember putting the ball on the spot and I stepped back and I looked up and the Park End was down. All I remember is seeing kids and people swinging in the trees, because it was a sell out and people were desperate for any vantage point whatsoever.

Anders Limpar: Graham scored for 2-1. That actually lifted us a little bit, because during the half-time in the dressing room we were so, so pumped up – nobody sat down. So we stood up for 15 minutes ready to go.

Graham Stuart: Again, silly things run through your mind. I remember looking up. I'm about to take an unbelievably important penalty and I'm seeing people swinging around in the trees! It was one of them, you go back to your basics and you think to yourself right, pick a spot, don't change your mind. Whatever you do, don't change your mind. If the keeper saves it there's nothing I can do about it, but make sure you hit the target and don't change your mind.

Stuart Barlow: We'd just got back in the game. We'd been battered; I felt as a player we'd been battered first half and then all of a sudden we are back in the game, so you can imagine the buzz of the players.

Anders Limpar: What I can remember is that we were actually all over them in the second half, we could have scored the equaliser much, much earlier. We got a little bit more frustrated because they were just defending, and then Barry Horne scored a cracker.

Barry Horne: Despite the team's failings, I'd come through a sticky patch. I didn't have the best of starts to my Everton career, in fact it was grim at times, but I was getting stronger and stronger throughout the season. I actually felt I played well and I was playing well, and I was really, really confident, and when you're confident you just do things. Twelve months earlier I would struggled to get that ball under control and pass to a teammate. But on this occasion the ball came to me and it just sat up, I just controlled it and my first thought was get there before Vinnie Jones. As it came to me I realised, 'I've got this now, so what's next?' I felt I was playing well, I was full of confidence, so it just happened.

Ian Snodin: We know Barry weren't renowned for his long distance passing, his shooting, his goal scoring ability, but in this particular game he smashed one from the Gods. He'll never strike a better ball. It has a little pop up as well as he's going to hit it, and he's let fly and it's gone into the top right hand corner. Wow! What a goal and the place erupted! The players went berserk because we realised then that we were back to 2-2, we've got a great chance.

Graham Stuart: I see Tony Cottee, so I bumped a little one-two off with Tony and he just laid it back into my path, and it was more of a 50-50 challenge, and I got a contact on it, that's about as much as I can say, contact. The rest is history: it bobbles over Hans Sagar's arm and nestles in the back of the net eventually. I've always said it's the best goal I've scored and the worst goal I've scored all in one. Nobody cared, nobody really cared one little jot. I remember the whole euphoria of the place; you don't even know what to do. I just got up off the floor and just started running. Everybody's jumping on you and what have you, but unbelievable atmosphere.

Stuart Barlow: Even the goal, watch it back now, it bobbles. You watch the goal and people say, 'Oh Hans Segers throws it in,' but first and foremost Graham has mishit it a bit, it's gone through someone's legs and when he dives it bobbles over his hand.

Dave Watson: When it went in, it was amazing. From where we were we were dead and buried. The old church, we never give in, we never give in, we never give in. We had that. Don't get me wrong Wimbledon came back at us and could have scored again. We got through it, amazingly. It's a situation you wouldn't want to be in ever, ever again. The pitch was invaded. We had to try and get off. It was just total relief. A few of the players had a few drinks together. Everybody was just physically and mentally drained. It was unbelievable. Bloody hell. I could eventually sleep that night because I'd had a few drinks but your mind was racing.

Neville Southall: As I said, there was never any doubt at all that we'd be saved and we were.

Ian Snodin: I remember getting off the pitch and all my kit, the boots, the socks the lot, and getting dragged into that player's lounge before I even got into the dressing room, by a couple of my pals and just anybody who had got in there. I had three bottles of beer before I even got in the dressing room.

Graham Stuart: The biggest emotion was relief, simple as that, I think the relief around the whole place, whether it be our dressing room, outside, I just think around the whole football club was relief; we'd dodged a bullet here, and we did. We really dodged a bullet that afternoon and I think it was kind of like the emotion was relief, but also to make sure we're never in this situation again. Unfortunately, we were a few years later. I think in our history I hope to god that's the closest we ever come.

Dave Prentice: I remember the final whistle. John Fashanu hadn't been playing on the pitch and was trying to usher the players down the tunnel because he was terrified there was going to be physical harm on the pitch. They were just wanting to get out of there as quickly as possible.

Tony Cottee: We come in after the game and I remember there were a few people cracking open champagne because we stayed up, and I was sat in the corner thinking, 'Why are we celebrating staying up?' It's not really good enough for Everton Football Club. I was a bit worried about the situation going forward into the start of the new season.

David Unsworth: Euphoria. You've won the cup final. I went along with that, because it's the relief. But if I was there now there's no euphoria at that. You can't be celebrating failure. But it was just champagne everywhere, like we'd won the cup.

Dave Prentice: That day a guy called Roy Wright was in charge of the [*Football Echo*] edition that day, and he had the biggest typeface I've ever seen in my life, ready for the front page. One said, 'Safe,' one said, 'Down.' And the final whistle had gone; I was in the press box – pre-internet days – and everyone is celebrating and going wild on the pitch, and I couldn't send the report until it was confirmed that other results had gone Everton's way. Eventually Phil McNulty looked at me – he was sitting next to me – and started screaming, 'We're safe, we're safe! Chelsea have beaten Sheffield United, they're down.' So I was able to send that paragraph over saying that Everton were safe. The pink *Echo* was on the street literally 20 minutes later and people were parading up and down Goodison Road holding the footy *Echo* like some banner. We're safe! It was just completely surreal, and quite shameful really, thinking about it. But it was such an incredible relief.

Neville Southall: After the game, there was lots of talk of never letting Everton fall into such a perilous position again, about fresh starts. It was a complete and utter disgrace that a club like ours were ever in such a situation. But I didn't hear many people taking the blame for it. Who was to blame for the mess? The players, because we were shit. But then it didn't help that we had Walker in charge either, because he was clueless.

Andy Hinchcliffe: I was playing a reserve game at Sheffield United, and we couldn't believe what we'd heard. We couldn't believe when we got back on the coach what had transpired.

Tony Grant: The reserve match was a nothing game. They're thinking about their first team; we're thinking about our first team. I don't even know what score it was, but I know as soon as the game finished everyone ran off the pitch and was in the tunnel. There was a small radio on the floor and we had the results coming in, and that day Sheffield United went down. We were there with them, so it was ironic.

Joe Parkinson: The match itself was quite nasty, because their first team could go down, and they actually did. It was a nasty game, and we all came off in the tunnel [at half-time] and it was close to even a bit of fighting because they were all taking a bit of mickey out of us because we were down, and they were up. By the end of the game we changed it round and we were up and they were down, and then we were giving them a bit. It was really quite tense there.

John Ebbrell: I played with the weight of the world on my shoulders, because I was a local lad. For me, I'll be straight, it was too much, and I'm not afraid to say that. But it at least it showed how much it meant to me. That's the way I analyse it now and look back. I wish I could have gone and played with freedom and no fear, but at least it meant that much to me.

Peter Johnson takeover

That summer, following the death of Sir John Moores, the Tranmere Rovers chairman and Birkenhead businessman, Peter Johnson, completed a takeover of Everton, seeing off a rival bid by a consortium led by the theatre impresario and director, Bill Kenwright. He issued a share rights issue, in the process raising £10million of much needed transfer funds.

Bill Kenwright: In the late-1980s I was asked to go and produce movies in LA by a particular Hollywood studio. The other big love of my life was movies: Errol Flynn, Alan Ladd in Shane; and this was a magical, magical moment for me. I was in my boardroom saying to my staff, 'Listen I'm going to LA, but this company will still exist. I'll be back every six months, you will run it for me regardless.' As I was telling them my private line went in my office, I walk back in, and it was Sir Philip Carter. 'Bill, are you coming to the game on Saturday?' I said, 'Is the Pope Catholic? Of course I am.' 'Is there any chance you could get there a bit earlier?' I wasn't surprised because there was talk of Paul McCartney doing a gig at Goodison and I was involved in the talks. I got there and Sir Philip, as I do now, has an office up there; went and sat in. He came in, said, 'Sorry I'm so rushed but we've had a board meeting, would you like to join the board?' Hollywood went out the window; everything went out the window. I mumbled, 'Yes please.' Philip had asked me to keep it quiet. It was a few weeks after Michael Knighton had done all that bouncing the ball on the head and was going to take over Manchester United. He said, 'You'll get a lot of publicity, and we are a private board, so just keep it to yourself till we announce it.' The game was against Millwall, that's how long ago it was; Millwall were in the First Division, and we beat Millwall and I became a board member the next week. It was an incredibly proud moment.

Lord Grantchester: Towards the end of Sir John's life, it was about how his various business interests and relationships would be dealt with in the best possible way from so many points of view. That didn't just involve Everton, it involved so much in the city of Liverpool and other aspects of life. Everton was obviously one feature of it. Littlewoods was another feature and through board connections and so many interests, it got tricky between the family and other personalities. It all got into difficult territory.

Bill Kenwright: My relationship with Everton didn't change as a board member, because I was absolutely the fan on the board; or the fanatic on the board. [The other directors] would sort of almost pat my head and go, 'Yeah, we know, we know.' I would cry at a defeat. I was very different from the rest of the board; I was very emotional but it's not true that they didn't love the club, because a lot of tripe is written about board members. They loved their club. But I lived for it.

Peter Johnson: I supported Tranmere when I was a youngster as I lived on that side of the Mersey. When I was about 18 I went across to Liverpool, which has been well documented, so there is no point in avoiding it, but it was only on the basis of a friend of mine having two season tickets and his father was getting on a bit so he asked me to go with him and really that's why I changed allegiances. In 1987, one of the directors of Tranmere came to see me and he asked if I'd like to save Tranmere. At the time I said no because I was too busy with Park Foods, but I thought about it and decided to go and have a second look which is when I decided to join them. It was the first time that I'd been in an administrative position at a football club and I found it quite interesting. But I found that after a number of years of success, taking Tranmere from the bottom of the Fourth to virtually the top of the Second Division and after about five visits to Wembley that I couldn't really move the club forward. The tradition and the history of the two clubs on the other side of the water really precluded Tranmere from breaking the mould.

Bill Kenwright: I was in my office in London, in Shaftesbury Avenue – it was quite a big office – and my PA came in to see me, and she said, 'There's a group of people here.' They hadn't booked or anything but it was the Moores family, three of them. They came in, they were lovely – Lady Grantchester, I think John Junior, there were three of them. I'm not sure, they'd either been to the funeral or they'd been to the reading of the will; and they said, 'Our Dad only wanted the club to go to the director with 'blue blood in his veins.' And that's you.' I don't know whether I was naïve, I don't know whether I was stupid, but I didn't understand what they meant. I thought, 'I can't own Everton. My Gran owned Everton; my Granddad, my uncles; those supporters that I travel up with every week on the train.' They talked about the shareholding, and they talked about how I could raise money, and they talked about different kinds of shares. They were just terrific; they were really lovely. They said, 'We want you to own Everton.' I was stunned. I had quite a few Evertonians that worked for me, and they came in and I said, 'I think I've just been offered to buy Everton'. To cut a long, long story short at the board meeting, I told them exactly what had happened, and I said, 'So guys, I'm going to raise the money, I'm going to buy the club.' Sir Desmond Pitcher said, 'It doesn't happen like that; there's going to be other bidders.' I said, 'But they'll only sell to me, they've told me, and they own the shares.' What happened was Desmond introduced Peter Johnson, and then the battle started between the pair of us, and I don't know how long that took – six, seven months.

Lord Grantchester: David Marsh was chairman, through the transition as I call it: what was going to happen to Everton, insofar as what the family wanted and what was the best way of making it happen. So it's got a multi-faceted angle to it. I got involved with my mother acting on behalf of Sir John in trying to manage this process of dialogue with the Board, what was required, how we were going to go about it, what was the best outcome to it. Eventually, as you know, it broke out between the Bill Kenwright consortium and the Peter Johnson bid. My involvement was trying to help as best I could in amongst all of that.

Peter Johnson: It was available and I couldn't afford Liverpool. It didn't really bother me. The white knuckle job moved to Goodison. I don't think I lost a derby, I think we had nine derbies and I don't think we lost one. I know football fans say they can't change their allegiances, but once it's your club you're stewarding that club for the fans, whose club it really is.

Lord Grantchester: The whole approach was to make the transition of Everton into what we call safe hands, respecting the traditions of the Club. Of course a lot of football has had some scurrilous aspects about it in terms of corporate governance, in terms of unofficial payments in terms of inducements. It's got important governance issues. So we were only looking to someone who had Everton's interests at heart; who was the best person who could carry on this tradition of making sure Everton continued being successful with the right culture in terms of youth development and in terms of everything the Club was doing in the community. Bringing forward youth players through the youth system, getting involved in the locality, encouraging boy's clubs, all that sort of stuff as I've suggested was in the background with Sir John. We still wanted to keep that background, that culture, that philosophy, with a new owner at Everton.

Dave Prentice: There was very much a PR war between Peter Johnson and Bill Kenwright to gain control of the club. I remember [the *Liverpool Echo* sports editor] Ken Rogers was very much a supporter of Kenwright; he'd worked with him for a long time, going back many years. He was a very high profile supporter of Kenwright. He basically nailed the *Echo*'s colours to that mast. All that turned out wrong because Johnson was the winner at the end of it.

Lord Grantchester: It was a very difficult time. As you know with football, everything is very high profile, there's few secrets. Transfers, players, everything, everyone knows what's going on, so it's very difficult to manage in terms of personalities, in terms of the formalities, in terms of legal proprieties, in terms of executors of the will and things like that. All that has to be paid attention to. I became involved to try and help clarify, help communicate, help find a way through all of that. It then became very difficult between the two competing bids and in the end, whether it worked or not, we tried to make everybody work together for a greater result.

Bill Kenwright: Towards the end of it it was coming to the Wimbledon game and because, if nothing else I'm a Blue, I felt responsible for every corner kick we lost, every throw in; I just felt responsible that we were in this state, and I thought, 'It's got to be sorted out.' I went to see Peter Johnson and I said, 'Look,' – because it was a total impasse, more than half wouldn't give their shares to him – 'You've got more money than me; if I stand aside would you love this club as much as I do?' He said, 'Of course I will; you and I together.' On the Friday before the Wimbledon game I went to see the family and I told them I was standing aside. They were not happy – this is Lady Grantchester – and they said, 'The club is much more important than the takeover battle. He's got the money; we can't go in tomorrow not knowing that the future of the club is secure, and this media battle can't go on.' That's what happened; and it was the best and worst day of my life. And we beat Wimbledon too; we all know it well.

Dr David Marsh: Peter Johnson had said that he would like to take over Everton and, from my recollection, that he was prepared to do so, I suppose not bankroll it [but], guarantee the share prices.

Peter Johnson: Lady Grantchester, John Moores' daughter, held the key, and there was me on one side and a consortium of four fans on the other side. In the end I was able to persuade Lady Grantchester that I should be able to do it. She kept moving the price up. And we had a few interviews in London and in Liverpool, and then that was it. Quite simple.

Bill Kenwright: The day after the Wimbledon game I went with our dog, and with Jen [Seagrove, Kenwright's partner], to the top of Hampstead Hill overlooking London, and my body was covered in psoriasis because of the stress. I got there and just broke down and cried; sobbed and sobbed and sobbed because of the relief of the previous day; because of maybe the relief that at least something had happened for the club. And I vowed to Jen that I would never put her – because everyone around me for that six months was ill with my illness – through that again.

Lord Grantchester: It's probably fair to say that the preferred candidate was Bill Kenwright and his consortium. But then in terms of the bidding process, Peter Johnson's counter offers brought other corporate responsibilities into play. I would say that I'm very pleased with how Everton has developed. I'm not too upset with Peter Johnson and that era, because he brought in fantastic players like Andrei Kanchelskis, and did a lot of investment into the Club. It's obviously been a difficult process, Bill Kenwright has been brilliant, trying to get the right ethos of the Club, the right managers and the long term aspects of success, taking the Club forward. It's been a long, hard process to bring Everton through to positioning itself touching on the doors of Champions League football. It's been a long, hard process and I've shared all of that by being involved, both on and off the Board, trying to make it happen. Nil Satis Nisi Optimum.

Dr David Marsh: Nobody at that stage – and this was early Premier League – could've envisaged the amount of cash they would have available. You had to do it on the back of your own money. I certainly did not have that kind of money available and I think many of the directors of football clubs are in the same position. Peter Johnson was enthusiastic, even though he was a Liverpool supporter. He sold his shares in Liverpool bought the shares from the shareholders in Everton and that was it. Some of us kept our shareholding and he brought in three people of his own group, Clifford Finch, Richard Hughes and himself.

Peter Johnson: It cost £10 million to complete a rights issue, which not many people went to buy, so it left me with £10 million to get control.

Lord Grantchester: Peter Johnson financed the initial bid but Bill Kenwright was still involved because he was on the board before. He was still a director and still carried on, even though he wasn't in full control. In time Bill took over stewardship of the Club. Now he has brought in more investment with Farad Moshiri, with more success to look forward to.

Alan Myers: Peter had some great ideas and he and his fellow director [Clifford Finch] were in many ways ahead of their time. They started the Megastore and wanted to do things with TV, they launched Radio Everton, and he wanted to do magazines, which in those days were not really done by football clubs. It was quite innovative by Cliff. He had a lot of foresight. But we had some crazy times, it was nonstop. We won two games in the Howard Kendall season; I think we beat Liverpool 2-0, and drew with Arsenal. The next day, little did I know that the commercial side of the board had commissioned a DVD called 'Turning the Corner.' We hadn't turned a corner at all!

Peter Johnson: I thought that Megastore was a statement. We bought a petrol station and a nightclub. Closed the road off. It was fantastic. When we turned the corner to win the cup, the megastore was still in carcass form. We were starting to build Rupert's Tower and the supporters were coming off the megastore like locusts and we had to have the job stopped on the Monday and structural engineers had to come in and check it to see no damage had been done by the people it was carrying.

Alan Myers: In the commercial manager's office there was a shirt with a number nine and where the name of the player is, it just said D I T T O. I said, 'What's that shirt?' He said, 'Somebody wrote in to the mail order and he said, 'Can I order one Duncan Ferguson adult, 'Ferguson 9' on the back and one junior, ditto?' I got this letter, and it started, first line was 'Are you taking the fucking piss." Someone had actually printed 'DITTO 9' on the back and sent it out, and genuinely thought that's what they wanted. It just summed up some of the things that went on at that time; it was comical at times, the way the club was run.

Peter Johnson: I was a bit surprised by fans' reactions to some things. They're so intense. I mean a fella was questioning me one time and he said, 'Do you like this?' 'Yes.' 'Do you like that?' 'Yes.' 'Do you like tomatoes.' 'Yes.' So he said, 'Well they're red you can't be a true Evertonian.' Well how bloody stupid is that?

The end of Mike Walker

Despite adding Daniel Amokachi and Vinny Samways to their ranks, Everton started the 1994/95 season abysmally and were bottom after going their opening 13 league games without a win.

Dave Prentice: I remember when Everton tried to sign [the Brazil international forward] Muller and one of my colleagues, Ric George, was very much a world football expert, he told me all these stories about Muller. He was a bit of a loose cannon in Italy and there were all sorts of lurid rumours about him. He just seemed like it was quite a risk as a footballer. This is pre-internet days when you didn't know as much about footballers as you do now. I remember going down to speak to Mike Walker about this and some of the concerns that we had about committing so much money on this player. And he was quite patronising to me, quite dismissive; and I thought, 'Well, if you're not the person to listen then fine; it's pointless going any further.'

Andy Hinchcliffe: I think you get a sense. It's hard to explain, but it's just like any business if you're on the shop floor or whatever, there's just a feeling in the air isn't there, that there's something not quite right. When you do have experienced players there, and they're maybe starting to raise eyebrows when certain things are being done and the training is a certain way. Sometimes you need the change to notice what was going on before. It's very true in life.

Graham Stuart: You look back at it and say to yourself, 'We've got a team here that has very nearly got relegated, and it's relatively the same sort of side as the start of the next season.' You think to yourself, 'Perhaps we were kidding ourselves that this was a one off; perhaps we're not as good as we thought we were.' Before you know it you're behind the eight ball again because we've started the season off so badly.

Daniel Amokachi: When a team is struggling, they kind of point hands to the manager. But all around you've got to look at the attitude of the players. You look at the attitude of the players: do they want to fight for the cause. Mike Walker, there's no doubt in my mind he was so nice. I always say he's too nice to be a manager, because in this modern era you've got to be tough to be a manager. You've got to be outspoken and let players know what you want, and if they are not ready they should get out. He's not that type of person, and that is why I think the team struggled a bit.

Graham Stuart: I think a lot of the players had totally and utterly lost any kind of faith with Mike. I don't mean that disrespectfully to the man, but I think that's just the reality. He wasn't getting a tune out of the players. It was a case of something's going to have to happen to change the direction of the football club and the dynamic of the football club, because it was blatantly obvious that it wasn't working.

Joe Parkinson: We were expecting it, and I think deep down we were hoping, because we could see things weren't getting any better, and for the sake of the club something needed to be done. I don't like slagging Mike off, I don't really want to, but he just wasn't up for the job really.

Neville Southall: The problem was less the personnel than the way we played and the way we trained. Tempers were boiling over in the dressing room. Walker would come in and rant and rave about us not being fit – it was always our fitness he questioned, oddly – and we'd just sit there. When Spurs beat us at White Hart Lane he lobbed a teacup at the wall and covered my CD player with tea. I'm not one to lose my temper, but I told him he was a prick.

David Unsworth: It's always tough when you're not winning games; and we didn't win anywhere near enough games that was expected of us. I was a young player and young players want to get in and stay in. And the bigger picture doesn't always come clear until you get a little bit older, more experienced, and you become a senior player. So I have no doubt that a few senior players weren't happy with the style and the way he managed. But at the same time I'd never have a bad word said against him because he was great for me.

Neville Southall: I remember someone saying that they only learned after Walker was gone that football was played in two halves of the pitch, because we only ever played in our own half under his management.

Peter Johnson: Mike Walker wasn't my pick, but I was asked whether if they appointed him would I object, and I said no. I was still an outsider. I think history would show that goalkeepers don't often make good managers, but he was the manager of the club when I got there and I was quite prepared to give it a go. It was a very bad start. We were bottom after 10 games and we had an opportunity to make a change of manager. It was an international weekend. After about 10 or 11 games the points total was just ridiculous.

The return of Joe Royle

Peter Johnson: Joe would have walked bare-footed over broken glass down the East Lancs Road from Oldham to Liverpool to manage his old club. He did a good job, a very good job. I got on very well with him.

Dave Watson: It was a breath of fresh air. I'd played with Joe at Norwich. The lads loved it. Joe had a massive personality. He'd walk in the dressing room and his face would light people up. He'd have people laughing and joking. It was like someone switched a light on. It had been so glum and dumb.

David Unsworth: He changed it overnight, because the first day he came in our training sessions just went up 100%. Our first session we had our shin pads on; it was like a game – we were kicking lumps out of each other; we were pressing; it was just like, 'Wow, what was that? It's like I've just played a game for an hour'; and that set the tone.

Willie Donachie: Everybody was nervous. But we had great professionals, like Dave Watson the captain; Neville in goal, who was crazy but a very good professional; Barry Horne. And they were the leaders of the other younger players and the foreign players. And without them it would have been very difficult. You know if you go into a club where they're not good professionals and they don't really want to work then you're struggling. But they all did want to work, so it was relatively easy.

John Ebbrell: I remember Joe talking about how we'd been a 'soft touch'. He said: 'I'm an Evertonian I've been looking at you from afar, and the days of being a soft touch are gone. We've got a limited number of games so training will now be exactly how we're going to play, everyone will wear their shin pads when we are training and if there's a tackle to be there to be won in training you're winning it, and I'll be picking the team on the training performance.'

Neville Southall: He showed us a video, I think of AC Milan, who were the top team in Italy and Europe at the time. He showed how they played a pressing game: getting it, giving it; closing opponents down when they were in possession; hitting them on the break. 'This is the best team in the world,' said Joe. 'They get more money than you; they work ten times harder than you lot at the moment. If it's good enough for them, it's fucking good enough for you.'

Andy Hinchcliffe: We were in training twice a day, three days a week, working with weights, it was like a sea change, from the Mike Walker days. I loved every aspect of it, because you became quicker, faster, stronger, more confident, literally in the space of 6-8 weeks, you could see. It was hard work, because it was such a change.

Tony Grant: Joe got the chance and took it, whereas Mike never. Joe came in, straight away identified what we needed to do to stay up. We were involved in the FA Cup still as well. He shored things up, he had a great coach in Willie Donachie, and Willie's not soft, he gets you fit, you all know what you're doing, and there was always good players there. It just needed someone to run the ship really. Joe took his chance and was a great manager for Everton.

Neville Southall: His assistant Willie Donachie was absolutely brilliant. He was the first holistic coach I'd come across and his routines were superb.

Willie Donachie: I did a lot of work on the training ground and Joe addressed people individually. I think that was the balance. I don't really like talking to the media or negotiating with the board. I just want to be involved in the game, playing football and with the players, whereas Joe was very good with the media and the board. He's good with people in general.

David Unsworth: He changed a few people around. We had Barry, John, Joe Parkinson sitting in front of myself and Waggy. Andy Hinchcliffe came back into the team; he took set pieces. Duncan started scoring goals; Graham chipped in; Paul Rideout chipped in; Anders went on this run of form that was just outstanding. Overnight he changed the ethos of how we were going to play.

Stuart Barlow: Joe would say to the players we would call him, 'Gaffer', but to the staff around Bellefield he'd say, 'Look you call me Joe. I'm Joe to yous,' and it was great to see he was just a normal person.

Graham Stuart: Big Joe Royle comes into the football club, and you go from a man who I never really felt got to grips with Everton Football Club in Mike Walker to a man who knew absolutely everything about Everton Football Club – as a player, as fan – and now he had the opportunity to show it as a manager. I think it totally and utterly transformed Everton Football Club from that moment on. That was it then, gone were the dicey moments, and I think Joe really, if he stayed, would have kept pushing us on, but that's another story.

Andy Hinchcliffe: The stuff we did in training, body shape, mediation, was the stuff people now would be taking for granted in terms of the science of the game. But what I found looking back, probably the most important thing was the trust they put in players. I remember Willie Donachie saying, one of the first conversations he had with the group of players was, 'We are men, and if you have a problem you speak to us. You don't go behind closed doors, you don't go sniping to your friends. We are honest and open. We're here to take criticism, and we will work together.' It's that togetherness and that trust from day one that was established.

Daniel Amokachi: The training was like 120%. You have to give 120%, the same way you play, the same we train. Willie, he's a tough character; he's tough, passionate, he wants you to give 100%. If you don't give 100% you re-take the drill and make sure we get it perfectly. The mind-set was right there: we are at the bottom of the relegation, we just have to give everything and go back to the old school, the basics.

Willie Donachie: I believe the way you train is the way you play. So if you're training sloppy, you'll be sloppy in the game. Every training session has to be like a game or it's a waste of time. So that is a big part of my job, just make sure they do things with the right intensity and the right focus, then it will be easy in the game. It is simple.

Andy Hinchcliffe: It was remarkable the way they took the bulk of that squad and actually turned it round – both mentally and physically – into believing and playing like a top six side, which is basically what Joe did. It was just by putting demands on the players, putting trust on the players, and saying, 'It's all about work.' And once you find the joy in working hard, chasing the ball down, closing down, and that's what we found. We couldn't get enough of it by the end.

Daniel Amokachi: [It was] The old school, one route football. Get the ball up there; you have Paul Rideout who can flick the ball, you have big Dunc who can flick the ball, and the other players jump in. So it definitely paid off very well, because if you have players that are willing to run for 90 minutes, the one route football definitely pays off.

Duncan Ferguson, Dogs of War, and avoiding relegation

In October, shortly before Walker's dismissal, Everton had brought in Duncan Ferguson and Ian Durrant on loan from Glasgow Rangers. Ferguson had been subject of a British record transfer just 16 months earlier but had struggled at Ibrox under the weight of expectation and disciplinary problems. While Durrant returned to Glasgow, Ferguson's loan move was made permanent in December 1994.

John Corbett: Ferguson was another exciting player but a man who came with a lot of baggage. He was almost tainted by the fact that he'd joined Everton because other clubs probably wouldn't touch him with a barge pole. He'd been involved in activities in Scotland on the pitch which had led to a prison sentence; he'd fallen out with Scottish FA; he refused to give interviews; he was an eccentric. But, many people thought that we were punching above our weight when we acquired him, and I think in a better Everton side Ferguson would have probably been one of the outstanding players of the late twentieth century.

John Parrott: What you've got to remember is that he engendered everything the Everton fans wanted to see. They wanted a hero. They wanted to see someone with passion, someone who kissed the badge and actually meant it. Someone who's got a tattoo on his arm to prove it. He's someone who loves the club through and through.

Willie Donachie: He could have been like a world star. But for one reason or another he didn't. He took some big knocks; going to jail and all that stuff. I was always trying to get him to play for Scotland again and he wouldn't, and I understood why. But it's a waste of time having grudges and holding things against people, because you've only got one career and you've got to get the most out of it. So that was the only thing frustrating with Duncan. To me he always tried and in the big games he was unstoppable, because he was big, and he could jump, and he was brave. He should have run riot in the world, not just at Everton. But I think he did everything he could.

Tony Grant: Duncan was great. I'm a big Evertonian, I remember Sharpy and that team, nearly all of them are legends for me. But we haven't had many. And for me Duncan is an icon. For what he done, he almost turned it around, he was that big, swashbuckling striker that defenders hated, he'd mix it with every defender he played against, no one liked playing against him. Around the training ground he was bubbly, good fun, great with the young lads, great guy really.

Neville Southall: Duncan's one of the nicest people that I know, the sort of person that would give you the last penny in his pocket. I think he's a terrific fellow, but an idiot at the same time. Duncan should have been – and I've said this to him on numerous occasions – the best player in the world. But he just wasn't motivated enough to do that.

Anders Limpar: My biggest assets were my speed and ability to cross the ball. I had a lot of assists in my four years at Arsenal to the forwards there, so that was my biggest asset. To put the ball in for Duncan Ferguson, that was quite easy for me to reach him, and he – as we know – was one of the best headers of the ball in Europe at that time. It wasn't just me; it was everybody who saw a good outlet in Duncan. It was easy, and it was nice to play with him as well because that brought the pressure off the rest of the players.

John Parrott: I met Tony Adams on holiday in Antigua in his drink phase, which started about 11 o'clock in the morning and finished about 11 o'clock at night. I'm having a beer with him most days and I said, 'Right I'll see you in the players' lounge when you come back.' Everton had previously had Tony Cottee playing and Arsenal had been coming and beating us every time. Anyway, Adams turned up to play against us and of course we've now got Duncan up front. Him and Duncan had a right royal battle all the way through and they've come in the players' lounge at the end of the game; a good game. Tony Adams has got a cut over his eye, a fat lip and bruises all down one side, and Duncan comes in. He's got a cut over his other eye, a fat lip and bruises down his side as well. Duncan says to me, 'That's a proper centre half!' I said, 'What do you mean?' 'I gave him a right bang and he said, 'Oh it's like that is it?' and he gave me one back.' He loved it. They had a drink and I saw them talking and as Tony goes to go, he says, 'John, see you later, and bring back Tony Cottee!'

Daniel Amokachi: When big Dunc came in it was a different ball game. You need players with character, players that believe in themselves, believe in winning and have all the mentality. He really brought that into the locker room, and it was amazing to see him, the kind of passion that he brings into the team, and definitely he contributed for the survival of that season and winning the FA Cup.

21 November 1994
Everton 2, Liverpool 0

Andy Hinchcliffe: That Liverpool game was classic. We practised and practised and then [Duncan] scored from a corner, and then Paul [Rideout] makes it 2-0. You win a game, you win a Merseyside derby again, belief goes through the roof doesn't it? So you're putting things into practise to win the game, and then winning the game you can't wait for the next one, whereas before that we were really worried game by game, we didn't know how it was going to go. But suddenly everyone believed.

David Unsworth: What we had worked on was our set pieces and Andy's delivery from set pieces was amazing. And Dunc came alive, didn't he? As Joe called it, the legend was born that night.

A wonderful, wonderful goal from Duncan. And then Paul gets a second right near the end, and we're off and running.

Neville Southall: He'd been a bit lost on the pitch in his first weeks at the club, but when we faced our neighbours in Joe's first game in charge he went to war.

John Ebbrell: I think Joe ignited Duncan. Because under Mike he was very much pass, pass. We had Vinny Samways, who was a really good player by the way, but a lot of it was sideways and pass, pass, pass and under Joe it was 'Right, it is going in,' so that enabled him to use his size and presence a lot more, and they worked with Duncan on being in the right places to score goals – between the posts basically, which was important.

Andy Hinchcliffe: I watch a lot of football now and it looks as if free-kick takers and corner takers are trying to individually pick someone out, and we didn't ever do that. It looks like we did, because if Duncan's on the end of a free-kick and he scores, it looks like I put the ball right on his head. But what we used to do was to attack three areas. We got players near post, central and far post, and we used to put the ball along a trajectory. But I couldn't guarantee that I wasn't going to slightly under hit it or over hit it. So to play the percentages we used to fill certain areas, and they knew the area I would be aiming for.

Graham Stuart: The fans took to Duncan from minute one, aided and abetted obviously by scoring one of the goals in the derby, the first goal in the derby, which was Joe's debut game. It couldn't have got any better for Joe, a derby in his first game, his new signing scores and we're off and running then.

David Unsworth: We won three games in a week [V Liverpool, Chelsea and Leeds United] and then we were out of the relegation straight away. Within a week we'd come in, we changed the way we started training; we were so fierce and competitive in training; it wasn't like that before. We changed a few personnel, we got the results, we got big wins, and then we just took off. We couldn't stop winning after that.

Anders Limpar: I just love that expression the Dogs of War. Don't forget the Dogs of War – as they were called – were unbelievably good football players as well. They were unbelievably good passing players; they could pass the ball so good. Then you have players that are grafting like Barry Horne, for example, who works his bollocks off to give the ball to you. My position and my thing was to attack, as a skilful player – I have to say – you just love to have players working with you in that way.

Willie Donachie: I never liked it, because they were very good players. Joe Parkinson, Barry Horne, an international, John Ebbrell. I think Joe regrets it a little bit, because it takes a little bit away from how good they were. If Joe Parkinson hadn't got his injury, he would have had a really, really good career. Barry Horne did, John Ebbrell did.

Graham Stuart: It smoothed out a little bit more and I think we got a lot easier on the eye once we got out of trouble and once confidence was flowing through the side again. But I think when Joe first came in, initially the requirement was to make us hard to beat and he did that and all of a sudden things began to turn.

Andy Hinchcliffe: I was more of a Chihuahua, wasn't I? I wasn't a Rottweiler. Joe Parkinson, he epitomised it for me. He was so unlucky with the injuries he had, not to play for England and have a greater career, he was a fabulous footballer. He was one of the toughest men, but funny off it. Going into a 50-50 with him, you'd be lucky to come out with your legs really. Not that he was dirty, he was just incredibly strong and powerful, and the timing of his challenges. He epitomised it all.

Tony Grant: Every day is like a relegation fight on the training ground. You've got to be on your mettle otherwise you're going to get put up in the air. So, training is hard. But you're like a family, you're just backing each other. You all know this game is an important game, we've got to do something to get a result. So, no one is tentative, we're all geeing each other up to get a result. We all know each other's qualities. If I was playing, Dave Watson would be saying, 'Granty, get on the ball, get us playing.' If it was Joe Parkinson playing he might say, 'Joe, win them tackles, win that header, get stuck in.' We all knew each other's qualities, and if you're playing, you need them qualities to come out.

Neville Southall: My Wales team-mate Barry Horne in particular came into his own. He had signed two years earlier, but hadn't really won over the fans until that goal against Wimbledon.

Joe Parkinson: We tackled everything. We saw a crisp packet blow across the pitch and we tackled it. That's what we needed. I don't care. We are still talking about it now, and talk about it in a fond way really you know, it's not derogatory to anybody really. He knew us players, what we were just decent, strong players, and it's exactly what we needed at the time.

John Ebbrell: The overriding thing about that was Joe, Barry, myself... we got on so well, the three of us. We were brilliant in the dressing room, we had the same humour.

Joe Parkinson: Barry gets a lot of adulation, but I think John Ebbrell was so underrated. I know he came onto the scene expected to do massive things, playing for England Youth and all that, but he was so underrated. I loved playing with both of them.

Daniel Amokachi: It's all about the character that Joe brought into the team, and Willie. Because when you have a manager that is old school, and then he made sure that the players believed in themselves, and got us to that level of fitness where we can run for 90 minutes. It is very difficult for any team to play against. I remember all the games we played against Manchester United, Chelsea; all the big teams. At Goodison we picked up all three points. That tells you how the team was really working.

Neville Southall: Without that kind of effort we would have sunk without a trace. But we became hard to beat, we were competitive, we got in peoples' faces and other teams didn't like playing against us. But we played some good football too. Which team wouldn't with a player like Anders Limpar in the squad?

Willie Donachie: Anders was just quite a complicated person. Unbelievable talent, but nervous as hell. And we had to reassure him all the time, and try to encourage him and help him believe in himself, which was strange for me, because he had everything except that real sort of mental toughness. But he was very talented. It was a bit of a bunch of crazy people. Neville at the forefront.

1995 FA Cup run

David Unsworth: Bristol City away was the one game where we had no right to win; we got battered, and Matt Jackson scored a screamer out of nothing. Nev made save after save, they hit the bar, the post. Jimmy Gabriel said after the game in the changing room, 'It's games like this you know your name's on the cup.' I always remembered that, and he was right; he was absolutely right. We dodged one that day.

Dave Watson: We went away to Bristol City and got battered. It was 0-0 and we scored late in the game. We came in at the end and Big Joe, with a big smile, went, 'You need a bit of luck to win this cup and we're on the march!'

Andy Hinchcliffe: It was never, 'It's a cup game so we will leave four or five players out.' We desperately wanted it, the longer we went on in that competition the more chance we knew we had. I think Joe probably realised what a cup win could do for confidence. And then to have everything to fall into place, to avoid relegation and win the cup, that would have clearly been the plan. They weren't saying, 'Right the cup's on the backburner.' Maybe if they had done that things would have worked out very differently and we could have been in deep trouble.

Daniel Amokachi: Nobody expected us to end up at Wembley, but then we just kept eliminating all those teams, and just kept moving forward.

Dave Watson: We played Newcastle [in the quarter-final at Goodison] and I scored the winning goal. It was a bobbly day. It was windy. I was 33-1 to score. Not that I had any bets on the game, I don't. My dad – he was called Alec, he's passed away now – and my family did. When I went in the lounge after the game they were all celebrating! I thought it was just because I scored a goal but they were saying, 'I had a tenner on you!' They forgot about getting to the semi! It was a header, no great goal or anything, my dad and my mates were all celebrating in the lounge. It was magic walking in there. I was so happy and I thought they were celebrating the game. They were all waving these tickets about.

9 April 1994
FA Cup semi-final
Everton v Tottenham Hotspur

Graham Stuart: I remember the bus turning into Elland Road and it was chockablocked with Everton fans. I thought to myself, 'This is our day, I can feel it already.' We were already super confident as a team because we were regularly winning games of football. It was all relaxed, everybody knew their jobs, as a team we trusted each other, and we turned up at Elland Road. As soon as we got off the bus it was all Evertonians cheering us, cheering us into the ground. We ran out on to the pitch and we had three quarters of the ground, and you felt like we were at home.

David Unsworth: We drove down the hill towards Elland Road, and all I could see was just a sea of blue everywhere. Everywhere we went there was Everton fans. And at one point we were outside the ground and I'm going, 'Where's all the Tottenham fans?'

Anders Limpar: It sounds silly, but we were pumped up with confidence. There was only one winner in that game.

Graham Stuart: We just knew it was going to be our day and we went out and delivered.

Tony Grant: When you walked out there, where the dugouts were, it was all Everton. And when you looked behind that goal, it was all Everton, and when you looked behind that goal it was all Everton. It was just surreal. They made a boobie really, the FA, by doing that, but it was great for us, because I've never heard noise like it. Warming up was unbelievable. Plus we were playing outstanding, and on the day we showed what we could do. We had got through the hard part of the season, this was the time to relax a little bit, this was a joy.

David Unsworth: We just knew that was our day. You just knew. I knew driving down the hill when I saw the sea of blue, and when I walked out onto the pitch before the game, to look at the pitch, and the Everton fans were behind both goals. There was just no way we were not going to win that game.

Andy Hinchcliffe: Once that first goal went in, we were never going to look back, because we just knew that they weren't going to out run us or outplay us, it just wasn't going to happen. It was our day.

Graham Stuart: We were on the front foot from minute one and then Andy Hinchcliffe whips a cross in and Matt Jackson scores with a header. So, we're 1-0 up, and it was 1-0 at half time. In the dressing room we're saying, 'Come on boys, we're 45 minutes away from Wembley here, don't give this up. Keep pushing on.' And then Paul Rideout breaks through, and I remember it as you do as a striker, as a partnership. If he's bursting forward, go in there and head for goal because you might get a rebound. As it happens Ian Walker saves it, but he palms it straight into my path and it's a nice, easy tap in to put us 2-0 up. From that minute on I'm thinking we're going to Wembley here and it's like a real great feeling.

Anders Limpar: They talk about the hard work and the hard grit of the players, but they always forget that they were good players – at the bottom they were unbelievable, good passing players, and you have to say that first. When it came to the semi against Tottenham we were such a good team as a whole unit. So I wasn't scared to play against Tottenham on the neutral ground.

Dave Watson: It was 'scheduled' for Tottenham-Man United in the final and then we upset the applecart by battering them at Elland Road. I'd been in bed all week. I had flu or something and I'd never been ill in my life. I was washed out. I dragged myself up and made the game. I was weak. It was a magnificent performance. If I couldn't have done a job I wouldn't have played. I felt I'd have a presence as the captain. We conceded one goal and that was Sheringham when he dived in the box and nothing happened and I was pissed off at that. I got over it after a bit! We had three sides of the ground and it was electric.

At 2-1, Rideout picked up a knock, prompting Amokachi to warm-up. Although the physio, Les Helm, eventually signalled that Rideout was fine to carry on, there was no stopping Amokachi, and he bounded on as a replacement.

Daniel Amokachi: It's normal when a player goes down and you play in the same position, you've got to go and get ready. I got ready and I just kept going because I was anxious; I was anxious to be on that field. That was the period where I was really, really feeling I was on top of the world. The signal I saw from the doctor was, 'He's done.' And then Joe said, 'Give him five minutes.'

Neville Southall: Les Helm, the physio, was busy treating him and signalled to the bench that he was going to be okay, but Daniel took it as a signal to come on and just wandered onto the pitch before anyone could stop him. He was bonkers.

Daniel Amokachi: I told Jimmy Martin to write the slips, he never knew that Joe never told me. And he just wrote it and I gave it to the fourth assistant. The fourth assistant just picked his changing board up and I stepped onto the field. And then I saw Joe rushing to the line and I just stopped back and looked at him, fixed my collar and it went in. If you bring me out, we've already done with our three substitutes.

Graham Stuart: Joe really wanted to see if Paul could recover, because me and Paul Rideout were tearing them to shreds on the afternoon and he wanted to keep that going.

Daniel Amokachi: The third goal we started off from the middle, I did combination play from Unsworth to Limpar, and then a cross and I headed it down. That was 3-1. And then the fourth one, it was I think a corner kick from Spurs, and then a break, the late Gary Ablett took the ball from the left, a good sprint, and I was far away on the right side. We just kept going, there was two Spurs playing running back too. Then he crossed it in and I just ended up jabbing it into the roof. It was sealed and done. The beautiful thing about it again, after the game Klinsmann came into the locker room and shook my hand and gave me his shirt. That was quality from him.

David Unsworth: Joe tells the story great, the substitution he never made. But Daniel was a great character, and actually should have had three that day, let alone two. A brilliant substitution.

Daniel Amokachi: The good thing about it was that in less than ten minutes I ended up scoring two goals. It was a beautiful day for all the blue side of Liverpool, but at the same time I never mention it to the world, it was Joe that mentioned it to the world that I substituted myself. And then he said, 'If you try that shit again you're leaving.' But it's normal. I tell that story every day to my players, but I tell them that I am telling you the funny side of football: if you're ready, if you really want to play, you show it, but it's not something you should try, because if I didn't score or we end up being knocked out, I'm sure that that would have been my last game at Everton.

Joe Parkinson: What a player, what a character Daniel was. He was just amazing in the changing room – I think we maybe got rid of him a bit too soon. I thought even when he was out the team you wouldn't know that, he was the same sort of person and he'd just come in the changing room and he'd light the place up and get everyone going – brilliant.

Daniel Amokachi: It was a special day. It's not just about the two goals that I scored, it's about me sitting back home in Nigeria as a young kid, watching the FA Cup every year. Every year the FA Cup, nobody misses it. It's watched globally, especially back home in Nigeria. And today I'm here helping my team to book a place to be at Wembley. That's special, that's too special a moment for me. In all the reminiscing of when I was watching the FA Cup on TV flew into my head after the game, even when I was in the locker room and all that. I just prayed that God should give me the grace to be part of the team when the final day comes.

1995 FA Cup Final
20 May 1995
Everton v Manchester United

Dave Watson: We made a record that week. 'Everton's gonna win the cup, big Dave's gonna lift it up, let's go!' It was the old Farm song. It was great. The Farm were Liverpudlians and there was one Evertonian in the Farm. He come down and did the song with us. I still sing along with them. It was great. It was a really good song. 'Remember boys back in 66 they won the Cup with Catterick, and Kendall's boys in 84, now big Joe Royle is coming back for more!' It was really good the way they did it. I've still got tons of copies! It was amazing.

Tony Grant: We weren't confident. We knew we'd done ever so well; we'd stayed up, we were in a cup final playing Man U, who were brilliant. We had a party all booked in London in a big hotel, and we would have enjoyed that no matter what, but we knew it would be so much sweeter with a trophy there.

Joe Parkinson: We beat them a month or so before, Duncan Ferguson scored, and we just knew we could beat them.

Willie Donachie: When we were at Oldham we played United in the semi-finals of the cup twice, and drew with them, took it to a third game. So I knew they weren't invincible. They had a good team, some very good players, but again, that's always been my attitude: If you work hard against somebody you've always got a chance.

Neville Southall: One of the great things about playing for Joe and Willie is that we always went out to win. They were both naturally positive people and they brought their attitude to life to the football pitch.

Andy Hinchcliffe: Even though we were clearly confident after beating Tottenham, we still felt, 'Wait a minute, this is Wembley, this is United, look at the players in their team.' We still had to be realistic and could we do the things we did at Goodison and around the country? Could we still do it Wembley? And we knew it would have to be the type of performance that we eventually did put in to win the cup. But that was probably the only time in the competition that we really needed to dig deep and grind out.

David Unsworth: You get what you deserve I think, and the week before we got to the Cup Final we beat Ipswich to stay up, and that was just total relief. So we went down a couple of days early to the Cup Final, went down on the Wednesday, and we trained. And there was just the relief about it all that we'd stayed up, and we were just going to enjoy it.

Peter Johnson: You're always in with a chance, but they were such a powerful side, Man United. Although Everton have always done quite well against Man Utd considering, better than Liverpool. I think they have a better record against them than Liverpool have.

David Unsworth: I remember Joe's team talk: 'Well we're here now lads, we might as well just go and win it.' And it was that simple, but that powerful. And we did. We got the goal. Alright, we sat back in the second half and we defended, and Nev's pulled off a couple of great saves but I thought we deserved it and it was just a wonderful icing on the cake of what was a great journey that started badly and changed when the manager came in.

Paul Rideout: The ball bounced up and it was so slow. It went up in the air and the way I approached it, I knew I had to generate some power to get it in there, but if I'd probably taken my eye off it a little bit and looked at Denis Irwin coming towards me, I might not have got such a clean header. But because it was so slow it probably helped me. And the focus was there just to head it. Fortunately it went in the corner. It kind of floated. If you see my reaction, even when I headed it it took a long time to go in. I looked almost surprised. It was like, 'Did that happen? Oh yeah, alright, I better do something now.' And off I went.

Tony Grant: It was supreme header against an unbelievable goalkeeper. I still don't know how he did it, but Rideout was one of the best headers of the ball I've ever seen. I still don't know how he generates that much power, standing still, to get that in.

Peter Johnson: Rideout's header was a brilliant header, it was from a standing start. He had to, because it came back off the bar, and we were fortunate with Bruce, I think his hamstring had torn. He couldn't get off the ground to stop the ball going in the net.

Graham Stuart: Second half of the game, you can't go 90 minutes against a Man United side with the quality they had in those days and not come under pressure. But when we did come under pressure, big Dave Watson and David Unsworth were solid at the back. Big Nev when required was there again.

Neville Southall: I made a good double-save at my near post from Paul Scholes, where I blocked his first shot and got a leg to the follow-up. Gary Pallister had a stooping header, but I dived and caught the ball. I also saved from Nicky Butt at the near post. Even as a veteran, the old reflexes hadn't left me. There was no way anything was going to get past me, no chance.

David Unsworth: As influential as he is on the pitch and off the pitch, he made two great saves at a key time, and it was what we needed, particularly as we were defending so deep. He made a couple of what I'd call 'Neville saves' where he made them look easy. He comes and picks one out of the sky right at the end as well. Joe was like, 'Oh, thank God for that.' I'd probably say Neville was the key man that day.

Daniel Amokachi: They just kept coming, kept coming, kept coming until the last minute.

David Unsworth: Everybody's performance was fantastic. I had a great battle with Mark Hughes, alongside Waggy as well. Waggy headed and kicked everything that moved that day. Barry and Joe covered every blade of grass; Anders for an hour was unplayable; and Paul gets his goal.

Andy Hinchcliffe: It's horrible. Absolutely horrible, you just can't wait. I know you're wishing your time away, and I was lucky enough to play at Wembley with England, but you're just wishing, because you just know...

Graham Stuart: I don't think I've ever been as tired in my life on a football pitch – my lungs were burning, and I was thinking, 'Please just blow the whistle.'

Andy Hinchcliffe: United players had the luxury of playing there many, many times, so they could afford to lose one final, because they might win three or four. But I probably knew, and many Everton players probably knew, that this was going to be our only chance, so if we had to wish away 45 minutes just to win a game, then we're quite happy to do that, because it's a very unusual set of circumstances. We just wanted to win. I think for the whole club, the fans, for Willie and Joe, for what they had done.

David Unsworth: I got really emotional. It was my dream to win the FA Cup as a kid. I'd played it over in my mind a million times when I was playing with a sponge ball in a terrace house in Chorley; kicking it against the wall you run away thinking that you've scored the goal in the Cup Final. The Cup Final was a big thing in those days, wasn't it? You'd sit down with your family in front of the TV for hours and hours. I got quite upset before we went up to collect the trophy. And then obviously you're trying to pick out your family in the crowd. It was relief more than anything, and then euphoria kicks in later on. And we had a great night.

Dave Watson: It was amazing to walk up the steps to pick up the FA Cup. That's the dream. I'd been with Norwich and picked the Milk Cup. I'd won the league and this was to complete my big three domestic ones. It was a really proud moment to walk up. Prince Charles and Harry were supporting Man United. They look devastated on the picture when I'm holding up the cup. They're all grumpy at the side. It was magnificent. I had a scarf around my neck. It goes back. Sometimes your dreams come true. As a young kid you watch the cup final, you think, 'It'd be great to do that.' To play for your country, make your debut against Brazil. It seemed to fall into place for me. I worked my nuts off. I was no great footballer but I had a great attitude. I was good in the dressing room motivating people.

Peter Johnson: We had a party for the team, for about 600 people at the Royal Lancaster. We had it planned that if we'd lost then the maître d' would call us in and we'd all go in and eat, but if by some chance we won the team would hold back and we'd go in and sit down and the cup would come in with Dave Watson led by a piper. That was incredible.

Daniel Amokachi: My first season, and [one of] the first black players to play for Everton, the first African to win an FA Cup final. It can't get better than that, it can definitely not get better than that. It was celebrated back home in Nigeria. It was really celebrated. I remember all the families were in London. We had a good night and then the next day, you know how it is, the rooftop open bus and all the Evertonians on the streets it was crazy day. It was a beautiful day.

Neville Southall: How did I celebrate, then? I drove home, got back about 10.30pm, and went to bed. But I'll tell you this, driving home all smug and happy, and seeing all the happy Evertonians heading back north, was one of the most satisfying experiences of my life.

Joe Parkinson: He just shot straight off, which is fine. I love Nev to bits and if that's what he wants to do then fine. But why did he have to tell everybody? Just go and do it. It's as simple as that.

Everton under Joe Royle June 1995 – March 1997

Dave Watson: Big Joe turned it round by his character and personality and having a great coach in Willie Donachie. He was magnificent. Well ahead of his time. He took no nonsense off anyone.

Alan Myers: Joe Royle had unbelievable talent to make you feel so special and part of the team. No matter who you are, whether you're the top striker or whether you're like me just running the press. On the day I started he called me into the manager's office, and he said to me, 'You're one of us now, son,' and I'll never forget it. It was brilliant working under Joe. I'll never forget the first time I did a match, and he wanted me to come away on the bus with the team, which I thought was great because it was almost like a dressing room, the bus; I didn't think I should be on there. We played Chelsea away, and I was sat at the back, out of the way, and we were going down the King's Road, and I heard this shout from the front: 'Where's Myers, where's Myers?' I put my hand up, and he said, 'Come down here,' and he asked Willie Donachie, his assistant, to sit over on the other side, and he said, 'Sit over here, son.' So, I sat on the front seat with Joe Royle, and we drove into Stamford Bridge, and there were thousands of Evertonians, as there always are, waiting for the bus. And that's one of the most special moments I ever had as an Everton fan, as an Everton employee. It was a little thing, but he made me feel ten foot tall.

Duncan Ferguson imprisoned for assault

Duncan Ferguson had arrived at Goodison with a twelve-match ban hanging over him following an off-the-ball incident in which he headbutted an opponent while playing for Rangers. He had also been charged with by Strathclyde Police and faced a custodial sentence. In October 1995 he became the first footballer to serve a jail term for an on-the-pitch assault when he was sentenced to three months in jail.

Graham Stuart: There was a sense of shock around the football club, and I think Joe took that hard, personally took it hard I remember him saying that in a modern-day society when you're trying to keep people out of prison, and help them, and stuff like that. For Duncan to go into prison for that; it just didn't feel right, it didn't sit right.

Anders Limpar: You expect the players to be professional off the pitch and on the pitch. It's not for me to tell him what to do, but you have to have the respect for the banner, for the club and everything. What he did, there's only Duncan who can explain why he did it. That was quite a shock for us, but I was actually in the same position with Tony Adams at Arsenal, who went into jail. Of course, we were in shock, our best player going to jail. That was a blow for us.

Peter Johnson: I think by the police in Scotland and the Scottish FA, he was seen as a naughty boy and it was almost teaching him a lesson. But I think doing two terms, then coming out with a twelve-match ban was a bit unfair. We supported Duncan, I went to see him in Barlinnie. But you can't win. We sent a car to pick him up, he's got to be whisked away because the paparazzi were outside. But it was looked upon by many journalists as a weakness, that we were pampering him. He's gone to jail and we're sending a posh car for him. Life's not like that.

Andy Hinchcliffe: Whatever happens on a football pitch, we didn't expect them to lead to custodial sentences. And you always think it's not going to happen to one of our guys. Knowing Duncan as we did, we know he could be fairly volatile and aggressive, but he's lovely. We knew him as the person he was around the ground. Obviously we'd seen the incident and everything else, but we thought it wouldn't happen.

Peter Johnson: We supported him in court then we appealed. He had been to jail and he was doing time off the pitch as well. That's not fair. I think the law has changed now in regards to double jeopardy, but that was double jeopardy. It was looked to be unfair and we won the case, but only by 2:1 in the courts. Two judges to one. It was close. It could have been the other way.

Everton return to Europe

Peter Johnson: I hoped we'd do something in the Cup Winner's Cup as it was the time. But we went past Reykjavik and then it was Feyenoord. Reggie Blinker scored over there. We were disappointed because we'd agree to buy Kanchelskis and there was a hitch, a contractual hitch, so he wasn't able to play against Feyenoord, who were not a bad side. It was a difficult one.

Andy Hinchcliffe: I think it was 0-0 in the first leg, and lost 1-0 in the second leg, Reggie Blinker scored. I think we were a bit unfortunate. They weren't two of the greatest games, but the atmosphere at Goodison and certainly in Rotterdam, I've never again experienced. You hear the stories and it's like, 'Yeah we'll be fine,' but the atmosphere, the crackle in the ground, you get it very rarely during your career. It's just a shame we got beaten, because you'd love to have more of that.

Anders Limpar: We were better as we showed in that game, and it was close – we had a couple of chances to score a couple of goals in the home games, so that was very disappointing to go out at that stage. We should have won that game, to be honest with you.

Tony Grant: I don't think there was much difference between Feyenoord and us. I came on for the last half hour at Feyenoord away, and I was a very technical player. We had two corners, and I remember them clearly now – they came straight out to where I am. I chested it lovely, and I just had to volley it at goal, I did it so many times. I put it wide. Two minutes later, the same volley wide, I couldn't believe it. Not even threatening the goal. And we had chances in that game. Ronald Koeman was playing. But I don't think it was a gulf, no.

Andy Hinchcliffe: That's what you really want, to play in those atmospheres. It was difficult to play in; it was threatening as well. I think that's what you hear about with certain grounds in the world. You do feel it, you feel it coming off the stands in waves, and we certainly felt it that day. You're there to do a job, and it's just a shame we lost out, but it was a close call over the two legs, that's just the way it went.

Andrei Kanchelskis

David Unsworth: I thought the Kanchelskis signing was a steal; I thought it was a real steal. Couldn't believe we'd got him; was delighted that we had.

Neville Southall: Kanchelskis was a truly outstanding player: fast, direct and a sublime finisher. He would have held his own in the class of 85, although I feel Trevor was probably a better defender than Andrei.

Andy Hinchcliffe: If you play against David Beckham, of course he could manipulate a ball around you amazingly well, but he didn't really have a trick and he didn't really have an awful lot of pace. So in a way, if you say I'm going to get close to you, you can maybe limit the damage. He can still hurt you, I remember at Old Trafford once he hit me in the chest with a ball, and it was like being hit by a howitzer. But you have that possibility of stopping the problem, because there is only one problem. You'd play against Kanchelskis and he's got the pace, the power, the height, he's good in the air. If you say, 'I'll deal with his pace,' then suddenly he'll get the ball into his feet and he'll run at you; he'll go inside or outside. So if you've got four or five problems with a player, what on earth are you going to do?

Tony Grant: He gets in all the top teams now, 20 years later. He was built for the modern day. 20 years' time from now, he'd still get in all their teams, because he was left footed, right footed, he had the biggest thighs ever, he could run like the wind, and he could score goals.

Willie Donachie: He's one of the quickest, most powerful players I've worked with. When he was shooting, it was like the ball flew in. Natural power. You need to see it and be close to it to appreciate it. It would be past the goalkeeper before they knew it. He was a very, very good player.

Graham Stuart: He was a strong boy Andrei, super quick. Set goals up, he scored 16 that [1995/96] season. So when you've got a wide man scoring 16 goals and probably setting up 20, that's a massive thing to have, that's a huge amount of armoury to have in your side. I scored 14 that season, and with Duncan chipping in, Paul Rideout pitched in with a few as well, Anders Limpar on the other side. All of a sudden your armoury is pretty good.

Peter Johnson: Two goals at Anfield, and then Fowler scored a goal with a few minutes to go. I was thinking, 'I can't believe this.'

Tony Grant: One was a header; a great header as well. He was an outstanding player. I think he was played in for the other one. You're not catching him are you? So you're not catching him, but you know something is coming at the end of it. There's lots of players that you can't catch, but nothing usually happens at the end of it. But with him something's always going to happen.

Andrei Kanchelskis: Everybody remembers these two goals, everyone speaks about the two goals in the derby, even though it's a long time. But it was a great result for us and the fans.

Anders Limpar: He showed the whole of England and the whole of the world what a player he was. Obviously, it's nothing to hide that you're over the moon to beat Liverpool at Anfield, especially at the time. They were really, really good. He scored two crackers actually, and he was a character as well.

Joe Parkinson: We had Kanchelskis on one side and Limpar on the other, and it was perfect for us. You get the ball and you try and find one of them two and they'll go and do the magic.

Andrei Kanchelskis: We had some good strikers, Duncan Ferguson, very strong and tall, very good in the air. Joe Royle told me when I came to the club, 'I need some crosses in the box to Ferguson, I need service.' Ferguson was very good in the air and strong, but if he doesn't get service he doesn't score goals because he is an attacking player. Also Anders Limpar was on the left side delivering a lot of crosses. Hinchcliffe's left foot was excellent, he had good passing and good vision for the diagonal to my side.

David Unsworth: The two of them together it was just a joy to watch them in front of me. Just brilliant.

Daniel Amokachi: He was good to have; him and Limpar, players like that who like taking players on and creating chances. It gave us two different dimensions. Limpar can start from the left, he can start from the right, or they change wings. It made my second season there sweeter than the first, because now players were comfortable: we're cup winners, we have players that want to keep the ball, that enjoyed playing.

Andrei Kanchelskis: Limpar played left side and I played right side. There was a lot of passes from the midfielder as well. I remember Tony Grant, he would play passes, he was very good technically. He had good vision and passing like Paul Scholes. Paul Scholes was excellent, the best for a long ball.

Tony Grant: I understood football. So I understood who your important players are and how they want the ball. I got put with Andrei, so even in training as soon as I got a half turn with the ball, I know where he is going to run, because that's where I would run if I had the pace. So I put the ball where I would want it, and where he would want it.

Daniel Amokachi: You remember we had Vinny Samways in that team, somebody that likes keeping the ball. And then Kanchelskis joined, Limpar and Unsworth were there, players that liked keeping the ball and enjoyed playing football. That's how it showed in the next season, because the next season we had a very, very wonderful pre-season and then everybody was just enjoying football.

Graham Stuart: Joe Royle's got to take a monumental amount of credit for the transformation that as a football club we made; from struggling like mad to winning the FA Cup, to signing the likes of Kanchelskis, to finishing sixth in that season as well and playing some really, really good football.

Anders Limpar: Arsenal came fifth and we came sixth, and we were so close. But over a season we weren't better than sixth place, that's the truth. The league table never lies. It never lies.

Andy Hinchcliffe: I think you can always say we're going in the right direction and we're doing things in the right way, but sometimes you need something tangible, something else. Something added to the following season, just to say there, that's proof that we're doing it.

Daniel Amokachi: That's how it is; that's football; that's life. It happens. It happens, but that is just football. That is just football. But I think that was a wake-up call to the rest of the Premiership teams: This Everton is a team to reckon with.

Gary Speed

In summer 1996 Joe Royle added Leeds United's Welsh international midfielder, Gary Speed, to his Everton team. Speed was a lifelong Evertonian.

Simon Hart: There's certain times when Everton buy a player, and it just feels right. Somebody you look at from the outside and think: 'Top player, good professional, somebody you actually want to sit down and have a drink with.' Although, Gary sooner probably would have had a tea, wouldn't he? It just felt right, and we knew the tales of him taking papers to Kevin Ratcliffe's house in the 80s. I really, really liked Speed.

Barry Horne: Joe said he would give me another contract, gladly give me another contract, but he knew that I hated not playing, and he said, 'You might not play.' Granty was coming through, John [Ebbrell] and Joe [Parkinson] were younger than me, and he said he was going to sign Gary Speed to play. Joe said, 'I'll do you a favour, I'll see if I can get you away cheaply.' I left too soon, I was really upset to leave but felt it was the right thing to do. I had played with Gary for Wales and he was everything that everybody said about him. He was charming, he was dedicated, he was a fantastic professional, made the best of himself. Good teammate, reliable. He did everything right. And he was a good footballer into the bargain…

Willie Donachie: Gary was a beautiful man. He was good looking, very skilful, fantastic work ethic, he had everything. But he was a good person too. I remember one game towards the end of our reign when Joe had left and Dave Watson was in charge and I was helping Dave. I think it was West Ham we were playing, and we weren't very good, so after the game I was having a bit of a go at the players, and he just turned round and said, 'Willie, you know we're all trying our best for you?' And it just stopped me dead in my tracks. That's all I've ever asked of anybody, but it's just the gentle way he said it, and he was very sincere. It's something you can always remember – they're always trying their best, no matter how bad they are. He was an Everton fan, everything about him was just great. Really good professional; brave, skilful, hardworking, everything. He was one of those that got the most out of his game, which I respected.

Richard Dunne: He was very talented but he was the best professional that you could've ever come across. He was one of those who put the extra hours in in training and he was determined to win. He had Everton in his heart he wanted Everton to be successful, you could see it not only in matches but every day in training. That there was a time and a place for playing about and everyone having a laugh but when you got down to it Gary was the one who would be always pushing people and making sure that everyone was trying to make themselves better.

Alan Myers: I got a call, and they said, 'We would like Gary Speed to model some Calvin Klein underwear.' So, of course, Gary was a good-looking man and I went to him, and asked, 'Gary, are you interested in this?' So, he says, 'I'll ask my wife,' because he was just newly married and it would've been him just standing in a pair of Calvin Klein underpants. Anyway, he come back, and he said, 'No, I don't think I should do it.' A couple of days later, he said, 'Did they ever come back?' I said 'I told them you didn't want to do it. By the way you know they were offering £10,000 for that.' He nearly fell off his chair! I think he thought it was a couple of hundred quid or something.

Abrupt Departures

Despite a promising start to the 1996/97 season, by Christmas form had dipped and results started to slip away and unhappiness started to manifest itself in the dressing room and on the terraces.

Phil McNulty: Joe did a fantastic job saving Everton from relegation, because they were, as he said himself, snookered when he took over. And then the other bonus was winning the FA Cup, and it's been proved since then how difficult it is for Everton to win the FA Cup. I think one of the biggest problems that Joe had was that he signed Andrei Kanchelskis, who was fantastic for one season, and then played at Euro '96 for Russia, and when he came back – for whatever reason – he was just never the same player again. He seemed unsettled, he was agitated, and clearly, in the end, he was angling for a move, which, in the end, he got – to Fiorentina. And Kanchelskis was such a huge part of that previous season when, I think, Everton only just narrowly missed out on Europe. To lose the influence of a player as good as that and someone who Joe rated so highly had a really bad effect on the team. And in the end, the football – and Joe will argue differently for this, forever and a day, and he's perfectly entitled to his opinion – was just a bit too predictable.

Andy Hinchcliffe: I got injured in a game against Leeds [on 21 December], I didn't know what I'd done, but then I found out that I clearly ruptured my cruciate ligament. I had surgery the next day and they actually give it to you in a jar. You're thinking, 'Wait a minute, your whole world has been ripped apart.' In an awful way I wasn't too concerned, I was concerned about Everton but I wanted to come back playing for Everton, and I was thinking 'Am I ever going to come back playing again?' So very selfishly I had to throw myself into getting myself as fit as quickly as possible, because the team needs you when things weren't going so well.

Andrei Kanchelskis: We started very good. Every season the big teams buy two or three players. At Everton we didn't. Joe Royle told the chairman that we needed some new quality players. Maybe there was no money, Everton weren't like Manchester or Arsenal, who are big, big, big clubs. There was no quality players bought, and therefore no improvement.

Tony Grant: That would have been nice wouldn't it? To bring a few players in with what we already had. I don't know. It's been a thing with Everton for years hasn't it? Where's the money? Where's the money? We've had so many young lads come through the academy, so where is it? I don't know.

Neville Southall: The assumption was that Joe had a lot of money to spend, and certainly by comparison to his successors as Everton managers he did. But despite being linked to all sorts of players he never quite seemed to pull off the deals he should have done.

Andrei Kanchelskis: Sometimes you play very well and you're unlucky with results in the game. This is true. Also, you don't have a big bench like the big teams. If some of the quality players are injured, like Graham Stuart or Limpar, there's no change. Young players come in, there's no quality and experience. This is a problem. If you have a good bench with good substitutes this is no problem. But when there are injuries there are no replacements. This was a problem for Everton.

Neville Southall: If I was brutally honest I'd say that we had a good system of playing and changed it too quickly. People wanted School of Science, not the Dogs of War, and didn't think we should be playing the way we did. But there was no point in fans looking down at a team of grafters, because we were winning that way and weren't able to play as successfully with the ball on the floor. The other factor was that other teams had started to work us out, which may have had a bearing on the change of tactics as well.

Andrei Kanchelskis: I had a few problems. I had played for Russia in Euro 96. I was very disappointed, very sad. At the start of the season it was okay, but after I had some problems and injury. I was very sad at the results for the Russian national teams, everyone was saying I played badly. Some press, especially in Russia, said bad things on every player, especially for me as I was playing in England. Everybody was waiting, Russian fans, for good results. I didn't play well like in my first season.

Alan Myers: I remember him leaving, which was a difficult situation, and we played away. I think he'd been substituted or something had happened, and we'd been beaten. We were all coming back on the bus, and he just kept saying to me, 'Oh, this is crap, crap, crap. Team crap, manager crap,' and he was clearly upset about what had happened at the game. He knew the writing was on the wall, and that he would go.

Andrei Kanchelskis: We went in the cars to the chairman's office. They said 'This is the situation, Fiorentina are interested in you. We sell you.' I said 'What sale? It's not possible, I have a contract.' The directors say we wait for your choice, give you some time. Fiorentina are willing to pay a lot of money for you. They said you have two choices: stay or move. I said, 'Okay I'll stay.' They said, 'It's difficult for you to stay, because there is no money, there is problems.' After me they sold other players. I remember seeing it in the newspapers.

Joe Parkinson: Andrei famously couldn't speak any English unless you spoke money and then he was fluent. Anything to do with money he was perfect at speaking, but if you wanted anything tactical, this that or getting told off, he couldn't speak, so the players had had enough of him. We got beat 4-1 at Newcastle away and we come in and we were absolutely destroyed, Willie Donachie tore the heart out of us. Joe Royle came in with Peter Johnson and said we've just sold Andrei to Fiorentina for about £7.5M, and I just went, 'Get in there!' with everyone listening. I think Joe Royle realised he had to get rid of him.

Alan Myers: We'd played at Newcastle away, and Joe Royle came out in the press conference afterwards, and someone asked about the move to Fiorentina, and the journalist said, 'Have personal terms been agreed?' Joe – as he would – replied, 'I think they have been some months ago.' I think that was the problem; I think he sort of wanted away for some time.

Andrei Kanchelskis: Fiorentina directly paid £8 million, not half and half. This is maybe why some chairman say this is good money. After I saw in the newspapers that other players were sold: Hinchcliffe, Speed, Barmby. I was disappointed, I was happy to play at Everton and for Joe Royle. I'm disappointed in the directors' decision.

Joe Royle Departs

Everton's depression hastened following Kanchelskis's departure. The normally affable Royle refused to speak to the press as Everton suffered their worst run of results in 25 years. Just as a corner seemed to have been turned, Royle unexpectedly resigned on the 1997 transfer deadline day.

Daniel Amokachi: In the football world you know it cannot be rosy every time. Sometimes you're lucky, you go for a beautiful run for a couple of seasons, and then you struggle a bit.

Alan Myers: The pressure went all across the club. But it's football. I used to always say to staff, 'It's Rock and Roll; it's not life or death.' We only know too well that it can be life and death, but what I mean by that is that the actual job is not a difficult job. But you never understand, until you've worked in a football club, what it means to you, what it does to you. It grips hold of you. I've done a lot of jobs in me time, but nothing has ever gripped me like working for Everton.

Phil McNulty: Joe is a larger-than-life guy, he's very, very witty, very shrewd, but he was sensitive to criticism – I think, as we all are, not just him.

Andy Hinchcliffe: Obviously what happened was really disappointing, because it was someone who had showed so much faith in me and was such a good guy. Somebody like that leaving the club, you think 'This can't be right.' But there's obviously things behind it in terms of results.

David Unsworth: I think Joe should have been given more time. I think Joe should have been given the funds to sign the players he wanted after what he'd done, because that was why he left.

Andrei Kanchelskis: This is life for the coach. I didn't like the situation for Joe Royle. It's the normal life for the coach. If they get good results everyone is like 'It's good, good, good.' Sometimes you get bad results. Joe Royle spoke with the chairman. He told the press, 'I need some quality players.' If we get no quality players and there are injuries, there is no bench. I remember him saying it.

Willie Donachie: It came to transfer deadline day, and Joe had gone to them and said I want to get these two players, Tore Andre Flo. But it wasn't going to cost a lot. Another one was a Norwegian player that we were getting for almost nothing [Klaus Eftevaag], and they wouldn't agree to it. So Joe sort of said 'If you're not backing me do you want to call it a day?' Simple as that. And the chairman must have said, 'Yeah, let's part company.'

Peter Johnson: I foolishly accepted the resignation. We spoke a couple of seasons afterwards and I said, 'I should have refused in that boardroom.' And put my arm round him. But I didn't, because I don't cuddle men very easily. It was a shame, a terrible shame. In fact, that could have been part of the Everton problem, caused by him leaving. I got on very well with him, worked well with him.

Barry Horne: Joe tried to sign me back on that day and I'd agreed to come back, everything was done. The contract was written up, [club secretary] Michael Dunford had prepared the contract, and I waited hours and hours and hours. I was away with Wales. Michael said, 'I'll get the contract drawn up, don't go training, we'll fax it down.' And the phone call I got was very different to the one I was expecting, because in the interim Joe had not been able to sign one of two players, it was Tore Andre Flo for £900,000, who then went on to be a multi-million-pound footballer.

Tony Grant: I was disappointed when Joe left. I just thought there was no reason to sack him, we might have been going through a bad time, but what he done previously it was like 'Just back him. Give him some money two bring one or two others in, and lets just build on what we've done previous.' I don't think we were ever going to go down, but I don't know why he went. It was a loss.

Peter Johnson: We got on well together, we worked well together, I liked him. We still have a banter when we see each other and our paths cross. But I think we both agree now that it was a mistake.

Alan Myers: I don't think anybody, including Neville himself, was aware of how close he came to becoming Everton manager. I was outside Bellefield with Peter Johnson the morning after Joe had left and we were discussing who should take over as caretaker boss. 'I have a shortlist of two,' said the chairman, 'Dave Watson and Neville, but I'm leaning towards Neville because a goalkeeper has less responsibility on the pitch.' At this point Neville pulls up in the carpark – it was early and he was always first in for training – gets out his car and heads to the Bellefield entrance. Seeing me he yells, 'Alright Alan, you fat cunt!' As he headed in through the doors, Peter, says very dryly, 'I think the shortlist is down to one.'

Dave Watson: Big Joe was promised so many players and it never happened. Peter asked me to take charge for the last seven games of the season. I looked at the last seven fixtures and they were daunting. Liverpool, Tottenham, Aston Villa. We needed four points to stay up. We got a draw at West Ham and we had an injury crisis. Michael Ball, Richard Dunne were playing in our team. Paul Rideout had gone to China on loan. We had a shortage of players. He hated flying. I called him and I said, 'I need you to come back.' He came back for the one game, played in midfield and he was magnificent. We won the game and it was happy days. That was a major moment.

Howard Kendall Mark 3

Peter Johnson promised Evertonians that they would be 'pleasantly surprised' by Joe Royle's successor. Yet the search was excruciatingly protracted. Attempts to hire Bobby Robson and Martin O'Neill were rebuffed and after it seemed as if Andy Gray would take up the role, he too rejected Everton. Three months after Royle's departure there was a familiar face in the manager's office.

Peter Johnson: I went to Barcelona and met up with Bobby Robson, watched a match, had a chat with him the next day. I think he was ready to go but not quite ready to go. But he was fantastic. I talked about the press in England, and he said 'Press?' He took me down into his office underneath the Nou Camp, and he said 'You call that press? Look at this! 12 pages, 20 pages. God it's fanatical. Fanatical.' But we couldn't nail it down.

Tony Grant: I wasn't an Andy Gray fan as a player, everyone else was, but I was a Sharpy fan. I looked at midfielders, but Sharpy was my striker. So when the Andy Gray thing came about, I'll be honest with you I didn't really bat an eyelid. I would have liked him, and I could have took it either way. I would have liked Waggy [Dave Watson] to have been given a chance. I'm not sure Dave would have wanted to be Everton manager at that time, but I would have loved him to have got a chance.

Neville Southall: I think the prospect of Andy managing Everton would have been really good. He knew enough about football, he knew enough about the players, he knew enough about coaching; he knew what we wanted. He knew the club inside out, he knew some of the players, he knew what he wanted to achieve.

Peter Johnson: We had a meeting right away with Martin O'Neill. After a board meeting I went down to meet him on the motorway. We couldn't get him to clinch it. I remember one club offering him or telling him, or putting it in the paper, that the jobs here, all you need to do is come up for it. But he didn't move.

Howard Kendall: I was in Majorca on holiday when I got a tip-off that I was under consideration. I knew that Andy was also in the frame, and the Sheffield United chairman understandably wanted to know what the situation was. I wasn't making a decision on the matter; I was waiting to see what would happen and who they wanted – me or Andy Gray. There was talk of a two-man 'dream team', but that possibility was never mooted to me. It's not one that I would have considered, nor is it one that Andy would have contemplated either. He wanted to be his own man and rightly so.

Andy Gray: I met Peter, and I met a couple of the other directors; not quite sure who they were at the time. I met them over in Tranmere over at his fast food place, and I spoke to them for hours. And they asked me if I was offered the Everton job what would I do? How would I see it? And I told them, and what we would need to spend I told them, they were rather shocked at what I told them. We talked for hours, and I said – I've said ever since then – had Peter Johnson ever turned to me and said, 'Okay Andy, we want you to take Everton on from here,' I'd have taken the job. I would have taken the job. I would have taken it and said, 'I don't care what Sky do, I'm taking it.' But he didn't. After two or three hours, he just said 'Thank you Andy, we have other people to talk to.' I was kind of left a little bit flat, because I was really excited, and my heart was ruling my head. I would have signed and said 'Well never mind Sky, I don't care. I've got a contract but I'm going, I'm resigning.' But he didn't. He left it and in the meantime he was leaking stories to the press about what we'd spoken about. And what he was doing was whetting Everton fans' appetite, and it was giving them the impression that I had been offered the job and I had accepted it, and that was unfair, it caused me a lot of problems with Evertonians. They felt that I was letting them down.

Graham Stuart: Andy had never been a manager. I loved Andy Gray and like him as a guy, but I remember thinking to myself, 'That's a risk because you're going into the unknown.' Because as you're a magnificent ex-Everton player, well you've never be a manager. It's a huge club to come into. Although Andy had been around football with Aston Villa, to take over the reins of Everton Football Club would have been a massive move for him.

Andy Gray: In the meantime Sky obviously found out about the meeting and offered me a contract. I hadn't heard from Everton so I signed the contract, and then about four days later Peter Johnson phones up and says, 'We'd like to talk to you about taking the job.' I said, 'Peter I can't, I've committed myself now and I can't change my mind.' And he'd left it too long, because I'd thought long and hard about it. He would like to talk to me again, and I thought, 'Well I can't, because I've signed a new deal with Sky and I've committed myself to that. I haven't heard from you, what can I do?' When I went to meet him I'd phoned a couple of guys in the game, I said to them, 'Listen, there's a chance that I might be taking Everton.' I honestly thought I'd get offered the job that day. And I said 'I want you to come with me,' I'd picked out my backroom staff, and then after it died a bit I thought, 'Okay, it's not going to happen and it didn't happen.' Admittedly it was the right club at the wrong time, that's what I would say, without a doubt. I don't think Peter at that time was doing all he could to take Everton forward, and the thought that I mentioned money to him, about transfers we'd need, Peter kind of baulked at it. That's the way it was, and it was proven that way, it was tough. Howard went in after that for a third time, and it was a real difficult time for him, and I understood why.

Andy Hinchcliffe: We just didn't expect Howard, it was completely out of the blue, because all the talk was of Andy Gray leaving Sky to come and take the Everton job, and that it was we presumed was going to be happening.

Graham Stuart: I must admit there was a smile on my face because I absolutely adore Howard, and he'd had a huge impact on my life, on and off the park. I wasn't upset to see Howard coming back.

Howard Kendall: I had no qualms about returning to Goodison, even if Andy had seemingly been Johnson's first choice. They say you should never go back, but this was the fourth time I was entering the club: once as a player and now three times as a manager. When Everton ask, as I know so well, it's very difficult to say no. The fact that I was third or fourth choice didn't really ever bother me. People say I was only asked back because I was the most successful ever Everton manager.

Neville Southall: I could see Johnson's point of view: He was a safe pair of hands and knew the club inside out.

Howard Kendall: Peter had a reputation as being an awkward chairman; meddlesome in some respects, completely hands-off in others. To me he was a stranger. I couldn't tell you what he was like because I didn't know him. I had virtually no contact with him at all. What contact I had was through the secretary Michael Dunford or his henchman Clifford Finch. It certainly wasn't the same cosy atmosphere that had predominated in the 1980s. At times it could be quite testing. I was, however, helped greatly that year by Bill Kenwright, who sat on the Everton board. He was a great ally to me, just as he remains a great ally to Everton Football Club to this day.

Tony Grant: I think with him coming back lots of us looked forward to it, I think Big Dunc was. I know I was. It was the first time I properly had him, he was only here a short while before and then went away. This time when he came back I was so looking forward to it, and I've only got great words for Howard. Training was great, everything about it was great.

Gareth Farrelly: I think the mood at that time with him coming back was always going to be a positive one. Football fans, everybody is quite funny like that – 'the king is dead, long live the king' – when a manager comes in. But I think from my side, I think if you had been subjective about it and you'd had looked at the previous seasons and the fact that it had been a struggle, you may have thought about something differently. But as I say, for me that was something that didn't even come up on the radar. It was just an opportunity to play for the club I supported.

Peter Johnson: I think we were interested in the silver haired Italian, Fabrizio Ravanelli. I was abroad to negotiate a salary and then his agent said 'Neto.' I said 'What does neto mean?' And it meant tax paid, which made a dramatic difference. You can always hide behind the pay structure, but that was ridiculous.

Howard Kendall: I took all the players to the Chinese restaurant. Slaven Bilic [who had joined from West Ham for £4.5 million while Everton were without a manager] was there, and I had a list of the other fines. And he said, 'I've got to go now; one of the kids has got to go to the dentist; I'll leave my card.' So he left his cash card in the Chinese and said, 'Give it back to me tomorrow.' Well, the Moet et Chandon came out, the lot came out. That's how much they loved him. I'm not talking about me having Moet; I'm talking about everybody having Moet. It must have cost him a small fortune, but with the amount he was earning he would hardly have noticed. That's how hard it was.

Gareth Farrelly: I think Howard was doing things exactly the same, and that was the difficulty to a degree, because the game had started to change – players had different demands, there were far more resources available. I had come from a very strict manager at Aston Villa, much more of an emphasis on lots of different things, whereas at Everton, Howard would probably say that it was a lot like the last time round, whereas the game had started to shift a little bit.

Tony Grant: Did some other clubs have better swimming pools? I mean we never had one. I'm sure they did, but I don't think it was looking back, I'm sure it was fine, training was fine. I've see lots of managers managing now, training and coaching; Howard was doing the same then. Training was fine. The top and bottom of it was that it comes down to players. How good are the players?

Gareth Farrelly: Would it be done differently now? I'd say yes, absolutely. But, that was how it was at that particular time. It wasn't something I was used to because I had been very fortunate that the people I had worked with had much more of an understanding of sports science, much more of an understanding of health, fitness and nutrition.

By November of the 1997/98 season, Everton were in deep trouble, four points adrift at the bottom of the table after a 2-0 defeat to Tottenham. After that match, 2,000 fans stayed behind to protest against Peter Johnson's ownership – it was a sign of the times. In January, Gary Speed and Andy Hinchcliffe were both sold.

Gareth Farrelly: Everyone will tell you a different story of how it can form a distraction, but it's not really one of the primary concerns for people. I think there's always a level of optimism when a manager comes in, players come in; everyone has good intentions and obviously that wasn't the case. Again, you look back and you see a demise doesn't happen overnight, there's obviously a period of years and different elements to that.

Howard Kendall: The one I get asked about today is the sale of Gary Speed to Newcastle United, then managed by Kenny Dalglish. All sorts of conspiracy theories have been bandied around about Gary's sale, most of which are nonsense. There was no real bust-up. It was a messy transfer, complicated by the fact that he was the club captain and a lifelong Everton supporter. I didn't want to lose him. He was one of my best players, my captain; someone I had made captain. It wasn't clear whether I would ever see the money his sale generated.

Thomas Myhre: I have the greatest respect for Gary, when I first came in and my girlfriend came over with me, he was the first one to say hello in the players' lounge, an absolute gentleman. But he and

Howard had their differences, and he was the captain, and of course the story of him not going on away game, because of their – what can I say? – they didn't agree on certain things. But I could never see that in the changing room, and I was new, I wasn't involved in that.

Gareth Farrelly: Gary Speed wanted to leave, which was difficult at the time. Andy Hinchcliffe was my room partner, I was sad to see him go and he was a great character around the place.

Alan Myers: I think what troubled me about Gary was that when he left, it was so misjudged by the fans. I'll never forget when he came back with Newcastle: I was on the side of the pitch, and he was getting booed as he came off back from the warm up. I went to shake his hand and put my arm around him, and he said, 'Oh, don't get yourself in bother.' I think he was really concerned how the fans would react to it. I didn't care because I knew the real Gary Speed, and I knew that one of the reasons he went is because he felt it wasn't as professional as it should've been. It was never spoken about that, and Gary genuinely did want to better Everton, because he was a real, true Evertonian.

Gareth Farrelly: Seemingly we didn't play well enough consistently enough. There were never games you went out in to where you thought you weren't going to compete or do well, but you slowly but surely got sucked into what would have been a difficult situation. Again for me, because I was younger at that time you see it differently, you're not experienced in any of that, you haven't encountered it before.

Roger Bennett: We signed Mickael Madar. No one in world football coveted this guy but he came. He was French, I think he played for the national team or was a fringe player in their international squad for the Euros, and no one coveted him until he came to Everton. As soon as he came you just pinned your hopes immediately on him, but that was the kind of players that came through. They were like the epitome of the period. Any other club he would've been some random, but when he arrived at Everton by God you were so desperate that somehow the genius would come.

Tony Grant: What I would say is that some of the young players he bought didn't hit the heights that he was expecting. He bought [John] Oster, Farrelly and [Danny] Williamson, who were three young players. So he was looking to try and build something, but they just never hit it. They found that step too hard.

Gareth Farrelly: It was a massive learning curve for me, it was incredibly difficult. It was full of contradictions – on the one hand you turn around and go 'I'm playing for the club I supported, it's the best thing ever,' but then on the other hand you're going to every game with a pressure situation like you've not really encountered before, so it creates a totally different challenge.

Tony Grant: There were some games that year where we had great games against good teams. And you're going 'Bloody hell we can play,' but we just couldn't sustain it. Sometimes that comes down to the quality of the squad. It's not actually as good as people think, and I think it catches up with you over a tough season.

Gareth Farrelly: You have to adapt, adapt how you play a little bit. Again, any given game you might start off playing really well but not score a goal and then concede one, which puts more pressure on. So, again all of those things will be thrown into the mix as to how and what. But it certainly wasn't ticky tacky, pulling your boots on and going 'This is going to be a great day today' – it certainly wasn't like that. Pressure brings challenges to different people.

10 May 1998
Everton 1, Coventry City 1

Back to back defeats to Sheffield Wednesday and Arsenal near the end of the season meant Everton needed to better the result of Bolton Wanderers – who were away to Chelsea – on the last day. Everton themselves had Coventry at home.

Thomas Myhre: We went to Wimbledon, drew 0-0, and everyone was like, 'Now we are basically clear.' Because we looked at the games we had left. But we just messed it up at the end. We lost at home to Sheffield Wednesday, who were bottom and had already been relegated, and then of course Arsenal. So it ended up going to the last day of the season, we could get relegated after looking quite safe four or five games before the end of the season.

Howard Kendall: Wins were hard to come by after Christmas. We drew a lot of matches, but there were some bad defeats as well. We lost 4-1 at home to Aston Villa and 3-1 to Sheffield Wednesday. In our penultimate game of the season Arsenal beat us 4-0 at Highbury, in the process lifting the Premier League title. That put us in the relegation places for the first time since Christmas. We were really in a lot of trouble.

Gareth Farrelly: There were different games weren't there? Sheffield Wednesday at home, I think we got beat 3-1. From my own side, Leicester City at home was a draw and I missed a chance. I joke with people now, it's one of them that comes back to me in the night – a side foot volley, and I put it over the bar. I remember thinking 'Oh my God, how?' Every game took on increased significance – Arsenal away, we got beat 4-0, which crowned them as Champions. There was that lead in where every game became 'this is a big, big game today.'

Howard Kendall: We went into the final game of the season against Coventry needing to get a result better than Bolton, who were away at Chelsea. If Bolton won, Everton were relegated.

Gareth Farrelly: Even that week was kind of surreal, because we'd obviously lost on the Sunday. There was a mini derby on the Monday, and we asked to play in it, I had only played a half against Arsenal. The irony is I'd played really well in the half but we got thumped 4-0. We beat Liverpool in the mini derby. One2One were the sponsors at the time and on Tuesday there was a corporate day out at Doncaster races, so we turned around and said 'We don't want to go the races because we want to train.' There was a day off after the races and then players were like 'We want to be in and train, Sunday is the biggest game ever.'

Alan Myers: We recorded two versions of the chairman's statement, because it was so volatile and so risky at the time: one if we'd gone down and one if we'd stayed up. And this was before the game, so you can imagine what it might have been like.

Rev. Harry Ross: One particular thing I remember about the Wimbledon and Coventry games is that the police used to come into the hall and also have their tea during the matches. After the Wimbledon game I just felt relief that we had stayed up, just pure relief. I remember being in the stand sat with the likes of John Bailey and Alan Harper. When it had finished I was grabbed by so many people hugging and kissing me, and when I got back to the church the police were there, also quite relieved that there hadn't been an problems. In contrast when I got back to the hall after the Coventry game there were the police dressed in full riot gear shields and everything, the full Robocop stuff. That rather felt like they were going too far and I think I made a complaint. It's not something the church should be used for. Alright the police can come in and use it to sit quietly and have a chat before going back on duty, but to use it as that sort of base didn't feel right, so I told them.

Howard Kendall: Sunday 10 May 1998 was the day of reckoning. Mike Walker had been in the same position four years earlier. Like him, I understood the enormity of our situation, but I think it would have been far, far worse for me than it would have been for him had we gone down given my association with the club. For me it would have been a killer. I was the most successful manager in the club's history and had a great record as a player. To be relegated was just unthinkable.

Gareth Farrelly: It was always a surreal day. From the time we left the hotel, the journey to the ground, there was people out on the street, Everton fans. The bus into the ground, there were people out already. We got into the ground – I say it to people now – the ground was full early, the women were on the pitch, the lads had won the youth cup, they were on the pitch and it just felt different.

Howard Kendall: The night before the match I had an epiphany. Gareth Farrelly couldn't find the back of the net all season. His form had been patchy and he was in and out of the side. I'd had a little meeting with my staff the night before – we stayed away from home the night before the game – and agreed on the team. Then I changed my mind during the night. I woke up and thought, 'He's due one,' and went back to sleep. I don't know for what reason, but I went down next morning to the staff and said, 'I'm playing Farrelly.'

Thomas Myhre: I had a long season in Norway and then no break. I basically played [for Everton] from November, I think I played 26 games. So I basically went on a run of 56, 57 league games plus cup games on the trot, without a break. So at the end I wasn't performing well, I was tired, at the end of the season I was looking forward to a break. But everything looked as if it was going okay, the result was going away, Gareth scored a cracking goal…

Howard Kendall: There was a tense and volatile atmosphere inside Goodison. We needed the crowd to get behind us and to do that we needed an early goal. Cometh the hour, cometh the man. Six minutes in Gareth Farrelly let fly with a shot from 25 yards that flew into the roof of the Coventry net. Goodison erupted, but we failed to settle.

Gareth Farrelly: I hit some brilliant shots that year and I hit some awful shots. Lots of awful ones, right. I made goalies look amazing, I made stewards look rather fearsome or scared. You look back now and think you have to keep going, don't you? It had been difficult that season, there was pressure but I obviously kept believing that something positive was going to happen.

Tony Grant: I was in the stands because I remember Gareth had played a few games that year, and kept shooting from 100 yards, and they were all hitting the stands. But that day it went in and it was like 'Wow.' But all that practice does pay off in the end. It was a great goal.

Alan Myers: The game swung one way, swung the other way. It was such an emotional occasion for everybody.

Gareth Farrelly: I got that opportunity by being selected, which is part of the story that Howard will tell, that I was due one or whatever. The story got better with his after dinner speaking. But if you keep going and do the right things there is a chance that it will come right, so it was massive for me. You don't think about it, or go into any great detail in your mind beforehand. There wasn't a set visualisation programme, that If I keep doing this, but it's just one of those things. You're only sat here realistically because of what happened with that.

Howard Kendall: Four minutes later Goodison was silenced. David Burrows went down the left and sent in a cross for - of all people - Dion Dublin, whose header slipped out of Thomas Myhre's grasp and into the Everton goal.

Thomas Myhre: At the end, when you could feel the atmosphere at Goodison, people are tense but the right result is coming in, but then Dion Dublin heads like a looping header which I would have saved 100 out of 100 times - I don't know what went on in my head. It was an easy save, and I basically dropped it in the goal. I was like if I could find the biggest digging machine to open the fucking ground I would have done it.

Gareth Farrelly: I look back now, we missed a penalty, Nicky Barmby, but for me that is part of the folklore around the goal. It's obviously better for me that he missed the penalty, but I would have taken the three points above that. But you obviously had what happened with Thomas then, the goal goes in and automatically everything shifts again to a state of panic. But it was a game that we should have won anyway, because if Coventry come to Goodison Park, Everton should beat Coventry. That was how you thought.

Thomas Myhre: Ball in the air, looping header, far away and I got my both my hands on the ball and it slipped through them. It went totally quiet at Goodison! I was like 'Oh, my, God, what have you just done?' But luckily it ended 1-1 and we stayed up, and I can remember all the fans coming out and tearing the pitch up: it was just weird.

Howard Kendall: The crowd howled for the final whistle and amid the screaming of whistles came another roar to signify that Jody Morris had scored a second goal for Chelsea. Moments later came the final whistle at Goodison and the players ran for the dressing room as the crowd stormed onto the pitch, singing and dancing in relief. I looked up to the stands and picked out Bill Kenwright, who gave me the thumbs-up.

Alan Myers: In the aftermath of that, when I was on the pitch with thousands of fans, and someone got hold of me by the neck and said, 'This isn't Everton,' and I'll never forget that moment. And he was right. He was being aggressive, but I had to agree with him.

Thomas Myhre: I'm just happy it didn't end up with us going down, because Everton had been up since the 1950s. So it's unthinkable, and thank God that didn't turn out to be something that sent us down, because basically I could leave Merseyside for good. Of course, it was a terrible mistake by me; no excuses. I could see Howard afterwards, the relief. He looked at me and I just held my hand up, but everyone one is buzzing in the changing room. We'd stayed up, that was it.

Gareth Farrelly: I remember sitting with the manager and just saying 'This can never happen again.'

Everyone will talk, 'Oh we went and had a brilliant night,' but it wasn't that. It was just like, 'This can't happen again, we have to be better.'

Tony Grant: I actually celebrated, I went out. I think I went down County Road. Because at the end of the day it was a crap season, and I wasn't going to go home and go 'That was a crap season.' We all know it was a crap season. But it's like winning a trophy that day, it was probably bigger than winning a trophy. So there was something to celebrate, we were celebrating staying up. In Everton's eyes that's not acceptable, but it was this year. It was acceptable this year, so we went out, and quite a few of us had a drink and enjoyed ourselves.

Gareth Farrelly: I didn't feel embarrassed, I felt relieved. At that particular moment you don't really think about the significance of the goal, you just look at it, the atmosphere was amazing, I'd never encountered an atmosphere like that because of the seriousness of the day – it's difficult to recreate or even try and articulate. But it was an amazing experience. To come through that was huge. It wasn't like lets go out and have a celebration, it was more this can't happen again.

Peter Johnson: I thought a draw would do us safe. Keeping the one point. I remember a fella running on to the roof just in front of the directors' box to attack me. I can't remember anything else.

Howard Kendall: The unrestrained joy of Goodison soon turned to anger. Before the Main Stand stood 10,000 angry fans calling for Peter Johnson's head. My team huddled in the dressing room celebrating our safety. There was, of course, nothing really to celebrate.

Peter Johnson: I think my car was attacked outside. But the board are not actively trying to get their teams down, they are trying to win. I suppose there was a flag going round, 'Agent Johnson, come home, mission accomplished.'

Thomas Myhre: He wasn't wanted by the fans. They didn't think he was an Evertonian, that he put his money in the club, things like that. When I came I didn't know much about it, but I knew it was in the background. As a player you don't get involved in that part of the business.

Gareth Farrelly: I think there was always that underlying current there, Johnson obviously had his own thoughts on that, which transpired after that.

Peter Johnson: I've been around football long enough to know sack the board is a demand. Of course Kendall and Carter had it, 'Kendall and Carter out.' And then they saved themselves at Oxford with an equaliser and the rest is history. It went from there to there.

Howard Kendall: Four weeks after the Coventry game, the board met and backed Peter Johnson in a decision he had made to sack me. The first I knew about it was when a journalist phoned me on holiday in Spain to ask me for my reaction to the rumours. News had been leaked to the press and Johnson was meant to meet or phone me to tell me it was all over but that never happened. It wasn't very nice being left to answer speculation about my own future.

Peter Johnson: I suppose it can always be handled better.

Howard Kendall: I was still in Spain when I received instructions to fly out to meet Johnson at a hotel near Lake Como. So I made the long journey across Europe to go and see him. I got there expecting the worst, but what followed was just the strangest meeting. There was a plate of sandwiches awaiting me, and he offered me one. I declined. We chatted in general terms for 20 or so minutes, and I sat there waiting for him to sack me. But he didn't. It was as if he was unable to face up to doing so. I returned to England in this kind of limbo. I had to wait several weeks for the telephone call that told me I would no longer be manager of Everton Football Club. A total of six and a half weeks had passed between the Coventry City game and the day of my dismissal, 24 June 1998.

Thomas Myhre: He was fantastic to me, I think everyone who has played with Howard and had a career with Everton absolutely adored him. What he has done for the club has been fantastic. I only had him for that half a season, a bit more, but he became like a father figure for many of the players. For me as well, that short spell in which he was there, so I was very sad to see him go.

Howard Kendall: I don't ever regret going back to manage Everton for a third time. What I didn't like was the manner in which I left. If Johnson and Clifford Finch didn't think I was the right man to manage the club then I felt the least they could have done was come out and say it to me. They didn't have to put me through that time. When people are coming up to you – your own players – asking what is going on, and you're not able to tell them, then it's a terrible thing. They're undermining you and your position as manager by not coming out and telling you their intentions. It got worse than that during the summer of 1998. I felt undermined not just as a manager, but as a person too. I was hurt, no doubt about that. It didn't sour my love of football or Everton – nothing could ever do that – but I do think it dimmed my relationship with managing.

Walter Smith

On 1 July, 1998, the former Glasgow Rangers manager, Walter Smith, was unveiled as Howard Kendall's successor as Everton boss. He brought with him his long-term assistant, Archie Knox. The pair had a formidable pedigree, having won seven consecutive Scottish Championships after succeeding Graeme Souness at Ibrox in 1991. Only in their final year had they conceded that crown.

Walter Smith: I was at the World Cup in France, and I got a contact from Sheffield Wednesday and on the same day Everton, so that was effectively the first contact we had. I made an arrangement to fly home and go and see the people at Sheffield Wednesday. On my way down there I got a phone call to ask if I would be happy to go to Everton to meet the people there. So I went and met the people at Sheffield Wednesday, and then I went to meet Peter Johnson.

Peter Johnson: I thought it was a good couple. Good pair. But one man's meat is another man's poison, so there were fans that didn't want him and fans that did – you can't do right for doing wrong. I thought it was a good coupling.

Walter Smith: I mean no disrespect to Sheffield Wednesday, but Archie and I were of the same mind that Everton were a traditional club, a football club that you respected from the outside. That for me was a big attraction.

Michael Ball: I remember Jimmy Martin going 'Bloody hell they're good aren't they?' Little staff comments here and there – they were totally different to what we'd had before; Mike Walker, Joe Royle, Howard.

Peter Johnson: I do believe if you're manager of Celtic or Rangers, you've got to work hard not to win the league and the cup between them. I could see him getting success at Everton as he had at Ibrox.

Michael Ball: You could see what they were trying to do. You could see the reasons behind the training methods, the training styles. But he was tough, pre-season was tough. They were doing it for the right reasons. We used to have to go in with suits on every day at Bellefield. 'A normal man would have to go to work 9-5 in a suit, so why should you be so different?' So he brought that in. I think he spent his first two days, looking out the window at Bellefield, looking on us coming in as tramps with shorts and flip flops and thinking, 'What the fuck have I got in here?' So that got changed after day one.

Richard Dunne: They were disciplined. They wanted us to wear shirts and trousers into training every day. But I didn't think they were over the top in any way, they were fair and they stuck to the rules at times and at other times they let them go and had a laugh with the players. I thought the two of them were sound; very approachable and dead chatty and nice. If you do break the rules or annoy them, well then, they're the manager and it's the right for them to have a go at them.

Tomasz Radzinski: I think it was a great pair; Walter Smith being a very calm guy and explaining everything calmly, and Archie Knox was the complete opposite, throwing some rather unusual vocabulary around. I had to get a dictionary from some guys! It was intense, which is a good thing. You're always looking up to the gaffer, you're always looking up to Walter Smith, he's the one who's choosing the team. He's the one who's placing the team on the pitch. And then you have a guy who is either running you silly or screaming at you, for no apparent reason sometimes, sometimes very rightfully so. So I did think it was a very nice combination of managers.

Peter Clarke: Were they a good cop, bad cop pairing? Both, I think, were tough: hard men, hard characters. Walter had a bit of a softer side, Archie was a real tough disciplinarian, a tough task master. But at the same time the two of them if you gave your all, if you gave everything, you gave as good as you got, were respectful and carried yourself in a right and proper manner, they had time for you. Certainly they were two tough men, two tough men to please, but perhaps that builds character.

Richard Dunne: Archie's baseball bat? I never saw it, thank God. The thing is is that they were so successful at Rangers that they wanted that same success and they were probably disappointed that we never achieved it. But they weren't bad people. They were nice fellas and they were strong. They commanded respect and they got that. But I wouldn't ever say that they were crazy with baseball bats or overdisciplined. They were good, they were just trying to do their best.

Michael Ball: He said, 'I haven't come down here to just be numbers, I want to be successful. I've got a good record in Scotland, I don't want to be ruining that.'

Walter Smith: When I went to meet Peter Johnson, he said to me that that he was under a bit of pressure, but he wanted to give it one last go. And he was prepared to spend. It worried me a little bit that a couple of other managers had turned down the job, but when I met him he seemed sincere enough in terms of putting more money into the club, which ultimately he did do. I think that was the start of his downfall. I think that behind the scenes he didn't have the money, but after saying he was going to spend the money, not just to me, but to supporters, to everybody else. So we went there hoping that we would have an initial spend to take Everton from the position they had been in – not just in the previous season, but they had been struggling in the bottom half of the league [for some years].

David Unsworth: Walter had come in, and he'd come in with a promise of a transfer kitty, transfer budget of whatever it was. Olivier Dacourt came in, John Collins came in, I came in. Walters' reputation in Scotland was second to none; I really enjoyed playing for Walter. Archie Knox, great coach. It felt like this was a team that was going to have a go.

Walter Smith: Initially we got an influx of players, and during the early part of that season, for having a new team, we actually started, I would have thought, fairly well. In fact really well, for trying to knit a new team together and get everybody together. And [Peter Johnson] did spend money, which he had promised to do.

Michael Ball: At the time I didn't really like it, because I was the young Scouser and the coach was turning French. I didn't know what was going on in team meetings. But I could understand it from their point of view as well. Olivier Dacourt, Marco Materazzi. Olivier Dacourt was a really good lad, he got himself involved with everyone. But I think English football or the club itself wasn't ready to embrace foreigners, to get them to settle. They sort of got left to their own devices.

Thomas Myhre: I'm not sure how many foreigners Walter had at Rangers, but I think he was used to having a few foreigners. He bought foreign players in that didn't settle in the team, it didn't matter how good they were playing wise, they didn't settle with the English players. It was an English club.

Michael Ball: When we were on the coach, it'd be John Collins, Materazzi, Dacourt, all taking French. So we tried to ban them: 'Speak English so we know what's going on.' But that's hard. Nowadays you just let them get on with it; whatever you feel comfortable with. But back then it was sort of like, 'You've got to do this, do it this way.' And Archie made sure they had to do it.

Archie Knox: Another handicap for these foreign players at that time, which I don't think will be the same now because they're all preparing to want to come to England, was that none of these guys spoke English. Materazzi, Bakayoko, Dacourt, they didn't speak English. We got a lecturer from Manchester University to go and live with these lads full time. He was absolutely remarkable. He had them writing and speaking in English inside a month.

Tony Grant: He brought Dacourt in, who I have lots of time for, I loved Olly and thought he was a great player. Big Marco [Materazzi]. I got on well with Marco. Marco was only young and I was young, and he was living in town. Marco was really homesick, that was the problem with Marco, he just mentally couldn't settle. And we never saw the best of Marco at all, he had all the ingredients, he was massive. It was a great buy, it was just that it didn't work, because the guy was really homesick.

Walter Smith: The whole thing for all these guys was new. The same situation still applies these days.

There's a lot more foreign players playing in every country in the world. Back then it was a change for all these guys, so the first three or four months that you're there and you're forming a team, there's a lot going on within your club that isn't just on the field. If you take the foreign players – Materazzi, Dacourt, Bakayoko – they weren't experienced professional players. A lot of clubs now are bringing in players at the very top level who are experienced and now can handle the circumstances of going and playing in amongst them.

David Unsworth: The shift in mental attitude, mental toughness certainly came in when some of the foreign players [arrived]. A lot of the players around that time wouldn't play unless they were a hundred percent fit. Now that's a real shift from the mentality of what I was brought up on, of, 'You just get on with it; you just take something for it or have a jab and you just get on with it, and you just do whatever you can to just get out there.' There was a shift in attitude to, 'Well, I'm not a hundred percent; I'm not risking it.'

Thomas Myhre: You can imagine Marco Materazzi coming in at Bellefield and into the canteen, and all they would have is poached eggs on toast and beans, and that was it. They were used to pasta and things, and I think the French guys couldn't even understand how people could eat what we ate up in that canteen, but that was typical English. Cup of tea, beans on toast, that was the thing. I think it was a bit of a culture clash.

Walter Smith: That was a part of every football club's circumstances at the time. I was at Rangers for instanc and you tried to give them reasonably healthy food, but the majority of the guys are British, right? They're British. You have what you were brought up with. Italians have different ways. The advent of sports science and nutrition, and all the different aspects of it, but at the time none of us had that. And you can say that foreign managers have brought it in, but that's not the case, it has happened on a natural basis.

Michael Ball: We were training twice a day as well, and it was difficult for Archie to try and get that transition, with where the club was at and what they wanted it. They had hit the heights with Rangers, a massive, massive football club. So they had the resources and experience of playing in Europe and the Europeans; they had a lot of foreigners up there. They knew, they had their experience. Down here we were still a typical English, traditional club.

Walter Smith: We knew the problem, the players who were already there and under contract, they were injured, not playing, or we were unhappy with. That's a major part of taking over a club. That's why the first season's always an extremely difficult one. You've got a dressing room that's a little bit unhappy, they know you're not really interested in keeping them, and the other half are just knew and want to get on and do well. But that's the circumstances we had.

Archie Knox: We had a circumstance at the club where we had a lot of players, about nine players when we arrived there, earning a lot of money. They had paid a lot of money in transfer fees for them, and the first two years Walter was there they hardly put a first team jersey on. Slaven Bilic came back from the '98 World Cup injured and hardly played at all, and there was a load of players like that.

Walter Smith: Materazzi and Dacourt went on to have international careers for their countries – they were younger then. They came to Everton the same way we came to Everton, thinking they were joining a really terrific club with a great background to it, and they were going to go forward and enhance their career. Obviously after a three or four-month period it was obvious to them that that wasn't going to be the case – it was obvious to everybody that wasn't going to be the case for a long period of time.

The sale of Duncan Ferguson and end of Peter Johnson

Not until 23 November 1998, did Goodison witness its first Everton league goal of the season when a Michael Ball penalty saw off Newcastle United in front of the Sky cameras. But behind the secnes another story was unfolding: the club's talisman, Duncan Ferguson, was being sold.

Alan Myers: The press room was going crazy with the rumours that Duncan Ferguson was being sold to Newcastle. So, I went down and spoke to [the club secretary] Michael Dunford, and I said, 'Is this right?' And he said to me, 'Rubbish, Mr Myers, rubbish!' I'll never forget those words. So, I went back up to the press room and I said, 'It's absolute rubbish. No, it's not true.' Everyone was quite shocked, because I was so strong about it. On the way back down the stairs, there's a little chairman's office, sort of a match day's chairman's office, which was hardly ever used, but it's on the first floor as you go up in Goodison Park and I saw the door was slightly ajar, which was unusual for that office, because it was private. I wanted to make sure nobody was in there messing about, so I pushed the door open a little bit more to look in, and sitting in the office was Ruud Gullit, Duncan Ferguson, and his agent, and they were actually signing a contract. And you can imagine how I felt after just literally seconds coming down the stairs, having told the media that it was absolute rubbish. Within 15, 20 minutes, during the second half, Duncan left reception, got into a car across the road by the Winslow and drove off, with people shouting after him, 'Don't go! Don't go!' It was proper emotional stuff.

Walter Smith: I was doing a Sky interview after the match and the guy asked me a question. He said, 'There's rumours here that Duncan Ferguson has been transferred to Newcastle.' Well it would be the first that I'd ever heard it as a manager, Archie was the same. So I went back into the dressing room where [Newcastle manager] Ruud Gullit came in for a drink. We never mentioned this transfer or anything. And we were going upstairs to get our wives and as we were walking up the stairs Duncan came down.

Archie Knox: His words were, 'I thought you would have tried harder to keep me.' And I'm saying 'Keep you where? What are you talking about?'

Walter Smith: We had no idea.

Archie Knox: He said he'd been transferred to Newcastle. So it was like: we need to go and have a word about this and see what happens!

Alan Myers: There was a press release sent over. Walter didn't want it sent out, and the chairman was telling me to get it out. I didn't know what to do for the best, and so I hid in the toilet! Everyone was looking for me, because the chairman was going mad, wanting to know why the press release hadn't gone out. I was too worried about what Walter and Archie would do to me if I put it out. The trials and tribulations of a press officer! I just literally didn't know what to do, so the only thing I could do was hide in the toilet.

Walter Smith: You felt foolish as the manager of the club. If Peter Johnson had sat us down and said 'I've made a pig's ear of this, I've got to transfer this player, we need this money' then I said I would have said 'Well okay, there's not a lot we could have done about it.' But not telling us, that was a different aspect.

Peter Johnson: Walter and I had a slightly different opinion on how it happened and what happened.

Walter Smith: I came back and said, 'Jesus.' I don't think either of us had ever experienced a position like that before. So the next day I was hauled into a board meeting, and I don't think anybody, even the other board members, believed that we didn't know anything about the transfer. It was one of those, it was a really awkward circumstance, and left me in a situation where I said to myself, 'What am I going to do here?' I'd never been in a position before where I didn't know what to do, to be quite honest with you. So I said to myself, 'He obviously doesn't have enough trust in me to tell me he had to transfer a player.' That was one thing. Then the overriding factor for us in all the talks, was we had bought quite a lot of players in to play at the club and then at the first sign of a problem you're being seen to get up and go off.

Alan Myers: I think as it transpired, whether it was right or wrong, the chairman got the blame, which put him in a weakened position – as weak as he'd been – and he had been weak at times. As far as the fans were concerned, and in terms of holding onto the club, I think that was the sort of the straw that broke the camel's back. I think he realised that the game was up.

Phil McNulty: In the office as that story was developing, you thought, 'Well, two things are going to happen here: either the manager will go, or the chairman will go.' The environment around the club at the time, the way people were feeling about Peter Johnson; Walter had only just arrived, so there was a reservoir of goodwill for him. He had brought quality players into the club in Dacourt, Collins, Materazzi, etc. So, the force was with Walter, if you like, rather than Peter Johnson. You sat there at your desk thinking, 'Well, either *he's* going to go, or *he's* going to go.' The town would not be big enough for the two of them. And in the end, it was the chairman who went, which is an unusual turn of events. But I think by that time, Peter probably had enough of Everton and the stress it was bringing him.

Dave Prentice: My acting editor at the *Echo*, Tony Storey, wouldn't believe that a player could be sold without the manager's knowledge. He said, 'The Echo's stance on this was the manager must have known. Unless you can prove that to me otherwise that's what we've got to write.' So I went down to see Walter and said 'My editor won't believe you didn't know anything about it.' His reaction was sensational. He just went insane. 'Get that fucking twit on the phone and I'll tell him what's going on!' And I'm sat there and there's this absolutely incendiary manager ringing and slamming the phone down, ringing and slamming the phone down. Either he was a sensational actor or he genuinely was so, so angry. In the end I said, 'Look, I believe you, I believe you. I'll go back, and convince the editor that you were unaware.'

Alan Myers: The next morning, we had an emergency board meeting over at Park Foods. I went over with Walter in his car, and I went and sat outside until they asked me into the boardroom, and Peter Johnson went in, and within five minutes, Peter Johnson come out and said to me, 'Okay, Alan, you come with me.' So, off we went in his car, up to Oxton, his house, and we then sat there – well, I sat there – for about four hours on the settee with nobody. The only person that came in was his housekeeper, and she kept coming in making me tea and biscuits and toast. I'm thinking 'What's going on?' I sat there for about four hours. So, then, Peter showed up again with [his partner] Lorraine Rogers and he said,

'What do you think?' I said, 'They're not happy, you know, because Duncan's gone,' and he said, 'Well, I'll be in Jersey in an hour,' and that was the last we saw of him. He went that day.

Walter Smith: We were in that awkward situation. After speaking to the board, and then finally clarifying everything, we played at Charlton the following Saturday, and I met Sir Philip Carter and Peter Johnson, and the chairman said he didn't tell me, he didn't want to tell me, he thought I'd hear from other people. Anyway, I didn't. So that was that, and after a bit of discussion between everybody, Archie and I felt that after bringing a lot of players together it would be the wrong for us to go. And the club was good wasn't it?

Archie Knox: Great club.

Alan Myers: Peter had a really good sense of humour and I had a lot of time for him. He had a home in Jersey and for some reason the *Liverpool Echo* was always popular on the island. He told me this story about how he used to go down to the port when the ferry used to come in and pick up the paper. One day he went down in a wooly hat and a big coat. The guy who was unloading the papers threw the bundle onto the quayside and they landed with the sports pages up and there he was on the back page. The fella looks down at the paper and says, 'This twat lives here!' Peter just mumbled something like, 'Ah, right!' and went on his way.

Everton in limbo: November 1998-December 1999

Peter Johnson put the club up for sale, but there was a surfeit of buyers. Bill Kenwright, whom he had defeated in a takeover bid in 1994, put together a consortium to buy Johnson's shares, but it was a full 13 months before a deal was concluded.

Walter Smith: The financial side of the club started to come to the fore. Peter left and put the club up for sale, and it was that way for about the next 14 months. So when the bank came in to take over, it was one of those things where we had to get on with it and we actually ended up having to sell players.

Bill Kenwright: Four years later, with Everton in more or less the same position, I said to Jenny, 'What would you think if...' She said, 'Listen, you're crazy but it's your life.' I just said, 'It's in trouble, and I've got quite a lot of letters from the fans, and in particular one group that I admired called the Independent Supporters. And the club was not in a good way.' So that's when that one started.

Alan Myers: There was a sort of an impasse. It wasn't long after that when Peter said that he would be selling the club now. And then it was Christmas Eve 1999, when Bill took over the club. It was an odd time.

Archie Knox: You look at the transfers we had at that particular time, and you think Materazzi, Dacourt, a wee bit later on Michael Ball, Richard Dunne, Francis Jeffers, a hell of a lot of money came in.

Walter Smith: We had a lot of good young players that I'm sure would have been happy to stay at Everton if everything had been okay. I think effectively Peter Johnson had just had enough. It's difficult when you're the owner of a club. I mean I don't think that he had any badness or anything like that.

He would have wanted Everton to do well in his initial stages. I must admit I was hoping that we could have formed a decent relationship, and maybe got the club back with his help.

Phil McNulty: Peter Johnson was someone who, ultimately, people were critical of, including myself, but I always felt that his intentions were good. He was genuinely out to make Everton a force and to do the things and provide the finances that would do so. It didn't work out, but I don't ever think at any stage Peter Johnson's intentions were bad. There was all this 'Agent Johnson' business. I don't believe for one second anyone would be as stupid to do anything like that.

Dave Prentice: They were strange times. Very very optimistic times at first under Johnson, but it got to the point where the banks could quite well have foreclosed on the club and they could have been grim and terrible.

David Weir: I think when there's a negative or a flux associated with the club, it's an excuse for the players. It's an excuse for the players not to perform. At a football club the focus should always be on the football, on the pitch, but it seemed like at the time that more of the stories where associated with what was happening off the pitch. It can be a distraction, but it can also be an excuse.

Patrick Hart: You wanted an end to the Johnson thing, because it had gone on for too long and the club was struggling, they were in a mess. They beat Sunderland 5-0 on Boxing Day, and it seemed a new dawn. It didn't last that long, the new dawn. At the time you thought 'Okay, that's the end of a dark time, and at least there's a possibility that something good will come'. But it didn't really materialise.

Mike Hughes: Peter Johnson gets some stick from Everton fans and if you look at what happened maybe with some justification. But it isn't anything he wanted to happen. He did a great job at Tranmere and he knew that Everton was a much much bigger job and he fell in love with the whole idea. I think he had great ideas for Everton but I think he actually saw that the writing was on the wall for him financially. Let's be honest, he was a businessman who made a lot of money. I know the word 'project' is used far too often these days but he saw Everton as a sleeping giant that he could reawaken. But a very easy way to lose money is to buy a football club. I think that Peter Johnson saw that he was haemorrhaging money and being criticised left, right and centre and I think he just wanted out.

Peter Johnson: I thought it was a good experience. I enjoyed being chairman. My two proudest moments are on photographs: holding the cup at Goodison when we brought it back, I was very proud of that, and very proud of receiving the freedom of the city on behalf of Everton. First time both the big clubs have been managed and owned by Scousers: Roy Evans, Joe Royle, me and David Moores. That was a super moment. I did enjoy it. Intense. And until it started getting nasty it was very enjoyable.

The class of '98

Although Walter Smith had an unwelcome inheritance at Goodison, he was blessed with Everton's most outstanding crop of youngsters in a generation. Led by legendary Colin Harvey, a team consisting of players such as Leon Osman, Tony Hibbert, Richard Dunne, Francis Jeffers and Danny Cadamarteri secured the FA Youth Cup crown with a 5-3 win over Blackburn Rovers on aggregate the previous spring.

Colin Harvey: When I went back there was some very, very good players. You're talking about Franny Jeffers, Danny Cadamarteri, Richard Dunne. Phil Jevons, who never went on to be really top class but was good. A kid called Jamie Milligan, who was one of the best footballers I'd seen. Adam Farley was a decent player as well. There were some very, very good players. We had a very good side.

Leon Osman: I'd played in the year above since I was 11, and then I went down into my own age group and it was so competitive and so good, the standard was so high all the way through. We used to win most of our games every weekend. We played our games on a Sunday. We used to win pretty much every weekend. You just become used to winning.

Richard Dunne: We had some very good players who didn't make football as a career but we were just a good bunch. We all got on well and I think that helps. We all respected each other and we all played for each other and we all enjoyed a good laugh in the dressing room. I mean we'd be there from 9am to 4:30pm, 5pm some days, doing little jobs around the place. But we all just got on with it, we were all similar sort of personalities and we all mixed well.

Adam Farley: Everton produce these players because they make you welcome. You enjoy your football, there's no cliques like at Liverpool like I can remember, it's just a nice place to be at Everton, and we all got on as a team. We knew we were going to win the Youth Cup when we beat Blackpool in the first round. We just knew that we were going to go all the way because you looked around at the players we had, it was unbelievable.

Tony Hibbert: When we won it I was playing the year above. We won it with Mick O'Brien and Phil Jevons. [Danny] Cadamarteri, and [Richard] Dunney, and I think [Michael] Bally could have played for us, but obviously he never. They had some good lads back then. My normal year I think we had a stronger team and we should have won it with the players we had, we had a great team. But obviously we didn't. But growing up through it was brilliant, a brilliant experience in the two years when we won it and got to the quarters with my year. It was a great experience, playing against some great teams as well.

Danny Cadamarteri: I remember our semi-final was probably tougher than the final itself. We played against Leeds in our semi-final and we did bully them, we outmuscled them, we outran them, we outfought them, and then when they got tired and ran out of steam we outplayed them. But the Leeds game was a lot tougher game than when we played in the final.

Leon Osman: The scouting department got a great bunch of lads in. We had coaches of the standard of Colin Harvey; being the first team manager, come down and be our under-18s coach, which was unbelievable for us as youth team players coming through, and that was one of the main things that happened to us.

Colin Harvey: Richard was probably the most successful, because he had a really good career at Man City. The others were very, very good, but they weren't as good as Kevin Ratcliffe [and his generation: Graeme Sharp, Gary Stevens, Kevin Richardson, Paul Lodge, Brian Borrows and Martin Hodge] Kevin Ratcliffe and them were top class. Really top class.

Leon Osman: We were sort of shifted from pillar to post at times. We went to Dunnings Bridge Road, in Netherton, where that Goals facility is now. We trained there for a while but the building was derelict and falling down. Some stories about things going on there are ridiculous, with the building, we should have never been allowed near it. So then we ended up moving over to the Civil Service Club at Thornton, where we got changed there and drove back to Netherton. Then it became too difficult, so we stayed at Netherton and got changed and ate there.

Adam Farley: We won the Youth Cup and Howard was manager at the time, and to be honest the majority of us knew we were going to get our chance the following year. Howard got the sack, Archie and Walter came in, and it was just a different set up altogether when they came in because we were training with the first team prior to all them coming in. We were sent down to a place in Netherton training with the kids. Gareth Farrelly, John Oster, John O'Kane: they were all sent down to train there as well. It was no good for anyone really.

Leon Osman: I was always frustrated certainly by the fact that you know you looked around at other youth teams – and I'm not saying we were as good as the '92 Youth Cup-winning team that Man United had or Liverpool's a couple of years later – and they then got a few players into the first team. Once you've won the Youth Cup there's obviously a few talented lads there that can make the grade. And at the time we were languishing at the bottom of the league regularly, so there was obviously the quality there to be brought through, but instead Walter Smith chose to separate us.

Tony Hibbert: I think the situation with the club financially wise and the managerial side of things round then, I think Everton were just looking for a quick fix, and I think there is a lot of pressure on a manager to let the kids come through. It's a big gamble. I think if you can go out and look for a quick fix, it's a lot easier as a manager.

Michael Ball: He just wanted to deal with the players who were going to do a job for him on the pitch. So as a man, or as a footballer, just take it, it's football's decision, so just get on with it.

Leon Osman: Walter used a couple of the youth team players that had won the Youth Cup, but it was to make up the numbers, it was usually when no one else was there, it was a last-minute substitution or what have you.

Tony Hibbert: I made my debut under Walter so I've got a lot to thank him for, obviously. Farls [Adam Farley] made his debut, there was a few, but not really – you would have thought more of us should have come through as a group, as a unit. There were dribs and drabs, but I think that was just the situation and the era the club was in.

Leon Osman: He ended up selling, or not using the Youth Cup players and bringing in the likes of Richard Gough, David Ginola. I've got nothing particularly against them older lads, but Goughy was 40. And to be honest to bring Goughy in, not a problem, because again you're learning from better players, but it certainly stopped the progression of young players. It was short-term players he was bringing in and stopping the progression of the long-term players that could have maybe had a chance.

Colin Harvey: I'm always a believer that if you're good enough and you work hard enough, you'll make it. I don't care what the manager thinks. If you're good enough, and you work hard enough, and you get your chance, you'll take it.

Campbell saves the day

Everton found themselves nine points from the traditional safety mark of 40 points with an entire ten games to play in the 1998/1999 season. But in the time honored tradition of the 1990s they suddenly became embroiled in a relegation battle. They were bolstered by the transfer deadline day signings of Scott Gemmill and, most significantly, the former Arsenal centre-forward, Kevin Campbell, on loan from Turkish club, Trabzonspor.

Kevin Campbell: I think it was experience that the team lacked. To get a short-term fix was the issue because at the time I think the team were doing okay but they had two youngsters upfront: Danny Cadamarteri and Francis Jeffers. So not really much experience – good young players but not really much experience for the run in of the season.

Walter Smith: I think in Kevin's case he wasn't getting paid in Turkey or something like that [he had been racially abused by the Trabzonspor chairman] and they were going to spark whatever legislation FIFA had in place, that if you don't get paid so many times you get released from your contract, but the club are still duty-bound to pay you. Whatever technicalities it was. So somebody came up and said you can get him on loan because Trabzonspor want to alleviate the wage bill. We got him over and he was terrific for us, he was a great lad. He did great for us.

Michael Ball: Walter bought in a lot of senior pros. I always had mixed issues with them all. I think we had two young kids from Barcelona on trial, two small stocky lads, and they ripped us apart in training. I went 'Bloody hell these are good.' I don't know if they were twins or brothers or something, but they were really good. Then the week after Kevin Campbell came in for a trial, he'd been training on his own at Lilleshall, and he didn't do anything. I thought 'He's not going to sign,' and next minute he's our saviour! That's why I'm not a manager, because I would have picked the two kids and we probably would have been relegated.

Kevin Campbell: The second game was Sheffield Wednesday at home. I remember we took the lead, Franny Jeffers scored. 1-0 at half-time but we gave two gifts to Benito Carbone. They beat us 2-1 and then we dropped into the bottom three then. But the actual makings of the team was pretty good. We had good experience in there, and as far as I was concerned it was just a matter of time, but then at that time we only had six games to go.

Archie Knox: Jeffers was a very clever player. He could stay clear of the physical contact and stuff like that and bop in round about the box. He was a really good finisher. Kevin Campbell would be able to hold things and maybe slip a pass in, or out wide and Jeffers was a fox in the box if you like who could get on the end of stuff.

Tony Grant: No one really plays with two up top now do they? In them days everyone played with two, or your number 10 was a proper number 10. They bounced off each other and worked really well together. Franny was bright as a button, and he could finish.

Kevin Campbell: At the time we were playing three at the back and five across the midfield. So there was plenty of support for the front boys, which really helped. Because a lot of the time what happens is, the front player or the front players get isolated, the team gets stretched and the defenders and the midfield sit back. So you know it's like two players against eight, and it never works. But it was quite an aggressive system and we did pretty well from there. It was quite an aggressive system, and that was good.

Thomas Myhre: Kevin came and scored goals straight away. He was the nicest man on earth, a really good guy. Successful from day one after coming from a bit of a bad period in Turkey. We were relieved to have them, and I remember that last game of the season we beat West Ham 6-0 at Goodison. We struggled scoring that season and suddenly we started scoring goals.

Kevin Campbell: The thing is I'm a bit of an all-rounder. Playing in the first half of my career, I used to hunt space. And then obviously when Ian Wright joined Arsenal I had to revise my game to be better with my back to goal. So I could do both, and that really worked out. So whoever I played with, I could be the opposite. Playing with Franny, I recognised he had a fantastic knack of playing on the shoulder. So if he's got a knack of playing on the shoulder I've just got to make sure to get the ball in that space. He's sharp and he's quick, so you've got to know your strike partner. That's what I know very quickly – what to do with him. Obviously if he's getting a lot of the ball where he's happy, he's going to give me balls where I'm going to be happy. So that's the sign of a good partnership.

Michael Ball: Kev just brought that experience in. He was a leader, Kev, but in a nice way. He was a gentleman, and he pointed everyone in the right direction. 'Just do this. This is what works for me, so if you try and do this for me.' And then Franny was his legs and his brains around him. Kev could hold the ball up; he was an easy target for myself to try and find and Franny could work off Kev, and they had a great little understanding and relationship.

Kevin Campbell: That's something that's kind of been forgotten in the game. When you're an older player you've got to put your arm around the youngsters and actually teach them, because unless you teach them and show them what's right, they're never going to know.

Leon Osman: He really did welcome you. You didn't feel awkward, you didn't feel out of place when you were in Kev's company. So I can understand how Franny and certainly Wayne Rooney sort of found it easy to go and play their football in the first team. They were under Kev's wing at that point because he's really good at that.

Kevin Campbell: Even when we hit the bottom three, there was still a good team spirit. The fans were amazing. It gives you give confidence when you've got good players around you, especially as a striker, I knew I was going to get chances. When you know you're going to get chances as a striker, you fancy yourself. Luckily enough I hit the ground running and after six games, after the final six games, I ended up with 9 goals in 8 games, which was great.

Bill Kenwright takes charge

On Christmas Eve 1999 it was announced that Bill Kenwright's True Blue Holdings Consortium – consisting of Kenwright, the builder, Arthur Abercrombie, software developer, Jon Woods, and businessman Paul Gregg – had completed their takeover of the club. The price was said to be £30 million.

Jon Woods: James Clement Baxter in 1892 lent a thousand pounds interest free to build Goodison. He is my first cousin thrice removed, so a blood relative and a founder shareholder. So there's your history, and the family have held shares ever since, and still do. There was only 2,500 shares but he had a fair chunk, which I eventually got. Whilst I held 200, I bought the bulk of them. But it pales into insignificance in to the numbers I bought in 2000. What it means is that the family have held a shareholding in this club as a founder member of the Football League, and here I am today and there's no one else, because every other founder club – the Accrington's and the Villa's and whoever else – they've all changed hands.

Mike Hughes: We were just ready to go home because it was Christmas Eve when the story broke that Everton were being taken over Bill Kenwright and his consortium. Bill had tried to put together different consortiums in the past and it hadn't happened but he managed to come up with the right sort of money this time. He'd scrimped to get the money in place that Peter Johnson wanted and it all became so very very different overnight. When Bill came in it was like – from an Everton fans' perspective – a breath of fresh air to have somebody who absolutely and utterly believed in the club. He was fantastic. It pains me to see the criticism that Bill Kenwright's had down the years by people who really really should know better because all he's ever had is the idea of making Everton better.

Jon Woods: The Johnson regime was selling his entire block of shares. And I knew Bill, but I didn't know him particularly that well, and it came about that I'd heard he'd done what he'd done, and so I joined the group, as did Paul Gregg, and Arthur Abercrombey. So, as a block, we held these shares as a block in one entity, giving us not quite 75%. In my case and in Bill's case and in Arthur's case it was for the love of the club. I'm not sure about Paul Gregg, I think he had another angle. But he'd just come into money, sold his business and was in entertainment.

Walter Smith was allowed to spend relatively freely in the transfer market during the summer of 2000 in lieu of an impending deal with NTL – a telecommunications company – who were taking a shareholding in the club. But in October the deal collapsed at the eleventh hour, leaving another gaping hole in the Goodison finances.

Bill Kenwright: Part of the thinking behind the takeover, was that it was the time when the media groups like Granada, Sky, VSB, NTL, were buying percentages of football clubs – ten percent, so they could have a good seat at the table, basically. We'd done a deal with NTL and we were getting an investment of over £30 million, exactly the same as Arsenal's. [Former Arsenal director] David Dein was my best mate and we did exactly the same deal – they did it with Granada I think, we did it with NTL; and they went bust, literally three hours before we were supposed to sign. These deals take months and months of legals and paperwork, and my office, my desk was falling to pieces under the weight of the documents. I always had Sky on, and I saw Keith Harris on the steps of somewhere – he was the chairman of Football League – saying NTL had pulled out of sponsorship of the Football League, and I thought, 'That's ominous.' Then I got the phone call saying our signing is off. So, we then had to go instantly and borrow that money, because we had no cushion, and for Walter to get players; and that's what we did.

Walter Smith: Bill's consortium took over; they were the only people that wanted to buy Everton at the time. Initially on the back of the deal with NTL, we brought in some other players. He brought that, and therefore they were hopeful. Almost immediately NTL withdrew the deal. So they had somewhere in the region of £50 million [it was reported to be £20 million at the time] I'm not saying promised to them; that was the deal that was withdrawn. They didnae have that. So we had tarted up the stadium, we had done everything else, and then all of a sudden that money wasn't there. So we were back to the situation we were in at that the previous time.

Jon Woods: We'd had the internet boom and bust by then, because that was March 2000, April 2000 when it fell off the cliff. NTL were taking stakes in Newcastle, various clubs. And I'm not sure quite sure we would have been top of the list then. They would have been knocking the door down at Leeds, perhaps, Newcastle and the obvious, Man United, but not Man City then and so on. And they were basically giving decent money for about 10% [stake]. It never happened. We didn't get it. We didn't do a deal.

Bill Kenwright: If you can imagine having your home and your mortgage with no income whatsoever. It's when you've got an overdraft, massive, and expectations, and you're losing money – because football clubs, not just Everton, lost money – and as the years progressed our losses were exactly the interest on our loans. So even when we did well under David Moyes and we got into Europe, we would lose at the end of the season four or five million with the interest on the loans. In some way, to breath a little, to live a little, you've got to stop the borrowing; you've got to stop. It's difficult because the question, the quandary, always is, do you go for stars, do you go for the top four?

Barmby crosses the divide

Everton finished a turbulent 1998/99 season fourteenth and after showing good form in the subsequent campaign they reached the FA Cup quarter-final but finished thirteenth – the lowest position they'd held all season. One of their catalysts was the club's record signing, Nick Barmby, who earned an England recall. However he shocked Everton by moving to Liverpool that summer. His wasn't the last departure.

Michael Ball: We were at England together, but he left for Liverpool. A week later he was on the bus at the front and I was walking past, and he just said, 'Michael I had to, I had to.' I was like 'No you didn't!' He said 'I had to for my career, I wasn't going anywhere at Everton, I've changed for my career.' I said: 'I'll get you in training.' Joking.

Tony Hibbert: It doesn't really happen. Especially as a Blue you can't help but think, 'Oh my God, what's he done?' I was surprised more by the fact that Liverpool allowed it to happen as well. I thought it won't be done. Obviously it been done with Beardsley and Abel Xavier as well. At first I was shocked that it actually got allowed to happen, but Barmby was a brilliant player, absolutely class, a great little footballer.

Michael Ball: Everyone's different – Nick's not from Liverpool. It's something I could never ever have done, but Nick's not an Everton fan, he's not a Liverpool fan. It was someone who didn't understand the passion in the city really, so it was his choice. I didn't really like it and I made sure I wound him up. I'd be playing against him, which I never thought I would, at Anfield. We clattered each other in the first three minutes of the game.

Kevin Campbell: When it comes to negotiations players and their representation and the club, it's a matter of negotiating and trying to get the deal done. Obviously he got a better offer somewhere else, and the fact of the matter is it is obviously tough to take sometimes when you're an Evertonian, but he done what he thought was best for himself. That's just life.

Walter Smith: Like all of these things, it's not a factor of, 'Did we want Nick Barmby to go to Liverpool?' No, we didn't want to let Nick Barmby go to Liverpool. Remember, we grew up in a Rangers and Celtic environment. So nobody had to teach us about fucking Everton and Liverpool. We didnae need to learn about that. So when Liverpool came in and put in a bid for Nick Barmby, no person at Everton wanted to sell him, but we had to.

Archie Knox: Every transfer of a player was through necessity.

Stagnation under Smith

With the collapse of the NTL deal, Everton faced more financial uncertainty. There was a high turnover of players, although Smith's perceieved preference for older players over youth brought some consternation among fans. Everton continued to struggle to rise beyond mid-table. In 2000/01 they finished sixteenth.

Kevin Campbell: I had Don Hutchinson, I had Scott Gemmill, I had so many good players in the midfield who could service the front boys, because as a striker that's what you've got to look at. You look at the number nine or you look at the strikers and you're paid to score goals, and you're paid to be the cutting edge. In one summer, all of those players were gone and we brought in two new players, Tommy Gravesen and Alex Nyarko, who were good but they've got to find their feet. So we absolutely ripped the heart out of the middle of the pitch and we put two new players in there who had never played before. It takes a bit of time. Sometimes that's tough to take but you've got to get on with it and try and make the best.

David Unsworth: I think it was a tough time. When I look at his first season when we had Nicky Barmby, Don Hutchinson, Dacourt, there was some good performances, and some good wins at that time. But it turned quite sour and nasty quite quickly towards the end. And I never quite got to the bottom of why that was the case because Walter's reputation was fantastic and he was a top, top guy; tough, hard, but very, very fair. Archie's coaching sessions were brilliant, really, really good. But it just didn't work for us; it didn't seem to click for us, and I think it turned quite nasty at the end.

Hana Roks: They were dire dire days of going to away games and not winning. Every single goal then meant so much because we obviously thought this was the year we were going down. I felt that Smith didn't have a clue what Everton were about. It was just horrible; a horrible, horrible time.

Richard Dunne: Walter came down and he saw me and Bally sitting together. We'd lost a game on penalties [to Bristol Rovers in the League Cup in September 2000] and we were sat with a couple of senior pros and they were telling us a joke while we were playing cards. He came down and gave me and Bally a rollicking but it was just one of them things. I'm sure he was just really pissed off and wanted to have a go at someone and, like it is in football and probably in other jobs, the young lads, the newcomers bore the brunt of it.

Alessandro Pistone: You can't really say for what reason you can express yourself on the pitch, but we always had the feeling that the team was a good team and could turn a season into a positive season.

Kevin Campbell: I think he was very frustrated at times, but Walter's a fighter. He knew he's got to do the best with what he had. Him and Archie Knox were putting the work in, putting the time in. I honestly don't think he got the credit he deserved. He was working with a handicap at times. To be able to do what he did at the club I think he was a very special man. I really liked him and I still do. I like him a lot.

Archie Knox: You've got to be realistic, we were realistic with things. We're going to be down among that lot. The squad that we had, similar to the other squads in that area. If you could win a game against them good and well, kept your head above water and stuff, but we never had the team that was ever going to, at that time, go above level.

Over a two-year period Paul Gascoigne, David Ginola and Mark Hughes all signed, aged 33, 35 and 36 respectively. Against this backdrop, in the summer of 2001 Francis Jeffers was sold to Arsenal £8 million, Michael Ball was sold to Rangers for £5.75 million and Richard Dunne joined Manchester City for £3.5 million. An increasingly injury prone Duncan Ferguson had also returned in 2000 but failed to start a game before Christmas and over the following four seasons averaged just 11 starts per campaign.

Walter Smith: These were opportunities we got, to take Mark Hughes, to take Ginola. All these guys in their time were terrific footballers. Fantastic footballers. We knew Gascoigne from Rangers. Ginola and Mark Hughes, you're looking at guys that were brilliant players, and they're ending their careers. So that was the circumstances. We took a chance with them.

Tony Hibbert: To be honest Ginola kept himself to himself. You could see he was a class player, but because of his age and the way football is he was slowing down, but he was still a fantastic footballer. Gazza was the complete opposite. He still had the ability of a world class player, he was unbelievable. But he was just nuts. You didn't know what he was going to do, what he was up to, and that was the mad part to him. He'd come in every day and he'd get into routines in his head where he was on this fitness regime, and he was 100% committed to it.

Alan Myers: I remember Walter calling me in the day before Paul Gascoigne arrived. 'Right, I've got a job for you.' So, I said, 'Oh, yeah?' So, he said, 'Yeah. Paul Gascoigne's signing tomorrow.' And I said, 'Really?' So he said, 'Yeah. He signs for us. It's going to be your job to look after him.' Little did I know what that entailed.

Peter Clarke: For me it was like a dream come true – growing up as a kid watching Italia 90 and seeing him upset because he was going to miss the final has a real effect on an eight year old boy. Although he was a Newcastle and Tottenham player he was someone that I liked to watch, I liked to see do well. He was a real icon for the English game after Italia 90. So although he'd perhaps had the better part of his career before he came to Everton he was still a phenomenal footballer. Just to be able to play and train with him was just as my little boy describes things now: it was awesome.

Alan Stubbs: Gazza was obviously a big name with probably his better years being behind him. But he was still a character, he was fantastic in the dressing room. He was a brilliant guy. And I probably saw [more in] the Gazza deal than the Ginola deal. I could see what that was, the Gazza one. There was probably more scepticism in the Ginola deal coming to the club. Whether that was Walter's deal, I don't know. It maybe had a bit of Bill in that deal. And to be fair, I think Gazza had more of an impact than what Ginola did when he came too.

Jimmy Martin: The things Gazza used to get up to were unbelievable. I remember him sending one of the staff to the shop for half a dozen eggs. We said, 'Gazza, we don't need eggs, we've got plenty.' What he'd done, was the staff member had a little Ford Fiesta which was his sister's, and he put a kettle whistle in the exhaust, so when he started the car up it started to whistle and whistle! He loved it that much he sent Jimmy Five Bellies to the hardware store and got 15 kettles just to get the whistle off them and stuck them in players' exhausts. So when everybody started all you could hear was a whistle, and the louder it got when they were driving away. And that was the funniest thing ever. We had a little wall at Bellefield and he sat on that wall and laughed his head off. Just sat there waiting for everybody getting off.

Peter Clarke: You'd see Jimmy Five Bellies around on a relatively regular basis. In my opinion Gazza just wanted to be loved. I was in the squad but I wasn't on the bench for this particular game. I remember him taking a free-kick and he's hit it and he's felt for his thigh and come off injured. He's gone into the dressing room. I'd come down and gone in there to go the toilet and he was there and was emotional. He wanted to give me some money to sit with him. He wanted love and he wanted some company. 'Put your dough away I don't want your money I'll sit with you kindly,' I said. I just sat with him and let him talk. He was a big hero of mine, it was amazing. But whether that was a sign of what he'd been used to, that people had been quite sinister in the way their friendship was with him I don't know. But I didn't want his money. He was Paul Gascoigne I'd sit with him all the days and all the time that he wanted.

Alan Myers: We were away at Newcastle, and we'd won 1-0, which was very unusual for us – Kevin Campbell had scored the winner. It was a great day. What people don't remember about the goal was that, as the ball comes out of our defence, Gazza makes this little flick out to Gary Naysmith, who was the left wing-back. And nobody really spotted the little flick, which, to be honest with you, made the goal; without that, it wouldn't have happened. For some reason, I was down by the tunnel and Gazza came over to the side, and – this is during the game – he shouts and screams, 'Myers, did you see the flick?' Although the game was going on, he was shouting to me – did I see the flick? He was so upset, because nobody spotted it. After the game we were waiting on the bus to leave St James's Park, but Walter and Gazza were still inside the ground. I went down to find them, and there's Paul Gascoigne sat on the physio's bench in floods of tears, literally. Like a broken man. He was distraught, and I thought, 'Oh, my word, what's happened here?' So, I said, 'What's wrong?' and he just started crying and said, 'I'm just so happy that we've won. I'm just so happy that it's been such a great day.' He was so emotional; he was a wreck, emotionally.

Tony Hibbert: It's strange when you see the press and the way it is now. That was probably his problem – he would give you the last penny that he had or the clothes off his back to help you out. He's the nicest fella I've ever met in football. Brilliant. Football wise he was still clever up there but absolutely mad. We had Mark Hughes and people like that, so it was crazy coming through and training with them. When Walter got sacked a lot of them left.

Michael Ball: I've always loved Paul; I think he's one of the best British players we've ever had.

In training he'd do something and you'd go, 'Yeah there it is,' but it wasn't enough, you needed someone who could do it all the time. We couldn't carry people. So on the football side of things I wasn't too impressed with him, but I loved being around him, his infectiousness.

Alan Myers: He was quite possibly the most amazing character I met in the game. I never met anyone who'd had such an impact on me as Paul Gascoigne did, both professionally and personally.

David Weir: Ideally Everton want to keep their best young players, especially the local ones and the ones who've had allegiances to the club, but it works both ways as well. The players have got to decide to leave, there's an element of that in it as well; you've got to be honest about that. But there's also got to be, with the club, a willingness to sell, and we were having to sell. It works both ways, and obviously I have been a player and assistant manager, so there are two sides to every story. There's a financial side, there's a career side, there's an emotional side. A lot of factors go into players actually staying or moving from a club, but obviously you want to keep your best players and you want to keep the local ones and the ones who have got an affinity, but it's not always as easy as that, as we all know.

Michael Ball: I'm not sure of Franny's situation, because I phoned Franny when he left. I was in Spain, and I phoned him, 'What the fuck are you doing?' He said, 'I just couldn't turn it down.'

Walter Smith: Franny Jeffers, £8 million.

Archie Knox: Every one of them.

Walter Smith: It kept the club going.

Archie Knox: Michael Ball, another one that saved the club.

Walter Smith: That was one of these things where, would you want to do that [sign older players and sell youngsters]? No disrespect to any of them, but no, you wouldnae. We didn't start out like that – we started out bringing younger ones in that were going to try and hopefully go up and flourish within your club. You ended up saying to yourself, 'Well, do we need a bit of experience to help you through the circumstances that are there?'

Kevin Campbell: They come through the ranks and they're Evertonians, they're the lifeblood of the club. So when you actually sell them, they're like selling the family jewels. But we understand that football is a business and books have to be balanced.

Richard Dunne: Anybody was for sale. Anybody that any other club wanted they could have. I actually went in and spoke to them and they said, 'Look we've accepted this offer from Wimbledon' and I went down and did a medical and all that at Wimbledon and I went back down the next day and they said, 'Oh we've got no money and the deals off.' So I went back to Everton and it was, 'Why are you going now? Why do you want to leave Everton?' I said, 'Because you want to sell me.' 'Yeah but don't go there.' As I left the office Joe Royle had just rejoined Manchester City and he rang me and asked me to come down. Once I'd been told I could leave it was just a case of, 'Well I don't want to really hang around now. I've said my goodbyes.' Once they had come back and they'd accepted it I knew where I stood.

Michael Ball: There was only three offers that Everton accepted: it was Liverpool, Middlesbrough and Rangers. And I wasn't going to Middlesbrough because they were playing against Everton. I wasn't going to Rangers because it was in Scotland, and I didn't think sort of that was the right move for me. But half of my dressing room was Scottish, so I spoke to everyone. And it was a three-week period of thinking, 'What the hell's going on?' I wanted to prove myself so that Walter might change his mind. He said, 'You get out of this club, or we'll let you rot in the reserves.' Those were his last words to me. So I trained by myself. I thought, 'I might prove him wrong, hopefully someone will get injured.' They bought Pistone.

Kevin Campbell: The manager's job is to manage. He needs to try and balance it out and keep the club in the top flight. It's not nice for fans, obviously, because everyone wants to see the home-grown boys come through and do great for the team, but again it is a business and sometimes it's a brutal business.

27 January 2001
FA Cup Fourth Round
Goodison Park
Everton 0, Tranmere Rovers 3

On 27 January 2001, Tranmere Rovers – fourth from bottom in the First Division – made the short trip across the Mersey to take on Everton in the fourth round of the FA Cup. Peter Johnson had returned to Tranmere as chairman, but perhaps wisely did not show his face at Goodison. After Steve Yates gave the visitors the lead in the 21st minute, Everton simply capitulated, losing 3-0.

David Unsworth: It was just a bad game, and day. They were up for it, we were poor that day. Just a horrible 90 minutes.

Michael Ball: I played against Jason Koumas and he was running the show. It was one of those games where I knew what he was good at and I was trying to tell my teammates – 'He's going to be the playmaker, just get on to him. If anyone's going to hurt us, it's going to be him.' I was playing centre-half, and it was just simple, basic goals. There was nothing… we were just giving it away to them.

Peter Johnson: I didn't think it was appropriate for me to go to that match. Just as well because they were fighting each other in the aisles.

Kevin Campbell: That's football for you, isn't it? We're looking at turning Tranmere over at home, let's be brutally honest. We didn't start the game too bad – so many of these games hinge on the first goal. They got the first goal, and it seemed like they rose a level and we dropped a level. We battled and battled, and they seemed to score at all the right times.

Peter Johnson: I had a place in the south of France. So I went down there, my daughter lives there so she speaks French. She went and booked us a table in 'La Gaffe' which is in Antibes. There was a 20-minute delay because the crowds couldn't get in on time. It kept going back, George Best was the commentator. I couldn't believe it. When it was 1-0 Georgey said, 'It won't be long before the Premiership club gets one back.' Then it was a shock, then a bigger shock, then a bigger shock.

Michael Ball: That was probably my worst feeling and my worst game, an embarrassment of a performance really. You didn't really do anything wrong, but we didn't do anything to stamp our authority on the game. We just sort of turned up and expected to win. That stupid big team mentality. We didn't earn the right to play against them. I can't really remember any player making mistakes but it was like we were playing in the park.

Kevin Campbell: I fancied that if we'd got back on level terms we would have won the game, but we keep seeing these giant killing acts going on, and that was one of the toughest days. That wasn't a great result for us and we got a lot of stick for that one, but rightly so because we didn't deliver.

Michael Ball: What I really remember of the whole game was afterwards, because there was no team talk after the game. That shows you how bad we were. They didn't even bother coming in. They went to the staff room. Dave Watson popped his head round the corner and went, 'That was Tranmere by the way boys.' Shut the door and went on. I think we needed that, in a weird way. It couldn't get any lower.

Peter Johnson: They beat Everton really fairly, and then they beat Southampton from 3-0 down. Then they played Liverpool. They were unfortunate to lose that. They had to succumb in the end.

The People's Club Reawakened 2002-2018

'When I took overI had a feeling that finishing just outside of relegation, avoiding relegation and staying up was going to be acceptable. And I could smell it. I smelt it around the club, and I felt that was one of the reasons why I had to try and make a big change."

David Moyes

David Moyes replaces Walter Smith

Everton had finished the 2000/01 sixteenth and, following the enforced sales of the club's best young players there was little room for optimism, going into the new season. Supporter unrest was already palpable and in one extraordinary incident a supporter invaded the pitch in a game against Arsenal and offering to exchange his shirt for Alex Nyarko's – the inference beng that he could do better and the Ghanaian was unworthy of it. By March 2002 Everton had won just once in the league in four months and had been ignominiously dumped out of an FA Cup quarter-final against Middlesbrough. The board acted to change.

John Corbett: I think we'd got to the point where we didn't want any more relegation battles, and we were heading in that direction in the early part of the twenty-first century. Under Walter Smith we seemed to stabilise, then we seemed to stagnate, and then we seemed to fall into a nosedive once again, and people still had memories of that awful sason when we had to beat Wimbledon. We thought, 'Is this where we're going again?'

Niclas Alexandersson: You could sense the frustration from the fans. For Alex [Nyarko], who was the one that was involved in that [shirt-swapping incident with the supporter at Highbury], it was really tough. You have to accept some stick when you're not playing well but that was, of course, way over the top. Something similar happened in the Swedish league in the last game with Henrik Larsson at his time when a fan ran onto the pitch but that was after the game and he tried to take the shirt off. That's a very strong symbol when you take someone's shirt. That was tough.

Phil McNulty: Walter Smith was not this sort of distant, miserable figure who didn't really buy into Everton that some people portray. If you got to know Walter Smith, he was an incredibly witty, funny man; he really wanted Everton to do well. It just wasn't a period when the club was built to do well: there was too much change; there wasn't enough money going around, he had to sort of cut his cloth accordingly. I know plenty will disagree with me, but I do think history does view Walter Smith harshly. I think he did a much better job than a lot of people will give him credit for. Although, I do accept, and I think he probably will, that at the end, it was time for him to go after that cup quarter-final defeat at Middlesbrough when they lost 3-0. I think his time had run out then.

Jon Woods: It was left too late, and we went to Middlesbrough and we lost 3-0, and then on the way home we decided that Walter had to go.

Tony Hibbert: When the results are going badly the manager is the first to get the blame, he takes the bullet, which isn't fair, but that's football. You had a feeling that it was going to happen but you didn't know when.

Alessandro Pistone: It doesn't matter how good you are or how good you've done before, or how good a person you are, if you don't get results that's the easiest thing to do for a club, is to change the manager. I've had a few in my career, I've had a few changes, so I know that's what happens in football. It's a lot easier to change a manager than players.

Alan Stubbs: He was a really good man manager. He let you know what you needed to know, and just wanted his players to get on with it. I think as players you read quite a bit about what's going on in the press, and at the time I think we knew that he was wanting more money from the club to bring in players, and it just wasn't happening. I think he'd lost out on a few deals as a result of it.

Kevin Campbell: It was a shock to all the players. But we know again that it can be a brutal business, and that happened. David Moyes came in, and to be fair to David Moyes, David Moyes came in and he made a good impact on all the players.

Walter Smith: Everton's whole circumstance was driven by a lack of finance at that time. It's not rocket science. We left, and Davy got a level of investment into the team. Now before he took the job I phoned him, and I would recommend him because I knew that they were going to be more stable financially when we left. As I say, the directors probably didn't trust us to handle their investment. So that's fine. For four years we did the best we could under the circumstances we were in, but the financial aspect of it improved greatly.

David Weir: I worked with Walter and Archie afterwards again, and their methods work. It was a complicated football club at the time, but Walter and Archie had a great deal of success at Rangers, previously working together with similar methods. It was a matter of the club being in a difficult positon, a great club obviously, but in a difficult period of its history, and Walter coming in to try and steady that. All the stuff with ownership and things that were going on round about it make that difficult. The off-field issues regarding the football make it difficult, [and affect] the actual day to day work in regards to the football. Some of the players that were coming in, came in quickly and went out quickly. It was never really settled enough to be successful, so that was probably the difficulty with that. But it was a good environment, it was a great working environment. Bellefield itself as a training ground is probably the best one I've been associated with.

David Moyes: I was watching a player for Preston, and we drove to Bristol to watch him. On the way down in the car I got a call from Bill to say, 'We're quite interested, would you like to meet?' I So I drove to Bristol, and then I drove to London with my chief scout in the car, and had a meeting with Bill in his house with Jenny, his partner. Partly I was trying to convince Bill as well, because I was relatively unknown. But Bill was the one who phoned me and invited me down. I think by the end of a couple of hours we had had in his house, I was probably going to choose to become the manager of Everton, if I got offered it. By what Bill was saying to me, it looked like that was going to be the case.

John Corbett: Moyes was a young manager from Preston North End who brought in different ideas. He was not an old timer like Smith had been; he was somebody who'd been and done all the coaching courses and he was a breath of fresh air, and brought about an instant change in the ethos of the club. And I think history will be kinder to Moyes maybe once he retires. As an Everton manager you've got to say that he did save Everton from, shall we say, joining the ranks of the also-rans.

At his unveiling, Moyes christened Everton 'the people's club of Merseyside' and instantly struck a rapport with the club's success starved fans.

David Moyes: It had been a hectic day and my brother was driving me into the city and we were driving in through this tight old part of the city. The kids were playing out on the street – it was nearly back to the old days in Glasgow – and all the ones I saw were in Everton kits. Maybe it was just my eye getting dragged to it, but everyone was wearing an Everton strip. It made me think that people on the streets support Everton.

Bill Kenwright: We were united in a need. David was hugely ambitious and wanted to make Everton his shining glory. I wanted to make Everton what they always had been to me – a top club; *the* top club. And we both needed it, and we both needed each other. We came through a lot together.

Niclas Alexandersson: He came in he came in with a lot of energy. He was young as a manager and I think very different compared to Walter. David Moyes wanted to be on the pitch more or less the whole time, to have a hand everywhere and he was very energetic in his coaching role. At the time I thought he was a good injection with the energy he brought in.

Tony Hibbert: The first thing I liked with Moyes from day one was his honesty. He came in after his first meeting and said to us that he's still learning, he's still learning the game and management, bear with him. He took it that way. I liked the way he came in and settled, before slowly working his way in and got to know the lads better, and obviously got his way across and how he wanted to play. But it was more or less a togetherness that he brought. His massive strength was creating a great team spirit.

Leon Osman: Looking back now David Moyes was the perfect man to come in and move us forward. He was relatively new, he'd done okay with Preston, showed promise. He was cheap because we were bringing him up into the Premier League.

David Moyes: I think when you come in as a young manager you come in with a little bit less fear, and you come in with a little bit less understanding or knowledge, which sometimes is a good thing. And it brings you in with a freshness, a freedom to go on and do things which I'd been doing, and I did.

Alan Stubbs: He brought a real energy to the club. He was a young manager on the up, and he had a real desire to succeed. At the time, when you look back now, he was probably a real good fit, even though the lads had a lot of respect for Walter. David Moyes comes in, he has a real energy and exuberance about him, a steeliness, and the first thing he wanted to do when he came in was probably make us hard to beat. And that had the desired effect on us avoiding relegation towards the end of that season.

Mike Hughes: We interviewed Bill Kenwright on the night he made the appointment. Bill talked about having met David Moyes and I think the famous phrase that he had that he said to me was, 'He had me at hello' – the line from the famous film Jerry Maguire.

David Unsworth: What David did, he got the club straight away; he nailed it straight away, and if you're not a former Everton player, or you're not an Everton fan or you're not someone who's connected with the club, sometimes it takes different people different amounts of time to understand what we're all about.

Tomasz Radzinski: He made the players aware of where he's going, how he wants everybody to play, what he wants to do, and there was a kind of a unity when David came. He put everyone on the same line, the same track and we played at home our first game [against Fulham], where David Unsworth scored the winner, and it gave us the belief again that everything is possible.

Kevin Campbell: It was a good move by David Moyes, because there was a lot of experience in that squad, a hell of a lot of experience. He was asking questions, which is fantastic, that's how the solutions and problems are solved, by asking questions. We were a very close-knit group and the management team were very close with us. We got through the tough times and then we started to excel in the second season.

David Moyes: I came in with a little bit of a 'my way or no way' attitude. We had a very experienced group of players. Walter's group and within that group there was David Ginola, Paul Gascoigne, Duncan, Tommy Gravesen. You could go on and on, senior players. So, probably at that time, they're looking to see how you handle yourself, how you carry yourself. I had to go in and really stick my chest out and get on with it. I didn't bring in an assistant manager at the opening part, I used Andy Holden as assistant manager, who was great, gave me an insight into what was around me. But really being on my own was just showing that I could stand on my own two feet and manage.

David Weir: He liked to be on the training ground, and he liked to walk through, in detail, what he wanted and how he wanted his teams to play. In my experiences in football, maybe other than internationally, I hadn't had as much of that. David was very much about moving players a yard, two yards here and there; he was very specific in regards to what he wanted and very hands-on in regards to what he wanted, whereas Walter was probably more trusting in regards to the players making the right decisions at the right times.

Dave Prentice: I remember there was one time Unsy told me that the players were really unhappy with him because he was basically working them too hard; he was running them too hard on the training pitch. And he found that out to his cost at Shrewsbury, in the third round of the FA Cup in 2003. He had them training on an absolute mud heap on the morning of the game, to get used to the pitch. But they were just leg-weary as a result, so got knocked out. He learned as he was going along.

Leon Osman: He had quite a few run ins with players in those first eighteen months, because he was unknown, the players didn't know him. The respect wasn't there at that point, because some of these players had played at the highest level and done things in the game and all sorts. And an unknown man had stepped in to manage them, who was telling them to do things that they couldn't quite understand.

David Moyes: I don't think everyone was receptive. My idea was to bring in a new, young team. Walter, who's a great friend I admire, and was one of the people I would go and speak to, and actually when Everton did offer me the job I went to Walter's house to speak to Walter, who said definitely. But I wanted to do it differently, I didn't want to bring in old players who I felt were nearing the end of their career. I wanted young ones, I wanted to get them energetic, athletic. And that really had to start, but it was also going to be a longer process doing it that way.

Alan Stubbs: He was was a very strong-minded person and if he had something in his head, he'd want to do it, no matter what. Whether it didn't make a few players happy, he would want to do it no matter what. He was that strong-minded: 'I couldn't care less if you're not happy, we're doing it, that's it.' And I think one or two early on probably had not heard that before. Or they'd probably heard it, but not for a number of years. And then suddenly David comes in and he was very on the front foot, wasn't afraid to tell people what he thought, no matter what, even if they liked it or not.

David Moyes: Paul Gascoigne had to leave, it was sad, he was a great guy. I kept in touch with him for a long time. David Ginola was undoubtedly a massive talent, but I had to find a way of starting to turn the club around, and unfortunately they were probably some of the early fallers at that time. It's always going to be like that in football, you're not going to keep everybody happy. I think when older players come to the end of their time it can be hard for them to accept and hard for them to take, but they have to move on and maybe they're not wanted. So I wouldn't have expected them to be overly happy, but I think in truth they probably accepted the decision.

Alessandro Pistone: He was a great manager. I'll always say he was probably one of the best managers I've had in terms of training, in terms of preparation of the game. I always reckon that he was a really prepared manager.

David Unsworth: I think the level of detail that David and Alan brought to the team, it made me sit up straight away. The level of detail, that he would go into the opposition about in the week leading up to a game. That was the biggest thing and the biggest compliment I can pay David is his detail in the opposition. We knew exactly what to expect and he and Alan Irvine left no stone unturned.

David Moyes: My style was to play with two centre-forwards. I've always enjoyed crosses in the box, if I could have got wide players to put the ball in the box. Because I had been a supporter I always thought it was exciting; wingers, crosses, centre-forwards heading it in. And Everton always had a great tradition of number nines. So I wanted to try and follow that tradition a little bit.

Leon Osman: He got Everton playing. He demanded that we run round, he coached a system. He was one of the new, modern managers, whereas years ago the manager would manage and the coach would coach. David Moyes came in and he did both. So he would be out on the training field and he would demand standards, and he showed people where he wanted them to stand.

Alan Irvine: I think there was this incident with Jesper Blomqvist coming off the pitch and David having a go at him. By the time I got in there [later in 2002] David was very much in charge, and there was a group of players who looked like they were ready to work the way he wanted them to. This was a team that had been fighting relegation in the previous seasons, and we got off to a really good start and finished that season in seventth position.

Lee Carsley: Straight away his standards were high in terms of the way that you conducted yourself on the training ground, the way you conducted yourself around the training ground, the responsibility you had when you were representing the club. Your body language when you were being substituted – I remember an incident with Blomqvist. The manager was shouting to him – but he was talking to everyone – 'Don't ever try and embarrass me coming off the pitch. You're playing for Everton, you aren't as important as the club and the team.' That was an, 'Ooh, bloody hell, he's not to be taken lightly.'

Tomasz Radzinski: He did actually work way, way, way more on sessions, on tactical stuff. We would definitely know every single play that we needed to do, whether it's a free-kick around the penalty area, whether it's in the middle of the pitch, whether it's throwing, whether it's a corner. Every single aspect of the game had been taken care off, so the guessing game and the uncertainty in the game was gone, in an attacking and a defensive way. The strikers had to be present at the defensive corners, defensive free-kicks, and the opposite as well.

Alessandro Pistone: I can't really explain why, but training with him was good, always at 100 per-cent. Maybe not a long session – an hour and a half maximum, but with a logic. He knew what he wanted to get from a single player from a single session, so it was good.

Leon Osman: It was in the period of change in football. Now managers tell players exactly where they want them to be. Years ago things were a lot more open to interpretation. A player would go out and express themselves and do things, but now you're sort of doing what the manager wants as much as everyone else. David Moyes came in and that's what we needed at the time. We needed to have a structure, and he tightened us up, got everyone working for each other. It definitely worked.

Lee Carsley: He was a big believer in picking teams to win matches and stopping the opposition. I remember one game playing right-wing against Manchester United because Mikael Silvestre was just bombing on as a left-back, and my role as a winger was to stop him. Our right-winger's job was to stop their left-back, it's usually the other way round, isn't it? But I spent all night at Old Trafford chasing Mikael Silvestre up and down that side. I think I had three touches, but I was willing to do that for the team because I tried to put the team before myself on as many occasions as I could.

Alan Irvine: Everybody knew what their jobs were and he built a very determined team. To be honest it was a team that was probably built to be difficult to beat. I think that was a great place to start, because you've got to make sure the foundations are right and the foundations of winning games are first of all being difficult to beat. Goodison became a difficult place for opponents to come once again. The team played with a lot of energy, and a lot of determination.

Louis Saha: I remember a time when I was with Manchester United [in February 2004] and I played my second game for the club, and I find myself a bit relaxed, I scored already two goals against Everton, but we missed two or three sitters. We were 3-0 up, and the manager [Sir Alex Ferguson] at half-time was fuming because he knew that the spirit of this club [Everton] could make them come back from anywhere. He shouted at us like we were not winning at all, because he knew that spirit. He respected this very much, and I understand it because at the end we needed to score an extra goal, because it was a 4-3 game.

David Moyes: I felt when I took over I had a feeling that finishing just outside of relegation, avoiding relegation and staying up was going to be acceptable. And I could smell it. I smelt it round the club, and I felt that was one of the reasons why I had to try and make a much big change.

Leon Osman: Colin Harvey was Everton coach years before he stepped into the manager's role, and he coached us. He showed us how to set up defensively. Very similar to David Moyes, I think that's why me and David Moyes worked together for so long, because he was very similar to Colin Harvey. Having been drilled so much in that youth team period under Colin Harvey, to make the step up to play for David Moyes was such an easy transition.

Alan Irvine: There was a reason for every session that we did and generally that reason worked towards how we were going to play on the Saturday. We watched the opposition very carefully, and we did a lot of work to try and make sure that we reduced the threats that they had. I was going to say negated them, but you can't do that with a lot of the very best teams. We had a plan for every game. That plan changed depending on the opposition and at the beginning, the plan was generally more about how we were going to stop them than how we were going to actually create things ourselves.

Tony Hibbert: I don't think we set out to be in the top ten or anything like that. He was bringing a squad together and we still had a couple of old players, but a lot of players that played in the Walter era were more or less moved on, so it was a bit of a new squad what he had. We never looked to see, it was a learning curve for all of us and we were enjoying it. It was a matter of sticking together. We never spoke about reaching the top ten or needing to do this, the club itself just felt different. It felt strong as a club and as a unit, so I think the feeling of that helped massively.

Wayne's World

Moyes's early period at Everton was helped by the emergence of the club's most outstanding yout player in living memory. On the opening day 16-year-old Wayne Rooney joined Tomasz Radzinski and Kevin Campbell in a three-pronged attack. He was soon to write his name in football immortality.

Howard Kendall: My final act as Everton manager had been the Coventry City game [at the end of the 1997/98 season]. My penultimate one had occurred at Goodison three nights earlier, when the youth team lifted the FA Youth Cup. Leon Osman, Tony Hibbert, Francis Jeffers, Richard Dunne and Danny Cadamarteri all played a part in the two legged win. Between them they would make more than 800 appearances for Everton and three of them would earn international recognition. The credit was all Colin's really, for he was youth team manager at the time, but it happened under my watch. I suppose you could say it was the final act of a partnership that lasted off and on for more than 30 years. I remember asking Colin at the time who he had coming up through the ranks. Colin doesn't mess about; he's very direct. If someone stands a chance of making it that won't be enough; it's got to be special for Colin to pay attention. He looked for something outstanding, extra special. 'Only one,' said Colin. 'He's twelve years old. His name's Rooney.'

Colin Harvey: I used to go on a Sunday Morning and watch the different age groups, and I usually watched the under 15s and the under 16s, because they were the next intake. Anyway, there was an injury in one of the games I was watching, I walked over and the under 10s were playing. There was a coach named Dennis Evans, who was a very good coach; coached basketball and other things, a good all-round coach. This kid picks the ball up on the halfway line and slaloms past about four players, lashes it in the top corner. I said, 'Who's that?' He said, 'Wayne Rooney.' And I heard of him, but I'd never seen anything of him. Anyway he does it again about quarter of an hour, 20 minutes later. I said, 'Dennis?' He said, 'He does that every game. It might be three or four times he goes past five or six players.'

Walter Smith: I always remember, Colin said 'You'll have to take a look at this boy we've got. He's playing in the Under 19 team.' We went 'Under-19 team?' He said 'Aye, he's only 15.' We were saying to each other 'How can a 15-year-old play in the under 19s?' We were able to sit in the manager's office and we used to go in and do a bit of training Saturday morning before our game. And there was a game on. They were playing Manchester City, and I'll never forget it. Archie and I were sat at the window looking at it, and I said to Archie, 'That boy's coming on that they are talking about, that lad Rooney.'

Archie Knox: He was a flippin' Roy of the Rovers at that level. Some of the stuff he could do; he would just get the ball and run right through the other team. From the half way line or something, run straight and score.

Michael Ball: I was still young and I loved going to the youth cup games. When I was a youth player I'd love when Tony Grant was watching or when John Ebbrell would watch. You want to impress the manager, but you want them to talk about you. To this day I don't know who I was talking to, I was sitting there. There was a free-kick ten yards inside their half – I can't remember who they were playing now– so normally a centre-half or a full-back would take it and this lad hit it and hit the bar. The ball bounced, he ran on, shot, and it went in. I'm thinking, 'Who's that? What's he doing shooting from there?' That's when they started talking. I never knew anything about Wayne. That's when they said, 'He's going to be a boy, this one.'

Tony Hibbert: He was doing well in the academy and playing in the youth cup. I remember watching some goals and as you're there you to get to hear about the next lads; 'This lad's this and this lad's that', being in the place you hear this. So when they come in to train you're looking for that, and to be honest with Wayne it was so, I wouldn't say easy, it was just so natural. Nothing fazed him. So with him stepping up as a fifteen-sixteen-year-old to playing with grown men in a first team was no different than playing on the park with his friends for him.

Colin Harvey: You see the background he's from, he's from the middle of Croxteth. I always used to go in early, and I was going in about 6am one morning, a summer's morning, and there were five kids crossing the road ahead of me. He was one of them. He didn't see me and I drove past. I phoned his dad up later that day and I said, 'Come in with him whenever you get a chance tomorrow, either before school or after.' So he came in with his dad and I said, 'Do you want to be a footballer or don't you want to be a footballer?' He said, 'What you on about?' I said, 'Well I saw you yesterday morning.' He said 'No you didn't.' I said, 'Yes I did. You were crossing the road not far from where you live.' He said, 'I'd been at a sleepover at my mates and we'd just got up early and went out for a walk.' And there were five of them, and if they weren't on pot they were going to be on it sooner or later. You just looked at their faces. I said, 'Well if you're going to knock around with them, knock around with them, otherwise get yourself away from them and you've got a chance of being a footballer.' And he went out then. His dad said, 'I've been dying to say that to him for ages.'

Kevin Campbell: I played with Wayne when he was fourteen, that was my first game with him. I think we were playing Southport in a friendly. I was just coming back from an injury, so I was going to play 65 minutes in a friendly at Southport. And there was just this young kid who looked like a baby on the bus. Andy Holden said, 'He's your strike partner upfront. Treat him like a first team player.' I laughed. He said, 'Kev, you'll see.' I played with him and by the time I come off it was 3-0, Wayne had got two, I'd got one and even at fourteen I was like, 'You're kidding me.' You could tell he was just special. Straight from school he came and joined the first team squad. It was uncanny that he was so good. But he was going to be the future of the football club.

Colin Harvey: I took him to Coventry for an under-18 game, and he'd be about thirteen. I took him as a sub, and we were getting beat 2-0. We had a lad called Nick Chadwick, who went on to score quite a few goals in the lower divisions. So I brought him off and put Wayne on, and within a minute he'd bent one and hit the crossbar, put someone else through and scored a goal. And Nick went, 'Who's this kid?' I said, 'It's Wayne Rooney.'

David Unsworth: John Murtagh [a long-term member of the Everton coaching staff] pulled me one day and said, come and look at these two goals that this fifteen year-old kid has scored for our youth team last night. He scored two goals against Tottenham. And I was like, 'Who the hell is that?' Before I knew it at 16 he was playing with our first team, and we couldn't even catch him to kick him let alone tackle him.

David Moyes: They were playing Tottenham in the FA Youth Cup semi-final. It was on at Goodison, a two-legged game at that time. They asked me to sit in the gantry, I was doing a bit for Everton. I was in the gantry looking down, and Wayne was stunning. I walked down, this would probably be about April time, and the boys had come back on the pitch for a cool down. I remember going up and tapping him on the shoulder and saying, 'You'll be with me next year.' I didn't know him, and he was a really shy, quiet boy. As it was we called him up, he was on the bench at Southampton that year. We had to get permission to get him out of school and all the things that went with it.

Colin Harvey: He was very, very mature. I remember we used to get him up Tuesdays and Thursdays. We were training at the Thornton, and I used to go back to Bellefield with him. He'd come in for his lunch; he'd have his school blazer on, and not a word was said to him. If it had been any other kid they would have got the mickey taken out of them, but no one said a word. He just walked in, sat down, had his lunch and then we'd drive back and I'd drop him at De La Salle, and if I didn't say something to him he wouldn't open his mouth all the way back. Just a dead quiet kid. Dead humble.

Alan Irvine: I think Wayne would have been a player wherever he was. Quite simply he had lots and lots of attributes. Bear in mind, he left school and came straight in to work with the first team, and wasn't out of his depth. That's almost unheard of. Other 16-year-olds who have broken through at Everton, left school and spent time with the academy before gradually breaking into the first team, whereas Wayne came in straightaway and stayed in then started to play a part in the games.

Jimmy Martin: I got to know Wayne quite well, I'd drive him into Bellefield. He used to come in to the kit room in the afternoon after training. 'Can I have a bag of balls Jimmy?' he'd ask. He was well-mannered, a good kid; very shy kid; and he used to just say, 'Can I have a bag of balls, and go and have a little kick.' And he'd go on the pitch in the afternoon, maybe an hour, hour-and-a-half, and just practice. That was Wayne Rooney. That's why he's a good as he is today.

Alessandro Pistone: I believe Moyes was clever to treat a player like Rooney as he did, because Wayne started training with us in pre-season, so we always had the sensation he was a great player. We knew that. We knew he was going to be a top player. But he did well, the manager, to let him play not every game. He gave him the time to grow by himself, not to try and rush him.

Tomasz Radzinski: To be honest his training sessions were way more impressive in the beginning than his games with the first team. I think he must also have been a little bit overwhelmed from being at this young age in the Premier League, although he didn't look like he was. But whatever he was showing us in training, he was still twice as impressive at it was when he was playing actually in his first minutes in the Premier League, this is how good he was.

David Moyes: He had childish behaviour, he'd run out and want to kick all the balls away, the sort of thing a kid would do, but we loved it. Wayne was then sixteen, seventeen, he was hanging about with real senior players. We had to make sure he wasn't led too far away from a path that a young player should be on. He was a really good boy; he loved his football, and that was the biggest thing for me. His love of football, the love of kicking the ball, the love of being on the ball was probably the thing. I think when you see people like that it really thrills you.

Jimmy Martin: He was the last of the street footballers. I'd drop him off and he'd go straight out in the street and play with his mates. He just wanted to play football.

On 19 October 2002, Arsène Wenger's Arsenal arrived at Goodison. The Premier League champions were undefeated in 29 league games. In the final minute Rooney's dipping curling shot from 30 yards beat David Seaman crashed off the underside of the crossbar and over the line. It was one of Goodison's finest-ever goals.

David Moyes: There's only a couple of times when I've left Goodison, when you're in the changing room at Goodison, down in the walls and you can hear the crowd a little bit going out. There's probably only two or three occasions where it was rapturous down the whole street, everybody. That was one of the days, because of the result and the introduction of Wayne as well. He was one of their own – probably half of the supporters might have known Wayne from playing in the streets with him, or bumping into him, or going to school with him. I think when it's like that and you know somebody who's so good and has scored that goal, I think it really means an awful lot to people.

Highs and Lows

Everton finished the 2002/03 campaign – Moyes's first season – seventh, having occupied a European slot until the final day. The following season was more challenging, however, and Everton finished seventeenth, having recorded just nine league wins all season.

David Moyes: This was a club that had only finished twice in the top half of the league since the Premier League had ever started. So this was a football club that was needing fixing, turning around, and it did, but there was always going to be dips with it until we got any level of consistency.

Alan Irvine: David made an impact when he came in and that impact gained momentum and that momentum carried us through the first season. But really the squad wasn't that much different from the squad that had struggled in the previous seasons and had been fighting against relegation. So it was then a case of realising that we were going to have to change things round a bit, and it was more about changing players than changing emphasis, because we'd always wanted to attack. We just weren't good enough at it at times.

Tomasz Radzinski: We didn't get many new players coming in, I think we lost one or two. Being in the same situation with David Moyes not changing the training, the same system, maybe we got a little bit of a repeat year, where not everybody's as sharp anymore, because we know the training already, we know what he expects of us, and since we know it we don't need to do it as well as we did last season. I think this was the biggest problem the second season in charge for David Moyes. It probably wasn't him, it was more the players; we didn't get enough fresh blood to get the hunger back on the pitch and try to make sure we stay away from the relegation zone in the early days of the season, and have a nice and easy season, hoping for the best.

David Moyes: Bill Kenwright said to me, 'David, I'll only be able to get you £5 million to spend.' He says, 'I'll promise you £5 million,' and that's going back to the start when I took the job. I said, 'Fine, I'll work with that.' I always remember saying to him: 'As long as you don't sell any players, and you let me prepare the players any way I want.' He said 'Deal.' Shook his hand on it, and me and him went with that. Lots of times I'd push for money, but when I shook his hand with the deal, I squeezed him for every penny, and any money we did generate we re-used it.

Alessandro Pistone: In that time, obviously, the board had to face up with a choice and I believe they did well because they have to maintain an equilibrium. You can get a top player, and I believe that's the right decision, you can't get one or two players and give them two times or three times the wages that you give to some other players, because the risk is that you don't get the results and you create a bad atmosphere inside the training ground. You have to grow step by step, and I believe that's what they did.

Nigel Martyn: Once you're down there, it's really, really difficult to claw your way up, it really is. Once I'd arrived [in August 2003] it was fairly obvious that it was going to be a tough campaign just to stay in the league.

Alan Irvine: I think that first of all as a coach or a manager, when you win, you move on really quickly to the next game. So you'll come in after the game, you'll say 'Well done' to the players, you'll go into the manager's room and you'll say 'Right, who's next?' You're immediately thinking about the next game. When you lose you dissect it, you dwell on it, you pour over it and think 'What if I'd done this? What if I did that?' So you continually look for ways in which you can turn things round, and quite often the solution is probably getting back to the basics and focussing on the things you do well.

Nigel Martyn: Your start is so important; if you can get a start going and you're in the top three or four, you tend to almost stay there. Alternatively, if you start really badly and start at the bottom, it's really hard to climb out. Every game just becomes a fight really; you can't throw off the shackles at all. You play so tightly that scoring goals and winning games ultimately become more difficult.

David Moyes: We lost 5-1 at Man City on the last day of the [2003/04] season, and that was probably the only time I thought, 'I could be in trouble here.' Not because I thought I'd done a bad job, but if you look at that season, we were safe by Easter, and I think we hardly won a game after Easter. And this is where my story about the team getting safe and having a mentality, 'That's us, we're done now.' I hated it. I hated it. And I felt as if I had to change to see if I could get us back to a winning level more often.

Dave Prentice: Everton had got safe by Good Friday, beating Tottenham, and then switched off. Totally went on their holidays, put their flip-flops on, got beat on the final day 5-1 by Man City, and I wrote a stinging piece about their attitude. I'd heard one of the players in Bellefield saying, 'We're going to get battered at the weekend and the manager deserves it.' They we were down on Moyes because he was working them so hard. I'd heard that, saw how not arsed they were at Manchester City. So I wrote this stinging piece and the headline was 'Taking the Piss' and it caused a major fight. Alan Stubbs was very clever; he actually got it reprinted and handed it round all the players and used it as motivation at the start of the next season. 'Alright, this is what they think of us, let's show them otherwise.'

Leon Osman: I'd come back [from a loan spell at Derby County]. Played against Wolves from Derby that first game back, didn't expect it, scored, played the last three games but we lost all three. And obviously Moyes went mad at us in the dressing room, as he should – 'Let's raise your standards.' I got the feeling that going into the next season, he wasn't that confident of lasting long in the job. And things became so much more relaxed.

Kenwright on the edge

In summer of 2004 Bill Kenwright had a spectacular falling out with one of his consortium partners, Paul Gregg, which culminated in Gregg calling on Kenwright to step down in order to attract new investment. Everton had debts of £40million, a proposed stadium move to Kings Dock had collapsed and rumours were rife about Wayne Rooney's future at the club. In the midst of this crisis, CEO Trevor Birch resigned just six weeks into the job. Kenwright would hold on to the club, replacing Sir Philip Carter with himself as chairman of a revised board, with the London-born American based millionaire Robert Earl buying Gregg's stake in Everton. The True Blue Holdings consortium that had bought the club was dissolved But a summer of mudslinging and misinformation – a baseless story on the front of the Sunday Times that a Russian billionaire was about to buy into the club; or the mysterious financier, Chris Samuelson, who disappeared as quickly as he appeared – made some fans suspicious of the chairman, despite his obvious infatuation with the club.

Jon Woods: It wasn't just Bill [who sought the dissolution of True Blue Holdings]. [Paul Gregg] wanted out. Well find someone to buy your shares and we'll tell you if we like them. But you see, what is the point of buying a stake if you're not in control? So Bill and I were in control without him. It was easier with the three, shall we call it. At this point in time I think we had 50.1% between us, I think with Arthur [Abercrombie]. Maybe without. So there's Gregg's stake 23% or something like that. What good is that? You can't even get on the board. You've got no right to be on the board unless now if you're over 50 or 75, that's different, you own the place, or control it. So what is its value? There is this massive stake, which isn't even enough to stop the function of the club for the sake of it. With companies, you know how the breaks work. So he needed to find someone who wanted to be involved.

Bill Kenwright: People can never quite understand, who don't know football, how a supporter who maybe earns 25 grand a year can worship a player who earns four times that a week, and not resent. Well, similarly, the supporters can't understand why we are not spending more, and they're not really interested that we haven't got it because they pay their money. And logic doesn't come into football all that much. But it was tough, because more than anything – this might be to my detriment, and it might not – I want Evertonians to be happy; that's what I want. Ask me one thing for Everton and that's it. David used to call it 'the Saturday Feeling.' I want Evertonians to have that Saturday Feeling every moment of their lives. It's impossible because football has highs and lows but that's why I do it. And there's no martyr in that; I'm an Evertonian, so I want it for myself, and I want it for them.

Mike Hughes: You look how Leeds have been taken over, Coventry have been taken over, Portsmouth, all these clubs have been taken over, why aren't Everton being taken over well? There's been lots and lots of people who have been interested in taking over Everton. Bill Kenwright wasn't prepared to sell it to just anybody, he wanted to wait for the right person. And if you look at what's happened at Leeds, at Coventry, at Portsmouth and lots and lots of other clubs that could've happened to Everton. But he waited and waited till the right guy came along and Everton got the right guy in Farhad Moshiri.

Simon Hart: He did have a plan, didn't he? He had a plan with NTL, Kings Dock, with Paul Gregg.

That was ambitious, and it was a positive move. The relationship with Gregg for whatever reason didn't work out, and that plan didn't come off – and maybe the council weren't as cooperative as they are currently. Of course, Kirkby was an awful idea and divisive, and Evertonians should thank the KEIOC group for leading the resistance to that. But Kenwright chose a very good manager in Moyes, and I think that relationship was beneficial for Everton, Kenwright and Moyes.

Mike Hughes: Everton fans should actually should get down on their knees and thank Bill Kenwright for what he's done. I've had fallouts with Bill Kenwright over the years when we've done interviews when things haven't gone particularly well and you have to ask difficult questions but he never ever held it against you because he knows you're only trying to do your job. But you know the integrity of the man and you look at what he's done and Everton fans who were critical of him are absolutely – for me – are way out of order.

Simon Hart: What got me was talking about Kenwright to people who were Evertonians who wouldn't criticise him in any way. To them he was this charismatic Evertonian and they're saying 'What else would you want? Be careful-what-you-wish-for.' It was hard to have a reasoned, balanced, nuanced discussion about him, because it was either 'Uncle Bill saved the club' or, 'Bullshit Bill - he's held us back', when the truth's somewhere in between there, isn't it? Somebody who cares about the club but also cares about himself and yet, at the same time, appoints a good manager who provides a stability which does help the club function relatively well for a period of time.

Jon Woods: How thick are they? How thick are they to think… places like this are so transparent, so transparent. You know, that's not the way we run the place. They say 'Where's the Pienaar money?' It's in the bank paying off the overdraft or it's gone to pay Lukaku's wages or whatever. What a stupid question.

John Blain: I think a balanced view would be, for a period time he was the right man and he did a good job, but for a while the business stagnated under his direction through his own lack of financial resources and his apparent inability to find others with deep pockets. He may have just about got away with it in the end with the investment from Farhad Moshiri before a small window of opportunity closed forever. For me, an A-minus or B-plus score, but with some missed opportunities in the past, Kings Dock being the most notable.

Joe Anderson: A lot of people knock Bill Kenwright for his tenure as chair. I've got nothing but admiration for the guy. He's given the club his heart and soul over many years and has continued to do so even through a period where he's not been in the best of health – I think people know that. His passion for the football club and his desire to find the right investor has been admirable. For all we know he might have had more lucrative sounding offers to take Everton off his hands but I know he was very wary about the wrong person taking it on and the impact it can have – just look at what Hicks and Gillett did at Liverpool and how David Moores, the former owner, ended up feeling about that – writing an open letter in a newspaper begging them to leave.

Kenwright was able to see off the challenge of Paul Gregg that summer, but retaining Wayne Rooney proved beyond him. A £20 million bid from Newcastle was rejected, but the boyhood blue would soon be wearing the red of Manchester United after a £27 million deal was agreed.

Bill Kenwright: The regret, and it's a big word but it has to be admitted, was when I bought the club with Jon, Arthur Abercrombie, Paul Gregg, because then that was pain on a level that I cannot explain. Some of the things that happened; if you can imagine what you believed was your family turning on you. It was not people on the board. Just the things that happened. There were times when it was the fan base, when the media and the fan base got it a million percent wrong with Wayne Rooney: [that] we wanted to sell him and the boy didn't want to go, which was a million percent wrong. And to cope with that, when they said you've got to have a police escort, I said, 'I ain't going to have a police escort at Goodison Park; you can forget it, it's not for me.' And then the later times, and I don't want to go on about this too much because the disaffected supporters, the ones with bile in there – we almost knew their names there were so few of them – trying to cause uproar and whatever, that was tough.

David Moyes: We were finding it hard to stop it. I was really protective of him, and protective of my club and I hated the thought. Every day I was picking up papers, Wayne's going here, Wayne's going there. I remember I went out to watch him in Portugal playing in the Euros, and everybody was saying 'Wayne's meeting people on yachts with his agent Paul Stretford.' And I knew Paul, and I was angry.

Kevin Campbell: We played Manchester United, I think we got beat 2-1 that day. That was Wayne Rooney's first game at Old Trafford for the first team, and he really showed up. He scared the life out of them at times, and I think that was the defining moment, because I think Sir Alex Ferguson said to himself, 'I've to go and get this kid. He'll be the mainstay of the club for years.'

David Moyes: I had met Alex Ferguson on two occasions at the Haydock Thistle Hotel and it was about Wayne, privately. We got a room, we met privately, and he said to me, 'I want Rooney.' I said 'I'm not selling him.' And to be fair Alex accepted it. He said, 'Ok, no problem David. Just don't let him go south.' I think there was a lot of talk at the time that Chelsea were after him. I said, 'Fine.' Met him again, he said, 'I'm hearing Chelsea are in for him, he's going to go.' I'm saying, 'No, he's not going anywhere, I'm not selling him.'

Tomasz Radzinski: Well this was the problem, this was the interview I gave. Me saying that Wayne should go to a club with ambition and obviously from my point of view from that moment, the moment I gave the interview saying, 'Everton has no ambition, Everton is not a big club.' It was silly. It was really stupid and silly from me. I still think Wayne should move a step up, even at this time, but I shouldn't have said it in those words. I think Wayne was ready to play Champions League, he was ready to play for the silverware, whether or not it was United or Chelsea, whatever team he was going to go to, I think he was ready. But this thing shouldn't have come from me, it should have come from David Moyes. He should have said to the press, 'Yes, he's ready and he should go.'

Alan Stubbs: Wayne was going to go from Everton, whenever it was going to be. Whether it was that season, whether it was the season after, it was literally going to be a matter of time. And as an Everton fan we didn't like to say it, but we knew it was inevitable. And even as a player as in the team, we all knew. We just came to the conclusion that we wanted to enjoy him as much as we could while we had him.

Alan Irvine: There's a certain price that any player at Everton would have been sold for, and that obviously included Wayne. I think everybody looked and thought, 'Finished seventeenth last year, just lost Wayne Rooney, this is going to be a disaster.' But in some ways I think it probably galvanised everybody, because everybody was writing us off right from the beginning, whereas the previous season they're saying, 'Oh, Everton will kick on now.'

Alessandro Pistone: I wasn't surprised, because that kind of money is a massive amount of money in that period. I believe Wayne wanted to fight for a league or play in the Champions League, so it's always a decision between the club and the player, but at that time I believe that money was a great amount of money and the club had to make a decision.

Tony Hibbert: I know a lot of people will go berserk at Wayne leaving, but he helped the club. If you need to sell a player to help the club, then sell a player to help the club – the club comes before anyone else, the club's bigger than anybody else. So I had no problem with Wayne going to Man United for 20 odd million pounds. It was better for all parties. I was sad to see him leave, because he was an unbelievable talent, but to me the club comes first.

Alan Stubbs: I think if you flip it the other way, would Everton have had to sell Wayne Rooney if they weren't in such a perilous position financially? And the answer would have been no. And I think that was probably the biggest deciding factor in Wayne going. The club were in a pretty perilous position and Wayne basically kept the wolves from the door for a considerable amount of time.

Patrick Hart: I felt terrible about the sale, because he was only eighteen. If the team was going to make progress, they had an eighteen year-old forward who was an Evertonian, who could have at least stuck around for a couple of years. I thought that he let them down. I don't know the financial story behind it, but he wanted to leave ultimately, I'm pretty sure of that. It was disappointing. It felt like the whole football industry needed him to leave as well, which was a bit depressing.

Kevin Campbell: Unfortunately, Everton weren't cash rich at the time. Sometimes what went on wasn't pleasant because it kind of turned the Everton fans against Wayne, when it shouldn't have been that. As captain I didn't like what was going on because it kind of hung him out to dry a little bit. Everyone knew that the club was in dire straits financially. They needed the money, and it would have been just nicer if they'd come out and said, 'Look, we'd welcome Wayne if he could come back but we really need to sell him. We do, because we haven't got the money to balance books.' I'm sure the Evertonians would have been gutted but they would have understood that a lot more.

David Moyes: In the end we really couldn't stop it, even though it was something I never wanted to happen. I remember it was actually at Old Trafford, we played Manchester United. The deal was concluded that night. I think we got £24 million plus add ons, something like that. It was sad, but Wayne probably at that time had nearly outgrown Everton and had to step on. And we weren't a good enough team, or in Europe, or really pushing on to suggest it was right. So it was always going to be hard to keep our best players at that time.

Jon Woods: Basically the club needed the money. He wanted to go, and his agent obviously advised him. They were paying him whatever a week, we could pay the same, but he's more attractive to Coca Cola playing for Manchester United. Simple isn't it, really?

Alan Irvine: There's a certain price that any player at Everton would have been sold for, and that obviously included Wayne. I think everybody looked and thought, 'Finished seventeenth last year, just lost Wayne Rooney, this is going to be a disaster.' But in some ways I think it probably galvanised everybody, because everybody was writing us off right from the beginning, whereas the previous season they're saying, 'Oh, Everton will kick on now.'

Nigel Martyn: I mean you obviously want to keep hold of your better players for as long as you can, but if somebody comes calling, you're not naïve enough to think, 'Oh well, he will turn that down to stay with us.' Man United were the biggest club in the country at the time, and it was a real opportunity for him.

Alan Stubbs: He was a teammate, but he was a friend and all. And it wasn't advice in terms of 'You've got to leave Everton.' Everton is my club, I grew up as a boy with it being my club, and the last thing I wanted was for us to lose our best player, because he was winning us games singlehandedly at times with his ability. But every goal that he scored, we knew that the clamour that was going to build around Wayne was only going to get bigger and bigger and bigger, up until the day came that he went. I would have loved him to have been there for another two, three years. I would have loved him to have been there for all his career if I'm being honest, but I think there was a reluctance at the time.

David Moyes: Looking back at the journey, we had to sell to be able to reinvest. I think going back, the way we did the work at that time was pretty shrewd.

Tim Cahill and Moyes's modern football miracle

Alan Irvine: Every summer, David and I would go and spend some time thinking right, 'What new practices can we make up? What can we change? How can we freshen it up?' In the first season we went to St Andrews for a pre-season training camp and we had meetings with the players in the hotel to talk about how the team would work together. In the first year those meetings were fantastic, and we actually laid down the ground rules about how as a whole team and playing staff we were going to work for the whole season. We tried the same meeting the next pre-season in St Andrews and I thought it was a disaster. I felt as if we didn't get any positive outcomes from them. And that was probably a situation which should have been ringing alarm bells for us. With hindsight I feel that some of the players thought 'Crikey that was hard work, getting to seventh. Not sure if we can do that again.'

Alan Stubbs: David had a way of how he wanted his pre-seasons to go, no matter what. And knowing the fitness coaches that were there, Dave Billows, they probably had heated discussions on how it should go. You've got Dave trying to bring in some new evolution of how pre-season training should go, and you've got David with his strong-minded beliefs of how or what he wanted to get out of pre-season. You can imagine the two of them going head to head, some interesting conversations. But David would always win, and they were really tough pre-seasons, probably as tough as what I've encountered.

Leon Osman: We went to [2004/05] pre-season in Houston – went to Austria first but then went to Houston. We'd worked under him for a while; he was very tense and very uptight. He didn't drop his standards, but his demeanour and manner just became more relaxed. It just really helped. We got there and he was usually very regimented but we got there in the middle of the day, say Friday, three o'clock, and we didn't train. We had that afternoon to ourselves, the evening, the full day the next day where we all played golf, and then had a night out. We didn't start training until the afternoon on the Sunday, because we had to acclimatise. That was so unlike David Moyes. It was usually get there, 'Right let's get your boots out and go for a run.'

Alan Irvine: By the third year we didn't have the meeting at St Andrews as we realised that it wasn't a magic pill. What we needed to do was find a way to reignite the feeling that we had before.

Leon Osman: We had pretty much two full days on our own, and we had such a good time. We did all sorts, it was ridiculous. Ice rinks and golf and drinking, everything. It was like a mini stag do. But then when we got ready two days later, started training, it was like 'Right, we've enjoyed ourselves here, this is it. Let's keep up, let's get back now.' And it just seemed to work. We'd had such a good time, up until then, so all of these stories lasted the rest of this trip, because you'd had your fun and every time in training something happened, you referred to something you'd done in the last few days. It just became such togetherness, such a close knit group, and just constantly laughing and yet able to do your work.

Lee Carsley: We were doing an evening session in Houston. It had gone dark because there was no floodlights on the pitch. We'd finished a running session, which was an outrageous session, he fucking ran us into the ground he did. He got us all together in the centre circle and he said, 'Listen lads, Wayne's going, I'm not bringing anyone in, this is going to be our squad for the season, so get your heads around the fact that we need to stick together and we need to pull together, and we need to fucking go for it.' That for me was one of them moments where the team just bonded. We got together. It was the best team talk he ever did whilst I was there.

Alan Stubbs: It probably brought all the lads together really quickly. I think it probably was a catalyst for us doing pretty well. I think it's difficult to turn round and go, 'That was the reason why the season went so well,' or 'that was the reason why the season went so poorly.' I think it's a number of factors that can ultimately lead to a good or a bad experience.

David Moyes: It was a play-off game. I said to Bill, 'Will you come and watch a player at Millwall with me?' We had already met a few players in Bill's office, we'd done it with a couple of other players – we met a couple who we didn't really like. We didn't like their attitude. The two of us worked on it together. I took him to Millwall and said, 'Come and look at this boy in the Championship who I really like.' We actually went to see three players: Lucas Neill, Steven Reid, Tim Cahill. And Tim was the one who I had my eye on. He was a midfield player who could get in the box and score. And I liked the thought of it. Anyway, we got him into the office as well, and Tim's charm and character, personality – he'd win over anybody, he really would – won over Bill, and it matters a lot to Bill. Bill wanted to see people who had big heart and a big personality.

Mike Hughes: I can remember speaking to David Moyes about Tim Cahill. Tranmere had played Millwall in a night game and David Moyes had gone over to watch and I asked about Tim Cahill and he said, 'No not interested in him. I've seen that in the papers we're not interested in Tim Cahill.' Obviously they then signed him. David Moyes would never tell you or wouldn't tell you much with regards to that sort of thing. I remember asking him on a Saturday after a match the transfer window closed on the Monday or the Tuesday in January, 'Do you think Everton will be signing anybody?' 'Er no, we won't be doing any business,' and they signed four players. That was what David Moyes was like.

Tony Hibbert: To be honest, with Tim, £1.5 million we didn't expect a world beater, we didn't expect a lad from the local park. We expected a normal player, we didn't expect anything. With him training, he was a normal honest lad and a good player, a very good player. He didn't light us up, this unbelievable kid, but as the games went on, he more or less bought into the whole idea, and I think it helped him that he was close to me, he was close to Ozzy, he was close to a lot of people that were close to the club. He bought into the fact that it's Everton Football Club, and we would die for this club.

Alan Irvine: It was a great move for Tim and he was a great fit for us. He wasn't ready to play in one of the top teams, but he had the chance to come and play every week for us. It was a great step for him and as I say a terrific signing from the club's point of view.

Hana Roks: He had the passion and he loved Everton. When you got a corner you thought, 'Tim Cahill's head's going on this.' And he had quite a little nasty streak in him as well which I always love. I always remember him losing his boot, I think it was at Blackburn away, and he's scored and he's had no boot and it was just great. He's just one of those players where you could be in the 97th minute drawing 0-0 and you think 'Cahill'll step up here.' Obviously we didn't know much about him he'd come from Millwall and I knew he'd played against United when Millwall got beat 3-0 [in the 2004 FA Cup Final]. I think that's really the only time I'd seen him play, but he came to us and the rest is history.

Simon Hart: Maybe the World Cup shouldn't be viewed as the ultimate barometer and the Champions League should be, but Tim Cahill went and scored in three different World Cup finals. I think if you put him on a big stage, he tended to grow on that stage, rather than the other way round. And he'd do it in the biggest games for Everton. So I would say he's world class, and I love the fact that Cahill, at a time when other players would leave Everton citing lack of ambition, not only remained, but bought into the city and the club.

Alessandro Pistone: They were always trying to discover these new and upcoming players, young players with great potential to bring to Everton and to build up a new team, a big team. Obviously not spending massive money to bring in players with already three, four, five seasons in the Premier League because you have to face up with the fact that you cannot compare with – at that time – teams like Manchester United, Arsenal, with massive money to spend. So they were always trying to do the things cleverly.

Leon Osman: Rooney hadn't gone at that point, but we all knew he was going. He'd injured his foot. We'd brought in this lad Tim Cahill who had scored a couple of goals for Millwall. Seen his goals, he was a good player but we hadn't met him yet, because he was at the Olympics. So we just had our little team and our little squad. I wouldn't say we were thinking, 'We're confident' and all that, but we had smiles on our faces. We were enjoying playing football with each other. And that always helps.

Tony Hibbert: The team spirt was unbelievable. Great bunch of lads, friends on and off the pitch. It was brilliant. The club itself to be honest, from staff in the canteen to secretaries, it felt good, it felt a good place as a unit. It was just a good place to be.

Leon Osman: We didn't start off the season too well. Arsenal were still 'The Invincibles' back then and we lost 4-1, but then we went to Palace, 1-0 down early again. Then their keeper – Julian Speroni – changed our season. Kev Campbell robbed him of the ball and from then we never looked back. The belief, the confidence, we just had all of it. Things fell into place, we went to Old Trafford and drew, we beat West Brom. The happiness and the excitement and the togetherness when we celebrated, every one of us got in a huddle. I think we were still referring to, 'Do you remember that in Houston?' It was a really good time for us.

Kevin Campbell: Again it was that toughness. Tinkered with the formation, we started playing 4-5-1, and what tended to happen was Tim Cahill came in, who had a fantastic ability to get into the box late. The striker had to lead the line, so when the striker's leading the line you tended to find that the strikers weren't scoring a lot of goals, but Tim Cahill, who was kind of joining in, was getting quite a bit of the goals. Moyes tinkered with the system and it worked. Hard to beat, tough, hardnosed club again, which the fans love.

Alan Irvine: As you've no doubt heard plenty of times goals change games and if you do get a goal and you are a team that is very determined, then there's a fair chance that goal might be enough for you. Tim's goals were one of the things he brought to the team, but you know he headed plenty of balls in our box as well.

Leon Osman: Tommy Gravesen was one of the most technically gifted players I have ever played with. Skill, range of passing, strength. But defensively, we called him, 'Mad Dog', because he just ran all over the place like a mad dog. So it was always difficult for Lee Carsley to play in a 4-4-2 with him because you need to work as a two, and Tommy would run all over the place, charge round people and leave big gaps. So it just fell perfectly for us because Tim Cahill could do both and Tommy could do both. So between them, they did half a job each to help Cars. So Cars did the main job and they did half a job each, and yet Tim got forward with his other half and Tommy created everything with his other half.

David Moyes: He was tough, Tim. He was tough, and he wasn't a great football player as far as midfield passers go. This is where his position developed into a bit of a number ten, in between a midfield player and a forward. Tim being what he was meant we had to try and find a way of playing which fitted Tim Cahill in. But at this time we'd started to bring in Mikel Arteta. We also had Leon Osman, a similar type, so you talk about style… I used to laugh when I heard people say it, because I used to think, 'Well, what style do you play with Mikel Arteta and Leon Osman?' Yeah we had another type which was a Tim Cahill, or in the past it was Duncan Ferguson, Kevin Campbell, but we were trying to evolve our style to become better with our football.

Danny Cadamarteri: Gravesen played like a man possessed. He was all over the pitch. He'd chase the ball into the full-back, and the full-back would play it to the centre half, he'd chase it to the centre half and that centre half would play it to the other centre half, and he would run it down and play it to the other full-back, he'd chase the other full-back and then he'd win the ball.

Lee Carsley: My role was to give Tim and Thomas the licence to get forward, get second balls, to keep the play moving simply, to plug gaps in defence when needed, just be a good team player. We'd done a lot of work on the back four and myself in front; defending, defending, defending, wave after wave of attack against twelve players, fourteen players, sixteen players, and we just developed a real resilience. Along with Richard Wright and Nigel Martyn behind us, we forged a great unit.

Alan Stubbs: You didn't know what you were going to get from Thomas Gravesen, and I think that was the thing that was good about him. But I don't think Thomas knew what he was going to give you, so if he didn't know, then we wouldn't have a clue! But when he did perform, he was, at times, excellent throughout the season. Kevin Kilbane was probably a typical David Moyes player. Very honest, really hardworking, run forever, big, strong, powerful; and he was a brilliant lad.

Kevin Campbell: Tim's got a great leap on him, so he's got a better chance of winning that ball. He mastered it, didn't he? He mastered getting in the box late, which was great.

Nigel Martyn: I think defensively we got better. He went with three in the midfield or five all the way across, and we had workers there that ran their socks off every game. With Marcus Bent up front that season, he was very mobile, so he could run into channels.

David Weir: I can remember winning a lot of games 1-0, and I can remember us having a lot of momentum and a good spirit about the place, and just a belief that we were going to win games. Definitely the pieces fell into place, Thomas Gravesen was a big part of it and the unity within the group was good. But again, you wonder if that comes from winning or vice versa. That's the kind of conundrum associated with football – what comes first? But the system itself, it wasn't revolutionary. We were hardworking, we were one upfront, and we played on the counter attack quite a lot, even at home sometimes, the opposition – especially the better teams – would have more of the ball. Marcus Bent was lightning quick, Tim Cahill could pop up with a goal, and defensively we were pretty sound, Lee Carsley being a big part of that, and Nigel Martyn I think was a goalkeeper at the time; top class players.

By the start of 2005 Everton had 40 points – more than they'd gained in the entire previous season – and were occupying a Champions League spot. In January they signed Southampton's centre-forward, James Beattie, for a club record £6million and Real Sociedad's midfielder, Mikel Arteta. Thomas Gravesen, however, was a surprise departure to Real Madrid.

Alan Stubbs: We would always be shouting and encouraging Thomas to get back in, whereas Mikel, he brought that discipline, but it was a controlled discipline. He was technically not as skilful as Thomas, but in terms of retention of the ball, distribution of passing, scoring a few goals, scoring goals and all from set pieces, he had a bigger influence on the team. He didn't have the dribbling ability of Thomas, even though Mikel was very good, but Mikel gave us something that at that time was more consistent with what we needed.

Leon Osman: We didn't really know much about [Mikel] when he came in, but what a good player he was. He seemed to fit in seamlessly, everyone took to him really well. I think we brought James Beattie in at roughly the same time, and he was another one. He came in and found his way in the team. Things just worked out for us at that point.

Tony Hibbert: Mikel was a brilliant player. Football ability-wise he was brilliant. To be honest I didn't realise how good he was until he came, but he probably gave us that football side of things.

Alan Irvine: Mikel had the reputation of somebody who was a nice footballer but didn't really work that hard, but he came in and fitted in brilliantly. I love players like Mikel, Steven Pienaar and Leon Osman and Leighton Baines, I've mentioned them enough times already for you to probably get that… Really talented footballers, technically very good, very aware of what is going on round about them, but they were all great characters as well. Fabulous footballers' and great professionals. The training was getting better and better which led to even better performances and results. So yeah Mikel was a huge addition.

Kevin Campbell: I'd left by the time he came in, I'd gone. But obviously I watched from a distance. Mikel Arteta was a fantastic player. He was a dictator of the tempo of the game, which Everton really didn't have. Being able to dictate the tempo means that you control the game. Everton tended to control the game a lot better, and once you can control the game and control the tempo, you've got a better chance of winning games.

Many factors helped Everton's ascendancy that season, including a resurgent Duncan Ferguson, who put years of injury problems behind him to play a telling part in the campaign – often from the bench. On 20 April 2005 Everton effectively secured Champions League qualification with a 1-0 over Manchester United; Ferguson's winner the high point of one of the finest performances of his career.

David Moyes: It was incredible the night Duncan scored against Manchester United. I always think of Everton as a hard-working, industrial football club. They always talk about the School of Science, and I can see the players that they had, but I don't think I saw any of the great Everton sides that weren't competitive. When I think of Everton of the past I would think of Andy Gray and Graeme Sharp upfront, Trevor Steven one side, Kevin Sheedy, maybe Reidy and Bracewell, whoever it may be. I wouldn't have said they were going into those games not at it every game. I still saw Everton in that picture, that was my picture of Everton. I wanted to try and get a team that could never be as good, never be the same but could follow that picture.

Tony Hibbert: From the minute you kicked off you just knew. From the changing rooms, leading into the game, you just knew, he'd tell you he was up for it, no matter what. And you just knew, 'Wow, we're going to get a game from Fergie here.'

Leon Osman: It was like winning the league for us. It was ridiculous. It was my first full season, and we'd done this, and who knows, imagine what can come next. It was really a good achievement. We got off to such a good start, we were in the top four pretty much all year, and really did deserve what we got.

Alan Stubbs: After that start, we just thought, 'You know what, we'll just keep doing our own thing, we'll just keep going and see where it takes us.' And we probably got strength from everybody writing us off. Because from early on, you see, 'Oh Everton have started off really well, but that will peter off, they'll probably finish in the top eight', type of thing, and it probably give us a bit of an extra incentive. As well as that, we had David driving it home all the time, because David would turn around and say he wanted to finish first. And we would all be like, 'Yeah, okay, good one.' But that was him. He brought not just a winning mentality, but a real desire to not take second best. And with that group he certainly just seemed to light the fuse paper with it. And for that season it worked.

Nigel Martyn: The season before was such a struggle and it was hard work. That's when it's a tough place to be, where you're going in every day and you've lost again the week before, you're down in a relegation fight. The following season you're up challenging for Europe, you're winning games, you're getting good results against big sides. Everything is brighter, your confidence is up, it's a much happier place to be. Training wise and on match day you feel a lot more confident, and it's not something that you can manually switch on and off, it's just literally how you feel. We, in that second season, were feeling better about ourselves, a bit more than we were the season before.

Kevin Campbell: Everton did so well to get into Europe, the Champions League. That actually bucked the trend, didn't it? That was like winning the division, because breaking into that top four was unheard of.

Leon Osman: You certainly look back now – and just think if we'd have done that now or if ten years ago Everton would have had the financial backing to go and support what we did… but we were a team; we'd just finished seventeenth, had to sell Wayne Rooney to pay the bills, couldn't invest any of it, got a great team together, managed to finish fourth, suddenly you've got all these extra games. And we brought in one player to strengthen. I think it was Simon Davies, who happened to be in my position, by the way. Imagine nowadays a team finishing fourth in the league and then buying one player? Without strengthening you're not going to be able to keep going.

After Liverpool's surprise Champions League triumph over AC Milan UEFA had to decide which of the two Merseyside clubs to allow into the draw. The rules clearly showed it should be Everton, but the governing body deliberated. In the end a compromise was reached: Liverpool would enter qualification at the first qualifying round; Everton would still enter in the final qualifying round. The draw would not prove kind though: the Toffees found themselves up against Villarreal, who had just finished third in La Liga and possessed the brilliant Juan Roman Riquelme in their ranks.

David Moyes: The build-up to it was obviously Liverpool winning the Champions League. I remember I was at home and the Liverpool game was on. I remember the staff were texting 1-0 Milan, 2-0, 3-0. The staff were all texting, 'Great, great'. And by the end of it I had booked a flight to get out of the country, because I couldn't stand the thought. We had finished fourth, Liverpool had finished fifth and Everton had very rarely finished above them in [recent] history. For us to do it and find we were sort of trumped by Liverpool was terrible. So I got of the country. I remember phoning Bill Kenwright and saying, 'Tell me there's not many people on the streets Bill,' when Liverpool were parading the trophy, and he said 'You don't want to know David.' So I was glad I got away. That was the build-up.

Nigel Martyn: Celebrating finishing above them was great and then they go and spoil it by winning probably the most exciting European Cup final in memory.

Leon Osman: There was talk of us not suddenly getting Champions League and them not getting Champions League, qualifiers and all that.

Alan Irvine: I remember Mikel's reaction to seeing the draw. He immediately went 'Oh no that's a terrible draw.' That was really quite poignant. For a player to react in that way is unusual, but when we started to do our homework on Villarreal it became clear how difficult a task it was going to be.

David Moyes: I always thought they never wanted five English teams in the Champions League. I didn't think it worked. Obviously we drew Villarreal, who were second in Spain that year. And we drew them. For me it was still a bit great – 'We'll take it on, we're in the Champions League' – but I knew we hadn't got a draw which would give us a real chance of getting in. We knew we had to do incredibly well. So it was an incredible blow to us, the draw that we got.

Tony Hibbert: We weren't afraid. It was all new to us and an experience, so we weren't afraid at all going and playing them. It was lik, 'Bring it on!' It was another game. So we did in a way, but not to an extent that we thought we were going to get turned over or we were out because we were playing them, it was a good experience.

Leon Osman: You put on a brave face, but as always happens with Everton, we get the toughest draw we can. To get Villarreal at that stage in a qualifier – you know there was teams out there I've never even heard of, and we get the biggest team in the qualifiers, barring us. It just was what it was, and you've then got to put a brave face on and get on with it.

Alan Irvine: They were a top, top team with really good players. They had [Juan Roman] Riquelme in their team, and he was like a quarter-back. Whenever he got the ball everybody ran, and he was capable of putting it on their toes. A lot of those players that played in that Villarreal team, made moves again that took them on to another level, for example, Marcos Senna, and players who people didn't know too much about became household names and top internationals. Any team that finishes where they finished in Spain, would have done extremely well in the Premier League. I believe they would have been a top four team.

David Moyes: The two games will always live with me because of the incredible atmosphere at Goodison. Riquelme playing for Villarreal, a stunning team, Villarreal. That year Villarreal got to the semi-finals and lost on penalties kicks to Arsenal to go to the Champions League final.

Nigel Martyn: They kept the ball a lot. We just didn't seem to be able to get around them as much as we normally would. Normally we would be in and around them a bit more. The passing was very crisp. I remember they seemed to knock it around us a lot of the time, and we were chasing but we weren't quite there. I just think if that game had been a week or two later then it would have been a much tougher game for them.

Leon Osman: I think it was a learning curve for everyone. It's not like we'd been in Europe before and had experience of it. I think maybe we came out and tried to go at them and get that goal, whereas they were quite cute. They'd been there before, they know just keep it tight and there will be opportunities there. And we opened ourselves up a little bit too much.

Villarreal won the first leg at Goodison 2-1. Back in Spain Villarreal took further control of the tie with a goal from Juan Pablo Sorin, but Everton were level in the second half – and in the ascendancy – after a brilliant Mikel Arteta free-kick. Soon afterwards Duncan Ferguson rose home to score a header from a corner, bringing the scores level on aggregate – only for it to be disallowed by referee Pierluigi Collina for a non-existent foul. With the momentum all but gone, Everton conceded a late goal.

Bill Kenwright: I just wasn't comfortable that night from my arrival at the ground. For starters, I was the only person in their box. They only had the chairman sitting there, so I was surrounded by all of their dignitaries sat in armchairs. And after about 20 minutes I said, 'I can't be here; I just can't be here. I don't want to be rude but I want to be with my people,' and I went and sat with James Beattie, who couldn't play that day. It was a jump for joy when the ball went in the net and we just looked at each other in massive disbelief when he thought it was a foul.

David Moyes: Duncan scores to take the game into extra time, and Collina doesn't give it, and it's incredible, still to this day. I remember it, outside I'm saying, 'There's no touch, no touch.' He said, 'No, no.' I remember standing outside the dressing room, Villarreal: 'No, no.' I look back – Collina never refereed another game of football after that game that night. My thoughts are that I don't think UEFA wanted five British teams in, I don't think it worked in the way it was configured.

Nigel Martyn: At the time I'm down the other end. I remember seeing Duncan jump and head the ball very cleanly. Then I see him give the foul, and I could only think it was for something else. It wasn't for what Duncan had done, it was for something else. Somebody pulling, blocking, whatever. I couldn't see what that could have been, that happens so often. You've got a corner, you watch the ball and you watch the guy that's going to head the ball, you're not watching everybody else. So I kind of thought, 'Right okay, he's seen something, so that's why he's disallowed it...'

Tony Hibbert: He give a foul on Marcus Bent. He said Marcus Bent fouled the lad, and we can't see a foul. We looked at it and looked at it, and we cannot see a foul. We didn't know on the pitch, at the end we were saying 'What was the foul for'? And he pointed to Marcus Bent. It was just one of them that was like, 'Wow.' We just could not believe it.

Bill Kenwright: I had that feeling all night; all night long; I'm saying no more. I had a feeling all night long.

Nigel Martyn: I can remember Diego Forlan was on the halfway line and he looked over at me and I made a gesture to him sort of saying, 'This is getting close now', and he was nodding, even sort of agreeing that they were in trouble at that point. But I've seen it on the telly a few times, and I'm not sure why he's given it.

Mike Hughes: That set Everton back because it shocked Everton. Villarreal ended up scoring another goal. As far as the goals are concerned, if you add them up, Villarreal won the game comfortably. But they didn't .

Leon Osman: We were certainly in the game, we had a chance. We were robbed by Mr Collina, but looking round at the draw... you're never amazed when you're an Evertonian...

Alan Irvine: I went in to see Collina after the game and he said it was a foul by Duncan Ferguson.

Nigel Martyn: I think a few of the lads were asking him afterwards, and he sort of very dismissively brushed them away really, he kept very tight lipped and just walked off.

Alan Irvine: Having worked so hard to get there, and then for it to be taken away in those circumstances was extremely hard to take. You go from the high point of finishing fourth and qualifying for the Champions League to the low point of being out before you've started.

David Moyes: We ran them really close, but they had a real star player in Riquelme, and I think sometimes that's the difference, you needed a player of that ilk. We were building a team, we probably didn't have a player who could maybe individually make the difference as Riquelme could.

Mike Hughes: As much as the four days that broke Everton in the seventies being pivotal, that decision by supposedly the best referee in the world actually set Everton back who knows how far. If Everton had gone into the Champions League that season – I think Villarreal got to the semi-final and Everton played really well and arguably should've beaten Villarreal – the money that Everton would've made through being in the Champions League what difference could that have made? It's another case of what might have been for Everton fans and a there's been so many of them down the years.

If the defeat to Villarreal was a steep learning curve, then the 5-1 loss away to Dinamo Bucharest in the UEFA Cup second round was a shock.

Leon Osman: We went 1-0 down, equalised, Joseph Yobo was credited with it but I nicked it off him on the line and never got the goal. And then we were 1-1, conceded, 2-1. And at that point 2-1 would have been fine for us, but being naïve, the manager made a couple of attacking changes to try and get us back into the game, and as a team we sort of went on the attack. And you don't need to do that in the first leg of Europe.

David Weir: Everything that could go wrong did go wrong. It just seemed to be that very early on it was clear that things weren't going to go our way, and that continues to be the case. Goals went in from different angles and from different methods. It was obviously a very frustrating night because we still wanted to do well in that competition, still wanted to stay involved in that competition. But you've got to give credit to them, they played well. We weren't at our best and we didn't give the sort of performance we'd have liked in that competition.

Nigel Martyn: I think one of the other managers had spoken to one of our coaches and he'd watched a game, and he said, 'If they're not on something I don't know what,' because they just basically ran us into the ground, and it was just like playing the best team you'd ever faced. I don't know, it was a bizarre situation, because they just seemed to be faster, fitter, stronger in every department really. There was more of a realistic game at Goodison, we sort of battered them without really creating that many chances, but the damage was done away. It was a real shame.

Tony Hibbert: There was a massive step in a way of technically ability in Europe. It was a lot slower, individual players were a lot better than what we were playing in the Premier League. In a way of, the Premier League was 100 miles an hour. Playing in Europe, it was a lot slower, and relied on individuals, players with the ability to pick a little passes and flicks and stuff like that, so that was all new.

Alan Irvine: I felt as if there was very, very little in the game in the first half and I thought that we were in a decent position at half time, but they got a couple of goals quite early in the second half and we probably got a bit too open, thinking that we needed to do something about that over there. In actual fact, probably with a bit more experience we might have just said 'Okay, we'll settle for where we are just now and take them back to Goodison and have a go.' Because we did take them back to Goodison and we did have a go! But we'd given ourselves too much to do.

Everton would finish in a disappointing eleventh in 2005/06, unable to scale the same heights as the previous season after their double European exit.

Tony Hibbert: We'd be going in to it and thinking, 'What the hell is going on with us?' We wouldn't know. We'd have a few losses and go back to the basics, we'd even have a meeting and say, 'Listen we need to change. Stop what we're doing and go back to basics and get it forward as quickly as possible, and we will play off the second balls.' We'd done everything, we just didn't know why it happened with us. Strange.

Nigel Martyn: At the start of that season he changed it, he brought James Beattie in and started playing with two upfront, which meant we just weren't quite as compact as we had been. The manager, I think, had recognised that people sort of said, 'Alright you've done well, but you're a bit dour in the way that you play,' and I think he genuinely wanted to be more of a threat going forward, and try to put other teams under more pressure than perhaps we did before.

Leon Osman: It was a mixture of a European hangover, the disappointment of how it was. You look at football today and you look at football back then. We had, what, a fourteen-man squad, would you say? We certainly didn't have a big squad. We had a fourteen-man squad, and we were now competing in four different competitions. The season before we'd managed to compete in the league, but you're playing, Saturday, Saturday, Saturday. You've got a full week to gather yourselves, everyone is fit, everyone's raring to go, whereas we were suddenly playing Saturday, Wednesday, Saturday, Wednesday, with a fourteen-man squad when everyone was fit.

Alan Irvine: I think sometimes the effort required to get to the position that you want to achieve is so great that you find it difficult to do it again, and that's when perhaps things need to be freshened up a little bit. But you may not have the money to do that, or the opportunity to do that. Of course people might also look at you and say 'Why are you breaking this up? It was really good last year.' So it becomes a very difficult situation.

Nigel Martyn: I think what happened was we left ourselves a little bit vulnerable, whereas we were solid before, we were probably a player light in midfield a bit more often, and that really caused us not to start the season too well.

Alan Irvine: It was a supreme effort to finish seventh in that first season, it was a supreme effort to finish fourth in the third season, and there was probably a little bit of 'Wow, we've got to do this all over again,' without people really consciously thinking about that. Otherwise it's difficult for me to put my finger on it.

Scouting for Moyes: Building a top six team

Steve Round: David and his staff, we went to games all over Europe, we'd scout the opposition. I was never at home for five years. You're watching opposition, you're watching players, you're watching recruitment, you're watching everything. So if you're not working at the club you're out watching games.

David Moyes: We worked really hard on the scouting – I demanded off the scouts all the time. Probably more importantly, I was at games three or four nights a week watching. And it wasn't always to see players, you'd be amazed how many times you go and say 'I've seen somebody I quite like.' It's a little bit less likely to happen now because of the knowledge of everything. We were still maybe just a little bit in front of a lot of the others in what we were doing. I wanted a really strong scouting network.

Joleon Lescott: David Moyes had thought about a process of, over the next two or three years, we can build something and push, because it was more to do with squads and players, there wasn't the money factor then was there? There wasn't a huge difference in money. Even the top teams weren't spending three times as much as everyone else, so it was more of a level playing field then.

Tim Howard: I've always said from the day I stepped through the doors at Everton [in summer 2006] it felt like home. I was there ten years, but I got there and then Joleon came, Andrew Johnson came, Tim Cahill and Mikel Arteta and Phil Neville were already there, and then Jagielka and Baines came, so we kind of all came at the same time within a three or four year period, which ended up making the backbone of that team for the next decade. We were all kind of transplants, and we fitted with that team very well.

Leon Osman: Phil Neville led by doing everything first. Warm-ups, he was in front. Going to do something, getting off the bus, he was first off the bus. Phil Neville led. Phil Neville was first into action. And he would never ask you to do something he wouldn't do himself, he was that type of captain.

Gerry Moore: I thought at the time he came, and I still do, that he was a great signing. Although he split opinions at United, on the pitch Phil was in charge. He would run his heart out for the club and it takes a lot after playing at a club like United for that length of time to come to Everton and to still give 100 per-cent. He was obviously going to be a captain because he was a leader on and off the pitch and that is very important.

Steve Round: One of the things you could never underestimate in my five years was the importance of Phil Neville. Phil Neville was the captain, he became captain during my first year, and he was the epitome of professionalism. He led from the front, he was a cheerleader in the dressing room for the coaches and the manager. You could rely on him to get the right messages out. He brought people together. He was an exemplary captain, he really was, and he had a massive, massive effect on the culture, the dressing room, and the way we played at Everton.

Tim Howard: We had a brilliant manager in David Moyes, and what he realised in his time at Everton was that you couldn't waste money, because there wasn't a lot of it to spend. So he was very particular on what type of players he brought in, the character of player he brought in, and at that time he was going round to clubs, and because of the way it happens in world football, players become surplus to requirements. It doesn't mean they're not good, it just means that money has brought in new players and they're forced out. So David really did a good job, financially, finding those players who were still at the top of their game and had a lot to offer, but for whatever reason weren't in favour at their current club.

David Moyes: Nev was someone who could play full-back, could play midfield, but also brought a level of professionalism which upped the standard of what we had. He gave us another [level] in how he prepared himself. He came with an incredible winning mentality. Phil brought that to us. One day, one of the players was getting booed, and in the dressing room at half-time he says, 'Look, if they're booing that player, they're booing us all. We're all in this.'

Alan Irvine: We signed Phil Jagielka [in 2007] for three positions as an example. We didn't have a lot of money, and when you don't have a lot of money you need to be really, really careful about how you spend that money, because if you get it wrong you don't have any reserves to fall back on.

Tim Howard: The formation we played the most was a 4-5-1. Very flexible, but a 4-5-1. And also, in his recruitment policy, not only did I say he brought the right characters in, he brought in players who could play a variety of positions, so he'd bring a centre-half who could play left-back, he'd bring a left-back who could play left-wing, he'd bring a winger who could play striker. So there were all these different positions – you came to the club and you had your position, but you could also be flexible enough. Jagielka played right-back, centre-back, number six for us. He was always a centre-back, but Moyes definitely recruited players who could play in more than one positon.

David Moyes: Joleon I must have watched live 24 times, and that was because we were also in for Robert Huth at that time, and the decision was 'Do we take Joleon Lescott or Robert Huth?' Robert Huth was at Chelsea, and in the end I just went for Joleon because I wanted a left-footed centre-back.

Tony Hibbert: We bought Lescott from Wolves, and again – the same as Tim – it wasn't like, 'We've got this kid, he's unreal, we've seen him play.' He was a normal signing until he started playing with you. Give Moyes his due, he got some great signings that did well for us. With Tim, I think he didn't have the best of starts at Man United, he wasn't the best, but I would probably say that Tim was the best keeper I've played with. [Moyes's] signings for Everton were spot on, money-wise as well as helping the club and the team.

Alan Irvine: I felt that what David had managed to do gradually – he could only do it gradually, because he didn't have the money to do it quickly – was to improve the quality of the team individually and collectively whilst retaining the same values which were important to him and fitted the culture of the Club.

Tim Howard: He always kept the team fresh by bringing in new players, but the thing with David Moyes is that he is full of fire. He doesn't take a day off and he doesn't say, 'This session doesn't matter.' You were quite literally on your toes every single day. I think when the team loses their passion and their hunger and their fight it is when the manager loses it, and the manager never lost it. Every single day he was on the training ground, in his boots, getting in players' faces, demanding the best. That's what you saw from him. Again, he brings in players he trusts. So when he brings you in and asks you to be responsible and take a leadership role, you do it because you don't want to disappoint him.

Tony Hibbert: The money the top teams were spending was frightening, and obviously they were buying people who had seen it all and done it before, they've experienced it. We obviously made some great signings, the likes of Joleon Lescott and Tim, but they were Championship players. We weren't buying elite players to get us through to that. That might have been just the theory at our club; buy players to sell them on. I don't know. We just needed someone in to change the philosophy of us and what we were doing; the way it's changing now [in 2017]: we've got a foundation, we need X amount of players to get us onto a next level.

The 2007/08 league campaign was another relative success: a top four place seemed attainable until a late season dip in form, and Everton finished fifth. There was a clear attempt to expand the attacking game, which was helped by the guile of Leighton Baines and Steven Pienaar down the left-hand side. The squad was further boosted in summer 2008 by the additions of Marouane Fellaini for a record transfer fee from Standard Liege and Louis Saha from Manchester United.

David Moyes: Baines we had brought in from Wigan. I was pushed really hard by the agent on Steven Pienaar, who had been at Ajax and gone to Dortmund where it hadn't quite worked, and I was thinking 'maybe not.' But the way I wanted to play at that time was with a little bit of false wide players, false wingers, which was maybe Osman or Arteta at the time, a little bit of both. And there was an incredible understanding between Pienaar and Baines.

Joleon Lescott: A big surprise for me, the way Mikel took to that [central midfield] role [having started his Everton career on the left of midfield]. It wasn't so much the ability, because that was never in doubt. It was the fact that he just had the willingness to get involved in the breakdown of play. I didn't expect it. I'm not saying I didn't think he could do it, because I'd never seen him to judge that, but there was a time when I thought 'Wow, he's really took to this.' And having that, again, that was a difference to Lee Carsley. With Mikel they had to respect the fact that he was a bit better on the ball, defensively obviously not as good as Lee, but on the ball they then had to respect that he can cause problems.

Steve Round: You're looking at developing and expanding cohesion and combinations. So while I was there we had arguably the best combination in the league, which was Leighton Baines and Steven Pienaar, who were almost telepathic. But people don't realise, we worked on that in training. We'd always pick them in the same team, we'd always put them together, we'd always do little combinations, we'd always do four against three in corners.

Tim Howard: I think when David Moyes was hired Everton weren't doing very well, and the idea for a lot of Premier League clubs is to stay in the league, solidify yourselves as a Premier League team, and then build from there. I think Moyes was brilliant at that. He got us to defend with vigour and with passion; even our best players, guys like Mikel Arteta at the time, who was a maestro with the ball, but learnt how to tackle, and fight, and get stuck in. But as the years went on David Moyes allowed us to become more expansive, and he taught us to become more expansive. With the likes of Leighton Baines, and Mikel Arteta, and Steven Pienaar: guys who could get on the ball and express themselves.

Steven Pienaar: At the time when I came into the team I had a few different left-backs behind me. I had Lescott a few times, I had Nuno [Valente] playing left-back so it wasn't quite settled. The following season Baines also started getting into the team. On the training ground was the main thing, because even in training we were working hard, and the manager always made a point and kept us in the team. I think that understanding from the training ground, we took to the games and that's what made it work.

David Moyes: He was an acquired taste, Steven, and maybe people were saying, 'What have we got here?' But I think it became one of the best partnerships in the Premiership at the end of their time. Those two had an understanding as good as the days when [Ashley] Cole was playing with [Florent] Malouda, where they had a great understanding together.

Leon Osman: They were a real unit. They were together, they sort of worked without having to even think about it, to the point at the time, I was playing midfield and I purposefully went and played on the left of the two central midfielders because I could get involved in that play. I would always gravitate towards them so I could join in, and the three of us would have a little pass. But ultimately it was them two who got into the attacking positons, I just kept feeding them with the ball in the right areas.

Steven Pienaar: It was just the honesty between the two of us. Working hard: when he overlaps I make sure I cover, I have to track my runners and make things easy for him as well defensively. He appreciated a player playing in front of him that also put in the effort so defensively. It wasn't something special that we did in training, it was just an understanding of working for each other.

Joleon Lescott: For some reason, the understanding of them two was instant, it wasn't like they had to wait six months – as soon as they played together they knew that they benefitted from each other. Straight away.

Steve Round: We did sessions to get in the final cubes of the pitch. Once we got in the final cubes, how do we create an opportunity to get Fellaini a header, or Cahill a header, or a cut back for Arteta, or whatever it may be. So we'd work on that training, but fundamentally they had this uncanny ability to understand where each other was all the time. Reverse passes, one touch passes; sometimes I don't think they even knew how they were doing it. It was uncanny, it really was.

David Moyes: The other thing people didn't realise, Steven Pienaar was a cross country champion in South Africa, which meant that he had brilliant energy, which people didn't quite recognise. And he was a really talented footballer.

Simon Hart: What's underrated is that team as a footballing team; the midfield with players like Arteta, Pienaar, Baines, Osman; clever players, clever footballers, really unlucky not to win a trophy.

Steven Pienaar: The camaraderie was so big in the dressing room that every player knew what was expected of each other, so it made it quite easy. Whoever the manager put in the middle, players like Mikky, would understand how to keep the ball. That was also the strength of our team. I think most of the neutrals didn't realise how well we kept the ball.

Joleon Lescott: We were taught different aspects, and we catered for every team. It wasn't a case of, 'Well we're going to do this and hopefully this works,' it was like, 'Well they're going to do that and so we need to do that.' I think that was different. I noticed the fact that he set us up to combat every other team. It wasn't just, 'Well, we're good enough to do this', or, 'We're going to do that' and be stubborn about it. It was generally, 'Let's try and [stop this].They're going to do one thing, we need to do another thing to come out on top.'

Steven Pienaar: I think from the manager's point of view when he signed players, he signed players that can play all across, so it was quite easy when sometimes Fellaini would play as a number 10, sometimes he would play defensive midfield.

Tim Howard: When Marouane Fellaini came in it was hard to figure out who he was and what was his best position and best attributes were, because he had that soft chest. You could put it up and he'd take it down very elegantly. He could battle in the air with the best of them, but he's a good footballer, a very good footballer, he's proven to be. So it was just trying to find out what the big man was all about, and it took us a little bit of time, but I think ultimately what was really good for us was that we could play him in the number six or number eight role, where he could maraud around the midfield and get the ball at his feet. But there were also times where we could say, 'Hey, go stick him upfront as a number nine', depending on what the game offered, and he could be the lone striker. There were some options there and a player of his calibre we hadn't had before.

David Moyes: Fellaini was a midfield player. He played a bit as an attacking midfield player. He wasn't a holding midfield player, was nothing like that. We actually had a little bit of a problem when he first came in trying to get Cahill and Fellaini in the team, because in a way they were both a bit similar.

Fellaini could play a bit deeper. In the end Fellaini became a little bit of the number 10 for us at times, and did a great job.

Everton in Europe

Everton were back in Europe for the 2007/08 season, playing in an expanded UEFA Cup that contained its own group stage. This time, it was clear that they had learned from some of their previous mistakes. They beat eventual champions Zenit Saint Petersburg, and topped a group of five with four wins from four. A particular highlight was a 2-0 win away to Nuremberg with 8,000 Evertonians invading the Bavarian city.

David Moyes: It was a massive priority. Going back to being non-negotiable, I don't see that only playing in one tournament was enough. I used to get asked the question a little bit, 'Are you prioritising?' No, we always had to play our best players. Of course you had squad players that played, but I wanted to win every trophy I entered.

Tony Hibbert: We felt a lot more comfortable and the players that he brought in in those year were a lot better technical wise, football wise, so we enjoyed it more and it wasn't a shock to us. No matter where we go, the fans were unbelievable, and to be honest it was a way for them to get out and have a party. That's how it was, my dad went on many of them and it was more or less a drinking weekend! It was crazy. The fans deserved it, they hadn't been away in so many years, so it was great for them to get out and experience it all again, like they should do.

Steven Pienaar: I think that was also one of the reasons the manager signed me, because he said to me, 'We're going to play in Europe, so we need players who know the pace of the game and in European competition.' To be honest we took it in our stride. We did quite well, the first season in the Europa League.

Tim Howard: We played some really good teams. We travelled well. We competed when we had away games. We were able to play a continental style and weren't really ever outmatched.

Leon Osman: We'd learnt a lot from our previous experience and we had a right good go.

After beating SK Brann in the Round of 32, Everton came up against Fiorentina in the next knock-out stage.

Tim Howard: We went away from home and played in Italy. It was 0-2. We came home and we needed to get a result, and we played open and free-flowing, and really put them on the back foot. It was an interesting game because we needed to keep a clean sheet, which I believe we did.

Leon Osman: I think we got it wrong against Fiorentina. I think we were going so well, 1-0 down away at their place and again we took a midfielder off to put a striker on to try and get an away goal. We conceded in the last ten minutes and suddenly [it was 2-0] instead of 1-0 back at Goodison, which we were certainly capable of getting.

Hana Roks: The away leg in Florence was horrible. Me and my Dad went over and it was just raining all day. We went via Rome as soon and as we got to Rome someone tried to rob my Dad. Then we got the train from Rome to Florence and we had the wrong tickets so my Dad got fined. Then it just went from bad to worse, really. The guards were horrible and our fans were put in this giant cage. We scored and it was ruled offside and we got beat. Everything went wrong. We got to the hotel where we were meant to be staying at and they said they were overbooked. By this time it was late and me and my dad are walking round town trying to find a hotel and couldn't get in anywhere and we seen these Evertonians walking passed and they said, 'What are you doing walking round?' and we said, 'We can't get into a hotel.' 'Come and stay in our room.' Me and my Dad went and stayed in their room and we couldn't thank them enough.

Joleon Lescott: That was probably the most hostile experience I've had away from home during that time. It was intense, the way they section the fans off. I think we were unfortunate at that game. If I remember, Tim [Cahill] scored a goal that maybe shouldn't have been disallowed. It was an overhead kick as well. We felt unfortunate; we didn't feel we deserved to lose 2-0.

Steven Pienaar: The pace of the game was totally different, it was much slower and obviously with the teams in Europe, they play slower and they don't go direct like some of the English teams. That was the big difference. For us also, we just thought, 'Yeah, we can slow it down, we can go direct, we can run for 120 minutes.' Even when we played against Fiorentina away we were poor that night, but when we played the return game I think we should have won that game. Unfortunately, if you don't take your chances you have to go to penalties. That was the big difference.

Tony Hibbert: Fiorentina were a very good side, but that's football, it's one of them things where you've got to take your chance. We messed up out there, we were controlling the game out there. We shouldn't have let that happen out there, we were really in control.

David Moyes: The [home] game against Fiorentina was an incredible night, another one of the nights you really remember. The effort the players put in. Those nights were what I wanted to bring back to Goodison, and they were starting to become a bit more often. Everton were beginning to get close in European competitions.

Joleon Lescott: Coming back to Goodison, we kind of knew that they wouldn't have experienced anything like that, the atmosphere there. I remember feeling like that was probably the height of my Everton time, due to the fact that I'd just signed a new contract. The ambition as well that was shown by the club, and the way we were playing, it was like a new lease of life. I remember going into that game thinking, 'We've got a real chance,' and we were really close to going through.

Leon Osman: They were patient. We were Premier League, we were English football, we were all action. You know, get the ball forward, now we've got it up here let's do something with it. Whereas they were patient. That was it. They were getting the ball forward, waiting for their opportunity. They defended for their lives. It was new, but it was becoming a part of what we wanted. We wanted to move forward, we wanted to play in Europe, and this is the way they play in Europe, so let's figure it out. For large parts in that run, pretty much all of it, we figured it out. We were good. Even the second leg against Fiorentina, you realise you get teams back to your place, you've got a chance. Teams don't travel well. So suddenly you need to give yourselves credit for going over somewhere and getting a 0-0 draw or losing 1-0. That's an okay result in Europe. That's something that we didn't quite understand, that losing a game in Europe away from home isn't a bad result, because you an bring them home to your place, where teams don't travel well.

Steven Pienaar: We always played in the same way, whoever we played against at Goodison Park. It was always make life difficult for them and put them under pressure from the word go. That's how we approached all our home games.

Joleon Lescott: The experience on the whole was good. I remember that was when Victor [Anichebe] announced himself on the European stage. It was just like a rollercoaster, and the momentum we had from certain league games going into the UEFA Cup, we combated each other. So we'd have a good result in Europe, then we'd come back and take that confidence into the week, it was just like a snowball effect, it just kept on rolling and rolling. It was a good time.

Lee Carsley: We had some really good nights in the UEFA Cup, the second season. Fantastic times when you think about going over to Nuremburg and Alkmaar. It was almost like travelling with the Republic of Ireland, where you go out to an away game and there would be green everywhere; it was the opposite, it was blue everywhere, home and away. Especially Nuremburg. The scenes from the Nuremburg hotel when the fans were hanging off the bus stops and hanging off trams, it was absolutely brilliant. We stopped the traffic. They were great, great nights.

Simon Hart: Moyes actually cracked the whole, 'How do you play the Europa League and league' question – I know it was the UEFA Cup then – but Everton were playing in the UEFA Cup, and yet, they were in this rhythm of playing a game on Sunday and winning that as well. There were no excuses or anything. That was to Moyes' credit that there was a 'no excuses' kind of mentality within the club. Moyes was a hard worker, and that came through with his players. I really liked that team, and Fiorentina was such a heartbreaker, because you think of teams like Fulham that have reached European finals.

David Moyes: Rangers got to the final that year against Zenit, and we had beaten Zenit in the group stage at home. So again, we had a really good team at Everton; we didn't have a strong enough squad. We were just lacking a real top number nine, and we were aware of that, and we were trying to keep the team going, but losing to Fiorentina on penalty kicks was sickening. But again, I think it was a sign of how far we had travelled, that we were getting to even later stages of European competitions and coming close.

Steve Round: We felt that with Everton we had a certain style, especially at homes, where we had to stick with that. We had to be aggressive with our play. You'd always have a game plan. Away from home there was more of an emphasis on possession, more of an emphasis on a slower tempo, because that's the European style, and it's being comfortable with that, whereas at home we still wanted to go front foot, fire balls and go for it. I think teams came to us and go 'Woah', and when that Goodison roar came in, I tell you what, there was a few of the foreign teams that couldn't handle that.

2009 FA Cup run

Everton endured a frustrating start to the 2008/09 season: sluggish in the league, knocked out of Europe by Standard Liege, and knocked out of the League Cup by Blackburn Rovers. For the first time in his reign, though, a domestic cup run proved to be the saviour for Moyes and his side. The catalyst was a 1-0 win over rivals Liverpool in an FA Cup fourth round replay, a victory which came in the dying moments of extra time, thanks to a brilliant curled finish from the young Dan Gosling. It came a week after Benitez had described Everton as a 'small club.'

Tim Howard: That was my favourite game. I think as a competitor, as a footballer, that's the game you lose sleep over. It gets your blood boiling. You become hero or a villain based on what year it is and what game it is. So those give me my fondest memories, because I really feel like there's been very few times in my career that I've had: being able to walk on to a pitch or into a cauldron with that type of emotion, and that type of anxiety. It's a beautiful thing.

Tony Hibbert: They got a player [Lucas Leiva] sent off early on. I remember, we couldn't break them down. We could not break them down. They were playing well in a way of keeping us away, and we were playing some good stuff, controlling the game, but we just couldn't find that little pass. I remember it going on and thinking to myself, 'How long is left, how long is left?' Constantly looking at the clocks and thinking, 'Right, come on, we've got this keep trying.' Then I remember just thinking, 'Oh my God, we're not going to do it.' And obviously Gosling gets that goal.

Joleon Lescott: I remember not being overly stretched in any way. I wouldn't say it felt easy, but as I said it was like we were comfortable, and we just kind of wanted for it not to go to penalties, because they had players that had probably experienced a lot more of them situations than us. We were kind of hoping that someone could step up. There's moments in players' careers that you can say, 'Well that kick-started it.' I think that was the moment for Dan.

David Moyes: One of the bigger nights. We beat them in extra time, and actually we'd never had a great record at Anfield, but we always went there and had a lot of draws, partly because we didn't have an individual player to completely make the difference, a centre-forward who was clinical. But we drew at Anfield in the FA Cup, and brought them back and won it, Dan Gosling scored the winner in extra time. So that was a great night, which got us on the run.

A 3-1 victory over Aston Villa in the next round and a 2-1 quarter-final win over Middlesbrough set up a semi-final tie with Manchester United at the new Wembley stadium. A tight game ended goalless and with a penalty shootout, which is where the real drama started. Tim Cahill missed the first spot-kick, but Tim Howard became the hero, denying Dimitar Berbatov and then Rio Ferdinand. Jagielka, despite his miss against Fiorentina, stepped up and scored the winner, sending the club to their first major final since 1995.

David Moyes: This was against a Man United side that were used to it, more used to that than we were. We had nothing to lose, really. But we were improving all the time, we were an up and coming team improving.

Tim Howard: His game plan, often in big games and big moments was to be compact, be hard to beat, soak up the pressure, but then be good with the ball going forward as well and trying to hit teams on the counter, because we had players capable of doing that. But we were also a very good footballing team.

Laura Smith: The United semi-final is without doubt the best football match I've ever been to for a full day experience. It was amazing.

Steven Pienaar: I remember the manager said to us, 'You guys have got an opportunity here to create your own history, just go out and enjoy the game.' As players we wanted to get into the final and we put everything into that game, and I think we deserved to win.

Steve Round: When we played Man United we knew that at Wembley with the pitch – I'd got a lot of experience at Wembley through the England connection [Round had previously been part of Steve McLaren's backroom staff during his tenure as England manager] – we couldn't open it up and have a complete end to end football game, we just couldn't do it. United had too much talent. So we had to go almost up against them, man to man and say, 'Right, it's me against you.' Let's look you in the eyes and say, 'Are you prepared, are you really prepared to do what it takes to win this game? Because you're going to have to run over my dead body to do it.' We made sure that that attitude and mentality was there.

Louis Saha: When you have that kind of understanding with the mentality of United, you know that everything needs to be really tight. That's basically what we done. In the first few minutes of the game we dominated, Tim Cahill had a great game. All those players understood the game plan of David Moyes. I think Jack Rodwell as well had a tremendous game. I do remember this game as one of the most accomplished ones. I think from the side everyone has a very big focus. It was like a final for us, the way we played. That's why I think we deserved to win the FA Cup that year.

Joleon Lescott: As a team we were confident: the big occasions never fazed us. We believed that what we're doing is right. We're not stealing wins – there was never a game when I thought, 'We were lucky there, we shouldn't have won.' It was like, 'We earnt that.'

Leon Osman: We practiced our penalties. After missing a good few years back [in a League Cup tie against Middlesbrough in 2003] Moyesy didn't want me anywhere near penalties. But we practiced them and I knew exactly what Jags was going to do. Obviously Tim Cahill missed the first penalty and you start to think 'Oh no, don't let this happen.'

Steve Round: I'd been at Middlesbrough through to a UEFA Cup final, where games were decided on penalties, I'd been with England where penalties were so, so important. I'd mentioned it to David, the importance, and I did a little presentation once about the importance of penalties and penalty shootouts, and how we needed to practice. David straight away, being David – his work ethic was the best I've ever seen of anybody ever – was on to that like a shot. He was like 'Definitely, we do it.' And he made sure that team practiced. So whenever we got to a penalty shootout I was confident. On the back side of that we had Tim Howard, who was so fast; he was so good penalties.

Tim Howard: Like anything else, I tried to study players who I thought I knew, who I thought I'd seen before, certain tendencies. I think you can tell sometimes penalty location based on how a player passes the ball and strikes the ball. So we did endless amounts of preparation, and it's in those moments that you hope to get lucky but you also hope that if you do enough preparation that it will shine through in the end.

David Moyes: We made a deal, if you were taking a penalty, before the game you had to tell us what you were doing, where you were putting it, so you couldn't change and it was non-negotiable again. Also we had looked at the Man United players who took them. Tim Howard knew where they had gone in the other final, so we just took the gamble that they would do the same as they did in the other final. I'm not saying that's the only reason we got through, but it was certainly was one of them.

Laura Smith: When it went to penalties I can remember just sitting down and putting my head in my hands and thinking, 'Oh well, we've had a nice day.' Tim Cahill went to take the first one and I turned round and was like 'I'm not watching this.' I turned round to face the back and he missed, so I thought, 'Sod it we're going out anyway I'll turn round and I'll watch it.'

Leon Osman: Tim made two good saves and then it comes to Jags, and we're all in a line, and I'm thinking, we know where he's going, seen him do this penalty last couple of days in training, I know exactly where he's going. So as he's running up, the second the keeper dives the wrong way, that was it. He's not missing the target. I was already up. For some strange reason, Jags ran one way, and I ran the other way, and I ended up celebrating on my own, celebrating in the middle of the pitch on my own.

Laura Smith: Jags hit that last one and everyone just went mental. I can remember I was looking at Leon Osman at the time and he just erupted. I sort of had a delayed reaction I didn't know what to do and everyone just went mental. It was just brilliant. Then all of a sudden it was like the red half of Wembley had just disappeared and we were still in there an hour later.

Tony Hibbert: To be honest, before playing at Wembley, I've never agreed with the semi-finals being at Wembley. Never. We get there and it's like 'Wow we're at Wembley here'; it was a nice emotion. It was the hottest day ever, and then having all the fireworks and standing there, it was crazy. The pitch wasn't the best, the pitch was terrible. It was solid. Coming to the penalties was just madness, knowing you're going back to play the final there was just chaos. Absolute chaos. It was a great feeling, but at Wembley it was good.

Cruelly for Jagielka, that penalty would prove his last involvement in the competition. Six days later, in a home match against Man City, he snapped a cruciate ligament and joined Mikel Arteta, Yakubu and Nuno Valente on Everton's long-term injury list.

Hana Roks: I remember looking at him and thinking, 'He's crying there.' Obviously I couldn't see the tears in his eyes from the stand but it looked as if he was crying. It was heartbreaking for that to happen to him after doing so well in that game and then obviously as a fan you're gutted. But as a player I imagine they go through the same emotions as us. But he looked devastated; it was soul destroying. I can't imagine what he felt, but it'd could've been different on the day of the final if he had played.

Simon Hart: Moyes went into the cup final without his best striker, his most creative midfielder, and without his first-choice centre-back. You know, their hands were tied, possibly even before they kicked off that game. That's like if you'd taken Frank Lampard, Didier Drogba, and John Terry out of Chelsea's team, and people tend to forget that.

Back at Wembley six weeks later, facing Chelsea, Everton raced into an early lead, Louis Saha netting the fastest goal in FA Cup final history with a half-volley after Fellaini's knock down. The game was just 25 seconds old.

Steve Round: It's not a burden, because you respect and honour the history of the club. So you actually bring that on board, and it's part of the club, so you're very proud of it when you work there. I think the biggest regret I had in the five years I was there is that we never won a trophy. That's the biggest regret, and we were very close. Very close. The priority for Everton was always finishing as high up as we could in the league because we needed to get the Sky money in for the resources to keep the club alive and floating, and to push on year on year. But there was a real desire within the club to try and win some silverware for the fans.

Tim Howard: We had won some big games that season. We knew we were going into it as underdogs, but I think when you go through the gauntlet of the FA Cup, when you get to the final and the sun's shining at Wembley, you feel like you have a chance, and boy did we ever with Louis Saha scoring within the opening 10 to 15 seconds or whatever it was. That was pretty awesome.

Jose Baxter: I was on the bench. It was surreal. It was a great memory walking up them stairs and being a part of a great day in the club's history; getting to a massive final at Wembley and seeing all the royal blue shirts.

Leon Osman: You know they're a good team. But you think, 'We've got a chance, come on let's give it our all. It's 50-50, off we go.' And then we score after 27 seconds. I don't think I'd even touched the ball and we're 1-0 up. And you start to think, 'Right, come on now. 90 minutes.'

Louis Saha: I always look at the time and the frustration that it brings me is huge, because I want to win. Whatever people say about the record I don't really care.

Joleon Lescott: When they kicked off again, it was like the kick-off for the game. There was no panic. I looked and thought, 'It's just gone back to the centre-half, they've gone to the full-back…' It was just literally like they had ignored the goal. They just ignored it and thought it's going to come. We believed that we could perform. There was a level of player that they had at their time, all in their prime, and that was the difference. If you're talking in today's market, the players they had in their prime, they're £150 million players. If you look at it, we did well to make the game so close.

Jose Baxter: When we scored it was like, 'Hang on a minute we're not just to make the numbers up we're going to win this.'

Steven Pienaar: I thought, 'This is the best way to start a cup final.' We were on the front foot, and slowly we started dropping deep, and Chelsea got back into the game. At times it looked like it was going to be one-way traffic, but we also had our opportunities in the game, but at the end I think you know when you go 1-0 up, you start defending deep, you're dropping off, you're allowing the other team and just creating pressure for yourself. I think that was our problem at the time.

David Moyes: We started so well. There was a strange level of confidence at Everton, where we might not have shown it but it was a bit of 'Well, stand up, we'll show them, we'll match them, we'll do whatever we have to do.'

Tony Hibbert: It was out of nothing, Louis' goal. It was a great feeling, it was like 'Right, come on, we'll kick on. As the game went on it was like, 'We've scored too early', because it was just the pressure. We had the mentality that we'd scored a goal and we sat back, and we allowed them to come on to us.

When you look at it, I think we scored too early.

Steve Round: We came out of the blocks firing which we knew. We scored a good goal. We had another opportunity to score a second. What you mustn't forget is Chelsea were the best team in the league then. They were magnificent and they'd got top players. We really needed just to hang in there and then we knew with our fitness and our competitive spirit, we knew that the longer the game went [we had a chance]. We needed to get to half-time 1-0. If we could get to half-time 1-0 then we could regroup, reorganise. And then I fancied us to see it through.

On a blisteringly hot day Chelsea's quality would soon tell. Didier Drogba levelled after 21 minutes, and Frank Lampard gave Chelsea a lead they would never surrender eighteen minutes before full-time. Everton did not have enough firepower to respond.

Tony Hibbert: I got booked early doors, it wasn't even a challenge. He's come across me, and I've jumped out the way to go across that way, and he's fell over and the ref booked me. That was five minutes into the game, so straight away that's in your head, 'I can't tackle, I can't do this, I've got to look after myself.'

Jose Baxter: It was roasting. I remember having cold towels on my head on the bench.

Joleon Lescott: My mouth was like a carpet. That's one thing I do remember from that day: the heat, and the intensity of the game. The concentration… it's not so much about the legs, it's just the concentration. You have to be on your mettle, because the players are so clever, you have to be aware for any possibility. Nothing's lucky. When it's that level of player, it's not luck, it's skill. So you had to cater for that.

Leon Osman: My overriding feeling of that was just how hot it was. If you asked me to watch any game back, I couldn't [watch this]. It's probably the game I would hate to watch back the most. Just the fact that it was so hot. I've said it a few times, the most difficult player I've ever played against was Ashley Cole, because I was not a right-winger, didn't have the pace to compete. So Ashley Cole ran me all game and especially first half we were in the sun all game. It was just so difficult.

Jose Baxter: I do remember them trying to triple up down one side and I remember one of the strikers drifting out left – I don't remember if it was Malouda or Kalou – and then obviously they had Ashley Cole as well. They seemed to have a lot of legs down that side.

Steven Pienaar: After they scored, at half-time when we got into the dressing room, the manager he was quite upset, because he was like, 'Why did you guys take your foot off the pedal?' We started off the second half and gave it a right go, but unfortunately, they had too much quality in their team and we conceded.

Tim Howard: It's almost inevitable, it's human nature, to try and protect what you have. As a goalkeeper you try and influence. First of all you try and organise your defence to make sure you're set up to take that barrage and to play your own part in it. Ideally you try and help the team as best you can with regaining possession and making the right passes out of the back, hitting long balls that are accurate, but ultimately you can't really affect the play up the pitch because you can't get a hold of the ball yourself.

Tony Hibbert: The lads that we had, it was probably us at one of our strongest points. I've played in a lot of games with the lads, and literally it has been wave after wave, and we've ground out a 1-0 win. So I knew deep down that our mental state was good and the lads would run the extra mile to do stuff, so it never came to a stage where it was like, 'Oh my God that's it, they're going to score in a minute.' It was always a mental state of ,'We don't care, we will dig in, we will just drop back and we will still be the same.'

David Moyes: The right-back Lars Jacobsen played [as a half-time substitute for Hibbert]. He got a bit of a chasing. Malouda and Cole gave us a bit of a difficult time down their left hand side. They had that level of ability; just better than we were. It wasn't heart, it wasn't spirit and we lost the final 2-1.

Louis Saha: I was really frustrated because I felt that we had a few chances and had a great game, but sometimes you don't take the right opportunities at the right moments, and that's what they do; the big teams, that's what they do. They score at the right moments, and we didn't manage to do that. At the end of the day I was really frustrated. Very angry because of the fans travelling; I really wanted to win the trophy for Everton.

Tim Howard: I think when you get so close to lifting a trophy, you want to lift it, and there's no bigger disappointment. I don't care what anyone says, it's a heck of a lot different if you lose in the final, and so I would have liked to have won silverware for Everton because it was a club I loved dearly. I think that's where the disappointment lies.

Player sales, fighting the tide, breaking the glass ceiling

The dynamics of the Premier League changed inexorably in August 2008 when the Abu Dhabi royal family bought Manchester City. While Moyes's Everton was built on prudence, hard work, good scouting and excellent management, so City in the same period had been the polar opposite. Moyes had a tiny net spend over his seven years in charge, but City, suddenly empowered by Gulf oil riches, spent a net of £327million over just three seasons. There was an inflationary effect on the whole of the Premier League and Everton not only found themselves struggling to compete but some of their best players were sold: Joleon Lescott to cash rich City in the summer of 2009, Steven Pienaar to Tottenham in January 2011, Mikel Arteta to Arsenal on deadline day, summer 2011, and Jack Rodwell a year later, once again to Manchester City. Not only were the club losing players – they were losing players to teams they aspired to compete with.

Bill Kenwright: When David joined we worked towards consolidation. With David the phrase was always, always, 'Sustainable growth'; we had to grow each year. From the first signing of Joseph Yobo, each year we had to make a signing that meant something. We had some bad days at the start but we started growing as a club, and we got into Europe. But still, I wasn't going to see the bank manager. I was going to see the head of Barclays all the time, who were great and who supported us, because we're a good club. You won't find any skeletons at all at Everton. We're just a bloody good club who hopefully do things right.

Simon Hart: It was hugely annoying, frustrating when the Abu Dhabi royal family bought Man City. I suppose it's what made those Everton/Man City games so special during the seasons that followed. Goodison is such a brilliant place when it's angry, and you had that kind of collective animosity towards

City suddenly; becoming the wealthiest club in the world, trying to take our best players, and being better than us, when they'd done nothing but gain the favour of a very, very wealthy man in the Middle East who wanted some soft power. It just felt wrong, and it was great that the players would kind of tap into that. I'm sure Moyes was firing them up in the dressing room on the back of the Lescott transfer. There were some pretty special results on the back of that, and even if we'd lost the war we were winning a few battles. It didn't feel right, but then maybe I'm just an old fashioned kind of Evertonians who has a certain world view of football.

Bill Kenwright: I'd been at Wembley a few years earlier for the playoffs when the place was empty because Citywere losing 2-1 to Gillingham and they won 3-2. It was near extinction time for City, wasn't it? I live in London, so I was very aware of the Abramovich thing, because a lot of my mates are Chelsea supporters. And I think I'd be the same, buying your way to the top – can it be right? Can it be? I can remember thinking that distinctly.

Louis Saha: The money was crazy. A team like Tottenham started to increase the volume of their transfers: A team who didn't have the wage sometimes to compete and be trouble in the Premier League were starting to spend £15 million on a player, or one striker. You're starting to say, 'Oh.' They narrowed the gap, and of course they make it really hard. Everton were not always the team that could be competing for Europe. They find themselves a bit surprised because the style had changed. You're even starting to have the introduction of Swansea, people who surprised us in the way that they play. They managed to get through and get into Europe.

Steven Pienaar: Obviously for the fans it was frustrating, because you always want to keep your best players at the club. But also from the club's point of view, at the time they needed the money, and obviously when other clubs come in you get an opportunity to go to a big club, I don't think any player will say no. It's quite understandable from a player's point of view. But at the end of day, it's like leaving a family behind. Life moves on.

David Moyes: That was tough because at that time we needed the money. Bill stuck to his word, but they were needing more money to fund it, partly because wages were rising etc. The Arteta one went through for £10 million, and we had lost Lescott. We were still a club – not because we wanted to – selling off because we didn't have enough to keep them, we couldn't do enough. And we were still fighting to get up, but in truth our record had been that we replaced the players quite well. Joleon Lescott left and we found a way, we moved on, we got on with it. We brought Sylvain Distin in, who did a great job for us in his time. So we did keep moving along.

Steve Round: During the course of my time there we had some big offers for players from some big clubs, and the players said no. The players said, 'No I want to stay at Everton, because of what we'd got within the dressing room.'

David Moyes: Bill took incredible criticism for loving a football club, being with it. I hope that if you go to the end point today, you would say, 'Look at all the people who have sold to people, at the moment Bill's looks like a good sale, an honest sale in the right interests of the club and doing right.' Sir Philip Carter was a brilliant man. If there was ever a chairman any manager would want, they'd went Sir Philip Carter. If there was an owner you'd ever want, it's Bill Kenwright, because he was supportive, he backed you up when you needed it. I think he knew, because of his business and industry. Some folks said 'Ah, we were too close,' well, me and Bill fought all the time, because I wanted more money. But I also respected what Bill said.

Tim Howard: A lot of big clubs with big money were coming in to take our players, but Bill Kenwright and David Moyes dug their heels in and got above market value for these players, and I always think that's a good thing. If a guy's going to go you get the most for him and you use that money and reinvest it, and I thought we did that well.

Steve Round: With Joleon, I think Joleon was the start of the modern day huge transfers, and it was the start of Manchester City's rise to where they are now. We couldn't compete with their resources, and we couldn't compete with what they were offering Joleon financially. To start with we tried to keep hold of Joleon, we didn't want to lose him, he was a fundamental part of our success and our team, but we also understood the resources we could gain from this would allow the club to be solvent and carry on for a number of months, or a year or two. And also it would give us the opportunity to rebuild in certain areas

Leon Osman: We were a team that didn't have the financial clout of others. We wanted to keep our better players but we were always susceptible to other teams coming in and stealing our players. Players want to play as high as they can and win things. We didn't have the financial backing to go and make that team stronger properly. We didn't have the real power to go out and improve ourselves, and players will spot that.

Steve Round: We managed to sell Joleon for £25 million, we brought in Sylvain Distin for about £5 million, and Sylvain Distin was a great player for us. So we didn't lose out much. And then we had another £20-odd million that we could put back into the club, and also use for recruitment. At the end of the day, sometimes it's a business. I wish we could have been in a position where, like they are now maybe, we could compete on an even keel. But we weren't, and we knew that. So to be honest, it didn't really effect us. It was just how it was.

Tony Hibbert: It was stupid money that they were spending left, right and centre. I wasn't stupid in thinking it was going to happen overnight, it's a progression of time and change, and making the club sound. I'd rather make the club debt free and healthy than be spending £50-60 million on individuals. I'd rather know that we are secure and then we can look at players at a certain value. I'm that way.

Leon Osman: Those who didn't have a real love-in with the club, say as myself or Hibbo will look to find somewhere where they can go and win stuff, and where they can go and make that step up or whatever it may be. Unless they see the club moving forward, and we didn't have the backing to do that at the time.

David Moyes: Mikel had been brilliant, and I'm going to say this: Arsenal were qualifying every year for the Champions League, we weren't. We were fighting every year to be in the Europa League, and at that time it was very hard if the big clubs came calling, very difficult to keep your players. They wanted to go to the bigger clubs. Partly for more money, partly because they were getting a level of European football. We were talking big at Everton, we wanted it, and we were probably delivering it in our own way through training, through management, through the things we were doing behind the scenes to try and give us a little bit of an edge which we didn't have because we didn't have the money.

Steve Round: It was transfer deadline day [in August 2011]. I think we'd brought in one or two players on very low money, almost a loan. But we also knew that we had a debt to the bank we had to pay. We were looking to sell one or two players that were our fringe players, but we couldn't. We were thinking we were going to get a bid on deadline day. Four o'clock comes and we're all in the office, there's a knock on the door and Arteta's at the window. 'Can I have a word?' He said, 'Look, I think Arsenal are going to come in for me in the next hour.' I mean you could of hit us with a frying pan across the face, you know what I mean? It was a massive blow. Such a good lad, such a good player. He said to David, 'I don't want to leave Everton, I love it at Everton. I absolutely love it, but this is Arsenal.' I think they were going to double or triple his wages. So David being David, being fair, just an honest man, said, 'Okay, Mickey, you've done your time here. I respect everything you've done for us, I respect you as a person. If they come with the right offer, I won't stand in your way.' And it took a lot for David to do that a lot, because he was such an important player to us. But he realised from a humanitarian point of view what this meant. In the back of his head he also knew we had to pay the bank. Anyway, an hour later we get a call off Arsenal and they offered ten million quid. Even then we tried to fight it, but in the end he went. That was that.

Everton soldiered on, owing much to the unity fostered by Moyes and the squad in a number of years together, and a sense of understanding of the club's financial situation. But the league was becoming harder to compete in, and Everton were now struggling to qualify for Europe.

Sylvain Distin: I can give five hundred reasons for our slow starts to the season, but will it be the right one? No, I can just make speculation. Some said we worked too hard in pre-season, some said we didn't work hard enough so we were not fit enough. It's only going to be speculation. To be honest, what matters is where you finish at the end. It's not really how you start or how you finish, it's the whole season as a whole, and what position you have at the end of the season. Even if people have big expectation, and the fans had big expectations, I think we did quite well.

David Moyes: If there was one thing we were short of at Everton in my time it was – and I'd have to be respectful – I would have to say a top striker. Because we didn't have the £20 million that was becoming required to sign a Fernando Torres

Steve Round: Because of the resources we had to spend, we had to get centre-forwards who were either up and coming, over the top, or were very good centre-forwards, don't get me wrong, but they weren't elite centre-forwards. They weren't at the likes of a Rooney or a Van Persie. Even when Man City signed Dzeko, we were in for Dzeko. We were in for Dzeko at £17 million, and he went to Man City for about £27 million; they came in at the last minute. Somebody like that would have helped us go the next level.

David Moyes: I had flown to Paris to meet Demba Ba, and on the trip I was going to meet Miroslav Klose. So I flew to Paris and met Demba Ba in the airport in Paris. The evening before Germany were playing in a friendly. Miroslav Klose's wife had been to Finch Farm to look round. From Demba Ba I was going on to meet Miroslav Klose in Germany, and he broke his wrist and couldn't meet me because he had to go and get an operation on his wrist. So I never got to do Miroslav Klose, and at that time Miroslav Klose was 33 probably, but if you look what he did at Lazio for the years and years after [over five seasons he became Lazio's seventh all time highest goalscorer and scored the winner in the 2013 Coppa Italia Final against the club's bitter rivals, AS Roma].

Sylvain Distin: We did have good strikers, you have to remember guys like Yakubu or even Louis when he was fit was an amazing player. You come back to the financial situation of the club; if you want a player who scores 20 goals every season you have to pay for it, and at the time we couldn't pay for it, so you have to gamble on players that you hope will perform as well as you think, but also have good potential. That's what they did with Lukaku, and season after season he just showed his potential. But it's difficult when you were in the financial position we were to get a player who would score 20 goals, and expect to buy him for ten or fifteen million.

Tony Hibbert: I think we cried out for someone with pace, real pace. Someone different. We had Yakubu, but he would score goals and you still had that belief in him because he would get something from somewhere and it would look so easy for him. As a player we did feel we needed that extra spark in us to get us scoring again.

Steve Round: We accepted it, but it was frustrating. I went out to watch Lukaku playing in Belgium, when he was eighteen years of age, before he went to Chelsea. I think I saw him three times. David saw him, the chief scout, Robbie Cooke at the time, was banging on about him, 'Here's a young player that we might be able to nick out.' But when it came down to it we just didn't have the money, just couldn't do it.

David Moyes: There will always be misses that you thought you had. We missed out on loads of players, but I've got to say we came close. People will tell you I had Phil Jones before he signed for Manchester United, I had him and his parents up in the house. I had Aaron Ramsey and his parents up in the house. At different times I had Craig Bellamy, I had Joey Barton, I had Roy Keane.

If one thing could be levelled at Moyes and his teams during his tenure, it was their inability to win away from home against the so called 'big four' of that era: Chelsea, Manchester United, Arsenal and Liverpool. Moyes oversaw 46 away league fixtures at the grounds of these respective clubs – Everton did not register one victory.

David Moyes: I'd put it down to us being lacking that one or two real creative players. We had creative players, but at that level we were behind. We didn't have a centre-forward who could nick us a goal out of anything. We had really well organised, well drilled, players at their maximum, but we were short of that quality. I'm going to say this, and I'm going to contradict a little bit, I didn't want spending to be the only way we could be successful, but we were lacking a wee bit of icing on the cake which would help us win away from home. It was a problem.

Steven Pienaar: Normally when we played at home against the so called top four we always were on the offensive and made it difficult for them. Obviously when we went away you had to be a bit more cautious and set up defensively and make sure we didn't concede. The longer we stayed in the game, we always had an opportunity to win the game or even get a draw, and most of the games it worked.

Steve Round: The style we developed was from David's time when he had to fight and scrap just to stay in the league. There was definitely a culture and a resolve born where we would be a resilient team. And the backbone of the team was built on defence. Mourinho's Chelsea, the backbone was built on defence, no question. We were always looking to keep that, but expand moving forward. To expand moving forward you need a better quality of player, and... it's very easy to say we either attack too much, that's why we concede, or we defend too much, that's why we don't score. At the end of the day you should have 11 defenders and 11 attackers – the whole team attacks and the whole team defends.

Tim Howard: Very few teams won away at Chelsea, won away at Manchester United, and won away at Liverpool. These are difficult places to play. I think at certain points we hadn't won at Chelsea, but no one had won at Chelsea for like three years, so I think it was a bit unfair that criticism. We knew who we were, we tried to go away from home, be hard to beat, and sometimes when you do that you don't always get a ton going forward.

David Moyes: I actually think other teams saw Everton as a real challenge when we came to play them. I think other teams saw Everton and said, 'They're going to have a right go here.' But I can't think in my time many times that we went to those grounds and were absolutely humiliated. There was no thing, we tried everything; to be more attacking, to be more defensive. I think at times it was just the level of the player against the top teams.

Steve Round: The dream for me at that time was that if we could have brought Rooney back to Everton, or if we'd got Lukaku, we had got a real chance. Real chance. That's how you felt. We were playing some great football. Our possession stats were way up, our creativity stats, our shots on target, all the things you look at. Our goals against record was still strong. I thought we were developing into a style, evolving into a style that we could really push forward.

Louis Saha: If you're a striker you need to score goals to be able to help your team win something at the end of the season – you have to score goals. My aim was to score 20 goals; if I could help others to score and assist, creating space for my partners, that was my thing. Of course you know it's going to be difficult at times, because you have big teams like the Man U's, the Man City's, the Arsenal's, the Tottenham's, they had more funds and could attract a striker that could score many, many goals because they're world class players. Of course that was not maybe what we had, like a Wayne Rooney, who is definitely one of the world class players, but it takes time for him to arrive here.

Steven Pienaar: The manager wanted us all to work hard for the team, and with the guys the mentality was right in the dressing room, so we didn't mind putting in a shift, but you always want to attack as well. Sometimes it was hard, tough, when we had the ball, from chasing so long you get tired and you don't have a lot of options going forward.

Everton 1, Liverpool 2
FA Cup semi-final
14 April 2012

Everton reached the FA Cup semi-final for a second time under Moyes, where they were drawn against a Liverpool team in the death-throes of Kenny Dalglish's secon managerial reign. Nikica Jelavic's first half goal gave Everton a deserved lead, but the game swung on a catastrophic backpass by Sylvain Distin on the hour mark, leading to an equaliser from Luis Suarez. The winner, two minutes from full time, had an aura of inevitability.

Tony Hibbert: I thought it was a massive opportunity. To beat Liverpool you probably would have picked that game, because I don't think they were anywhere near their best.

Leon Osman: In any game of football the opposition are going to have a moment, a period in the game. And we dominated in the first half and they came out, and they got the bit between their teeth and got on top for ten minutes. We rolled it out, we rolled it. We got through that ten-minute period, we'd suddenly got out of our half and got into their half. That's it, we've got over their period, let's us get back on top of the game, we'll dominate the game again now. And that was certainly my feeling. But then Sylvain obviously made that mistake. The back pass, Suarez got them back into the game.

David Moyes: It was a day where we were better than Liverpool, I believed we were better than Liverpool. But on the day we made a couple of bad mistakes, Sylvain had a short pass back and Suarez scored. We were, at that time, the better team.

Sylvain Distin: It's extremely difficult. Obviously, no matter who you play against, that's not the type of mistake you want to do, but that was a semi-final of an FA Cup, and that was against Liverpool, so I would say that's all the possible worst conditions for me. Everybody knows how focused I am and how passionate I am about Everton. It was a very difficult time for me, but you have to react, there's no choice. I have to say my teammates helped me a lot through it. You're always going to have some bad reactions from fans, some of them feel like you did it on purpose, which is completely insane to even think that, but I have to say in general the fans had a really good reaction. They were upset, of course, but as a fan you have to remember the one who was the most upset and the one who is going to suffer the most is the player – depending on the player, obviously, but considering my personality I can tell you it was a very difficult time for me. The only thing you feel is I want to try and repay and fight if I can, and all I can do is give my best from there.

Steve Round: I knew all about Andy [Carroll] because I worked with him at Newcastle when I was a coach there. I used to take him out on the field every morning before the rest came out and do heading practice and all the rest. I wish I hadn't after that. There's not much you can do – if a ball comes in the box, and he's got a run or a jump on you… you coach them about getting under him, about stopping him from jumping, about making sure he doesn't get a clean header. But there are certain times in the game when a centre-forward who is exceptional at one thing, does that one thing, it's very difficult to stop.

David Moyes: Unfortunately we lost 2-1. It's certainly got a chance of being the darkest day of all, to lose. We at that time, I thought, were the better side than Liverpool, and we didn't win on the day.

Steven Pienaar: I flew in from Amsterdam to watch the game [Pienaar was cup-tied having rejoined from Tottenham in January], and I think the guys played really well that day. One mistake from Distin brought Liverpool back in the game. I think that was the best we'd played against Liverpool since I was there. In that FA Cup semi-final, only that one mistake and Suarez got in and scored. After the game we were really down, because we knew we had a good opportunity to go to the final.

David Moyes: Strangely enough the next game was when we went and drew four each at Manchester United [and effectively cost United the title]. So we were a good side, and we just didn't perform as well as we could on the day in the semi-final, which for me would probably come as the biggest disappointment.

Steve Round: I think the biggest disappointment in the whole time I was there was losing to Liverpool in the semi-final. One mistake. I thought we had the better of the game for the 90 minutes, but one mistake, one goal. And that was a real sickener.

Sylvain Distin: I could say that the FA Cup was my only regret, but actually no, because I really saw the true face of some fans, of some players, of some of the staff, and they got me closer to a lot of people as well. It was a difficult time, but I learned a lot through it as well.

Tim Howard: It was just such a disappointment, that was a game we should have won. It's always incredible when you play your biggest rival in a Cup match like that. To go 1-0 up and not be able to at least see the game out to penalties or win it ourselves, it was heartbreaking. It was one of the tougher losses I had been part of, simply because I felt that we were on the day the better team, and we didn't get our rewards.

David Moyes: I remember after the game at Old Trafford Alex spoke to me, and I said 'I'd had given everything to beat Liverpool in the semi-final of the FA Cup, I'd have done anything,' because there was so many Evertonian supporters down against their rivals. At that time we were on the rise. I think we finished above Liverpool in the league that year, so there was signs that we were improving

Moyes's last stand

The biggest disappointment of the 2012/13 season would prove to be in the FA Cup once more. Everton got a home draw against a Wigan Athletic side that would be relegated from the top flight that season. It was another golden opportunity. However, the Blues were completely outclassed on the day – a rarity at Goodison Park – as Roberto Martinez's side ran out 3-0 winners. They would go on to win the trophy that season with a surprise win over Manchester City in the final, but were then relegated a week later. Moyes's departure, after more than eleven years as manager, had been confirmed at that stage as he succeeded Sir Alex Ferguson as Manchester United manager.

Steve Round: In the FA Cup anything can happen. We went into that game full of confidence and life, thinking we were going to win. In the FA Cup things like that happen, and we got beat. Respect to Roberto, he set his team up perfectly, completely different to what we expected. He caught us by surprise, and I think they actually deservedly won the game.

Laura Smith: It's just one of the things with Everton. They build you up and they build you up and promise you everything and then bring you back down to earth, a little with bang. I can remember just walking out and thinking, 'Whatever!'

Roberto Martinez: Did that game get me the Everton job three months later? I don't know; obviously I'm the wrong person to ask that question. But it was a game that had a big influence on myself too. I got the feeling of the expectation on that day for Everton to go through, the feeling around the crowd; I felt that it was a big, big club, like a sleeping giant. Trying to win silverware in that environment would be something very, very special. And I think that day I realised that it would be an interesting project that I would be interested in.

Tim Howard: In our last season under David Moyes we were undefeated at home I believe [they lost just one league game to Chelsea, in December]. I think what the idea was, was from minute one, when it came to Goodison, just be a force: press teams, get in their face, make it difficult, put them on their backside. Just brimstone and fire, until we had the ability to get the game settled. We would try and put them under as much pressure as possible. And I think that showed and paid dividends.

David Moyes: I think the supporters might have got to the stage where they said, 'Why's this not getting any better?' To be fair, I did as well, because I wanted to finish in the top four. And actually I think in my second to last season I remember saying to Bill Kenwright, 'I think we've got a good chance of winning the league.' We were a centre-forward short, but I felt we had a really good team. And I was confident, I was feeling good about the team, but I just felt the supporters were beginning to get bored, because we were finishing fifth, sixth, seventh. But I don't think until today anything's changed. If you're being honest you'd say they've not broke that ceiling. Everton, before I took over, had hardly finished in the top half of the league. And then obviously since the Premiership has started I think they've only finished a couple of times above Liverpool.

Leon Osman: I'd seen us progress. I think it stayed the same, quite similar, during his tenure, but the quality of players he managed to bring in [improved]. You can only manage what players you've got. We suddenly started to get a really good team. By the end of it, some of our play, some of our players and the way we played was just brilliant. And you're starting to think, 'Right, again this is it, we're back now, we're moving forward,' and then the Man United job came in. It's difficult to turn down something like that, and off he went.

David Moyes: I was at the end of my contract. We had been speaking about it all through the season, but I didn't want to feel as if that I was going to overstay my welcome at Everton. I think the supporters did want something else. I knew that there wasn't going to be any more money coming the following season, and the players, I thought, we were starting to get close to needing to replace them again. I felt like when I first took over, and the players we'd got in, Sylvain Distin was getting older, Tim Howard was older, so there were two or three players that were beginning to get a bit older, and I'm saying, 'We're going to need money to replace these boys again,' and I knew there wasn't going to be an awful lot of money on the horizon.

Bill Kenwright: He absolutely wanted to join Manchester United. Always. It's not something he carried round with him, and I'm sure during the years he was so successful with us he had other overtures, but Manchester United was what he wanted.

Tony Hibbert: I was angry in the way that the whole thing was done. I was really, really, really angry. Fair enough if Man United want him and yeah, okay, he goes. But to make us pay for another manager, I didn't like [Moyes's contract had run down by the time of his departure]. The whole situation of him going to Manchester United – I didn't think he was good enough from day one, I knew; but as a manager you'd be stupid to turn it down. But to make Everton, where you have been there so long and been so loyal to, go out and fork out for another manager is a joke. If United want him that bad then United should buy him. Buy him out of his contract. Don't let your contract run down and then leave us in a situation where we've got to go and buy a manager. I didn't like that as a player; clubwise, I just didn't like it. I think that was out of order.

David Moyes: A month before the end of the season, it was a month, not even a month. April 26th, 27th, I got a call from Alex and that's when he said to me about the job. So really I hadn't known anything about it. A lot of people think I did, but 100% didn't. Because of that, it gave me a chance to leave Everton. My contract had run out, I hadn't had to be sacked and I hadn't had to be pushed.

Steven Pienaar: It doesn't matter if you're a carpenter or whatever, when you get an opportunity to work for a bigger firm – a bigger firm or a bigger club, whatever way you want to put it – in life you have just to stand open, if you want to push yourself and challenge yourself. At the time I think he made the right call and all the players were happy for him. It was part and parcel of the players' and managers' relationship, we had an understanding and he put a lot of work in, and we put a lot of work in for him. We were all happy for him, and obviously we all wanted him to succeed.

Tim Howard: I thought that after the service he had given our club, the loyalty that he had gave to the players, the fans, and the club, I think that it was very tough to begrudge him. In fact I would challenge anyone to make a different decision. That happens: it's football. It happens with players, it happens with managers. I have an incredible admiration and respect for David Moyes, I always have. He's very dear to me, and I wished him well. All the players at the end of the season wished him well. And then he went down the road, and we had to compete and fight each other for points.

Steve Round: I think that's one of the things you always try and do as staff, is if you leave the club in a better state than you took it, then you've done a half decent job. Definitely. And you can see that, by the legacy which we left, the following season Roberto had a great season. He added the Lukaku that we never had, which was a shrewd move and a smart move, and he had the resources to do it. And they had a terrific season. The foundations and the legacy that we'd left carried them through for a long period of time. From my perspective, I thought that was great to see.

Steven Pienaar: He told us he's got an opportunity to go and coach United, and the players were happy. He told us, and we all went out after that with the manager for dinner, and we all said our goodbyes.

Louis Saha: How did Moyes and Sir Alex Ferguson compare? They both had the eye to progress, maybe in a different way. Of course success helps, when you have two or three titles in your belt as manager it's always a help for getting players. I would say David Moyes struggled to attract those big players without the money. So he had less facilities, but I think that he had the same philosophy. Maybe the difference between them as well was the fact that Sir Alex Ferguson was a striker, and David Moyes was a defender. You can see that in their style of management. They were looking for a different base I would say.

Simon Hart: The David Moyes we saw later at Sunderland [where he was manager for the 2016/17 season] was sadly a pale, kind of, shadowy imitation of that flame-haired, immensely-driven fellow who arrived at Goodison. I remember speaking to [Everton's former director of communications] Ian Ross about him, and he was saying he couldn't have a conversation anymore because he was so utterly focused on the job. I think that was hugely helpful for Everton – somebody like that who wanted to make a name for himself as a manager and, in the process, reignite something at the club and drag them out of that mediocrity.

Martinez's mantra

Moyes' departure left Kenwright in an unfamiliar position – he had to appoint a new manager. Not since 2002 had that been the case. Kenwright clearly had the 3-0 defeat to Wigan at the front of his mind, as it was soon announced that he agreed a deal with the bold and innovative Roberto Martinez. The Spaniard – the first manager of Everton from outside of Britain and Ireland – was given out a four-year contract, and set about making Everton more expansive.

Roberto Martinez: I think Mr Kenwright and I had a couple of meetings. It wasn't at that point a formal interview to me, but it was. Bill Kenwright is used to meeting a lot of people in his business, and is probably a magician in terms of getting feelings right in the first time that he meets a person – it could be in the acting world or in football world; he's a person with an incredible social intelligence in that respect. So looking back I'm sure that I was 'interviewed' a couple of times, when we met. But it worked both ways; you're intrigued about a new project, you're intrigued about what's behind the football club, and I think in those meetings we got to know each other on a human level. We both found out about the opportunity of working together.

Alan Myers: He was such a nice guy. You'd think, 'How are you so nice?' Some people think it's to the detriment of him. I disagree with that, because I think he was able to cut that off when he needed to. I'd never met anyone, any manager, who was so clued up commercially and marketing wise. He just knew what to do.

Laura Smith: I went to one of the fan events when he had very first come in at Aintree Racecourse and I met him. I don't know whether or not he had a script or something in front of him but everything he was saying was the right thing. He won everyone over with his words basically. He was a lovely, lovely man, but probably too nice because the players went soft on him.

Roberto Martinez: It was fascinating to find out about Everton. I did study from the first day that I took the job; I wanted to know about Everton. It shocked me straight away when I realised I was the fourteenth manager of Everton. Sometimes in the modern game, clubs go through that number of managers in five years. It is not something that I took lightly. So at that point I was very intrigued by this very beautiful football club that I was going to manage, and tried to understand the fans. I always feel that as a manager I need to understand the fans first and foremost. And I didn't want to hide the fact that, as Everton, you have to fight for silverware, you have to be competing, you have to be able to win against anyone at Goodison. I wanted to do it with a certain style that could replicate the best feelings of our fans and the best years of the clubs history. But it was a fascinating period with reading books and watching DVDs, and getting familiar with the history of Everton.

Tony Hibbert: With Martinez coming in, we had seen him at Wigan and knew about the relegation, but as a player looking at him and in the stand looking at him he looked like a manager that you wanted to play for. He was so positive and so nice that you couldn't not like him. It was strange because when he came in and spoke to you, you couldn't help but feel ten foot tall. He was that type of person, and I do think the club needed that. He changed a hell of a lot of stuff and a lot of stuff wasn't working, and it didn't work, but I knew about his concept and I bought into his concept, he had great ideas. He was clever, and I do think the club needed this new fresh idea of how to play football.

Steven Pienaar: The manager came in with new ideas. The way he wanted us to play was the right way. I think with the core of the team that was there before he came, in our first season we basically just carried on, and we played more attractive football and he brought some players in, and we played quite well. And we were unfortunate that we didn't finish fourth.

Roberto Martinez: For me the signing of Gareth Barry was essential. We had good experience in the dressing room. When we faced Manchester City with Wigan, he was the most influential player. I knew that he was the difference between being able to dislodge Man City or not, that it was full of stars. So he was very important for, first, developing a training culture where the young players could learn and learn standards, and then in games that they could have that environment that they could make mistakes and enjoy the football in the same manner.

Tim Howard: We did a lot more. Roberto is a coach who does a lot of unopposed ball work, meaning a lot of playing in a team formation without opposition. But his ideas are it doesn't matter about the opposition, it's about you and it's about how quickly you can move the ball, how concisely and crispy you can get on the ball and play forward. It was different training than I had done, whether it be with the national team, with Everton or Man United, but it was good. It was different, it was a change. I think he brought a few players in that he thought mirrored his style, to go along with what we already had.

Sylvain Distin: I think it was a mix of what Moyes implied to us. I think we could have played some games without David Moyes on the bench, because everybody knew what he had to do; everything was clear, everything was straight, and we had a lot of habits. Everybody knew his job. So we still have some of that left, that David Moyes spirit, and Martinez came as well with a new type, new style of football, and the mix of both I think worked really well. This season everyone felt really comfortable, I think we adapted really well to his style of football that was completely different than what had gone before. But at the same time we kept that team spirit and that defensive toughness that we had from Moyes. So I think the mix of both worked really well.

Roberto Martinez: We needed a finisher. When I arrived at Everton we lost Marouane Fellaini [Moyes bought him for Manchester United having at the same time been rebuffed in his attempts to sign Leighton Baines] and he was the top goal scorer, and the clear goal scoring threat that the team had was relying on his position on the pitch and how he was playing. So we needed a finisher and Romelu Lukaku was that, an outstanding finisher.

Alan Myers: Lukaku came in, and he was a real shy lad; he was quiet; he was polite; he was really nice kid. I remember talking to him, and he was so articulate. He was 19 but you thought you were talking to a 28-year-old. He sounds about 28, you know, and then, you realise he was a kid. You felt he was a real talent. I remember speaking to Roberto about it and Roberto said, 'He's played so much football for his age.' He had so much experience for someone so young, and I think that was what really fascinated Roberto about him.

Leon Osman: For me, he's such a big guy, yet when he's in and around the penalty area – the D at the edge of the box, anything where he's through one v one or has a strike – I'd put money on him to score. The only one who came close to that was Yakubu. But Rom's a lot more mobile than Yakubu.

Tim Howard: We didn't have that £20 million striker who would bang in 20 goals a season [under

Moyes], and Romelu was special. He scores goals anywhere he goes, whether it be Chelsea, West Bromwich, Everton, now Man United, Belgium – he is a goalscorer. Get the ball up to him and he is going to put it in the back of the net more times than not. So, for us as a team, going as we've just chronicled, finally getting to the era where he's up top for us you're like 'Woah, this is going to be special.' It was fun to be a part of that. We do our dogged defensive duty back here, it's not going to be pot luck at the top once we get up there. He's going to score.

Roberto Martinez: With John Stones I tried to sign him [for Wigan] in the previous window, and we were very close; so at that point I knew that I saw him as a future centre-half. When he was at Barnsley he was playing at right wing-back, he was playing right-back, he played with the Under-21s as a right-back, and when I arrived at Everton that was the position that he was given. I almost started in an advantageous position because I could feel that I wanted John to play more centrally, play in a centre-half role. With Ross Barkley in the first training that we had I will always remember the way that he scored two goals from outside the box, one with the right foot and then the next one with the left foot. I knew he was a special talent. But, a young player; he needed understanding and he needed fitting in and a way of playing that could enhance those qualities.

Tony Hibbert: The first year was all about playing football, passing, that's all it was. Nothing to do with fitness, just passing. The first year we still had the nucleus of David Moyes' side, and to be honest that's solely why we did so well, because we had the nucleus of that side that were set up to not got beat. Then we had Martinez's new way of playing; getting into these positions and knowing how to break people down, it was working for us.

Mike Hughes: If you look at how good Roberto Martinez was in his first season in charge at Everton he couldn't have been that good if it wasn't for David Moyes. That was largely David Moyes' team, the backbone of it. We know that he brought in Romelu Lukaku on loan, Gareth Barry on loan and he made changes and he made Everton a really really good team, but he'd been left a really really good team. If Roberto Martinez had been left the team that had been left for David Moyes there was absolutely no chance whatsoever of him being able to do what he was able to do.

Leon Osman: What happened at first was Martinez took the David Moyes team and just allowed the full-backs mainly to attack a bit more, get in the box. You seen how many goals the full-backs scored that season, the first season [Seamus Coleman scored 7, Leighton Baines scored 6 and Bryan Oviedo 2]. He allowed them to release themselves. But the mentality was still for everybody to get back. We'd had that, we'd drilled that into ourselves over the previous two seasons.

Steven Pienaar: We definitely had the balance right. The manager basically implemented small things, attacking wise. Because as a team we always knew what our first duty was to make sure we don't concede.

Tim Howard: I think we played really well that season. We had already a very strong foundation, some top quality players. The additions he brought in, in terms of Gareth Barry and James McCarthy and players like this, also with his own tactical thoughts on how the team should play; I thought we surprised a lot of people.

Tony Hibbert: Going through that season, I spent a lot of time injured and I spoke to Martinez a lot, and I remember saying to him, 'I honestly can't believe the way we're playing, it's unbelievable.

We're controlling games like I've never seen us control games before.' It was frightening, the stuff we were playing was unbelievable.

Roberto Martinez: You always look on that season: could we have done anything more in order to get more than 72 points? The truth is no. We gave everything we had; we played with incredible flair and big heart. What I loved, was that combination of real passion but a real quality in what we were trying to do.

Defending without honour

Roberto Martinez's honeymoon period hinted at a bright future. In his first season at Goodison Park, his team had built on their defensive discipline under Moyes with an increased understanding of how to keep the ball and attack with penetration. In his second season, though, the first part of that well-balanced jigsaw disappeared. In the previous three campaigns, Everton had conceded 40, 40, and 39 in the league. This time around that number rose to 50, and included a 6-3 home defeat to Chelsea and a 3-0 loss at Southampton.

Roberto Martinez: Behind the scenes we put a very strong plan to try to bridge that gap that we saw on the pitch with a long-term strategy, bring in what we thought were exceptional young players and giving them the opportunity to develop. Giving a young player the opportunity to develop means it's going to cost you points; they're going to make mistakes, and it's normal. But I think it was the long-term strategy to try to get a value into the club that could allow us [to progress]. If we were going to polish these players into world-class players and could keep them, we would get the benefit. If we couldn't keep them – because that's also what happens in the game – it would be for the valuation that we need and we could reinvest that, and we could use it to bridge that gap.

Steven Pienaar: I think in the second season he wanted us to play more openly. Sylvain [Distin] left [Distin was actually dropped], a younger player came in [John Stones], and obviously it takes time to gel, and that's why we had a poor second season.

Tim Howard: I think teams found us out a little bit, which happens to any good team. They began pressing us high up the pitch, and that led to some inconsistency across the back. Again that was on us as players, to try and figure out the best way to manage it, and I don't think we adapted as well as we could have in our second and third season.

Sylvain Distin: I went from checking how many clean sheets and how many goals we conceded to checking how many passes I make in the game. Yes, it was satisfying to see, 'Oh yes, I made 100 passes,' or, 'I've got 90% completion on passes,' but I'm a defender and I'm a bit old school. I like the defensive challenge. For me that's my job. It was very different as well to be able to play this type of football. You need as a centre-back to put yourself in positions that are good to play football, but maybe not good to defend. If you lose the ball sometimes you feel uncomfortable, but at the end of the day you need to listen to the manager. If you want to play you need to do what the manager wants you to do, so I did it and I think I adapted quite well as well. But did I enjoy it? We finished for three consecutive seasons being the second or third best defence in the league, I take more pride in that than making 100 passes as if I was an entertainer or midfielder. It was satisfying to know I could do it, but I won't get any pride out of it.

Tony Hibbert: He was too nice. He would have a go in the changing rooms, but he was never blaming someone or putting a finger on someone. It was never that, which was far from what we had last time, and if it wasn't him doing it, it was the players doing it to each other, that's how good a knit group we had – if the manager wasn't doing it, the players were having a go at each other. With Martinez there was none of that, and it snowballed in a way. Players were saying 'Well, hang on, if that players' not doing it, and you're not having a go at him, then I'm not having a go at him. There's no point.'

Laura Smith: There was only so many times that you could switch Sky Sports News on and hear him say, 'Phenomenal.' I think in the end the fans got really really annoyed at that.

Leon Osman: I had a moan or an instruction or a shout and was told that he would do the talking. So basically, pipe down. So then you start coming in the dressing room and everyone's quiet until you start listening to the manager. And that real confrontation between the players, which had obviously been there for years, sort of filters out because that's what the manager desires.

Tim Howard: Each manager's entitled to have their style, and when that happens you have to adapt. Roberto was the manager the first season too. We didn't pick the bones out of that season, so surely it's not all just down that. Each manager has their ideas on how they want the team to conduct themselves, and that's okay too.

Steven Pienaar: Some games the manager would come in and he would say, 'Yeah, I think we played well,' and the players were like, 'Fucking hell, that was shit from us, we played shit and you come in now, were you watching the same game?' Slowly like that, the players started not believing things anymore. When you lose that belief you think, 'I don't care if we conceded three goals, I think we still played good.' Sometimes the guys that were there longer obviously were just like, 'Fucking hell, can you just tell us, have a go at us. We're grown men, you can criticise us and tell us.' That's where I think it went wrong, the manager was too nice at some stages.

A saving grace during the 2014/15 campaign proved to be Europe. Everton had once again qualified for the Europa League and set about their work in impressive fashion, finishing top of their group. A double win over a Wolfsburg side containing Kevin De Bruyne was particularly noteworthy: Everton dismantled their German counterparts 4-1 at Goodison and 2-0 in Lower Saxony. An aggregate 7-2 win over Young Boys of Bern in the next round followed. Europe, it seemed, had not worked Martinez's Everton out.

Roberto Martinez: We had outstanding performances in the Europa League, beating Wolfsburg home and away, beating Lille. They were Champions League teams the season before. Many people forget that we were the last British team to be knocked out of Europe, so it was a really good season in Europe. Bearing in mind that English teams will find it very difficult to be successful, and it's been the case in the last few years because the demands of the Premier League put an extra difficulty in doing well in Europe. We dropped a few points in the league, but it wasn't a case of having a problem internally, not at all, no.

Leon Osman: Maybe the consistency wasn't there, but game to game he could get a team firing in cup competitions, and we did well. We went to Wolfsburg and won home and away; they were considered the best team in our group, and a top team across Europe at the time. Kevin De Bruyne was one of their players, and we deserved to win both games, we played really well. We defended well, we scored two good goals away from home, scored four I think at home.

After defeating Young Boys in the Round of 32, Everton were drawn against Dynamo Kyiv in the next round, and faced them first at Goodison. They soon went 1-0 down, but a Steven Naismith leveller and a late penalty from Romelu Lukaku gave them a good chance travelling to Ukraine. What followed, though, was a frantic game indicative of the second half of Martinez's era. The Toffees simply couldn't keep Dynamo from scoring, finding themselves 4-1 down inside the hour.

Leon Osman: We just came up against it away in Kiev. Dynamo Kiev, which brought back memories of Bucharest. Blinking heck.

Brendan Connolly: They had had some issues with their crowd the round before, against Guingamp from France, and there were some ugly scenes then. With a combination of that and with the conflict that was still going on in the Ukraine [Russia had invaded the Crimea in 2014], I think a few people must've thought we were mad to even think of going. But the conflict was some way away in the Crimea, in the Eastern Ukraine, so – as supporters – we thought we'd be alright. But it was quite sobering to see the memorials to those who had lost their lives in the conflict only 12 months earlier in Kiev. There'd been over 100 people killed in the demonstrations in Kiev and the political ongoings.

Tony Hibbert: The mentality was different. It was always, 'Well, okay, score a goal, score another goal.' It was always that. It was never, 'Score a goal, have a rethink and go again.' It was always, 'Score, score, score' – that concept. It was never a concept of, 'Okay, we've gone behind, we need to do something different.' It was never Plan B or Plan C, it was Plan A constantly. If things weren't going right, we were still doing it. That was the problem.

Leon Osman: I think we gave a sloppy goal away at home, and if we take a 2-0 lead over there you've got a chance. I think the game just slipped away from us, the crowd play a big part. I think they released half the army barracks to go and stand in the stand and they were all fully kitted out in that. They made a hell of a noise. There was a whopper or two, goals scored. We were just too open at the time. We needed to go out and outscore teams to win games.

Tim Howard: I thought we played well in the first leg, and I thought we were poised quite well and set up quite well to certainly get something in the second leg, and it all kind of fell apart. It's weird when you look back on those games and you think how did all of that happen? But it does.

Roberto Martinez: It was a difficult place, full stadium; difficult political moment at that time in Ukraine, and it became a crazy game. It's hard to explain. Two or three goals were outstanding from Dynamo Kiev, especially the one from the left-back; if he tries a hundred times it will only happen once. And it was a game that went away from us for the right reasons at times, because we got a little bit fearful of losing the opportunity of getting through, and that stopped us from doing certain things better. And probably we played a little bit to the occasion rather than to do what we did in the second half against Lille. But the team never lost the desire to keep trying and we scored a late goal in the first half. The problem was it wasn't going to be for us.

Brendan Connolly: We ended up chatting to a few of their supporters and had an enjoyable evening after the game. But the mood of the Everton fans was pretty bleak, understandably. Having gone over there quite optimistic and even making quite a positive start to the game, but then ending up getting beat 5-2 on the night with a late consolation goal.

Although there were good individual games, Martinez was unable to halt a wider malaise and Everton's defensive vulnerabilities plagued them. In 2015/16 home defeats included 3-0 to Manchester United, 3-2 to Leicester, 4-3 to Stoke and 3-2 to West Ham – when Everon had led 2-0 with 12 minutes left, having also missed a penalty. The most embarrassing defeat of all, though, came at Anfield, where the Blues were routed 4-0. According to BBC statistics, Jurgen Klopp's side registered 37 shots that evening.

Roberto Martinez: We had to play with ten men for a large part of the West Ham game. We had a player sent off in the first half. Even with that we were superior to West Ham; we scored a second goal, then we had a penalty and that became a turning point. And it's almost that missing that penalty [the players] felt the fear – it's almost that you could feel it, that we had at that point something to lose. Then West Ham all of a sudden threw everything forward and we couldn't defend the box. If you look at the specific actions, from being able to score the third goal, to lose the game 3-2 is unthinkable. And that's probably the last bit that we needed to solve, but as a team that had an incredible bravery and an incredible desire to win things, and [in] the process we were learning how to do it and how to cope with those expectations.

Simon Hart: The West Ham game for me, was kind of the nadir, it was the high point of everything that was wrong about Martinez. In the press conference afterwards, he was talking about how Everton had lacked experience to hold onto a 2-0 lead at home against West Ham. This was the man who had Leon Osman on the bench and sent on Oumar Niasse who had never played Premier League football, and was the least-experienced player on the bench. The fact was that he just talked to us as if we were idiots, and you can't really do that for too long and get away with it.

Tony Hibbert: The lads wanted him to have a go at us. That was the biggest problem, instead of coming in and saying little bits, the lads wanted him to have a bollock at us and tell us how crap it was and how this and that, to really go at us. Because we knew playing the game and with certain individuals not doing stuff, we'd come in and it'd just be like, 'Okay we got beat again.' It was one of them. The lads who had been there a while and knew the club didn't like that, didn't like the fact that we can come in and nothing what happened.

Leon Osman: We'd had our first season, we'd finished fifth, playing some great football, dominating games. Because we were what we were, we were Everton, we got the ball forward, we played some great football, but we got the ball into the other half and tried to work an opportunity. Under Roberto Martinez we passed it more at the back and sucked teams into us and then hit them with the openings. Whereas what happened next, the following season, we would pass it at the back and teams would say, 'Fine we'll just sit back here and take a draw.' We were just encouraged to pass and pass and pass, and not get the ball forward and into certain areas quick enough, and it just became quite boring if I'm honest.

Steven Pienaar: I would agree we lost that mentality, the will to defend. After that, most of the players basically just wanted to attack and forgot that our first duty was to defend. Obviously they say the best way to defend is to attack, but sometimes I think we were open like a Dutch cheese at some stages. I think that as soon as we concede you could see the guys drop their heads, there wasn't that fighting spirit we had under Moyes.

'If they would call somebody, let's say, 'a bastard', they would call me a 'black bastard'. It was proper racism, there's no two ways about it.' Everton's first black player, Cliff Marshall trains under the shadow of Liverpool's Anglican Cathedral. [*Getty*]

'The blue side has always been painted that they are the most racist part of Liverpool. But being there and experiencing what I did, I don't agree with most of what I've heard before.' Everton's first black signing, Daniel Amokachi. [*Getty*]

'There was an education needed there that these were the things that couldn't be said and it was right and proper that the club were taken to task over it.' John Barnes backheels a banana that was thrown on the pitch during Liverpool's FA Cup tie with Everton in 1988. [*Getty*]

The hunt for a new stadium: There were failed moves to [top left] Kings Dock and (*top right*) Kirkby. Will a proposed move to Bramley Moore Dock come to fruition? [*Authors' collection/Getty*]

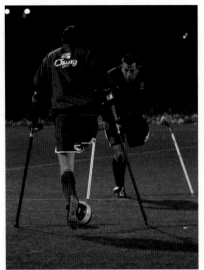

'Everton in the Community is not about football, it's about education and about providing facilities. It's the idea of belonging and being part of it and I suppose working on the mentality of the People's Club.' *Clockwise from top left:* Everton's disability team kickstarted EitC's recognition; 'The People's Hub' has embedded Everton into the heart of the L4 community; reformed addict Lee Johnson, pictured with Roberto Martinez, is one of EitC's many success stories; a drum band perform ahead of a game during the 2016/17 season. [*Getty/Alex Baillie*]

Seamus Coleman in action in a friendly against CD Everton of Chile in 2010. Everton v Everton was the longstanding dream of the Ruleteros Society, which fosters links with Everton's South American cousins. [*Getty*]

Dr David France with one of the Everton ledgers, which forms the heart of the Everton Collection, an unparalleled single club collection of documents and artefacts. [*David & Elizabeth France*]

The Everton Former Players' Foundation was another of David France's initiatives. Here he is (*right*) pictured with Alan Ball, Alex Young and Duncan McKenzie before a dinner in 2006. [*David & Elizabeth France*]

Everton's managerial mastermind Mo Marley during the 2005 Premier League Cup final defeat to Leeds Carnegie at Spotland Stadium, Rochdale. [*Getty*]

Everton celebrate their 1-0 win over Arsenal in the 2008 Premier League cup final, their first victory in a final over the Gunners. [*Getty*]

Dowie, who scored a 119th-minute winner in extra time to give Everton a 3-2 victory, kisses the cup. [*Getty*]

Michelle Hinnigan leads her side out in the 2014 FA Cup final against Arsenal, a re-run of the 2010 final. [*Getty*]

Lindsay Johnson heads the ball off the line as the ball loops over Brown-Finnis. Despite their best efforts, Everton would lose 2-0 on the day. [*Getty*]

Everton celebrate winning WSL 2. It would later be confirmed that they were to be promoted after Notts County folded, and that the players were to become full-time. [*Getty*]

Andy Spence and Gabby George pose next to the Everton crest, after the latter becomes the first full-time Ladies professional to sign for the club. [*Getty*]

Going to the Game: 'It was a tremendous event for a lad of eleven. It was my first time in London and my eyeballs were popping out when I got my first sight of all the glass.' Everton fans before the 1906 FA Cup final at the Crystal Palace. [*Getty*]

Going to the Game: 'My father went to the 1933 FA Cup Final and was back in the house at 9.30pm – they laid on 40 charter trains from Wembley to Liverpool.' Evertonians congregate ahead of the 1933 FA Cup final at Wembley. [*Getty*]

Going to the Game: 'When I saw Goodison that first time, I was just amazed at the enormity. It sends a shiver up my spine on match days now, hearing the horses going through the stadium, and looking at the size of the horses and the smell of the match day. The noise, and the colour, and the atmosphere.' Fans approach Goodison in 1964. [*Gerry Cranham/Offside*]

Going to the Game: 'It was the clichéd moment; it was very true to it the moment you walk up the steps and you inhale that unique smell of spilt beer, dodgy fried products and police horse urine, which kind of surrounded the ground.' Fans outside Goodison in 1964. [*Gerry Cranham/Offside*]

Going to the Game: 'Everton gave me a sense of safety. If you're in love or you have a relationship, you can't describe it, can you? It's difficult to say what that one person, that one thing, what that one moment, gives to you that nothing else does. And nothing but nothing in my life has got near it; not near it.' Everton fans watch their team take on Manchester United in 1964. [*Gerry Cranham/Offside*]

Going to the Game: 'It was absolutely insane! I'm getting goosebumps now just talking about it, just thinking about the experience. The Gwladys Street was absolutely nuts for at least five minutes after they restarted play; it was just amazing.' Everton fans celebrating in 1978. [*Getty*]

Going to the Game: 'Seeing Goodison for the first time was, I imagine, like a Muslim going to Mecca, or someone visiting the moon.' Goodison in 2017. [*Alex Baillie*]

The Changing face of Goodison: A demonstration baseball game, during the second leg of a post-season tour by the New York Giants and the Chicago White Sox, at Goodison Park football stadium, 30 October 1924. Ray Schalk of the White Sox is at bat, with Hank Gowdy of the Giants catching. [*Getty*]

The Changing face of Goodison: Tottenham's Ted Harper leaps high to aim a header towards Billy Coggins' goal during a Second Division match in October 1930. The Bullens Road stand in the background was constructed four years earlier and still stands today. [*Getty*]

The Changing face of Goodison: An aerial photograph of Goodison dating from the late-1940s or early-1950s. [*Getty*]

The Changing face of Goodison: In 1966 Goodison was one of the main host stadiums for the World Cup, staging matches up to and including the semi finals. The USSR's legendary goalkeeper, Lev Yashin, in action [left]; Pele, who was kicked out of the tournament faces Bulgaria [right]. [*Getty*]

The Changing face of Goodison: A view from the newly constructed Park Stand in 1994. [*Offside*]

The Changing face of Goodison: The iconic wooden seats remain an unchanging part of the Goodison experience in several parts of the stadium. [*Offside*]

The Changing face of Goodison: The Archibald Leitch designed balustrades remain an iconic part of the Goodison experience. [*Simon Stacpoole/Offside*]

The Changing face of Goodison: St Luke's Church remains part of the fabric of Goodison. The Everton board even rejected an approach from the ecclesiastical authorities to purchase it, believing it wasn't appropriate to deconsecrate a church. [*Getty*]

The Changing face of Goodison: The Old Lady in 2017. [*Simon Stacpoole/Offside*] [*Getty*]

Roberto Martinez: I think it's true that defensively we weren't good enough at home. I think in football you cannot generalize. The first six months in the third season we were outstanding; some of the football was the best that we ever had, better than the first season. But at home we had to do too well to win football games. We were being controlled from 60 minutes and then one action that for whatever reason we couldn't defend well and properly, and we end up in the back of the net. The amount of points that we dropped at home, it cost us. So did we make mistakes defensively? Were we a fragile team defensively? No. Did we defend well enough at Goodison? No. That's the truth; we didn't. [In 2015/16 Everton conceded 30 league goals in 18 home games under Martinez, recording just five wins] But away from home, if you look at the stats we had a very, very impressive away record in the Premier League [Everton recorded 24 league points from 54 available, the eleventh best record in the league]. The problem that we had is that we couldn't replicate that defensive play that we had away from home at Goodison. So there is a combination of aspects of why that happened.

The 2015/16 season's hope for redemption came in the FA Cup, a competition in which Martinez had already triumphed as Wigan manager. Everton reached the quarter-final stage, and was given a tough tie in the form of Chelsea at home. With the game in the balance, Romelu Lukaku scored one of the finest goals Goodison Park has seen. Picking the ball up, Lukaku drove between Branislav Ivanovic and Cesar Azpilicueta, ghosted past Mikel, tied Gary Cahill in knots and slotted the ball past Thibaut Courtois. Lukaku would soon add a second on the night, cementing his reputation as the club's talisman.

Roberto Martinez: The whole approach towards that game was of a really confident team. You would never have guessed what happened in the previous game [the 3-2 defeat to West Ham]. And that's where we were. We were trying to build a winning team with taking risks on the pitch, because we wanted to be a team in control of our own fate, which means we needed to know how to score goals and try to win games. But there were key moments that we couldn't cope with, in terms of defending specific actions that almost caused a little bit of having something to lose.

Everton 1, Manchester United 2
FA Cup semi-final
23 April 2016

Roberto Martinez: I stayed at Everton because I truly believed that we could win silverware, and we could develop a squad that could take us somewhere. Obviously in the third season we made the two semi-finals of the two cups; so it means that we were getting close to being able to cope with those expectations, to be able to cope with going somewhere you're expected to win in a knockout phase like we did at Middlesbrough, and places that you are expected to win and progress would be Man City at home, at Goodison, in the first leg. So we were getting very close.

Hana Roks: Personally I think Martinez should've been sacked before that. I'd have had Rhino [David Unsworth] and [Joe] Royle in then. But I don't understand people booing Martinez at half-time. It was vile. At half-time it was 0-0, wasn't it? It was so dejected, so subdued. It wasn't bouncing like it was on previous occasions when we've been. It was like in our heads, 'Oh we're not going to win here.' It's horrible to go to a match feeling like that. Obviously when we scored everyone was going mad.

Roberto Martinez: I will always remember driving with the bus to Wembley, seeing everything in blue; the fans were incredible. The memories of the games at Lille, and the European games in Switzerland, it was almost taken over, the blue sight of the city in a foreign place – when I say foreign, away from Goodison. It was an incredible feeling of a big occasion. We didn't [know] how big it was. I think the first half carried that responsibility.

Leon Osman: My family were in the crowd, my kids, and it become very negative at that point. Quite scary, a little bit, how the feeling around Everton and the manager was at the time. To go the game and feel intimidated in your own end showed everything about where the club was with regards to where the fans were and with regards to Mr Martinez. It was sad to see.

Roberto Martinez: Second half was almost all the work in the last three years in understanding how you can break a team down, how you can play against a team that has got the pedigree and experience like Manchester United, and winning big games and winning trophies. I thought we showed in that second half period all the work that was invested in three years, in terms of mentality, in terms of tactical knowledge, in terms of the technical quality. And that was a real shame that we couldn't get the rewards of what that second half performance deserved.

Dave McDougall: When we were awarded the penalty, everybody was saying 'Baines! It should be Baines!' and then Lukaku steps up – 'I'll take it.' And he missed it! I think that spurred Man United on. You can't give teams a second bite.

Simon Hart: Lukaku was a player who repeatedly told us he had to leave Everton because he needed to win trophies. But there were five or six great chances and a penalty against Man Utd; he didn't score any of them in that game. He could've put Everton into a cup final against Crystal Palace singlehandedly.

Roberto Martinez: The second half against Manchester United we had no lack of understanding how to break a top team down. And I could see signs that they were coming together, but in those two cup competitions we should have won the silverware if we wanted to carry on with the understanding of the fans.

Exit Martinez

After Lukaku missed a succession of chances, including his missed penalty. Anthony Martial's last minute winner saw the end for Everton. Three weeks later Martinez was sacked following a dire 3-0 defeat to Sunderland. Joe Royle and David Unsworth took charge for the final day of the season.

Roberto Martinez: I think it happens in football when you don't win. The reason you don't win is because of the way you're working, so if you're a negative guy the reason that you don't win is because you're negative; if you're a positive guy that's the reason why you're losing. I understand that; I've been in the game long enough. When you win everything is fantastic; when you lose everything is wrong. I understood very, very early that's it not like that. You could lose and you could play really well and create something behind the scenes really powerful and strong, and at times the opposite. We could win but it's just the short term and you don't know what's round the corner. It's part of football. I don't see it as anything different.

Mike Hughes: He was criticised for being stubborn but all the best managers are stubborn. Alex Ferguson – there was nobody more stubborn than him. You've got to stick to what you believe in and in the end what Roberto Martinez believed in at Everton wasn't working and it was right that he was removed from his job. But if you look at some of the football that Everton played under Roberto Martinez, even in the seasons that things didn't go so well, they were playing some great football. That home record was really really poor and I was commentating on matches that Everton should've been winning and they weren't winning them. They were drawing too many and they were losing too many but you just thought that it only needed slight modifications. I think his absolute belief on playing out from the back as the only way to go when results weren't going Everton's way; he should've been able to see that it wasn't working. And you always have to adapt, don't you?

Simon Hart: How far can you get by just talking a good game? Donald Trump got to be the President of the United States, and Martinez was only Everton manager– so, I don't know. Maybe I'm just scarred by the way he would talk complete and utter nonsense to us whenever things went very wrong. People were expected to still believe that. It was just insulting, really.

Roberto Martinez: I look back on my time at Everton with a lot of pride. It was an incredible period. I will always feel very close to Everton. I was the fourteenth manager of a glorious football club, and the way I see it, extremely proud and privileged, and the memories that I collected I will never forget them. And as we always do when you move on you always keep all the good memories and you forget about the bad memories very quickly. I think Alan Ball's famous saying that, 'Once Everton touches you nothing is ever the same again' is true. I wanted that quote to be in the dressing room, and we put it there because it's very true. I think Everton as a football club carries that charisma and that grand feeling that has been there forever, and I think you get moved by it, the intensity of it. I am very proud, and it's true that I always check the results and there is something in me, I can't wait to see Everton with silverware and deep down, celebrated.

Moshiri stakes his claim

For years Everton had existed in a perpetual state of being best of the rest, able to trouble and test the top four, but never able to truly worry them. Even putting aside the angst of an increasingly frustrated fan base, Bill Kenwright was acutely aware of this, and had tried to find a buyer as far back as November 2007. His careful nature meant that became a slow, somewhat arduous process, and perhaps with good reason. But eventually his found his man: on 27 February 2016, it was announced that Fahrad Moshiri had purchased a 49.9% stake in Everton. The British-Iranian, who had recently sold his stake in Arsenal to partner Alisher Usmanov to free himself up, promised a new era of investment. In September 2018 Moshiri increased his stake in the club to 68 per cent, with a promise to up that shareholding to 77 per cent by June 2019.

Jon Woods: Bill was very picky. We've talked to lots of people over the years. He was very picky who came in, and I think he got the right guy in the end.

Bill Kenwright: You are looking for someone with money; that's where it starts. He's got to have the money. And then of course I've got to feel he's got the right DNA. I met most people, and three people I turned down because I had bad feelings about were disasters for other clubs; absolute disasters.

And I met two groups of people and one individual over the final year maybe, and I was happy with each of them. But there was an instinct about Farhad; his knowledge of football is as good as anyone I've ever come across. His love for football is all consuming; and I had to make that love of football include Everton, and hopefully take over from the love of football to the love of Everton. That took a year; and that was the challenge. It was David Dein who introduced us. Farhad is an Evertonian now.

Denise Barrett-Baxendale: One of the most wonderful things about the investment and the welcoming Mr Moshiri here and the new directors on the board is that it helps serve the club's community programme. Obviously our board continues to be led and managed and directed by our chairman Mr Kenwright. We've managed to maintain the Everton essence. It's very important to our new owner, it's very important to the board that we continue to operate in the way that Evertonians expect us to.

Ronald Koeman, building blocks for the future

If Everton fans were looking for a sudden cash splurge with their new owner, it wasn't going to come immediately. However, there was one clear statement of intent: Ronald Koeman was announced as manager in June 2016. Koeman had already managed a host of big European clubs: Ajax, Benfica, PSV, Valencia and Feyenoord, and his move from Southampton to Merseyside showed Everton's increased financial muscle. In partnership with a new Director of Football, Steve Walsh, Everton set about rebuilding their squad. They finished the 2016/17 seventh, qualifying for Europe, and over the following summer invested heavily, buying Jordan Pickford, Gylfi Sigurdsson, Michael Keane and others. There was a return too for the prodigal son, Wayne Rooney.

Denise Barrett-Baxendale: If I you were to ask me to capture the best time or the best occasion to be an Evertonian, it had to be last year [2016/17] for me. Everton Ladies were promoted, our U23s won the league, fantastic performance from Everton first team, an aspirational new manager, investment into the club, progression for the stadium and the redevelopment of Finch Farm. It's always a magnificent time to be an Evertonian, but at times it can be magical. That season for me was a defining time, whereby we're making real progress and we're doing it the Everton way.

Becky Tallentire: The thing is for success you need all the planets need to align. You need to have the manager, you need to have the team, you have to have the financial backing, you need to have the stadium; so all of these things need to be in a row. And I don't think all our ducks are in a row just yet. One day it will be, and that will be our time. I just don't see it coming for a long time. There's always something missing from the equation. I don't think that it's great for us right now. I don't know when it will be great in the foreseeable future.

Dave Prentice: Ronald Koeman is absolutely 100 per-cent straight with people. And media as well – he's not interested in having a relationship with anybody in the media, but you guarantee his press conferences you will get good lines from him because he answers questions honestly, candidly, probably a little bit more forthright manner than he ought to. There's an organisation about the team, certainly defensive that wasn't there; there was an energy in the attacking third, you wanted to see pressing high up the pitch. A lot of very, very good things. The concern of course is that he wants to be a successful manager and he wants to go as high as he possibly can, and whether that's higher than fourth or fifth place in the Premier League, he might have ambitions elsewhere. But for that to happen he's got to be successful at Everton first, and if he isn't he's not going anywhere else.

Everton's start to the 2017/18 season was deeply disappointing and after just two league wins in the opening three months of the campaign and facing an ignominious exit from the Europa League, the board sacked Ronald Koeman. David Unsworth was placed in temporary charge, but despite an upsurge in form, after six challenging weeks he was himself replaced by Sam Allardyce who joined on an 18 month contract. Allardyce, who had a reputation as survival specialist and advocate of direct football, had never managed a club to higher than sixth place in a managerial career that had taken in Bolton, Newcastle, West Ham and Crystal Palace. A spell as England manager had ended after just a solitary game and in disgrace. His was not in any way a popular appointment among Evertonians. 'Big Sam' built on Unsworth's mini-revival and despite the stultifying football and dreadful away record, Everton finished the season in eighth position and were bolstered by the signings of Cenk Tosun and Theo Walcott in January. The manager, however, was alternately a figure of derision or ridicule among the majority Evertonians and his departure shortly after the final game of the season was no surprise. The summer of 2018 was one of great change at Goodison. The Portuguese Marco Silva succeeded Allardyce and he was joined by Marcel Brands, who left a glittering record at PSV Eindhoven to replace Steve Walsh as Director of Football. Denise Barrett-Baxendale was a popular replacement for Robert Elstone as chief executive. On the pitch there was a clear out of the dressing room with Wayne Rooney the most notable departure. In came the Brazilians Richarlison and Bernard; Barcelona's Andre Gomes, Lucas Digne and Yerry Mina, a star of the 2018 World Cup with Colombia; and Chelsea's man mountain centre-half, Kurt Zouma.

Patrick Hart: I'm more hopeful now than I have been since 1990 in terms of actually winning a trophy, a cup. It looks like they are going to build a stadium that will be a genuinely top stadium on the docks. It's possibly the best thing that's happened to the club since winning the cup in 95, but possibly since the mid-80s team, just in terms of re-establishing Everton in the city of Liverpool. On one level it's re-establishing them in the city, but also re-establishing them as some kind of force in English football, or at least presence.

Phil McNulty: I think the future's very optimistic. I think the slight problem they will face is that it will take them three or four windows to really get to where they want to be in terms of the squad, although they made a fantastic start to it this summer. Other clubs aren't going to be standing still, waiting for Everton to catch them up. But I just think now, with the new owner, the money, the prospect of the new ground, the better players arriving, I think Everton can be more optimistic about the future than they could've been for a generation. I'm not suggesting they're going to emerge as title winners, but you can see them winning something, and you can see the progress of the club being on a very upward curve now, barring something catastrophic happening. I know some Evertonians will say, 'Well, this is Everton; something catastrophic will happen,' but I think the curve is upward. I think there is only one direction the club is heading in now and that's a very positive, upward one. The new owner has changed the expectations and standards.

Simon Hart: I look to the future with mixed emotions, because for me, Everton will always be Goodison: going to that wonderful old stadium. I was there with a German journalist a few months ago, and he absolutely loved the place, and he couldn't understand why we'd want to leave there. There are reasons why, of course. For me, the future is exciting, but something will be lost in the name of progress, and hopefully, it'll be a proper football stadium where we can get angry, and which will be the place where referees and opposing players don't really liking playing at. Hopefully we'll have that; there couldn't be a better location for it. I just hope that Everton's new stadium retains that kind of anger, to be like Goodison where a bunch of miserable bastards can turn up and have a moan. I don't want it to be a fun; we're not Americans.

Tim Howard: I'm excited about where the club's going and how forward-thinking they are, the money that's being spent on top quality players. I really do think there's exciting times ahead for Everton, and obviously as a former player but as a lifelong fan, it's beautiful to see.

Mike Hughes: These are the most exciting times that's there's ever been for the young Everton fans who never witnessed Everton winning the FA Cup in 1995 or Everton winning the league in the mid 1980s, playing the most glorious football that's ever been seen. They were glorious times but a lot of Everton fans never ever witnessed that they are told by their Dads and their Granddads and their Uncles and their cousins about the great Everton teams of the past, but the signs are good that Everton are going to be able to compete.

Part 2

Changing Face
of Football

'When I first started at Everton, everybody had one set of training kit. They used to go to a local launderette where the young players used to take it down and wash it all. Of course, it's got a lot bigger now. Players have got 4 or 5 training kits; and we've maybe got 70 – 80 players altogether with the 23s, 21s, and first teams as well. There's a lot going on now.'

Jimmy Martin

The inception of the Premier League in 1992 initiated the biggest period of change in Everton's history since the club's formative years. Not only were the club founder and continuous members of the richest, most globalised league in the world, but because of the Premier League's popularity they found themselves in a rapidly changing environment. Football became a more tolerant game and barriers were broken. Meanwhile the evolution and professionalisation of the sport saw facilities improve inexorably. In 2007 Everton left the club's historic training base of Bellefield for Finch Farm in south Liverpool. Ten years later it seemed as if the club's decades long search for a new home had been realised with a heads of terms agreement in place for a stadium switch to a site in Liverpool's north docks.

Racism

From the 1960s an increasing number of black and mixed race players began to have an influence in the English game. Everton's 1966 FA Cup hero Mike Trebilcock was one such player, and the club's first black player, Cliff Marshall, came through the ranks to make a handful of appearances in the mid-1970s. Alas, racist chanting was a feature at Goodison until the late-1980s and this, combined with a failure to sign a black footballer until 1994, tarnished the club's reputation.

Martin Dobson: We just looked at Cliff as one of players. You don't look at him as someone different. He's a player and a great guy; that's it.

Cliff Marshall: It wasn't a thing I focussed on at the time because I didn't see colour as an issue with the environment I was in, although there was racism on the opponents' side and, to be honest with you, some of the Everton fans. When I think back over that period there was some not nice things that were said by my own fans. Ignorance again, wasn't it? When I speak to some of me Aunties and me Uncles who went the game supporting me and what they had to put up with in the stands is unbelievable. I had the same banana treatment, monkey chants and all that carry on, but it wasn't just Everton; that was what it was like in those days. You've either got to be strong and get on with it or weak and crumble. Well, I wasn't a crumbler. I just got on with it. When I had it with players, mainly full-backs, I just used laugh at them and torture them. When I say torture them, I'd do my best to nutmeg them and run away from them and they'd never catch me. I was so quick I could give them ten metres and they still wouldn't catch me; that's how quick I was.

Emy Onoura: In a way, Cliff Marshall played in an era before the real viciousness of racism kind of started. Cliff was more of the exotic kind of generation. It was more like 'Look at him'. That's not to say he never got racist abuse. I didn't really hear it. I mean you kind of heard people around you describing him, fans describing him, but it was more using racist language, the n word usually, but it wasn't systematic, all parts of the ground shouting abuse or anything like that. In a sense he was more of an era where it was more of a novelty than anything else. That's what I remember of it, he might tell a different story.

Cliff Marshall: Was it proper racism? If they would call somebody, let's say, 'a bastard', they would call me a 'black bastard'. It was proper racism, there's no two ways about it. To put me off my game, obviously, but they are using bad words.

Martin Dobson: Cliff was the first black player to play for Everton. A great lad, Cliff. He didn't play many games because we had competition in those wide areas. But again, you're concentrating on your own game. We must have had conversations with him, but then you're not trying to highlight it. We've all got certain things we've got to come through to be better players or to adapt to situations, and presumably Ciffy had to get through similar situations, but more difficult.

Brendan Connolly: I don't remember any racism being directed towards Cliff, but maybe that's because it was just part and parcel of the game in those days and sadly you accepted it. There was a famous incident at Goodison with Clyde Best, a black player for West Ham, who was getting some abuse from the crowd, and then he scored a goal. Credit to the more sensible or more balanced Evertonians that he actually got a round of applause because it was a cracking goal and I think there was an element of them giving their disapproval to the racism by applauding his goal. Sadly, it was part and parcel of the game in those days and sadly most people seemed to find it humorous.

Clyde Best: I'd had plenty of stick when we played away from home about the colour of my skin. I'll never forget going to Everton on one occasion [in November 1972] and hearing perpetual monkey chants. I knew who they were directed at. After all, I was a novelty. Most people had never seen a black player before. I also knew the best way to silence the perpetrators. I picked the ball up on the halfway line with Terry Darracott hanging on to my shirt, trying to pull me down. I dragged him literally all the way to the penalty area and when the keeper came out I sold him a dummy and clipped it over his head. After the game Joe Royle came up to me and said it was the best goal ever seen at Goodison Park. It was my way of making a statement.

Cliff Marshall: The only black player that played before me that I can recall was Clyde Best. Big bad Clyde. And he took a lot of stick. That was the only one I knew. It's not like nowadays where you have all of these people and groups where they can help you. In those days we didn't. It was different times. Even in the England Schoolboys you had it. We went to play in Germany and it was terrible over there in Germany. You just got on with it.

Emy Onoura: We beat Stoke [in the FA Cup third round in January 1977], and Garth Crooks came on as sub. That was the first time I really remember wholesale racist abuse of somebody at an Everton game. I wasn't a regular attender at the time, I was an intermittent attender. I might have gone to that game because it was a cup game. So I would have been about 12 or something like that when that game came about. I remember that distinctly. I just remember him getting loads and loads of abuse, loads of monkey chants in particular, but also loads of verbal abuse as well. He'd come on quite late in the game as a sub. I was kind of intrigued by him anyway – me and him were probably the only two black people in the whole ground.

Tony Kellaher: My first home game was in 1971. I suppose racism was rife in those days, not so much homophobia and sexism. But being from a very quiet family in a quiet area of Litherland going to the game for the first time was quite an adventure for me and I was quite alarmed even then at some of the comments that were shouted at the players.

Eric Brown: I always admired Cyrille Regis. I saw him in a game at West Ham once, and somebody threw a banana at him. He picked it up, peeled it, ate a bit of it and threw it back, and he got a huge round of applause. They were on his side after that. It was a sad thing.

Brendan Connolly: I must say Everton had a reputation for being a racist club and I do think that genuinely was misguided and unfair. I think every club had its following of racists and again I think football crowds are just a cross section of society and sadly as there are racists in society every club had them. I do genuinely feel– and I'm not being defensive – that the reputation that we had as being worst than most, I don't think was justified.

Emy Onoura: There was quite a racist undercurrent already at the game, at the games I had gone to, and as I started going to matches I was kind of really aware that the levels of racism were kind of to the point where you'd expect it, it was just part of the match. Then when John Barnes signed [for Liverpool in summer 1987] I just knew it was just going to be another level. That's what happened. It was inevitable. Funnily enough, the racism at Everton started to crank up as soon as John Barnes arrived – it started to crank up before that famous derby game [an FA Cup fifth round tie in February 1988], which I refused to go to. I knew what was going to happen and I couldn't bring myself to go to that derby game, so I didn't go. When John Barnes came, the people who decided it was unsavoury decided it was no longer unsavoury, it was alright to behave like that because he was 'one of them'. So people who knew better all of a sudden had *carte blanche* to behave in a just really obnoxious, poisonous way really. Derbies in particular became poisonous atmosphere. Any team who had maybe three or four black players in it, it just became toxic really quickly.

Graham Ennis: It was horrific the abuse that Barnes got. I was at the League Cup game [at Anfield in October 1988]. I certainly remember feeling that I was the only person at the end of the game that wasn't chanting – it was that bad. I think some of it was bravado, I think some of it was, 'Let's have a go at Liverpool,' and some of it was probably genuine racial hatred. There was an FA Cup game at Goodison, later, that was a minor incident by comparison. And Barnes had bananas thrown at him by supporters of his own club, in his first game against Arsenal. There was an education needed there that these were the things that couldn't be said and it was right and proper that the club were taken to task over it. We played them again a few days later [in the league] and it was a lot better. I think it shocked everyone.

Bishop Tom Williams: There was always black players in the past but people never understood the difference between humour and sarcasm and wit and then skitting. Some people used mockery, but there's a difference between a sense of irony and seeing the funny side of something to people were saying things which were just objectionable.

In the early-1990s When Skies Are Grey, edited by Ennis, led the way with an anti-racism campaign, adopting the Italian slogan No Al Razzismo. Neville Southall posed in a T-shirt promoting the slogan and it seemed like a big moment in Everton's evolution to being a more tolerant club.

Graham Ennis: As a magazine, *When Skies Are Grey* has never sought to be a campaigning publication. We've never hitched our tent to any particular campaign. We've always taken the view that we're a forum for all fans, we'll print articles for and against everything but we'll never take an editorial stance. Racism is different. Everton at the time was in a strange place. They didn't say anything and they'd never signed a black player, which added fuel to the fire and there were some fans who gloried in that. We didn't believe the club was inherently racist but that some supporters were. What we tried to do was balance it out. Racism was starting to be a stick that Liverpool beat us with and an unfair one because had John Barnes signed for Everton it would have been exactly the same, but the other way around. There was something strange about football supporters in Liverpool. There was an intimidating atmosphere in football grounds and black players still talk about it now. It was important for us to set our stall out. It was very important to us to set out an agenda that all Evertonians weren't like this.

In August 1994 Everton signed the Nigerian forward, Daniel Amokachi, for a club record £3million from Club Brugges. His immediate acceptance both among players and fans seemed to alter the reputation Everton had suffered from.

Neville Southall: He was a good lad, Daniel. He was a clever lad and had earned a law degree in the USA before becoming a professional footballer. He was an exporter/importer and had all sorts of things going on. His obsession was with 'sexy football'; he was always banging on about 'sexy football', and he just couldn't understand why we played like we did because it wasn't 'sexy football'. He'd occasionally wander on and do something brilliant or wander on and do something that was just a waste of time. Like Duncan he was another one of those players who on his day was fantastic, and on a bad day was just dreadful. There was no in-between with him. But he loved playing the game and this bizarre idea of 'sexy football.'

Daniel Amokachi: When you look at the red side of Liverpool, they always had African Americans, African players playing in the team [Howard Gayle, a Scouser with a father from Sierra Leone became Liverpool's first black player in 1980; he was followed by John Barnes in 1987 and Mark Walters, Michael Thomas and David James in the early-1990s], and the blue side of it has always been painted that they are the most racist part of Liverpool. But being there and experiencing what I did, I don't agree with most of what I've heard before. All the fans that I met in the stadium or on the street or in the bar, they were always passionate. However, I had an incident, a racial incident, in the hotel. I didn't see the person, I never met the person. I came downstairs in the morning to go for training, and my bumper was peeled of, and there was writing on the car, all sorts ... this N word, get out, you know. But it had nothing to do with the fans. That is the world that we live in, and we can't do anything about it. We just have to keep educating the people and keep ignoring whatever they do, and we just keep seeing the world moving in the perfect direction.

Amokachi's arrival was followed four months later by the full-back Earl Barrett. In 1999 Kevin Campbell joined from Trabsonspor and went on to become Everton's first black captain.

Emy Onoura: Amokachi came and things kind of died off a little bit, but they didn't really. The sea change didn't really happen until Kevin Campbell came. He was a good player, he kept us up almost single-handedly. He was club captain. It wasn't until he came until changes started to happen. In fact, it wasn't until post-Eric Cantona [Cantona in 1995 attacked a Crystal Palace supporter who racially abused him] that nationally new laws were brought in against racism. Obviously clubs were kind of forced to adopt these new laws, guidelines and regulations. But we could have pre-empted some of that to be honest. The best that we had, the only thing we had coming out of the club was, 'We're not as bad as other teams'. What other teams? Chelsea? Millwall? We're not as bad as Millwall – is that the yardstick by which we were judging the club by?

Kevin Campbell: I became Everton's first black captain in 2001. To be captain of a fantastic institution like Everton was obviously a very proud moment for me. But it wasn't a matter of me changing who I am to be captain. I just carried on doing what I was doing anyway. Because fans ain't stupid: fans know if you're being honest or not. I've always been honest, I've always tried, I've always spoken highly of the club, I'll never bad mouth the club. It was always just a matter of really carrying it on and wearing that armband with some distinction. Hopefully I did that.

Denise Barrett-Baxendale: We have a zero-tolerance around anything like racism, sexism, homophobia and hooliganism, so we have a magnificent safety and security team here. We have fantastic installation of cameras, whereby if you're going to behave in a way that we think is inappropriate in our stadium, we will see you. We're very clear in being able to identify you, and we will deal with that. There's no place for anything like that at Goodison Park, and we'll take a robust response. Obviously, we follow all the 'Kick it Out' campaigns, and anything from a league perspective in terms of campaigning and awareness. But really, we deal with things at source, so if there's an issue, we're going to deal with it. We don't expect anybody who comes to Goodison Park to feel unwelcome, to feel intimidated, to feel different. This is an inclusive stadium, and we apply a very robust response to any issues like that.

Henry Mooney: What was acceptable the 1970s is no longer acceptable in the 2017/18 season and I think that is right across the board. You still get the odd isolated incident, sadly, but hopefully we'll be able to eradicate that over the next decade or so, although I'm not totally convinced we will do as you always get some idiot who wants to shout something. The FA, Premier League, Football League, PFA, Kick it Out, Show Racism the Red Card; they're all working in the right direction but you still get the odd one.

Emy Onoura: When I started watching footy there were no black managers, there were no black journalists. There'd be more black people on the pitch than there were in the crowd. I'm very confident that you'd get a crowd, they'd watch 22 players, and there'd be a crowd of 30, 40,000, I could guarantee I'd be the only black face in that whole crowd amongst everybody. Fundamentally, that hasn't changed a lot. There are more black players on the pitch now, that's changed. And a lot of them from abroad, that's kind of changed. But there's not many black people in the press box, there's not many coaches – not a lot's changed apart from the fact that now players aren't called black bastards or use the N word against them. Fundamentally that's the only thing that's changed.

Hooliganism

Football began to be tainted by hooliganism in the late-1950s and by the 1970s it was a feature of English football both at home and abroad. Supporters began staying away from games in their droves, which, in its way, exacerbated the challenges the game was already facing. English football's nadir came in 1985 when rioting Liverpool supporters caused the deaths of 39 fans before a European Cup final against Juventus in Brussels. Now dubbed 'a slum sport for slum people', the British government banned English clubs' participation in Europe. Not until the early-1990s, with the implementation of all seater-stadia, did the problem largely leave the English game.

Emy Onoura: A lot of the time, going away from home, the danger was from the local police force. They just shoved you around and battered you from pillar to post. If you didn't move quickly, if they asked you to move and you didn't move quickly enough, you'd get smacked. If you didn't follow their instructions, even if they never told you what they were, you'd get smacked. If you were walking along a road on your way to the ground or from the ground and you were on a pavement and you stepped out on the street, you'd get a smack because you wanted to avoid or something. If you lagged behind to nip into a shop to buy a drink, or ciggies, or sweets or anything you'd get smacked. It was just like a really poisonous, hostile atmosphere. So what it did was, I think, all of the decent fans kind of went 'I can't be arsed with this. I just can't be bothered going, why am I going to travel the length and breadth of country to face hostility?' It kind of left going away to a few diehards who always went home and away, and a few hard core lads who looked for trouble.

James Mossop: It all seemed to begin with a core in London of National Front people and they were deliberately causing problems. On Merseyside Everton and Liverpool they work alongside each other so there was very little or nothing there, similarly in Manchester. But there was some bad stuff, you'd hear about trains being wrecked. West Ham had a group of fans known as the 'Under 5s' because they were young hooligans and Millwall were always notorious. Whether it was a generational thing I don't know, but you'd have to say now that it's not entirely gone but it's a lot better than what it was.

Eric Brown: I was working for a national news agency, and quite honestly I spent more of my time writing about hooligans than I did about football, which I absolutely loathed. But I did understand why that was necessary, it was a big news element in the game. Let's face it, we'd all rather be writing about what's happening on the pitch, or even round the pitch, like transfers for example.

John Corbett: I think possibly the reason was that people didn't travel as much as they do now; they weren't as worldly and they tended to be more parochial than perhaps you might imagine. People tended to possibly resent the fact that some clubs were starting to form an elite towards the end of the 1970s into the '80s, and I think when you went to away games you were always aware of the fact that this was their cup final and you were intruding on their turf. And if the result went against them you were always in danger of being pelted by bottles, being spat at, or even being squared up to in the street.

Martin Dobson: I think as a player, what you tend to do is concentrate on the game. You can't bother about these things. I think this the thing about being focused now, isn't it? You're in the zone, you don't get too bothered about what is going on, because you like to think other people are sorting that out. And unless the referee blows his whistle and says, 'Right lads, it's dangerous we're going back into the dressing room, that's it,' You've just got to concentrate on what's going on in the field and see it through.

Bob Latchford: Football in the 1970s was beset by hooliganism problems. Barely a Saturday passed without stories emerging of trouble at football stadiums. Travelling Everton supporters had been caught up in a few nasty incidents, at Newcastle on Good Friday [in 1978], and against Chelsea on the opening day of the 1978/79 season. At the so-called Battle of Kensington High Street, Chelsea hooligans barricaded an underground carriage and indiscriminately attacked Evertonians. Police were taken by surprise by the scale of the incident and when they arrived with reinforcements several had been stabbed and many more need hospital treatment. I played most of my career against a backdrop of what seemed – if you believed the press and politicians - like endemic football hooliganism problems. It might seem strange, but as players we were largely removed from it. A lot of it was being done outside of the ground so in many respects it didn't really affect what was happening on the pitch. You knew it was going on but if I'm honest I don't think I was ever in a match where fighting broke out, like in a derby match, and police dived straight in and pulled the people out. I never encountered hooliganism getting out of control, where the game was actually stopped. But you were always aware that at any time something could go off.

Emy Onoura: [At Goodison] we used to go in the Enclosure, and the Enclosure was right next to the away fans. I remember thinking, 'I like it here', because there was that air of violence around the place, and you were right next to the away fans and everyone would be shouting abuse at each other. I quite liked the atmosphere in there, I suppose. It was exciting. I was kind of aware of the underlying hostility and violence and a lot of things would be thrown: golf balls, cricket balls, coins. There was always an undercurrent that it was going to kick off and you kind of learn to predict when it did go off. You could kind of feel it. And then occasionally something would happen completely out of the blue.

Charles Mills: Stoke City was notorious. They used to park the coaches on rubble-strewn wasteland behind the Victoria Ground, half-bricks all over the place. You knew if you were from the city you'd get bricks. We had that. And I remember the year we won, 1969/70, we played Stoke City away on Easter Monday; we won 1-0, and I remember just getting a boot on my shin. A chap a few years older than me, obviously a Stoke fan. I just ignored him. He was leaving at final whistle, I got another boot; I ignored that as well. So you let slip little things like that. I never wanted to be anywhere near trouble, and I still don't.

John Corbett: If you went to away games you tended to feel a little bit threatened, particularly going to places like Old Trafford, or even obscure places like Stoke City, where very often you got gangs of youths hanging round outside squaring up to whoever might emerge wearing an Everton scarf.

Dave Lewis: [As a police officer] if you went into the crowd, if you imagine that swaying mass, it must've been hugely difficult to try and get in there to get anyone. The CCTV cameras were nowhere near as good as they are now, so how you would pick someone out of the Gwladys Street or on the Kop? It is pretty mind boggling really. But bear in mind in those days the police ran the stadium; we didn't have stewards. It was a 100% police operation so whatever needed to be dealt with they dealt with on their own.

Charles Lambert: As a fan and as a reporter you were aware of hooliganism. When I went to away games I'd go to, say, watch Everton play Spurs away, I'd get off the tube at Seven Sisters and I'd make sure that my Radio Merseyside tape recorder was carried in such a way that the Radio Merseyside stickers were not on view. You were just sensible, really. You say, 'Did you ever think anybody would be killed at a football match?' I suppose you don't think that but obviously in hindsight when you see there is mass brawls breaking out and there's no proper crowd safety in place. A friend of mine lost an eye because somebody had thrown a dart. How far is that from somebody losing their life?

Brendan Connolly: If we're talking about the 70s and 80s, it was a working class man's game. I know if I went for a job interview and if they asked you what your interests were you'd be very reluctant to say that you were a football supporter and God forbid you said you travelled away to watch games or even abroad – people immediately labelled you as a hooligan. Now it's changed so much; it's becoming more a middle class game. You hear all the talk about the prawn sandwich brigade and the expectations have changed. I think people go expecting to be entertained and they just sit back waiting to be entertained and as a result there isn't the same atmosphere. I think back to when we had a pretty awful team, early-70s, early-80s, awful teams, you'd very rarely hear the team booed off. They'd have to be really bad, week after week after week, to be booed off or for the cushions to be thrown from the Top Balcony. But now we could play brilliantly one week we could go the next week and if they don't perform first half they can be booed off at half time; it's just a total change in expectation and it's that expectation of people just sitting back waiting to be entertained. The money has a lot to do with it Because they've paid so much to get into the game expect to be entertained and then when it doesn't happen then they're not happy.

Emy Onoura: When you went to home games you could kind of avoid it, but away games you just couldn't. You travelled down on the train or on the coach, typically if you travelled on the coach you'd be stopped by the police miles from the ground. You'd have to walk miles to the ground, literally a two or three mile walk. You'd be searched; the atmosphere from the police would be hostile, the atmosphere from the away fans would be hostile and all of that kind of stuff. And then typically you'd be kept in the ground after the game as well. You'd have a police escort but then fans following the escort on the other side of the road or behind you. You'd have lads breaking off, occasionally you'd get ambushed. Once or twice we'd have to fight our way out of a tricky little spot to be honest.

Jimmy Martin: In the days when I was coach driver [the 1980s], the coach always parked outside the ground. They never took them out anywhere because there was a hooligan [element] then, so the coach got as near to the dressing rooms as you could, otherwise you'd get bricked if you parked somewhere. I remember going to Millwall and we parked across the road; it was like a scrap yard type of place and they had a railway line at the top; I remember just pulling out and the coach just getting bricked and I hear all the windows getting smashed. So ever since we had that problem it was always parked near the ground after that.

While there the spectre of hooliganism hasn't entirely left the English game – Manchester City fans attacked Evertonians at the 2016 League Cup semi-final at the Etihad Stadium – incidents today tend to be isolated. However, still suffering from their reputation as the bete noires of European football in the 1980s, English fans – and Evertonians – have found themselves targeted at European games.

Sergei Tomashevskii: They are stuck in the past all these Eastern Europeans. Football hooligans in Russia, Ukraine, Poland, Croatia, Serbia they have read too many books about football hooliganism like Dougie Brimson books and about the Green Street hooligans. They just can't realise and understand that it's an old story and it's different now in England. They just copy the English fans from the 1980s and, of course, for them, it's like a challenge when their teams play against English teams. They see it as a challenge to check how good they are.

Hana Roks: Athens [when Everton played AEK in a Europa League tie in 2009] was quite spicy. There was a bit of fighting on the train there, which was to do with them trying to pick pocket people. I remember in Athens their fans grabbed an Everton flag and they burnt it. Well they tried to set it on fire but it'd been raining again – rain seems to follow Everton everywhere we go – but they were trying to set it on fire in the away end, and we were laughing our heads off.

Brendan Connolly: We went to Dresden for pre-season in 2016 and we were talking to some of the Dresden supporters. They said they'd done their research into Everton as to whether they had a hooligan following and they decided that Everton didn't really have one, so a lot of their hooligan supporters decided not to bother going to the game. They thought it would be a fruitless task so they didn't even bother!

Hana Roks: We travelled to Lille [in October 2014 for a Europa League group game]. I was in the square and we'd taken three coaches to that one so there was a lot of us in the square all standing together.

What we tend to do, which is what a lot of Evertonians tend to do, is get a load of beer, stand in the square have a sing song. I've not noticed any trouble whatsoever and I remember just hearing a massive bang and everyone kind of moving out the way and we are just thinking, 'What is it?' Obviously I had no idea it was tear gas that made a big massive bang like that and I remember looking up and there was smoke everywhere. My Dad hadn't moved as he was just minding all the ale for everyone as if nothing had happened, but I said, 'What the hell was that?' There was rubber bullets as well. My wife Tasha got hit by one in the leg and my mate picked it up and said, 'What the hell are they?' Once they did that they made a big line [of police] all suited and booted to the top. It was just a weird thing to see because as I said I hadn't seen any trouble. [Note: Everton FC and two local MPs issued a formal complaint about 'disproportionate' and 'heavy handed' police tactics at that match. Lille police never had the courtesy to respond.]

Fan media

The 1980s fanzine culture belatedly arrived at Goodison in 1988 with the publication of the iconic When Skies Are Grey fanzine, which was swiftly followed by several others, including Blue Wail and Gwladys Sings The Blues. In the noughties a succession of fan-run websites emerged, followed by podcasts.

Graham Ennis: Every club from Merthyr Tydfil to Arsenal had a fanzine in the late 1980s. Everton were quite late to the party. Liverpool too. Back then for supporters of football on Merseyside the only place to express your opinion in print was the letters page of the *Football Echo* – which was overseen by the former Liverpool captain, Tommy Smith! This might have something to do with *The End*, a magazine that had been producing issues sporadically through the eighties. I think people were afraid of being compared to *The End* – with some justification. I had toyed with the idea myself but the idea never got past the planning stage. Maybe there were others but as Christmas 1988 approached Everton did not have their own fanzine. It took a lad from North Wales to start an Everton one. His name was Chris Collins. Chris' stated aim was to get a magazine out there and see what happened. The first issue was described by the ever sympathetic Len Capeling of the *Liverpool Daily Post* as looking like it had been written by a 'vicar on speed'. I think that was a compliment. This was in December 1988. Chris' timing was impeccable, the first issue sold out and more importantly, almost immediately after he received a deluge of mail from potential contributors. I was one of those people who got in touch with Chris after the first issue and offered to help. I also sent a piece I'd written about ugly Liverpool players which had been printed in Off The Ball and said he could use it in *When Skies Are Grey*. He had seen the piece and he was made up to receive it. He gladly took up my offer of help and posted some handwritten articles and letters he'd be sent to me and asked if I could type them up. Yes, back in those days we used to correspond almost exclusively by post. Chris would receive articles via the post and he would send the handwritten ones to me. I would type them and send them back to him alongside any pieces I'd written myself. Bit different to today's technological world. I was fortunate because the job I had at the time allowed me certain freedoms, shall we say, and therefore I had the time to do this. As each issue passed I was doing more and more – including adding 'acerbic' comments to the letters I was typing up. Chris decided that this additional work merited promotion to 'co-editor'. *When Skies Are Grey* was quite prolific in the early days and had already become essential reading for Evertonians. After something like six or seven issues we were selling five thousand copies. We were the 'only show in town', there was nowhere else for the voice of the average supporter to be heard other than in the highly edited letters pages of the *Pink Echo* on a Saturday. To be fair, I think we were all surprised by the early success of

When Skies Are Grey and Chris began to struggle in terms of having the time to keep it going. As the 1991/92 season started, we agreed that he would hand over the magazine to me. This was just after issue 14. A few months earlier, I'd met Phil Redmond – not that one – through *WSAG* and we'd instantly connected with each other. Over the years we'd read the same magazines and gone to the same concerts, not to mention following Everton home and away – in some ways it was incredible that we hadn't met before. It was, therefore only natural that Phil was the first person I'd turn to now I had to do it all myself. The first issue we did together was issue 15 which we threw together quickly after we'd set up a new PO Box and got a new printer based in Liverpool. I think it took us a few issues to settle down but we were lucky; we already had an established pool of contributors who could be relied upon to regularly send articles and cartoons.

Simon Paul: It was 2004, I enjoyed Everton. I was interested in web design; always enjoyed writing about whatever I was interested in at the time. I spent quite a while in my younger years writing about dance music on a freelance basis in the south west and south coast of England then moved back up to Merseyside, got back into my football again and wanted to write about it. I was excited by this new technology of the Internet and the fact that you could reach people. I could write and have control over what I was writing rather than writing on a forum or writing on someone else's fanzine or on someone else's website, I wanted complete control over what I was putting out there. So NSNO.co.uk came to be. The thing that helped us gain a following was the fact that YouTube hadn't been invented yet. At the time we were the place where you could get the video of Everton goals, and download Match of the Day when it was available on video, then edit it so it was just the Everton bits and upload that to the website and let people download that. Before broadband existed trying to upload a ten-minute video for Match of the Day with a 56k modem was not the most fun. But we got there, and that gained us a following, and quite a loyal base that would return to the forum time after time. People wanted to contribute to the site, so they were welcomed and we got lucky with a few exclusive stories. We started up when Wayne Rooney was still at Everton Football Club and we were the first people to tell people what his tattoo was after he'd walked out of a tattoo parlour to be mobbed by hundreds of people at Aintree. It kind of grew unexpectedly from there.

Graham Ennis: We used to get up to the ground about two and half hours before kick off, dropping all the boxes of fanzines off at the traffic island opposite St Lukes'. There used to be over 20 of them. A friend of my wife's had arranged for us to have a parking permit outside her mother's house so we were able to park up close to Goodison, which is just as well as we wouldn't have been able to carry that much. Then over the next hour our loyal sellers would arrive and take their own boxes to their pitches at each corner of the ground. We were lucky that we had a group of lads who had been with us for years so we could trust them implicitly. We owned the Island and we'd get so busy on there that we often needed four sellers on there when there was a new issue. In short, from about 2.30pm it would be pandemonium. We'd have queues. We'd be selling right up to kick off – Evertonians are notorious for arriving at the last minute – and then we'd cram everything into a single bag and take that into the match. I think people sat around us were genuinely unaware that the bag they kept falling over as they tried to nip to the toilet had over a thousand quid in it. Mainly in pound coins. Afterwards, we'd go back to ours, count it up, make sure all the bills were paid and then divvy out any slummy. Happy days.

Simon Paul: From what started as something that was basically 'I'll write on this every now and then' became a daily task. Now, when I either get up before work or after the day job to work on it. I'm still doing that now. The things that it's given me the opportunity to do have been fantastic – working with Bob Latchford on his book *30* and creating the website that raised money for the Everton Former Players' Foundation; getting involved with other books, people like David France and the Everton Hall of Fame. There was the Everton Former Players' Foundation tenth anniversary dinner at the Park end, and there was me and [my NSNO collaborator] Ian Ball, stood in the Captain's Table lounge in the Park End, and we were the only two people in that room that had never kicked a ball for Everton, and there were 75 of us in the room. We each said to each other, we could never have had the opportunity to do this without NSNO. Something that started as just an idea of writing something, keeping control of what I wrote, to being able to do that with it, it's just amazing.

Eric Howell: There were various other podcasts about my MLS Club, Kansas City, and I realised that podcasting hadn't really picked up in England yet. There was one podcast that was about Everton that was very sporadic, it didn't have very much of an international feel to it, it sounded like two guys that were sitting in a bathtub talking about Everton. So I decided to put feelers out there on Twitter looking for somebody, a man on the street, local to the ground to see if they wanted to help me out with it. That's where Ped [Peter McPartland] reached out to me and he said, 'Yeah I'll help you out, but if I'm going to do it I want to do this'. So, what I thought was going to be an Americans' view of Everton with the support of somebody local turned into the Followtonians. We came up with the tag line, 'Same club, different accents,' and it just really worked. But at first I couldn't quite understand Ped because I hadn't had much interaction with a Scouse accent at the time, so there were words and definitely phrases that I had to have translated to be able to speak. After just a couple of times of doing the show we had a whole lot of fun and we just kept doing it.

Graham Ennis: There were a number of reasons that we moved to digital in 2013. It was declining opportunities to sell, rather than sales. We used to bring a magazine out one week and then mop it up a week later. You'd get that sort of time period potentially within a week or two weeks. But when Sky started messing around with fixtures it seemed to be that the gaps between games got longer and you ended up selling an issue that could be three or four weeks old. Add to that with the internet being around and that increased presence the news comes a lot faster, so your issue dates a lot faster. So, if you're selling something that's three or four weeks old it really is three or four weeks old, whereas when we started it could still be fresh a few weeks later. We did used to sell out, but it was hard hard work. I want to do so much with *When Skies Are Grey* and being digital allows that freedom. The paper issue used to be 48 pages. If you wanted to add pages you have to go up in fours. The more you add, the more expensive it gets. Working digitally we are allowed to produce what we want. The standard issue is 64 pages but often it stretches into the seventies. Our largest issue was something like 120 pages.

Simon Paul: I think we're definitely busier on the website when things are going badly. I think the forums, if we're to analyse the number of forum posts when Everton are playing well and when Everton are playing badly, you've definitely got more people online, you've definitely got more people ranting and raving about Jose Baxter getting a game over another player, or whatever. From when we had the sit-ins in the Gwladys Street at the end of Roberto Martinez's reign, the site's probably the busiest it's ever been in the three months from April to June when we finally got Ronald Koeman as manager. It gives people the opportunity to go online, spout off, and then carry on with their daily lives and forget what they've written. They can complain about Everton rather than having to wait until they go down the pub and see their mates, or rather than having to bore their missus with it who's completely not interested because she wants to watch the latest Love Island episode. I think when things are going poorly then things are much, much busier on websites like NSNO.

Graham Ennis: I'm proud that we've been producing a fanzine for almost thirty years and in that time we have given a platform for people to write or draw cartoons. We've had some legendary contributors over the years and if it wasn't for us they might not have found a vehicle to get the stuff out of their heads, on to a page and in front of the Evertonian public. That is an amazing achievement – even though I say so myself.

Bellefield

In 2007 Everton left their historic – and ageing – training base at Bellefield for a new purpose built facility in Halewood, called Finch Farm. The expansion of the Everton squad, advances in sports science and a need for more modern facilities precipitated the move.

Tony Hibbert: From the day we [knew we were] moving nothing got done at Bellefield. It was, 'Listen, we're at Finch Farm tomorrow,' and that was it. Nothing got done at Bellefield in terms of, 'This our last day, let's cheer it off or something.' The history of Bellefield is unbelievable. To leave it just like that and not even do anything, I was hurt. Seeing it as a kid, to playing on it, everything about Bellefield. I was hurt.

Leon Osman: Bellefield was just so small: one corridor; two, three dressing rooms; one bootroom; one gym; canteen upstairs. I could stand in the main reception, shout at the top of my voice whoever I wanted, and they would shout, 'Yeah, what's up?' Whereas suddenly you went to Finch Farm and you could spend 25 minutes looking for someone and not find them there. It was so foreign, it was just strange. It was so big.

Jimmy Martin: When I first started at Everton, everybody had one set of training kit. They used to go to a local launderette where the young players used to take it down and wash it all. Get all the £1 coins in the machine, and then put as much stuff in the machine so they had a few £1 coins left for the chocolate and the newspapers, and they used to just sit down and read the papers. It was good. Of course, it's got a lot bigger now. Players have got 4 or 5 training kits; and we've maybe got 70 – 80 players altogether with the 23s, 21s, and first teams as well. There's a lot going on now.

Tony Hibbert: Moving to Finch Farm, we were getting told it was 'unbelievable', 'state of the art', 'this is the way it's going'. But walking in there, it's literally nothing to do with Everton. There was nothing to do with Everton in there. You wouldn't know. There were no pictures, no blue, nothing. It was terrible. All of the state of the art stuff was fantastic, but it lost the feel, it lost the good times, it lost the soul of the club. It just lost it, and to be honest from when I was still there a year ago, it's just not right, it hasn't got it.

Danny Cadamarteri: I've grown up at Everton, I've grown up at Bellefield and although I do love going over to Finch Farm now I still drive down past Bellefield, where all the houses are now, and look back and think 'Flipping heck I just remember running round there.' That's ingrained within you once you've been there and spent time there and become a part of the club. There's no taking it out of you.

Leon Osman: It wasn't Bellefield, it wasn't where I had played football for the last 17 years or whatever it might have been. It wasn't where I had been every day. I knew Bellefield like the back of my hand,

I loved the pitches. Suddenly you got to Finch Farm and the pitches were slippy, they weren't quite right. They weren't the same as Bellefield. And the dressing rooms were too big, I couldn't find anyone. [I thought] 'I don't like this, I want to go back.' But the facilities were top notch, and actually it's alright this, having a swimming a pool to do my fitness work in, and actually this gym's well better. And actually this video department's top class. Oh look at that canteen. So suddenly you start to appreciate what it is and how much it can benefit you. Suddenly the next thing you know it becomes part of your everyday life.

Lee Carsley: Getting a state of the art training ground really kicked the club on to another level. In terms of when you're trying to attract players and show them your training facilities, even though Bellefield had a great presence, you walk round Finch Farm now and it's as good as you'll find, training ground wise. It was fantastic for us. David Moyes always made a point of making sure that if we were training on a Sunday that the kids would go in, so the kids were in and out of the swimming pool. It was a proper family club.

The search for a new home

Everton have been toying with the idea of leaving Goodison since the late-1980s, when a joint stadium with Liverpool on Aintree Racecourse was mooted. In 1997, via a contested fan poll, Peter Johnson received a mandate for a new stadium, despite the details being vague and the location – Cronton on the outskirts of Widnes was a possibility – unclear. These plans died when Johnson left the club. A subsequent move to the Kings Dock fell through in the early-noughties.

Martin Dobson: It must have been such a burden, trying to locate to a new ground. Because, when you think about all the new stadiums now, hospitality is one of the main factors. People want to come to the ground, meet their mates maybe an hour before the game, have a drink, have a snack and then after the game discuss what happened in a nice lounge, in that kind of environment and then disappear when the crowds have gone, but we can't do that at Goodison. Does it take away from the intimidating factor? When we get a night game and it's full on, the place was rocking. The crowd inspire the players, the players react and all of a sudden there's a lot of noise. We've seen a lot of games like that at Goodison, at a new ground it takes a bit of time, as they've seen down at West Ham.

Dave Prentice: Dixie Dean is the great grandfather of my children and if you look at pictures of him scoring his sixtieth goal, you'll see the Bullens Road stand is virtually the same. That is what made Goodison what it is; why people love it as a stadium. It breathes history and tradition. And whilst it might not be fit for purpose as a modern football arena, there's something about it that's quite magical that other stadia don't have. I love that. I look at the pictures of Dixie's sixtieth and you see the Archibald Leitch criss-cross. Okay, the seats at the bottom part are slightly different but to all intents and purposes that side of the ground is still exactly the same.

Jon Woods: There's a lot of restricted views here, hardly any corporate boxes. It is wearing out. How long before you'd have to change Bullens Road? There's a lot of wood in it. That's fine, but how do you try to change the Gwladys Street? You can't build it any higher because there's houses across, or maybe not even as high as it is. [That said] I love it here.

Laura Smith: Biggest mistake, the one that that never happened, was the King's Dock Stadium. A stadium on the waterfront right next to the Albert Dock would've just been amazing.

Hana Roks:: I would love it if we got a new stadium, but until I see that first brick get laid I won't believe it. I believed that we were moving to the King's Dock. Pretty much everyone thought we were and then the next thing you see is the Echo Arena. I think that would've been an amazing opportunity.

Bill Kenwright: How close were we to a new stadium on the Kings Dock? I think close. The legend is Everton could not come up with the money – that's not true. Other people dropped by the wayside at the end and we had a written letter saying we had the money. I think that was close. But it was a big deal and for the funding partners on Merseyside, it was just too big at the end of the day.

Jon Woods: There's all sorts of talk about the King's Dock, but, essentially, I don't think we'd ever get a price to do it. I don't think anyone could tell you how much it would have cost. With a roof, which I don't think anyone had then. Maybe there was a few in Germany. We did go for it, the Kings Dock, we spent money. The council obviously wanted it. They want it in the city and it does benefit the city, doesn't it? As much as Albert Dock, and however many years that took, but it's now an important part of the city.

Patrick Hart: At the time it seemed a big missed opportunity and it remains a big missed opportunity. There seems to be a thread through a lot of these missed opportunities from 2000, which is that Bill Kenwright has wanted to have a measure of control, and was unwilling to cede any control. That seems to have been a strong factor in a lot of the stuff that has gone on. It's probable that Farhad Moshiri's takeover is going to work out well for Everton – we don't know for sure – but we might have been spared a bit of suffering along the way.

Jon Woods: We didn't have any money. We'd bought quite an impoverished club [in late-1999] with all the wrong players [and] it depends who you are, maybe the wrong manager… If you think about it now, it was never going to happen. Now it's different; there's more money in this game. Obviously, the more money in the game the more money a player's going to cost and the more wages they're going to want, and we can see all that. But looking back it was unrealistic, the Kings Dock.

David Moyes: I was involved in all of the stuff. Everything going on at the club, Bill involved me in. Obviously, I didn't know about the money situation, I didn't know the buyers, but all the time we were always hoping for investment in Everton. My hope was that we redevelop Goodison. I wanted us to redevelop Goodison. In the way that Brian Gray at Preston [Preston's chairman when Moyes was manager at Deepdale] redeveloped Deepdale. I thought if we could redevelop Goodison, build one stand at a time… but we didn't, we weren't getting the money. And if you ask me personally, I still think I'd like to redevelop Goodison.

After the collapse of the Kings Dock project in early-2003, the Everton board struggled to find an alternative. A highly contested and unpopular option was a move to Kirkby, where the stadium would form part of a supermarket development. Despite the divisiveness of the proposal, in 2007 a fan vote gave the board a mandate of sorts to pursue the proposal.

Dave Kelly: I watch Everton home and away and in the last eleven years, I've missed only one game.

Of the seven ever-present clubs in the Premier League's history, we have been the least successful. While other clubs have invested lots of money in stadiums and infrastructure, we did nothing. Yet as Kirkby unravelled over weeks and months and years, it became clear the destination was not in the interests of the many and rather the interests of the few, particularly Tesco. For Everton, it would have given a quick short term fix to a longstanding problem, certainly not the long-term solution.

Jon Woods: I think it came in through Keith Wyness, this enquiry, or he pushed it along. I don't know to what extent. Of course, there's always objectors; if you had a chip shop in this road you'd object, because you don't have a chip shop business anymore. That's the one end of the scale. There's people who object for the sake of it, who don't want change. Kirkby was out of the city, that was the first excuse.

Laura Smith: I lived in Kirkby for eight years so I've got nothing against Kirkby. It wasn't necessarily because it was in Kirkby it was that it was going to be on a Tesco car park. I've been to Wigan. It's one of the worst football stadiums ever. There's no atmosphere, there's no pub outside. Obviously Goodison and Anfield there's houses all round them, pubs, there's a row of shops, whereas if you're on a Tesco forecourt there's no atmosphere there. You're literally just walking to the game and walking back again and that's not part of going the Everton match day out.

David Moyes: I was involved a little bit, but Kirkby was never really accepted. It was Terry Leahy from Tesco who was involved. Terry Leahy was a big Everton supporter and was helping the club, because we didn't have anything. We were sort of doing it on our own, with very little help from the council or anything. But my undivided hope was that we redevelop Goodison, I always wanted it to be. I used to think one side every season, build on top or whatever we need to do, but it never got to that stage.

Dave Kelly: We decided to stay with Keep Everton In Our City [KEIOC] because it felt like we were vacating the city of our birth and we were handing over our city entirely to our neighbours from across the park, though that wasn't the sole reason for my objection to it. I'm a lifelong Evertonian and a more or less a lifelong Kirkby resident. I've lived for 55 of my 59 years in Kirkby. I've never believed you can force a pint pot into a quart. The reality is, the population of Kirkby would have increased by more than 100-per-cent on a match day. Its population was around 45,000 and the new stadium would have held 55,000. Kirkby is a relatively small town on the periphery of Liverpool. It would have meant that on match-days the whole of the town would have become a no-parking zone. Though the plans claimed it would be served by a park and ride scheme they were dreadfully flawed. It was estimated that it would take 14 seconds for a bus to park near the ground, for every fan to disembark the bus and then leave again reversing out. The transport plan was unrealistic. I took great offence at the terminology being used, it was abhorrent. They were talking about crush loading fans onto trains [considering 96 Liverpool supporters were crushed to death at Hillsborough in 1989 and Kelly has long supported the affected families campaign for justice]. They were talking about fans queuing for anything up to an hour-and-a-half to get fans out of Kirkby after a match. The store that Tesco were proposing to build would have been the biggest in the UK but it would have been 107-per-cent bigger than what they were legally entitled to. It would have dominated the town and other stores would probably have ended up closing as a result. It would have killed Kirkby town centre dead in the water. It was fundamentally flawed on so many different points. There was talk of cross subsidies and finance coming in from different places but nobody could really explain how the ground was going to be funded.

Joe Anderson: I can understand why Everton considered Kirkby because there was a fantastic business case. They were going to get Tesco paying huge amounts for a stadium that would have cost Everton very little. Given that Everton had very little, that's why it was so attractive. Ultimately I think there would have been resentment for moving outside of the city boundaries.

Dave Kelly: I submitted a resolution to Liverpool City Council asking the council to support the campaign to keep Everton in Liverpool. I told them that if the city council allowed Everton to abandon Goodison Park and move to Kirkby it would have been akin to the decision to demolish the overhead railway, or to destroy the Cavern or to flatten one of the cathedrals. It would have been an act of urban vandalism. It would have been municipal neglect of a grand scale.

John Parrott: I thought we were going when they mentioned Kirkby. I thought it was absolutely ideal. What's the difference to me if they go to Kirkby? Why would I have minded? I would have loved to have gone there with my son. Obviously there may have been objections from the people who lived in the area, I don't know the ins and outs of that, but the ground was there it was all set to go. I'd have been more than happy.

Dave Kelly: People like us have long been referred to as the vocal minority. We shout the loudest. We're rent-a-mob. But we realised, it's all well and good getting out on the streets and making a big noise – you have to be organised to get what you really want in life. So we started a political party called First for Kirkby and stood as candidates in the town. Knowsley Council had 62 councillors at the time and 61 of them were Labour. Its MP had a 38,000 majority in parliament and Knowsley was the safest Labour seat in the country. But we came within 16 votes of winning a seat. If this had happened in any other town or city in the country, Kirkby First would probably have had people elected onto the council. I think this took fan activism and people defending football clubs to a new level.

Jon Woods: It failed planning because, apparently, of the size of the complex Tesco were building, which by the way, now wouldn't happen because it just wouldn't. It may have now been built, but it'd be pretty empty. It was absolutely enormous, almost two thirds of the size of the Trafford Centre, and you'd only get this by having a football ground attached to it. So it didn't happen.

Dave Kelly: We took on the biggest retailer in Europe in the shape of Tesco. We took on our own local authority. We took on a Premier League football club. And we beat the three of them.

Bill Kenwright: Was Kirkby a mistake? I don't know. It wasn't for me, that's all I can say. But I think it came out of the best intentions. Terry Leahy, Evertonian; I think it came out of the best intentions. But I shed no tears.

After the Kirkby plans collapsed in 2009, the search for a new home continued. In 2015 the club entered into a partnership with Liverpool City Council to move to a new site in nearby Walton Hall Park. While more palatable to most Evertonians than Kirkby the plans never came to anything and the club withdrew the following year. By then a new site had been identified at Bramley Moor Dock in the city's north docks, an iconic site less than two miles from Goodison.

Bill Kenwright: Kirkby was never the love of anyone's life, especially me. Joe Anderson has been a big plus, and first of all we had Walton Hall Park which was a great, great location, and when that didn't prove possible – nothing to do with Everton, just wasn't possible – we were presented with a list and one was Bramley Moore Dock, and we went, 'Oh my God!' We went to see it, but the cost of something on the dock – certainly on a dock that is a floating dock – is colossal because you've to drain everything for starters. And so it is a massive challenge. We started a beauty parade of architects; we came up with the team that we thought was most right. I hope, I think, I believe I've made them Evertonians; you'd have to ask them but they are seeped in it. And we are hopeful that we are progressing.

Laura Smith: When it first got announced I got excited again because I think that's a great location, it's an historic location, as well, which I think it what I want for Everton. The worst thing they could possibly do is build a fish bowl with a running track round it and put it in the middle of a car park. Because it's in an historic location and it's all brick and obviously that'll be incorporated into it I allowed myself to get a little bit excited. Then when it was announced that it was actually going to happen I was delighted. Obviously it's going to be heartbreaking to leave Goodison, because this is all we've ever known.

Barry Horne: I've been a long-standing advocate that Everton should try to stay at Goodison. Looking back the Kings Dock opportunity was a missed opportunity, I've no idea what happened politically or why it didn't happen. Imagine that now. But I've come to accept now that we all know a move is inevitable unless somebody's going to spend the equivalent amount of money rebuilding Goodison. And if this new project is to come off I think it will be fabulous; I think it will be absolutely fabulous. I always felt it was really important that if we did move from Goodison that they were as near to the city centre as they are now. And, of course, if they were nearer it would just be amazing because everything's in place, just got to put the stadium there. I think it would be absolutely amazing, much as I'll be sad that Goodison's gone, thing change, things move on, I accept that now.

Denise Barrett-Baxendale: Moving to a new stadium on the banks of the royal blue Mersey – how spectacular is that? People talk about new stadia effect and a new stadium regenerating a community. But not only will we regenerate the northern side of the dock, we will also regenerate the north of the city, which has been our spiritual home, and that's really important to Everton Football Club. It is part of our value system, we would never abandon Liverpool 4, that wouldn't be right or proper. There's an investment strategy, a long-term investment strategy, and a philosophy which will mean that Everton will live on in this community for generations to come.

Mike Hughes: Everton fans had heard enough about moving grounds. Bill Kenwright desperately wanted them to move to the Kings Dock. Ultimately that failed because he wasn't able to get the financial backing. Then the plan to go to Kirkby was something that he thought would work out but it never had the backing of the fans to the extent that the Kings Dock did. Farhad Moshiri comes in, and there is this talk of a new stadium – one in Croxteth [a proposed site by Liverpool City Council that was never pursued] or the one that ended up being the one they are going to build down at Bramley Moore Dock.

Denise Barrett-Baxendale: Robert [Elstone, Everton's CEO] leads the stadium project and I am part of the wider stadium team. I lead the legacy project for Goodison Park because they're important as one another. They're parallel plans. Obviously, planning for the new stadium will depend on what happens here, so they're interlinked and of equal importance: what happens at Goodison Park will be as important to our fans as the new stadium, they will expect the Club to continue to have a strong connection with the community. The Goodison Park footprint will be what is used to animate the community programme moving forward. That will be a mixed model; it will potentially have housing, sports facilities, health facilities, semi-independent living, educational facilities. I can't say much more than that at the moment, but it would replicate what a community needs and wants, and it would be managed by a trust, by Everton in the Community. In terms of big strategic projects, Robert and I are leading those as executives on a day-to-day basis but we have very clear and regular contact with our Chairman, fellow Directors, and owner.

Dave Lewis: Everyone will miss Goodison when it's gone. People will be in tears and people will want seats and this and that. I keep saying to the stadium manager now, 'You've got to have a plan in place because really we don't want people dismantling the stadium.' West Ham did at the Boleyn Ground, and they said, 'Right if you want to buy your seat, we'll box it up and send it to you, you can have your seat.'

In 2017 a 'heads of term' agreement was signed. Liverpool City Council agreed to guarantee the project in exchange for an annual fee of around £4million from Everton. Although, at the time of publication [October 2017], stadium plans have neither been released nor submitted for planning approval, after four aborted moves in 20 years, it is the closest Everton have been to securing their new home.

Joe Anderson: It's very similar to a mortgage. Everton are going take a loan to build the stadium and in order to secure that, they require a guarantor. Liverpool City Council will offer that security. I've met with independent financial organisations, which have scrutinised the council's position and our capability to act as security and they are fine with the arrangement. We wouldn't be allowed to risk the city council's future. In other words, the city is protected. We're essentially the bank of mum and dad, helping the kids out. Meanwhile, the beauty of it is we receive quite considerable revenue income for securing the loan, at around £4m a year.

John Corbett: I think a new stadium if it happens quickly will bring more investment; more investment will of course keep Everton in the top end of the Premiership. I mean, there's talk now of having a top seven rather than a top six in the Premiership; and I think the evidence of the 2016/17 season is that Everton are a country mile ahead of the rest of the pack, and close on the heels of Man United and Arsenal at the moment. So Bramley-Moore Dock I suspect could be a kind of beacon for Everton for the next few years. It could draw in better players, it could bring in the money to pay for these players, and hopefully a successful run maybe in Europe in the coming season and maybe in the season after that could make a huge difference.

Bill Kenwright: I wouldn't use the word fearsome for the new stadium but it's got to be family orientated and it's got to be awesome. We don't want the seats to be far away from the pitch. The design is wonderful. That is the quest – to make this have all of the qualities of Goodison on the Mersey. We want to give them Goodison plus plus plus. But never ever lose the feel of the blue and white palace.

More Than a Club

'The club are courageous. We're pioneering in our own DNA.'

Denise Barrett-Baxendale

Everton in the Community

Created as the Everton's Community Department in 1988 and formed as a charity in 2004, Everton in the Community is the club's multi award-winning community arm. From providing a huge range of sporting opportunities to the people of Merseyside, to its successful health, education, social inclusion and employment projects, Everton in the Community is internationally recognised as a model for a football club's community outreach scheme.

Henry Mooney: If you look at this football club, it's 140 years old and Liverpool is 125 years old. They are the centre of the community, like a church, like a school and a university and we should be giving things back. If you look at the city we are both probably among the oldest businesses. You'd have to go some way to find a business that's been going 140 years successfully, most of the time anyway. And so we used the club as a vehicle to engage people in the community. We should be making it more accessible, which we have been over the last few years.

Amanda Chatterton: We have a commitment and a duty of care to our communities. Every football club has a commitment. We don't want to take out of the community and obviously match days are impactful, as everyone knows. We want to say, 'Look, we are doing great things. We are engaging with our Blue Mile, with the businesses around here, with housing. We do care if someone is parking in front of someone's house where they shouldn't be on a match day. We do care about noise levels. We are a community and a charity that listens.' I think that a club to have and to align its own charity, as in Everton in the Community, is a massive statement. It's the club saying, 'We believe in our community.'

Denise Barrett-Baxendale: The community programmes were first established in 1988 and had been set up following some significant issues in football: hooliganism, the loss of the game from families, the Bradford fire, Heysel, [a year later] Hillsborough. The government was almost saying to football, 'You need to take control of the game, and if you don't, we will.' Football had to reclaim the game for fans, for families. So, what clubs did at that time was to reach out into communities, it was really all about reputation and brand. Today, Everton in the Community is a very substantial social programme that stands up as sustainable in its own right and serves the needs of the community of Merseyside. It is an example of good practice, nationally and internationally, and demand has never been greater for our services. It's been a terrific time at Everton, and there are greater things to come as we look forward to a new stadium and the Goodison Park legacy, which will just give even greater opportunity for the expansion of Everton in the Community.

Ted Sutton: Everton didn't have any charitable or community work when I arrived in 1988. As time went by I sort of moved into another direction. Back then it was Everton 'Football in the Community' and the onus was on football, it wasn't on athletics, it wasn't on cricket, it wasn't on basketball, but I think what the line was, 'What happens if you're not good enough for football? You could play cricket but still support Everton.' They were looking for an all-encompassing programme but when I went there the main emphasis was just on football. It was always football when I was there [Sutton worked for Eveton in the Community from its inception in 1988 to 2007] but when I started off there was me and nobody else. When I left we were in a position where I had ten full time members of staff, one of them was Mo Marley. I brought her in for women's football and we had a diverse programme of community work that was looked upon very well. We've been to presentations in London at the Albert Hall and every time we went Everton's name was always synonymous with football in the community.

Denise Barrett-Baxendale: When the community programmes were developed in 1988, they had a very clear remit. It was about regaining a positive reputation in communities for football. So, it was about working in areas of high deprivation, areas with anti-social behaviour targets and sending coaches out with the crests on their tracksuits, to go into areas to build cohesion, to get young people active in sport, and to get people to feel positivity about football.

Ted Sutton: With social inclusion I worked closely with the police. There was a lot of vandalism around the Everton/Anfield area so we did some coaching sessions in Anfield Boys Club to try and get the kids from around the area to come and play some football and have some coaching rather than hanging round the street corners and getting themselves into trouble. The biggest one was the kids who were sagging off school. They weren't getting to school for one reason or another and what we decided was that if they came to four of the sessions they'd get a ticket. The club was fantastic in terms of that; I used to get 200 tickets. If you can go into a school and say 'There's thirty tickets here but you must have four weeks full attendance and you must take part', kids went wild. So, football's a tool whereby you can stimulate and generate interest in kids who have got social problems.

Carena Duffy: Back then it was football focused; going into schools, going into areas that were quite deprived, taking coaching sessions. But the disability project then took it to the next level, whereby we were the biggest disability engagement project in Europe. It was giving people with disability the opportunity of being equal and that was through the power of football, the power of Everton football club. We had Steve Johnson [Johnson won 130 England caps for its amputee football team, winning three World Cups] who is in the National Football Hall of Fame in Manchester next to David Beckham. I think that project took it to another level. We were a registered charity by then and we had Chris Clarke [an Everton in the Community officer] who was very savvy and he's really committed to the third sector; he then started to look at other social issues, mental health, anti social behaviour, crime and various other things.

Ted Sutton: There was no fundraising as such. I wanted at one stage to go into and talk to the people in the lounges and try and get sponsorship and things like that, but it was frowned upon. At the time we were never instructed to become a charitable organisation. What happened [in 2004] was because we had that many members of staff and we were finding it increasingly difficult to maintain that number we had to look for another means of support. Dave Connor [EitC's business manager from 1997-2005 and a key figure in amputee football], who was absolutely brilliant, was there twelve, fifteen hours a day putting this document together and we got it through to become a charitable organisation. If you read the players' contracts they were supposed to do two hours a week. It was never really implemented. I was fortunate that I'd have lads that would come and do stuff for me, the likes of [Danny] Cadamarteri, [Richard] Dunney, Michael Ball. But it was difficult at the time. They must be in heaven now, because Denise makes them do it and they've got to do it. I've never seen so many first team players. I went to see David Moyes and said to him about player appearances and he went, 'Go and ask them yourself!' The Community programme has changed completely now. I think the players are more approachable to go and do stuff than what they were years ago.

Denise Barrett-Baxendale: When I arrived [in 2010] I was very clear that there was a social strategy that underpins the value system of this football club; its heritage. What that meant was that we should be far more ambitious. We should be delivering in line with what the Merseyside community needs. Whether that's services for mental health, support around testing for testicular cancer, bowel cancer, stroke recovery. Whether it's about domestic violence – those really hard to reach communities. That messaging is alive in our communities on Merseyside. Everton Football Club has been exceptionally courageous and progressive when it comes to social responsibility. Setting up your own school is a ambitious thing to do – you don't just pop a school up. It's a Department for Education submission, which has exceptional scrutiny, and you're taking the responsibility of educating young people into your hands. But the club is courageous. We're pioneering in our DNA.

Bishop Tom Williams: Everton in the Community is not about football, it's about education and about providing facilities. It's the idea of belonging and being part of it and I suppose working on the mentality of the People's Club. But it's a very fine line about what you mean by Everton in the Community. It's not social work but it is about identity and belonging and the sense of pride.

Denise Barrett-Baxendale: I felt very much at the time that Everton in the Community was a hidden gem. What I wanted to do was take it out of the shadows and allow Evertonians to absolutely understand what their club was involved in and embrace the community, and help the community help us to understand how we could assist with even more substantial and impactful programmes.

Matthew Foy: I think it's more to do with what Everton is in general. We've worked with Liverpool fans, for example, and they say, 'Well, I'm a Liverpool fan but the work that you do is absolutely brilliant I'll never forget it.' And that's great to see, that's it's not all just football, football, football and they are seeing for themselves what we can do.

Denise Barrett-Baxendale: We wanted to make sure that Everton in the Community was embedded in every community, whether it was a school facility or a church hall, or our own facilities here at the stadium, we wanted as much coverage across Merseyside as possible to give access to the services and resources of Everton in the Community. So that was the aspiration really. And when I look now, almost eight years on, it's just terrific to see we've smashed any target we had: 157 delivery sites across Merseyside, and showing no signs of slowing down. So, we've certainly exceeded our initial expectations and strategic intentions, and we go from strength to strength.

Carena Duffy: If you think back to what it was like, in 2008/09 we raised a profit of unrestricted fundraising of £24,000. In the last financial year (2016/17) we raised in excess of £400,000; that's just me and my team of Julianne, who is my assistant, with, of course, the help of the fans.

Amanda Chatterton: When you look at some of the negative press around football clubs – around player wages and around issues in football – I think having a good solid CSR strand and a productive sports community demonstrates good practice.

Henry Mooney: Was there a positive knock on effect with the fanbase? I think maybe initially there was but not now because how Premier League football sells. You don't need a community programme to help sell out. We are selling out: we've sold out every single home game season 2017/18 and we've sold out every single corporate space.

Rev. Harry Ross: The work that Everton does behind the scenes is tremendous but a lot of it is confidential and it's part of what the club is about and its caring side. I think a lot of the big clubs don't have that type of idea. But Everton have always been that way and a lot of it comes from the top with Bill

Kenwright being a Merseysider. I think he's always had the community at heart. He's not just a football chairman, he's a man that cares about the local area.

Matthew Foy: When I was growing up, being a boyhood Evertonian you don't notice it. Whereas you see Everton Football Club in the media, the eleven players, the manager, you don't notice the work that goes on behind the scenes. You expect it as a kid, 'Oh it just happens'. Obviously I have an insight into what Everton in the Community do and when you realise how much goes on you think, 'Wow, that's absolutely amazing the stuff that goes on and it's something that I'll take pride in.' I was in the first ever batch at Everton in the Community to have an apprenticeship, which I take pride in. Five years later I am still here, so I must be doing something right.

Amanda Chatterton: I think we are the 'Peoples Club' in so many ways. Even on a personal level it's been like a family. It's about doing great things, it's about caring about the community, it's about caring about other people, it's about not everything having to have a commercial value. It's about doing what's right and if people have perceived is as right it's because we want good things in the community. Liverpool is a very tight community. People help people and are very friendly. I think people at the club always go out and over and above to offer fans, partners, everyone connected to Everton, and in the local area, whatever team they support, to make it really inclusive. I think that's where it possibly comes from and how its legacy lives on.

Matthew Foy: I've seen the lads over the three or four years, from where they started to where they are now. It's staggering. Now they are like the mentors of that group, like the veterans helping the new people coming through showing them what they are doing. Obviously in a few years time they'll be in that role.

Lee Johnson: It's hard to put into words how Everton have helped me on my journey of, firstly, getting clean, secondly, getting accommodation, thirdly, getting an education and progressing into work. It's quite an amazing turnaround from the way I was living. My life was homelessness, drugs, hostels; a chaotic life really. The first time I experienced homelessness I was touching 16 and that lifestyle went on until I was 32. It was actually eighteen years of having no fixed abode and nowhere to live at all. I was a drug user and the Whitechapel Centre [a Liverpool-based housing and homeless charity] got me into accommodation. They told me they didn't want me to be isolated in a house, so they suggested that I went and played football for the homeless football team. Everton in the Community were doing coaching for the football team, so I started playing for them. I was the only chaotic drug user who played for the team but Henry Mooney was the coach at the time and that was the first time I came into contact with Everton in the Community. I had never heard of it, it wasn't in my sort of vocabulary or in my circle. I played football when I was younger so when this came round I thought I would give it a go because it's a football team. My physical and mental health wasn't good and I couldn't adapt to living in a flat at the time. I just knew I had to do something to get out and help myself. It was just a matter of fate that I started going. The lads I made friends with there I am still friends with now and I've been round the world with some of them and they still play in my football teams today. We won the league and at the end of the season the Whitechapel Centre had got me a place in detox. When I came out I went into supportive housing because I didn't have any of the life skills to live on my own in a flat. I didn't know how to cook. I didn't know how to clean. I didn't know how to look after myself. I didn't know how to pay bills. All the life skills that most people take for granted. I was in supported housing in Anfield, called the Bridge Project. It's for ex homeless people, drug addicts, alcoholics. I was in there for fourteen months and stayed totally abstinent. I remember it was Christmas Eve and I was walking past Goodison and Henry Mooney was one who I knew from playing football for Everton in the Community and the Whitechapel Centre. I just said to him, 'I've got nothing to do with my life. I've got clean but there's nothing happening.' Henry said, 'We'd love you to come here and volunteer for Everton in the Community and just help out on coaching sessions and things like that.' I started volunteering here and then got my first job here as a tour guide. It was like second nature, talking about Everton Football Club. I was quite good at that and it built my confidence because when I came in I had no confidence or self esteem as I had never worked.

Matthew Foy: Everton in the Community is life changing, saves lives. I've still got the picture of Duncan McKenzie with the scissors in his hands opening up in 1988, so to be part of that and to help people, to save people's lives, to help people change and to have people come up and say, 'Thank you so much' – money can't buy that. Each day is a completely different day to the day before and that's what you take pride in. Every day is a different day and that's why this job is brilliant because you don't know what's going to happen. It's so unique.

Lee Johnson: Everton in the Community is amazing. When they sat me down, obviously I'd been on drugs, I had been homeless, I'd been in trouble on the streets and they told me it was a risk. But now I've been told I'm one of the most trusted people in the workforce. I've worked for all the managers since I've been here. I've worked for them on different projects and to be told I'm one of the trusted people that works here – you have to pinch yourself.

The Finch Farm and Goodison Chaplaincies

Reverend Henry Corbett was asked by Howard Kendall to be chaplain to Bellefield in the 1980s, a role that later became officially recognised by the board. Reverend Harry Ross, formerly of St Luke's Church on the corner of Goodison Park, assumed the role of chaplain to Goodison in 1977.

Rev. Henry Corbett: I remember Howard Kendall saying, 'My players have problems but they won't always come to me – I'm picking the team!' And he then gave me very good advice, that I should start with the apprentices and then when they get into the first team they would know that I am a genuine person, there to help. The only problem was that a lot of apprentices are let go, but the likes of David Unsworth, John Ebbrell, Leon Osman, Tony Hibbert are examples of players who I got to know in those early days as apprentices and who went all the way through to the first team. I've been involved at Bellefield and then Finch Farm ever since, and Harry Ross has been chaplain to Goodison Park and the staff there, as well as doing important work with the Former Players Foundation. One big difference between Bellefield in the 1980s and 1990s when I started and now Finch Farm today is the huge growth in support staff, as well as the academy being now on site with the first team. There are so many people around compared to the Bellefield days that I am aware that I don't manage to see everyone when I call in, whereas at Bellefield it was much easier to get around everyone from Harry and Norman on the gate, to apprentices cleaning the boots, to first team players in the canteen, to the manager and coaches.

Rev. Harry Ross: As vicar of St Luke's, there was a very good relationship with the club because they would talk to me about various things that were happening and would ask my advice if someone was ill or if somebody wanted a funeral. A lot of the fans would have their funerals in the church right next to the ground. The club have also helped in many ways and, of course, they also hold a Christmas carol service in the church.

Rev. Henry Corbett: Players do have problems, as we all do from time to time! In the early days I remember being told, 'There is no sentiment in football' and it was sometimes a case of 'Well, I had it tough, so these guys should have it tough!'. Now there is much more support for problems and issues off the field, and one obvious practical example is the care needed for foreign players coming to Everton, maybe with families, young children, language issues, and there is excellent care at Finch Farm for those issues. I still think however that there is great value in having a chaplain around, because I am a bit of a safety net as someone who is confidential – except when something needs to be communicated further – unshockable, and I can be a sounding board for issues on players' or staff's minds. So, for example, when there is a bereavement I can be of help both with practical questions and also with emotional and pastoral issues, or with weddings, baptisms, but also with family issues or simply with questions about daily life that as a vicar in a parish I may well have come across. And I am keen to be available and of help to people of all faiths and none, and to encourage a respect and understanding of different faiths. My chaplaincy is in practice one day a week, usually a Tuesday and with other meetings, visits, occasions as they may come up. I am a full time vicar in two parishes in Everton and I also remember making the decision that I would never ask for signed shirts, footballs, autographs, match tickets every Saturday, so that when a player or staff member see me coming they don't think, 'What does Henry want from me this time? A shirt, a football...?' I am there to offer them something, not get something, and that something to start with is a listening ear, a concern for them and their life off the pitch not just on it. A wise old manager said to me, 'Don't talk about the match last weekend, and definitely not about the tackle or goal they missed: you are interested in the person, not just the player, how they are, not how they played: that is the coach's area.'

Rev. Harry Ross: Staff would talk to me about problems and worries that they had, in their own families mostly. If there was a wedding or funeral I would take it for them. I would also visit members of their families who might be ill or need some help in some way. Some of them would talk to me knowing that anything that was said was just between me and them and I remember during the worries we had about the team being relegated very often the staff would be worried that they may lose their jobs as had happened at other clubs. But that never materialised and I never heard anything said that they would actually do so.

Rev. Henry Corbett: The chaplaincy has been very good for me as hopefully it has been useful for the club – and people do say and have said encouraging things about what I have offered in help and support. It has been good for me once a week to be out of my two busy parishes with all the joys and sorrows there, to be in a different setting, listening, learning, engaging in conversations about all sorts. A coach said to me once 'You'll see all of life in a football club' and that has been very true, from a tragic early death of a young player to a great wedding in the Anglican Cathedral; from family issues to worries about relationships; from so many engaging conversations at Finch Farm to the dedicating of the discovered and then renovated grave of the Rev. Ben Chambers, the minister who started it all off in 1878 with St Domingo's football team. I hope and think he would approve of what I try and do as chaplain at Finch Farm.

The Everton Collection

Also known as the David France Collection, the Everton Collection encompasses the largest single club collection of artefacts in the world. Housed in Liverpool's Public Records Office it includes 78 years of club ledgers, more than 6000 programmes, 40 medals that cover all of the competitions won by Everton, tickets, photographs, cigarette cards and other documents. Many of these items were accumulated by France himself.

David France: If you look back at the time when I did it, the only thing we had going for us was our heritage. 114 seasons in the topflight – absolutely unparalleled. When people talk about Manchester United or Chelsea they're Johnny-come-lately's. When I ran an oil company in Houston, I used to talk to people about football, and they used to talk to me about baseball. I remember chatting to this guy one time and saying, 'In 1888 we were playing organised football.' He looked out of the window and said, 'God, in 1888, here in Texas we were playing Cowboys and Indians.' It's shows you the depth and the richness of our history. We pioneered so many things and we were always a big force. We've been a household name, now that's not the case unfortunately, during a time when football is more popular worldwide than ever before, and we've missed that. We missed the boat that we helped launch, and we need to get back on the pilot ship and catch the boat up. When it comes to the Everton Collection I'd gone to Everton because my mum was going to throw out my programme collection and I asked her to send them to Houston. I thought, 'I'll give these to the club', but they weren't interested. I thought they had archives and this would compliment what they had. But the club didn't, they weren't interested, for whatever reason. So, I thought 'Someone needs to do this, because this is part of the history of football and the history of Merseyside'. So I set about doing it. I'm not a collector, I don't collect things. I collect friendship. I'm appreciative of our history and our heritage and I have an intellectual curiosity in that, but I'm not interested about collecting. I decided what I would do is secure the knowledge base of our club, and that has to be paper. I was interested in programmes, any documents. That's what I went after. I developed a strategic plan, and I found out that there were dealers in this kind of stuff like there is in everything, and I went over and told them that I'd pay whatever they wanted for the stuff. This was before the internet. What I was surprised about was the quality of the stuff that came in. I didn't think this stuff existed. Of course, it hadn't existed in accumulation, it had existed tucked in people's attics and in the backs of drawers, and now it was all coming together, and we were putting together a jigsaw puzzle. And it was incredible the stuff that came in, it is incredible. There are documents that show Everton being invited to the first meeting of the Football League, prior to the Football League – 'Come to Manchester and we're going to discuss starting the Football League.' What price do you put on those things? That's the history of football, the world's game. We had the first season of Everton programmes in the Football League. We had them all, plus 30-40 friendly games they played that season as well. We also have the same for the season before when they played non-league football, and that to me is just incredible – Everton going to Northwich Victoria or going to Bootle, or Paddingham or Blackburn Rovers or Blackburn Olympic, the big clubs in those days. It documents where it was. We've got the biggest collection of Liverpool's information that there is, because we've got all the programmes from 1904-1930 odd, which were joint programmes between Everton and Liverpool. One week Everton at home, one week Liverpool were. I like to call it all the Everton first team and reserve team programmes, but the reserve team programmes are the Liverpool first team programmes. So, it's got all that documented.

David France's dream was always that the collection would eventually rest in the hands of Everton FC, to which end negotiations opened with the club in 2003. The collection was conservatively valued at between £1.2million and £2million, but France did not want to see it split up among private collectors. The club said they could not afford or justify the outlay. Instead it helped launch a charitable trust to help raise funds. In November 2007 it was revealed that a £1million bid for lottery funding was successful. The collection was made available to the public in September 2009.

David France: It reflects that is a passion, it reflects that it was a project that you just get on with. I had no idea where the project was going. I wanted knowledge. In the early-90s Christies and Sotherby's realised that there was a business here. Football was big time and there was a business in football relics lets; antiquities, treasures, football gold. So it was a natural extension for me, after I got the knowledge base put together, to go after these glittering pieces. I got one of every medal that Everton had ever had. I wasn't keen on shirts, balls or books. It was a question of stories, and a question of the fact that I lived in the United States. But it was a great honour to buy people's medals. And when you add that into the former players foundation, people wanted to cash in on the medals and they wanted to do it with some discretion, so I was an outlet for that. I always paid more than what they would have got at Christies. I always took pride in that. I was protective of our reputation as a club and me as an individual that we looked after them as well. I always paid people what they wanted for it, and if they undersold themselves I always paid them more, because I wanted them to feel good about it and I wanted them to feel like that the medal is going to go on display one day at the museum, and it is part of a collection that will never ever be broken, never been sold off, and it is there for posterity. That was important to me and to them. I think it must be heart-breaking to sell your medals, I really do. It must be heart-breaking to sell your father's medals: it's not an easy decision. Surely it isn't. A lot of players sell stuff because they have more children than they have medals, and what do you do? It only causes family problems. But I was there at the right time and scooped them all up, and we had to pay ridiculous amounts of money. But I was fortunate and I could, so why wouldn't you? My good wife was very tolerant, and she thought it was better than riding round on a Harley Davidson. It was a mid-life crisis, maybe.

EFC Heritage Society

Founded in 2008, the EFC Heritage Society was created to promote and preserve the rich heritage of Everton FC.

Brendan Connolly: The society was yet another initiative of David France. He has a lot of initiatives, a lot of them to do with the welfare of former players and the history of the club, particularly around the collection. He wanted to ensure that there was a body of people who would promote the Everton Collection, who would work together with the Everton Collection to enhance that. But more than anything to promote the history of the club. David invited me to join as I collect Everton memorabilia. I knew David from that line and the early members were a combination of collectors, authors, historians and statisticians. I think David wanted to cover every aspect of the history of the club.

Everton Former Player's Foundation

Formed in 1999, the Everton Former Player's Foundation was the first such organisation to raise money for the physical and pastoral care of former players. It subsequently formed the benchmark for other such organisations globally, notably Barcelona's.

David France: Brian Labone would say to me, 'Oh someone is down on their luck, I bumped into someone and gave them a few bob.' He said to me that someone had seen a certain player in Bootle Strand with no laces in his shoes, hobbling round and I said, 'Let's go and see him'. Next time I came over we went to see him, and it was very sad. Fame is a terrible thing. To have fame and then all of a sudden you have no skills and you can't get a job, and you're depressed, it's terrible. Most of the footballers of that generation didn't have skills or job prospects. They had money for the time but they didn't have discipline with it. If they got divorced then they don't have that structure, which was the case with this individual. So we sorted him out in a nice way, without embarrassing anyone, showing compassion and making life easier. He was in a terrible state, about 20-odd stone. A handsome man who had lost his confidence. He had a long career and married a concert pianist, which didn't work out for him. His life hadn't been good to him, and he was huge. His television didn't work, so we sorted him out in a nice way. I was quite forceful with him, saying, 'Look at the state of you, you need to lose some weight.' I put him on a diet of Lentil soup. 'Next time you come back you need to have lost some weight, because I'm going to weigh you, and I'll know.' He lost weight, we took him to the clothes shop. What you take for granted is that you reckon somebody has a shirt, but you've grown so big that you don't so we had to get him everything. A whole wardrobe. He went out in public for the first time and he loved it, because people loved him because he was so funny, charming and sarcastic and appreciative of people. We did that privately, but Brian came back and I said, 'I'm going to form a charity, a proper charity, and do it right. You don't have to force this on people, but people just know it's there and you haven't forgotten them, and that's the most important thing. People who have fallen on hard times, people in poor living conditions and people who have injuries, and people who have been forgotten, that was important. Remind them that they are still loved and admired and that they are still wanted.' The Charity Commission knocked us back too many times: three times, four times, but that was just a challenge for me, so I paid to have it done and we went and raised money.

Rev. Harry Ross: When David France was establishing the Foundation I was asked to form part of the group that set it up and was to run it. I got to know a lot of the former players personally and I got to know their problems and they knew that they could come to me if they had any financial difficulties or mental or physical problems where they needed help. People think because they're the players they don't have any needs, but they do. They're just ordinary people and they would just ring me up and still do and nowadays they text me or email me with any problems and they will tell me their problems and I will talk to them or to their family and see if I can help.

David France: That's when you realise what a great club it is. It wasn't that hard to raise money, personal donations from some of the celebrity Evertonians. The club also gave us a testimonial for old players every other year, half the money to the player and half to the fund. We've done 100 hips and 100 knees [operations] we looked after people, and it is tremendous. The PFA were happy to help us and were very generous. Other clubs saw what we were doing and embraced it in their own ways; the likes of Real Madrid, Barcelona and Anderlecht, they picked it up and they make it into bigger, better things.

Rev. Harry Ross: Many years ago I remember I and another Trustee visited one player in what used to be called a doss house. We knocked on the door of a vey run down house in not the best of areas and this man, who I can only say looked like a tramp, answered and I asked if this player was in. 'Yeah come in.' So, we went in and was told he was in basically a bedsit up the stairs and after a while of knocking on the door he eventually answered and he was in a right state. He'd been drinking. In fact, I think he'd wet himself. He had no money and he was in a real state of distress and he got a bit aggressive. After finding all this out I immediately rang round the other Trustees and we managed to get him out of that place into a better flat. We got him some clothes and we got him fed and then because of his obvious drink problems we got him a place at the Sporting Chance clinic and the PFA also helped. We got him back on his feet again and we continued to look after him until he died, which was caused by his problem, and at his funeral his former teammates made sure his funeral was well attended. So that is the kind of thing where players need help of some kind, and not only them some of their families also. We helped in many ways with any mental or financial problems and when they lapsed we got them going again and if they needed help we were there for them.

Henry Mooney: I think we've moved away from the health and wellbeing of former players, although that is still a big part of the Former Players' Foundation. We are moving more towards helping people who have made the wrong decisions in their lives. We've had a few that have been in the media that we've helped; a number who have made the wrong decisions in life and we are doing more to help them. I think one or two of them are doing really really well. I just think we continue to help where we can and when we can.

Tony Kellaher: I think we are working towards more helping with the mental health issues as well as the players get older and older.

Henry Mooney: I think your modern day footballer won't need to access the Former Players' Foundation for physical health reasons but maybe for mental health. I'm sure that will happen and we are working with a number of former players that have mental health issues and we are trying to deal with that, along with the PFA, because we are not the only club that has that. We are doing some work with the PFA on a project about former players – and even some current players – that have mental health issues.

Tony Kellaher: As part of being a trustee of the Former Players' Foundation I have attended many players funerals over the years, the likes of Tony McNamara, Tom Gardner, Bobby Collins and Alex Young. What comes across is how playing for Everton has defined their lives. Tom Gardner, through injury, was only able to play one game but that one game was the making of his life and his widow and family were rightly proud of that and of how Everton and the Foundation had looked after him. Whenever I talked to Tom over the years he was very very proud to have worn the blue shirt. Going up to Scotland for the funeral for Alex Young it was the same but also it was noticeable how highly respected Everton are in the game itself, even in Scotland. Listening to a marvellous speech by Scott Gardiner, the Chief Operating Officer of Hearts, he couldn't speak more highly about Everton and how they are regarded as a leading club in community and former players matters.

Rev. Harry Ross: I went around to many clubs up and down the country and I said to them, 'What are you doing for your former players?' Many weren't doing anything or nowhere near as much as what we were doing at Everton. So, we went and talked to them in the Midlands, other clubs in the North West.

We went up to Scotland and also held a meeting at Goodison that was attended by Robert Elstone, who had just become the CEO at the time, and we helped a lot of the other clubs either set up a former player association or gave them ideas and help in improving what they did. Everton were excellent. They helped the Foundation in many ways and they helped with tickets for the players to go to the matches. I remember for the 2009 FA Cup Final Bill Kenwright paid for the Former Players to go to the match at Wembley and he also invited them to the after match party at the Grosvenor and put the players up at a hotel overnight.

The Ruleteros

The Ruleteros Society is an autonomous supporters association which aims to encourage links and friendship between Everton FC and its Chilean counterpart, CD Everton. It was founded in June 2002 by John Shearon, an Evertonian who had visited Chile on a number of occasions, and Evertonians based in both the UK and Chile. Its name translates to 'the roulette players', because Vina del Mar, where CD Everton play, is full of casinos. Its motto is, 'Once an Evertonian, twice an Evertonian'. It has also forged links with Club Everton La Plata in Argentina and Club Atlético Everton in Uruguay.

John Shearon: The Ruleteros was set up in 2002. I'd made several trips to Chile and in 2002, at the prompt of the people in Chile, we formed this group, which was not just to be a Liverpool based supporters club but to be a pan-Everton project. It was the Chileans and us and it would be set up by members of both camps and we've been plugging away ever since. The main aim is to keep and maintain the contact between the fanbases of Everton in England and the clubs in South America. If anything between the clubs comes along that's just a bonus, but that's not our driver. Our main aim is that when we go over to South America, any Evertonian can come to us and we give them advice on anything: hotels, tickets and there'll be people there who see them. And when they come here we do the same. In 2009 we visited South America and went from 'Just Everton' and CD Everton to Everton and Everton. So we went to Chile, Uruguay and Argentina and we made contact with two clubs in those countries, one in Rosario in Uruguay and one in La Plata in Argentina. They are amateur clubs, they started in the twentieth century but they've been going for something like 100 years. They still do the same thing they did a hundred years ago which is look after their particular barrio. In 2010 a pre-season friendly was played between Everton FC and CD Everton. That had always been the dream. We didn't care whether it was at Goodison first or if it was in Chile first, but we got Goodison. Everyone laughed at it when we first mooted the idea, but that's one of the reasons why we set up the Ruleteros, so that we could get a game between the two clubs. There's four Evertons at the moment and we hope to go out to Argentina and make contact with a couple more. We have a Facebook page, so that's the principle way for fans to talk to each other, as well as Twitter and a web page, but we have direct contact with the clubs, with fan groups, which we do through email or phone. It's more than a hobby, it's like an extension of Everton FC. We keep an eye on them and they keep an eye on us. We watch the matches, we discuss the matches, we keep the news and we do a match report every Monday on our Facebook page for the game that has taken place on that weekend.

Everton Shareholders Association

Founded in 1938, the Everton Shareholders Association represents 350 of Everton's 1500 stockholders and is considered to be the club's 'watchdog'.

John Blain: The Everton Shareholders Association is the oldest such club body in world football. Historically, it was perceived to be almost like a watchdog, which was independent of the club per se, and just observed and engaged with it as best it could; to make sure things are done the right way I suppose. I can't really say what it did 40 or 50 years ago but from a power point of view it had very little, if any influence other than the power that comes from how long it's been in existence and how it's perceived as being representative of what is often referred to as 'minority shareholders'. Fundamentally the Association, depending on your view, represents between 15 per-cent and 30 per-cent of the shareholding in the business. With that in mind we don't have representation at board level. At the moment we don't have great dialogue and engagement with the club because it goes through phases of whether it thinks it needs to engage with the Association or not. Certainly membership of the Association ebbs and flows depending on whether there's something of significance going on. The club went through a period of not holding general meetings after the Companies Act changed. When I became the chairman of the Association in 2012, one of the things that was sitting on the 'to do' list was getting those general meetings reinstated. I think that was probably an example of where the Association, despite being a modest organisation, took on the football club and the guys who had 68% share in the business, and overturned that huge voting power that they had in a populist sort of way and got general meetings reinstated. That's an example of our 'watchdog' behaviour. It's right for the club to have general meetings every year. The incumbent owners didn't want to have them because they found them an inconvenience, but we do have them. That's probably what we're there for. It seems like the new stadium might have the potential to become something where the Association might get up on its hind legs and say, 'Guys, we need to do things in a slightly different way'. Hopefully the Association spends most of its time being quite quiet; it doesn't have to rattle any sabres or anything, and does the other work that it does around forums and charitable things.

Everton Ladies:
A Short History 1983-2018

'I've won the league with Everton. If I was to go tomorrow, I'd go happy.'

Andrea McGrady, Everton Ladies player from the 1990s.

Beginnings, early league successes

All teams start somewhere, and the origins of Everton Ladies – like most other football teams – are typically humble. Effectively run as a pub team in the 1980s and early-1990s, Leasowe Pacific formed when Billy Jackson, who ran five-a-side sessions at Dolphin Youth Club in Birkenhead, teamed up with June Gordon, who ran Hoylake WFC. Hoylake had been struggling for players and would merge with Dolphin in 1988. When the five-a-side team led by Jackson started playing 11-a-side, it took on the name of the Wirral pub from which it was based. Leasowe Pacific was born.

Billy Jackson: One of my daughters, Michelle, was always with me at football on a Saturday or a Sunday. We were asked to go up to the Dolphin Youth Club in Birkenhead. They were playing five-a-side there, and we got all that going; five-a-side. That's where we basically started. I think it was June Gordon, they had a team out in Hoylake, and they were looking for players. They asked me if I would manage them and take the five-a-side girls up and form a team. They were losing players, and that's what we did. We started off as the Dolphin, playing five-a-side, we went up to this Hoylake team and then we became Leasowe Pacific, from the Dolphin.

Cathy Gore: Billy Jackson did not poach me, but came after me when I was playing for Kirkby Ladies, so that's how I came. I came to Leasowe as it was then. They were just training … They were a five-a-side team at first, then they went 11-a-side. I joined them when they were an 11-a-side team. The girls didn't even know I was coming. I was the enemy originally. So that's how I started.

Maria Harper: How it came about, me playing for Leasowe, was actually through playing five-a-side football. I used to play for a team called The Belvedere, which was in Liverpool 8. And we got through to the finals. We played The Dolphin in the final, and they asked me to come and play for them, which I did. That's how I got to play for them.

Billy Jackson: We trained on a Thursday. Before we played the five-a-side we used to get up there early and we used to train outside, come back, do work inside, and we ended up playing five-a-side for half an hour on Thursdays and Sundays. When we weren't playing it was Thursdays and Sundays we trained.

Maria Harper: They played from a local pub, which was The Leasowe, and from there it progressed and went on to be Everton. That's how initially I got to meet all the Everton players. They all lived that side – over the water I say – so they were all over from the Wirral, and I lived in Liverpool. My ex-husband at the time, he lived over that side, so that was the other reason for going over to join. So it started off as five-a-side, and then it became Leasowe, and we played from the local pub.

It didn't take long for Leasowe to blossom, in fact, they would go on to completely dominate the north west region for the years to come. Between 1988 and 1992, Billy Jackson's 'pub' team would win five straight regional titles, a cut above their opponents in every aspect.

Louise Thomas: I used to play for a different team called Deeside Ladies and I played against the then Leasowe Pacific Ladies. Basically, I started to play for them instead because they were younger and had a lot more quality.

Maria Harper: Do you know what, honestly, it might sound a bit of a cliché, but it was a really good team spirit. There was always Louise Thomas, who scored goals by the minute. Cathy Gore was ruthless in the middle, Mo Marley was really good. I could go through the whole team; there were really, really good players.

Billy Jackson: We had really good players playing five-a-side, and we just built up from there. The more we got recognised, more players wanted to come. It just escalated from there. We were training five-a-side, and then we started playing in Birkenhead Park through the summer. It just escalated, players started coming, they wanted to come because of the success we were having.

Louise Thomas: We had a cracking group of players. We had plenty of pace, we also had your tacklers. We blended in well as a good team, and most of it came from playing five-a-side together, because we played touch football.

Cathy Gore: Being good at five-a-side didn't mean you were good at 11-a-side. They trained hard, and Billy Jackson as a manager, he worked us hard, and we reaped the rewards then. Then we became dominant, and more wanted to join us. Success breeds it, doesn't it?

Mo Marley: It was a lot of the strongest players in the north west. It's a bit similar in other sports, one team dominates at that level, and it attracts the best players at that moment in time. I had played for a team in Runcorn called Darsbury, which was quite low-level, whereas Leasowe was seen as one of the better teams. It was a step up for everybody, so it was almost like now, the way everyone wants to go and play for Man City Women or Man City men, it was the natural progression for everybody at that time to make that transition, step up, and go to play for Leasowe.

Keith Marley: We always had the best players in the area. We had a slight rivalry with Knowsley United, who are now Liverpool Ladies, and players used to flit from team to team, which they always have done down the years. When I was involved they were already established as a good side. We continued to do that and recruited the best youngsters when they were coming through.

FA Cup glory, national recognition

If success on a regional level was all but guaranteed, success on a national level was always going to be a trickier proposition. Playing against teams like Doncaster Belles and Friends of Fulham – who had a host of England internationals – meant Leasowe were considered underdogs in the Women's FA Cup. That would not deter them though, and in 1988 the team reached its first final. They would lose 3-1 to Doncaster Belles that year, but at the end of the next campaign they got their hands on the most coveted trophy in the game after a 3-2 win over Friends of Fulham.

Mo Marley: That's the day I signed for Leasowe. I went to watch that day. I think it was about March 1988 at Northwich Victoria. I'd gone to watch them play in that game, and Doncaster were far superior that day. I joined them and a year later, which was 1989, we went and won the FA Cup at Old Trafford.

Billy Jackson: It was building and building. We had a bit of bad luck in the FA Cup previously, but we got another couple of players who wanted to come, and that year we had a really good team. We beat the odds, put it that way. Basically, none of our players played for England at all, none whatsoever. Doncaster Belles – whom my daughter went to the season before – I would say about 80% of that team played for England. We ended up playing them in the [1989] quarter-final and knocked them out. When we knocked them out we thought 'Well, we've got a good chance.' It wasn't a fluke game either, we deserved the win. It was really a good game.

Maria Harper: The other thing I remember is Billy Jackson, who was the manager, his daughter played for us the year previously. She said 'I'm leaving this year, I'm going to Doncaster Belles,' who were a very, very strong team. 'I'm going to play for Doncaster Belles, I want to win trophies,' and this type of thing, and 'I think I've got a better chance there.' Lo and behold, the year she left us, we played Doncaster Belles. I don't know whether it was the semi-finals or the quarter-finals, and no one expected us to beat them, and Billy's daughter, who had left us, was playing for Doncaster Belles, and we beat them 2-1. She was devastated.

Mo Marley: Don't underestimate it, that Friends of Fulham team were on paper, potentially stronger than Leasowe. That's a big debate, loads of people will debate that one, but they had Hope Powell, Brenda Sempare, Marieanne Spacey, Linda Curl. They had a lot of what you would perceive as English internationals at that time, they were dominating the England team then. I'd never even heard of an England team at that point! So that victory was really quite unique, and a massive landmark in the transition in women's football at that time.

Maria Harper: Friends of Fulham were the superstars, and I think it was Marieanne Spacey who said, 'They're the Wimbledon of women's football.' Literally we were just a gang of thugs! I don't know whether they underestimated us in the cup final.

Billy Jackson: We were given that nickname. We were just basically a pub team. That's what we were; a pub team, like a fella's team.

Cathy Gore: We worked hard. I always said if we could match them on fitness we'd have a chance. Personally, that was my thing: if I was fit enough I'd give anyone a run, as long as I was fit as them. The England players were all super fit – I say 'super fit' – not like nowadays, but in those days compared to the rest of us, they were. So if we could match them with that we could certainly match them with playing then.

Louise Thomas: We were all down to earth players, and Friends of Fulham were a cracking side then as well. They had your Brenda Sempare's and what have you, but I think it was a good bit of management too. I won't say exactly what he [Billy Jackson] said to us in the changing rooms when we played them like!

Billy Jackson: Everybody rooted for everybody; we were all together.

Cathy Gore: The week before the cup final, a few of us had been to Hillsborough. So they put it to us whether to cancel or not. But it wasn't about that, we just got on and played. The TV [stations] were really interested in certainly myself and the people who were at Hillsborough. Rightly or wrongly it added spice to the thing.

Louise Thomas: The Hillsborough disaster was quite a shock to everybody. It was good of them, Friends of Fulham, as they were called then, they felt it as much as us. I think it just brought everybody closer. Half of us were reds and half of us were blues.

Cathy Gore: Billy was a big Liverpool fan. There was about half a dozen of us who were actually at Hillsborough, and knew each other through the football, but there were three of us who were in the squad who were there. It was quite poignant, and it brought us together. Still to this day we're all still friends and pals.

Becky Easton: I remember I played for a local team called Rivacre Ladies in Ellesmere Port and we were a few divisions below Leasowe. There used to be a Channel 4 programme on, which back then was unusual for women's football, to be on the TV. Leasowe got to the final and they won it the next year. I remember watching that and thinking, 'They're not too far away from where I live, I'd love to play for them one day.' I remember some of the players – Maria Harper was there, Louise Thomas, some big players.

Mo Marley: I think it was about 1990, Leasowe went to an international tournament in Sardinia and played against international teams, other club teams. One of them was the US national team. So you've gone from playing in an FA Cup final at Old Trafford, winning the FA Cup final and playing as a club team against national teams in Sardinia, representing the country. Then, not long after that, I think that's when the better, stronger players got a bit of a sense about wanting to go and play in the new National League.

Admittance to the National League

After well and truly conquering the north west, and having proved their capabilities on a national scale in the FA Cup, it was soon time for Leasowe to face teams like Doncaster Belles and Friends of Fulham on a more regular basis. Jackson's side were admitted to Division One North for the 1992/93 season, having initially declined to play in that league in the 1991/92 season. After their first season, they gained promotion to what was then the Women's Premier League.

Keith Marley: When the National League first came in, you would have to travel the whole of the country. In the first season, probably for financial reasons, we refused to join. But then the second season, because we'd won the league again, we had to go in it, which really was a good thing, because it ended really well. We should have done it in the first year, but we had chosen not to.

Louise Thomas: It was great; it pits your wits against them, doesn't it? The only bugbear was that everything was coming out of our own pockets at the time. It's not like it is now where they have a wage and what have you; all the girls had to dig deep into their own pockets to pay for accommodation and travel, so I think the commitment was there from everybody.

Andrea McGrady: You were one of the first to play in the newly-found league and everything. It was exciting. You were playing against teams not just from the north west. You did travel as far as Milton Keynes and teams like that. Teams like that were actually put in the northern division. Experiencing all that travelling as well, it didn't faze you one bit. It was just exciting: 'This is the start of something now.' You feel a little bit more professional.

Billy Jackson: It was a bit harder, obviously. In the north west league that we were in, without being conceited or big-headed or anything like that, we were basically winning everything, year in, year out. And that was a step up then, better competition. We held our own, and we did really well.

Mo Marley: We had had a taste [of national competition] with the FA Cup building up to that point, so that team were ready for that kind of challenge. It was high level. You still had your strong dominance; you still had Arsenal and Doncaster Belles, who were still dominating at that moment in time. I think Everton were just pretty consistent all the way through that league.

Maria Harper: I left then, because there was teams over [the Liverpool] side of the water [River Mersey] who were setting up. A lot of my friends were over this side, and I thought, 'We've maybe done as much as we can here, it would be good to go over to this side of the water.' That was my reason for coming over this side of the water. It was hard; it really, really was hard to leave the team I had been with for so long, but I just wanted a new challenge. I went to Knowsley then, who would become Liverpool.

From Leasowe to Everton

At the start of the 1994/95 season, Leasowe had no affiliation with a professional club, despite their early success. That, however, would soon change after a meeting with Everton chairman Peter Johnson.

Billy Jackson: We ended up going to Everton. I'm a Liverpudlian myself. We were going to try Liverpool, but when I got in touch with them a month or so before, they had taken on a Ladies team. Then Louise [Thomas], June Gordon and myself, we got a meeting with Mr Johnson. He owned Park Hampers and he was Everton's chairman then. We had a meeting with him and he was quite keen to take us on, which we were grateful for.

Mo Marley: Initially, it was really more of a brand. You've got to remember that as Leasowe Pacific we were running out of a pub. That's the reality of it, and it was great. The pub funded us, a lot of the sponsorship come from that. Leasowe Pacific is a pub on Corporation Road in Birkenhead [The Pacific Pub on Price Street in Birkenhead is now closed]. And we were training regularly at the YMCA, so there was no real kind of identity for the club – or real formal structure behind it, so that's when Peter Johnson came in, because of his world connections and his Everton connections. To be fair he came and watched us quite a few times over at Moreton, we used to play at Moreton over at the snooker centre. I think it's a housing estate now.

Andrea McGrady: It was that brand name of Everton; known worldwide. For me personally as an Everton fan, it was wearing that kit. It was on loan. We had to hand it back. On the Monday morning, all dirty and everything, it would get washed for us. It was washed by Jimmy Martin, who's still the kit man there now. And then we'd pick it up on the Friday night ready for the weekend.

Billy Jackson: It changed me because I had to wear blue! It's one of them things, I was Liverpudlian, but it's like everything else, you do what you do for the club you're playing for and you're running. It was good; we got noticed. It was a good feeling really, having a Premier League club backing you, which they did.

Andrea McGrady: I would probably say it was 50-50 [split between Everton and Liverpool fans on the team]. There were a few hard-core Liverpool fans as well. It was always great banter between everyone, but once you put the shirt on, on the Sunday, no kind of Everton/Liverpool thing came about. Leasowe used to play with the Liver Bird on their shirt, so it didn't bother me. Once you put that shirt on and you cross the line, that's it, everything's forgotten. You're one team, you work for each other, and you die for each other really.

Keith Marley: There was a time when we were going to leave Everton. We basically didn't get anything off them bar a name. We weren't demanding the earth, but we just needed a little bit of help. I think in the early years we used to even pay for our own kit – an Everton kit – and we used to pay for training. It was poor to be fair, but obviously they were the dark days. It's so much different now. The only good thing about it was that you were called Everton, and wore an Everton kit. Again, here was a bigger attraction to sign better players. So it worked in that respect.

Mo Marley: Everton came on board and the brand changes a little bit then. We then switched playing pitch to Marine [in Crosby], so being part of the club at Everton, we had more financial backing. We then started to train at Netherton [Everton had a training base there in the late-1990s]. So we had more of a home, more of an identity and more of a brand, which opened and created more opportunities for us really.

Louise Thomas: We still weren't getting paid, but we had the facilities for training – Everton's training ground and what have you. I think that helped us. We were bringing the odd couple of little coaches to help.

Mo Marley: Part of that is Everton Ladies had a youth structure. There was Everton Girls before we were Everton Ladies, so we came across to Everton Ladies and merged with the youth section, so we had a fully functioning club structure and a clear pathway for all players from eight right the way through to the seniors. So we were quite smart.

Andrea McGrady: We didn't get any financial reward from Everton. We still paid our own subs and the cost of the minibuses were spread out between us. A fair whack between each and every one of us.

Billy Jackson: They gave us all the kits and tracksuits and whatever. We had the coach now and again, they paid for the coach for the League Cup final. They paid for the coach for that, and that was very appreciated.

The road to glory

Leasowe and Everton's first three seasons in the Women's Premier League resulted in three mid-table finishes: sixth, fourth, sixth – solid, if unspectacular. But it was perhaps elsewhere that they showed their most obvious signs of progress. In 1997 they reached the Premier League Cup final, where they would face Millwall Lionesses. Although Everton would lose a tight game 2-1, they were beginning to hint at what was to come.

Billy Jackson: We got beat in the League Cup final because we lost our goalkeeper and didn't have a stand-in. We had someone who could play in goal, but we were rather unlucky in that game. We could have won it. We were unlucky.

Mo Marley: We recruited quite a lot of players just on the back end of that cup final. Yes, it was a loss, but we actually recruited some really good players after that. Again, your success brings the better players, doesn't it? That's what continued to happen.

Andrea McGrady: During that season you'd probably say we felt a little bit that something that could be happening here. That was the first national final we'd gotten to for quite a long time. We should have won the game. We were 1-0 up, we were denied a penalty when it was 1-0, and should have gone on to win the game. How we lost it I still don't know, but I'm blaming the slope at Barnet's ground.

Becky Easton: I remember some of the players there and I knew there was a good squad. A cup final's a great occasion and a great day, and it's tough to get there, especially in those days in the women's game. So I thought we're not far away from winning something, and I thought – with the addition of myself and maybe a couple of other players – there was a chance.

That near miss against Millwall would prove to be a stepping stone for greater success. A year later, Everton would become champions of England, seeing off competition from Arsenal, Doncaster and Croydon to clinch the Women's Premier League.

Andrea McGrady: Louise Thomas was the best centre-forward in the league, in my opinion. We used to play to her strengths, and when Mo came in, Mo was the best centre-half in the business. We used to work on Louise's delivery of corners, and Mo's strength in both boxes. Mo was probably one of the joint top scorers at the time, because she was so lethal in the opponents' box as well.

Mo Marley: We had a really good balance and some really good individual players. Again, we didn't necessarily have the best players on paper, but we had players with a real team ethic. We could rely on them 100 percent to play for the team, not for themselves.

Billy Jackson: Arsenal were the top dogs. We beat them at home, and that was the turning point. We beat them at home and then went on to win the league. We had good spirit, good players, all together. We did really well.

Andrea McGrady: I absolutely loved every minute of playing upfront with Louise Thomas; this is probably one of the reasons why I wanted to join Leasowe. She was a complete player: quick, strong, and could score goals. She was a born footballer, who was a natural. I loved every minute of playing with Louise.

Louise Thomas: We had a good bit of management off Billy, because they [Croydon Ladies] had a cracking girl in the middle, called Brenda Sempare. We had Cathy Gore, who was like a Peter Reid. In the changing rooms Billy said 'Cathy, as soon as Sempare gets hold of that ball, hit her. Not nasty, but go right through her, and let her know you're there.' That first tackle, straight away, that was Brenda Sampere not interested, because Cathy Gore hit her. I don't mean actually hit her, but she made a cracking tackle on her and it actually put her off.

Cathy Gore: I'm a Liverpudlian at heart, so I was compared to Graeme Souness as well. You can picture the type of player I was. I was a bit rough and tumble compared to some of them.

Becky Easton: We had a lot of aggressive, tough players in midfield. There was Cathy Gore. I played there myself, and they didn't like it. They [Arsenal] were a flair team, and they had a few little egos, if you could say that. They didn't like it if you were tough, physical and stopped them playing. I think that was the way to play against them back then, and it seemed to suit our game, and they didn't like it very much. I would say it stifled their flair.

Cathy Gore: There was only one or two that would do that type of football, who played that sort of way, the hard tackles. The rest were really good footballers. There were a couple of physical players, but that was not the main feature of the team; they just worked ever so hard for each other.

Andrea McGrady: We had the hardest start ever; we had Arsenal away, who were the champions, and then Croydon and Doncaster in our first three games. We managed to get seven points out of nine – the confidence just grew from them first three games, it really did. We just went on a roll. We probably had won the league by Christmas, because we were that strong up until Christmas. Having England internationals helps. When you play with better players it makes you become a better player as well. You're working with them in training and you're playing with them on Sunday. You pick up little things from them, because they've been away with international football and have picked up little tricks of the trade.

Mo Marley: It was a tight league all the way through. I think we won 50% of our games 1-0. That was pretty special, because we didn't have the experience at that level, and I don't think really people believed that we could sustain it and maintain it. I think everybody thought we might have wobbled or buckled at the end, but we sustained it. We actually won it with a game or two to spare in the end as well.

Becky Easton: I remember that campaign probably more clearly than anything. We were just a really hard-working team: we fought for each other, we scrapped. We probably won most games 1-0. We weren't full of goals, flair, or anything, we just really grafted for each other. We won it through guts and hard work, and sweat, and it was great to beat them [Arsenal]. I think it was the first time in ages they hadn't won the league, or somebody from the north had won it, so it was a great time. It was probably sheer hard work that won us that league, and looking back now at the players we had and the players they had, it's crazy to think that we won it.

Keith Marley: Teams we should have beaten easily we'd struggle against a little bit, maybe win 1-0, but we'd always get the win. I always remember playing Arsenal at Marine, and we hit a little bobbler. It went through about 17 people and nestled in the back of the net, and we beat them 1-0, which virtually won us the league. That was quite amazing. We won quite a lot of games, like the old Arsenal. '1-0 to the Arsenal,' that's what we used to sing. We got through everything and won it, but we had a feeling that we could win it, because they were dropping silly points.

Andrea McGrady: One of the final games – the game I think we [essentially] clinched it – was away at Croydon. We'd had a player sent off, and we never seemed to get a result away at Croydon. It was one of those grounds it had a running track around the pitch, and it was a horrible ground to play on. Usually, we never came away with anything, but we did that day, so it wasn't until then we knew. But Arsenal were a fantastic side, and it went down to the very last kick of the game I think.

Maria Harper: I think I was the loudest supporter. I'd stopped playing then, and went [to watch the game at Croydon]. It was just phenomenal. Everton just needed to draw to win the Prem, and we got a player sent off really quickly in the game: down to ten against literally the England team – Hope Powell, Brenda Sempare, Kerry Davis. It was ironic; it was like the FA Cup final all over again, and they only needed a draw. We got a player sent off, and I'm sure the referee played 15 minutes of extra time. Honestly, I'm not exaggerating.

Andrea McGrady: It's difficult to put in to words. It's just a dream come true. When you look back at it now, you're actually part of the best team in the country. That's the only way you can describe it. Being an Everton as well, and winning it with Everton. Ask any Everton fan what it would be like to wear that shirt week in, week out. I'm still a season ticket holder now, and whenever the guys I go the game with now, they still talk about it: they still introduce me as 'Andrea, she's won the league with Everton.' We're talking 20 years further down now. It's still a huge part of my family's life as well; they still talk about it.

Louise Thomas: We were always the underdogs, weren't we? The little northerners playing against the big southerners.

Andrea McGrady: I've won the league with Everton. If I was to go tomorrow, I'd go happy.

The Marleys

Following their surprising and brilliant title win, Everton did not disappear from the picture, but they certainly did not reach the same heights. They would finish the next three seasons in fourth position, and the campaign after that in fifth. Things just didn't appear to be quite the same.

Becky Easton: What I remember happening was that the season after we won it, we started developing a reserve squad, and a lot of effort and focus was put on developing the club rather than trying to retain our title. I think we lost a little bit of focus. Before that, it was just about the first team, and all the resources went into the first team and looking after them. Then, we expanded into having first team players going to play for the reserves. I think we did lose a little bit of focus; it became a bit of a one-season wonder, which is a shame to say. We should have pushed on really; we should have kept players or even strengthened, signed more players, because we'd proven we were a good team. It was a bit of a shame.

Billy Jackson: One or two players left, for reasons you don't know. Other players started playing for England as well, like Mo Marley herself. We had players picked then; once we got recognised as Everton, and doing what we did, we had players picked for England as well.

Mo Marley: People had this unity about wanting to win the league. I think after we won it, that's when things changed a little bit. I think people expected to win it again, and that's when the team started to drift a little bit: people were questioning people's motives, and we lost a couple of players – some went to Liverpool again, some went to Donny.

Becky Easton: I was in the England team then, and there were probably six or seven England players at Doncaster – all great girls who I got on with well and all great players as well. The chance came to go to Doncaster, I thought 'It's such a big name in women's football.' I think it was two years after we'd won the league at Everton, and because we didn't push on, things went a little bit flat. The timing just felt right to move to Doncaster.

Mo Marley: If we could have kept that together, we would have been a special team for a longer period of time, but people get their heads turned, don't they? They think the grass is always greener.

Andrea McGrady: Players came and went, we lost a couple of the internationals. I don't know the reason for it really; I can't put my finger on it. Other teams strengthened. Even in the men's game, it's so difficult to retain a league title; everybody wants to beat you the next season. It was disappointing that we didn't do anything.

Keith Marley: Other teams were probably showing a lot of interest in their women's team whereas we'd led the way for quite a while; we were sort of pioneers in the game. It only takes a fashionable team to come along and you end up losing [players]. Nobody got paid, so you could do whatever you pleased. As soon as one had a little problem with the club, four or five would walk away in one go.

Billy Jackson: I never had any qualifications as a coach. It was just my experience of playing football over the years and then teaching the girls what to do in the best way I could. But then, players went to England and it was like 'Shall we get a coach in?' We tried it; it partly worked, it partly didn't. It started getting more professional, without players being paid. The girls wanted to be more professional with a coach, and we got a first aid chap in. We still did well, we still won five-a-side competitions with that team, but as we got going with the league again, it fell down a little bit.

The 2002/03 season would see Everton finish just one place above the relegation zone, but a significant change at the club had been made. At the turn of the century Billy Jackson stepped down as manager, and was briefly replaced by Keith Marley. However, it wasn't long before Mo Marley – so vital as a player in the previous years – stepped up after working on her coaching badges. Everton had a boss to take them forward into the new age.

Billy Jackson: I was working. It was taking a lot out of me. I was an ACD driver. When you're going down to Southampton to play on a Sunday and having to get all the way back home, often not until midnight or one o'clock… I was going to work at five o'clock in the morning. It started getting a bit too much. Mo's husband came in and helped out, and then I decided not to carry on, and then Mo took over with her husband Keith.

Keith Marley: I was determined – I knew what was required – that I would do the best I could. I used to fund quite a lot of it as well; I was probably the main sponsor. But I just loved it, the effort all those girls used to put in for nothing. I would do the utmost that I could do to make it easier for them. So I paid for quite a lot of things, and it didn't bother me in the least. I have a running joke with my friend now, who's the manager of Everton Ladies, that Everton owe me about £30,000. I used to pay like £1,000 for a hotel bill or something like that. I just left it. I loved it. That was the way it went.

Louise Thomas: I'd gone with Billy because of my ankle. I thought, 'Enough's enough, we've done our time. We'll just pass it on now.'

Keith Marley: There was one stage where they didn't want me to be the manager. I was expected to just pass it to someone else, to one of their friends. We were like 'Excuse me it's now Everton football club' – unlike Liverpool, who would change managers every five minutes because the girls all kicked off – every season they had a new manager. But I was determined that I wouldn't give it up. If there was someone who could do it better than me then I would have stood to one side, no problem. But to actually ask somebody who didn't have a single clue to take over from me… But to be fair to them, the vast majority of players had a big vote and a big meeting, and the majority voted that I should stay as manager. So that's how that stayed.

Mo Marley: Billy resigned, and the way the club management structure worked at that moment in time, he was just voted in, my husband. At the time I was the only person who didn't want him to take the job. I was strong on this. He didn't have the right qualifications, he hadn't managed previously, and he'd almost fulfilled too many roles in the club to then become the club manager. I was outvoted, but in the meantime, as he took charge of the club, him and I spoke. I was doing my coaching qualifications, and due to the restructuring, I was working with him but playing, and then as a club we decided he would manage the development league team and then I would continue to manage solely the first team.

Keith Marley: Eventually when Mo was coming towards retirement, that was the natural progression, I was happy. Mo took over. Mo had kudos, being an ex-England Captain. Again, we managed to get the best young players. Even at that time we were getting the best young players from various parts of the country.

Mo Marley: We had a great turnover of players while my husband was in charge. I remember the League Cup final against Arsenal at Tranmere, and I think we needed to change the players. I think the whole club needed a clear direction, so from then we lost a few players. A few players weren't happy with the management structure change, that upset a few people. That point then was probably the right time for me to go in as a coach. I was quite a young coach at the time, coming to the end of my playing career and my international playing career as well.

Becky Easton: It was becoming more professional. I remember speaking to Mo before I signed. She set out the plans that she had, the players that she was targeting, and it just seemed like a whole new ball game really. There was Fara Williams that she targeted, and Rachel Unitt. When I came she brought in six or seven – maybe more – and it just took the squad to another level really. I'd known Mo, and I'd had a lot of respect for Mo as a teammate at England and Everton, and as a player and a person as well. She just kind of sold the club back to me.

Mo Marley: We just recruited what we thought were the best players, that we were familiar with. I knew what was happening in the Centre of Excellence programme, because that was my work role, and we just recruited the best players who had come out of the Centre of Excellence programme in the region, and tried to build up a team over the next couple of years. That's what pretty much happened, and that's been Everton's backbone and structure consistently, still to this day. They rely on the strength of the Girls' youth project, which is now called the Regional Talent Centre. Everton have got one of the best returns in terms of producing players from youth into the first team. And that pretty much all happened the following ten years, while I was in charge.

Keith Marley: It was Mo's kudos that was bringing those type of players in. She didn't use her England connections – she wouldn't do that – she was just asking them to come and play for Everton. We had Jill Scott, Lucy Bronze; Toni Duggan was a local youngster who we had always known about. All those players, we enticed them to come and play for Everton. At that time, other than Arsenal, Everton were the best team to come and play for. That was because we'd emphasised so much about the coaching side of it; it was so important. That was always going to be our pulling point; not so much money. We had Fara Williams come up and live in Liverpool from London all those years ago; it was unbelievable. Rachel Unitt, Lindsay Johnson, etc. were all absolute top draw players. But Mo was the draw for them to come and play, because of the coaching we gave. I don't think Arsenal did much coaching to be fair, they were off the cuff type players – good quality players – but the coaching we did was unbelievable for years and years. It continues to this day, that side of it.

Rachel Brown-Finnis: We had a quality side, and I think every player who has played under Mo Marley has massive respect for her. As a coach, she's fantastic. She eventually went on to take the England under 19s job, and has been really successful in developing players.

Andy Spence: My first age group was the under 12s, and I remember it being on a real cold, poor, Astroturf pitch in Kirkby. It no longer exists, the Astroturf, but we had some real superstars in the making in that first team that I got to coach. It was the likes of Toni Duggan and Michelle Hinnigan, who obviously have gone on to have really good careers themselves. I had a really good impression of women's football and girls' football from the very start, because I was working with two super-talented players amongst a lot of talent within that little under 12s age group.

Rachel Brown-Finnis: She wanted to use her love of the game, starting with the very youngest – the under 9s at the academy – and bring those through to the first team. Again, at that time there wasn't the money to buy players, nor was there the capacity to offer full-time training – or anywhere near that really. It was three pairs of Umbro boots and club kit, free travel, all that kind of stuff. It was literally the things you were bargaining for. And Mo was quite clever in using [other avenues]. The example I gave was of Liverpool John Moores University [Marley put Brown in touch with the university on her return from the US, and Brown was granted a scholarship]. That was a great lure for me to come to the club; that was a massive selling point. You had to really think outside the box, because money and material things just weren't at the club's disposal. Mo Marley was very conscious of that, but wasn't perturbed by it; she didn't think it wasn't fair. She worked with what she had, she believed in the young players, and always brought those players through.

Michelle Hinnigan: Mo Marley implemented new coaches at the Centre of Excellence and at the younger ages – from under 9s upwards to the development team, which is the reserves now. I think she implemented her style of play, of getting the ball down, wanting to play and limiting touches and stuff like that. What still goes on now is what she implemented through all the youth teams and the ages.

Re-emergence and Arsenal's shadow

After a couple of seasons of consolidation, it did not take long for Mo's method to start paying off, and Everton would soon emerge as the real contenders to Arsenal's long-standing supremacy. With a mixture of signings from around the country and starlets from the academy, the Blues would finish second in the Women's Premier League five times in a row, from the 2005/06 season to the 2009/10 campaign.

Mo Marley: At Everton we were completely amateur and could not offer the players anything. At Arsenal, their players were paid to play a role: they had a job within the programme, so they were recruiting the best players from around the country to be able to go and play for them, whereas we were recruiting the best amateurs in and around our region. Of course we couldn't bring the best players from London at that time to come and play for us, but in the latter years we started to do that. Obviously we were fortunate enough …The big turning point for us was when we signed Fara Williams and Rachael Unitt. That was difficult for someone like Fara. Fara used to travel up from London on a Thursday, Friday and travel back on Sunday night or Monday morning. She lived the weekend in Liverpool and then the rest of the week down in London. Signing players of Rachael Unitt and Fara Williams' calibre then attracted the interest of a lot of other internationals, and a lot of up and coming players for the future, the likes of Jill Scott and Lucy Bronze. And it helps them from an international point of view as well, because the playing philosophy [at Everton] would help them improve as an international.

Lindsay Johnson: Liverpool were in a lower league than Everton. I knew Don Scott, who was the England sports scientist, because we're both from the north east. She asked me to play in a tournament one weekend, and it was an open tournament. Mo was actually playing. She didn't play much; I think it was all kind of set up really. I had a conversation with Mo then – she said she was retiring from playing, and being the manager she was looking for a centre-half. I said, 'Well I'm not a centre-half,' and she said, 'Yeah, you are a centre-half; I've seen you play, you're not a centre-mid, so I'm going to play you centre-half.' It's Mo Marley – if she's going to tell you where to play, you just do it, don't you? If I could go there and learn from one of the best centre-halves in the country, then I was going to do that.

Rachel Brown-Finnis: [Mo] used all the video analysis of our games, video analysis of the opposition you were going to be playing, any set pieces. I can't imagine she did anything other than watch football games at her house, in between coming to our training sessions and telling us everything that was going to happen. She'd go to as many live games as she could as well. She really was the eyes and the ears for the team. Yeah, we set up slightly differently against certain teams, certainly defended slightly differently on set pieces against other teams. But she created a real good team spirit, and that was the strength of that team at our peak in 2008, 2009, 2010, and 2011.

Natasha Dowie: Charlton folded, so I had to find a new team, and Arsenal wanted to sign me. I met with [Arsenal manager] Vic Akers, he showed me around the training facility, and it was out of this world to be honest. But I've always been that kind of player who has never wanted anything to be too easy, and I kind of felt like Arsenal at the time; they were just the team to beat. They were dominating, and I thought that it wasn't going to be a challenge. They were the best, and I wanted to beat the best. My manager at England under 19s was Mo Marley. I spoke to her and asked if she'd be interested in signing me. She said she would, so I signed for Everton. I was very excited; I didn't really know what to expect.

Andy Spence: I think if ever there was a team who were going to push Arsenal, it was well accepted that it was going to be Everton. We always felt that we were very close. We were training twice a week, I think it was a 9pm to 10.30pm slot at Everton, the old training academy ground. We had players that were travelling three and four hours to get to training and three and four hours to get home. Arsenal were almost ahead of their time in the sense that they had players who were working within the club, who could almost treat it as a full-time job just to play football. So we were almost competing against a professional team, and to run them as close as we did...

Becky Easton: When we won it back in the 90s, we were all a little bit agricultural maybe. We were just hard workers and not really great footballers. Then, we brought in a little bit more flair, more attacking options. We were always strong in defence, but there was more attacking flair that we brought in, and we played good football. Mo had her own style: she liked to get the ball down and play good football, and that's what we did.

Lindsay Johnson: We were known throughout the league as a good footballing side. With Mo, we spent a lot of time trying to move the ball quickly and play it into feet. We weren't a long ball team at all; she didn't focus on that. We had it in our locker because we had a lot of pace upfront, but we liked to move the ball quickly, and that's what we were known for.

Michelle Hinnigan: I think everyone really believed in ourselves because of the quality of the players we had in the team. We had a brilliant team; from Rachel Brown in goal, all the way up to Natasha Dowie up front. It was a really, really strong team. Arsenal had always been that team back then, champions of England and always winning the trophies, and always getting the limelight, but I think [at] one time we believed we could do it.

Becky Easton: They were still probably signing players from all over, the best players who were available. They'd had a squad together for a long time: Rachel Yankey, Emma Byrne, Jayne Ludlow, those kinds of people. They knew each other's game inside out. It seemed to go on for nine or ten years, and it was hard to break that dominance, even though we tried and tried. On numerous occasions we got really close to them, but it was really hard.

Rachel Brown-Finnis: I think it was the winning mentality they had, that mentality to get the job done. They had the likes of Jayne Ludlow, the old guard of Arsenal; I think Katie Chapman was playing for them too. Rachel Yankey, Alex Scott, Kelly Smith – they were well respected. The ones who'd been at Arsenal for years, the ones who had who'd won the FA Cup millions of times, and won the league millions of times. They knew what it took, and they were also well up for giving each other an absolute rollicking on the pitch, which I liked; not every player was happy to manage a game that way.

Lindsay Johnson: Sometimes in the early days, we weren't as ruthless as we should have been. We got on – we were a really, really close squad at one point, and I think that sometimes went against us. When we played Arsenal, who were our biggest rivals at the time, they hated one another, and they were ruthless with one another. At times we lacked that ruthlessness with each other; I think we could have had a bit more of it. We were definitely a footballing side and played some really nice football, but we just never did enough to win the league. We were always second or third, we never did quite enough.

Natasha Dowie: We had a lot of talent, and a lot of young talent as well. I never once went into a game against Arsenal scared or frightened of their dominance. It was more that we had nothing to lose. We were always going to be the underdogs, and we definitely were their biggest rivals in the league, so they always upped their game as well, because they knew it was going to be a tough game against us.

Among the near misses in those years, one season particularly stands out: 2008/09. Everton, undefeated all campaign, went into the final match of the season against Arsenal needing just a point to clinch the title. However, a goal from Suzanne Grant gave the Gunners a 1-0 win, cruelly snatching the title away from the Toffees. Both teams had dropped just five points in 22 matches.

Lindsay Johnson: I remember it all, it was at Widnes. It was at the big stadium; this was before it was a 3G pitch – it was a lovely grass pitch, actually – and all we had to do was draw with them; we could afford to draw with them and have the point. This was definitely our best squad, we were so confident, playing good football. It was early on in the game, it came from a corner. Suzanne Grant, a Scottish girl for them up front, she got free. I even remember who was marking – it was Tash Dowie – and she got free from Tash and scored a header. But it was so early on in the game I was confident that we were going to pull at least a goal back and maybe get the win. It was really early on and we just couldn't [score]. They shut up shop. We said if we couldn't get a result at home playing as well as we did then we didn't deserve to win the league, but that was the closest we came, so it was so frustrating, and that was our time. I was gutted for us as players, but it was for Mo really, the amount of effort and she put in; it was Mo I felt most for really.

Keith Marley: You've got to look back at that with pride, because we should've won the league that day. We were playing them at home, we only needed a draw. We just lost 1-0, which was unbelievable. You look at the history books now, Arsenal won that league, but we should've won it, hands down.

Rachel Brown-Finnis: We did run them close. It was neck and neck; we beat them, and they beat us. They seemed to have that winning mentality; they kept on winning things, which they were used to doing. Tactically, Mo was excellent, but she was limited, because we only got together twice a week or three times a week towards the end of her being club manager. The team we were playing against was one who were training five days a week.

Lindsay Johnson: I think we always went into the games with Arsenal as underdogs. There was a time when that worked in our favour and we really did take the game to them. You just always knew with Arsenal that they were going to come at you with waves. We didn't have as big a squad as Arsenal, we never did. They had internationals on the bench, and we didn't. But it was our team cohesion, our work ethic, and our football that we that got us through the games.

Mo Marley: We let ourselves down by dropping points against the perceived weaker teams, or lesser teams. The year we lost out on goal difference, if it was head to head we would have won the league, but the fact is that that Arsenal scored more goals than us against the so called weaker teams. That was our inexperience over a number of years, it wasn't because we weren't as good as them. We built our teams on a consistent playing style: very well organised, hard to beat, and with a real strong physical output. Our players took complete physical responsibility of their own performance, because they were amateur. That was the dedication of the players at that moment in time.

Natasha Dowie: Truthfully, we probably deserved to win the league in the end. To lose that last game 1-0… It was just on goal difference that they beat us to win the title. That was a killer blow, but maybe their experience, and having won it for so many years, maybe that just tipped them over the edge to beat us on that day. We were just a little bit naïve, or not used to that occasion. But it was definitely a game you'd always want to play in against them, and we definitely, in every game we played them, gave them a great game.

European adventures

By virtue of being England's second-best team, Everton would soon find themselves competing in Europe on a semi-regular basis, which brought excitement – and its own challenges. In their first outing in the 2007/08 UEFA Cup, Mo's side progressed through the first group stage with a 100% record, but were unable to overcome Frankfurt and Belgian outfit Rapide Wezemaaal in the second group stage. A return to Europe beckoned in the 2009/10 campaign, this time in the Champions League, and Everton would once again sail through the group with a 100% record. This time they would come undone in the round of 32, losing narrowly to Norwegian side Røa IL. Their last appearance in this competition, the 2010/11 campaign, saw more progress. After sailing through the groups once more, Everton enjoyed knockout success against MTK Hungária and Brøndby IF before eventually succumbing to Duisburg in the quarter-final. Everton remained trophyless, but had certainly made their mark on a European stage.

Lindsay Johnson: Mo would be able to get some sort of footage because of her links with England; it was the smaller teams we struggled with. Say Frankfurt, we'd be able to get clips of [Birgit] Prinz and the like, from England playing the German team. So most of us knew what the likes of Birgit Prinz were all about, but Mo was very good on her organisation and her preparation.

Becky Easton: I think the first time we were in Europe, because we didn't know what to expect as a group of players, it was probably a little bit like a holiday. I think we went to Croatia. We were delighted to be there in the first place. It was a massive thing to be in Europe, and we just enjoyed it really. We did well because we were up against lesser teams in the qualifying group.

Mo Marley: I think people underestimate the travel, that's the biggest thing for me. We didn't have a lot of money, so the budget was quite tight. So to travel, to come from work, to travel match day minus one, train in the stadium after travelling all day, and then play the next day against one of the best teams in Europe is a big, big request. On reflection now, as a coach in the Champions League, I would go two days before, not one. But finances dictated whether we could afford to do that or not. We sometimes struggled on the road. Without telling you all the things we had to deal with, we were inexperienced when we went to our first group stages. We played Frankfurt without any pre-match food in us, because the hotel hadn't organised it. We took for granted that it was, and certain things like that, that's where we were inexperienced as a club.

Rachel Brown-Finnis: I wouldn't say we were going out there for a holiday. Initially we went out and played a round robin of four games, or something like that. Second-class citizens is maybe the wrong term, but we did feel a bit underprepared. The kits and leisurewear we were provided with, you didn't begrudge any of that, because it was all new stuff, but it was some stuff from last season—some almost like fake stuff, some sort of random kit. Mo wanted us to be in Everton stuff all the time, which is the right thing to do, but we didn't get the allocation of leisurewear from the club that the men or the boys got. So the kit was kind of cobbled together; not the match kit but the leisure kit. But we were dead proud to have all of this kit, you got your kit in like a bin bag, your leisurewear, and that's what you toddled off to Lithuania with, or wherever it was.

Becky Easton: It was difficult to go away. I think it was a week – maybe over a week at a time – cooped together in not the best hotel, and I think we played something like three games in a week, so that was tough. Fortunately, they weren't tough games, but we weren't used to it. At international level, if you play in tournaments you're used to that. I played for England, so I was used to going away with the squad and playing a couple of games in a week; but a lot of the girls were not used to going away with the team and playing a few games in a week. That was a tough part of it.

Rachel Brown-Finnis: We were super proud to have got to go and play in Europe, because we had never experienced that before, and we did alright. Frankfurt was one of the teams we played, and I remember the German forward [Prinz] absolutely smashed two goals straight past me. You just thought, 'They are another level.' But you look at how most of those players were professional players, or trained every single day with their clubs, so that's when you could see the difference in level between outfits. But as I said before, we always maximised what we did have, and not moan about what we didn't have, and I liked that positivity.

Mo Marley: In the first year of the Champions League we lost to Røa. We went out to Røa and I think we were 3-0 down after 20 minutes! We'd had sickness in the camp: we had a bug in the camp, somebody had got food poisoning. Our players are quite inexperienced; we're trying to win it and left ourselves exposed rather than tightening up. To this day, we should have won that home game. There's a picture of Toni Duggan and Natasha Dowie on the line, and to this day I still don't know how that ball did not cross the line. But there's loads of little things there you take for granted until you experience it and you live it, and we were just inexperienced when it came to the Champions League.

Becky Easton: I think technically and tactically we were fine; we were probably ahead of the others. But in those days fitness was a big aspect of it. We were beaten by German teams and knocked out by a German team and a Norwegian team once, and they were just a bit fitter and stronger. We'd do well in patches, and then probably towards the end they'd be a bit stronger and a bit fitter than us. That's come along way now [in English football].

Lindsay Johnson: It was just a great experience, and it was that point when we were at our best. We were going away in these summer breaks for our qualifying tournament, because we'd finished second, and it was like a little pre-season. There'd be two teams in there that weren't really good, and one team and ourselves. It was like a little pre-season tournament, we'd go there, usually qualify, and then hit the better teams in the knockout rounds. That was great development for everyone, and I think by this stage we were really gelling and playing some good football, but unfortunately again we didn't get past the quarters, which is still a great feat for a team and a squad that we had, but there was some opportunities missed there as well.

Rachel Brown-Finnis: At stage, a lot of infrastructure of training programmes came from England. So if you had, say, half your squad were in the England team, we were all doing five, six days a week because we were following England training programmes, and then you maybe had other players who didn't get the chance because they worked full-time and didn't get the chance to train every day. They just didn't have the contact time on the ball. So, as a team, you were less prepared. We knew that women's football overall was making progress, but then when you played against the likes of Duisburg, you realised, 'Wow, we're still a long way behind,' and we were. As an England team compared to Germany, in 2008, we were still a long way behind, and it always was physically against the Germans; they were bigger, faster, stronger.

Mo Marley: If you look at the home leg against Duisburg, we made two identical mistakes in the first half, and it was a case of, 'Right, tighten up.' It was more about tightening up and using it. We did exceptionally well away at Duisburg, but knowing we had to win the game, it was still a close encounter.

Rachel Brown-Finnis: Some of the best stories are from Europe. The team camaraderie was absolutely brilliant. You'd go to somewhere in Eastern Europe at the back of absolutely nowhere. When we stayed in Lithuania, we stayed in a high rise. I don't think anyone else stayed in this hotel, and there were literally bullet holes in the outside of the building. On the top floor where there was 'the games room', there was a balcony with no wall, so you could literally step off, with like some brown velvet, weather worn sheets on this balcony. The game was a made-up ping pong table, with these handmade bats. But we had the best time. They're still some of my fondest memories, from those European trips, just because they were so random. You didn't go to Paris, you didn't go to Munich, or any known cities. I think we were in Serbia one year, and nobody really wants to go to Serbia, you would think, but you got to learn the history about it all, because it was all so recent as well. So it was really, really interesting, and really close to the cultural bone of the place.

Cup success

Given their role as bridesmaids in the league, and the power of rivals on the continent, Everton's golden generation were in danger of being viewed as the 'Nearly Women'. That would change in 2008, however, as the Blues finally overcame their arch nemesis, defeating Arsenal 1-0 in the Premier League Cup at Brisbane Road. If that game wasn't a classic, the 2010 FA Cup final against the same opposition certainly was. In normal time Everton twice led through goals from Natasha Dowie and a Faye White own goal, but were pegged back on both occasions. That meant extra time at the City Ground, against an Arsenal side who had mastered the art of winning trophies to the point where it seemed a mere formality. This time was different. One minute before penalties, Dowie secured a famous victory. In three seasons, Everton had defeated Arsenal twice in a final.

Becky Easton: It was beginning to change. We'd had a few close games, and then we had the League Cup final where we actually beat them; I don't think they'd been beaten for two seasons, and we beat them 1-0. That signalled a change, I think, for the whole of women's football, because it wasn't just us on their shirt tails, it was everybody else. Everybody came up against them ... Not that you expected to lose, but it was unusual for teams to beat them or even get a draw, so once we beat them in that League Cup final, I think everybody looked at that and thought, 'They are beatable if you get at them. They're not this dominant force that they have been for years.' That was a big turning point.

Keith Marley: When we won the League Cup final, 1-0, we were a bit lucky that day, because we did get battered at times. We survived with thanks to the crossbar, and off the line saves and various different things, but we won the game.

Rachel Brown-Finnis: 2010 was amazing, because it was a first for the club, and that group of players was a special group of players. 2008 was making our way up to that point, and we weren't quite at full tilt, but it was still the first piece of silverware, and still pretty magical for everyone.

Mo Marley: For me, that's one of the most exciting games. It helps when you win it, but I think that was a proper, proper cup final – people still make reference to it as one of the best, for sure. It had everything. Because it was extra time and so late, I think that made it even sweeter.

Becky Easton: I still watch the video back now, that was a brilliant day. It was a great game as well – it was a great game for a neutral to watch. We were 1-0 up, then it was 1-1, then 2-1, then 2-2, then into extra time.

Natasha Dowie: It went into extra time and I thought, 'Please don't let this go to penalties,' because it's just the worst way to win a game. Jill Scott went up for a header in midfield, knocked it down to Brooke Chaplen, and I just remember peeling off Gilly Flaherty's shoulder and Brooke slipping in a great ball to me. I thought it was a little bit too far ahead of me, but I saw Emma Byrne coming out of her goal and she made my mind up for me. I thought, 'I'm going to have to dink this over her.' It might have even been Faye White. I peeled off her shoulder, Emma Byrne came rushing out, I saw Gilly running back onto the goal line to try and clear the ball. I just got enough on the dink over Emma Byrne, and Gilly couldn't get there. When I saw it going into the back of the goal, I actually couldn't believe it was happening. I just remember running into the crowd, grabbing the nearest person to me, jumping over the bannister, and just hugging this kid. I don't know who he was. All the girls were going crazy. I didn't even realise how long we had left. It was the longest two minutes of my life. I remember they actually piled the pressure on the goal as well, and Mo Marley was just telling us to get back in and to defend for our lives.

Becky Easton: I remember Tash scoring in injury time, and it was just an amazing game – probably one of my favourite games I've ever played in. Again, I think it was because of 2008 when we won the League Cup, I think we thought, 'We can beat these in this cup final.' They'd won a lot of FA Cups, I think they'd won it more times than anybody – way more than anybody – so when they turn up to games like that, I think they expect to win. That spurred us on a little bit, and I remember thinking – even though we were up twice in the game and they'd got it back – 'We can do this,' even going into injury time and extra time. I was in my late 30s then, and I played the full game and extra time. For the whole time I thought 'We can still do this,' and everybody in the team had that feeling then that 'This is our day, they're very beatable'. That was a great day, a great win that. I look back on that day very fondly.

Michelle Hinnigan: It showed us that we were bridging that gap and getting closer and closer to Arsenal. I think on the day we just believed in ourselves, and every game was getting closer and closer against them. I think it was a fair result for us, I'd say. About time.

Mo Marley: It was almost like breaking a little bit of a hoodoo as well, wasn't it? We'd played Arsenal in a couple of finals and we'd let ourselves down, I'd felt, on the previous occasions. We had a few heavy defeats against them. I thought it was really sweet that that was the only real time they've lost the FA Cup final. We're the only ones to do that, and that will stay with me. I think they had won it something like twelve times on the bounce as well [between 1998 and 2010 Arsenal won eight FA Cups. As of 2017, they have never lost another FA Cup final]. We were the underdogs, no doubt about it.

Natasha Dowie: When the whistle blew, it was like a dream come true. You always dream of playing in an FA Cup final, and I played in a final for Charlton when I was 18, and Arsenal smashed us 5-1. So to get the opportunity to play in another one and score two goals and the winner was by far one of my highlights of my career, and I don't think I'll be able to top that day to be honest.

Women's Super League, a new boss and player exodus

In 2011, Everton were one of the eight founder members of the Women's Super League – a new semi-professional competition with the backing of the FA – and entered into it with high hopes. Indeed, the Blues would record two third-place finishes in a row at the start of a new era for the women's game. However, things would not continue in the same vein for the club. The advent of the WSL meant increased expectations from players, yet Everton began to lag behind other professional clubs. In 2012, neighbours Liverpool raided the Blues and signed Becky Easton, Lucy Bronze, Natasha Dowie and Fara Williams. Jill Scott and Toni Duggan would both join Manchester City in 2013. Liverpool would go on to win back-to-back WSL titles, while Everton began to falter.

Rachel Brown-Finnis: [The WSL] set about that structure that you had to have, and it started to leap into the right direction. It wasn't without its flaws, and anything where you're starting without a blueprint is going to have teething problems, but I think the FA's done a brilliant job in addressing those things, not being afraid to change things, and make some quite bold and big decisions. And where it is now compared to where it started five, six years ago, it's unrecognisable, and for the better.

Mo Marley: It was a big push. We as a club were a little bit concerned about how that would look. There was an expectation of a lot of financial backing, which we never really had. We were based on our club philosophy of producing our own, so heavy financial investment was expected, and we didn't feel that we were at the point where we could actually compete with the big clubs, never mind if they were all starting to put more money in.

Andy Spence: Those first couple of years, clubs were testing the water, and obviously, certain clubs then took the decision to go full-time or close to full-time. Players would naturally gravitate towards those clubs, because for the first time ever they were giving girls the chance to become almost professional footballers in England. Naturally, there was a lot of movement in players between clubs, and it's well documented that we lost a lot of our senior international players during that period. It was difficult in that girls wanted to train every day, and at that stage we weren't in a position where we felt we were ready for that, for a number of reasons.

Keith Marley: The financial demands they were putting in were ridiculous. I was always against it, and I think I've been proven right. Then you get… Not so much player power, but everything then is all about money; it's not about football, it's not about sport, it's all about money. I didn't really like it. Within a year or so we had lost quite a lot of our best players, because Everton were a little bit asleep in that respect. It was only after all the players had gone that they decided to say, 'Hang on a minute, you need to keep your best players here we need to sort of put more money in.'

Lindsay Johnson: It was really difficult. I don't care what anyone says, how hard you train … I was there the whole time, and you're training at eight o'clock at night. You put 110% effort in, you do, but it's going to impact on you. You can't recover as well as other teams, it becomes tiring. Sometimes training can become a chore, because you're hanging about, you've been to work all day, you've got a job. It was really difficult, and we'd lost some really, really good first team players to clubs, and then you're playing against these players who are professional, or at least semi-professional, where they're training through the day, and getting the recovery and resources they need, and you're not getting that. It did become really difficult.

Natasha Dowie: We trained at Finch Farm, but we were the last ones that were allowed to train there. We had to wait until all the kids were finished, so we used to train really late at night – it was about 8.30pm until 10pm at night – which wasn't ideal. But at the time when I was there we weren't allowed any other access to the gym or anything like that, so to be honest the relationship with regards to the men … They invited us to their end of season awards do's, they seemed to support the women's team, but I do think they could have done a lot more.

Rachel Brown-Finnis: It was frustrating every single day of the week, it drove me mad. The fact that we literally had to wait. Sometimes we couldn't even go into the physical building of Finch Farm until everyone had left. The rules seemed to change weekly. Sometimes we couldn't go in the gym beforehand. Sometimes training wouldn't start until quarter past eight, and it would be going on until half past ten. Most of us were working either full-time, or virtually full-time jobs. So your days were ridiculous, but you just did it. It wasn't ideal, but I think the frustrating thing was that you felt the lines of communication between the women's side and the club weren't really progressing. Thankfully, things have changed.

Keith Marley: We used to train at eight o'clock at night until ten o'clock, after most of the girls and us have done a full day's work. It was difficult, but that was just the way it was. We always tried to change it and implement different things, but then you've just always got your little jobsworths, 'No, you can't train on that pitch.' We'd have sessions ready to go on a grass pitch. There must have about ten or fifteen pitches and it was, 'You can't go on that pitch, you can't go on that pitch and you can't go on that one.' It'd just drive you nuts. They're better now; they are full-time. That's the reason a lot of people left I suppose. We were just caught a little bit short.

Natasha Dowie: I'd worked under Matt Beard at Charlton when I was 17. He rang me up and said that Liverpool were going to be going full-time, training every night, offered me a very good deal as well there. At the time Everton were only training twice or three times a week, and didn't have any ambitions to go full-time. The money I was earning just wasn't enough to live on at all.

Becky Easton: I was released by Andy Spence. Andy was the assistant to Mo, and I think he was the head of the Centre of Excellence, so he had a big thing about youth and youth development, which is fair enough, and when he took over, I must have been about 38, which I know is old, but I felt like I could still perform. But he made quite a few changes and one of them was he said he was releasing me, so that was when I went to Liverpool. I asked Liverpool if I could trial for them for six weeks, and I did. Luckily, they signed me. It wasn't because I wanted to leave Everton, if he'd have offered me a contract I would have stayed there. But it turned out well for me, because Liverpool won the league two seasons in a row!

Mo Marley: Obviously there's a big push now: they're talking about the club going more full-time [Everton have since announced they are to go full-time], but that's taken a good six years of consistency and sustainability in doing what they've been doing, and I think Everton have got the plan right. You can argue they haven't got the plan right because they haven't won anything and got relegated, but I actually think Everton's original plan was prudent and realistic with regards to what it needed to look like long-term. Now they've got some stability, and now they're looking at the next stage. I think it's great, but I'd like to think it's definitely still sustainable.

Andy Spence: I think people always think it just boils down to finances. We wanted to see if this was something that was actually going to be here for the long-term, because it takes a big financial commitment, and you've got to make sure that you're committing the right finances to the right situation. We took our decision to stay part-time, to look at it. Yeah, we lost some players, but you know what, you could go full-time and still lose players, so that happens. Yes, we lost senior internationals, but again where did we call upon? It was our youth set up, and that was then very much our mind-set – 'Right, okay we've lost a lot of senior talent, but we knew we had a lot of youth talent.'

Those losses were compounded by the fact Mo Marley stepped down from managing the side in 2012, in order to concentrate on England duties. Andy Spence, who had been assistant to Mo, was left to manage a decimated squad.

Rachel Brown-Finnis: Andy coming in was a change in style; he hadn't really managed before other than with the reserves. He's a brilliant coach, but I think he was still finding his feet in management. When you have some very strong personalities in the team, like in any industry managers need to manage personalities to get the best out of them, and I think he was still finding his way of managing. Some of those ways weren't that successful: he couldn't quite control the bigger personalities; some of those personalities almost got out of hand, and it started to go sour a little bit. Players moved on because they got the opportunity to go to Liverpool, which was training full-time, so it was a professional job. Why wouldn't you move on if it's round the corner and you get the opportunity to do that? I can completely understand why all those players did move on to a club that was providing a better opportunity, and a fresh start for some of them.

Michelle Hinnigan: I had been with Andy since he started at Everton. I think it was the under-12s when he came in as a coach. He had the same motto as Mo to be honest with you, because he had worked alongside her for that long. He just instilled the same foundations that Mo did. He wanted to develop all the young players, but without the experienced players it's a hard job to do, especially with all the other teams. They were building on their teams and strengthening, because they had a lot of money and the full-time basis. I think that's where we struggled.

Natasha Dowie: My main reason to leave was the players they were talking to – the likes of Fara Williams, Lucy Bronze, and Becky Easton – so I knew that Liverpool were going to have a very, very strong team. They had some amazing international players, which had never happened in the league before: the likes of Whitney Engen, Amanda Da Costa, the Germans Nicole Rosler and Corina Schorder, Louise Fors, the Swedish player. It excited me, being able to play with international players. To be honest, it was a pretty easy decision for me. I loved Everton as a club, and I knew I would get a bit of grief moving to their rivals, but from a selfish point of view, I knew it was going to better me as a player, and being able to train full-time was a really exciting opportunity.

Lindsay Johnson: It was really difficult for Andy. He was making that transition from being an excellent assistant coach, and he was learning his trade next to, for me, the best manager in the league. It was difficult. Whoever the manager was, they were going to find that difficult. I've got a lot to thank Everton for. In the heyday, we got everything we needed; it just didn't go along with the rest of the league when that went [professional], and for me, that was the biggest thing. They needed to do that quickly.

One last cup final and the spectre of relegation

Given the sheer exodus of players, it was perhaps inevitable that Everton would succumb to relegation. That season was 2014, as the Blues failed to win any of their 14 league games. Everton did somewhat surprisingly reach the FA Cup final in the same year – following impressive wins over Liverpool and Notts County – but were eventually defeated by Arsenal once more.

Andy Spence: The whole competition was brilliant for us. We had a great run, again, in a difficult season. It was a bizarre season, because we got to an FA Cup final, but we also got relegated, which is quite unique in many respects. It was a season of real disappointment and frustration, but the FA Cup run was incredible. We beat league champions Liverpool, 2-0, and beat them really convincingly, and deserved to win. Two of our local Academy graduates, Nikita Parris and Alex Greenwood – who have both gone on and are now senior internationals – both scored in that game. They're special moments that will always stick out. Against Notts County, Nikita scored two goals in the semi-final to book a place in the final for us. We played Arsenal and on the day it was 2-0, and being honest it could've been three or four, but Arsenal were in a far different position than us. We were a team scrapping for points, week in week out, to try and stay in the division, ultimately, and it was difficult.

Michelle Hinnigan: When I was growing up I had 20 to 25-year-olds to look up to. I think I was one of the oldest, and I was still only 23 when I was made captain. It was a little bit more difficult. There were a lot more younger faces, because Andy wanted to develop the younger players. That was his motto, where we didn't really have the experienced players as much as when I was a youngster. It was a bit difficult, but I've enjoyed every part of leading along the way.

Andy Spence: We knew we had the super talents like a Nikita Parris. People forget that during the season we got relegated she was second top goal scorer in the whole league. We weren't a million miles off, even in the league campaign. Small moments make big differences. I remember we were 1-1 against Chelsea and missed a penalty, and in the Birmingham game we missed pretty much an open goal, and suddenly those six points would've kept us up. That's what happens, they're the fine margins at elite level sport.

Rachel Brown-Finnis: It's certainly not down to Andy; it's down to the fact that clubs like Man City and Liverpool, just around the corner from any player based in Liverpool, were offering full-time contracts, full-time training programmes. So any of your best players, any of your England players were going off to play for those clubs, because all of your England teammates and all your England players were having that opportunity, and you needed to keep up. It was simply because Everton couldn't even offer training every day, whether they paid you nothing or whether they paid you something – they couldn't say 'Right, we can offer a pitch every day, and we can offer to do your training sessions every day.' So they couldn't compete in that respect. That's what became frustrating, but that's really why they slid backwards, because players moved on, players left. A few of us decided to retire, so they really lost a lot of England players.

Michelle Hinnigan: I think at the time you just think everything's against us; the luck just wasn't going our away. I always remember back to one game where we had a goal disallowed. If you look back at that, it would have won us the game: little things like that where you think it's just not with us; silly fouls being given or silly penalties being given away, all little bits that didn't add up. Once you know you're at the bottom of the table you put that pressure on yourself even more, because that's not where you want to be. There were eight teams in the league, which was really hard for us: 16 games is not enough for a league, and that's one of the other reasons why there was relegation.

Promotion back to the promised land, going full-time

There was to be no quick redemption for Everton, and it wasn't entirely expected either. Two third-place finishes in WSL 2 with a young squad was no disgrace, but it showed the increasing competition they now faced. Everton would go on to top the Spring Series of WSL 2 in 2017, winning seven of their nine games. No promotions had been scheduled between the two leagues, but with Notts County folding in April, WSL 2 teams were given the chance to apply to replace them. Everton and Doncaster Belles – who finished runners-up behind Spence's side – applied, and the Toffees would eventually win out, with applications based on five criteria: finance and business management; marketing and commercial; facilities; player, staff and youth development and on-pitch performance in the 2016 season/2017 Spring Series. 18 days later, it was announced that Gabby George was to become the club's first full-time professional player, signing a two-year contract. The club's step to professionalism is a welcome one and hints at a bright future, but Everton know the fierce competition that awaits in the top flight.

Michelle Hinnigan: This time I think the atmosphere was different, and we believed that we could go and win the Spring Series. But we didn't expect to be promoted at the time that we were.

Andy Spence: Youngsters were almost trying to compete in an adult league with an under 19s team, and so we knew it would take its time. But those under 19s are now under 21 and under 22 players for us. So we knew it would take a bit of time, and you know what, for the quality we had we probably really should've gone up a year earlier, but we didn't. We did really well in the Spring Series, then unfortunately there was Notts County's situation. We got the promotion via that route, which isn't ideal, but nobody could tell me they wouldn't accept it if they were in the same position.

Michelle Hinnigan: I think it was the attitude and the togetherness of the squad towards the end. After a few results that we got our way, we didn't really realise how good a team we were together and how good we were playing. We were creating a lot of good attacking options and there were a lot of goal scorers on the sheet. I think it was something that just clicked. That's why we were so good this year.

Lindsay Johnson: They're doing everything right now, they've gone professional. It's in its infancy. Andy's been hard at work making a lot of signings, and I've just seen they've signed another striker, which is definitely what I think they needed. I think this squad is young, and I'll think they'll do really well, not just to stay up, but just to solidify that position in the league this season, and then next season, when people know what Everton are about...

Michelle Hinnigan: I think it's really good and it shows the direction that Everton are actually going, and it shows the club itself want us to go even further this year by backing us even more, and I think now, compared to back then, we're getting a lot more help and support off the club, and we're really one team at the moment.

Becky Easton: There's new ownership now at the club itself, which seems to have more financial clout behind it, and hopefully that will filter through to the women's team. That needs to happen. As well as looking at the youth that they've got and bringing young players, they might need to sign some real quality players. The game's gone worldwide now, and people are signing from all over the place, and you need to be in that market to succeed. Maybe they need one or two world class players to add into the youth as well.

Andy Spence: Anything is possible, anything is achievable. Get the right group of players together, the right team spirit, and obviously top quality mixed in with that, that gives you a chance. City and Arsenal or Chelsea don't frighten me; in fact they inspire me. They're ahead of us now, and rightly so, but who is to say that within a couple of years we can't talk about Everton being ahead of them? That's always the ambition of a top club like Everton.

Going to the Game: The Match Day Experience

'The noise and the music as you come up the steps, you can hear it building up and building up. When you hit the top step and come out it's a brilliant environment, and obviously Z-Cars is the theme.'

Kevin Sheedy

Initiations

Bill Kenwright: I had a lovely, lovely schoolteacher in primary school; his name was Mr Parry, and he became Chairman of the Shareholders Association, who I got to know very well 40 or 50 years later. He was a season ticket holder, and the season tickets then included the reserve games, which were every other week. And he took me in the stands, so I sat up above in the stands to see Everton reserves versus Chesterfield reserves. There was no-one there, it was freezing cold, and it was 0-0, and I thought, is this it? What everyone goes mad for? That was my first game.

Keith Tamlin: The first match I went to was with my father who was a keen Evertonian ands a seafarer. Whenever he came home he liked to go and watch and he took me to a game at Goodison and we stood in Gwladys Street. I was very young, very small so he sat me on the top of the wall separating Gwladys Street from the church with a lot of other kids – this was the end of the 1940s around '47. I always remember it because a police sergeant came along with a big stick calling us all sorts of names 'You little Bs' and trying to hit us with his stick. Mind you it was a stupid thing to sit on that wall because there was a big drop! There was a huge crowd, well over 68,000, and it was a wonderful game, which Everton won. Everton played brilliantly and I was a fan for life.

David France: I was born into an Everton family. I am a fifth generation Evertonian: my father was an Evertonian, my grandfather was an Evertonian. I was indoctrinated as a child. I was brought up in a rugby league town, where we didn't play 'soccer' (we called it 'soccer' not 'football') at school. The only school pal I had who played soccer was Ted MacDougall, who went on to play for Manchester United and Scotland. My Dad told me, and my grandfather confirmed, that my great, great uncle Billy bought three of the original shares of Everton football club in 1892. I can't track that down, and I don't know what happened to the shares, but I've no reason not to believe that. So I was brought up in an Everton home, and my Dad used to say, 'This is my gift to you, David.' We were brought up in poverty, in real poverty. We had one electric lightbulb and one cold tap. They were Methodists, very strict. We didn't drink, we didn't smoke, we didn't gamble, we didn't do anything like that. The one thing my Dad used to say to me was that the greatest gift I can give to you is Everton. We didn't get things for Christmas or birthdays, I never ever got a birthday card or cake. We never had those things. We didn't miss them – a lot of the kids around us didn't have them either, so it wasn't like we were unique, but we didn't have them. I would say to my Dad, 'I'd really like a bike for Christmas' and he would reply, 'Son, I've given you the greatest gift of Everton', and I'd say, 'I'd still like a bike.' But I never got one.

Charles Mills: My memory is from Dad going to the match. I think my first game was a public practice game in 1956 when I was three. But the one I remember most clearly as a first game is Everton against Blackburn Rovers, which I think was 1959/60 season. Dave Hickson scored two goals and I thought if we won that game we'd won a cup; obviously we hadn't, it was just a game.

Eric Brown: Lots of people ask me, 'Why Everton?' It all dates back to an early match I went to at my local club Charlton Athletic. I live in Kent, I was born in Kent, and had absolutely no connection with Merseyside. I started to go and see Charlton Athletic, and in 1959 they were drawn in the FA Cup against Everton, in the fourth round. It was one of the first matches I went to. Charlton happened to be leading 2-0, and fairly near the end, Dave Hickson roughed up the Charlton goalkeeper Willie Duff a little bit. Duff responded by flattening him with a left hook, and he was then promptly sent off. Very clever move by Hickson, because it then meant Charlton were down to ten, and Everton scored twice in the last ten minutes or so. I found this so exciting – I was aged ten – and Everton must be such a great team to come back from 2-0 in the last ten minutes that I, in future, would support them as well as my local club.

Dave McDougall: My first home game was in 1966, against Arsenal. Nobody in the family was interested in football so I jumped on a bus, which was the 56, and went into town, got off at the terminus, and asked somebody the way to Goodison Park, because I'd never been there. They directed me and I've been going ever since. My lasting memory was walking up Scotland Road and looking up and seeing the old big steel gantry floodlights.

Gary Jones: I remember my first day, I was so excited. I got the bus to training, and my first day in I saw Alex Young, the great Alex Young. Alex was jogging around the perimeter of Bellefield, and I was just in awe. I then met all my idols. I was working with them, which was unbelievable. A really, really exciting time in my life that was.

Gary Imlach: My father [Stuart Imlach] became coach in 1969 and we just parachuted into that amazing time at Goodison, with that amazing team. On the days that my Dad would take us – me and my two brothers – it was extra special. He didn't always take us because he had his youth team duties or he might be off somewhere else, but if he was taking us we'd head into Liverpool in the Volkswagen Beetle that we had then, and as we got closer to the ground the traffic would get greater and we'd be nosing our way through it. We weren't having to park up at the Mons pub or two miles away, like everybody else and hiking in; we nosed our way all the way into the official car park. Then you'd enter at the corner of the ground and walk across the pitch and down the tunnel to get in. That was the way we went in when we arrived with my Dad. It was just an astonishing experience. If my Dad was off with the youth team we'd go with one of the other coach's wives, Margaret Casey, Tommy Casey's wife, and that would be a different experience, but still we would present ourselves at the main doors and Jack the doorman would nod and let us into the players' lounge to watch Football Focus or whatever was on the telly in the run up to the game.

Denise Barrett-Baxendale: When I saw Goodison that first time, I was just amazed at the enormity. I think I've spoken about this in the past, where I've said as a childhood memory, and it sends a shiver up my spine on match days now, hearing the horses going through the stadium, and looking at the size of the horses and the smell of the match day. The noise, and the colour, and the atmosphere. Even now on match day, when my window is open, or if I am on my way to the boardroom, and I hear the police horses, my heart races. That anticipation; it never fails to excite me.

Mavis Spurgin: I've lived in the area since 1946 and still do, and I can remember when I was little minding people's bikes in the back yard. Lots of people had bikes then because most people didn't have cars and so that was a nice little earner as a child. I lived in Goodison Road from 1946 to 1964 so that's how I made some extra pocket money until I was old enough to go to work. People were always nice and polite in those days, win or lose, they were polite when they came back to collect their bikes. I remember it was always very very noisy when they were passing our house, win or lose. In fact it I don't think it was any quieter when they lost but you could always tell if they'd won or lost as it was obvious when you saw them going past. When I was very young I remember I used to run in to Goodison when they opened the gates at half time.

Graeme White: I went to my first game when I was five, around 1979. It was exciting and it was frightening, because everyone stood side by side and we had the big railing. At that sort of age I always remember being put on my uncle Bob's shoulders because for some strange reason my Dad didn't want me on his shoulders because he wanted to watch the match and not have this five year-old little boy wriggling around. I remember looking round and seeing everyone enjoying themselves and really enjoying the atmosphere. It was brilliant, the togetherness of standing side by side with someone and the cheering and the chanting, trying to sing the songs. That's what I remember of the experience when I was a very young boy. It was mouthwatering when you used to stand there and you'd go, 'Wow this is Goodison Park'.

Frank D'Arcy: I was captain of Liverpool Schoolboys and I used to live in Anfield at the time, so all my football was played in Stanley Park. My mother came over to Stanley Park and said, 'Quick, get home.' I said, 'What for?' 'There's an Everton director there.' I always remember the name, Mr Baker. All the children in the street are all looking at his car, a big black limousine I said, 'Well what do you want me to do?' She said, 'I don't know just get back home.' When I got back home he turned round and said to me, 'We'd like you to take an apprenticeship at Goodison as an apprentice footballer.' When you are fifteen all you want to do is get back to your mates in the park don't you. I said, 'Okay, okay, yeah, yeah, yeah.' So he said, 'Just sign there please.' I signed and he left me ma £300 – that was a lot of money in those days – and I got £150. I still don't know what happened to it.

Roberto Martinez: Growing up in Catalonia, it was a very significant moment when Gary Lineker signed for Barcelona. Obviously, he came from Everton, and that was a big moment in trying to understand what Everton was and why Barcelona was signing a player from Everton. That was the first time I heard about them. As a young person, you're just concentrating on the Spanish players and the Spanish League and it wasn't so much from abroad, but the moment that Gary Lineker signed for Barcelona is the first time I was aware of Everton. There were images of Goodison Park where you see the pattern on the stand, and that was quite a strong image. And once you get that image then Howard Kendall became a really important figure in Spanish football, with Athletic Bilbao, one of the few foreign managers that had a massive influence in the Spanish league. That almost linked the two together, because Howard Kendall was the one who sold Gary Lineker, and in a way it gave me a piece of the history of Everton.

Sergei Tomashevskii: When I was a boy in the Soviet Union I loved the Beatles and my Dad explained to me that English football was the best, so I decided to pick a team and somehow I picked Everton because they are from Liverpool. The decision was between Everton and Liverpool, because of The Beatles but I just loved the blue colour. I think when you pick there is no explanation. My Dad used to collect football programmes and there was a programme article, Portsmouth away from 1988, about Everton being the champions and I just liked it and I thought I would follow. There was no English football on TV for the first few years, I just checked the results in the newspapers and that was it.

Lennart Roth: About 30 years ago Unilever in Sweden asked me to relocate and go and work at the Unilever Research Laboratory in Port Sunlight. During that time I had to choose which club to support, Liverpool or Everton. I choose Everton because of their more family oriented approach and the team playing with heart and dedication. Liverpool FC was then more of a business than a club so my choice was easy.

John Corbett: My first memory is probably late September 1962. I was eight years old and we had just moved from Essex to Merseyside. My father had been appointed Plant Security Officer at Ford, he'd already worked at Dagenham Ford plant for some fourteen years, and we all moved north to Liverpool. While standing in the corner of my new school, which was St Joseph's Prep School on Menlove Avenue, I was approached by a gang of boys who said, 'Which team do you support?' Having previously been to West Ham I thought that was not a good team to promote, so I knew the two local sides were Everton and Liverpool and instinctively I just said, 'Everton'. They said, 'You're in our gang'. And that was how it all began.

Fred Kwong: It's something like 30 years, since I was a boy and Hong Kong started showing highlights or showing the full matches on the TV of the English league. I supported Everton because I liked the colour Blue and at the time Everton were champions; it was 1987. So that is the start of it and since then I have told people that I support Everton, although when I was a boy I didn't really know why and what was behind it all.

Per Malmqvist Stolt: I'm born and raised in the north of Sweden and at that time [the 1970s] we did not have a football team that was even close to being in any of the higher divisions in Swedish football. Furthermore, there were no live football on TV from the first division in Sweden. In the 1980s and early 1990s football had a hard time competing with, for example, ice hockey and the attendances were quite low. Not because of hooliganism, which is worse today than back in the 1970s to early 1990s. But the interest was just low. Today the Swedish First Division (Allsvenskan) have very high attendances and in the bigger towns in Sweden many fans live for their football team. So, back when I was a small boy in Boden [a small garrison city up in the north of Sweden], English football was the only live football we could see, except for the national team and when a Swedish team advanced in the rounds of the European Cups. The English clubs became our favourites on the schoolyard. I watched them on TV and remembered a player called Dave Thomas who played without skin pads and the team was Everton. I was quite young and I probably played on the floor when my Dad watched Tipsextra. When me and my friends at school took English clubs as their favourites, I took Everton.

Alan Myers: I think the earliest I can go back was when I lived in a place called Old Swan in Liverpool, and I was one of eight children. I was the sort of middle boy; we were six lads and two girls. I was the only Evertonian out of all of them: my Dad was an absolute staunch Red, and the reason I became an Evertonian was a little bit bizarre. There was a lady across the road who, as a kid, I used to cut hedges for for a bit of extra money. She was a cleaner; she happened to be a cleaner for Harry Catterick's office in Bellefield, and that was her thing. One day she was talking to me; she said, 'You should be an Evertonian.' I must've been about eight or nine, or maybe ten, and this one day, she said, 'Do you want to go to the football?' I said, 'Yeah, I'd love to.' So, she gave me a ticket to the reserves – because in those days a season ticket used to also have a stub which was for the reserves games, which were always played at Goodison. She gave me this one, and I went for the first time on my own. And that was it... But living in a house of Liverpudlians, you can imagine the stick I took, because we didn't win anything. This was the early-70s.

Joe Royle: I was actually on the terraces when Alex Young made his debut. I was there that night against Tottenham. I had been coming with a regular friend of the family over the road, who was a tugboat captain on the Mersey. They now live in Australia and I am still in touch with them, although he died a number of years ago. So yes, I was a blue. My father was from Manchester, and he had a leaning towards Manchester United, but I was a blue from way back. My grandfather, who was a policeman in Chinatown, was a rabid blue, and his son, who was also a policeman and later chairman of the shareholder's association, Norman Dainty – Chief Superintendent Norman Dainty – he too was a rabid blue. I wouldn't say I had no choice, but it was certainly in the blood.

Dave Lewis: My first memory was standing on a box in the Park End in 1970 when we beat West Bromwich Albion 2-0 the League Championship winning season. I think my uncle took me to that one. What did I think of Goodison? I didn't, I could only just about see over the wall!

Ric Wee: Back in the 1980s in Malaysia, we were watching the weekly Football Show on TV, called 'Big League Soccer' and the live FA Cup matches. I watched the FA Cup final in 1984 when we defeated Watford. I was only eleven years-old and can't remember much except the natural desire to support Everton. I know this sounds cliché but back in 1984, as a boy then, it just felt right to support Everton. In Malaysia, I support Perak. I do follow other clubs in other European countries too. For example, I have been following Juventus since 1985, Barcelona since 1986 & Olympique Marseille since 1989; but the team I absolutely support, is Everton.

Joe Royle: I saw Dave Hickson second time around when he was probably past his best, but I did see him. I saw a young Brian Labone coming through. I went to Everton regularly and Everton reserves, I used to go in the boys pen there for a couple of coppers in those days. I spent a lot of my early life watching Everton as well as playing. The boys pen is exactly what it was: a pen in the corner. It was just a place where the kids could go and watch for coppers. Sometimes, if nobody was watching, you could climb out, and get into the real part of the ground, which I'm sure we all did at some stage. My friends were Reds, so we would sometimes go and watch the Liverpool reserves, and they would come with me to Everton. My leanings were always strongly towards Everton.

Bill Kenwright: My childhood was not hugely happy; I was a shy, insecure boy. My paradise was my Gran's on a Saturday where a small terraced house in Vallance Road in Anfield became Disneyland, New York, Los Angeles. On that day all of the aunts, all of the uncles, all the nieces, all of the nephews, would meet in this small house and we would all have whatever lunch gran had cooked together, and the men would all walk off to the football together. My Gran's was equidistant between Anfield and Goodison, literally a mile away – probably less, from both. And the day that they took me, the uncles and the elder cousins, was a day of a sort of manship for me; I would have been six or seven. We used to go each week to Liverpool or Everton. I stood on the Kop or the Paddock. I had a bigger affection to the Blue but I used to just love my uncles and being with them. Specifically, 20 October 1956 – you've got to remember in those days you didn't travel, you didn't go to away games, it was a big deal to go to an away game – we played Man United at Old Trafford, and Albert Dunlop made his debut. They weren't top of the league at the time; the Busby Babes were certainly up there, and Everton were just considered no-hopers. We won 5-2 at Old Trafford, and that was the moment. That was like the spark; the light bulb went off, and the next week we beat Arsenal at home 4-0, and that changed my life. From then on in it's been the love of my life; just all-engrossing, all-encompassing, total love affair, absolute love affair.

Sergei Tomashevskii: It was only when the Soviet Union broke up in the 1990s we started to watch some highlights from the western European championships, like the English Premier League and Spanish and Italian football. So from the early-90s I could see some highlights but the only 90 minute games were the FA Cup Finals. So it was only in 1995 that I got to see Everton for the first time for a full game.

Eric Howell: It was a night match on a Tuesday, the last day of January 2012, so it was pretty chilly, and Everton were facing Manchester City. It was deadline day so we trotted out Nikica Jelavic at half time and then some guy decided to handcuff himself to the Park End goalposts [the demonstrator was staging a protest against Irish airline, Ryanair], so I got to experience that. I was sitting in the Gwladys Street with Ped McPartland and his family and friends, so I had a very great view of the cross by Royston Drenthe to the feet of Landon Donovan who trapped it and laid it off to Darron Gibson, who smashed it right past Joe Hart. It was absolutely insane! I'm getting goosebumps now just talking about it, just thinking about the experience. The Gwladys Street was absolutely nuts for at least five minutes after they restarted play; it was just amazing.

Joshua Corbett: I saw my first Everton game in March 2013. I remember walking up to Goodison with my Dad and Grandpa and seeing the pictures of all the players on the Goodison timeline that goes around the ground. I knew that first visit was a chance for me to become part of the game. Stoke were a good strong side, but Everton passed it around and got a winning goal [from Kevin Mirallas] – though I don't actually recall seeing it as everyone was standing up in my way!

Eleanor Corbett: I went for the first time with my brother, Dad and Grandpa in 2015, but I didn't see Everton win for another two years. That was the game I really remember, a 3-1 win against Burnley. Goodison Park was just enormous and very loud and they served the biggest hotdogs I had ever seen. It was really exciting when Everton scored. I'd owned shirts and met some of the former players, like Neville Southall, but I think that was the moment I became a real Evertonian.

Davide Ghilardi: It was 2013/14 season that I saw my first Everton game. I was there with my group's mates, Everton Italia. It was a dream come true. One of my favourite days of my life. I appreciated everything about Liverpool. People were really kind with us, regardless of whether we were Evertonians or not. They liked a lot the fact that we organized a long trip to follow our passion.

Michael Lecluyse: I started following Everton when I was a young kid because of FIFA the football game. That's how it started, but it really kicked off when [Marouane] Fellaini joined Everton, that was the first Belgian player back in 2008. I was sixteen, so I could find on the internet more information about Everton and then I also started following them on Teletext back in the day and the internet. I started following them that way and then when Facebook came it was one of the first things I started following, so that's how it all started it started.

Sergei Tomashevskii: It was always a special feeling but the thing was that if I planned to go to Goodison [from Russia] it was better to plan to go for a week or better two or three, because it's so expensive; it's pointless to stay just for one day because it's such a long distance. You spend a lot of money anyway only going for one day so it's best to come for a few. Before I visited Goodison I already visited an away game, Stevenage away [in 2014], and I had been in the home end because I couldn't get a ticket for the away end because the ground was so small, but I enjoyed it so much. And of course the first experience of Goodison, it was hard to describe. You've seen Goodison so much on the telly, on the internet, but when you see it live then it's absolutely different. The atmosphere is great. I was in the Lower Gwladys when Everton played Aston Villa, they were 1-0 down but got back to 1-1.

Fred Kwong: Seeing Goodison for the first time was, I imagine, like a Muslim going to Mecca, or someone visiting the moon.

Per Malmqvist Stolt: It was quite late in life when I first visited Goodison. I was 28 years old. I had never before had the money to go and my parents were not interested In football and my father could not travel due to his MS. But in 1998 I had my own money and went to Goodison Park with a few friends. It was not the best of times for the club and it was a goalless encounter against Newcastle. It is a very strange and almost religious feeling when you arrive to a club and an area you know everything about. You have read everything about it, but you have never been there. I had a plan to walk down Spellow Lane, as Tommy Lawton had done when he first came to the club and the bus conductor said: 'Good luck lad, but you will never be as good as Dixie.' I had tried to find out which pubs you should go to and I wanted to walk all the way from the train station to Goodison. I knew everything about Goodison being in the city. But the walk was longer than I had thought.

Michael Lecluyse: You'll never forget the moment you enter Goodison Park for the first time. It's all pure magic. You hear it from other people and when you experience it yourself and Z-Cars comes on, it's goosebumps all over your body.

Simon Hart: I've got cagey memories of being taken up to the Top Balcony and just seeing the huge, or what felt like a huge, escalator at the time; going up and up and up, really high, and looking down on the Goodison pitch. I don't remember specifics from my first game, but there's the escalator; there's me in the players' lounge because of my Dad's connection with Mick Lyons, and kind of being excited because my Dad's name was in the programme.

Danny Cadamarteri: I only had one thing running around my head when I made my debut [against Chelsea in May 1997] because I lived with a family of Evertonians and my landlord was a proper Blue. He always said when I was in digs, 'If you ever make it and you play against people like Dennis Wise or you play against Liverpool, make sure you smash somebody in front of the Park End and the fans will love you.' So that kind of popped up in my head when I was sat there on the bench. I came on at half time and then after about ten or fifteen minutes this opportunity had come and I chased over and Dennis Wise was in the corner, right by the Park End where the away fans were, and I just jumped in. It wasn't a bad tackle and I won the ball, but I've lifted Dennis Wise at the same time and sent him flying. I can't tell you the exact words he said but it was a bit explicit, but he said it in a good way: 'I loved that son.' He picked me up and he shook my hand and as it happened the whole of the Park End just erupted and goes, 'Wayyyy!!!' It was because it was Dennis Wise and he was a nasty little southerner. It went down a treat with the fans.

Rev. Harry Ross: I started by going to watch Everton and Liverpool in the 1950s. I used to go in the Boys' Pen on the corner of Bullens Road and Gwladys Street, because I had relatives who lived in Gwladys Street and others who lived in Netley Street; relatives who lived up by the other lot's ground in Anfield, so I went to both games. I went once on the Kop before they had any of the barriers. You started off at the top and you ended up at the bottom, but what made it worse was when they used the rolled up *Echo* because there were no toilets and I got soaking wet. I decided I would never go anywhere near there again so I ended up going to Goodison on a regular basis.

Joe Royle: [The toilet facilities] weren't in any part of the ground. That's why you had the famous situation at Anfield when there was a tide at halftime. No one could get to the toilets, and everything, shall we say, flowed downwards.

Rev. Harry Ross: Later I became a curate and eventually when I was to get my own parish, which was in 1977, the Bishop of Warrington, Michael Henshall, had a whole long list of places I could go. I looked at it and got to the second one and he said, 'It's St. Luke's Church in Walton.' I said, 'I'll take it.' He says, 'You haven't seen it.' I said, 'Yes I have it's in the corner of my favourite ground I haven't seen inside it I don't care what condition it's in I'll take it over.' So I became priest in charge and then the Vicar and that's when I started my really strong connections with Goodison.

Roger Bennett: It was 1 April 1978, a morning game because the Grand National was that afternoon, against Charlie George's Derby County. I was seven and I went there and I walked into the ground and it was the clichéd moment; it was very true to it the moment you walk up the steps and you inhale that unique smell of spilt beer, dodgy fried products and police horse urine, which kind of surrounded the ground. And when you see that green – I've never seen anything greener in my life – it seared my eyes. Now, when I look at footage of games from that period, the grass was actually half mud it's not as green as you remember it. We walked to our seats surrounded by huge guys; I couldn't see a thing to be honest. It was freezing cold and I was surrounded by enormous guys. I was with my Dad and this stranger to my right was wearing a sheepskin coat, which was very popular amongst managers of the 1970s, it was full on Malcolm Allison. He just looked at me and realised that I just couldn't see because of these huge men in front of me and in one movement he'd picked me up full into the air with one arm as he took his coat off and folded it with the other and he just stuck his coat on my seat and put me on top of it. Suddenly I was about four foot taller and he gave me a kiss and he goes, 'We're all one big family here at Goodison'. That was it. I was already hooked. My Grandfather was an Evertonian, my Dad was an Evertonian, but that was the defining moment.

John Parrott: I remember the green pitch and horse manure all over the street. The ones I really loved were evening games and there's something special about evening games midweek. I can remember coming up, seeing the floodlights on and walking up to the top stand at the Gwladys Street and coming out and seeing the pitch and being absolutely gobsmacked.

Ric Wee: I visited Goodison Park for the first time in February 2014. My daughter and I, plus a Malaysian friend, Mohd Ridhwan, had arrived at Goodison at about 6pm. We wanted to walk around the grand old stadium before the match but alas, the weather was prohibitive. It was 12 February 2014 and we were supposed to play Crystal Palace. I was in UK then as it was Chinese New Year back in Malaysia where there was a long holiday. At about 6.30-7pm, the match was called off but just before that, I had uploaded a selfie on Twitter, excitingly sharing with my friends that I was finally going to watch an Everton match at Goodison. That tweet became viral after the match was postponed. Everton staff looked for me and when they found me, we were taken on a tour of the stadium and met many players (including a surreal chat with Leighton Baines). They also arranged to meet Roberto Martinez. Nice chap. The following day, I was invited back to Goodison to meet the press, but I didn't realise and anticipate that there were so many. Upon return to Kuala Lumpur the club contacted me to arrange a return to Goodison. I was touched. I agreed to return with the condition that I be permitted to help out and contribute to Everton in the Community during the said trip back to Goodison. We eventually arranged for me to return to watch us play City in May 2014 (our last home game for that season), which we unfortunately lost 2-3. Notwithstanding that defeat, the entire trip was humbling and appreciated.

What a club, to help make overseas fans like me, have our dream to watch a match at Goodison, come true.

St Luke's Church

Rev. Harry Ross: When I took over it in 1977 it was not in a good shape as the previous Vicar had not been too well for quite a while. So the church was a bit neglected. I remember not long after I was made Vicar I had the bailiffs come to the vicarage demanding that the Church repay so much of their debt and I managed to hold them off. Anyway, we paid the debt off but the Church roof also needed mending so I set up a church roof fund and that roof is famous for the amount of fans that have sat on it to watch the match. In fact if I had a pound for everyone that said they had sat on it we could've easily mended the roof. One time in particular I remember not long after I joined the church there was a fan on the roof and he was holding onto the cross. Nowadays people who look up won't see it because he gripped it that tightly we had to get it taken down because it became too dangerous to leave it up there. The cross is now in the memorial garden.

June Scott: I joined the church when the Rev. Ross was there and it's not as good as it was as there is a lot of older congregation and not as many going. The 'teas for the fans' used to be very popular and still are, but there used to be more of us to serve years ago. I can remember it wasn't busy when we first started it but it soon got very popular as more and more people got to know it was there. There has never been any problems with the fans and we have had away fans come in on many occasions. It was a good way for the Church to be open to the community and the fans, because we would get many people who would ask if they could go into the church and the wardens would take them in to have a look around. Then of course the Rev. Ross opened the memorial garden at the back of the church and people would come to visit where their loved one's ashes are.

Mavis Spurgin: I actually got married in St Luke's on a match day. It was 8 October 1960 [Everton drew 0-0 with Preston North End] and the wedding was at St. Luke's at 3:15pm. We had a policewoman and a policeman to mind the spaces for our wedding cars as I lived on Goodison Road and in those days cars could park on either side of the road. I can remember it was raining heavily. It was harvest festival and the church looked beautiful and I remember seeing a few of the fans who had gone late to the match stop and look to see what was going on. But it was funny that as we were taking our vows you could hear the crowd booing and shouting. I hope that was for Everton, not me and Ron, my husband!

Rev. Harry Ross: One of the things I set up to raise money was 'teas to the fans' which we opened in 1978 and at the start we only sold teas and coffees and biscuits, so I remember we made £7. We didn't advertise it then but as time went on we of course got more and more known, so, as you can imagine, we were making a lot more. Fans from all over came to have their cuppa before the game and even away fans came in. When we first opened the only food you could get before you went into the ground was from the chippy opposite the church and there also used to be hotdog carts that went round. I remember that the carts used to turn up in a van and the vendors used to get the carts out with the hotdogs already in them. And of course I did see the odd time when the cart would tip its contents onto the floor and nobody cared about health and safety in those days so all they did was get a shovel and tip all the contents – probably horse muck as well – back into the cart and wheel it away to sell them.

Mavis Spurgin: We have 'teas to the fans' on a match day and we get really busy. We don't open it as much as we did because the congregation is getting older now and it's harder for us to man it, but I do remember we used to sell out on most match days when Everton were doing really well. We still have our regulars: there's four people who come up every home game from Devon, but we have had people who come from all over the country and from abroad as well.

Rev. Harry Ross: I used to scatter a lot of the fans' ashes around the pitch and they used to come into the church first. If they weren't really church goers I would do a service next to the pitch and we would do the interment of ashes. Some of the players, for instance Brian Labone, was done on the penalty spot at the Gwladys Street end. Davey Hickson is on the side of the pitch and the fans, including my own father in law's, are right around the edge. I would get calls from all over the country saying they would like ashes out on Goodison. I got to meet so many fans from all over the country and we built up a relationship with the club that way. Then when they changed the pitch Everton decided that it had become too full and I had a think and told them that I would open a memorial garden at the back of the church, in about 2004. I think I had to go through all the legal permissions from the Diocese to allow us to do it and we had it dedicated. I can't remember how many there are now but there are a lot of people who have had their ashes interred at the back of the church and they can put a plaque up on the wall that separates the church from the ground. On match days fans would go into the garden to remember their loved ones

June Scott: When my husband Billy died, he was the Churchwarden for quite a long time and he loved the church and he loved Everton so we thought that would be the natural place for him to go. When Everton move the garden will still be there, but if something happens to the church that's what will be a worry.

Going the game

Barbara Garner: It was family and happy, and people talked to each other. Strangers talked. There was no sort of abuse. They'd say, 'Ah ref', or things like that, but they'd never throw abuse at anybody. All they'd do is when the ball came out, everybody used to shout, 'Our ball!' if it was the other players. Like in one voice: 'Our ball!'

David Hart: You could smell the cigarette smoke. Very different today's game, today's game is very sanitised. But the crowds were terrific. In later years I used to go with my brother, first on his scooter, and we'd get right to the ground and push it between the cars and we'd go in the Gwladys Street End.

Emy Onoura: I would never romanticise the old terraces. Lots of the time they were uncovered, depending on where you went. I remember there were lots of times, Hillsborough for example, when you'd be soaked to the skin, uncovered. Norwich I remember because it's a seven-hour coach journey, and it was an evening kick-off so we'd had to leave about midday, or late morning, got to Norwich for a seven, half seven kick-off. It was an FA Cup game or a League Cup game, I can't remember. It chucked it down all day, and on the terraces we were soaked to the skin. I remember sitting on the coach on the way back, and it was cold and wet. Fortunately we'd won, but we didn't get back home till about two in the morning, freezing cold and wet. I wouldn't want to go back to those days or anything like that, but I am a supporter of safe standing. I just think there's ways in which we can stand in safety and have decent toilets, and not have people squashed into pens like sardines.

Charles Mills: It could be an experience before you even got into the ground. Goodison Road would be so jammed and and you'd find yourself with your face up the backside of a police horse. There were some quite frightening experiences. I actually got locked out in 1967 when we played Burnley in the [FA Cup third round] replay. I didn't get in, got locked out. They closed the gates and I was just relieved to be out of the way to be honest with you. I got in the last twenty minutes.

June Scott: I moved to the Everton area around about sixty years ago when my elder daughter was only a little baby. It was much as it is today, but in those days they used to park on both sides of the street and it was a bit awkward if you were going out, especially if the children wanted to go out and play. I lived in Bardsay Road in those days and if I wanted to take them to see their Gran in Neston Street it was awkward to get the pram and the kids through the crowds. There wasn't any hooliganism then and the crowds were quite good and got out your way but they were noisy. There were always very big crowds but after the match everybody left quite quickly, so it did clear fast. The pubs used to always be busy and as they are nowadays as well. I didn't open my backyard to let people put their bikes in because I needed it for the children to play in but many young boys and girls in the area could earn some pocket money that way and when there were more cars it became, 'Mind your car, mister?' and they used to get some money to watch the car and very often they would be standing at the car when the owner came back and they'd get a copper or two for it. I remember if you had anybody visiting you'd have to put out chairs or ladders to keep a parking space before the council brought in a residents parking scheme, so that helped. Now the parking is okay but you have to time it if you want to get in or go out as a lot of the roads now are one way and, of course, you can't always get out when the match is on.

Father John Ashton: As a young seminarian in the early-1940s it was forbidden to go outside the grounds. They clamped down on the seminary students going out. I was in love with Everton and we'd get bits of news from handymen around the place – the groundsmen and people like that would tell us exactly what happened. Somewhat exaggerated but nevertheless they would tell us, 'Oh, we should never have lost.'

David France: My Dad let me go on my own aged eleven. I was a schoolboy – just a young kid. In order to show that I had gone I had to buy a programme. If I could travel from Widnes to Liverpool – a train and a bus – they thought I could then go to places like Burnley, Blackburn and Preston, because it was just an extension. By the time I was 13 I was able to hitchhike – a lot of kids hitchhiked in those days – there were so many trucks going to places that you could just hop in. Initially we went to places like Stoke and Leeds, I would never go to the north east. My mum was a Geordie but she never wanted me to go there, and we rarely went to London because it was a long trip. I got a season ticket from when I was about 14, and if I didn't go to the away games, I went to the reserve games. So, I went every week, it becomes a way. For me it was an escape, because I loved the people. It was my something special. The fact that we enjoyed success at the time was another thing, but I enjoyed going there. I loved going to the big city, it was the time of The Beatles, everything was going on. It was a great enhancement and enrichment of my life at that time. It was at the core of my life.

Andrew Corbett: Having a deep-rooted family history of Evertonians going back to the nineteenth century, familiar traditions and routine of a match day have been passed through the generations down to myself. I often think of my grandfather doing exactly what 'we' do now when he was our age. Waking up with high anticipation of the day's fixture ahead, a hearty breakfast or lunch to set you up before a pre-match pint, a quick punt at the bookies on the way to Goodison Park. Then we're set: The roar of the crowd as the Z-Cars theme plays, bringing senses of nostalgia, pride and identity. The anticipation and high expectation to get a result bringing emotions of both excitement and anger – depending on how the boys in blue deliver. At the full-time whistle, those emotions hit a peak. Whether it's ecstasy, satisfaction, or disappointment, all will be discussed analytically in the pub after the game. This is the same pub – the Edinburgh Castle in Crosby, better known locally as the 'Bug and Bite' – that my Dad and uncles introduced to me, and my grandfather introduced to them, and consequently all my siblings and cousins. We gather with the older generations to review the day's events. After the pub, a pit stop at the local chippy, and home in time for Match of the Day highlights. This is the match day I always had every other week for nine months of the year for as long as I could remember.

Carena Duffy: I worked in the ticket office from 2007-09. I loved it. I remember working the first week on the season ticket renewal process whereby the phones were literally ringing off the hook and the staff in the ticket office were counting daily hundreds of thousands of pounds when people were coming up to the counter and renewing their season tickets. It was the days before it went mostly online. It was still mostly people coming up to the counter and paying for the season tickets. It was chaotic, but that's how you learn by getting literally thrown out in the deep end. There was not much training, we were just learning from each other and there were quite a lot of new staff at that time in that part of the business. It was an exciting time for Everton because we were playing in Europe, so I ended up travelling around Europe watching Everton.

Dave Lewis: I've not been able to watch a game as a fan for a long time. You can't do it in the stadium control room. You can celebrate a goal being scored if you see it, but your focus has got to be that if someone scores a goal there's always the potential for something to be happening. I always say if there's five goals in a game I'm lucky if I see two. That's not what we are there for. You can't be a fan in the control room, you've got to be doing your job.

Richard Dunne: I loved it. It's a great stadium. It's one of the old school ones, of course, but it was brilliant once you had the jersey on the fans supported you. I had some bad games but I never felt like I was getting picked on by the crowd or 'owt like that. They always wanted to support you and if you met anybody out on the street it was like, 'Go on, you've done well, keep it up.' They are just very very supportive of their team and of their players and I found that even going back I was always fine with the crowd, they were always kind enough to me. It was a great stadium to play in the derbies. It was amazing. The atmosphere was very hard to replicate wherever I went after that.

Graeme White: Even if they had said they wouldn't pay me I'd still have said yes to becoming the Everton stadium announcer. From being that 5-year-old kid to becoming the stadium announcer and saying, 'Welcome to Goodison Park,' and announcing the team and saying, 'The goal scorer is...' and hearing 39,000 fans cheer – I was living the dream and still am to this day.

David Hart: One of the highlights from my memories was when Everton played a friendly with Club de Regatas Vasco da Gama [in April 1956]. They'd just been to see the Pope, and they were all playing with these lovely medals. And they played the most lovely football but couldn't score. Everton played Cyril Lello at centre-forward, and ran out 6-3 winners. I remember going on my friends' shoulders after the game, we used to put our autograph books in the coach windows, and they'd pass them round. It came back and I had Vava, Santos, about eight internationals. Somebody said, 'I'll get you some more autographs', and that was the last I saw of the book. I'm really annoyed I lost that. I remember that game, first time we'd seen the Brazilian style strips, with the sashes across.

Emy Onoura: When I was a kid going, the match was different. You kind of went for the atmosphere and because you could see from close up, and it gave you a different perspective. Now the atmosphere is almost part of the furniture you sell abroad as part of the TV rights. Nobody wants to watch football, it's part of the match day experience that you sell, a full ground where they create an atmosphere. Especially Champions League games.

Denise Barrett-Baxendale: We give a warm Liverpool welcome when people visit our club; they're our guests, and we treat them with that respect. We have really high standards right across our organisation. Whether it's our Academy, under 23s, Ladies team, our community programme, etc. we expect the best. We are referred to very fondly as 'The People's Club', which is a wonderful accolade and our staff strive hard day in day out to live up to that reputation. I will regularly meet Liverpool fans and fans from other clubs who will say to me 'Your club is a proper club and we respect how you support the Merseyside community,' which is exceptional, isn't it? When a fan from another club is prepared to commend us like that.

Following Everton from afar

Davide Ghilardi: It's never been difficult to follow Everton from Italy. When I was young, I used to buy football magazines with information about the Premier League. With the internet, it's been easy to follow the club. I'm lucky to reach Liverpool from Milan because I have the possibility to reserve a direct flight to Manchester and, there, to arrive in town with bus or train. It's been crucial, the existence of low cost airlines like Ryanair.

Lennart Roth: I live in Thailand now and mainly follow via TV and football websites. I am not a fan of either Twitter or Facebook. Since I watch most games live on TV it's a similar experience as a match day visit to Goodison but at a much-reduced intensity and atmosphere. Nothing can compare to being at Goodison when Z-Cars theme starts playing. It transports you to another dimension of reality where the game becomes part of all your senses. Since you sit so close to the game at Goodison you can feel the pain of the tackles and participating in heading the ball.

Jan Loudin: There is not much of an Everton following in the Czech Republic and Slovakia. I would say the number of people in the Czech and Slovak Fan Club is around 30, and seven to ten people posts regularly on our website, but the Facebook page of our fan club has more than 4000 likes. I follow Everton through TV a lot. Of course, I read various websites (Official, Toffeeweb) follow internet streams or TV in the pub during matches. Occasionally Twitter or Facebook (read, not react). I usually watch games on internet streams at home, because I don't have access to the local TV channel that holds rights to Premier League matches. Usually I am calm, occasionally complaining. A few times a year I watch TV in restaurants or pubs with the fan club, rating our performances immediately. In 2016 I made my first visit to Goodison. Memories? Beautiful stadium, nice printed programme and the whole old-feel look, which I like.

Aarkash Chandon: India doesn't have too much football. We have the ISL now, but back when I was a kid [in the early noughties], there wasn't much Indian football to follow. Being a kid who played football for school I was always taught how team work and chemistry is essential, and Everton was one of the few clubs that felt like a proper team. Using the youth academy well, not just buying a big money player to build a team around. I loved the sport, so I used to watch as many games as possible. Everton was one of the clubs I watched on TV. It honestly feels a little odd how invested I am in a team that plays on the other side of the world, in a place that I haven't ever been to. I can't explain how or where the passion comes from. I can hardly remember exactly when I became as emotionally attached to the club as I am today. While I'm watching the club play, nothing and no one else matters. My mood over the week depends on how the club fared over the last weekend. A question I'm asked very often in a country that only watches the 'Big Four', is why Everton? A club that's won one just one piece of silverware in my lifetime, and honestly there's no concrete answer for that. Maybe I was born blue? Maybe its just in my DNA? I'm not sure. All I know is that I've been an Evertonian for a large chunk of my life, and will be for the years to come.

Per Malmqvist Stolt: I follow Everton every way I can from Sweden. I watch as many games I can on TV and spend too much time on the internet and social media. Listening to the commentary from Darren Griffiths with Graham Stuart, Ian Snodin or Graeme Sharp is a firm favourite. I have also read quite a lot of books about Everton and Evertonians. For a long time I was the only Everton supporter I knew, so it was always a quite lonely thing. I have watched many FA Cup finals alone without anyone to share the feelings, or with people who did not support Everton. If Everton played on Tipsextra it was a very serious thing. A loss was catastrophic for days to come. These feelings level out with age and nowadays I'm not alone supporting Everton (I was always known as Per – he who supports Everton), thanks to the internet and Swedish Toffees. But due to the fact that I'm a family man I still watch many games at home alone, or with my eldest son, who's also an Everton supporter. Sometimes you watch with other Everton-supporters or at a pub.

Ric Wee: Malaysia's cable TV, ASTRO, usually will show live games and we would watch Everton matches via that cable TV. It's usually a mixture of anxiety, anticipation and excitement, whenever Everton games are shown live. Sometimes, I would join the Malaysian Toffees, who would meet at one of the cafes in town, to watch the matches. We have a healthy number of members in the Malaysian Everton Supporters Club all over the country, and watching the match together builds comradeship and friendship. The advent of the internet and arrival of cable TV to Malaysia in the early 1990s changed the way we connect with Everton. Nowadays, its rather seamless to gain news about the club.

Sergei Tomashevskii: I can remember that when the Soviet Union broke up that there was more information in the papers. There was not much on telly but in the papers there was quite a lot about European football and, of course, about English football. I knew about the players, so I could follow the team. and I knew who the manager was and the players and who scored the goals and about the starting line up. I was made up when Andrei Kanchelskis signed for Everton.

Andrew Corbett: For the past five-and-a-half years, I've been living in South Korea – roughly 9,000km away – teaching English at a university. Since then, my matchday routine has undergone a vast change. We are eight or nine hours ahead of the UK, depending on the time of year, so a 3pm kick-off is either 11pm or midnight. I was lucky enough to meet a great group of British lads in my local football team. Our camaraderie stems from our mutual love of the beautiful game. Without this, there is so much lacking in a matchday experience. We try to replicate a matchday like we would back home: we would meet for dinner around 7pm, usually a Korean BBQ which compliments beer so well. The first kick-off would be the midday televised game, which would be 8.30pm Korean time. Gambling is illegal in

Korea and thus, there are no bookies, so we bet against ourselves, picking players in turn out of the starting line-ups for goals and assists during the game - $4 a goal, $2 an assist. This trend continues throughout the night and keeps the interest whatever game we are forced to watch. The evening could turn out to be very cheap or very expensive, depending how well players did in the game. By the time the 3pm kick-off comes around, we are never too sure who is playing.

Fred Kwong: I would say that is easy for everyone to watch Everton. Hong Kong has a large Premier League following – I once read somewhere that it has the highest viewing figures of the overseas Premier League broadcasters, but I'm not sure about that. They are now showing nearly every game live on six or seven channels, so you can almost pick whatever you want. I think the TV selection in Hong Kong is even better than in the UK. The oddest match I remember? Once, during a vacation, I went to see some friends in some rural areas, and they had an outdoor barbeque. At that time, I think Everton were playing Man United, and somehow, I sneaked away from this place and managed to watch the second half through someone's window. It wasn't a bar or house; it was someone's workplace in an industrial estate, and luckily, they were watching the game. So I just stood outside and watched the whole of the second half. It was like UK-based fans not actually going into Goodison, but just watching through someone's window outside.

Roger Bennett: How would I watch the games? I'd watch them mostly in the pub at that time. I was the only Everton fan in that time period [Bennett moved to the US in 1991]. So Everton has always been there but what's been fascinating in America is there's this new immense fan base who have fallen in love with the game. 2010 it really went over the top and the Premier League started to be broadcast in a very aggressive way and there's so much league football that's broadcast live in America. New York is one of the greatest places to watch live football. You can watch more live football in America than you can in England and so a real football culture started to grow and, especially post 2010 World Cup, you had this immense American sports fan base that became hooked on Premier League football. What grew fascinating was watching this enormous fresh eyed support and they'd all fallen truly, madly, deeply for the sport, and none of them had geographic links for any team. When you grew up in England where you are from is mostly the team you support. I know now it's changed and it's fine for some kids to support super teams in London or Manchester United or whatever, but by and large you pick teams that are in your familial DNA or through geographic links. In America the majority of fans here have been able to choose with fresh eyes and just pick or just have that team choose them almost. It has been fascinating watching Everton – watching all the clubs – kind of fumble in that new reality. Everton, funnily enough, had one of the best cases to be America's team.

Michael Lecluyse: There were no Everton supporters in Belgium as far as I know when I started supporting. I searched on the Everton website for any Belgian contact but there was none and there was no Belgian supporters club so that was the reason why I founded it myself. Last year I met Stefan, who was supporter of the year at Everton. He's a Belgian and he has a small community around Brussels and the other side of our country, because here you have Flanders and Walloon. The old part speaks Dutch, while the other speaks French, and there was a little French community [who support Everton], whereas in Flanders, there was no such thing. So, back in the day, I thought I was the only Evertonian. When I spoke to my friends about football, I used to say I supported Everton, and they would all wonder, 'Why would you support Everton?'

Stuart Appleby: When I upped sticks and moved to Dubai back in September 2015, I was prepared for the fact it was now not going to be as easy to see my beloved Blues – especially in the flesh. Television-wise, I soon realised it wouldn't be a problem to watch Everton, though. In fact, I found it easier to watch my team in the United Arab Emirates than at home! Every single match here is broadcast live and then seemingly repeated non-stop, so you never miss a trick. Indeed, if we lose, there's no way of getting away from re-runs of the match. The days where you'd look to see which Toffees matches Sky Sports and BT Sports had picked to televise, quickly felt like a thing of the past for me. While I realised how big the Premier League phenomenon was away from UK shores – with the Middle Eastern audience being absolutely fanatical about it – it almost felt like I had gone back in time, too.

Eric Brown: I actually had a weekend in Liverpool with a couple of my mates [in the 1960s]. We went to a club, and it was hilarious how we were all dancing away and it got to 10pm or whenever it was, and all the music stopped and the lights came up. My mates and I looked at each other blankly, and televisions dropped down from the ceiling, and everything stopped so that everybody – the girls as well as the boys – could watch Match of the Day. Unbelievable, in this night club. That lasted just over an hour, then the televisions disappeared again into the ceiling, the lights went down, the music came on everybody carried on as if nothing had happened!

Roger Bennett: I was on the Syrian border in the mid-eighties, hitchhiking, totally lost and a Volkswagen camper van came over the hill and slowed down. I was in the middle of nowhere. I was in a valley, no one around. I could see it coming for miles and to be honest I did crap my pants because these were the days of Walid Jumblatt, Hezbollah, crazy things. The door opened and inside it was like out of central casting, just a group of mysterious men. I had no idea who the hell they were and they were looking at me, they cased me out, this Englishman and they are as suspicious as I am. One voice goes, 'Where you from?' and I said, 'Liverpool,' and there was a silence for about five seconds and they all went, 'Oooh Graeme Sharp, Gary Lineker, Kenny Dalglish.' They pulled me in and rode to the nearest city just talking about each of the finals in micro detail. There's been many life moments like that, where you realise what the city means to people worldwide. I just thank God that I'm not from Birmingham or Manchester or Leicester or cities that completely blur into one. You realise in that moment, that 1980s team that plundered that league win and the European Cup Winners Cup what that did not just for Everton, not just for the particular players, but just etching those shared memories in the profile of football fans around the globe. It's remarkable.

Merseyside derbies

Neville Southall: Just as Everton needed a strong Liverpool, Liverpool needed a strong Everton. When Everton got miles better in the mid-1980s, that made Liverpool pull up and overtake them again. It was like two competing brothers: one improved, the other had to get even better. It was brilliant to have the two teams as genuine rivals. If it's a level playing field then it's positive, because it means that both teams are striving to get better, and that can only be good for both of them. You can't have one team that dominates the city, because it's no good for anybody.

Geoff Nulty: I thought it was a case of there's no animosity between the two clubs. I think at board level there's always been a coming together of the boards and they've never been at daggers drawn and the same applied with the managers.

Frank D'Arcy: We used to go to a club in town called the Royal Tiger. You'd meet half the Liverpool side in there on a Saturday night after the match. You'd have Liverpool players down there and Everton players there. Obviously you got on well with them. You didn't ignore anybody. Their ground was just at the top of our road, so I used to just walk in and talk to the players and if you had any injuries you'd see their physio. You'd just talk to them. Not now though.

Bishop Tom Williams: Remember that quote Shankly made once? 'There are two clubs on Merseyside: Liverpool and Liverpool Reserves.' That was banter and I think people always appreciate banter. Once you start taking banter seriously then you'll get tribalism and that's the one thing I think is developing. It has become like the London clubs fighting one another or the Manchester clubs fighting one another. We were always from the same roots and I think we need to get back to that. That's why I think if any city in the world could have had the same ground it should've been us, but Liverpool supporters would go spare with you if you suggested that.

John Corbett: I had been to several derby matches before 1970 with my older brother, Bill, who is a Liverpool fan. Whilst I was fourteen or fifteen he would have been nineteen or twenty, so he used to try to bribe me to support Liverpool by buying me a ticket to go to Anfield on alternate weeks. Between 1968 and 1971 I saw quite a lot of Liverpool as well as Everton, including every derby match, which of course involved queuing for tickets, usually weeks in advance; and on one occasion involved bunking out of school and joining the queues down Priory Road at about 11.30 in the morning and waiting till six o'clock in the evening to actually buy a ticket. Crowd violence usually involved banter, usually involved people sort of harmlessly slagging each other off; there were some fights but not that many. It was friendly to an extent but people were often divided, not necessarily by families but sometimes divided within families, like my own. My old fella supported Manchester United, my brother Liverpool, and me Everton, but we of course would not physically assault each other on the basis of this. But, you would see people pushing and shoving in the street sometimes, but to be honest I saw very, very few examples of physical violence between Liverpool and Everton fans.

Gary Imlach: They were horribly nervous affairs. They were great in retrospect if you won, and there was a great excitement in the week or two weeks building up to them. But it was an excitement heavily flavoured with anxiety. Every time Liverpool got the ball and started pressing forward into the Everton half just induced terror. I don't know if any relaxed fan exists, but I certainly wasn't a relaxed fan.

Gerry Moore: The derbies always annoy me. We have always seemed to play like we are frightened of them. When we used to put the old Liverpool teams under pressure they didn't like it it's as if they would say 'What are you doing? Hang on slow it down we don't play that type of football' and I think in derbies we are beaten before we get there. Referees haven't helped us in derbies either – there was that brilliant goal by Don Hutchison a few years back, which everyone knew was a goal, but the only person in the ground that decided it wasn't was the referee.

Becky Tallentire: I always thought there was a discernible difference between Evertonians and Liverpudlians, apart from Gordon West's astute observation that 'They're really ugly' – which is quite true. I used to teach in a prison in Liverpool and I always found there was a lot more Liverpool fans in there than Evertonians, and if you can draw your own conclusions from that I'm not really sure. I always thought that Evertonians were more reserved and more dignified, whereas Liverpool supporters were quite crass and just gobshites, really; just shooting their mouths off all the time, not just about football, but about life in general. I don't know whether that comes from being a Liverpool fan, but I always thought that we were a little more reserved and a bit more dignified than them.

Hana Roks: I remember standing at a bus stop one year when we were facing relegation and some fella walked passed me. I must've been about eleven or twelve and I was waiting to go the match. He goes 'Ha ha yous are going down today' and walks away shouting, 'Liverpool'. That's always stuck in my memory. Every time we beat them since then I've thought of his face. I've never seen him again but I can always recall his face. I always think the worst ones are the ones who don't go the game and I just think, 'Do you know anything about them?'

Simon Hart: I've not lived in Liverpool for nearly twenty years so tend not to give Liverpool too much thought. The 'bitter' thing I don't like, though. They seem to have a problem with Evertonians not wishing good things for more successful local rivals who like to look down on us and lord it over us. If that's bitter, then how do we describe their hatred for their more successful local rivals in the north west, Man United? When they're ripping up the toilets at Old Trafford, or singing Munich songs in pubs... is that not bitterness?

Dave McDougall: Someone said to me that the atmosphere has deteriorated since Heysel and I agree. I used to go to Liverpool and Everton every week. If I wasn't at Goodison I'd be at Anfield and, by the way, shouting for Liverpool because I was supporting the city. But you wouldn't get that today. I haven't brought my children up to hate Liverpool, I've brought them up to love them but somewhere along the line they've made their own minds up. It has deteriorated, sadly, you can't go sit in the Kop with your blue and white shirt or scarf. I went to Ronnie Moran's testimonial with my blue scarf on and I sat in the main stand and I got absolutely ripped to bits. I was saying, 'Behave! He's been a great servant to the city of Liverpool and to Liverpool Football Club and also he was a personal friend of mine.' When you look at English football, not just Everton and Liverpool, the rivalry has always been a friendly rivalry and not the hatred and bitterness that is there now.

Rev. Harry Ross: I went to Anfield when I was Rural Dean of Walton and I took Bishop David Sheppard because he was paying a visit to the Walton Deanery. Everton were away and Liverpool were at home, so I had no option but to take him to see Liverpool. Who should be sitting right in front of me? Ian Rush. It was when he had just come back from Juventus and what was used in the *Liverpool Echo* but a photo of him and there was me sat behind him clear as day. Well the amount of leg pulling I got from that one photo I can't begin to tell you. I even got a signed photo of him sent to me and you can tell where I keep that, can't you?

Barbara Garner: I went to the Charity Shield to see Everton play Liverpool in 1984. A wonderful year 1984, dream year. When you looked round Wembley, everybody was mixed in, Liverpool and Everton supporters, families mixed half and half. At the end both teams ran round together. We won, by the way. Both teams ran round the pitch together waving to the crowd – blue and red balloons went up. There was a terrific atmosphere between the two lots of supporters.

Bishop Tom Williams: My father was an Evertonian and he was aggressively anti Liverpool. I bought him a season ticket for his 25th Wedding Anniversary in about 1970 and there was only one game he wouldn't go to and that was the Derby. He wouldn't watch Liverpool. He said he wouldn't watch them even if they played in our street. He had a thing about it and his brother was the same way about Everton.

Laura Smith: I won't go out my way to go the derby because I just don't enjoy them. I've never ever been to Anfield in my life. I won't go. I'm never going to go. But I can remember when we were on our way down to Wembley in 2012 [for the FA Cup semi-final against Liverpool] there being like a police instructionto say that Everton and Liverpool would be separated, that you weren't allowed to drink together, and there'd be no drinking on the streets. That was never going to work because brothers were going down: one is Everton, the other Liverpool. It's not like London or anywhere where it's completely separate. You've got people in the same household who obviously support both teams and when we got there none of that happened. There was a mixture in the pubs everyone was taking the piss out of each other and it's all lighthearted. But for that 90 minutes it's pure hatred, and there's no other words for it.

Bishop Tom Williams: I was doing a funeral at Anfield Crematorium and it was due at 1pm. I got there at 12.55pm and the place is empty, no sign of anyone. The same at 1.10pm, 1.15pm, 1.20pm. Soon after, these cars came screeching up, and the funeral director, John Coyne comes in. 'Sorry we are late; this family wanted to drive around Anfield and three times down Anfield Road. I couldn't change their minds, and they want that song as they come in.' I said, 'Fine, no trouble with that.' Next, they bring in all these wreaths, and every wreath was a red and white football. The women were all in black with red blouses on and the men were in red shirts with black ties and they are playing 'You'll Never Walk Alone.' As they come in, a woman comes up to me and says, 'Alright Father will you do us a favour?' I said, 'Certainly.' She said, 'Could you mention he was a Liverpool supporter?' I replied, 'Well, do I need to say anything!' She said, 'Oh you're not a Blue, are you? Oh God, he'll be turning in his grave.' So I said, 'Well he's getting burnt in ten minutes.' There was a bit of humour there and she said, 'So you don't mind then?' I said, 'Not at all I love burying Liverpool supporters.' And half the congregation were saying, 'You tell her Father, she made us wear these bloody things; we're Evertonians.' About two years later I had the opposite. I went in and they had all the Everton stuff and they had a picture in front of the coffin of an Evertonian urinating on a Liverpool fan. I said, 'You can take that away for goodness sake.'

Denise Barrett-Baxendale: In my 46 years, I've never considered our club in the shadow of Liverpool Football Club. I intend to live my life out never ever considering it either, we are a pioneering club, we have and will continue to shape the game.

Z-Cars

Rev. Harry Ross: I have it on my mobile phone and it just stirs you when you hear it. I remember it on TV and never thought it would be Everton's tune. I've heard it at funerals, weddings and when my time comes it'll be at my funeral as it's been important to me as well. Z-Cars is Everton.

Eric Linford: We had a funeral at our church a few years back and the guy came in or went out to Z-Cars and someone said, 'Was he a policeman?' Well today it means we're not far from kick off

Barry Horne: I will never forget the first time I ran up the tunnel as an Everton player, and the first time I ran up the tunnel as Everton captain. When I go back now, when I hear it, it's bizarre, because it's a strange piece of music to make the hairs on the back of your neck stand up. But of course it's not the music, it's the association, isn't it?

Hana Roks: Wherever and whenever it's played I get shivers down my back. Whether it's at Goodison because that's where I've heard it first; or I've played it in my bedroom; or when Tony Bellew walked out to it; or at Wembley after we won against United; whether we are on our way to an away game we hear it; and we heard it at Watford because obviously they play it as well; or when someone's phone goes off – you hear that song and it's just unbelievable. It's been played since I was a kid and it's just associated with Everton and Everton means that much to me. At Goodison, especially, when it sounds like it's played on vinyl and you can hear the beat kicks in, there's nothing better.

Gary Jones: You've heard the expression that it chills your spine. Like anything else, when you're playing, I don't think you appreciate it as much as when you're finished.

John Parrott: It's fantastic, it's what it should be about. What are Watford doing with Z-Cars? It's got nothing to do with them, it was set in Kirkby, for goodness sake! Why, why why? It annoys me intensely when Watford come out to Z-Cars, it's not their song.

Bishop Tom Williams: It does a lot more than 'You'll Never Walk Alone'. I don't call it 'You'll Never Walk Alone' I always call it 'That song from Carousel.'

Pat Van Den Hauwe: What does Z-Cars do for me? Bugger all. People ask me that. You know when we went down that tunnel, was that thing playing? Well I didn't hear a fucking thing. I was in another world. I was thinking about the match.

Duncan McKenzie: You're in the tunnel and the guy switched the thing in the tunnel to turn on the music and you're thinking, 'Wow, here we go'. There was a bit of clarity involved in that as well, in terms of your mentality towards the game, because I played with lots of people who would be throwing up before the game, and they got really nervous.

Graham Stuart: Z-Cars means to me I'm walking down the tunnel, and I'm excited. The hairs on the back of my neck are standing up, and I'm going out to play for Everton Football Club. The first thing that comes into my mind is that I'm in the tunnel, as soon as I hear it, wherever I am. People have got it on their phones, and it just sends you back to the tunnel.

Kevin Sheedy: It means you're getting ready to go to battle, it means you're getting ready to get into the best arena. The noise and the music as you come up the steps, you can hear it building up and building up. When you hit the top step and come out it's a brilliant environment, and obviously Z-Cars is the theme.

Laura Smith: There's goosebumps every time, even if someone's phone goes off when you're on the train. When we went to Lisbon there were thousands of us in a square the night before the game it was absolutely pouring down. In fact it was raining upwards it was that bad, but there were these three fellas in the middle of the square with a ghettoblaster and they were playing Z-Cars and everyone was singing it, so that was it then for the rest of the night.

Peter Clarke: When you get in the tunnel and you can hear Z-Cars it always gives you a buzz. You feel like anything is possible and you get the hair standing up on the back of your neck.

Terry Darracott: I loved that. That was part and parcel of your day, to run onto that and hear the crowd; they loved it. And they still play it now.

Colin Harvey: My wife Maureen came to a game with me a couple of months ago. I think my grandson was playing a game so he couldn't go and my other two daughters have got season tickets, so they were alright. So I said, 'Come the game.' She said, 'I haven't been the game for years.' So when we went out and sat down about ten minutes before kick-off, and obviously when Z-Cars came on, she said 'Blinking heck, I can feel the hairs on the back of my neck! I haven't heard that for years!' It does that to you, without doubt.

The Everton Faith: Reflections On Royal Blue Identity

'My Dad was an Evertonian. My mum was an Evertonian. Both my grandfathers – although I never met them – were Evertonians. What else was I going to be? It is the greatest gift I've ever received. And the greatest gift I've given. My son is an Evertonian.'

Graham Ennis, *Editor, When Skies Are Grey.*

Jon Woods: You didn't have a choice. The first word I ever spoke, and the first word I listened to on what was then called the wireless, was 'Everton'.

David France: You've got that companion with you through life, and for me and a lot of us, it is an important thing to have. It adds joy and matures you, unless you're a glory hunter, and I can't imagine what that's like. It adds something to your life that no one can take away. I'm thrilled that my Dad made me an Evertonian. I've always said that the pursuit of happiness – one of the American ideals – is a great cause of unhappiness. It's the pursuit of fulfilment, and when you have Everton in your life you're fulfilled. It enriches you it, it develops your character and qualities that prepare you for life.

Hana Roks: The Everton experience has been, for me, a rollercoaster ride. I hope things are changing now but we've had some terrible horrific times, like getting beat by Shrewsbury in the cup. I love going to the games. I love being with my mates, my family, going home and away, abroad with Everton. I'll always do it. My wife, Tasha, has got Everton tattooed on her arm, she goes to all the games, she's got a season ticket. She knows it's a big thing in my life and it's a big thing in her life so it's like something we do together. She'd been to Goodison but I took her to her first away game. It's a big part of our lives. Most of our friendship circle is mostly all Everton, most of my best friends all follow Everton. You get people who say, 'I haven't seen my mates for months. I think it's a great pleasure to see my mates every week. Whether we win lose or draw, we are in it together and the emotions are indescribable. I know people on our coach and Everton is their life and without it they would be really lonely people and the people on the coach they're their family. Everton is really special and, I know it's really biased, but I think we are like no other football club.

Rev. Harry Ross: I never ever thought that I would build up such a relationship when I was only a youngster. Seeing all the players, they were just far away from me. Now that I know them all and have got to know the club and how it works, I see the human side of it. It makes such a difference and I thank God that I was called to be the vicar of St Luke's. I was there for 33 years and I'm still the Chaplain of Goodison Park after 40 years. It's been a great privilege.

Denise Barrett-Baxendale: Coming back in 2010 to the club, it was late January. I was in the community office, and it was very late, probably about half seven at night. I was going home, I'd had a very busy day. I had an office with no windows at the time, so I'd been in the office since very early in the morning until very late that night. And as I walked up the stairs into the stadium the floodlights were on, and it had been snowing all day, the pitch was covered in a white blanket of snow. That will always be one of the most magnificent memories for me. I couldn't get my phone out quickly enough to take a photograph. It was a once in a lifetime opportunity to view my club and the internal workings of the club in the most romantic way. To some people it may sound ridiculous, but to me it was just beautiful to see the pitch snow white and the floodlights down, it was haunting. I walked up past the pitch and thought, 'Wow, I'm a girl from the city...' I'd been away to university and got my qualifications and had always been committed to coming back to work in the city because when I was educated in the city and when I was a young girl in this city, graduates left, and they didn't come back to Liverpool. It wasn't a place, sadly – politically and economically – to stay. I'd always committed – I wanted – to come back to my city; I wanted to invest back into Liverpool whatever skills and qualifications I had. However, I never thought for one minute I would be doing that at my club.

Eric Moonman: When you think about your own lifestyle, what's your *raison d'etre*? It's going to be your family and with me, as a Labour MP, it was socialism. But underpinning all that was Everton.

Denise Barrett-Baxendale: I've got a very romantic association, a love affair, isn't it? It's something that you're obsessive about. You wake up in the morning and it is the first thing you think about, it's the last thing you think about before you go to sleep at night. This is such a special place to be. The staff who work here are incredible, everybody shares a common purpose – wanting the best for Everton. To have the opportunity to influence how we deliver the games for our fans, the experience of the game for our fans, or to discuss things about building a community through Everton in the Community programmes, it's just amazing to have that privilege, they are opportunities that people dream of. What Evertonian wouldn't want the chance to work at this football club?

Graham Ennis: My Dad was an Evertonian. My mum was an Evertonian. Both my grandfathers – although I never met them – were Evertonians. What else was I going to be? It is the greatest gift I've ever received. And the greatest gift I've given. My son is an Evertonian.

Danny Cadamarteri: My overall feelings for Everton FC are totally summed up by the fact that I've got Nil Satis Nisi Optimum tattooed on my arm. It's become a part of me from when I was a kid. I left West Yorkshire as a young kid to embark on a dream and moved into a family of Scousers who were Evertonians and became, as people would say, a 'Born-again Evertonian'. It's part of the blood, isn't it?

Tony Kay: I still can't believe it, that people, after all this time, 50 years, that they still stop me in the street and say, 'Tony, come down and see me and say hello.' One match I went into a pub near the ground, The Brick I think it's called, and I went in there. I was having a drink, and these two old fellas, must have been 70, twins, and they were all kissing me and hugging me. I think to myself 'I must have been a better player than I thought I was, I can't believe all this adulation, it's incredible'. But that's what Evertonians are.

Becky Tallentire: I guess that every fan feels the same thing, because they would say, 'This is our gang and it's very tribal, and we've been through all this together.' But it seems that when players come here they kind of back that up and say, 'I've played at such-and-such a place, but Everton is always going to have a special place in my heart.' They're outsiders looking in, if you will, and you don't seem to hear the same accolades from players who play at other clubs. It seems at Everton it always touches the players, and they always have that bond and connection. You can see that at the former players' nights when they all come back. I don't know what it is. There must be something there that makes it true.

Lee Carsley: The best thing I can say is that people always know me by what I did at Everton in my career; it's almost like I only played for Everton. They forget that I played for Derby, Blackburn, Coventry, Birmingham, and I'm really proud of that. Everton was by far the best time of my career, with the best fans, at the best stage as well. At one point we had a really, really good team, a solid Premier League team that was exciting to watch and resilient, with good characters as well. It was a special time for myself and I'm sure for a lot of the other lads as well.

Tony Cottee: The Evertonians were fantastic. I did, and still have, a great rapport with the Evertonians. They could have not have been any nicer to me, they could not have made me feel any more welcome. I think a lot of the reason for that is that Cockneys and Scousers are very similar in terms of being working class people, they work hard during the week, they pay good money to watch their football and they want to be entertained. They've got a great sense of humour and the Evertonians were always brilliant to me. I go back to the club, albeit once a season now if I'm lucky because I'm living so far away, but I always get looked after and the fans are so kind to me. I don't ever, ever regret signing for Everton Football Club. I wish I could have achieved more and I wished I could have scored my 100th goal, but I don't regret signing for the club. It was a fantastic experience.

Elizabeth France: Supporting Everton Football Club has never been easy but has provided some of the best times of my life thanks to the camaraderie of the Everton family. During the good times and especially the not-so-good times, our beloved club is supported by some of the finest people on earth. The fidelity, compassion and generosity of spirit of the Blues who follow the club across the globe irrespective of the team's fortunes coupled with the dedication of the enthusiasts, plus the fact that we have a die-hard Blue as chairman and local lads in the starting line-up and pushing for places in the first-team squad make us extra-special in this day and age. This leads me to my other half's farewell dinner at Liverpool Anglican Cathedral in late-2016. I can picture him standing in front of the High Altar and explaining what Everton means to him before inviting others to do likewise. Subsequently, directors, ex-players, shareholders, season-ticket holders, international fans, Everton authors, blue-blooded journalists and even a reformed Category C hooligan provided equally heartwarming speeches. When it came to my turn, I joked, 'Behind every good Evertonian is a woman rolling her eyes.' Then asked the ladies in the gathering, 'Why do we allow something we can't control impact our lives to the extent that it does? Could it be that Everton family is the type of community that people advocate but rarely experience? If so, I'm delighted to be accepted as one of us.'

Mick Lyons: I had a season ticket from the age of about nine, and me and my brother used to get into the ground at about 1:45pm. We used to stand in the old Paddock. I was very lucky to be given the chance to play for my home team and then it was a massive honour to be made captain. All I ever do these days is wear Everton shirts. My mate's the kitman and he always gets me the latest shirt. I live in Australia now and I've always got the shirt on.

Michael Lecluyse: I compare Everton to having a wife. In the beginning you just fall in love and accept everything that's wrong, then you have your bad times – like we had with Martinez – but it's still your wife you still support it and you still get behind it. You still support your club whatever happens and you only remember the good times; that's what you should do. Everton for me is still pure magic. I don't go on holiday for example; I just want to save money to go back to Everton, because that is my holiday, even if it's only a weekend. It's just to belong back there because it's everything.

Paul Power: I absolutely adored my time at Everton. People said it was an Indian summer to my career, which it definitely was. To win the league and then to win the supporters' player of the year award. I really enjoyed my time. I enjoyed working with people like Howard and Colin, Terry Darracott, Mick Lyons, who were, in my opinion, great people. We had a great camaraderie amongst the coaching staff, as much as the players did when everything was going well. I absolutely loved it. Even though I've always been – since four years old – a Manchester City fan, and then played for City for thirteen years and led them out at Wembley. I just loved my time at Everton.

Pat Nevin: Everton fans were always brilliant to me, and are still extraordinarily welcoming, and I still meet a lot of Everton fans who say I was one of the players they really enjoyed watching play. You know this old School of Science thing, what Everton fans wanted was a cultured win. They like to win, but they want a cultured win as well and you could kind of feel that. The expectation was slightly different to certain other clubs; at other clubs they didn't give a stuff how you won. Everton fans obviously wanted an ugly win now and again, but there was something else in there, and I admired and liked that, and reacted to it.

Graham Stuart: It's still the best football club in the world for me. The people of Everton Football club are exceptional. There's still the same feeling around the place, the same sense of friendliness. That was epitomised to me the first time I spoke to Howard Kendall. This is a proper, proper football club. Not only is it a proper football club, it's a proper football club that's surrounded by good people, and I think that's more important than the football itself in some respects; the manner that Everton football club is thought of around the world is the most important thing to me.

Neil Pointon: Everton made me. It gave me all the insights that I wanted to get in football, it pushed me right up to the top level. It gave me something that nobody could give me in life, which is a League Championship medal. I loved my time at Everton, met some smashing people. I still go back, see the stadium, listen to the music coming down the tunnel, hairs on the back of my neck go up every time.

Kevin Sheedy: Everton have given me everything. They've given me my best moments in the professional game. I'm just so fortunate to be able to play so long in great teams, to have won trophies, and just to have left memories for people that enjoy the team and my performances. It is ust an absolutely privilege to have played and to have coached there.

Gary Stevens: I was very very fortunate to come down to Everton because it's a terrific club. To be part of such a successful side meant the world and the fans who watched would always support the club. In some way we've given the modern day side a bit of a problem because those fans are always going to want the same. And I don't think there will be another side like that Everton, because we were all UK based and it was nice there was a lot of Liverpool born players so the fans could recognise that. When you go back to the club and you appreciate how well you're thought of it's quite nice.

Pat Hart: I'd put my time supporting Everton in three sections: up until 1990 and Harvey's best season; then the decline, briefly illuminated by Joe Royle; then Moyes onwards. I thought the club was a different animal under Moyes, at least there was life there. The club was dying before Moyes, in various different stages and various different levels of doom, but I always separate them in my head. I'm glad that the best times happened when I was a child, when things are going to be more magical anyway. Maybe you could say that it hasn't helped in that I've always got those standards set back then. But life's never always going to be perfect. It's great to have experienced those moments of joy. I can deal with the dark times. You've got to do that anyway in life.

Derek Mountfield: I'm a local lad who got lucky, an Everton supporter who lived the dream, playing football and then signing for the team he'd supported all his life. People say 'What's your greatest achievement ever?' I say, 'You can play in FA Cup finals, European finals but I've got a piece of paper. It's a contract that says Derek Mountfield has signed for Everton Football Club.' That was good enough for me. What I did after that was a complete and utter bonus. Just that contract that says I'm an Everton player, on £125 a week, was enough for me.

Graeme Sharp: People can be attached to a football club and say this and that, and sing its praises, but

I do think Everton is special. This is a special place. It's just got something about it, a family feel, and the right passion and desire and demands. Sometimes fighting against all odds, everybody sticking together, and that's the most important thing. When I first came down, and Jim Greenwood put the contract in front of us, and I didn't know what to do, my Dad turned around and said, 'This is a proper football club. This seems like a proper football club that will look after you.' He was absolutely spot on – from the top to the bottom, it was a proper football club.

Graeme White: Everton Football Club is the best club in the world. I hold them dear to my heart and have done so since five years of age. I lost my Dad recently and he was the reason I became an Everton fan. When we walked into the church we carried him in to Z-Cars. Everton Football Club means a lot because every time I think of them I think of my Dad and when I think of my Dad I think of Everton, so Everton will be with me until I leave this world. Everton has brought me so many memories and so many friends and that's most important because most of my dear friends I've found through being a fan or working there. I also met my wife after being persuaded by an Everton colleague to go out after a match and our three children are all Everton fans.

Laura Smith: I don't know whether it's just because I am an Evertonian but I feel like it's different to any other club. I think that Everton as a club does more for the fans than any other club seems to do. I think they really realise that the fans are the club.

Mike Pejic: I look back with happiness and sadness really, because I felt like I would have ended my career there on a better note of playing hundreds of games for them and winning trophies. I hope I just gave the fans what they wanted to see, and they hold true to my heart, the fans of Everton, they really do. It was a great sadness that I had to leave.

Andy Gray: How do I look back on it? Gloriously. I can't look back on any time at Everton without a smile on my face. The moment I walked through the door, to the minute I got my first goal, to the minute we got to the cup final for the first time, to the minute we clinched the league and then won a European trophy, to the disappointment of losing to United at Wembley and that amazing journey home after the FA Cup final in 1984. That will live with me forever.

John Parrott: Howard summed it up: it's a marriage, isn't it? It's something that never goes away. It doesn't matter where it is or where I go. I remember being in Thailand. We were playing a cup quarter-final against Newcastle at home in the FA Cup and it was about 3am and Dave Watson scored in front of the Gwladys Street. 1-0, and I was shouting 'Yes, yes, yes!' and then I realised where I was. I was in Thailand in a bedroom and I thought, 'I think I better shut up now.' That's what Everton does to you.

Roger Bennett: It's been the greatest gift. It's the core of my identity. It is, I think, the greatest gift any father, any parents could give their child. I've got four kids who've grown up in New York and as a father I've worked quite hard on many things and there's nothing harder than making sure that all four of them are loyal dedicated Evertonians. It is very hard from afar, when Americans have the impulse to support the best. We want to support the best but my kids are all Evertonians and that is so important to me. I tell you what the values of the club are: collective endeavour, loyalty, tenacity and passion. Those four values to me are the most important; they all transcend football; they're the most important values in life and that's why I love Everton. They are less a club being an Evertonian, it's more a way of viewing life in which honour counts as much as glory. I've got a feeling the glory is about to come but within that reality you constantly create reasons to refresh, to restock your optimism. Being so gullibly optimistic I do believe that Everton will be amongst the leading clubs.

Alan Irvine: Everton's my club, and my family are all Evertonians now. It's the first result I look out for. I still have friends there in all different areas of the club. I love going back. Every time I go back I get welcomed in a way that's very humbling. The fans are brilliant with me whenever I walk down the street. It's a very special club for me. I wouldn't have left management to go back to any other academy other than Everton, and it's a brilliant club. I don't know the new owners; I hope that doesn't change the club in any way. I know that people will say, 'Hold on we want some money to buy players'. If that's the only way it changes then great, that's a positive. But Everton's been a special club, it's been a club that's done things with a load of class and a load of dignity. I think under the leadership of Bill Kenwright it's been a great club, certainly a fantastic club to work for, and I wouldn't like to see any of that being lost.

Bill Kenwright: Everton gave me a sense of safety. If you're in love or you have a relationship, you can't describe it, can you? It's difficult to say what that one person, that one thing, what that one moment, gives to you that nothing else does. And nothing but nothing in my life has got near it; not near it. It's like when I listen to certain songs of the time, or certain movies; I don't see the movie, I see where I saw the movie. Whether it was the Kensington, the Casino, the Lido, and when I heard the song. The Boys' Pen was rowdy, and it was a pen. It was like you see the hideous cages that they have animals in in zoos. It was a cage; a great big cage. And it was rowdy. There were fights. But I used to go there every week and feel at home, and safe. On my own – I didn't go with anyone. I never for one second felt scared, worried. And fights would happen round about me and I'd go, 'Yeah, fine.' I was a little boy, young boy. If I couldn't afford it, when the gates would open with 20 minutes to go, I'd wait, and I'd go in for the 20 minutes, or if I couldn't afford the whole money there was a half-time gate, and I used to go to the half-time gate, stand outside. It was like, and still is, a drug. It just pulled me towards it. Like Harry Potter's magic wand, Goodison just pulled me.

Derek Temple: It's the history, isn't it? It's the history of the club. School of Science, always known for the quality. Always had great players. The fans: they're very loyal, Everton fans. I think it is true: once a blue always a blue, you don't change. And you stick with them. You stick with them through thick and thin. I still go and watch the boys, and they are inclined to disappoint an awful lot. But, there will be other times when they turn it on and it is great.

Denise Barrett-Baxendale: It's one of those things that's addictive, it's compulsive, it's impulsive. It's irrational at times. It is that thing that is passion. It's about a passionate connection with something and then sharing that. When Z-Cars plays on a Saturday, and sharing that with the people in the stadium through the highs and the lows, people holding their face, people screaming and shouting. All of that emotion and passion just drives you on. It's that thing that makes you think, 'Wow, what a privileged position I'm in, and thank you to all the Evertonians and the participants on our programme that get behind us and support the club.' There are people that literally give their last penny for this football club, and we don't forget that. That's something that our staff are reminded of every day, and our staff understand. They're from the city; they're Evertonians. They are people who know what it means to be the first to get your shirt, or to be out there asking a player to sign a programme. They understand what drives Evertonians, and I hope that that comes across to

Evertonians with every interaction they have with the club.

Joshua Corbett: When I go to Goodison or even if I'm far away, knowing that I support the club makes me feel part of something, as if I'm always with a group of friends.

John Hurst: Unless you've done it you'll never understand it. It's just one of the great experiences not only playing but running out onto the pitch being met by that noise and knowing that there's sixty odd thousand just wanting you to do well. It was a great feeling.

Lennart Roth: Everton is more than a football club. It is a way to live your life. Strive for perfection in what you do but ensure that you care for the less fortunate.

Colin Harvey: I grew up an Evertonian, and I used to watch the game from the boys' pen. If somebody said to me, 'You're going to end up playing there, and they're going to end up building a statue of you' you'd think, 'Ah, don't be stupid'. Stood in the boys' pen, herded in with a load of other kids, to actually go on and play – which was the best part of it. You don't want to grow up being a manager or coach, you want to be a footballer but then to coach and manage and go back another time, it's just been absolutely amazing.

Father John Ashton: If God supported a football team would he be an Evertonian? I think he'd have to be, wouldn't he? He's the only one who knows where they are at.

Who's Who

Interviews

Alan Ainscow: Everton player, 1981-83.

Niclas Alexandersson: Everton player 2000-03.

Daniel Amokachi: Everton player, 1994-96.

Joe Anderson: Everton supporter from the 1960s. Mayor of Liverpool 2012-.

Stuart Appleby: Everton supporter from the 1990s.

Father John Ashton: Everton supporter from the 1930s.

Ray Atteveld: Everton player, 1989-92.

George Bailey: Everton supporter from the 1900s. Founder of Everton's first officially recognised supporters club and Goodison steward.

John Bailey: Everton player 1979-85.

Michael Ball: Everton player, 1997-2001.

Stuart Barlow: Everton player, 1991-95.

Denise Barrett-Baxendale: Everton supporter from the 1970s; club official and board member from the 2010s.

Jose Baxter: Everton player, 2008-12.

Roger Bennett: Everton supporter from the 1970s.

June Bernicoff: Football 'widow' from the 1950s.

Leon Bernicoff: Everton supporter from the 1950s.

Clyde Best: West Ham player, 1968-76.

John Blain: Chairman, Everton Shareholders Association, 2012-.

Tom (Tiny) Bradshaw: Liverpool player, 1930-37.

Cliff Britton: Everton player 1930-39; manager 1948-56

Eric Brown: Everton supporter from the 1950s.

Rachel Brown-Finnis: Everton Ladies player, 2003-14.

Charles Buchan: Arsenal and Sunderland player, 1909-28.

Matt Busby: Manchester City player, 1928-36.

W.J. Byton: Everton supporter from the 1880s.

Danny Cadamarteri: Everton player, 1997-2002.

Kevin Campbell: Everton player, 1999-2005.

Lee Carsley: Everton player, 2002-08.

Raich Carter: Sunderland player, 1931-39.

Aarkash Chandan: Everton supporter from the 1990s.

Amanda Chatterton: Everton in the Community official since the 2010s.

Peter Clarke: Everton player, 2001-03.

Wayne Clarke: Everton player, 1987-89.

W. R. Clayton: Everton supporter from the 1880s and longstanding director and committeeman.

Brendan Connolly: Everton supporter from the 1960s; chairman of the EFC Heritage Society.

Andrew Corbett: Everton supporter from the 1980s.

Eleanor Corbett: Everton supporter from the 2010s.

Rev. Henry Corbett: Chaplain to Bellefield and Finch Farm from the 1980s.

John Corbett: Everton supporter from the 1960s.

Joshua Corbett: Everton supporter from the 2010s.

Tony Cottee: Everton player, 1988-94.

Warney Cresswell: Everton player, 1927-35

Sam Crosbie: Everton supporter from the 1880s.

Will Cuff: Everton supporter from the 1880s; shareholder, director, secretary, chairman (1922-1938); Football League President.

Terry Darracott: Everton player, 1968-79.

Frank D'Arcy: Everton player, 1966-71.

Dave McDougall: Everton supporter from the 1960s.

William Ralph 'Dixie' Dean: Everton player, 1925-37.

Sylvain Distin: Everton player, 2009-15.

Martin Dobson: Everton player, 1974-79.

Willie Donachie: Everton assistant manager, 1994-97.

Millie Donovan: Wife of Everton's 1950s full back, Don Donovan.

Natasha Dowie: Everton Ladies player 2007-12.

Carena Duffy: Everton in the Community official from the 2000s.

Richard Dunne: Everton player 1996-2000.

Peter Eastoe: Everton player, 1979-82.

Becky Easton: Everton Ladies player from the 2000s.

John Ebbrell: Everton player, 1987-97. Youth coach, 2015-present.

Ernest 'Bee' Edwards: Liverpool Echo sports editor in the early-twentieth century.

Graham Ennis: Editor, When Skies are Grey Fanzine.

Adam Farley: Everton player 1999.

Alec Farrall: Everton player, 1953-57.

Gareth Farrelly: Everton player, 1997-99.

Matthew Foy: Everton in the Community official from the 2010s.

David France: Everton supporter from the 1950s. Author, and founder of the Everton Former Players' Foundation and the Everton Collection.

Elizabeth France: Football widow and supporter of many Everton-related endeavours.

Jimmy Gabriel: Everton player, 1960-67. Coach, 1990s.

Mick Gannon: Everton player, 1962.

Tom Gardner: Everton player, 1947.

Barbara Garner: Everton supporter from the 1950s.

Davide Ghilardi: Everton supporter

Gerry Glover: Everton player, 1965-66.

Arthur Goddard: Liverpool player 1902-14.

Cathy Gore: Everton Ladies player from the 1990s.

Tony Grant: Everton player 1995-2000.

Lord Grantchester: Everton director from the 1990s.

Andy Gray: Everton player, 1983-85.

Colin Green: Everton player, 1960-62.

Norman Greenhalgh: Everton player, 1938-48.

Victor Hall: Everton supporter from the 1880s.

Bryan Hamilton: Everton player 1975-77.

Sam Hardy: Liverpool player 1905-12.

Maria Harper: Leasowe Pacific player from the 1980s.

David Hart: Everton supporter from the 1950s.

Patrick Hart: Everton supporter from the 1980s.

Simon Hart: Everton supporter from the 1980s.

Jimmy Harris: Everton player, 1955-60.

Colin Harvey: Everton player 1963-74. Coach, assistant manager, youth coach 1976-2003. Manager 1987-90.

Joe Hewitt: Liverpool player, 1904-10.

Tony Hibbert: Everton player, 2001-15.

Dave Hickson: Everton player, 1951-55 & 1957-59.

Mark Higgins: Everton player, 1976-83.

Andy Hinchcliffe: Everton player 1990-97.

Michelle Hinnigan: Everton Ladies player 2007-17.

Barry Horne: Everton player, 1992-95.

Tim Howard: Everton player 2006-16.

Eric Howell: Everton supporter from the 2000s. Host of the Followtonians podcast.

Mike Hughes: Journalist and Broadcaster from the 1980s.

Gerry Humphreys: Everton player, 1966-69.

John Hurst: Everton player, 1965-76. Youth team coach 1994-97.

Jimmy Husband: Everton player, 1965-73.

Gary Imlach: Everton supporter from the 1960s.

Alan Irvine: Everton player, 1981-84; assistant manager 2002-07; academy director 2011-14.

Billy Jackson: Co-founder and manager of Leasowe Pacific/Everton Ladies.

Iain Jenkins: Everton player, 1991-92.

Lee Johnson: Everton in the Community official from the 2010s.

Lindsay Johnson: Everton Ladies player 2003-15.

Peter Johnson: Everton chairman 1994-98.

Gary Jones: Everton player, 1971-76.

T.G. Jones: Everton player, 1936-49.

Andrei Kanchelskis: Everton player, 1995-97.

Tony Kay: Everton player, 1963-64.

Thomas Keates: Everton supporter from the 1880s and the club's first historian.

Tony Kellaher: Everton supporter from the 1960s, trustee of the Everton Former Players Foundation.

Dave Kelly: Everton supporter from the 1960s Fan activist.

Howard Kendall: Everton player 1967-74; manager 1981-87, 1990-93, 1997-98.

Bill Kenwright: Everton director 1989-; Chairman 2004-.

Dan Kirkwood: Everton player 1889-91. Chairman 1909-10.

Archie Knox: Everton assistant manager 1998-2002.

Fred Kwong: Everton supporter from the 1980s.

Charles Lambert: Journalist from the 1970s.

Bob Latchford: Everton player, 1974-81.

David Lawson: Everton player, 1972-77.

Tommy Lawton: Everton player, 1937-45.

Michael Lecluyse: Everton supporter.

Gordon Lee: Everton manager, 1977-81.

Dave Lewis: Everton Head of Stadium Safety and Security.

Joleon Lescott: Everton player 2006-09.

Anders Limpar: Everton player 1994-97.

Eric Linford: Everton supporter from the 1950s.

Paul Lodge: Everton player, 1981-82.

Jan Loudin: Everton supporter from the 1990s

Mick Lyons: Everton player, 1971-82. Coach, 1987-90.

Keith Marley: Everton Ladies manager and coach.

Mo Marley: Everton Ladies player 1988-2002; manager 2002-12.

Dr David Marsh: Everton chairman, 1991-94.

Nigel Martyn: Everton player, 2003-06.

Cliff Marshall: Everton player, 1975.

Jimmy Martin: Everton coach driver 1979-90; kit manager 1990-present.

Roberto Martinez: Everton manager 2013-16.

Derek Mayers: Everton player, 1953-57.

Andrea McGrady: Leasowe Pacific and Everton Ladies player from the 1990s.

Jimmy McDougall: Liverpool player, 1928-38.

Duncan McKenzie: Everton player, 1976-78.

John McNally: Everton supporter from the 1930s.

Phil McNulty: Journalist from the 1980s.

Tony McNamara: Everton player, 1951-57.

Mick Meagan: Everton player, 1957-64.

Joe Mercer: Everton player, 1933-46.

Charles Mills: Everton supporter from the 1950s.

Charles Mills senior: Everton supporter from the 1920s.

Peter Mills: Everton supporter from the 1960s.

Eric Moonman: Everton supporter from the 1930s.

Henry Mooney: Everton supporters from the 1960s; club official from the 2000s.

Gerry Moore: Everton supporter from the 1950s.

Johnny Morrissey: Everton player 1963-72.

James Mossop: Journalist from the 1960s.

Derek Mountfield: Everton player, 1983-88.

David Moyes: Everton manager 2002-13.

Alan Myers: Everton supporter from the 1970s. Press officer, 1996-2001. Director of communications, 2013-15.

Thomas Myhre: Everton player, 1997-2001.

Henry Newton: Everton player, 1970-73.

Pat Nevin: Everton player, 1988-91.

Len Norman: Everton supporter from
the 1930s.

Geoff Nulty: Everton player, 1978-80.
Coach 1980-81.

Emy Onoura: Everton supporter from the 1970s.

George Orr: Everton supporter from the 1950s.

Leon Osman: Everton player, 2003-16.

Arthur Parker: Everton supporter from
the 1950s; brother of John-Willie Parker.

Joe Parkinson: Everton player 1994-97.

Roy Parnell: Everton player, 1961-63.

John Parrott: Everton supporter from the 1970s.

Simon Paul: Everton supporter from the 1980s;
Editor nsno.co.uk.

Jim Pearson: Everton player, 1974-78.

Mike Pejic: Everton player, 1977-78.

Fred Pickering: Everton player, 1964-67.

Steven Pienaar: Everton player 2007-11
& 2012-16.

Alessandro Pistone: Everton player, 2000-05.

Neil Pointon: Everton player, 1985-90.

Paul Power: Everton player, 1986-88;
coach 1988-90.

Dave Prentice: Journalist from the 1980s.

Preki: Everton player, 1992-94.

Tomasz Radzinski: Everton player 2001-04.

Alex Raisbeck: Liverpool player 1898-1909.

Kevin Ratcliffe: Everton player, 1979-91.

Kenny Rea: Everton player, 1956-58.

Paul Rideout: Everton player, 1992-97.

Stuart Rimmer: Everton player, 1982-83.

Hana Roks: Everton supporter from the 1990s.

Rev. Harry Ross: Chaplain to Goodison Park.

Trevor Ross: Everton player 1977-83.

Lennart Roth: Everton supporter
from the 1980s.

Steve Round: Everton assistant manager,
2008-13.

Joe Royle: Everton player 1966-74;
manager 1994-97.

Dolly Sagar: Wife of Ted Sagar.

Ted Sagar: Everton player, 1929-53.

Louis Saha: Everton player, 2008-12.

June Scott: Goodison local resident
from the 1950s.

Graeme Sharp: Everton player, 1979-91.

Jack Sharp: Everton player 1899-1910.

George Sharples: Everton player 1960-63.

John Shearon: Founder of the Ruleteros.

Kevin Sheedy: Everton player, 1982-91.
Youth coach, 2006-17.

Laura Smith: Everton supporter from the 1990s.

Walter Smith: Everton manager, 1998-2002.

Ian Snodin: Everton player, 1987-94.

Neville Southall: Everton player, 1981-97.

Andy Spence: Everton Ladies manager 2012-.

Mavis Spurgin: Goodison local resident
from the 1940s.

Gary Stevens: Everton player, 1981-88.

Alec Stevenson: Everton player, 1934-49.

Per Malmqvist Stolt: Everton supporter
from the 1970s.

Graham Stuart: Everton player, 1994-98.

Alan Stubbs: Everton player, 2001-05 &
2006-08. Coach, 2008-14.

John Sutherland: Everton player, 1956-57.

Ted Sutton: Everton official from the 1980s.
Founder of Everton in the Community.

Becky Tallentire: Everton supporter from
the 1960s; author.

Keith Tamlin: Evertonian, lawyer and
Everton director from the 1970s.

George Telfer: Everton player, 1973-81.

Derek Temple: Everton player, 1955-67.

Sergey Tomashevskii: Everton supporter
from the 1990s.

Dave Thomas: Everton player, 1977-79.

Louise Thomas: Leasowe Pacific and
Everton Ladies player from the 1980s.

Mike Trebilcock: Everton player, 1966-68.

David Unsworth: Everon player 1992-97 & 1998-2004. Coach and under-23 manager, 2013-present.

Pat Van Den Hauwe: Everton player, 1984-89.

Dave Watson: Everton player, 1986-2000.

Ric Wee: Everton supporter from the 1980s.

David Weir: Everton player 1999-2006.

Norman Whiteside: Everton player, 1989-90.

Jack Wildman: Everton supporter from the 1880s.

Bishop Tom Williams: Everton supporter from the 1950s

Dick White: Everton supporter from the 1920s.

Graeme White: Everton Stadium Announcer, 2003-.

Graham Williams: Everton player, 1956-59.

Jon Woods: Everton director from 2000.

Tommy Wright: Everton player, 1964-73.

Note: Playing careers are measured from a player's first team debut to their final game for Everton.

Bibliography

Every part of this book from 1946 onwards is based on original interviews, the vast majority carried out for this book. James Corbett collaborated with Howard Kendall, Neville Southall, Dave Hickson and Bob Latchford on their autobiographies and their contributions are taken from dozens hours of transcripts from the production of those books. The late Tony McNamara and Tom Gardner were also interviewed as part of Dave Hickson's autobiography, *The Cannonball Kid*. The quotes attributed to Paul Rideout came from an interview James Corbett conducted for *FourFourTwo* magazine in 2008. The interviews with Gary Stevens and Mike Trebilcock were conducted by Philip Ross and Gerry Moore on behalf of the Everton Former Players Foundation. The late and much missed Charles Mills senior and Dick White were interviewed for *Everton: The School of Science*. Joe Anderson and Dave Kelly were interviewed by my colleague, Simon Hughes, for *On The Brink*. The other 200 interviewees spoke for the express purposes of this work.

The passage of time has meant that there are few alive who witnessed Everton prior to the Second World War and surviving players only have careers extending back to the mid-1950s. As such, the chapter, The Making of a Modern Football Club is based on primary and secondary research across a range of sources. These are listed here:

Books

Corbett, James, **The Everton Encyclopedia** [deCoubertin Books, 2012]

Corbett, James, **Everton: The School of Science** [deCoubertin Books, 2010]

France, David & Prentice, David, **Virgin Blues** [Skript, 2003]

Johnson, Steve, **Everton: The Official Complete Record** [deCoubertin Books, 2015]

Keates, Thomas, **History of Everton Football Club, 1878-1928** [Desert Island Books, 1998]

Keith, John, **Dixie Dean: The Inside Story of a Soccer Icon,** [Robson Books, 2001]

McVay, David and Smith, Andy, **The Complete Centre Forward, The Life of Tommy Lawton** [Sportsbooks, 2000]

Orr, George, **Everton FC Champions 1914-15 'Over The Top'** [Lulu, 2014]

Platt, Mark, **The Red Journey: Liverpool An Oral History** [deCoubertin Books, 2017]

Sawyer, Rob, **Harry Catterick: The Untold Story of a Football Great** [deCoubertin Books, 2014]

Sawyer, Rob, **T.G. Jones: The Prince of Centre Halves: The Life of T.G. Jones** [deCoubertin Books, 2017]

Smith, Billy, **The Blue Correspondence [3 vols]** [Countryvise, 2007-10]

Tallentire, Becky, **Real Footballers Wives** [Mainstream, 2012]

Publications

Websites

The Athletic News

Everton Official Matchday Programme

The Illustrated Sporting and Dramatic News

Lancashire Daily Post

Liverpool Mercury

Liverpool Echo & Evening Express

Liverpool Daily Post

The Wellington Journal and Shrewsbury News

Bluecorrespondent.co.uk

Britishnewspaperarchive.co.uk

Toffeeweb.com

Evertonresults.com

Acknowledgements

My role in Faith of our Families is as its curator; someone who shaped and crafted around 2 million words of interviews and historical documents into a book. It was a colossal undertaking, but would have been nothing without the 200 or so players, managers, directors, chairmen, members of the media, club officials and fans who consented to be interviewed for this book. First and foremost, each and every one of them is owed a debt of gratitude for giving freely of their time and making this book what it is.

The Reverend Harry Ross was instrumental working behind the scenes, opening his contacts book, talking up the project, gently cajoling people to put themselves forward for interview and even proof-reading as we entered the last mad days of production. His 40 years as chaplain to Goodison Park has been characterised by his kindness, dedication to his mission (both the church and Everton) and hard work. These virtues are carried on by his son Philip who carried out or assisted with many of the interviews that formed the raw data of this book. His diligence, persistence, love and knowledge of Everton FC, as well as his excellence as an interviewer helped carry this project forward and enabled this work to be a more ambitious and wide-ranging book than I could ever have imagined. He also had a detective's knack of finding long lost gems relating to Everton's distant past in archives. Thank you also to Andrew and the rest of the Ross family for all that they have done.

My colleague, Jack Gordon Brown, shared many of these virtues and roles, and, in his first job in the media, handled himself like one of the old pros that he himself interviewed. Again, his ambition and persistence really added another dimension to this book. In particular he deserves all the credit for the Everton Ladies section which is the first comprehensive history written about a ladies club side in this country.

Thank you also to Simon Hughes for his work with copy-editing and contributions to the interview tally, to Megan Pollard for making things tick behind the scenes at deCoubertin, and Daniel Lewis for his faith and belief. I am indebted to George Chilvers for allowing us to reproduce his superb colourised image of William Ralph 'Dixie' Dean on the cover. The artist Paul Town was commissioned to produce an original artwork for the endpapers for the hardback edition of this book – the match being played is my own first game, against Arsenal in November 1985 – and he has produced some lovely work. Leslie Priestley has once again put together a magnificent design inside and out, while putting up with constantly shifting deadlines and the happy chaos of collaborating on another of my books.

Lots of people helped in little ways and large to enrich this work. Sam McPartland came up with the title after a lengthy Facebook debate. Adam Farley unlocked many doors with the 'Class of '98'. Henry Mooney, David and Elizabeth France, Brendan Connolly, Jim Buckley, Darren Griffiths, Thomas Reagan, Rob Sawyer, Billy Smith, Becky Easton, Jenny Seagrove, Tony Grant, Mo Marley, Stefan Van Loock, Louis Saha, Charles Mills, Michael Ball, Rachel Sutton, Gerry Moore, Ceylan Hussein, Kate Highfield, Martin Hardy, Sabahat Muhammad and Carena Duffy all provided helping hands along the way.

My own family in both England and Ireland have provided magnificent support and patience beyond the call of duty over a chaotic 18 months, in which I've often been absent either physically – I've made around 100 international trips during that time – or mentally. The cause for these absences is usually the same: my work. I have pursued this with the sort of relentlessness and passion that comes from knowing, befriending or being inspired by many of the characters who made Everton the great institution that it is today. I hope they all take pleasure in the end result.

James Corbett
Liverpool and Ireland
September 2017.

deCoubertin
B O O K S

www.decoubertin.co.uk